POWER Spelling

Ready-to-Use Lessons,
Spelling Skills, Memory Tools,
and Activities to Help Your Students
Master Any Word!

Linda Skerbec
Kris Yenney, illustrator

Take the S

T

Forever!

Library of Congress Cataloging-in-Publication Data

Skerbec, Linda
  Power spelling : ready-to-use lessons, activities & memory tools to help your
    students master any word/Linda Skerbec; Kris Yenney illustrator.
   p. cm.
  Includes index.
  ISBN 0-13-040884-0
    1. English language—Orthography and spelling—Study and teaching. 2. English language--
    Orthography and spelling--Problems, exercises, etc. L. Yenney, Kris, ill. II. Title.

  PE1143 .S54 2002
  428.1--dc21

                 2001052805

The spelling skills, memory tools, and activities in *POWER Spelling* began their development in 1971 when Linda Skerbec wrote *Let's Learn Spelling* for teachers and students in the Palo Alto School District. This original book has grown and been refined by classroom teaching, tutoring, and research; and as those using it have contributed and made requests. Today, *POWER Spelling* organizes the entire spelling process into seven complete *Spelling Skills* with corresponding *Memory Tools* that students can use for clearly understanding and remembering every word. Please share your requests and ideas, and those of your students. They are truly welcomed.

Attention: Schools and Corporations

The Center for Applied Research in Education books are available at quantity discounts with bulk purchase for education, business, or sales promotion use. For information, please write to Prentice Hall Direct Special Sales, 240 Frisch Court, Paramus, NJ 07652. Please supply: title of book, ISBN, quantity, how the book will be used, and date needed.

POWER SPELLING

As students learn these **POWER SPELLING SKILLS** *and* retain them with **MEMORY TOOLS**, they will be able to truly understand and master the spelling challenges that come their way.

POWER CLUES
PHONICS POWER
PRONUNCIATION POWER
POWER RULES THAT WORK
POWER OF ANCIENT ROOTS
VISUAL POWER AND PATTERNS
POWER OF THE BEAT AND SYLLABLES

Our Strange Language

When the English tongue we <u>speak</u>
Why is <u>break</u> not rhymed with <u>freak</u>?
Will you tell me why it's <u>true</u>
We say <u>sew</u>, but likewise <u>few</u>;
And the maker of a <u>verse</u>
Cannot rhyme his <u>horse</u> with <u>worse</u>?
<u>Beard</u> sounds not the same as <u>heard</u>;
<u>Cord</u> is different from <u>word</u>;
<u>Cow</u> is cow, but <u>low</u> is low.
<u>Shoe</u> is never rhymed with <u>foe</u>.
Think of <u>nose</u> and <u>dose</u> and <u>lose</u>;
And think of <u>goose</u> and yet of <u>choose</u>.
Think of <u>comb</u> and <u>tomb</u> and <u>bomb</u>,
<u>Doll</u> and <u>roll</u> and <u>home</u> and <u>some</u>.
And since <u>pay</u> is rhymed with <u>say</u>,
<u>Mould</u> is not pronounced like <u>could</u>
Wherefore <u>done</u>, but <u>gone</u> and <u>lone</u>?
Is there any reason <u>known</u>?

And, in short, it seems to me,
Sounds and letters disagree.
–Anonymous

Dedication

to my mother, Helen Woolery, my first teacher,
whose brilliance was always there to encourage my writing
and to give me the tools I needed to learn and remember spelling,
and
to my son, David,
whose love and profound commitment to truth in thinking and writing,
continues to inspire me to challenge students to seek truth, achieve excellence,
and keep learning joyful.

Acknowledgments

Thank you, Joe, my husband. You helped with so many practical necessities, and your meticulous editing of my early writing helped me raise this book to a much clearer level.

Thank you, Joyce Burich, a true teacher. You have *always* understood, encouraged, and *celebrated* my teaching and writing, as I have created learning materials to inspire and help students achieve excellence.

Thank you, Fred Dunbar. Your inspiration, profound understanding of my intuitive process, and your commitment to excellence in your work has kept me going and made this book possible in so many ways.

Thank you, Allison Arrigoni. Your young eagerness and joy of learning has been so often in my heart as I wrote this book.. You are the first student for whom this book is written.

Thank you, Kris Yenney. You gave your time to collaborate, as a musician, artist, and teacher, while we worked together to further understand the rich ways that the spoken language and music parallel each other. Also, your unique artistic gifts and wonderful drawings truly bring these lessons alive.

Thank you, Win Huppuch. You are the finest and most supportive mentor in education whom I have ever known. You've always been there with deep insights to inspire my thinking to a higher level. Your respect for spelling and hands-on writing keeps me creating the materials students need to learn and produce their best.

Thank you, David Berson. Your brilliant computer programs greatly enriched my research for the *Book of Lists*.

Thank you, Craig Masonek. You patiently read my writing and skillfully typed the exacting lists for this book...

Thank you to my students. Your desires to truly learn inspire me to create and teach the clearest and finest curriculum I can. Thank you, teachers and parents, especially Mary Lou Fisher, who came to me and expressed the desperate spelling needs of children, and kept asking me to write a spelling book until it became a reality.

Awesome! This is the most complete and wonderful Spelling Book I've ever seen (and I've looked for 15 years).
Every skill is covered, plus it's full of memory tools, fascinating information, and delightful drawings.
I just wanted to read it from cover to cover. Everyone should have a copy on a shelf close at hand.
-Mary Lou Fisher: Mother, Researcher, PTA President, School Volunteer

About the Author

Linda Skerbec has taught and created dynamic and comprehensive learning materials for over 30 years, as a classroom teacher, psychologist, tutor and mother. She holds a Masters Degree from Stanford University in English Education, a Lifetime Teaching Credential in Languages Arts, and Masters Degrees in Counseling and Psychology. Her inspiring materials make learning come alive for numerous students with differing gifts and abilities: from learning challenged, to academically gifted, to students who have "turned off" and lost the drive to learn.

Dedicated to understanding what inspires students to truly learn and retain the skills needed for excellence, Linda develops Language Arts Materials to meet three goals:

- ◆ Make learning so clear and accessible that students will see, from the start, that their efforts will result in individual achievement and excellence;
- ◆ Help students learn dynamic skills and also learn and develop the tools to organize and retain these skills: and
- ◆ Inspire curiosity and motivation in learning, and help students find joy and truth

Actively involving students in the energetic process of understanding and retaining what they have learned, Linda continues to find that if you clearly teach students the skills they need and ways to remember these skills, students will feel empowered. Then, they will continue to put effort into their studying, and they will experience the joyful confidence that comes from truly learning!

Her ongoing research emphasizes developing learning materials that access the brain's power to perceive, organize, and associate information so that it can be used and retained on a lifelong basis. Her materials draw on the structured dimensions of the left brain as well as the more conceptual, intuitive processes of the right brain. Her curriculum also fully integrates the three senses: auditory, visual and kinesthetic.

To make spelling come alive, Linda has created *POWER SPELLING*, an exciting and complete program that organizes the process of spelling into seven clear and dynamic *Spelling Skills* with corresponding *Memory Tools* that students can use to organize, learn and retain spelling forever: *POWER* Clues, Phonics *POWER*, *POWER* Rules, *POWER* of he Beat and Syllables, *POWER* Pronunciation, *POWER* of Ancient Roots, Prefixes, and Suffixes, and Visual *POWER* and Patterns. This program also includes *POWER Spelling Games*, intriguing *Special Lessons*, and *The Book of Lists*.

In addition to her unique spelling program, Linda has written *Imagination and Language*, and other Language Arts materials, to help students enjoy learning structured writing, creative writing, poetry, journaling, and grammar. She also writes poetry and fiction, and is doing ongoing research on how each child's unique personality type affects the way he or she learns. This research is furthered by Linda's work as a licensed therapist where she concentrates on helping both children and adults heal and grow by using and sharing their unique gifts and abilities. Linda also enjoys her family and pets, dancing, swimming, collecting shells and rocks, playing the piano, calligraphy, and drawing (she contributed the artwork on pp. vii, xii, 2, 269, 280, and 303). She savors the time she gets to discuss significant issues with her family and a few precious friends.

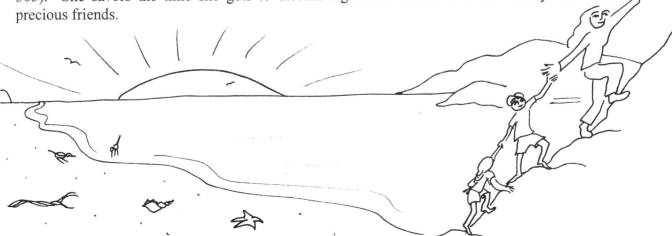

About the Artist

Kris Yenney has been drawing for as long as she can remember, beginning at the knee of her mother, Dorothy, a painter and sculptor. While in middle school, Kris was a student in Linda Skerbec's English and Creative Writing class. A few years later, she and Linda collaborated on a book, *Understanding and Valuing Other Cultures*, for the Palo Alto (California) School District. They have since completed several books together, including *Imagination and Language* for Prentice Hall, and other books of language arts curricula covering spelling, structured and creative writing, grammar, and poetry. Over the years, Kris's illustrations have proven very popular with both students and teachers.

Kris's whimsical line drawings of musicians have appeared in numerous magazines, on stationery, t-shirts, mugs, and on concert posters and programs for Arts organizations throughout North America. Her original works hang in private collections of musicians and music lovers throughout the world.

Music is a favorite theme in Kris's art because she is an accomplished musician herself, having studied the cello since the age of eight and earned a Master's degree in cello performance from the New England Conservatory of Music in Boston. Her music has taken her to foreign lands and has provided her with memorable and rich experiences, from performances in Jamaica, France, and New York's Carnegie Hall, to Raga studies in India and residencies at the Tanglewood Institute, Yale's Norfolk Summer Chamber Music Festival, and the Banff Centre for the Arts.

Currently a member of the San Francisco based contemporary "Left Coast Chamber Ensemble," Kris is also a founding member of the popular Celtic/Medieval/Magical quartet "Broceliande," in which she plays cello, double bass, viola da gamba, percussion and sings.

Kris complements her performing life with a full studio of private cello students, three youth orchestras which she directs, singing in a choir, and continuing studies of world music, natural healing modalities, and Middle Eastern dance. She tries – often in vain – to find quality time to tend her garden, dote on her cat, keep in touch with friends, read the occasional book, compose (she's an award-winning composer), and keep up with her very active mother.

The drawings herein are joyfully dedicated
to my cello students,
who went without regular lessons while I finished this project,
and
to Dottie Yenney, without whose love and support and artistry
I would not have such a sweet life.

What People Say About Learning Spelling

I memorize easily by seeing. I can just look at a word, and then picture it in my brain... Also, I can look at a word and know if it's right or wrong. I remember *chocolate* by pronouncing it the Spanish way: *cho-co-la-te*. I like the sound of some words... My favorites are *fluff* and *tickle*. (Allison Arrigoni, student)

I learn spelling by seeing little words inside of words, like *Mary* and *land* in *Maryland*... I can also put some words into a beat like: $e - l - ec - tion$ and $a - rith - me - tic$. (Michael Bench, student)

I've always simply sounded most words out by syllables. Good old phonics, I guess you'd say.

I simply feel how words are spelled. For a challenging word, like *argument*, I immediately create a way to remember it, like: *You can't have an <u>argument</u> with <u>gum</u> in your mouth*... I pronounce knee, *k-nee* and climb, *clim-b*... Also, I remember that *balloon* has 2 sticks and 2 balloons. Then I keep using my memory tools forever... Like any art, though, you need to put in effort to master spelling. (Linda Skerbec)

I just picture the word in my mind. I have some kind of visual association inside of how the word should look. (Paul Woolery, counselor)

My spelling is Wobbly. It's good spelling, but it Wobbles, and the letters get in the wrong places. (Pooh to Owl in *Winnie the Pooh* by A. A. Milne)

I've developed lots of spelling ability from reading and reading... As with music, though, I also believe that spelling has a genetic component to it... I have this innate ability to just look at words and know if they're spelled right. I also think it important to build spelling skills. (Dr. Tina Castanares, physician)

As I'm writing the word out, I can kind of feel whether or not the word is right.

Old English is a much simpler and more reliable language, with every letter distinctly and invariably related to a single sound. There were none of the silent letters or phonetic inconsistencies that belabor modern English spelling. (Bill Bryson, author of *Crazy English*)

I see words in my mind and then write them. As a kid, I was told that typing gave a consistent look to words. Now, I picture words and watch them unfold as I type. (Bill Phair, Book Production manager)

I remember some words just by the way they look, like the three parallel lines in *parallel*.

Constantly reading, associating words with their roots, employing little pronunciation tricks such as, "Wed-nes-day", have all contributed to my spelling ability. I can also visualize the correct spelling of a word in my mind. (Helen Woolery, mother)

Let us extend a word of encouragement to poor spellers. The inability to spell is not an inherited disease or due to malnutrition... It is indeed a curse, but the curse can be lifted – one is tempted to say – by the use of proper spells! If you've been a bad speller, you must begin again by refusing to admit defeat. Spelling can be learned. You can learn it! (*Macmillan Spelling Handbook*, 1939)

POWER Spelling: What this Book Contains
A Dynamic Ready-to-Use Spelling Program and More...

Over 30 years of teaching and research has gone into creating **POWER Spelling**, and I am now excited to share it with you. The *POWER Spelling Program* stands out because it covers *all* the spelling skills, plus it teaches your students to connect their words to *Memory Tools* so they can truly remember them. **POWER Spelling** provides: a Teacher's Guide; a Spelling Book (that covers and surpasses *all* state requirements in 36 lessons) with weekly Spelling Lists; Ideas for *Memory Tools* (a page for each list); 4 Special Lessons, *The POWER Spelling Book of Lists*, plus special wonders to discover.

POWER Spelling Teacher's Guide: In this guide I share insights and ideas I have learned for introducing lessons in ways that actively involve students. Also, with every lesson, I have included a *Learning Box* of information you can create on the board to reinforce the lesson's spelling concepts. This guide also provides unique ways to inspire and excite students about learning and retaining words. Finally, it suggests *Special Lessons* and *Lists* that can enhance the weekly lessons

Spelling Book: At the heart of this program is the **POWER Spelling Playbook** with 36 weekly lessons you can photocopy for direct use by your students. The *Playbook* is an intriguing, multi-sensory spelling manual that organizes spelling into 7 *Spelling Skills* that students can use to understand words – with 7 corresponding *Memory Tools* they can use to remember the spelling of words for a lifetime. As students do each lesson, they're building a valuable, personal spelling manual they can use forever. Wonderful drawings (which some students color) reinforce many concepts.

Spelling Lists: A 20-word spelling list (with bonus words) goes with each lesson, plus more. Every list is organized so that each of the 7 *Memory Tools* is used at least once (Suggested Memory Tools are listed by each word.) Also, each list has at least one *Clue-in-a-Row*, *Word Search Word*, and *one set of Homophones*. At the end of each list, you'll find *Other Word Forms* (that show noun, verb, adjective, and adverb suffixes for words). These lists, called **POWER Spelling Games**, can be used like traditional lists or be played as a game where students detect ways to use *Memory Tools* to retain words. A *Guide to Playing the Power Spelling Games* and a *Summary of Spelling Rules* help students play these games.

Ideas for Memory Tools: The *Suggested Ideas* for *Memory Tools* provide specific examples of one or more ways to use the 7 Memory Tools to remember every word in each Game: *Clues, Phonics, Rules, the Beat and Syllables, Pronunciation, Ancient Roots,* and *Visual Patterns*.

POWER Spelling Special Lessons: Four *Special Lessons* are included: *Do Geese See God and Other Palindromes…; Aardvarks, Llama and Other Double-Letter Words; Looking at Nouns, Verbs, Adjectives, and Adverbs; and Discovering What's Inside the Amazing Dictionary*. These lessons can be used at any time to add a unique spark to your spelling program or to enhance specific lessons.

The POWER Spelling Book of Lists: These intriguing Lists correspond to the 7 *Spelling Skills* and *Memory Tools*, and provide ways to remember words for a lifetime. They can be used as extra lessons or to enrich weekly lessons in the *Playbook*. These lists include: *Clue-in-a-Row, Lists of Words That Fit a Beat, Visual Clues…* There is also a section of unique lists: *Names and Their Meanings, Lists of the Most Frequently Misspelled Words,* and a *Timeline of English Words and Their Spelling*.

The **POWER Spelling Program** spans a school year, and the weekly lessons can be used with students of all abilities in a structured classroom, in small group programs, and individually. Also, the *Playbook* is such a complete spelling manual that it can easily be used one year and then be reviewed the next. For schools that are currently committed to other programs, the *POWER Spelling Lessons* and *Lists* can add enrichment. I hope this program brings joy to you and your students. *Linda L. Skerbec*

Linda L. Skerbec

The Purpose for this Book and Its Organization
A Lifetime Approach to Learning Spelling

The purpose for the **POWER SPELLING PLAYBOOK** and the **POWER SPELLING GAMES** is to provide students and teachers with a ready-to-use approach to learning and remembering spelling that is so thorough, so clearly understood, and so readily reinforced that they can use it throughout their life. This complete program presents all the *Skills* that students truly need to learn spelling and powerful *Memory Tools* to retain each word they meet! The weekly *POWER Spelling Lessons* (which include and surpass state guidelines) and the *POWER Spelling Games* go together to dynamically reinforce each other, as they help students become **POWER SPELLERS**!!!

The POWER Spelling Playbook
Where Students Gain the Skills and Memory Tools to Learn and Retain Spelling

The *Playbook* is a comprehensive, upbeat spelling manual with thirty-six weekly lessons that teach students seven *Spelling Skills* with matching *Memory Tools* that they can use to organize, learn and remember every word. Each one of the seven categories (which use auditory, visual and kinesthetic ways of learning) empowers students with *Spelling POWER* to use for these lessons and for spelling forever!

THE 7 POWER SPELLING SKILLS AND MEMORY TOOLS

- ◆ **POWER CLUES**: Students learn to create *Clues* for the difficult parts of words: by finding *Smaller Words in Words*: ju<u>ice</u>, arg<u>um</u>ent; *Clues in a Row*: <u>a-bun-dance</u>; *Letters in Words*: jewe<u>lry</u>, at<u>hle</u>te... *Other Word Forms where they can better hear a letter*: crum<u>bs</u>-crum<u>b</u>le, rec<u>e</u>ive-rec<u>e</u>ption; and *Same Pattern Clues*: m<u>ain</u>, pl<u>ain</u>, r<u>ain</u>...
- ◆ *Examples*: I would like <u>ice</u> in my ju<u>ice</u>; It's hard to have an <u>argument</u> with <u>gum</u> in your mouth; With our <u>abundance</u> of food, we even got to see <u>a bun dance</u>; If my cookie <u>crumbles</u>, I eat <u>crumbs</u>; The <u>athlete</u> did a <u>high</u> leap; I looked in my <u>jewelry</u> for the <u>lost ring</u>...
  Students also learn to create *Clues* for *Homophones* – to retain the differences in spelling and meaning: <u>Peace</u>: I know <u>each</u> soldier wanted <u>peace</u>. <u>Piece</u>: I ate a <u>piece</u> of apple <u>pie</u>.

- ◆ **PHONICS POWER**: Students learn that knowing the sounds of phonics provides great spelling help since *85% of the words in English are spelled like they sound*. They're first introduced to phonics in Lesson 2 where they discover in *The History of the English Language* the reasons why some words aren't spelled like they're pronounced. Then they learn about the different sounds that consonants and vowels create and how these sounds are spelled. As students truly understand phonics, they realize that the spelling of most words and syllables makes sense because they follows phonics rules. *Memory Tools* help with the rest of the words.

- ◆ **POWER RULES THAT WORK**: Students learn that most words follow dependable *Spelling Rules*: Qu Rule, Contraction Rule, Compound Word Rule, Prefix and Suffix Rules, Rules for Adding Plurals, Rule for Doubling Final Consonants... By understanding these *Rules That Work*, students can gain control over numerous words in the English language. The lessons give them clear, concise ways to remember the rules, as well as their exceptions. Students are also taught to group words together that have the *Same Patterns* and follow the *Same Rules*.

"these really work!"

- ◆ ***FEELING THE POWER OF THE BEAT and SYLLABLES***: Students find that hearing the *Beat* (accent), helps them divide words into syllables which enhances their ability to spell. Students learn ways to put rhythmic words to a *Beat*: <u>d-e-s-s-e-r-t</u>, <u>h-o-pp-i-n-g</u>, <u>r-h-y t-h-m</u>, and <u>e-n c-y-c l-o p-e-d-i-a</u>. They also learn that putting syllables to a *Beat* helps: <u>cho-co-la-te</u>, <u>a-rith-me-tic</u>, <u>math-e-ma-tics</u>, <u>ac-ci-dent-al-ly</u>. This tool is fun to use, and it can be drawn on to retain a number of challenging words. Students also learn that they reinforce *Motor Memory* each time they correctly write a word because their hand learns to FEEL the correct spelling.

- ◆ ***PRONUNCIATION POWER***: Students learn ways to handle Spellings' two main *Pronunciation* challenges: words that are phonetic, but misspelled because they're mispronounced; and words that are misspelled because they're no longer spelled like they're commonly pronounced.

   Students learn 7 keys to correctly pronounce words spelled like they're pronounced, like <u>every</u> (ervry), <u>library</u> (libary), <u>jewelry</u> (jewelry). They also learn *Memory Tools* to retain these.

   For the second group, students learn that until the 1400's, all the letters in words were pronounced; but today, there are Silent-Letter Words and other words that get misspelled because they're no longer spelled like they're commonly pronounced. Students learn to use *Special Phonics Pronunciations* (*SPP's*). For an *SPP*, they pronounce every letter for spelling: *<u>clim-b</u>, <u>k-ni-fe</u>, res-<u>ta-u-rant</u>, Wed-nes-day*. Words are pronounced in a way similar to Old English.

   Students can even speak their own *SPP Language*: *I k-noc-ked my k-ne-e o-n tha-t lar-ge roc-k.* It sounds a bit like Old English, and really helps with spelling.

- ◆ ***THE POWER OF ANCIENT ROOTS, SUFFIXES, and PREFIXES***: Students discover ways that Latin and Greek *Prefixes, Roots* and *Suffixes* work together to build words like *dis-<u>agree</u>-ment, trans-<u>port</u>-ing, and sub-<u>mar</u>-ine*. They also become familiar with their meaning and their consistent spelling, and have fun building their own words. They also grow in their ability to spot *Roots, Prefixes*, and *Suffixes*, and to identify words that have the same roots. This enriching skill helps build both spelling and vocabulary.

- ◆ ***VISUAL WORD POWER***: Students learn to train *Visual Memory* so they can picture words in their mind. They also discover *Special Visual Words* where letters in the word look like objects they can draw (2 sticks and 2 balloons in ba<u>ll</u>oon; 4 candles in bri<u>lll</u>iant). Students then learn about unique *Visual Patterns* in words: *Palindromes* (<u>racecar</u>, <u>kayak</u>); *Reversals* (<u>deer</u> – <u>reed</u>; <u>drawer</u> – <u>reward</u>), *Echoes* (<u>sen</u>se, <u>deci</u>de); and *Bookends* (<u>onion</u>, <u>museum</u>). They also discover *Word Search Words* (5 words in <u>heart</u>, 10 words in <u>information</u>); *Special Visual Words* (4 e's in <u>dependence</u>; all 5 vowels in <u>sequoia</u>), and words with the *Same Visual Pattern*: *cough, bough, through…; does, goes, hoes, toes…* Finally, students are encouraged to READ… which visually stores correctly spelled words again and again in their mind.

The POWER Spelling Games
Where Students Use the *POWER Spelling Skills* and *Memory Tools* They've Learned

Espelier, an Old French word from which *spelling* is derived, means *to comprehend; to puzzle out*. This is what the **POWER Spelling Games** are all about. As students look at their weekly spelling list of words, in a very real sense, *they're playing a game*. They're *the detectives* who use the *POWER Spelling Skills* and *Memory Tools* to understand and *puzzle out* ways to *learn* and *retain* each word.

The weekly *POWER Spelling Game* (20 words plus Bonus Words) is like a traditional spelling list, plus more. *Every game* has words specifically chosen to go with each *Memory Tool* so that all seven *Tools* are used. Also, each game has at least one *Clue-in-a-Row*, one *Word Search Word*, and at least one set of *Homophones*. *Other Word Forms* (*OWF's*) are listed at the bottom of each list. The *OWF's* show the noun, verb, adjective, and adverb suffixes for many of the words.

Also *The Guide to Playing the Power Spelling Games* and *The Summary of Rules* are included for students. It helps to read these with your students before the first *POWER Spelling Game*. Then they can refer to them when they play a game. (The words for the *Games* were chosen from: The Most Commonly Used and Misspelled Words; Recommended Grade-Level Words, Homophones, and Words Commonly Confused.)

A good time to play the *POWER Spelling Game* is after students have completed the corresponding lesson in their Playbook; although, some teachers like using the games to introduce lessons. The only rule is: Each *POWER Spelling Tool* must be used at least once in every game. For the rest of the words, students can choose the *Memory Tools* that work best for them. Some words are best retained by using *Clues*; others follow the sounds of *Phonics*; while some words can be mastered by using a *Rule*. Some words are remembered by *Feeling their Beat* or spelling them by *Syllables*; while others need a *Pronunciation Tool*. Finally, there are words that are truly retained by detecting their *Prefixes, Roots* and *Suffixes* or by using *Visual Tools*. The reason for using all the *Memory Tools* in each game is that this process keeps reinforcing the ways that students are learning to remember spelling.

A teacher can simply play a game with the whole class; or, for some students, it helps if they have first worked on their own, or with another person, and written down their own ideas. To play a game, simply write *The Power Spelling Game* and the words where everyone can see them. Then ask students to share their ways of remembering the words. What is most important is to *truly encourage students* and write down *their ideas* as they brainstorm and offer different ways to use the *Memory Tools* (Each game can be played on as basic or as advanced a level as a teacher chooses for a class).

Suggested Ideas for the Games provide specific ways that one or more *Memory Tools* can be used for *every word*. After playing a game, many students enjoy reading these *Ideas* to find out even more about the words and tools. As students continue using these *Memory Tools*, they will gain an ease in applying them and a comprehensive knowledge of spelling that they can draw on forever…

The Teacher's Guides
Inspiration and Ideas for Teachers

The *POWER* Spelling Program provides *Teacher's Guides* for the *POWER Spelling Lessons*, the *Special Lessons*, and also for *The POWER Spelling Book of Lists*. This introduction to these guides first offers suggestions for structuring the *POWER* Spelling Lessons and Games into your weekly schedule (This program can also be structured in a traditional way with the *Memory Tools* added for reinforcement.) Then, two examples of *Ideas for Introducing Lessons* are shared to give you a sense of what each guide provides. Finally, information is given on the lists and activities in *The POWER Spelling Book of Lists*.

Since the same seven *POWER Spelling Skills* and matching *Memory Tools* are at the heart of the entire *POWER* Spelling Program, the *POWER Spelling Lessons*, *Special Lessons*, and *Lists* will always reinforce each other. Each *Teacher's Guide* includes specific information on how the lessons and lists can best enrich each other.

Structuring POWER Spelling into Your Weekly Schedule

Most teachers use forty-five to seventy minutes a week to cover a *POWER Spelling Lesson* and *Game*, depending on the teacher and students' needs (Lessons 1-2 take longer.). A suggested process to follow is:

Monday: Introduce the lesson and the game that goes with it. The *Teacher's Guides* provide insightful ideas for introducing the lessons (and lists) in ways that will capture your student's attention. Work on the lesson with your students, or ask them to read and do the activities on their own or with a study partner in class, or for homework. Also, read the 20 words (and Bonus Words if you're including these).

Tuesday: Read *The Guide to Playing the Power Spelling Games* with students (Then review this for the next 2-3 lessons.). Then write 5-6 words from the Game on the board. Ask, "What *Memory Tools* can you use to remember these words?" Write their ideas on the board. Also ask, "How do you think these *Memory Tools* can help you?" Listen as students explore their ideas. Then, share, "These *Memory Tools* give your brain special ways to remember words. Keep using your *Memory Tools* for words, and you'll have ways to remember words for the rest of your life!"

Next, read the rest of the game words, noting the *Homophones*, plus the *Other Word Forms* at the end of the page. Then say, "Use your *Lesson, Guidelines*, and a dictionary to play this game. Discover ways to remember these words and write your ideas by each word. Then clearly write each word twice." Add, "The only rule is to use each *Memory Tool* at least once per game. For fun, try to detect a *Clue-in-a-Row* and see how many words you can find in the *Word Search Words*." Encourage students to work with a study partner or family member. This helps them be prepared to share *their ideas* when they play a game in class. (Feel free to choose the words you want your students to learn, and this can vary among students.)

Wednesday or *Thursday*: Play the *POWER Spelling Game* with your class. Write the words on the board and ask students to share the *Memory Tools* they used for the words. List their *Clues, Rules, Visual Tools*, etc., staying very open to all the ideas they offer. What is most important is to truly encourage their brainstorming process as they determine ways to use the *Memory Tools*. (Each Game has a page of *Ideas* with *Memory Tools* written out for every word. These help a lot when you play the games with students. Many students enjoy having these *Ideas*, but only share these *after they've done their own discovery process*, so essential to their learning.) A spelling test can be given on Friday. (Some teachers first review the *Memory Tools*.)

(For Lesson 1, also hand out the title page for the *Playbook*, and the first page, so your students can start building their *Playbook* (or give them a complete *Playbook*). Then read the first page with them.)

Inspiration and Ideas for Introducing the Lessons

The goals for the *Teacher's Guides* are to inspire teachers and provide insightful and intriguing ways to introduce the lessons and lists – ways that will capture your students' interest. Let's look at ideas for introducing the first two lessons. (Objectives for each lesson are also included.)

Lesson 1: *Getting to Know Your Power Spelling Tools*. *Objectives*: Students will be able to use the *7 POWER Spelling Skills* and *Memory Tools* to understand and complete the activities in this lesson.

To intrigue students, try this. First, assure them, "This is not a test." Then say, "Please write these words as I read them: *attendance, staccato, museum, sense, hanger* (clothes), *lamplighter*, *limb*, *astronaut* (words different than in the lesson)." Ask how they spelled the words. Write these on the board and create a little debate over which way is right. Then erase everything except the correct spelling.

Now ask questions to help students discover ways to retain the words. Ask, "Can you find any small words in *attendance*?" Help them detect a *Clue-in-a-Row*: At ten, dance... For *staccato*, ask, "What do you *see* in the way the letters look?" They might see taccat (a palindrome). Inquire, "What else do you see in *taccat* ?" Someone will suddenly discover *2 cats back to back*. For museum, help them create a *Clue*: Use the museum, and see the *Bookends*: museum... (Continued on page 2.)

Lesson 2: *Discovering the History of the English Language*. *Objectives*: Students will discover intriguing information about the history of English... and appreciate the many cultures that have made English such a rich language. They'll also understand why many words aren't spelled as pronounced.

Since this is usually the second lesson of the year, a special way to introduce it is to ask students, "Do you know what your name means or about your ancestors?" During this week, have students introduce themselves by sharing their name's meaning, the language from which it came... plus any words this language has added to English. (*The List of Names* enriches this lesson and is interesting to students.)

The *POWER* Spelling Lists

The *Lists* provide examples of ways to use the 7 *Spelling Skills* and *Memory Tools* to retain words. They can be used to enrich spelling lessons, plus many lists can be used as spelling lessons. The *Lists* include:

- ◆ *POWER* Spelling Clues
  Lists of Clues-in-a-Row, Clues for Homophones, Clues for Confusing Words...
- ◆ Phonics *POWER* and Patterns
  Lists of All the Consonant Sounds
  Lists of All the Vowel Sounds
- ◆ *POWER* Spelling Rules that Work (plus Ways to Remember Exceptions)
- ◆ *POWER* of the Beat and Syllables
- ◆ Pronunciation *POWER*
  POWER Pronunciation Keys
  Special Phonics Pronunciations for Words not-Spelled as Pronounced
- ◆ *POWER* of Ancient Roots, Prefixes, and Suffixes
  Lists of Special Roots: Star, Heart, Hand, Foot... and Clues for Roots
  Lists of the Prefix and Suffix Patterns
- ◆ Visual *POWER*
  Lists of Words You Can Draw, Palindromes, Reversals, Echoes, Bookends...
  List of Sight Recognition Words and Clues for Sight Recognition Words
- ◆ *POWER* Spelling Special Lists
  List of the 1,000 Most Commonly Used Words (and Most Commonly Misspelled Words)
  POWER Spelling List of Names and Their Meaning
  POWER Spelling Timeline of the English Language and Its Spelling

The Brain's POWER To Learn

As students learn the seven Skills and Memory Tools in their **POWER Spelling Playbook** and use them to play the **POWER Spelling Games**, they are accessing three senses through which the brain perceives and learns: HEARING, SEEING and FEELING. Also, they are training their brain to organize, associate and retain spelling information as it develops Creative Memory. Concerning the **Brain's *POWER***, it is key to know that research on how the brain works and how students learn has been incorporated into the Skills and Memory Tools which are presented in **POWER SPELLING**.

Current research shows that much of the Brain's POWER to learn spelling is organized in the following way:

- A—LEFT HEMISPHERE: This linear part of the brain understands structured approaches to spelling like Phonics, Spelling Rules, and the Prefixes, Roots, and Suffixes used for building words.

- B—RIGHT HEMISPHERE: This creative, spatial and intuitive part of the brain understands words from a more creative and intuitive approach that involves skills and tools like discovering Visual Clues in words or the use of the imagination or rhythmic and Kinesthetic ways of retaining words.

- C—FRONTAL LOBE: This speech and movement part of the brain is involved in speaking words with clear and accurate Pronunciation.

- D—TEMPORAL LOBE: This area of the brain involves Memory and Auditory Learning.

- E—OCCIPITAL LOBE: This visual processing part of the brain perceives and can even *photograph* the way the letters of a word are laid out.

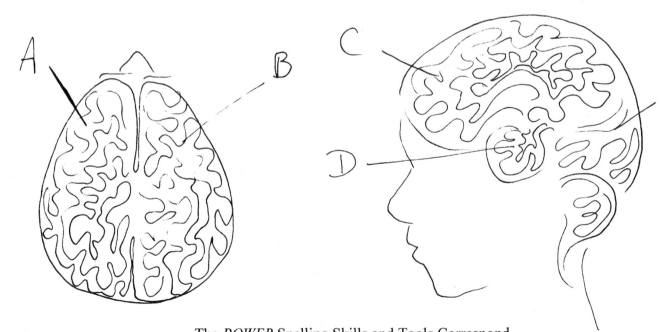

The *POWER* Spelling Skills and Tools Correspond
to the Ways the Brain Learns and Remembers Spelling Information.

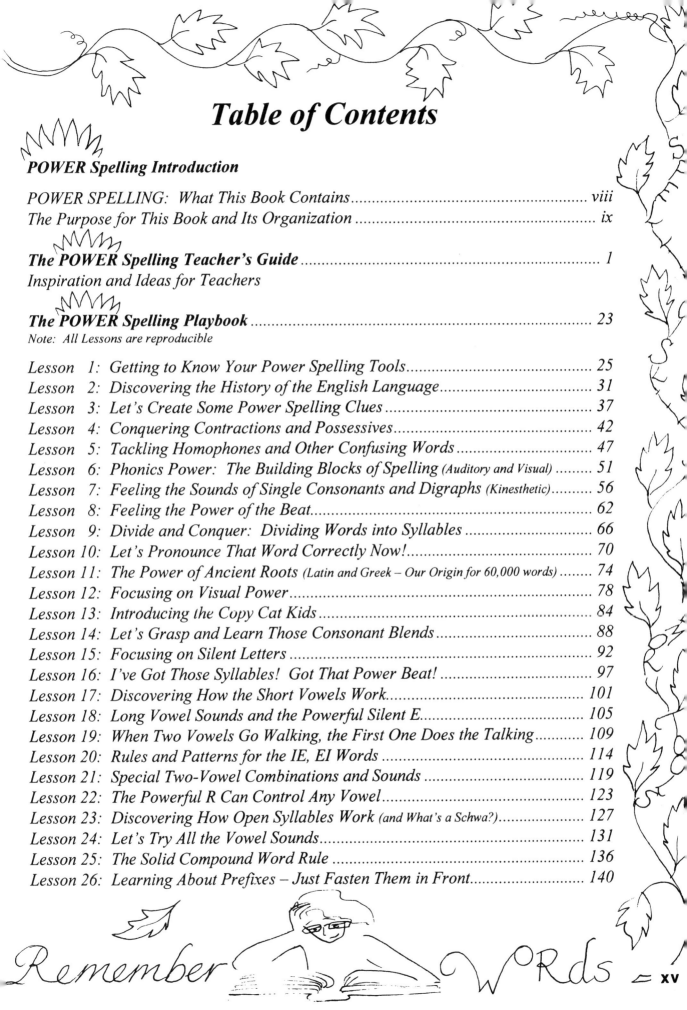

Table of Contents

POWER Spelling Introduction

The POWER Spelling Teacher's Guide

Inspiration and Ideas for Teachers

The POWER Spelling Playbook

Note: All Lessons are reproducible

POWER Spelling Games 191

Note: All Games and Ideas are reproducible.

POWER Spelling Special Lessons 267

Note: All Lessons are reproducible

POWER Spelling Book of Lists 297

Note: All Lists are reproducible.

POWER Spelling Certificate of Achievement 489

POWER Spelling Index 492

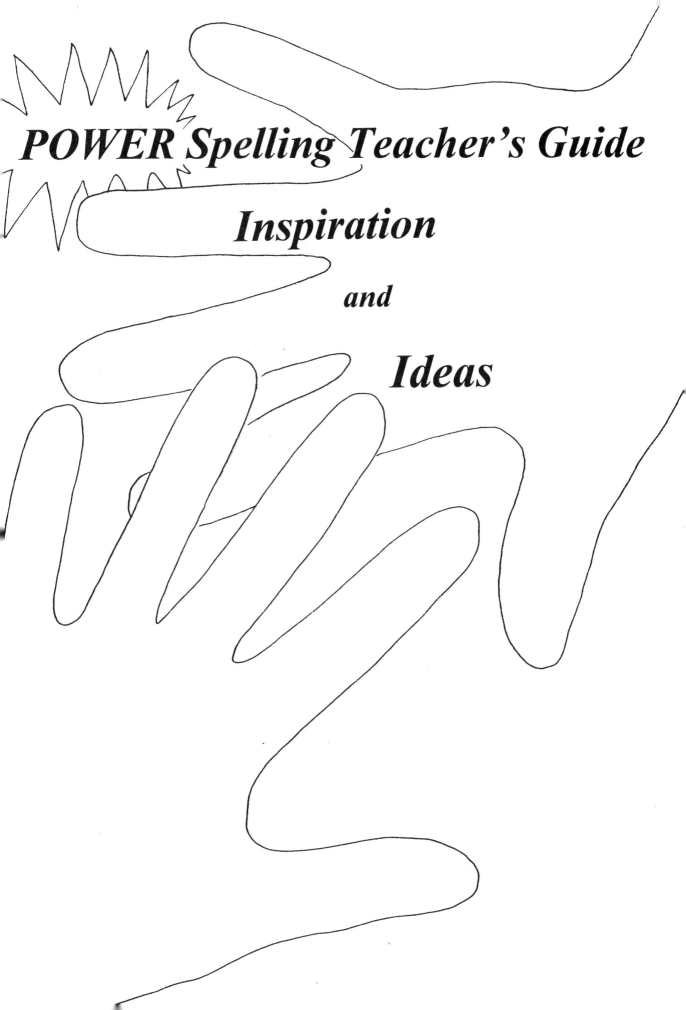

POWER Spelling Teacher's Guide

Inspiration

and

Ideas

The Teacher's Guide
for the POWER Spelling Lessons

The goal in writing *POWER Spelling* has been to provide teachers with a dynamic, ready-to-use program that organizes *Spelling* into seven complete *Spelling Skills* with matching *Memory Tools*. This book shares ways to take spelling from boring to *exploring* by actively involving your students in using these dynamic *Skills* and *Tools* to *understand and remember every word they meet!*

POWER Spelling seeks to provides everything found in a traditional spelling program plus more, while covering and surpassing all state requirements. There are 36 ready-to-use lessons, each with a weekly spelling list and reinforcement activities. These materials cover *all the Spelling Skills* and *Memory Tools*, plus they help students build a *complete spelling manual (called The POWER Spelling Playbook)* that they can keep and draw on for everything they need to know about spelling.

Each spelling list (called a *POWER Spelling Game*) directly corresponds to the words taught in the weekly lesson; plus all the words on the list have one or more *Memory Tools* that students can use for retaining them. Also, every spelling list draws on all seven skill areas so they will be reinforced each week. Additionally, every weekly list has at least one *Clue-in-a-Row*, a *Word Search Word*, one or more sets of *Homophones* (plus *Other Word Forms* at the end). These lists are both thorough and stimulating, and it's fun for students to discover what's on their spelling list and to detect ways to remember the words. A page of *Ideas* for remembering the words is provided with each spelling list. You can simply give these to students or use these for your teaching. What is great is that the *Memory Tools* empower students because they *truly learn ways to retain words forever*.

You can use these spelling lists like traditional lists, or you can use them like *games* and play weekly *POWER Spelling Games* with your students. To play a game, simply write the spelling words on the board and help your students detect and share ways to remember the words, using their *Guide to Playing the POWER Spelling Games* when they need help. Students become increasingly skilled at discovering ways to remember words as they continue doing lessons in their *POWER Spelling Playbook*. Above all, students gain spelling ability as they work to discover their own ideas for retaining words, plus draw on other suggestions, to find the *Memory Tools* that work best for them.

POWER Spelling is reinforced by *The Book of Lists*, which uses the same *Skills* and *Memory Tools*.
May this program truly enrich and inspire you as you use it with your students.

Inspiration and Ideas for Teachers

This guide contains inspiration and ideas for introducing the *POWER Spelling Lessons* in ways that are full of discovery for students. As you follow these plans, or create your own, above all, have fun teaching your students spelling. Help them discover interesting and fascinating things in words and excite them about learning and retaining them. Whenever possible, use the Socratic method of teaching where you ask questions, and let your students feel the joy of discovering answers.

The information for each lesson includes a *Learning Box*. Initially, just write the bold words in the *Box* on the board, since you will add the rest of the words as you introduce the lesson. Also, keep this *Learning Box* where students can see it for the week. It reinforces the *Skills* and *Memory Tools* that students are learning in their *Playbook* and using for the weekly *POWER Spelling Game*. (If you prefer for students to work on their own, note that the lessons in the *Playbook* introduce themselves and clearly present all the necessary skills and tools students need to learn and retain words.) Insights and ideas for presenting each lesson now follow.

Lesson 1: Getting to Know Your POWER Spelling Tools (Same *Skills* and *Memory Tools* in *Book of Lists*)
Objectives: Students will find that the *POWER Spelling Skills* and *Memory Tools* can be used to learn and remember words, and they will use these to do Lesson 1. They will also see some of the fun in words: *Clues in a Row, Palindromes, Beats, Visual Discoveries, etc.* Students will read *The Guide to Playing the Power Spelling Games* to play a game or to reinforce ways to remember words.

Begin Lesson 1 by saying, "For fun, try spelling these words (Read them.): *initiate, argument, brilliant, drawer, hangar* (plane), *newsstand, often, photograph, rhythm*." When students finish, ask how they spelled the words and print their different spellings on the board. Create a little debate over which way is correct. Then erase everything except the correct words, and write *The POWER Spelling Game* above the words. Ask students which parts of the words are challenging and underline these.

Now say, "Let's try a Game, and discover some *Memory Tools* you can use to remember these words." Ask, "Can anyone find any small words in *initiate*?" Help them see and write a *Clue-in-a-Row*. (See below.) Next, ask "Do you see a clue word in *argument*?" They'll see *gum* and be able to use it to create a clue. Students will see *ant* in *brilliant*; but also ask, "Are there any letters that looks like something you could draw?" They might see <u>illi</u> (a palindrome); but, also, ask, "Does <u>illi</u> resemble anything <u>brilliant</u>?" Help them see 4 <u>brilliant</u> candles (<u>illi</u>).

For *drawer*, ask, "What does *drawer* spell backwards?" They'll see: <u>*drawer*</u> – <u>*reward*</u>. For *hangar*, note that an <u>airplane</u> <u>hangar</u> has an <u>a</u>, while its homophone, a cloth<u>e</u>s <u>hanger</u>, has an <u>e</u>. *Newsstand* follows the *Compound Word Rule*. Just add both words: <u>*news* + *stand*</u> = <u>*newsstand*</u>. For *often*, suggest they use a *Special Phonics Pronunciation* and pronounce all the letters: <u>*of-ten*</u>. For *photograph*, ask questions that help students see the two *Roots* and their meaning and that <u>*ph*</u> in Greek = <u>*f*</u>. Next, ask, "Can anyone put *rhythm* to a *Beat*?" Write out their *Beat*: <u>*r-h-y t-h-m*</u>, and ask what's unique about *-thm*. Finally, ask, "How many of you think that these *Tools* can help you remember how to spell these words?" Briefly review, read the words, and see how they do on spelling them. They'll probably do well and feel encouraged. Now hand out copies of Lesson 1.

The *POWER* Spelling Game	
init<u>ia</u>te:	*Clue-in-a-Row*: We decided to <u>init</u>iate a trip to a pizza parlor, and <u>in it I ate</u> a lot.
arg<u>u</u>ment:	*Clue*: It's hard to have an <u>argument</u> with <u>gum</u> in your mouth.
brilliant:	*Visual*: <u>Brilliant</u> has 4 candles (<u>illi</u>) and also an <u>ant</u>.
drawer:	*Visual*: Reversal: <u>*drawer*</u> is <u>*reward*</u>.
hang<u>a</u>r (planes):	*Clue*: <u>Hang</u>ar has an <u>a</u> for <u>a</u>irplane.
new<u>ss</u>tand:	*Rule*: <u>Newsstand</u> follows the *Compound Word Rule*: <u>news</u> + <u>stand</u> = <u>newsstand</u>.
of<u>t</u>en:	*SPP*: <u>of</u>-ten. *Clue*: I am <u>often</u> one <u>of ten</u> who fish (dance, spell, climb trees…).
photograph:	*Phonics*: <u>ph</u> = <u>f</u>. *Roots*: <u>photo</u> (G. light) + <u>graph</u> (G. map) = <u>photograph</u> (light map).
rhythm:	*Beat*: r-h-y t-h-m. *Visual*: The syllable: *-thm* has no vowel.

(Also, before students play the *POWER Spelling Game* for Lesson 1, read *The Guide to Playing the POWER Spelling Games* and *The Summary of Rules* with them. These three pages show student ways to use the *Memory Tools* for a spelling list or game. The more they work with these tools, the better they will use them.)

Lesson 2: Discovering the History of the English Language

Objectives: Students will be intrigued about the development of English from Old English to the present (noting that in Old English all consonants and vowels were pronounced). Students will also realize that many words have come into English from other languages, including names. They will have fun sharing and learning the origin and meaning of names of students in class.

Lesson 2 reveals intriguing information about the development of English which helps students: grasp its breadth of history; understand why many words are not spelled as they are pronounced; and see that words from other cultures have helped make English a rich, expressive language. Since this is usually the *second lesson* of the year, a special way to introduce it is to ask students, "Do you know what your name means and do you know anything about your ancestors?" Give students time to collect this information. Then, over several days, have students introduce themselves by sharing what their name means and the language from which it came. Also, have them tell a few things about the country from which their ancestors came, plus share any words that this country added to English. As each students share, write their name, its meaning and country on the board. Also make a list of words from other countries. (*The List of Names*, in *The POWER Spelling Book of Lists* (section 8), helps with this introduction, and is intriguing to many students.)

   Another way to introduce Lesson 2 is to first create the *Learning Box* below on the board. Then say, "Today we're going to learn about some words that have been contributed to English by other countries. There's a list of countries and categories on the board. Now, write down words you can think of that have come from other countries." After a few minutes, ask students for their words, and write these under the categories.

Countries and Cultures		Food	Clothing	Holidays	Other
Amer. Indian	Indian (India)				
Arab	Italian				
Chinese	Jewish				
French	Japanese	(List words that students give below these categories.			
German	Russian	During the week, let students think of and add other words.)			
Greek	Spanish				BONSAI

It's also interesting to look at the 3 Stages of Development of English and the countries that came to England. Ask students to give you words that came from these countries and list these on the board.

Stages of Development of the English Language

Old English:
(A.D. 499-1066)

Anglo-Saxons: DETERMINER: the; PRONS.: you, me, he, she it; VERBS: is, can, will; PREPS.: after, in, of, for; CONJS.: and, but; NOUNS: barn, calf, brother, earth, father, mother, friend, hand, home, love, seed, work...; **Latin**: alms, altar, candle, creed, disciple, martyr, prophet...; **Vikings** (Denmark, Iceland, Norway, Sweden): get, hit, skin, shirt, sky...

Middle English:
(A.D. 1066-1485)

French-Latin: adore, ballet, beautiful, constitution, equality, fashion, feminine, government, jury, labor, liberty, magnificent, mansion, masculine, palace, soldier, throne, triumph...

Middle-Modern:
(1485-present)

Latin: altar, alter, amorous, image, maximum, merciful, scribe, verse, hurry, leapfrog
Greek: phantom, apothecary (pharmacist), arithmetic, antiseptic, photograph, psychology...

Exploration:

Spain: chocolate, ranch, tomato, vanilla...; **American Indian**: canoe, moccasin...

Modern: Space and Computer Age: astronaut, debug, joystick, microchip, satellite, Internet, e-mail...

(The *History of the English Language* in *The Book of Lists*: section 8, enriches Lesson 2.)

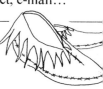

Lesson 3: Let's Create Some Power Spelling Clues

Objectives: Students will discover the fun and value of creating *POWER* Clues to remember the spelling of words (especially words that are not spelled like they sound). Students will try five different ways of creating these *Clues*. (See *Tool 1: POWER Spelling Clues* in *The POWER Spelling Book of Lists*).

Write the bold and italicized words on the board. Then ask, "Can anyone create a *Clue* for one of these words?" As students share clues, organize them into the categories below. Truly encourage your students as they try writing these different kinds of clues. Also, review each kind of clue and challenge students to create more during the week. (Collect these on the board.) Finally, hand out a *List of Clues-in-a-Row* (*See Tool 1, Book of Lists.*) Students especially enjoy these since they're fun and intriguing.

POWER Spelling Clues

WORDS: *athlete, beginning, courage, calendar, column, rain, separate, tired, thumb, tried, significant*

1. **Words in the Word Clues**: At the <u>beginning</u> of our trip, we stayed at an <u>inn</u>. When I tried to <u>separate</u> the apples and oranges, <u>a rat</u> jumped out. I <u>tried</u> to help <u>Ed</u>. When I am <u>tired</u>, my eyes get <u>red</u>.
2. **Clues-in-a-Row**: It takes <u>courage</u> to live in <u>our age</u>. This will is <u>significant</u>; please <u>sign if I can't</u>.
3. **Single letters or 2-3 letter Clues**: The <u>athlete</u> did a high <u>leap</u>. A <u>calendar</u> has a list and <u>dates</u>.
4. **Other Word Form Clues**: A <u>columnist</u> writes a <u>column</u>. <u>Thumbelina</u> was no bigger than a <u>thumb</u>.
5. **Same Pattern Clues**: <u>Rain</u> in Spain falls <u>mainly</u> on the pl<u>ains</u>. I <u>tried</u> eating <u>dried</u> fruit and <u>fried</u> bananas.

Lesson 4: Conquering Contractions and Possessives (See *Tool 3, Rules: Contractions with Bigfoot, Book of Lists*)

Objectives: Students will learn that for Homophones, the *Contraction* ALWAYS gets the apostrophe, and that this *Contraction Rule* always works. Students will discover lasting ways to remember the difference between 4 sets of *Contractions* and their *Homophones*.

Write just the *Contractions* on the board (Add a few cute apostrophes.). Then ask, "What's the apostrophe doing?" As students answer, "Replacing a letter," ask, "What letter?" Then write out the words for each contraction. Emphasize that *only an apostrophe can replace letters!* Next ask, "What are the *Homophones* for these contractions?" Add the homophones. Then state, "These 4 sets of homophones get confused more than any other words in English. Let's learn and remember the differences now!"

Stress that *the contraction ALWAYS gets the apostrophe.* Add that the possessive words have their own special forms that never need an apostrophe: *my, your, his, her, its, our, their* (also, whose). Finally, ask questions that help students discover the ways to remember the differences between the contractions and their homophones that are listed below. Go over these all week.

The Terrible Trio plus Whose: The Contraction ALWAYS Gets the Apostrophe!

1. **they're** (contraction): <u>They are</u>: NOTE: All 3 of these homophones start with <u>the</u>.
   their (possessive pronoun): <u>Their</u> has the possessive word, <u>heir</u>, in it.
   there (adv. telling where): <u>There</u> has <u>here</u> in it which tells w<u>here</u>.
2. **it's** (contraction): <u>It is</u>. <u>It's</u> a beautiful day.
   its (possessive pronoun): The bird <u>sits</u>, eats <u>its</u> <u>bits</u> of fruit, and sp<u>its</u> out p<u>its</u>.
3. **you're** (contraction): <u>You are</u>.
   your (possessive pronoun): <u>Your</u> has the possessive word, <u>our</u>, in it.
4. **who's** (contraction): <u>Who is</u>.
   whose (interrogative pronoun): <u>Whose</u> <u>hose</u> is this? (Interrogative pronouns ask questions.)

Lesson 5: Tackling Homophones and Words That Get Confused

Objectives: Students will learn that *Memory Tools* truly help for learning and remembering the difference between *Homophones* since Spell Check can't correct these. They'll also learn that English has many homophones since words were added from different places or were pronounced differently at one time. Students will use *Clues* and other *Memory Tools* to remember homophones.

It really gets students' attention to introduce Lesson 5 by giving them *The News Report* where all the incorrectly-used homophones got through *Spell Check* without correction (Lesson 12, p. 3). Students enjoy being *Bionic Spell Checkers* and catching all the funny errors.

   To show that English has homophones from different places and times, write the bold words on the board. Ask what the words mean and write this on the board. Then ask, "Does anyone have an idea where any of these words came from or when they came into English?" (Except for *gnu*, this is difficult.) Tell students that many dictionaries contain this information. Have students look up these words in dictionaries with this info. Finally, ask students to think of *Memory Tools* to remember each word. Write these next to the words. (See *Tool 1: Clues for Homophones and Confusing Words*, *Book of Lists*.)

Homophones: Where They Came From and When

1. **gnu** (antelope): 1770-1780, S. Africa. *SPP*: g-nu
   knew (past of to know): before 900, OE, knawan (know, knew). *SPP*: <u>k</u>-ne-<u>w</u>.
   new (fresh; not used): OE neowe (new). *Clue*: We watched the <u>new</u> <u>dew</u> on the lawn.
2. **capital** (city): 1775, modern American word. *Clue*: <u>T</u>allahassee, Florida is a capital city.
   capital (letters): 1775, modern American word. *Clue*: Our cap<u>it</u>al letters are <u>tall</u>.
   Capitol (from Temple of Jupiter on Capitola Hill in ancient Rome). *Visual*: A <u>Capitol</u> has a d<u>ome</u>.
3. **peace** (no war): 1125–1175, Old French, pais; Latin, pax. *Clue*: <u>Eac</u>h country was at p<u>eac</u>e.
   piece (a serving of an item): 1175–1225, Welsh/English. *Clue*: I want a p<u>ie</u>ce of p<u>ie</u>.
4. **principal** (first in charge): 1250, Latin, principal (first chief). *Clue*: The princi<u>pal</u> was his <u>pal</u>.
   principle (rule; standard): 1350, French, principle (first standard). *Clue*: A princi<u>ple</u> is a ru<u>le</u>.
5. **stationary** (stable): 1400-1450 Latin, statimarius (stays). *Clue*: Something st<u>a</u>tion<u>a</u>ry is st<u>a</u>ble.
   stationery (paper for letters): 1670-1680, Latin. *Clue*: Stationery is for a lett<u>er</u>.

Lesson 6: Phonics Power: The Building Blocks of Spelling

Objectives: Students will learn that Phonics teaches you about the sounds that consonants and vowels in an alphabet make. Also, students will discover that Phonics uses Hearing, Seeing, and Feeling.

Write PHONICS on the board and ask, "Can anyone see part of a word you know in *phonics*?" When you're given *phon*, underline it.. Then ask, "What does this root mean?" As students answer, add *Greek for sound* and *Phonics teaches you about the sounds that letters in an alphabet make*. Then ask, "Which senses does Phonics use?" Explore how Hearing, Seeing, and Feeling are involved in learning a language by asking questions that lead to the ideas in the *Learning Box*. For a reflective discussion, ask students what they think it would be like to live without hearing or seeing, or without both.

PHONICS: Greek for <u>sound</u>. Phonics teaches you about the sounds that the letters in an alphabet make.

HEARING: You *hear* sounds even before you're born. Then you hear words, and speak them. Later, you learn how sounds are spelled so that you can spell words.

SEEING: You *see* the letters of the alphabet. People used to use picture language, and some languages, like Chinese, still use pictures. You can see a person's mouth form letters.

FEELING: You can *feel* letters as they're formed in your mouth. (Lesson 7 covers: *Feeling Phonics*.)

CONSONANTS: Single Sounds, Consonant/Vowels, Digraphs (ch, sh, th, wh, ng (sometimes), zh, Blends.
VOWELS: Long, Short, 2 Special Sounds, R-Controlled Sounds, Schwas.

2nd Idea, Lesson 6: Look at the chart, *Sounds: The Building Blocks of the English Language* with your students. Then ask, "What kinds of letters does English have? As students say, "Consonants and vowels," list the sounds on the chart on the board. Ask students to think of sound words: bark, honk, oink, etc. (onomatopoeia), and write these by the sounds. Try to get a word for each sound.

"TOOT!"

Lesson 7: *Feeling the Sounds of Single Consonants and Digraphs*

Objectives: Students will say and feel the sounds of the consonants and digraphs so they can better identify them for spelling. Students will learn that sound begins with a vibration, and then travels in waves until it hits against the eardrum, and the brain translates it into a sound they can understand.

Begin by saying, "Let's be silent for a minute. Try to detect sounds you hear and write them down." Then ask students what they heard and write their sounds on the board (See below.). Then ask, "How many of you have dropped a stone into a still pond?" Then add, "What happens?" When you get an answer like *circles move out from the center*, say, "Sound waves are similar to these circles."

"Something starts a sound, and it moves out in waves." Ask, "Can you think of ways that sounds start?" If they have trouble, ask, "How about the sounds on the board?" Help students feel the 3 main ways vibrations start: *striking, bowing*, and *blowing*. Then have them think of sounds and figure out if they're *striking, bowing*, or *blowing*. Tell students, " you speak or sing and sound starts. Vibrations move out in waves until they hit the eardrum. The brain translates the vibrations (words, music…) into sound you can hear. Finally, have students say and hear the sounds of consonants and digraphs (pp. 2, 4).

SOUNDS HEARD: clock ticking, horns, other car sounds, bird singing, voices, water, crickets

The Three Main Ways That Sound Occurs:
1. **Something <u>strikes</u> something**: ticking clock, drumstick striking a drum…
2. **Something <u>rubs or bows</u> across something**: A violin bow moves across gut; crickets rub their legs together...
3. **Air <u>blows</u> through something**: Voice: air blows through and across vocal chords; air blows through a flute…

Lesson 8: *Feeling the POWER of the Beat* (See *Tool 4: POWER of the Beat and Syllables, Book of Lists*.)

Objectives: Students will discover that both music and language have beats. They will learn and be able to hear the beat (accent) and mark it in words. They will put some spelling words to a beat. They will also learn a little about students in the class who play instruments, dance, sing.

Begin Lesson 8 by playing some music students like. (Have a few students bring in their favorite music.) Then ask, "Can you feel the rhythm, and beat it out, or move to it." As students start tapping or moving to the music, ask, "What do you call *what* you're feeling?" As they say, "*Rhythm, Beat…*" have them feel it a little longer. Then ask, "Do any of you play an instrument, or dance or sing?" (Have a few students share what they do musically, and during the week include the rest.)

Ask, "What do music and words have in common?" Write their ideas on the board, including: *Music and Words have a Beat* (accent). Then write and say the words in the left half of the *Learning Box*. Ask where the strongest beat falls. Put an accent mark above the beats. Also, point out that letters can be spelled to a *Beat* to words. Ask, "Can someone put the letters in *possession* or *encyclopedia* to a beat?" Then do the same for syllables for *a-rith-me-tic* and *math-e-ma-tics*. Finally, ask student to suggest words and put their letters or syllables to a beat or combine them as in *a-c-c-i-dent-al-ly* and *e-l-ec-tion*.

Music and Words Have a Beat (accent)			POWER of the BEAT		Spell Letters and Say Syllables to a Beat	
mu-sic	drum-mer	gui-tar	Letters:	p-o-s-s e-s-s i-o-n	e-n-c-y-c-l-o-p-e-d-i-a	
har-mon-i-ca	pi-a-no	rhy-thm	Syllables:	a-rith-me-tic	math-e-ma-tics	

Lesson 9: Divide and Conquer: Dividing Words Into Syllables

Objectives: Students will learn eight ways to divide words into syllables. Further, they'll learn that dividing words into syllables helps with spelling because it creates lots of little words they can spell one syllable at a time. Finally they'll see that *dictionaries* show words divided into syllables.

Begin Lesson 9 by writing the bold words on the board. (Don't divide syllables yet.) Then ask, "Are there any ways you can divide these words so that you have smaller words to spell, rather than one long word?" As students give input, divide the words and help them discover *8 Rules for Dividing Words*, one after each set of words. Also, tell students that a *Dictionary* always shows you where to divide words (*Special Lesson 2*: *Aardvarks, Llamas and Other Double Letter Words* is great after this lesson.)

The 8 Rules for Dividing Words into Syllables		
camp-fire	snow-flake:	Divide between Compound Words.
dis-ease	trans-port:	Divide between a Prefix and Root.
cool-ly	shin-ing:	Divide between a Root and Suffix.
har-bor	lit-tle:	Divide between Two Consonants.
am-ber	phon-ics:	Divide after Consonant Following Accented Short Vowel
a-mong	di-vi-sion:	Divide after Single Unaccented Short Vowel.
fi-nal	a-pex:	Divide after Accented Long Vowel.
squig-gle	pud-dle:	Divide right before Consonant + LE.

Lesson 10: Let's Pronounce That Word Correctly (See *Tool 5: Pronunciation POWER* in *Book of Lists*.)

Objectives: Students will again note that before 1400 A.D., all letters in words were pronounced, but this is no longer true. They will then learn *Skills* and *Memory Tools* to conquer the two *Spelling/Pronunciation Problems*: *POWER Pronunciations* for words that get misspelled because they are mispronounced. *Special Phonics Pronunciations* (*SPP's*) for words no longer pronounced as spelled.

(Don't write on board yet.) Begin by asking, "Can anyone explain how words were pronounced before 1400?" As students answer, state that *once* (in Old and Middle English), *every vowel and consonant was pronounced*. Then say, "For pronunciation today, there are two main reasons words get misspelled." Add, "Do you know why?" State, "First, *they're spelled like they're pronounced, but people don't pronounced them correctly*; or second, *the common pronunciation no longer matches the spelling*.

Now say, "I'll pronounce some words two ways, and I want you to write the pronunciation you think is correct. Is the pronunciation *athlete* or *athelete*; *exacly* or *exactly*?" (Mix and say remaining words.) Then ask, "Which word did you spell? Write their spellings on the board.

Next, say, "Now I'm going to say some words that are no longer pronounced like they're spelled, so do your best to spell them (Read the list that begins with diamond.). Then add, "Now I'm going to say a *Special Phonics Pronunciation* (*SPP*) for each word where I pronounce every consonant and vowel like people did in Old English (Say *SPP's* twice). Write spellings students volunteer on the board. Ask if the *SPP's* helped. Also ask, "Does anyone say any words this way for spelling?"

Spelled as Pronounced	Mispronunciation Monster	Common Pronunciation	Special Phonics Pronunciation/Spelliing	
ath-lete	athelete	dimond	di-a-mond	diamond
ex-actl-y	exactly	ervry	e-ver-y	every
jewel-ry	jewelery	ment	me-ant	meant
min-i-a-ture	minature	offen	of-ten	often
pro-bab-ly	probably	restrant	res-ta-u-rant	restaurant
sur-prise	suprise	Wensday	Wed-nes-day	Wednesday

Lesson 11: The POWER of Ancient Roots: Latin and Greek - Our Origin for Over 60,000 Words

Objectives: Students will see that knowing Latin and Greek roots (and some Old English roots) builds spelling power because most roots are *spelled like they're pronounced*. Also, students will see that knowing roots builds vocabulary. (See *Tool 6: POWER of Ancient Roots, Book of Lists*.)

Write bold words on the board. Introduce Lesson 11 by asking students what each root means. Add, "Some words contain two roots: astronaut, photograph. For these, you just add roots together." Then, say "Roots often exist in a *Word Sandwich* with a prefix before the root and a suffix after it." Finally, ask student to think of some words that contain these roots (Write words by each root.).

POWER of ANCIENT ROOTSv

anim (L. alive): animal, inanimate

aqua (L. water): aquarium, **aqualung**

audi (L. hear): audio, auditorium

astro (G. star) + **naut** (G. sailor): = **astronaut**

bio (G.. life) + **logy** (L. study of) = **biology**

magni (L. enlarge): magnify, magnification

ped (L. foot) pedal

thermos (G. warm) thermos, thermal

photo (G. light) + **graph** (G. map) = **photograph**

tele (G. distant) + **phone** (G. sound) = **telephone**

Roots often exist in a **WORD SANDWICH: PREFIX   ROOT   SUFFIX**

Lesson 12: Focusing on Visual POWER

Objectives: Students will learn a way to build Visual Memory. They'll find that the letters in some words look like objects they can draw. They'll also discover unique patterns in words: *Palindromes, Reversals, Anagrams…* Students will see the value of knowing homophones since Spell Check can't check these. They'll also learn that by reading, they *see correctly spelled words* again and again…

Write the bold words on the board. Then take *dinosaur* and *career* and have students do the *Visual Memory Exercise* (p. 1). Say, "Write *dinosaur*. Now, look at *dinosaur*: dino (terrible) + saur (lizard). Also, close your eyes and picture *dinosaur* in your mind. Open your eyes and write *dinosaur* again." Also do this for *career*. Students usually see care in career, which helps with making a clue.

  Then have students find letters that look like objects they can draw in *luggage, brilliant*… Have them create a *Clue-in-a-Row* for *initiate*. Then help them see a reversal in *reward-drawer*; *4 e's in dependence*; all 5 vowels in *sequoia*; and palindromes in *reviver* and *DO GEESE SEE GOD*. (Now, See *Special Lesson 1: Do Geese See God? and other Palindromes*. Also see: *Tool 7: Visual POWER, Book of Lists*.)

Visual POWER

dinosaur: di-no-saur (terrible lizard).

career: *Clue*: See care in career.

luggage: *Visual:* See a sack and 3 bags.

brilliant: *Visual*: See 4 candles: illi

initiate: *Clue-in-a-Row*: In it I ate a lot.

reward: *Reversal*: reward-drawer. My reward's in a drawer.

dependence: *Visual*: See 4 e's.

sequoia: *Visual*: Only word in English with all 5 vowels.

reviver: Word Palindrome.

DO GEESE SEE GOD? Sentence Palindrome.

Lesson 13: Introducing the Copy Cat Kids

Objectives: Students will learn about the single-letter Copy Cat Kids and the letters they copy. Students will also meet the two-letter Copy Cat Kids and the letters they copy. They will review this information each day during the week.

Write the bold letters and words on the board. (Draw a few cats with the letters.). Begin by stating that there are 4 single-letter Copy Cat: *C, G, S*, and *X*, and introduce the cats: *Cisco, Gidget, Susanna,* and *Alex*. Then ask, "What letters do the c's in Cisco copy?" Write *C copies S and K*. Then ask for the letters that the g's in Gidget copy? Write, "*G makes its own sound and copies J*." Do the same for *S* and *X*. Then ask for words with *c, g, s,* and *x*: ask what sounds the letters copy (Add to the board.).

Do this same activity for the 2 letter Copy Cat Kids. Review the Copy Cat Kid sounds all week.

Single-Letter Copy Cat Kids	Two-Letter Copy Cat Kids
C: <u>C</u>is<u>c</u>o (copies K and S): <u>c</u>o<u>c</u>oon, <u>c</u>y<u>c</u>le, <u>c</u>ity	**CH** – **<u>Ch</u>risty** (copies K and SH): <u>ch</u>ord, <u>ch</u>ef
G: **<u>G</u>idget** (makes G sound, copies J): <u>g</u>oes, <u>g</u>ym, <u>g</u>em	**GH** – **Rou<u>gh</u>y** (copies F): tou<u>gh</u>, lau<u>gh</u>
S: **<u>S</u>u<u>s</u>anna** (makes S sound, copies Z): <u>s</u>ings, <u>s</u>ong<u>s</u>	**PH** – **Kristo<u>ph</u>** (copies F): <u>ph</u>one, <u>ph</u>antom
X: **Ale<u>x</u>** (copies KS and Z): e<u>x</u>cel, bo<u>x</u>, <u>x</u>ylophone	**QU** – **Ra<u>qu</u>el** (copies K and KW): <u>qu</u>een, <u>qu</u>ay

Lesson 14: Let's Grasp and Learn Those Consonant Blends (See *Tool 2, Lists of Blends, Book of Lists*.)
Objectives: Students will review all the separate sounds consonants make. They'll learn to carefully say *Beginning* and *Ending Consonant Blends* to hear each letter. They'll think of words for each blend.

Write the bold words on the board. Then state, "These are *all the <u>separate sounds</u> consonants make*."
(OPTIONAL: If you want more detail, ask questions to bring out the non-bold information and add it.)

All The Single Sounds Consonants Make

17 Single Consonant: (B, D, F, G, H, J, K, L, M, N, P, Qu (works like a single consonants), R, S, T, V, X, Z

2 Consonants/Vowels: W and Y

5 Digraph Sounds: Two-letters make one sound: CH, SH, TH (with air), TH (without air) WH

2 Special Sounds: NG (digraph: sing; sometimes two sounds: e<u>ng</u>ine);   ZH: azure, treasure

4 One-Letter Copy Cats: <u>C</u>is<u>c</u>o copies K, S; <u>G</u>idget-G sound, copies J; <u>S</u>u<u>s</u>anna-S sound, copies Z; Ale<u>x</u> copies KS, Z

4 Two-Letter Copy Cats: <u>Ch</u>risty copies K, S; Rou<u>gh</u>y copies F; Kristo<u>ph</u> copies F; Ra<u>qu</u>el copies K, KW

Beginning and Ending Blends: Blends are not single sounds. Each letter has its *own sound* and also *blends with other*

Now ask, "What are *Blends*?" Help students see that *Blends are not separate sounds.* Stress, "*Blends* need to be carefully pronounced so you can hear each letter." List the *Beginning* and *Final Blends* on the board (lesson, p. 1). Ask students for words with *Blend*s and add these to the board. Share that to find words for *Beginning Blends*, you just look under the letters in a dictionary. For *Ending Blends*, rhyme words. Finally, ask students to choose a *Beginning Blend* and make a tongue twister, or take a *Final Blend* and create a rhyme. Ask them to share these. (Lesson 14 has 2 POWER Spelling games.)

Lesson 15: Focusing on Silent Letters
Objectives: Students will learn to spot and hear *Silent Letters* in words and to use *Special Phonics Pronunciations (SPP's), Other Word Forms, Clues,* and other *Tools* to retain these words. Students will understand three reasons why English has silent letters.

Write bold words on the board. Ask, "Who can detect a *Silent Letter* in one of these words?" As students give answers, <u>underline</u> the *Silent Letters*. Then ask, "Who can think of a *Memory Tool* to remember one of these words?" On the board, write the *SPP's, OWF's, Clues, etc.,* that students create, and be sure to affirm them. (Some ideas are below.)

CLUES and MEMORY TOOLS for SILENT LETTER WORDS

thumb: *OWF*: <u>Thumb</u>elina was no bigger than a <u>thumb</u>.

sign: *SPP*: sig-<u>n</u>. *OWF*: We watched for a <u>sign</u> or <u>sign</u>al.

ghost: *SPP*: g-host. *Clue*: A <u>g</u>-host was our <u>host</u>.

knife: *SPP*: <u>k</u>-ni-<u>fe</u>. *Clue*: A good <u>knife</u> lasts for <u>life</u>.

calf: *Clue*: My <u>calf</u> was h<u>alf</u> the size of its mother.

column: *OWF*: The <u>column</u>ist wrote a <u>column</u>.

could: *SPP*: cou-l-d. *Same Pattern*: would, should.

raspberry: *SPP*: rasp-berry. *Clue*: ...rough as a <u>rasp</u>.

castle: *Clue*: The <u>cast</u>le <u>cast</u> lengths of reflection.

answered: *Clue*: <u>Were</u> your questions answe<u>red</u>?

island: *Clue*: There <u>is land</u> on an <u>island</u>.

whistle: *OWF*: We were <u>whist</u>ling with <u>whist</u>les.

Lesson 16: I've Got Those Syllables! Got That POWER Beat
Objectives: Students will learn about the 6 kinds of syllables found in words. Students will see that these 6 syllables are like the different ways vowels work: *Open Syllables; Closed Syllables; Silent E Syllables; Two-Vowel Syllables; R-Controlled Syllables; Consonant + LE Syllables.*

Write the bold words on the board. Then ask students, "Does anyone see a pattern that any of these groups of words follow?" As students give answers, write information across from each group of words. Tell students that most of the syllables in English words fall into the six categories below. Finally, help students identify the syllables in the words on the last page of the lesson which include:

red	yel - low	blue	green	white	pur - ple
closed	closed vv	vv	vv	silent e	r. syl. cle syl.

THE KINDS of SYLLABLES FOUND in WORDS in ENGLISH

1. **ta-ble, e-qual, ti-ger, mo-bile, mu-sic, a-like, di-vide**   OPEN SYLLABLES: always end in a vowel.
2. **ant, egg, pin, frog, sun**   CLOSED SYLLABLES: end in consonant(s); has a short vowel.
3. **face, these, kite, rose, flute**   SILENT E SYLLABLES: always end in Silent E.
4. **rain, peach, pie, boat, fruit**   TWO VOWELS SYLLABLES: always have two vowels together.
5. **star, fern, bird, fork, turn**   R-CONTROLLED SYLLABLE: R controls the vowel before it.
6. **pic-kle, pur-ple, squig-gle**   CONSONANT + LE SYLLABLES: always have C + LE.

Lesson 17: Discovering How Short Vowels Work (See *Tool 2: Phonics: Short Vowel Sounds, Book of Lists*)
Objectives: Students will experience how it sounds and feels to make each of the five short vowel sounds. Students will also learn how short vowels work and be able to write a rule for short vowels.

Write the rhyming phrases below on the board. Introduce Lesson 17 by having students read the lines on the board. Then ask, "Which words have short vowels?" Underline the words as students say them. (Note: *All* the words have short vowels. If students don't notice, point this out.) Then, ask, "What do all these words have in common?" Some of the answers you'll probably get are: *They all have short vowels. They all end with one or more consonants. They're all Closed Syllables.*

SHORT VOWEL SOUNDS

A	Cat with hat is up at bat.	A	Scram, Clam, you swam on Pam.
E	Sled on Fred, bed on Ted.	E	Red sled on Fred and Ted.
I	Pig with wig did a jig.	I	The ship felt the tip and the rip on *that* trip.
O	Hog with frog on dog on a log.	O	Frog on dog in fog on a log.
U	Hum and strum and drum that drum.	U	Hug a bug in a rug. (The ship *that* trip = Titanic)

Now write: **A SINGLE VOWEL STAYS SHORT** – and ask, "Who can complete this sentence and make a *Short Vowel Rule*?" Help students write a *Rule* like the one below. (Leave on board for the week.)

SHORT VOWEL RULE
A SINGLE VOWEL STAYS SHORT – WHEN IT IS FOLLOWED BY ONE OR MORE CONSONANTS WITHOUT A VOWEL COMING RIGHT AFTER THE 1st CONSONANT (V + C) and (V + CC)

Another way to introduce Lesson 17 is to play the *Sun Game* on the 2nd page of this lesson.

Lesson 18: Long Vowel Sounds and the Powerful Silent E *(Tool 2: Long Vowels with Silent E, Book of Lists)*
Objectives: Students will experience how long vowels make their sounds. They'll also understand how the powerful *Silent E* makes vowels long, and they'll learn some exceptions to the *Silent E Rule*.

Introduce Lesson 18 by helping students create the long vowel sounds (page 1). Then write the bold letters and words on the board. Ask, "What do you notice about these words?" They'll note the short vowels. Then ask, "Who can turn a word into a long vowel word?" Add their answers.

CHANGE SHORT VOWELS TO LONG VOWEL WITH SILENT E				
A	**glad**	glade	**stag**	stage
E	**met**	meet, mete (measure out)	**them**	theme
I	**kit**	kite	**slid**	slide
O	**hop**	hope	**rob**	robe
U	**hug**	huge	**us**	use

To make the point that silent e͟ makes the vowel before it say its name, have students come to the board and change the *silent e͟* in each word into a *person making the vowel before it say its name.*

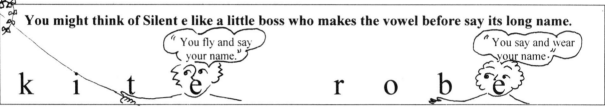

Later in the week, go over the *Silent E͟ Exceptions* on the last page. Point out that since no English word ends in v͟, silent e͟ just ends some -ve words rather than making the vowel before it long. <u>2nd Idea</u>: Begin Lesson 18 by playing the *Star Game* (page 2 in lesson).

Lesson 19: When Two Vowels Go Walking, the First One Does the Talking (and Says Its Name)
Objectives: Students will learn that often: *When Two Vowels Go Walking, The First One Does The Talking*. Students will also learn *Exceptions to the Two Vowel Rule* and ways to remember these.

Write bold words on the board. Then ask, "What do these words have in common?" Answers you may get are: *Each word has 2 vowels. The 2nd vowel's silent and makes the 1st vowel say its name...* Explain the *Rule* below, and ask for words where the 2nd vowel makes the 1st vowel long. Then for

LONG VOWEL DIGRAPH (2 Letters) RULE		
When Two Vowels Go Walking, the First One Does the Talking		
A	maid	nail
E	meal	beep
I	pie	cries
O	coat	blow
U	glue	cue

each word above, have students draw the 1st vowel saying its name while the 2nd vowel's silent. Later in the week, go over the exceptions (pp. 3-4 of lesson). See *Tool 2: Long Vowel Digraphs, Book of Lists.*

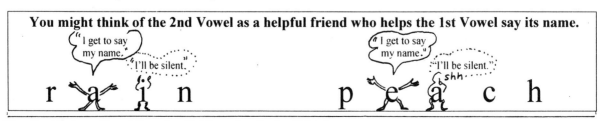

(See *Tool 2: Long Vowel Sounds with Digraphs, Book of Lists.*)

Lesson 20: The Rules and Pattern for the EI/IE Words (See *Tool 2: Phonics: IE/EI Sounds, Book of Lists*.)

Objectives: Students will clearly understand the *IE/EI Rule* and its exceptions. They'll use *Clues* and other *Tools* to learn and remember some challenging EI/IE words. (*Tool 4: Rules: IE/EI Scramble, Book of Lists*.)

Introduce Lesson 20 by asking, "Does anyone know the *I before E Rule*?" As someone says it, write out the bold words below, leaving room for the remaining words. Then ask, "Who can explain this *Rule* or give examples of words that fit each part?" Write down correct information and the words that students give. Then tell students that there are two points that are always true about the EI/IE Rule (Ask if anyone knows them.). Point out: Part 3 has no exceptions, and for Part 2, the spelling is always ei when c copies the s sound. When *c* makes the *sh* sound (as in *ancient* or *conscience*), the spelling is ie (Add Part 2 and 3 to the board.). Finally, add Part 1, and tell students, "Many words follow this part, but there are also exceptions." Add, "*Clues* will truly help with these. To conclude, have students use *Clues* and Other *Tools* to remember EI/IE words (pp. 3-4 of this lesson).

EI/IE RULE

Part 1: **I before e**
Many Words Follow this Rule: believe, chief, field, friend, niece, piece…
Some Exceptions: either, neither, foreign, height, leisure, weird…

Part 2: **Except after c (EI after C Sound)**: No Exceptions
Spelling is ALWAYS ei when c copies s: ceiling, conceit, deceit, receipt…
Exceptions: When c makes sh sound

Part 3: **Or when sounded as a - as in neighbor or weigh**: No Exceptions
eight, freight, sleigh, vein, weight…

Lesson 21: The Special Two-Vowel Combinations and Sounds

Objectives: Students will learn the *Special Two-Vowel Combinations* and be able to think of five or more words that make each sound. Students will increase their ability to identify, spell, and remember words with these sounds when they hear them. (*See Tool 2: Special Two-Vowel Sounds, Book of Lists*)

First, create the *Learning Box* on the board. To introduce Lesson 21 to students, say, "Let's play the LAUNCH INTO THE VOWEL POOL GAME." Read the game (1st page) with students so they'll understand it. Then have students work alone or with a partner for 5-10 minutes to put together some words. Finally, have students volunteer words, trying to include everyone. Write the word under its 2-Letter Vowel Sound: au and aw; oi and oy; ou and ow; ew; oo (moon) and oo (book).

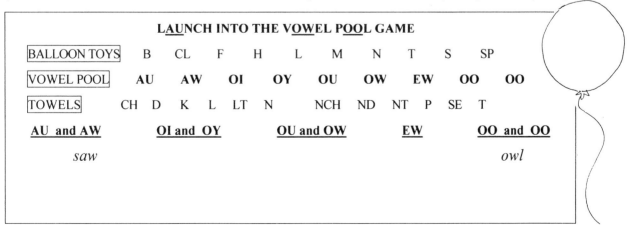

LAUNCH INTO THE VOWEL POOL GAME

BALLOON TOYS	B	CL	F	H	L	M	N	T	S	SP
VOWEL POOL	**AU**	**AW**	**OI**	**OY**	**OU**	**OW**	**EW**	**OO**	**OO**
TOWELS	CH	D	K	L	LT	N		NCH	ND	NT	P	SE	T

| **AU and AW** | **OI and OY** | **OU and OW** | **EW** | **OO   and   OO** |
| *saw* | | | | *owl* |

Another way to introduce Lesson 21 is to have students write lines using the words on pages 2 and 3 in the lesson. Then have them share their lines as you write them next to their Special Vowel Sound.

Lesson 22: *The Powerful R Can Control Any Vowel* (*Tool 2: R-Controlled Vowel Sounds, Book of Lists*)
Objectives: Students will learn how *Powerful R* affects vowel sounds. They will discover that in words like <u>fore</u>, <u>horse</u>, <u>more</u>, <u>there</u> and <u>where</u>, that when <u>R</u> is added, it is so powerful that Silent <u>E</u> loses its power to make the vowel before its long. They will also see that <u>R</u> can take words: <u>hail</u>, <u>pain</u> and <u>peal</u>, where two vowels make a long sounds, and remove the long sound: <u>hair</u>, <u>pair</u>, <u>pear</u>.

Write the bold and italicized words on the board (Draw a few Power R's). Begin this lesson by slowly reading the *Dinosaur R-Article*, pausing so that students can underline words and syllables where <u>R</u> follows a vowel. Then ask, "What did you notice about *R-Words*?" Write their ideas on the board.

   Then say, "Let's look at how <u>R</u> affects vowels." Ask a student to pick any word on the board and say it without <u>R</u>. Then have the student add <u>R</u> and say the new <u>R</u>-Word (as you write the new word below the word). Finally, ask how <u>R</u> affected the words. (*Tool 2, R-Article: Art of Musical Storytelling, Book of Lists*)

HOW POWERFUL R AFFECTS VOWELS

Short Vowels (*Put R after a single short vowel.*)

am	**bid**	**spot**	**bun**	**ham**	**gem**	**skit**	**con**	**spun**	**pa**	**ma**	**fa**
arm	*bird*	*sport*	*burn*	*harm*	*germ*	*skirt*	*corn*	*spurn*	*par*	*mar*	*far*

Long Vowels Together (*Put R after the 2 Vowels.*)

pea	**peal**	**tea**	**bee**	**he**	**sou** (ancient Chinese coin)
pear	*pearl*	*tear*	*beer*	*her*	*sour*

Long Vowels Together (*Put R between two vowels.*)   Note: With R, Silent <u>E</u> can't make the vowels long.

hee	**thee**	**whee**	**foe**	**hose**	**nose**	**cue**	**Sue**
here	*there*	*where*	*fore*	*horse*	*Norse*	*cure*	*sure*

Another way to introduce Lesson 22 is to play *Elevator Loader* on page 2 of this lesson.

Lesson 23: *Discovering How Open Syllables Work and What's a Schwa*
Objectives: Students will discover that *Open Syllables* ALWAYS end in a vowel. They will also find that knowing about open syllables helps with spelling because you can hear where one syllable ends and the next begins. This helps prevent double-letter errors. Finally, students will learn about *Schwas*, and join the unique few who know what *schwas* are. (*Tool 2: Phonics: Open Syllable Words, Book of Lists*)

Write the bold words on the board. Introduce Lesson 23 by asking, "Who can give an example of an *Open Syllable*?" (Write their words on the board.) Also, point out that <u>o-pen</u> is an open syllable. Then help students discover that *all the vowel have Long Vowel Open Syllables*, while *only 2 vowels* (a, i) *have Short Vowel Open Syllables*. Have students help label the open syllables below: L (long) and S (short).

   Then turn to the *List of Open Syllables Words* at the end of this lesson. Have students read some of the words and underline the open syllables. Note: Since open syllables NEVER end in a consonant, they are NEVER followed by double consonants. State that this is extremely important to spelling.

   Finally, introduce schwas on the first page of this lesson. Have fun with these upside down <u>e's</u>.

OPEN SYLLABLE WORDS

LONG/SHORT	LONG	LONG/SHORT	LONG	LONG
a	**e – go**	**I**	**cel – lo**	**ac – tu – al**
a – mong	**e – qual**	**cri – sis**	**go**	**Cu – pid**
ha – rass	**he – ro**	**di – vide**	**ho – tel**	**men – u**
ma – trix	**re – a – lize**	**im – i – tate**	**o – pen**	**u – nit**
ta – ble	**wle**	**pi – a – no**	**po – em**	**Y: my**

Lesson 24: Let's Try All the Vowel Sounds

Objectives: Students will name objects in a room and write each word by its vowel sound (out of 25 vowel sounds). Students will observe many different ways that vowel sounds in English can be spelled.

First, list all the vowel sounds in the *Learning Box* on the board (2ⁿᵈ page of Lesson 24 is the *Learning Box*.). Then, introduce Lesson 24 by using the fun activity: *What Do You See Inside and Outside This Room?* Ask students to look around and name things they see in the classroom and outside. As students name things (d<u>e</u>sk, b<u>oa</u>rd, win<u>do</u>w…), ask them to match the word to its vowel sound (*desk-<u>e</u> in egg; board-<u>or</u> in horn; win-i in pin; dow-<u>ow</u> in bow*). Try going around the class, having everyone name things. Then ask students to look at drawing of the room in the lesson, and to name objects and write them next to their vowel sound. Add that it's also okay to imagine things outside this room.

Later in the week, read together: *The Many Ways the English Language Spells Its Sounds*.

Lesson 25: The Solid Compound Word Rule *(Compound Words that are one solid word)*

Objectives: Students will learn that for hundreds of *Solid Compound Words*, all they need to do is add two words together. They will learn the few exceptions to this *Solid Compound Word Rule* and use *Clues* and other *Tools* to remember these.

First, create the top section of the *Learning Box* on the board. Then, ask students, "How do you think these Compound Words were created, and why are the dates so different?" Simply let students explore their ideas: *Someone said my head aches and simply put the words together and made <u>headache</u>. People stored cups on a board and decided to call it a: <u>cupboard</u>. Sports words, like <u>basketball</u>, were added later.* During the Space Age, inventors decided to call their space-travel machine a spaceship (Why not a *spaceplane*?). *Today, we have new words like database and Internet.*

Share that English has more Compound Words than any other language, and that a lot of these were created in America. Ask students why they think this happened. Also, ask their thoughts about some of the dates that words came into English. Finally, ask student to think of other Compound Words and look up their origin (*baseball, raspberry, etc.*).

Now, ask, "What's the *Rule for a Compound Word*?" Just state that you simply bring two words together without making any changes. Finally, say, "There are just a few exceptions to this rule. Can you think of any?" Help them think of the exceptions in the lower part of the *Learning Box*: shepherd, awful, pastime, until, welcome… Ask, "What letters have been left out?" Help your students think of ways to remember these: An <u>l</u> has been dropped from: *full, well,* and *till; Alphabet* and *shepherd* are spelled as pronounced; A *Clue-in-a-Row* for *pastime*: <u>Pa's time</u> is for his <u>pastime</u>…

SOLID COMPOUND WORDS
Just Add Two Words Together
(Origin and Date When Some Words Came into English)

basketball (America, 1890)	**lamplighter** (Eng., Amer., 1740)
bodysurfer (America, 1940)	**lighthouse** (Amer. 1655; Egypt 283 B.C.)
cupboard (ME, 1275)	**newsstand** (America 1870)
cupcake (America, 1820)	**spaceship** (America 1940)
headache (OE, before 1000)	**sunset** (ME 1350)
heavyweight (Amer., 1850)	**windmill** (ME 1250)

SOLID COMPOUND WORD EXCEPTIONS

shepherd (sheep + herd): Spelled as pronounced.	**alphabet** (alpha + beta): Spelled as pronounced.
awful (awe + full): Is something <u>awful</u> <u>lawful</u>?	**careful** (care + full): <u>One l</u>.
pastime (past + time): <u>Pa's time</u> is for his <u>pastime</u>.	**until** (un + till): <u>One l</u>.
welcome, welfare (well + come; well + fare): <u>One l</u>.	**wherever** (where + ever): <u>Here</u> or <u>wherever</u>.

Lesson 26: Learning About Prefixes - Just Fasten Them in Front

Objectives: Students will see that prefixes change or add to the meaning of a word, and that words with prefixes are easy to spell because you simply fasten the prefix in front of the word and spell the prefix and then the word. Students will also learn the meaning, of some common prefixes and create words by adding them to roots.

Introduce Lesson 26 by first writing PREFIX on the board. Then, ask, "What does prefix mean?" As you get answers: *fix before, put before*, write these next to PREFIX. Then ask, "How are prefixes helpful to a language?" Let students explore their thoughts. Let them know that English uses prefixes more than any language. Also, ask, "What's the rule for adding a prefix to a word?"

Next, write the five bold prefixes on the board. Then ask students to give you words that go under these prefixes. Have them spell the prefix and then the word. List words under the prefixes:

PREFIX – prae (L. before) + **fixus** (L. fasten)

(Simply *fix or fasten* a prefix *before* a word. Don't add any letters and don't remove any letters)

dis- (not)	**mis-** (wrong)	**pre-** (before)	**re-** (again)	**un-** (not)
disagree	mistake	prescribe	reclaim	unnatural
disease	misspell	prevent	reread	unfair
discuss	mistreat	preview	return	uncover

Finally, ask students to look up a few of these prefixes in an Unabridged Dictionary and see the long lists of words that use these prefixes. (*Tool 6: POWER of Ancient Roots, Same Prefix Patterns, Book of Lists*)

Lesson 27: Three Prefixes That Have Different Forms: In-, ad-, and com-

Objectives: Students will see that these prefixes: in-, ad-, com- (and also -ex) follow the *Prefix Rule* just like other prefixes. These prefixes simply have different forms they use, depending on the first letter of the root. Students will also review 2 pages of common prefixes and some words that use them.

First, write the bold words on the board. Then read pages 1-2 of Lesson 27 with your students. Then ask them to give you words with these prefixes. Write these on the board. Point out that *most of these words have a double consonant because the prefix matches the letter with which the root begins*. These words fit the: *One + One Rule*. Finally, help students learn the difference between **im**migrate and **e**migrate.

THREE PREFIXES THAT HAVE DIFFERENT FORMS (plus ex-)

in- (not, in, into): **illegal**   **immature**   **immigrate**   **inactive**   **irregular**

ad- (to or toward): **absent**   **accident**   **acquire**   **allot**   **annual**   **appear**   **arrange**   **assistant**   **attend**

com- (together or with):   **collect**   **commune**   **compete**   **connect**   **correct**

ex- (out or away from):   **extra**   **excited**   **emigrate**

emigrate = <u>e</u> (L. prefix: from) + <u>migrate</u> (L. root: move) = <u>emigrate</u> (When you *emigrate*, you *exit* a country.)

immigrate = <u>im</u> (L. pre: in; into) + <u>migrate</u> (L. root: move) = <u>immigrate</u> (When you *immigrate*, you go *into* a country.)

Lesson 28: *Magical Suffixes: Just Add Them at the End*

Objectives: Students will learn that suffixes have a magical quality! When they're added to the end of a word, they can change the word into another part of speech; make the word singular or plural; past, present, or future; or show comparison. (*See Tool 6: Roots, Words with the Same Suffix Patterns, Book of Lists*)

Write bold words in the *Learning Box* on the board. Begin Lesson 28 by asking students, "What does a prefix do?" Write their answers on the board. Then, ask, "What does a suffix do?" Again write their answers. Establish that what is special about suffixes is that they can turn a word into a noun, verb, adjective, or adverb. Ask students to try this for the word, *cheer*, using the suffixes below. Then have them do this for the rest of the words on the board. Point out to students that *people who have spoken English all their life can add suffixes very naturally.* Then encourage them to suggest other words to try. Note that some words can be 4 parts of speech, while others can't.

	NOUNS dom, ment, ness, tion, er, s The _____	VERB er, or ed, ing, s I _____	ADJECTIVE able, al, ful, less, ly, ness A ____ person	ADVERBS ly. I worked _____
cheer:	*cheer, cheerfulness*	*cheers, cheered, cheering*	*cheerful*	*cheerfully*
care:	*carelessness*	*cares, cared, caring*	*careful*	*carefully*
comfort:	*comforter*	*comforts, comforted*	*comfortable*	*comfortably*
great:	*greatness*		*great*	*greatly*
play:	*play, player*	*plays, played*	*playful*	*playfully*
love:	*love*	*loves, loved*	*lovely, loving*	*lovingly*

PREFIX: Added before a word to changes its meaning; simply add the prefix; don't change the words.

SUFFIX: Added after a word to change word into a noun, verb, adjective, or adverb; just add it, unless word ends in <u>e</u> or <u>y</u>.

Lesson 29: *The Rule for Adding Suffixes After Silent E*

Objectives: Students will learn and use the *Silent E Rule*, understanding how it works before consonants and vowels. They will also learn how the *Exceptions* work and use *Memory Tools* to retain these.

Write bold words on the board. (Draw a few <u>e</u>-people.) Begin by asking students to complete the 2 sentences for Consonants and Vowels. Then have them add ending to the *Silent <u>E</u> Words* on pages 1-2 of the lesson.

THE FINAL SILENT E RULE

When a CONSONANT comes before Silent E:
    Keep E before suffixes that begins with a consonant: amusement, excitement, likeness, lovely…
    Drop E before a suffix that begins with a vowel: amusing, excitable, lovable, pleasure, writing…

When a VOWEL comes before Silent E: Keep E before all suffixes: canoeing, freer, happiest, hoeing, seeing…

Finally, go over the *Exceptions*. Leave the information on the board and review it during the week. Also, go over a few *Clues* each day and review the other ones so students will truly learn this rule.

THE FINAL SILENT E RULE EXCEPTIONS

<u>CE</u> and <u>GE</u> Words keep E before <u>a</u> and <u>o</u> to keep C and G soft: *noticeable, courageous, marriageable, outrageous*

A few Words change <u>IE</u> to <u>Y</u> before **-ing**: *dying, lying, tying, prying, vying*. These words end with **<u>YING</u>**.

<u>UE</u> words drop <u>E</u> before both consonant and vowels: *argument, bluish, duly, rescuing, truly…*

Some Exceptions that <u>drop E</u> before a consonant: *argument, awful, doubly, judgment, ninth, possibly, twelfth, wholly*

Lesson 30: The Rule for Adding Suffixes After a Final Y

Objectives: Students will learn and use the *Final Y Rule*. They'll learn some *Exceptions* and use *Memory Tools* to retain these. Finally, they'll meet and remember *Ying* for -ing words.

Write the bold words on the board. (Draw y-people around it.) Ask, "Can anyone complete the sentences for the *Final Y Rule*. Write this on the board. Then say, "Meet Ying!" Note clearly that Y ALWAYS stays before -ING. Ask students for words where Y is preceded by a consonant. Add these on the board. Ask for words where Y is preceded by a vowel. Also add these. Review this info all week.

THE FINAL Y RULE

When a CONSONANT comes before Final Y,
   Change the y to i before all endings: *carried, busier, business, happiness, hurried, readiness*
   -except for those beginning with -ing: Y and ING stick together to create **YING**: *busying, carrying*
When a VOWEL comes before Final Y,
   Keep the y: *buyer, buying; stayed, staying; enjoyed, enjoying*

Discuss the *Y Rule Exceptions* and write examples of these. (Leave this information on the board all week.)

THE FINAL Y RULE EXCEPTIONS

Y words preceded by a consonant that keep Y when a suffix is added that begins with a consonant: *busyness* (act of Being busy), *babyhood, crybaby, ladybug, ladyship, shyly*
AY words that change Y to I before a consonant: *daily, laid, paid, said*

Lesson 31: Discovering How Suffixes Create Nouns

Objectives: Students will learn the different ways suffixes can turn a root into a noun, verb, adjective and/or adverb. Students will then look at the many suffixes that can be used to build nouns.

Write the bold words in the *Learning Box* on the board. Begin by asking students to use the suffixes and patterns below to turn the words on the board into nouns, verbs, adjective and adverbs. Give students 5-10 minutes and challenge them to see how many words they can create. Then write the words they share on the board. Also, ask students to suggest their own words and see what parts of speech these words can become. (Leave the *Learning Box* on the board for the week.)
Finally, read the pages in the lesson with students where *Noun Suffixes* turn words into nouns.

	NOUNS -dom, -ness -ion, -ity, -er, -or The_____	VERB -ed, -ing, -s I _____.	ADJECTIVE -ful, -less -ive, -ly, -er, -est The _____ person	ADVERBS -ly I worked _____.
act	*action, activity, actor*	*acts, acted, acting*	*active*	*actively*
free	*freedom*	*frees, freed, freeing*	*free, freer, freest*	*freely*
live	*life, liveliness*	*lives, lives, living*	*lively*	*lively*
play	*playfulness*	*played, plays, playing*	*playful*	*playfully*
rest	*restfulness*	*rested, rests, resting*	*rested, restless*	*restfully, restlessly*
thought	*thoughtfulness*	*think, thought*	*thoughtful, thoughtless*	*thoughtfully, thoughtlessly*

(Also, see *Tool 6: Roots: Word Building with Prefix, Root, and Suffix Blocks, Book of Lists*.)

Lesson 32: Suffixes Create Adjectives, Verbs, and Adverbs

Objectives: Students will learn and review the different ways suffixes can turn roots into nouns, verbs, adjectives and adverbs. Students will use suffixes to create nouns, verbs, adjectives and adverbs.

Write the bold words in the *Learning Box* on the board. Introduce Lesson 32 by asking students to use suffixes to turn the nouns below into *adjectives, verbs*, and *adverbs* by using the pattern under each part of speech. Challenge students to see how many words they can create. Then write their words on the board. Also, ask students to suggest their own words. Then have them see what parts of speech they can turn these words into with suffixes. Finally, read the pages with students where suffixes turn words into Adjectives, Verbs, and Adverbs.

It's fun to follow this activity with *Word Building with Magical Suffixes, Tool 6: Roots, Book of Lists*.

NOUN	ADJECTIVE	VERB	ADVERB
The _____	The _____ person	I ____ you _____	We worked _____
beauty	beautiful	beautify, beautified	beautifully
determination	determined	determine…	determinedly
happiness	happy		happily
help, helpfulness	helpful	helps, helped	helpfully
hope, hopefulness	hopeful	hopes	hopefully

Lesson 33: The Doubling Final Consonants Rule (for One-Syllable and Two-Syllable Words)

Objectives: Students will learn that the *Doubling Final Consonants Rule* is very powerful because this rule ALWAYS works, except for 2 words: *excellent* and *excellence*. Students will practice these two rules until they have clearly learned them; including knowing how the beat works in the *Doubling Rule for Two-Syllable Words*. Also, students will be introduced to the *Inserted K Rule*.

First, write the two Rules on the board (bold words). Then introduce Lesson 33 by telling students that the Doubling Final Consonants Rule is very powerful because it ALWAYS works (except for *excellent* and *excellence*). Add that these rules are quite easy to learn, and they cover many words. Review this rule all week. Have students discover more and more words that fit the rules.

The Doubling Final Consonants Rule (for One-Syllable and Two-Syllable Words)

Doubling Rule for One-Syllable Words
  If a word has one syllable:
  If a word ends in a single consonant: fan, swim, hop, run, star
  If a single vowel comes before the consonant:
DOUBLE the final consonant before a vowel suffix: fanning, swimming, hopping, running, starred

Doubling Rule for Two-Syllable Words
  If a word has more than one syllable:
  If a word ends in a single consonant: allot, begin, occur, refer
  If a single vowel comes before the consonant:
  If, when you pronounce the completed word, the accent falls on the last syllable of the original word, then
DOUBLE the final consonant before a vowel suffix: allotted, beginning, occurred, referred

Word that Don't Double the Consonant: difference, glistening, hoped, signaled, stared, traveled

Inserted K Rule
Words that <u>end in hard c (k sound)</u> insert <u>k</u> before suffixes that begins with <u>e, i, or y</u> to <u>keep the k sound</u>
frolic-frolicked; panic-panicky; picnic-picnicking…

Lesson 34: Suffixes Make Nouns Plural in Many Ways

Objectives: Students will discover different categories for making words plural by learning how plurals were formed in Old English and in some different cultures: Italian, Spanish, Algonquin Indian, French, and Latin. They will use *Clues* and *Other Tools* to remember challenging plurals.

Introduce Lesson 34 by simply asking students, "What do you know about plurals?" As students give answers, write down the 2 headings and 8 categories below (bold letters), and sort the plurals into these. These eight categories cover all the plurals. Since the first group (*-oes* and *-os*) are so challenging, emphasize that many *-os* words are Italian Musical Words (or can in some way be connected with music): *altos, sopranos, contraltos, cellos, pianos, solos, banjos, videos, studios, stereos.* Also: *avocados, Eskimos, hellos, ponchos.* Help students use *Clues* and other *Memory Tools* to learn these words. Finally, *The Lists of Collective Nouns* at the lesson's end is lots of fun to read.

BASIC PLURALS FOR NOUNS - just add S: *dogs, cats, horses, penguins*

SPECIAL PLURALS FOR NOUNS - 8 MAIN FORMS:

1. **-OES** (nouns end in o): *buffaloes, canoes, echoes, heroes, mosquitoes, potatoes, tomatoes, tornadoes, volcanoes*
   -OS (incl. Ital. musical pls): *altos, sopranos, cellos, pianos, solos, videos, studios, stereos*

2. **-FS** (Old Eng): *beliefs, cliffs, dwarfs, roofs*
   -VES: *calves, halves, knives, loaves, wives*

3. **-IES** (Fr. and Lat.): *babies, cities, families, ponies*
   -YES: *journeys, keys, turkeys, valleys*

4. **-ES** (Nouns ending in ch, s, sh, x, or z): *benches, boxes, bushes, catches, dishes, losses, passes, taxes, watches*

5. **Irregular Nouns** (Old Eng. before 900, and Lat. and Gr.): *children, feet, men, mice, teeth, women, crises, hypotheses*

6. **Nouns that Stay the Same in Singular and Plural**: *bear, cattle, chicken, deer, fish, milk, moose, sheep*

7. **Compound Words**: *buttercups, lamplighters, snowflakes, roller coasters, mothers-in-law, passers-by, vice-presidents*

8. **Numbers, Letters, Signs**: *100's, 6's, ABC's, m's, s's, t's, x's*

Lesson 35: The Challenging L Endings: -al, -el, -le, -il, and -ol

Objectives: Students will discover special ways to detect if the spelling for an ending is *-al, -el, -le, -il* or *-ol*. Students will learn *Clues, Other Word Forms, SPP's, etc.* to retain these endings.

Begin by saying, "Write these 12 words as I read them: *bridal, Capitol* (bldg.), *civil, council*(group), *counsel* (help), *jewel, nickel, parcel, tickle, total, towel, triangle.* After students write the words, put the correct spelling on the board. Then ask, "What *Memory Tools* can help you remember these words?"Tools that work are: *Clues, Other Word Forms* (you can hear *al, el, le, il, ol*), and *Special Phonics Pronunciations* (*SPP's*). Help students create and learn these *Memory Tools* (See lesson).

-AL: Note that -AL means concerning. Point out that *-ly* can be added to all AL words (except *bridal*).

-EL: Share that names like *Del, Mel, Nel, Vel* can be used for EL *Clues*. Note that -elle was once added to some words: *chapel, parcel, satchel, trowel, vessel...* to mean *small*. Think of an *elf* using these small things.

-IL: State that there are only 5 -IL words: *civil, council, evil, pencil* and *stencil*.

-OL: Add there are just a few -OL words like *capitol, symbol*.

-LE: Finally, note that the rest of the words end in Consonant plus LE.

(See *Tool 5: Pronunciation: Pronouncing Other Word Forms for L Endings, Book of Lists*.)

THE CHALLENGING L ENDINGS

AL (means concerning): *bridal*: concerning brides; *nautical*: concerning ships; *royal*: concerning kings, *total*: concerning totals. Also, *-ly* can be added to these words (except bridal): *medically, nautically, royally, totally.*

EL *Del, Mel, Nel…* make great *Clues*. Also *-elle* was once added to some words to mean *small*: *chapel, hovel, morsel, novel, panel, parcel, satchel, towel, trowel, tunnel…* (Perhaps think of an <u>el</u>f using these small things).

LE (the rest of the words): *castle, cuddle, riddle, snuggle, tangle, tickle, triangle*

IL (just 5 words): *civil, council, evil, pencil, stencil*

OL Just a few words like *Capitol* (building), *symbol*

(See *Tool 5: Pronouncing Other Word Forms To Hear L Ending, Book of Lists.*)

Lesson 36: Words with the Roots: Sede, Ceed, Cede, plus Old Seed

Objectives: Students will learn that: one word ends with the root, sede; three words end with ceed; eight words end with cede; and *there's just one seed*. They will also learn some noun, verb, adjective and adverb suffixes that can be added to these words.

Write the bold words in the *Learning Box* on the board. Introduce Lesson 36 by asking, "Does anyone know what some of these words mean?" As students respond, add brief definitions to each word. Then, ask, "Can anyone think of a clue that uses *proceed, succeed*, and *exceed*. Put their ideas on the board. Finally ask students to give you *Other Forms of these Words (OWF's)* and write these on the board. End by saluting *Good Old Seed*.

WORDS WITH THE LATIN ROOTS: Sede, Ceed, Cede, plus Good Old Seed

1 word has sede (to sit)
supersede: be above in power (sit above) *supersedes, superseded, superseding*

3 words have ceed (go; move):
proceed: continue moving forward: *process, procedure*   {As you **proceed** through life
succeed: move to goal: *succeeded, success, succession*   {And seek to **succeed**,
exceed: move beyond goal: *exceeding, excess*   {Don't let your wealth **exceed** your goodness.

8 words have cede (go; move):
accede: agree to; accept: *accedes, acceded, acceding*
antecede: to come before, like an ancestor: *antecedent, anteceding, ancestors…*
cede: to surrender land: *cedes, ceded,* ceding
concede: to yield to; give into; concede victory: *concedes, conceded, conceding, concession*
intercede: to go between to help: *intercedes, interceded, intercession, intercessor*
precede: come before or go before in rank: *precedes, preceded, preceding, precedent*
recede: to move back - receding waves or hairline: *receded, receding, recession*
secede: to withdraw from a nation, group: *secedes, secede, seceding*

seed: (Basic Old English): The part of a plant that reproduces it: *seeded, seedling, reseeded*

An Invitation: Because *POWER Spelling* involves so much individual creativity, we anticipate and truly welcome your ideas and involvement. We invite you and your students to send *Memory Tools* you've created and any thoughts you have for enhancing this book, as well as ideas for Special Lessons you'd enjoy, etc. Please send these to Linda Skerbec, c/o The Center for Applied Research in Education, 240 Frisch Court, Paramus, NJ, 07652. Thank You.

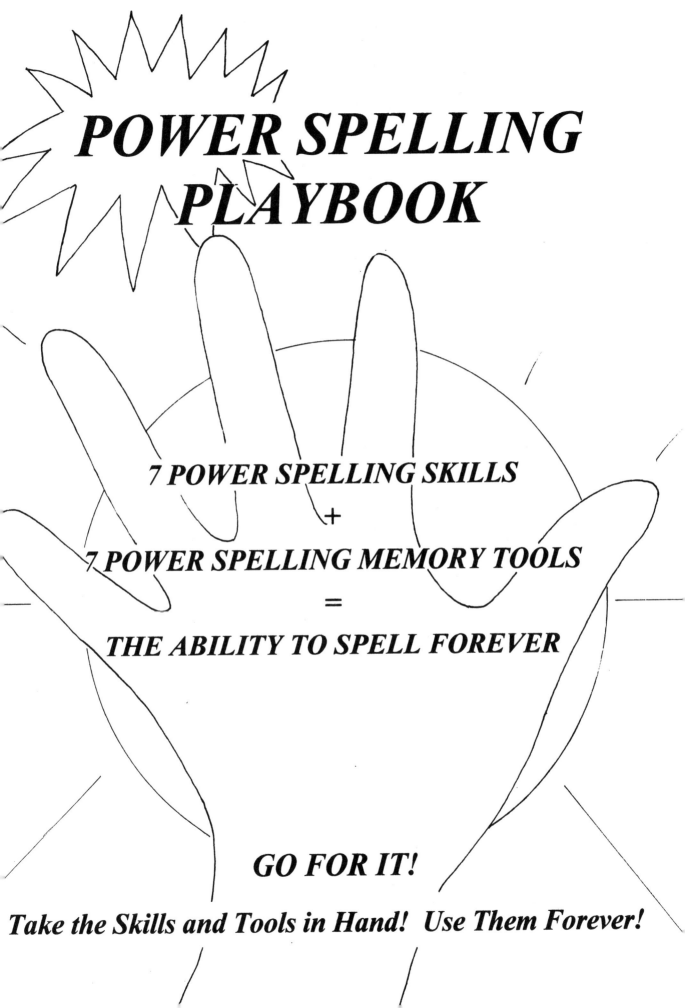

POWER SPELLING PLAYBOOK

7 POWER SPELLING SKILLS

+

7 POWER SPELLING MEMORY TOOLS

=

THE ABILITY TO SPELL FOREVER

GO FOR IT!

Take the Skills and Tools in Hand! Use Them Forever!

THE POWER SPELLING PLAYBOOK

Welcome to *POWER SPELLING*. *Finally*, there's a way to learn spelling that will teach you the skills and tools you truly need to succeed at spelling for the rest of your life!!! As you study the weekly lessons in your *PLAYBOOK*, you will learn fun and challenging ways to use seven great *POWER SPELLING SKILLS* and *MEMORY TOOLS* to understand and remember every word you meet. These seven *Spelling Skills* and *Memory Tools* are: *POWER CLUES; PHONICS POWER; POWER RULES; FEELING the POWER of the BEAT and SYLLABLES; PRONUNCIATION POWER; POWER of ANCIENT ROOTS,* and *VISUAL POWER and PATTERNS*. These will help you use your hearing, seeing, and feeling to investigate, detect, and find ways to remember *every* word. Now **YOU** can learn and gain the *POWER* **to truly know how to spell**!

As you keep using *MEMORY TOOLS*, you'll find that you're not forgetting how to spell the words you've learned. This is because *Clues* and other *Memory Tools* help you use and strengthen your **BRAIN'S *POWER*** to organize and remember spelling. Keep reinforcing your *MEMORY TOOLS* for words, and you'll soon find that your brain can automatically recall them. You'll truly know that YOU are training your brain to store and remember words for the rest of your life!

Also, with each weekly lesson, you get to play a *POWER SPELLING GAME*. For the game words, you're the detective who uses the 7 *POWER Spelling Skills* and *Memory Tools* to solve how words are put together and to discover the best tools for remembering them. As you keep doing these lessons and building your **Playbook**, you'll increase your detective ability and *GAME POWER* by learning more *Skills* and *Memory Tools*. The more *Spelling* knowledge you've gained, the more *POWER* you have for playing each game. Soon, you'll find that you're truly mastering spelling, and that **YOU** have become a *POWER SPELLER!*

So, without wasting any time, *LET'S GET GOING!*

Getting to Know Your Power Spelling Tools

Right NOW, in your **PLAYBOOK**, you can start using the seven **POWER SPELLING SKILLS** and **MEMORY TOOLS**. The skills will teach you ways to detect and learn the difficult parts of words, and the tools will help you remember the spelling. Keep using these skills and tools, and you will truly master spelling. So, let's learn **POWER SPELLING!**

"cha cha cha!" *snap*

TOOL 1 – *CRAZY POWER CLUES*: CLUES help you remember how to spell the hard parts of words. For example, the word <u>friend</u> can be difficult to spell because you can't hear how the vowels are spelled. However, if you look for small words in <u>friend</u>, and create a clue like: *On <u>Fri.</u>, the <u>end</u> of the week, I see my <u>friend</u>*; then, when you want to write <u>friend</u>, you can remember your clue. Each time you make a clue for a difficult word, you're giving your mind a Memory Tool.

Now, that you're warmed up, let's try the word: <u>argument</u>. Is it spelled *arguement* or *argument*? If you have a clue like: *It's hard to have an <u>argument</u> with <u>gum</u> in your mouth*, you will always remember how to spell <u>argument</u>.

❑ **NOW**: Underline the challenging parts of these words and create clues to remember them.

attendance   island

together   tomorrow

Another way to create clues is to use *OTHER WORD FORMS* where you can better hear the spelling of a word. You can use *signature* to hear the *g* in <u>sign</u>. For the silent *b* in *dumb*, you can use the clue: *<u>Dumbo</u> was not <u>dumb</u>; he could fly.* Keep using your clues, and you will easily remember them.

AT – TEN – DANCE!

HOMOPHONES: Clues are great for learning <u>Homophones</u>, words that are pronounced the same way, like <u>hear</u> and <u>here</u>, <u>peace</u> and <u>piece</u>, but their spelling and meaning is different. Clues truly help out because they help you remember the differences in the spelling and also in the meaning.

❑ **TRY THIS:** Create clues for the homophones below.

hangar – *a <u>garage</u> for <u>airplanes</u>.*   hanger (for clothes)

hear (listen)   here (place)

peace (no war)   piece (serving)

Keep making up *POWER CLUES* for challenging words and you'll be able to remember them forever!

♦ **TOOL 2 – PHONICS *POWER***: Phonics teaches you about the sounds the letters of a language make. Knowing these sounds gives you great spelling *POWER*, because *about 85% of the words in English are spelled just like they sound.* To get an idea of how PHONICS can help your spelling, let's meet the Copy Cat Kids: C̲isco, G̲idget, S̲usan, and X̲avier, who'll show you the four letters in English that copy other sounds: C, G, S, and X.

❏ **NOW**: To get to know the two sounds each Copy Cat Kid can make, write down two or three words for each sound.

C (Cisco) copies the sound of **k**-*c̲at*:	C also copies **s**-*c̲ity*:
G (Gidget) has her own **g** sound-*gum*:	G also copies **j**-*gentle, gem*:
S (Susan) has her own **s** sound-*s̲un*:	S also copies **z**-*ros̲e, treasu̲re*:
X (Xavier) has his own **x** sound-*x̲-ray*:	X also copies **z**-*x̲ylophone*:

You will learn more about Phonics in Lesson 2 as you read *Discovering the History of the English Language.* You will find out why some words are not spelled like they're pronounced. You will also learn why English has so many HOMOPHONES (words that sound the same with different spellings and meanings) and SYNONYMS (words that mean the same thing).

♦ **TOOL 3 – *RULES that WORK***: Understanding and using RULES that WORK really builds your spelling *POWER* by helping you correctly spell hundreds of words. Even though there are a few exceptions to some of the rules, they are not that hard to learn. Let's read some of these rules.

❏ **NOW**: The **Qu Rule** says: *Q must be followed by u, unless q ends a word*, and it ALWAYS works. There are no exceptions: *quack, quiet, quite, quill*... Add a few q̲u̲ words:

❏ **TRY THIS**: The **Compound Word Rule** says: To make Compound Words, simply add two word together without making any changes to either word: c̲up + b̲oard = c̲upboard and r̲ace + c̲ar = r̲acecar It has very few exceptions: *alphabet, almost, always, pastime, shepherd, until, welcome,* and *wherever*. Connect the words below to make compound words.

class + room	= *classroom*	ear + ring	=
news + stand	=	snow + flake	=

❏ **WOW**: The **Prefix Rule** works just like the Compound Word Rule. *simply add or glue the prefix to the word, without changing or adding any letters,* as in u̲n + u̲sual = u̲nusual. Now add these words.

dis (not) + agree =	re (again) + read =
mis (wrong) + spell =	un (not) + happy =

WOW! You can really feel your spelling POWER go up as you start learning RULES that WORK!

♦ **TOOL 4 – *FEELING the POWER OF the BEAT* and *SYLLABLES*:** Sometimes it really helps to put some words to a beat, especially when the words just naturally fit a beat, like:

M-i-s-s i-s-s i-p-p i,   r-h-y t-h-m, and **s-n-o w-double-u f-l-a-k-e**

FEELING the BEAT gives you spelling *POWER* for both letters and syllables in words with a beat.

a – rith – me – tic,   math – e – ma – tics,   cho – co – la – te

❑ **FOR FUN:** Take some words and put them to a beat. You might try double-letter words like *happy* or *committee*, or compound words, like *anyone* and *racecar*. The word *encyclopedia* easily fits a beat.

❑ **FEELING *YOUR MOTOR MEMORY*:** As a toddler, each time you practiced walking, your legs kept developing motor memory until you could walk automatically. In spelling, your hand develops motor memory. As you write a word again and again, your hand learns how it feels to write the word correctly. To feel how strong motor memory is, write your name below. Now, write your name incorrectly. How does it feel? Also, write the words *and* and *the* correctly and then incorrectly. What do you feel? *Each time you write a word correctly, you build motor memory* until *you know how the correct word feels.*

Name:_____ and:_____ the:_____.

TOOL 5 – *PRONUCIATION POWER*: You get instant PRONUNCIATION POWER by learning the right way to pronounce a word from the start. Lots of words get misspelled simply because people don't pronounce them right. They leave out letters, put in one letter for another, or even add extra syllables.

❑ **NOW:** For the 3 words below, learn the clues so you'll remember the correct pronunciation!

CORRECT PRONUNCIATION	MISPRONUNCIATION MENACE	CLUES AND TOOLS FOR PROPER PRONUNCIATION
dif<u>fer</u>ent	*diffrent*	Since we are different people, we differ on favorite foods.
Feb<u>rua</u>ry	*Febuary*	Is it <u>rude</u> on <u>February</u> 14 to forget to give Valentines?
lib<u>rar</u>y	*libary*	Don't be a <u>brat</u> in the <u>library</u>.

SPECIAL PHONICS PRONUNCIATIONS (*SPP's*): *Special Phonics Pronunciations (SPP's)* truly help for words with silent letters where the pronunciation is different from the spelling. This is because *SPP's* give you a way to *pronounce every vowel and consonant* similar to the way people said words when they spoke Old English. Then <u>climb</u> was pronounced *climban* and the <u>t</u> in <u>often</u> was pronounced.

❑ **NOW:** For the words below, say the *SPP's* aloud. Learn the clues to remember the pronunciation.

WORD	COMMON MISPRONUNCIATION	*SPECIAL PHONICS PRONUNCIATION (SPP)* and CLUE
<u>ever</u>y	evry	*SPP*: e-<u>ver</u>-y: <u>Every</u> true friend is for<u>ever</u>.
me<u>a</u>nt	ment	*SPP*: <u>me-ant</u>: They <u>meant</u> to look for <u>ant</u> and <u>me</u>.
o<u>ften</u>	offen	*SPP*: of-ten: I am <u>often</u> one <u>of ten</u> students dancing.

♦ **TOOL 6 – *POWER OF ANCIENT ROOTS***: You're truly becoming a POWER SPELLER when you can discover PREFIXES, ROOTS, and SUFFIXES in words. These word parts are great: *They build spelling POWER, because they're spelled like they sound,* and *they also build vocabulary.* You'll learn more about prefixes and roots soon, and you'll also discover the magic of suffixes. The ROOTS and PREFIXES below have come from Latin and Greek.

❑ **NOW**: Write all the words you know that have these Latin and Greek roots and prefixes (Gk. *ph* = *f*).

ROOT and PREFIXES	MEANING	WORDS CONTAINING THESE ROOTS
bio (G)	life	*biological*
geo (G)	earth	
graph, graphy (G)	write	
logy (G)	study of	
phon, phone (G)	sound	
port (L)	to carry	
vision (L)	see	
auto (L Prefix)	self	
tele (G Prefix)	far, distant	
trans (L prefix)	across	*transport*

♦ **TOOL 7 – *VISUAL POWER***: Perhaps you have the natural ability to just look at a word and see it in your mind (photographic memory), or you've learned to picture words in your mind. If you don't yet have this skill, you can develop it, and it will add a very valuable tool to your spelling *POWER*.

❑ **NOW**: Let's build VISUAL *POWER* with **climb** and **dinosaur**. First, carefully write **climb**, and look at climb and underline any difficult parts. Now, close your eyes and in your mind picture **climb** letter by letter or as a whole word. Finally, open your eyes and write **climb** 2 more times. Now, try your Visual *POWER* for **dinosaur**. Using this tool develops your Visual Spelling *POWER*.

climb:

dinosaur:

You can also use your Visual *POWER* to discover PALINDROMES (words spelled the same backwards and forwards): racecar, kayak, banana, and divide. REVERSALS (words you can reverse): deer-reed and reward-drawer are also fun. Then you can find words that are unique in some way: sequoia has all 5 vowels. Also, can you list 10 different words in heartbeat?

Finally, the more you read, Read, **READ**…, the stronger your Visual *POWER* will become since you keep seeing words correctly spelled! ALWAYS keep a good book handy!

❑ **TRY THIS**: Another way to use Visual *POWER* is to discover words that are easy to remember because of the way the letters look. Draw Visual Clues based on something you can see in these letters.

balloon   cycle   shampoo   parallel

The Power Spelling Tools Give You Ways
through the Maze to the Brain

Research shows that the belief *"I just can't spell"* is not true. Spelling is a learned skill, which means: <u>You can learn ways to spell</u> and <u>you can remember the words you have learned</u>. In other words:

You can **TRAIN** you **BRAIN** to **GAIN** and **RETAIN** the spelling of words.

Knowing ways *to gain* and *retain* the BRAIN'S *POWER* to SPELL is like discovering paths through a maze to the gold. While some people get lost in the maze, people who have learned ways to spell have grooved in memory paths that they use, moment by moment—to go back and forth to the brain, storing and taking out spelling information whenever they need it.

Four Important Points about Your BRAIN

To help you spell, your BRAIN needs to: **take-in** spelling information, **organize** it, and **remember** it by **connecting** it with something you know. Then your Memory Tools need to be **used** again and again.

1. Your BRAIN TAKES-IN spelling information by HEARING, SEEING, and FEELING.

2. Your BRAIN LEARNS by ORGANIZING this spelling information into CATEGORIES like: *Clue Words*, *Words that Fit Rules*, *Words that Fit a Beat*, *Visual Words*.

3. Your BRAIN REMEMBERS a spelling word by creating a MEMORY TOOL to CONNECT the word with something you know : <u>*Balloon* has *2 sticks* and *2 balloons*</u>. *A <u>hangar</u> is for <u>a</u>irplanes.*

4. Each time you USE these CONNECTIONS, you groove MEMORY PATHS more deeply into your brain, so that you can zip back and forth – to store and retrieve spelling information.

POWER Spelling Skills and Tools Match the Way the BRAIN Learns

1. The *POWER* Spelling Skills and Tools use HEARING, SEEING, and FEELING to TAKE-IN words.

2. These SKILLS help you ORGANIZE words into 7 great CATEGORIES: Clues, Phonics, Feeling the Beat and Syllables, Words that Fit Rules, Pronunciation, Roots, and Visual Power.

3. The SKILLS help you create MEMORY TOOLS that CONNECT the words you are spelling with something you know and can remember.

4. Finally, as you USE these MEMORY TOOLS again and again, you strengthen the MEMORY PATHS to your brain until they are automatic, like walking and talking.

NOTE: Research shows that good spellers know phonics rules; pronounce words correctly; understand roots, prefixes, and suffixes; develop motor memory from writing words; and use visual memory. Whether they know it or not, good spellers use many *POWER* Spelling Skills and Memory Tools! Also, good spellers usually keep a DICTIONARY within arm's reach...and they READ. "By George!

To **TRAIN** your **BRAIN** to **GAIN** and **RETAIN** the spelling of words,
MAINTAIN motivation, study, and read **AGAIN**...and you'll learn and feel great!

Your Power Spelling Master List

List words here that you have had trouble spelling, plus challenging words for which you've created memory tools. Briefly write down the POWER SPELLING TOOL(S) you've used to remember these words.

1. _____
2. _____
3. _____
4. _____
5. _____
6. _____
7. _____
8. _____
9. _____
10. _____
11. _____
12. _____
13. _____
14. _____
15. _____
16. _____
17. _____
18. _____
19. _____
20. _____
21. _____
22. _____
23. _____
24. _____
25. _____

26. _____
27. _____
28. _____
29. _____
30. _____
31. _____
32. _____
33. _____
34. _____
35. _____
36. _____
37. _____
38. _____
39. _____
40. _____
41. _____
42. _____
43. _____
44. _____
45. _____
46. _____
47. _____
48. _____
49. _____
50. _____

51. _____
52. _____
53. _____
54. _____
55. _____
56. _____
57. _____
58. _____
59. _____
60. _____
61. _____
62. _____
63. _____
64. _____
65. _____
66. _____
67. _____
68. _____
69. _____
70. _____
71. _____
72. _____
73. _____
74. _____
75. _____

Discovering the History of the English Language

Have you ever wondered where the English language and all its words came from; or why English has so many words that mean the same thing (synonyms); or why some words are not spelled like they sound? As you read this lesson, you will discover the answers to these questions. First, though, let's see how much you know about the countries from which our words have come.

THE RICHEST VOCABULARY IN THE WORLD: The words in English have come from all over the world. Tribes and conquerors who settled in England brought their languages with them. Later, English added words from Latin and Greek. Also, as English spread around the world, it welcomed many new words into its vocabulary. The number and variety of words that the English language has makes English the language with the richest vocabulary in the world.

❑ **NOW**: As you read the words below, after each word, in pencil, write the language or culture from which you think it came. As you read this lesson, you can check your answers. *CLUE*: These words are from the following languages and cultures: African, Algonquian (American Indian), Arabic, Australian, Chinese, Dutch, French, Greek, Hebrew, Japanese, Italian, Latin, Norse, Sanskrit (India), and Spanish. (*NOTE*: It is helpful to know that many dictionaries include the language or culture from which a word came, so just check a dictionary for information.)

arithmetic	**friend**	**phantom**
alter (to change)	**hamburger**	**photograph**
bagel	**karate**	**rodeo**
banana	**kindergarten**	**safari**
beautiful	**liberty**	**Santa Claus**
boomerang	**moccasin**	**scribe**
candle	**mother**	**skate**
candy	**neighbor**	**spaghetti**
chocolate	**origami**	**tea**
father	**pajamas**	**volcano**

❑ **WHAT DO YOU THINK?** Write down words, now in the English language, that you think came from another language or culture. To get started, think of words for food, clothing or holidays that have come from the cultures below or from any other cultures you wish to add.

American Indian:

Arab:

Chinese:

French:

Greek:

Indian (India):

Jewish:

Japanese:

Russian:

Spanish:

BONSAI

A Little History of the English Language
WHY SOME WORDS ARE NOT PRONOUNCED LIKE THEY ARE SPELLED

At times, everyone comes across words where the spelling is difficult. The reason is that there are many words in the English language that simply are not spelled like they sound. There are even some words where the consonants and vowels are silent. Since, for many languages, most words are spelled like they sound, it's important to ask—Why are words spelled in so many different ways in English, and why are there silent letters? What is the history of the English language and what caused the spelling difficulties to occur?

As you are learning the answers to these questions, you will discover that the history of the English language is like a great adventure. It is a story about daring tribes, fierce conquerors, castles and kingdoms, monks and monasteries, and awesome writers and dedicated printers.

You will also find that the history of the English language can be divided into three important time periods: Old English or Anglo-Saxon (449-1066); Middle English (1066-1400s); and Modern English (1400s-present). As you look at spelling, it's important to know that before the 1400s, all the vowels and consonants in English were pronounced, including silent e. Words were spelled just like they sounded.

❑ **WHAT DO YOU THINK?** As you start with Modern English, and read these four versions of a part of the "Twenty-third Psalm," you can see how much English has changed as you go back in time to Old English. Underline any Anglo-Saxon or Middle English words that you can figure out. Also, between which two time periods do you think the English language changed the most?

Modern English Today: Even though I walk through the valley of the shadow of death, I will fear no evil for you are with me. Your rod and your staff, they comfort me. (New International Version of the Bible, 1985)

Modern English (about 1600): Yea, though I walk through the valley of the shadow of death, I will fear no evil: for thou art with me; thy rod and thy staff they comfort me (King James Version of the Bible, 1611).

Middle English (about 1300): For gif that ich haue bon amiddes of the shadowe of deth, y shal nought douten iuels, for thou are wyth me; thy discipline and thyn amending comforted me.

Old English or Anglo-Saxon (about 900): Yeotudlice ond theah the ic gonge in midle scuan deathes, ne ondredu ic yfel, forthon thu mid me erth; geird thin ond crycc thin hie me froefrends werun.

"good morrows sweet allison!"

32

It Sounds Like Latin to Me, But Is It German?

English is called *a German language* because its basic words and the ways its sentences are built came from Anglo-Saxon, a German language that was *spoken* in England by A.D. 449. At the same time, over half of the words and the alphabet used for English have come from Latin.

It's interesting to know that the German tribes even brought a little Latin with them when they came to England. History tells us that in the first century B.C., Roman soldiers were in the area that is now called Germany. These soldiers brought things that the Germans had never seen – so when the German tribesmen "bought" these things, they called them by the Latin words the Roman soldiers used. In this way, Latin words like *butter, cheese, chest, pillow wine* were added to Anglo-Saxon.

Also, in the first century (A.D. 43), Roman soldiers conquered England and stayed there for nearly 400 years…but the English people never spoke their Latin. So, what do you think. Should English be called a German, or a Latin language? Read on…

Three Periods of English Development

OLD ENGLISH (449-1066): Around A.D. 449, three tribes (Angles, Saxons, Jutes) sailed from their homeland (now Germany), invaded England, and drove out the Celts and Britons. They brought their language, now called Anglo-Saxon (Old English), which was soon *spoken* in England.

English has gained most of its basic words from Anglo Saxon: *the*; pronouns: *I, you, me, he, she, it*; verbs: *is, can, will, eat, sleep, drink…*; and other basic words: *in, of, for, with, and but*. This language of the farm and kitchen has also given us: *barn, cow, calf, pig, sheep, stove, pot…* and more nouns: *child, brother, earth, father, friend, hand, heaven, home, love, man, mother, neighbor, seed, sister, water, woman*. Although many words have been added from other languages, the most common words in English, plus half the words in most sentences, are Anglo-Saxon.

LATIN RETURNS: Even though Anglo-Saxon was spoken in England, a problem remained. Since only the priests could use the letters (secret runes) in this alphabet, the common people <u>needed an alphabet</u>. In A.D. 597, Latin made its greatest contribution to English. St. Augustine and missionaries from Rome brought Christianity and schools to England. Many new words for things were added to English from Latin: *alms, altar, candle, creed, disciple…* This rich Latin influence continued for over 450 years, until the Normans invaded England in 1066.

The missionaries also brought their <u>Roman alphabet</u>, and soon they taught the common people to write their Anglo-Saxon words with the Roman alphabet. Around A.D. 700, the first great English book, *Beowulf* was written in Anglo-Saxon. It described the adventures of the mighty warrior Beowulf, who slew the savage monster, Grendel, for his king and people. Beowulf had all the qualities that the Anglo-Saxons admired: courage, generosity, loyalty, and strength.

VIKING WORDS: Meanwhile, from 750-1050, Vikings (from Denmark and Norway) invaded and settled in England. They added close to 1,500 words from their Norse language: *dazzle, cookie, freckle, get, hit, husband, leg, shirt, trust, skin, skate, sky…* They also added important pronouns: *they*, *them*, and *their*.

MIDDLE ENGLISH (1066-1476): In 1066, the Normans, led by the fierce invader, William the Conqueror, sailed across the water from Normandy (now France), conquered England at the Battle of Hastings, and established their kingdom. From 1066 until 1204, the Normans ruled England. This educated class spoke an elegant French language that came from Latin. Some of the words they brought into English are: *ballet, beautiful, constitution, elegant, equality, fashion, government, feminine, jury, liberty, magnificent, marriage, masculine, palace, soldier, state, throne, triumph.* These words are much less humble than the basic Old English (Anglo-Saxon) words, and also much more difficult to spell.

The steadfast language of the Anglo-Saxons remained strong, however, because the common people spoke it, so at least 4,500 Anglo-Saxon words have remained in English. Also, since both the common people and the conquerors kept their own language, each group often had a word for the same thing. Therefore, English has many Anglo-Saxon and French-Latin synonyms like: *home* and *mansion*; *work* and *labor*; *love* and *adore*; *hearty* and *cordial*.

Another reason Anglo-Saxon words have stayed so strongly rooted in English was that Chaucer, the greatest writer of his time, wrote in Anglo-Saxon. From 1387 until his death in 1400, Geoffrey Chaucer worked on his masterpiece, The Canterbury Tales, writing it in the language of the common people. In this great book about a journey from London to Canterbury, Chaucer tells his tale through his characters. The knight, the parson, the plowman, and others tell stories that show what their daily life is like, what they believe, and what they have been learning during their life on Earth. The Canterbury Tales is still read and loved today,

What is important about Chaucer's English is that at the time he wrote, words in English were spelled just like they were pronounced. Every vowel and consonant was spoken, which meant there were no silent letters. For years after Chaucer died in 1400, writers still copied his spelling, even though the way English was pronounced had changed.

❑ **TRY THIS**: For these Anglo-Saxon words, pronounce every vowel and consonant like people did at that time, and try to figure out the words. Write today's spelling next to the words you detect.

heofun	faeder	neahgebur	berern
modor	frend	niht	deathes

FROM MIDDLE ENGLISH TO MODERN ENGLISH (1400's to 1600's): During this period, many new words came into English; but, *alas,* things also happened that caused English to have many words that were no longer spelled like they were pronounced. In 1400, when Chaucer had died, people still pronounced all the consonants and vowels, including *final e*. By 1500, though, *final e* had become silent, along with other vowels and consonants in words like *climb, love, neighbor...* Middle English was changing into the Modern English you speak and spell today. Some of the reasons that words were no longer spelled like they were pronounced were:

◆ THE PRINTING PRESS: When William Caxton set up the first printing press in England in 1476, he used a lot of Chaucer's spelling, even though English was no longer spoken that way. As printing presses produced more and more books, people got used to this spelling. Then, in 1596, a schoolmaster named Edmund Coote wrote a spelling dictionary for the common people. Even though he wanted words to be spelled like they were pronounced, Coote chose the spelling people already knew. His dictionary was so popular and so many copies were printed, that it set spelling standards for people and schools all over England.

◆ THE RENAISSANCE and LATIN: During this time in history (which was going on when Queen Elizabeth I ruled England), people were very excited about ancient Latin and Greek writing and about new ideas. Some people got so excited about Latin that they changed English words into Latin spelling, which added more silent letters: *iland* became *island; dout – doubt...*

New words were also added to English because great writers like William Shakespeare (1546-1616) used words from Latin to express their ideas: *alter* (to change), *amorous* (loving), *image, scribe,* and *verse...* Shakespeare also created over 2,000 new words: *hurry* and *leapfrog,* and phrases like: *To be or not to be* and *vanish into thin air.*

◆ THE RENAISSANCE, GREEK and SCIENCE: Also during the Renaissance time, people in England began talking about the writing of Greek philosophers like Plato and Aristotle (who lived around 400 B.C.). Many new Greek words were added to English: *phantom* (ghost) and *apothecary* (pharmacist). Greek words were also used in math and science: *arithmetic; photograph* (phos: *light* + graph: *writing*); pneumonia (pneumo: *lungs* + nia: *disease*); *psychology* (psyche: soul + *ology*: study of). Since Greek spells *n – pn; f – ph; ; s – ps,* more silent letters were added to English.

Still today, new words are created from Latin or Greek. Words are also made by adding words from two languages: *television* (G. tele: *talk* + L. vision); *astronaut* (G. astro: *star*; G. + L. naut: sailor); *internet* (L. inter: *between* + O. E. net). Most of our basic words are from Anglo-Saxon (also called Old English) and most of our roots, prefixes, and suffixes are from Latin and Greek.

"bzzz..."

♦ EXPLORATION AND COLONIZATION: During the 1600s, as the English explored and established colonies, many new words were brought in from other languages. From the Canadian and American Indians, English welcomed words like: *chipmunk, moccasin, moose, potato, powwow, raccoon, skunk, squash, teepee, toboggan,* and *tomahawk.* From the Mexican-Spanish influence, we have gained words like: *bronco, cafeteria, chili, cigar, corral, mosquito, patio, quesadilla, ranch, rodeo, tomato,* and *vanilla.*

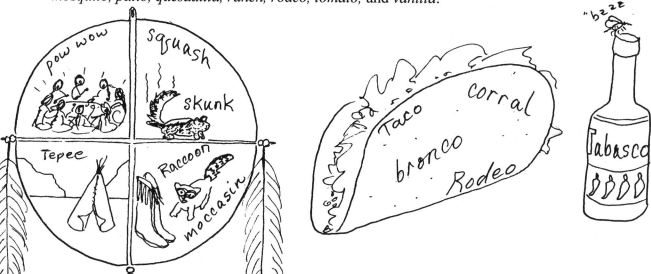

As English continued to spread, it brought in words from all around the world. From Germany (since 1600) we've added: *delicatessen, frankfurter, hamburger, kindergarten, noodle, pretzel, quartz, sauerkraut, stein* (beer mug)*,* and *waltz; boomerang, koala,* and *kangaroo* from Australia; *zebra* from Ethiopia; *limbo* (How low can you go dance) from Jamaica; *bazaar* from Persia; *cosmonaut* and *czar* from Russia; *sherbet, shish kebab,* and *yogurt* from Turkey. Although the English language has become richer in words, some of these words contain silent letters, or they are challenging to spell.

AFRICA: *banana, gnu (antelope), safari, tangerine* (Morocco)*, yam, zombie*

ARABIA: *algebra, chemistry, coffee, magazine, sofa*

CHINA: *chow, chow mein, soy, tea, tofu, typhoon, wok*

DUTCH: *cookie, pickle, Santa Claus, skate, sketch, sled, wagon, yacht*

FRANCE: *bizarre, boulevard, democracy, lieutenant, migraine, picturesque, restaurant*

INDIA: *candy, cashmere, catamaran (sailboat), cheetah, curry, jungle, pajamas, shampoo*

ITALY: *aria, balcony, gondola, mustache, opera, pasta, piano, solo, spaghetti, volcano*

JAPAN: *bonsai* (miniature tree)*, haiku, judo, futon* (bed)*, karate, origami, sukiyaki, teriyaki*

YIDDISH: *bagel, chutzpah* (rudeness)*, kibbutz, pastrami*

The language we use and spell is truly a melting pot of words from many languages and cultures.

Today, the English language continues to grow as new words are brought in from the space industry and computers: *astronaut, debug, joystick, microchip,* and *satellite.* Who knows what words will be added to English tomorrow – as new discoveries are made and new sciences are developed? We can only wait and see how the English language will continue to be enriched.

(TRY THIS answers: heaven, father, neighbor (near by farm), barn, mother, friend, night, death)

Let's Create Some Power Spelling Clues

Now that you have read some history of the English language, you have probably discovered that there are a lot of words in English that do not follow phonics or rules. You could say – NOT ALL WORDS ARE SPELLED LIKE THEY SOUND! As you have learned, English has many spelling challenges because our language has been built with words from many countries. Also, the way that English words are pronounced has changed over time.

One kind of challenge is that usually when words are spelled alike, they rhyme: *hop, pop, stop,* and *top…, bee, knee, see,* and *tree*. But, what about the words: *does* and *goes*; *doll* and *roll*; *boot* and *foot,* and *boots* and *feet*; *horse* and *worse…* WHOA! One person asked about this crazy spelling problem in the poem below:

Our Strange Language

When the English tongue we <u>speak</u>
Why is <u>break</u> not rhymed with <u>freak</u>?
Will you tell me why it's true
We say <u>sew</u>, but likewise <u>few</u>;
And the maker of a verse
Cannot rhyme his <u>horse</u> with <u>worse</u>?
<u>Beard</u> sounds not the same as <u>heard</u>;
<u>Cord</u> is different from <u>word</u>;
<u>Cow</u> is cow, but <u>low</u> is low.
<u>Shoe</u> is never rhymed with <u>foe</u>.
Think of <u>nose</u> and <u>dose</u> and <u>lose</u>;
And think of <u>goose</u> and yet of <u>choose</u>.
Think of <u>comb</u> and <u>tomb</u> and <u>bomb</u>,
<u>Doll</u> and <u>roll</u> and <u>home</u> and <u>some</u>.
And since <u>pay</u> is rhymed with <u>say</u>,
Why not <u>paid</u> with <u>said</u>, I pray?
We have <u>blood</u> and <u>food</u> and <u>good</u>;
<u>Mould</u> is not pronounced like <u>could</u>
Wherefore <u>done</u>, but <u>gone</u> and <u>lone</u>?
Is there any reason known?

And, in short, it seems to me,
Sounds and letters disagree.
–Anonymous

Homophones are also a challenge because they sound the same, but they're spelled differently and have a different meaning, like *desert* and *dessert*; *stairs* and *stares*. English also has confusing pairs of words like *tired* and *tried*. So, what can you do? ***POWER SPELLING CLUES*** to the rescue! They're a great tool for remembering the confusing and challenging words that don't follow phonics or rules(over 15%). Try creating clues like: A de<u>ss</u>ert is <u>s</u>omething sweet; and: When people de<u>s</u>ert you, you're all alone, like one lone <u>s</u>. Try these *Clues* too: When I'm <u>tired</u>, my eyes get <u>red</u>; I <u>tried</u> <u>Ed</u>; and: It's <u>rough</u> to walk *through* a door.

Creating POWER Spelling Clues with Real POWER!

And the list goes on… *ache* and *mustache*; *dearly* and *early*; *four* and *tour*, *through*, and *rough*…
You need **POWER SPELLING CLUES** for words like these – *Clues* that will give your brain a
POWER CONNECTION!   Then, each time you use your *Clue*, you'll remember the spelling.
Soon you'll master the word forever!!! For example: He has a chest ache helps you remember ache.
Once you know ache, you can create the *Clue*: Your mustache must ache when someone pulls on it.

Steps for Creating POWER Clues

Try these 5 key steps and create *POWER Clues* for **again, athlete**, and **castle**.

Underline or highlight the part of the word that's challenging for you: again, athlete, castle.

Look for helpful | Words in the Word. | Maybe you'll find a | Clue-in-a-Row |: a-gain, castle.

Create | Letter Clues | or use | Another Word | with the same letters: athlete-high leap; castle-length.

See if | Other Word Forms | help you hear letters more easily: athlete-athletic; castle-castling.

Think of words with the | Same Patter | again: main, train; athlete: mete, Pete; cast: last.

Choose the *Clue* that's easiest for you to remember. Learn it NOW and keep using it forever!

| again |: Practice again and again, and make a gain in ability (*Clue-in-a-Row*).
To make gains, go through the pain and train again and again (*Same Pattern*).

| athlete |: An athlete did a high leap (*Letter Clue*). That athlete is athletic (*OWF Clue*).

| castle |: I am castling my king with my castle (*OWF Clue*).
The castle cast lengths of light across the lake (*Word in the Word; Another Word*).

Summary of the Different Kinds of Clues

Knowing about different kinds of *Clues* EMPOWERS you to create your own **POWER Clues**.

| Word in the Word Clues |: Please add my address to your address book.

| Clue-in-a-Row |: This is significant, please sign if I can't. It takes courage to live in our age.

| Letter Clues |: A calendar has a list of dates. A straw is straight.

| OWF Clues |: A columnist writes a column. That athlete is truly athletic.

| Same Pattern Clues |: The rain in Spain falls mainly on the plains.

You can even try a Greek ***Clue-in-a-Row***: My bicycle has bi (G. two) cycles (G. wheels).

Create Your Own Crazy POWER Clues for Challenging Words

❑ **TRY THIS**: Now that you've learned about *POWER CLUES*, <u>your mission</u> is to take on the words below; detect and <u>underline the difficult parts</u>; and then conquer their challenge with *POWER SPELLING CLUES*. You will be gaining valuable experience in using different kinds of *Clues*. Above all, create *Clues* that will help YOU conquer each word. Examples are below. Good luck! ★

Some of these words are from the *Lists of Most Frequently Misspelled Words*. They get misspelled because they're not spelled like they sound; they have double letters; or because they're homophones.

Clues-in-a-Row

Be sure to look for small words, and just have fun writing *Clues-in-a-Row*.

abundance:

beanstalk:

meteor: Can you <u>mete or</u> follow a <u>meteor</u>? (mete: measure)

noticed:

o<u>ften</u>: I'm <u>often</u> one <u>of ten</u> guys who sing (fish, run, do spelling. Fill in *your* interest.)

<u>weather</u>: Why are <u>we at her</u> house when the <u>weather</u> is so strange?

Letter Clues and Words in the Word Clues

beautiful: _ _ _ <u>beautiful</u> person inside and out: <u>Be + a + utiful</u> = <u>beautiful</u> (*Letter Clue*).

argument:

begi<u>nn</u>ing (Try *inn* in your clue):

business:

de<u>s</u>ert (abandon, leave alone): When you _ _ _ _ _ _ someone, you leave them all alone (like one lone s).

de<u>ss</u>ert:

fami<u>li</u>ar: It's not good for a <u>family</u> to be f _ _ _ _ _ _ _ with a l _ _ _.

separate:

through:

tired:

Clues That Use Other Forms of the Word

For these words, use *Other Forms of the Word* (*OWFs*) where you can hear some of the letters better. *Remember*: You can always find the *Other Forms of the Word* in a good dictionary.

eagle (Check the dictionary.):

giggle: In giggling, you can hear the gl in g _ _ _ _ _.

sign:

Same Pattern Clues

Some words with the *Same Pattern* are suggested, but feel free to use your own ideas.

certain (*pain, rain, train*):

does (*able to do*): You can find two d _ _ _ (female deer) in d _ _ _.

horse (*hose, worse*):

goes (*foes, toes*):

stairs:

stares:

threw (*toss*: *brew, crew, flew, stew…*):

tried:

More Clues-in-a-Row

amiable (*friendly*: In French, *ami* means *friendly*):

nightingales:

pigeon: My pigeon has love my pig (an) eon.

weeknights:

Let's Review Some POWER Spelling Clues

1. **ache**: I have <u>a chest</u> a _ _ _ : _ + _ _ _ ~~st~~ = _ _ _ _ .

2. **address**: Add my a _ _ _ _ _ _ to your a _ _ _ _ _ _ book.

3. **a-gain**: You make _ _ _ _ _ in ability if you do something a _ _ _ _ and a _ _ _ _ .

4. **ar-gu-ment**: It's hard to have an a _ _ _ _ _ _ _ with g _ _ in your mouth: arg<u>um</u>ent.

5. **beautiful**: B_ _ b _ _ _ _ _ _ _ _ person (Say: <u>Be a</u> <u>beautiful</u> person, and hear *the silent e and a*).

6. **be-gin-ning**: At the b _ _ _ _ _ _ _ _ of our trip, we stayed at an i _ _ : beg<u>inn</u>ing.

7. **bicycle**: _ _ _ _ _ _ _ is made with 2 Greek words: <u>bi</u>-2 + <u>cycle</u>-wheel = _ _ _ _ _ _ _ .

8. **busi-ness**: I need a b _ _ _ _ my b _ _ _ _ _ _ _ : <u>bus + in + ess</u> = _ _ _ _ _ _ _ _ .

9. **calendar**: A c _ _ _ _ _ _ _ has a list of d _ _ _ _ . Can I <u>lend Art</u> a <u>calendar</u>? <u>ca</u>~~n~~ + <u>lend</u> + <u>Art</u>.

10. **certain**: I think it's c _ _ _ _ _ _ to r _ _ _ .

11. **desert** (dry place): Sometimes the d _ _ _ _ _ _ can feel silent and alone: one <u>s</u>.

12. **desert** (abandon): There's just one s in d _ _ _ _ _ (to abandon).

13. **dessert** (treat): I love <u>s</u>trawberry <u>s</u>hortcake for _ _ _ _ _ _ _ (something <u>s</u>weet; <u>s</u>econds).

14. **eagle**: The mother e _ _ _ _ cared for e_ ch little e _ _ _ _ _ .

15. **does**: Where _ _ _ _ a buck go when _ _ _ _ are with their fawns?

16. **goes**: When he g _ _ _ driving, he keeps his t _ _ _ ready.

17. **horse**: She cooled down her h _ _ _ _ with a h _ _ _ .

18. **sep-a-rate**: As I tried to s _ _ _ _ _ _ _ the oranges and apples, <u>a</u> r _ _ jumped out.

19. **stairs**: We climbed the _ _ _ _ _ _ in p _ _ _ _ .

20. **stares**: The actor practiced _ _ _ _ _ _ and gl _ _ _ _ _ .

21. **straight**: A _ _ _ _ w is right if it's _ _ _ _ _ _ _ _ .

22. **threw**: We _ _ _ _ _ out the b<u>rew</u>.

23. **through**: It's <u>rough</u> to walk _ _ _ _ _ _ _ a door.

24. **tired**: When I'm _ _ _ _ _ my eyes get r _ _ .

25. **tried**: I _ _ _ _ _ to reach Ed. *Same Pattern*: dried, fried

➤ **night-in-gales**: Even at n _ _ _ _ i_ g _ _ _ _ of wind, the n _ _ _ _ _ _ _ _ _ _ sing.

LESSON 4

Conquering Contractions and Possessives
Learning How the Tiny, Powerful Apostrophe Works

Tiny, but incredibly powerful, the **apostrophe** is really very easy to understand. The apostrophe takes on just two responsibilities, but they're very important.

1st: CONTRACTION: The apostrophe replaces missing letters in a noun + verb contraction: *Paul's hiking. Tina's climbing...* and also in a pronoun + verb contraction: *He's hiking. She's climbing...*

2nd: POSSESSION: The apostrophe shows possession for nouns: *Jim's bicycle*; *Laura's skis...*, but not for the Personal Pronouns: *me, you, he, she, it, we, they.* They have their own special *Possessive Pronouns* that don't use an apostrophe: *mine, your, his, hers, its, our* and *their* (also *whose* has its own form)

Contractions

Around A.D. 1400, when the English language was making great changes, people began using words called contractions. Words that people often ran together: *I am; it is; she will; you are; they are...* became connected and shortened: *I'm, it's, she'll, you're; they're...* The apostrophe was simply put in where the letters were taken out.

Like an ant, the apostrophe takes on and replaces letters much larger than itself. It replaces four missing letters in the contractions: *o'clock* and *they'd*, and five letters in: *he'd* and *she'd*. An apostrophe is so easy to use in contractions. *It simply goes in the place of the missing letters!*

o'clock	**they'd**	**he'd**	**she'd**
of the clock	they would	he would	she would

Overall, using contractions is easy. There's just one challenge that really confuses people: 4 sets of *Homophones* where the words are both a *Contraction* (pronoun + verb) and *a Possessive Pronoun*.

it's,	**they're,**	**you're,**	**who's**	**CONTRACTION**: 2 words (pron. + verb) come together.
(it is)	(they are)	(you are)	(who is)	The apostrophe ALWAYS replaces the missing letters.

its,	**their,**	**your,**	**whose**	**POSSESSION**: These special *Possessive Pronouns*
				NEVER use an apostrophe (also: *mine, his, her, our, their*).

They aren't that difficult to spell; you just need to discover ways to remember the difference. So, let's meet: "The Terrible Trio + Who's," or you can could them "The Quizzical Quartet."

THE TERRIBLE TRIO: *they're, it's* and *you're* + *who's*
(All four words are a *Contraction*: pronoun + verb.)
(All four words have a *Homophone* that's a *Possessive Personal Pronoun*.)

Now's the time to learn these four sets of challenging words: they're and their; it's and its; you're and your; and who's and whose. Take time to understand the difference between the *Contraction* that ALWAYS use an apostrophe (to replace missing letters) and the *Possessive Pronoun* that NEVER needs an apostrophe because it has its own special words. Also, these sets of words follow a rule that ALWAYS works!

Learn these words once and for all! Be a *POWER* SPELLER who NEVER mixes them up!!!!

42

The Terrible Trio and Who's Starring on Their Own Page

THE TERRIBLE TRIO: they're - it's and you're + who's

(All four words are contractions consisting of a pronoun and a verb)
(All four words also have a homophone that shows possession.)

Of all the words in the English language— they're and their, it's and its, you're and your, and who's and whose are probably the most often confused and misspelled. The reason is, that in addition to being contractions, these words also have a homophone that shows possession. (*They're* also has an adverb *there* that tells where).

Well, it's *Show Time*, and the *Apostrophes* are here and ready to help you –
Learn these *Contractions* and *Possessive Words* NOW!!!!

1. **they're, their,** and **there** NOTE: All three of these homophones begins with <u>the</u>.

    <u>they</u>'re = contraction meaning: <u>they are</u> (pronoun + verb). <u>They're</u> at school (They are).

    <u>their</u>   = possessive pronoun: <u>their</u> book (<u>Their</u> has <u>heir</u> in it). The <u>heir</u> rode <u>their</u> bikes.

    <u>there</u>   = adverb telling where: over <u>there</u> (<u>There</u> has <u>here</u> in it). They ran here and <u>there</u>.

2. **it's** and **its** REMEMBER: Apostrophes replace missing letters in contractions: <u>it's</u> (it is).

    it's   = contraction meaning: <u>it is</u> (pronoun + verb). <u>It's</u> a beautiful day. (It is).

    its   = possessive pronoun: <u>its</u> power. When he hits the ball, he watches its power.

3. **you're** and **you're** REMEMBER: Apostrophes replace missing letters: <u>you're</u> (you are).

    you're = contraction meaning: <u>you are</u> (pronoun + verb). <u>You're</u> my friend (You are).

    your   = possessive pronoun: <u>your</u> book (<u>Your</u> has <u>our</u> in it). I put <u>our</u> bats with <u>your</u> bat.

4. **who's** and **whose** ask questions. REMEMBER: The contractions gets the apostrophe (who's).

    who's = contraction meaning: <u>who is</u> (pronoun + verb). Who's on third base (Who is)?

    whose = possessive pronoun: <u>whose</u> hose?   <u>Whose</u> <u>hose</u> has been watering my r<u>ose</u>s?

Learn the *Clues* above to remember these words. Confused? Just ask: Is the word a <u>contraction</u> or does it show <u>possession</u>? Try this no-fail test. Take a sentence: When he hits a ball, he watches *it's* power. Try to fill in the missing letter in *it's*: He watches *it is* power. If the sentence makes sense, you have a *contraction. Keep the apostrophe.* If it doesn't make sense, you have a *possessive pronoun. Throw out the apostrophe,* but *keep the ball!*

So... Who's on first?

Conquering Pronoun plus Verb Contractions

❑ **NOW TRY THIS:** Since most contractions have a pronoun plus a verb, it helps to organize them across from the pronoun and under the verb that they go with. You may know most of these contractions; but, for review, write out the 2 words for each contraction below

Pronoun	am, are, is	would, had	has, have	will
I	I'm	I'd *I would*	I've	I'll
YOU	you're	you'd	you've *you have*	you'll
HE	he's	he'd	he's	he'll
SHE	she's	she'd	she's	she'll
IT	it's	it'd	it's	it'll *it will*
WE	we're	we'd *we would*	we've	we'll
THEY	they're	they'd	they've	they'll
WHO	who's	who'd	who's *who has*	who'll
	who're *who are*		who've	
THAT	that's	that'd	that's	that'll
WHAT	what's	what'd	what's	what'll
THERE	there's	there'd *there would*	there's *there has*	there'll
(adverb)			there've	

❑ **DO YOU KNOW THESE?** The rest of the contractions below contain a verb, plus a Word like *should, might,* or *not…* (A few contractions that go with pronouns are also listed.) For review, write out these contractions as two words.

ponoun + will	pronoun + is, has	verb + not	wouldn't	hadn't *had not*
these'll	here's *here is*	can't	aren't	mustn't
those'll	one's	don't *do not*	doesn't	didn't
this'll	**verb +have**	isn't	wasn't	needn't
	could've	won't *will not*	weren't	
let + pronoun	should've	shouldn't	hasn't	
let's *let us*	would've	couldn't	haven't	

"I haven't got a dime"

WHAT DO YOU THINK? Two meanings for *contract* are (1) *an agreement between two or more parties* and (2) *to draw two parts together as you do when you "contract" or shorten a muscle."* Do you think the word, contraction, is a good name for these shortened words? Explain why or why not.

The Terrible Trio plus Who's Go to the Beach and the Fair

❑ **TRY THIS**: The Terrible Trio + Who's have all gone to the beach and the fair today. Their problem is: They can't always remember which *Homophone* they should be, so they need your help. For each sentence, choose the correct *Homophone* and write it in the blank.

REMEMBER: *Contractions* ALWAYS get the apostrophe. The *Possessive Pronouns* NEVER do because they have their own little words to show possession: *their, its, your*, and *whose*. (While they're at the fair, our *Homophones* want to learn about the largest and fastest roller coaster in the world. Do you know where it is?)

1.   (They're, Their, There) _____ all going to the beach together.

2.   They saw giant waves crashing over _____ (they're, their, there), by _____ shoes.

3.   The *Contractions* wondered how they got sand in _____ (they're, their, there) shoes.

4.   Their sand castle had a flag on _____ (it's, its) turret and a moat around _____ base.

5.   Together, they shouted, "(It's, Its) _____ great fun to run and play in the waves."

6.   "(You're, Your) _____ a great wave jumper," the *Apostrophes* exclaimed to each other.

7.   "Yikes! (It's, Its) _____ already time to go the fair," they all yelled.

8.   "Don't forget (you're, your) _____ shoes," the *Pronouns* reminded the *Contractions*.

9.   (You're, Your) _____ really going to ride the Fastest Roller Coaster in the World?

10. "(It's, Its) _____ our turn to get on the roller coaster," the *Apostrophes* shouted with glee.

11. (Who's, Whose) _____ jacket fell while we were on the Ferris Wheel?

12. "(Who's, Whose) _____ going on the Merry-Go-Round?" the little *Apostrophes* asked.

(The Fastest and Tallest Roller Coast in the World is at Magic Mountain in Valencia, California: 415 feet tall; 100 mph. The World's Largest Ferris Wheel is in London and measures 500 feet in diameter)

45

For Nouns: Contractions and Possessives Use Apostrophes

There's no confusion about apostrophes for nouns because *both* contractions *and* nouns showing possession get to use the apostrophe. Nouns don't have special possessive words like pronouns do.

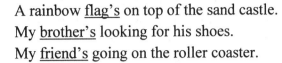

A <u>flag's</u> stars

My <u>brother's</u> shoes

My <u>friend's</u> jacket

A rainbow <u>flag's</u> on top of the sand castle.

My <u>brother's</u> looking for his shoes.

My <u>friend's</u> going on the roller coaster.

Apostrophes Show Possession for Singulars Nouns and Plurals Nouns

SINGULAR NOUNS: To show possessive for a singular noun, add 's.

the <u>wave's</u> height; a <u>friend's</u> sandcastle; my <u>mother's</u> shells; <u>Joe's</u> jacket; my <u>sister-in-law's</u> sons

POSSESSIVE PLURALS: To form the possessive plural of a noun, first write the noun in plural form. If the plural noun ends in s, add an apostrophe. If the plural noun does not end in s, add 's.

<u>children's</u> beach toys; my <u>sisters'</u> homes; the <u>owners'</u> carnival rides; my <u>sisters-in-law's</u> mom

SINGULAR	POSSESSIVE SINGULAR	PLURAL	POSSESSIVE PLURAL
My friend	My friend's sand castle	My friends	My friends' sand castles
Her horse	Her horse's reins	Their horse	Their horses' reins
The woman	The woman's jackets	The women	The women's jackets
Son-in-law	My son-in-law's shovel	sons-in-law	The sons-in-law's shovels

Apostrophes Show Individual Possession and Joint Possession.

INDIVIDUAL POSSESSION: For individual possession, add an apostrophe to the name of each owner.

<u>Marti's</u> and <u>George's</u> sandcastles;   <u>George's</u> and <u>David's</u> bikes;   the <u>seals'</u> and <u>penguins'</u> food.

the <u>lark's</u> and <u>nightingale's</u> songs;   <u>Lara's</u> and <u>Heather's</u> dad;   the <u>horse's</u> and <u>colt's</u> barn;

JOINT POSSESSION: For joint possession, use an apostrophe only with the final owner.

<u>Joe and Linda's</u> Beach House;   <u>Ron and Richard's</u> Roller Coaster Rides;

<u>Frank and Farley's</u> Ferris Wheel   <u>Maynard and Mary's</u> Merry-go-round;

Use Apostrophes for the Plural of Letters and Numbers

We carved <u>9's</u>, <u>10's</u>, and <u>12's</u> in the moist sand.   <u>M's</u> and <u>W's</u> have a wavy, ocean shape.
When I write my story about the beach, I'll be careful not to use too many <u>and's</u> and <u>very's</u>.

Tackling Homophones and Other Confusing Words

Homophones, words with the same sound but a different spelling and meaning, can be challenging (along with *Confusing Words* that are similar). Since *spell check* can't check them, *you* need to *know the difference*. So, exercise your spelling muscles, learn these words, and become a ***POWER SPELLER!***

❏ **TRY THIS**: Since the <u>Terrible Trio</u> + <u>Who's</u> are *Homophones*, let's review them. For each set, label the word that's the *contraction* and write out the full word (we've = contraction: we have). Then label the *possessive pronouns*. Also, write down the *Clues* you're using to remember these words.

1. <u>they're, their, there</u> (Never Forget: All three words begins with <u>the</u>.)
   they're =
   their =
   there = adverb:

2. <u>it's and its</u>
   it's =
   its =

"hee, hee, hee!" 3. <u>you're and you're</u>
   you're =
   your =

"Whose hose is this?"

4. <u>who's and whose</u> (These words ask a question.)
   who's =
   whose = interrogative pronoun:

❏ **NOW TRY THIS**: Create *Clues* for remembering the difference between these *Homophones*.

1. peace (n. harmony)
   piece (n. serving)

2. principal (n. person who runs a school, business, etc.)
   principle (n. rule)

3. to (prep. toward)
   too (adv. also)
   two (adj. number)

4. capital (n. city; money)
   capital (adj. letter)
   Capitol (n. Congress building)

5. stationery (n. paper for a letter)
   stationary (adj. stable; permanent)

Homophones, Homographs, and Words That Get Confused

This list includes *Homophones* (same sound, different spelling and meaning); *Homographs* (same, spelling, same sound, different meaning); plus sets of *Words that get Confused* because they're similar.

❑ **NOW**: Carefully read these words, and mark or highlight the ones you find challenging and need to work on remembering. Use these *Clues* and *Tools* to remember the differences, or create your own. You'll be learning one or two sets of these words in each lesson that follows. Also, be sure to look at the *POWER Spelling List of Homophones* in the *Book of Lists*.

1. **accept** (v. agree to; take what's offered)   I agree to accept your offer to teach me spelling.
   except (prep. to eliminate, to x-out)   There's no excuse except illness.

2. **advice** (n. helpful information or counsel)   The vice-principal added good advice.
   advise (v. to give advice or counsel)   Be wise when you advise.

3. **all ready** (adj. all of us prepared)   We are all ready (all of us prepared).
   already (adv. previously; by this time)   We were already there (The prefix *all* is spelled al-.).

4. **all together** (pron. all in one place)   We were all (all of us) together in the gym for the game
   altogether (adv. entirely, totally)   Your algebra homework is altogether (entirely) too late.

5. **altar** (n. altar in a church)   The altar area rises up in the shape of an A.
   alter (v. to change)   You can alter the terms of a contract.

6. **angel** (n. a heavenly being)   She cut a pink angel out of gelatin.
   angle (n. point where 2 lines meet)   He drew an angle with a ruler and put an e in the angle

7. **assistance** (n. help or aid)   They gave dance assistance.
   assistants (n. helpers or people who aid)   I assist ants who are assistants to the queen.

8. **bare** (v. take on; adj. nude)   You can't bare too many cares.
   bear (n. wild animal)   Don't be a bear.

9. **brought** (v. to bring)   I thought I brought enough chairs.
   bought (v. to buy)   I ought to have brought the book I bought.

10. **buy** (v. to purchase)   Can you buy a guy a flower?
    by (adv. near)   By is short. We walked by the park. Pattern: by, my, try
    bye (exclamation. Farewell)   Good-bye. Draw out the e… Good-by-eee… or by-eee

11. **capital** (n. city; money)   Tallahassee is the capital of Florida. Cash is capital.
    capital (adj. capital letter)   Capital letters are taller than some lowercase letters.
    Capitol (n. Congress building in Wash., D.C.)   The U.S. Capitol has a dome in the shape of an O.

12. **choose** (v. pick out)   I want to choose the biggest goose.
    chose (v. past tense of to choose)   He chose a green hose to water a red rose.

13. **close** (adv. near) She put her nose close to the rose.
    close (v. shut) Close the refrigerator so it won't lose cold air.
    clothes (n. clothing) Clothes are made from cloth: cloth + es = clothes.

14. **coarse** (adj. rough) Coarse with an a is an adjective. That oar is coarse.
    course (n. route, school subject) Our course was difficult, but we finished it.

15. **council** (n. legislative group) I use a pencil for notes at the council meeting.
    counsel (n. advice verb) He gave select words of counsel.
    counselor (n. one who advises) A counselor plays many roles. (*Roles* last five letters of coun*selor* reversed.)

16. **dear** (adj. kind; n. kind person) My dear, have no fear for I am near. Pattern: hear, gear, tear.
    deer (n. animal) A deer was nibbling on a reed. *Reversal*: deer – reed.

17. **desert** (n. dry place) He felt alone and deserted in the desert (one s).
    desert (v. leave alone) Desert means to abandon, leave alone, one lone s.
    dessert (n. treat) A dessert is something sweet like strawberry shortcake.

18. **flour** (n. grain made from wheat) I need four cups of flour. *Pattern*: hour, our, sour
    flower (n. bloom) April showers bring May flowers. *Pattern*: flower, tower.

19. **forth** (adv. forward, onward) He set forth – forward on an adventure.
    fourth (adj. concerning number four) Four + th. He is in the fourth grade.

20. **hangar** (n. place for storing airplanes) A hangar is a garage for an airplane.
    hanger (n. for hanging dresses) She put her dress on the hanger.

21. **hear** (v. listen) You hear with your ear.
    here (adv. this place) Here, there and everywhere.

22. **hour** (n. 60 minutes) I checked the hour hand on the clock.
    our (poss. adj. belonging to us) Our cat and your cat both are named *Shadow*.

23. **knew** (v. past of know) I know I knew before the new year. *SPP*: k-new.
    gnu (n. African antelope) Don't shoot a gnu with a gun. (*Same Letters*: gnu – gun.)
    new (adj. opposite of old) I bought a few new things.
    know (v. to be acquainted with now) I know you now.
    now (adv. at this time) How now brown cow? (*Same Letters*: now – own.)

24. **later** (adv. after some time) I ate later. Later comes from late.
    latter (adj. coming after) What's the matter with the latter batter?

25. **lead** (n .a metal; adj. metallic. *Homograph*) I read what he'd written in lead.
    lead (v. to show the way. *Homograph*) He likes to lead the group in reading.
    led (v. past of to lead) He led Ed to the school.

26. **lightening** (v. make lighter in color or weight) I was lightening her ten-pound load (from verb, to lighten).
    lightning (n. light flash before thunder) The lightning made a light zing across the sky.

27. **loose** (adj. not tight, able to get away)　The goose got loose.
　　lose (v. to suffer loss; to not find)　If you lose your nose, can you find it?

28. **meant** (v. past of to mean)　He saw me and the ant.　We were meant to be friends.
　　met (v. past of to meet)　I met my pet each day after school. *Pattern*: get, jet, let.

29. **passed** (past tense of v. to pass)　She studied and passed the test: pass + ed = passed.
　　past (n., adj. former, last. *Homograph*)　I wish this past year would last forever.
　　past (prep., by. *Homograph*)　He drove past the fast lane.

30. **peace** (n. quiet, harmony)　We wanted each nation to have peace.
　　piece (n. a serving)　I would like a piece of pie.

31. **peal** (v. to ring)　The bells begin to peal for the noon day meal.
　　peel (v. to remove the skin)　Orange peel feels bumpy.

32. **principal** (n. person in charge of a school)　The principal of the school was his pal.
　　principal (adj. main)　Three principal parts of a palm are: roots, trunk and leaves.
　　principle (n. rule, adj. main)　A principle is a rule of conduct.

33. **quiet** (adj. still)　She was quiet about her diet.
　　quite (adv. a certain size)　He ate quite a bite. (*Rule*: qu works as one letter.)

34. **stairs** (n. steps)　We climbed the stairs in pairs. *Pattern*: chairs, fairs
　　stares (n. looks; v. keep looking at)　Do you care if he stares? *Pattern*: dares, mares, wares.

35. **stationary** (adj., fixed, permanent)　A stationary object stays stable.　Stationary is an adj.
　　stationery (n. writing paper)　You write letters on stationery

36. **steal** (v. to take, to hide)　Make a deal; never steal. *Pattern*: heal, meal, peal, real.
　　steel (n. a heavy metal)　Steel feels smooth and cold. *Pattern*: peel, reel, wheel.

37. **threw** (v. to toss)　His crew threw out the brew.　He threw in a new ball.
　　through (prep. by means of)　It is rough to walk through a door.

38. **tired** (adj. fatigued)　When my eyes are tired, they get red.
　　tried (past of verb to try)　I tried Ed. *Y Rule*: try, change y to I and add ed = tried.

39. **to** (prep. toward)　To is short so you can use t' for to.　I walked t' the park.
　　too (adv. also, excessively)　Too means too much.　Stretch the sound.　I ate too… much.
　　two (adj. number)　The number 2 (two).

40. **weather** (n. climate)　I eat her meals outside when the weather is nice.
　　whether (conj. either or)　The surgeon had to decide whether or not to use ether.

41. **which** (adj. which one)　Which person is rich?
　　witch (n. rides a broom)　A witch had an itch that she scratched with her broom.

42. **write** (v. to enscribe)　I liked to write my stories at a peaceful site.
　　rite (n. a ritual)　Marriage is a rite or ritual of joining for life.
　　right (adj. correct)　If an action is right, you can do it in the light.

Phonics Power: The Building Blocks of Spelling

Once upon a time, maybe before you can remember, you began learning Phonics (the sounds that the letters of your alphabet make). Perhaps you learned that BBB… was the sound you hear in BALL and BUBBLES…, C you hear in CAT, and D in DOGS and DANCE…

Probably you learned to sing or say: ABCDEFG…HIJK…LMNOP…QRS…TUV…WXY and Z, where you learned a name for every letter in your alphabet. Soon, you began to recognize or read words and you learned CONSONANTS and VOWELS were the building blocks you put together to build words of all sizes…

BALL   FLUFF   HORSE   TICKLE   SEASHORE   EXPERIMENTALLY

Phonics Uses Your Senses of Hearing, Seeing, and Feeling

Since you can hear, see, and feel the letters of the alphabet and the sounds they make, you could say:

PHONICS IS AUDITORY, VISUAL, and KINESTHETIC.

AUDITORY means you can HEAR the sounds of letters in words and how loud or soft they are. Your ability to hear these sounds began even before you were born. After birth, you kept hearing and copying people – and you developed your ability to hear, detect, and spell the sounds in words.

VISUAL means you can SEE letters and words and can see the objects they name: FROG, SUN… Also, if you watch carefully, you can see people's mouths form sounds and words when they speak.

KINESTHETIC means you can FEEL sounds, letters, and words. You can touch and feel your lips, tongue, mouth…when you say and read words. You can feel motor memory, which is the shape of letters and words in your hand motion as you write. You can *feel* the difference between loud and soft tones, and between angry words and laughter – because you can feel sounds make vibrations.

Knowing that most people hear, see, and feel, can truly help you appreciate people who have to learn without one of their senses. What would it be like if you could just feel and hear? How would you learn if you could just see and feel? It's amazing to think about someone like Helen Keller. When she was born, Helen could hear and see. Before she was two, however, both her sight and hearing were destroyed by a brain fever. With the help of her tutor, Anne Sullivan, Helen learned to speak and identify objects and words through her sense of touch. She also used touch to feel Braille and to learn to form letters and words. By age 16, Helen Keller was able to go to school, and then on to college where she graduated with honors. She later lectured and wrote books.

The chart on the next page will show you The Sounds That Build the Words in the English Language.

Sounds: The Building Blocks of the English Language

26 LETTERS exist in English: **19 CONSONANTS, 5 VOWELS, 2 CONSONANT/VOWELS.**
These 26 letters and their combinations create all the different sounds in the English Language.
15 CONSONANTS MAKE THEIR OWN SOUND – B D F H J K L M N P R T V Z and Qu.
  2 CONSONANTS: G and S make their own sound; and G copies J (gem); S copies Z (sunrise).
    CONSONANTS: C just copies **K** (cat) and **S** (city). **X** just copies **KS** (box) and **Z** (xylophone).
  4 SOUNDS: W and Y are **CONSONANT/VOWELS** – w in wind/ bow ; y in yes/sky; bunny.

5 SHORT VOWELS	**CLOSED SYLLABLES**		**OPEN SYLLABLES**
a /ă/ as in **baa**	cat	**apple**	**acorn**
e /ĕ/ as in **eh**…	bed	**elephant**	
i /ĭ/ as in **ick**	pin	**igloo**	**divide**
o /ŏ/ as in **ah**	frog	**octopus**	
u /ŭ/ as in **ugh**	sun	**umbrella**	

5 LONG VOWELS	**SILENT-E**	**2 VOWELS**	**OPEN SYLLABLES**	
ā /ā/ as in **ace**	face	rain	table	
ē /ē/ as in **bee**	theme	peach	zero	
ī /ī/ as in **ice**	kite	pie	tiger	
ō /ō/ as in **oak**	rose	boat	banjo	
ū /ū/ as in **cube**	flute	fruit	music	**(few)**

5 R-CONTROLLED VOWEL SOUNDS (<u>ire</u>: like long <u>i</u>: f**ire**; <u>ure</u>: like long <u>u</u>: l**ure**)

ar /är/ as in st**ar**		
er /èr/ as in f**ern**	**ir** /èr/ as in b**ird**	**ur** /èr/ as in t**ur**tle
or /ôr/ as in h**orn**	**ore** /ôr/ as in **ore**	
air /âr/ as in h**air**	**are** /âr/ as in squ**are**	
ear /ēr/ as in t**ear**	**eer** /ēr/ as in d**eer**	

1 BROAD O VOWEL SOUND

au /ô/ as in **auto**   **aw** /ô/ as in s**aw**   **al** /ô/ as in b**all**

1 SPECIAL VOWEL COMBINATIONS – DIPHTHONGS

ou /ou/ as in cl**ou**d   **ow** /ou/ as in **owl**
oi /oi/ as in c**oi**l   **oy** /oi/ as in b**oy**

2 DOUBLE O SOUNDS

oo /o͞o/ as in m**oo**n   **u** /o͞o/   as in r**u**ler
oo /o͝o/ as in b**oo**k   **u** /o͝o/   as in b**u**sh

SCHWA SOUND /ə/ (Unaccented Neutral Vowel Sound in par**a**de, po**e**m, penc**i**l, lem**o**n, circ**u**s)

5 CONSONANT DIGRAPHS (2 CONSONANTS = ONE SOUND: Together Teams You Never Separate)

CH as in **chair**	bea**ch**	
SH as in **shell**	fla**sh**	
TH as in **three**	pa**th**	(voiced: with breath)
TH as in **feather**	smoo**th**	(unvoiced: without breath)
WH as in **wheat**	**wh**at	(HW sound)

1 NG as in so**ng**   e**ng**ine   (1 sound in song: 2 in engine)

1 ZH as in trea**s**ure (not spelled zh)   vi**s**ion.   a**z**ure (blue). mira**g**e (not real)

Hearing the Sounds of Phonics

Let's play a game where you truly *hear sound*. It's called *Onomatopoeia*. What? Sounds like Greek to me. In fact, *Onomatopoeia* is Greek and means *to make words* (-*poeia*) where the *name of the word* (*onoma-*) *is the same as the sound*: *bong, creak, choo choo, roar, splash, zoom*, and even, *ah choo.*

❏ **NOW**: *Hear* each word and write it next to its matching vowel sound: **baa**, **bar**k, **bl**a**re**, **bo**ng, **bo**w **wo**w, **bur**p, **ca**w, **chu**g, **cli**p, **clo**p, **croak**, **eek**, **eh**, **grate**, **groa**n, **grow**l, **meo**w, **oi**nk, **patter**, **pitter**, **pur**r, **roar**, **screech**, **sn**o**rt**, **ti**ck, **to**ck, **too**t, **wh**i**r**, **woo**f, **yu**ck, **zoo**m. Also, add sound words that *you* like.

Short Vowel Sounds

- ă as in **a**pple — *ah choo*
- ĕ as in **e**lephant — *eh...eh*
- ĭ as in **i**gloo
- ŏ as in **o**ctopus
- ŭ as in s**u**n

Long Vowel Sounds

- ā as in f**a**ce — rain
- ē as in **ee**k — peach
- ī as in **i**ce — kite
- ō as in **oa**k — rose
- ū in **u**nicycle — cube

R-Controlled Vowel Sounds

- är as in st**ar** — *"arf"*
- ĕr /er/ as in f**er**n
- îr /er/ as in b**ir**d
- ôr as in h**or**n — ore
- ûr /er/ as in t**ur**tle
- âr as in h**air** — square
- ēr as in t**ear** — deer
- ĩr as in f**ire**
- ūr as in l**ure**

Special Vowel Combinations

- au as in **au**to — saw — ball
- ou as in cl**ou**d — flower
- oi as in c**oi**l — boy
- o͞o as in m**oo**n — ruler
- o͝o as in b**oo**k — bush

Consonant/Vowel: y as in **y**es/sk**y**, e**y**e — w as in **w**ind/bo**w**

❏ **NOW**: Write these words next to their matching vowel sounds: **air**plane, **a**maze, **a**nt, **au**thor, **bir**thday, **e**lephant, **fue**l, **i**dea, **i**gloo, **loo**ked, feath**er**, **loo**se, **lo**se, m**er**maid, m**ou**th, n**oi**sy, **o**ctopus, **oi**ntment, **o**pened, pl**ai**n, pl**a**ne, p**ar**ty, p**au**se, s**e**ven, s**oo**n, st**or**e, s**ure**, t**ear** (to rip), t**ear** eyes, th**e**se, t**ur**tle, **u**mpire, and v**o**yage. If you wish, create *Clues* for some words.

From the Spoken Language to the Roman Alphabet You Use Today

Once, very long ago, before alphabets were developed, people gestured, spoke, and made pictures to communicates. Egyptians carved hieroglyphics (word pictures). The Chinese created characters. *Then* in 3000 B.C., the Hebrews created their alphabet by using *the first letter of an important word for each consonant*. From 1500-1000 B.C., Phoenician traders developed an alphabet of 22 consonants. The Greeks learned this alphabet in 800 B.C., dropped some consonants, added vowels, and in 600 B.C. passed their 24-letters to the Romans who added capitals to complete the 26-letter Roman alphabet.

It's interesting to trace how some letters developed. Each letters below began with a hieroglyphic picture. The Hebrews took the hieroglyphic for ox, drew a simpler ox, and made letter <u>A</u> for *aleph* (Heb. ox). The Phoenicians and Greeks each turned the horns, and the Romans wrote the <u>A</u> you use today. <u>B</u> stood for *beth*, the Hebrew one-room *house*. The Phoenicians added a doorway; the Greeks drew *beth* like their 2-room house; and the Romans rounded <u>B</u> into the shape you write. The Hebrew took the hieroglyphic with the shape of ocean waves and created <u>M</u> for *mem* which meant *water*. <u>O</u> stood for *eye* (omicron), and some ancient alphabets even added a dot for the pupil. The Phoenician letters *aleph* and *beth* later became *alpha* and *beta* to make the Greek word *alphabet*.

| Egyptian Phoenician Greek Roman | Phoenician Greek Roman | Hebrew Phoenician Roman | Egyptian Phoenician Rome |

Now let's discover how English got its alphabet. In 450 A.D., three German tribes (the Angles, Saxons and Jutes) conquered England, and Anglo-Saxon became the spoken language. It's interesting to know that Anglo-Saxon also had an alphabet. It was made of straight letters called runes (*rune*: secret), but *only the priests* could carve these letter for their *secret messages* and *spells*. Therefore, when Christian missionaries came to England in 597, they taught the common people to write Anglo Saxon with the *Roman Alphabet*. Note that if the common people had been allowed to use the *Anglo-Saxon Alphabet* you'd probably be writing letters like the ones below rather than using rounded Roman letters.

Write your full name with Anglo Saxon letters: _____. Also, write down any letters that look like the Roman letters you use. Why do you think these runes are straight?

ᚠ ᚠ ᛗ ᛦ (ᛉ)ᛁ ᛈᛟ ᚾ ᛒ ᛃ ᚻ ᚴᚷ ᛉ ᚾ (ᚦ)ᚻᚻ ᛝ ᛘᛗ ᛏᛉ (ᚹ)ᚱ ᛋᛏ ᚦ ᛈᚱᛗ

a ae e ea eo i o oe u b ch d f g h j k l m n ng p r s t th w y

- ❑ **NOW**: To learn more about hearing and seeing Phonics, choose one of these activities:

1. On the next page is the *Roman Alphabet* with a drawing for each consonant and vowel. Make an *Alphabet Chart* (any size, even miniature) and draw something important to you for each sound.

2. Today, Chinese still uses characters (about 50,000 word pictures) which often look like what they mean: *eye* ◎, *mouth* ▭, and *water* ⌇. Choose at least 15 Chinese characters or create your own language with at least 15 word pictures. Then write a letter or story using characters or your word pictures (Add English words if you need them.).

3. Turn all or some of the letter of the alphabet into a picture that begins with the letter (examples below

54

Let's Feel the Digraph Sounds (*Two Letters Make One Sound*)

Each digraph (CH, SH, TH-with air, TH-no air, and WH) makes its *own* sound. This sound is not a blend of sounds, but it's one single sound made by 2 letters (Gk: di: two + graph: letter). Digraphs are TOGETHER TEAMS that *must stay together* to make their sound. The NG sound acts like a digraph in the middle and at the end of syllables (ringing, singe), but NG can also be two separate sounds (engine, language). There's also a special ZH sound that acts like a digraph (not spelled ZH, but you hear it in azure, treasure). GH and PH act like digraphs (make one sound, but not their own. They copy F).

❑ **NOW:** Just like you said the consonant sounds, say these digraph sounds (plus NG and ZH). Try to FEEL how your lips, tongue, mouth, teeth, and breath work to make each sound.

CH (child, church) Say *church*. Feel your TONGUE touch the front ridge of the ROOF of your MOUTH and a little AIR goes between your LIPS.

SH (shore, shush) Say *shush*. Feel you TONGUE near the front of the ROOF of your MOUTH as your BREATH makes a *sh...ush* sound between your TEETH.

TH (thud: voiced: air) Say *thud*. Feel your TONGUE touch your top TEETH and air burst out your MOUTH.

TH (that: unvoiced: bit of air) Say *that*. Feel your TONGUE touch your TEETH and a bit of air come out.

WH (when, why) Feel your LIPS round and open more fully as they release air to make a *whh...* sound.

NG (bong, ring) Say *bong*. Feel your TONGUE round upward as an *ng* resounds in your THROAT.

ZH (mirage, azure) Say *azure*. Feel your MOUTH slightly opened and hushed breath between your TEETH.

Different Ways Digraphs and Sounds like Digraphs Are Spelled

❑ **NOW:** Read the digraph sounds (plus NG, ZH, PH, GH), and add 2 words for each sound. (Exceptions to phonics spelling are in *italics*.)

CH child (*cello-Ita., special*)   **CH copies K:** **ch**ord, **ch**orus (Gr.)

SH shell, sugar (*ocean, machine, conscience*)

TH that, path (voiced: air)

TH thin, smooth (voiceless: little air)

WH wheat (also called HW sound)

NG ring, singing (*tongue*) (NG can also be separated: engine, language.)

ZH azure, division, mirage, pleasure

PH and GH: physics, cough (PH and GH copy F sound.)

❑ **NOW:** Write each word by its matching digraph sounds. Underline the sound: athlete, **ch**ime, choose, **ch**ose, enough, establi**sh**, hush, measure, **ph**ysical, pit**ch**er, **ph**onics, ri**ng**ing, rough, **sh**adow, shark, shape, **sh**one, **sh**own, si**ng**, thought, tough, treasure, vani**sh**ed, **wh**en, **wh**ich, **wh**istle, young.

Let's Hear Single Consonant and Digraph Tongue Twisters

You've probably heard tongue twisters like *Peter Piper picked a peck of pickled peppers...* and *She sells seashells by the seashore*. A great way to hear and feel the sounds of consonants and digraphs is to say tongue twisters since the sounds get repeated again and again. Follow these steps:

First, choose a single consonant: _____.
Then write down words you know that begin with this sound (You can always find more words in a dictionary listed under the consonant.).

Now, put your words together until you create a tongue twister you like. Write it here.

Now, choose a digraph _____ .
Then write down words you know that begin with this sound.

Again, keep putting your words together until you like your tongue twister. Write it here.

A big black bug bit a big black bear.

For fine fish, phone Phil.

Fuzzy Wuzzy was a bear, Fuzzy Wuzzy had no hair. Fuzzy Wuzzy wasn't fuzzy, was he?

How much wood would a woodchuck chuck if a woodchuck would chuck wood?

Girl gargoyle, guy gargoyle

She sells seashells by the seashore.

Peter Piper picked a peck of pickled peppers. A peck of pickled peppers did Peter Piper pick. If Peter Piper picked a peck of pickled peppers, where's the peck of pickled peppers Peter Piper picked?

In Conclusion: The Greeks Did It Again with Some Help from the Italians

Now that you have read this chapter on feeling the vibrating sounds of phonics, here's a bit of history about how these sound vibrations were figured out. As early as 500 B.C., an ancient Greek mathematician named *Pythagoras* did experiments with the sounds produced by vibrating strings. Then, in 400 B.C., the Greek philosopher *Aristotle* suggested that the movement of air carried sound to our ears. Almost 2,000 years later (near 1500 A.D.), the amazing Italian artist and inventor *Leonardo da Vinci* developed the theory that sound travels in waves. Discoveries about sound continue to go on, as more and more is learned about how we hear, see, and feel the words we spell.

!!!It's amazing to know how much goes on for sound to be heard and for words to be spoken!!!

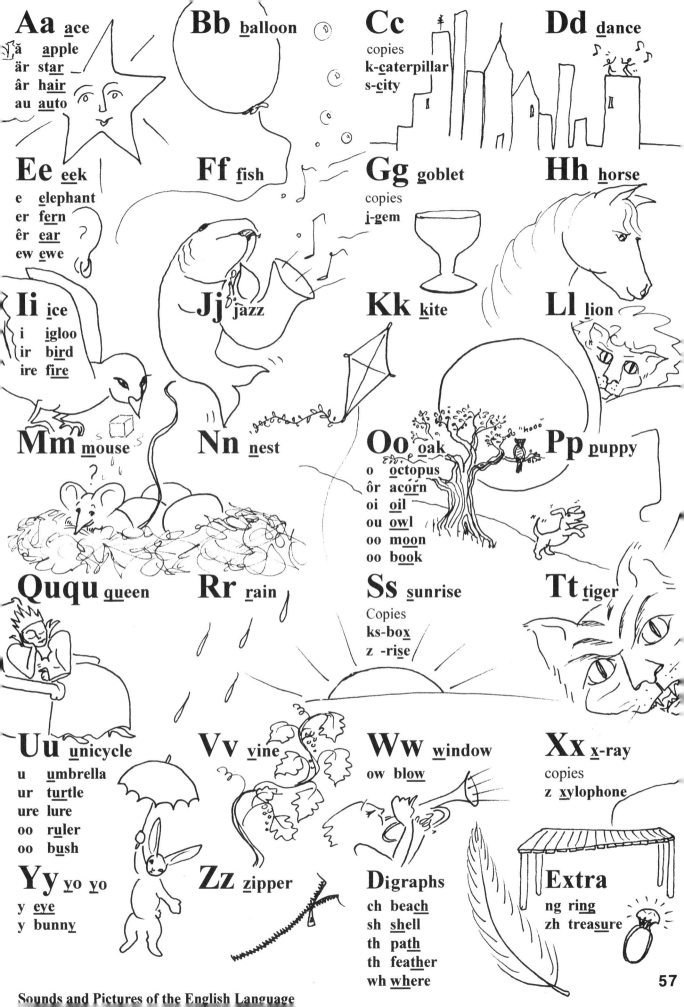

Aa <u>a</u>ce
ă <u>a</u>pple
är st<u>ar</u>
âr h<u>air</u>
au <u>au</u>to

Bb <u>b</u>alloon

Cc
copies
k-<u>c</u>aterpillar
s-<u>c</u>ity

Dd <u>d</u>ance

Ee <u>ee</u>k
e <u>e</u>lephant
er f<u>er</u>n
êr <u>ear</u>
ew <u>ew</u>e

Ff <u>f</u>ish

Gg <u>g</u>oblet
copies
j-<u>g</u>em

Hh <u>h</u>orse

Ii <u>i</u>ce
i <u>i</u>gloo
ir b<u>ir</u>d
ire f<u>ire</u>

Jj <u>j</u>azz

Kk <u>k</u>ite

Ll <u>l</u>ion

Mm <u>m</u>ouse

Nn <u>n</u>est

Oo <u>oa</u>k
o <u>o</u>ctopus
ôr ac<u>or</u>n
oi <u>oi</u>l
ou <u>ow</u>l
oo m<u>oo</u>n
oo b<u>oo</u>k

Pp <u>p</u>uppy

Ququ <u>qu</u>een

Rr <u>r</u>ain

Ss <u>s</u>unrise
Copies
ks-bo<u>x</u>
z -ri<u>s</u>e

Tt <u>t</u>iger

Uu <u>u</u>nicycle
u <u>u</u>mbrella
ur t<u>ur</u>tle
ure l<u>ure</u>
oo r<u>u</u>ler
oo b<u>u</u>sh

Vv <u>v</u>ine

Ww <u>w</u>indow
ow bl<u>ow</u>

Xx <u>x</u>-ray
copies
z <u>x</u>ylophone

Yy <u>y</u>o <u>y</u>o
y <u>ey</u>e
y bunn<u>y</u>

Zz <u>z</u>ipper

Digraphs
ch bea<u>ch</u>
sh <u>sh</u>ell
th pa<u>th</u>
th fea<u>th</u>er
wh <u>wh</u>ere

Extra
ng ri<u>ng</u>
zh trea<u>s</u>ure

57

Sounds and Pictures of the English Language

Feeling the Sounds of Single Consonants and Digraphs

As you think about FEELING the sounds of phonics, first, stop for a minute and listen. What do you hear…? Sounds are going on around you all the time. A brass bell is ringing… People are saying words to each other… A violinist is playing to a hushed audience… Crickets are humming… A waterfall is tumbling over rocks… and a single bird is trilling sweet melodious tones.

For each sound to happen, something has to hit or rub across something else, and create a vibration that starts sound waves resounding through the air. The clapper strikes the bell, and ringing sounds vibrate out. Air moves up and across the vocal cords and people's words move out. As the bow is drawn across the violin's strings, clear tones vibrate and flow out to the audience.

If you've ever dropped a stone into a still pond and watched the circle move out, you have a very clear picture of what sound waves do. For example, when you say, "Hello," or ring a bell, your vocal chords and the bell vibrate and set sound waves in motion that move through the air, just like the stone starts circles moving through the water. These sound waves vibrate to your ear, and strike against your eardrum. When your eardrum is struck, it then starts to vibrate and send out waves. In order for these waves to be understood by the brain, they are changed into nerve impulses. These nerve impulses then continue moving to the hearing part of your brain, where the brain translates the impulses into sounds and words that you can hear and understand.

| VOICE vibrates MUSIC vibrates | Sound vibrates out in waves | Sound waves hit your eardrum | Eardrum sends out waves that are changed to nerve impulses | Brain translates impulses into sound you can understand | YOU |

When you speak, air is forced up from your lungs and through your windpipe. Then, as the air is forced between your vocal chords, they vibrate and send out sound waves. Also, when you speak, you stretch your vocal chords across your voice box (larynx) like two rubber bands. The more tightly these chords are stretched, the higher the sound as the air goes between them. The more relaxed your vocal chords, the lower the sound. You can feel the tightness in your chords if you say *Hello* in a very high voice. You can feel the difference, if you relax and say *Hello* in a low voice. You can experiment with a rubber band. If you pull it tightly and ping it, you get a high tone; if you loosen it and ping it again, you get a low tone. You can feel your vocal chords vibrate when you press your fingers against your Adam's apple and say a word like: *Hello, thanks,* or *birthday.*

Finally, as you think about *feeling* sounds, note that when the tones of someone's voice vibrate to your eardrum, you can FEEL the tones in their voice, and they can feel joyful, sad, afraid…. Also, you can usually tell more about what people are feeling from hearing and feeling their tone of voice, even before you hear their words.

An Orchestra of Living, Feeling Instruments

When you hear birds twittering, frogs croaking, crickets humming, rabbits thumping, you are hearing a living orchestra where creatures are making sounds by blowing, bowing, and striking.

BLOWING: Birds, frogs, and most mammals (like you) force air up a tube so that it vibrates over the vocal chords and sound comes out a mouth or beak. This way of making sound is like woodwinds (flutes, clarinets, bassoons) and brass instruments (trumpets, trombones, horns) in an orchestra. Players blow into a tube, or the lips of the players create vibrations that create the instrument's sound.

BOWING: Crickets "sing" by rubbing sharp scrapers across files on their front wings in much the same way that a person plays a stringed instrument like the violin, viola, cello, bass.

STRIKING: Rabbits thump, woodpeckers peck, hummingbirds and bees beat the air, and whales slap the water with their tails in much the same way that people strike an instrument like a drum or a xylophone. Also, some shellfish strike their claws together and otters hammer shells like cymbals.

In a famous piece of music called *Peter and the Wolf*, the Russian composer, Sergei Prokofiev (1891-1953), uses the tones of instruments to show what the people and animals in his story are like. He uses the high oboe for the duck, the flute for the trills of the bird, and clarinet tones for the cat. Prokofiev captures the walk of the boy, Peter, on the violin; his stern grandfather's walk on the deep bassoon, and the booming of the hunters on the kettledrum. The French horn makes the frightening sounds of the wolf. The music always tells you who is coming into the scene.

❏ **NOW:** To hear and feel more about sounds, write down sounds made by the people, animals, and objects below that begin or end with *single consonants* or *digraphs* (CH, SH, TH, WH, and NG). Since the human voice is the instrument that can make the most sounds, say each sound as you write it.

people	animals	birds	reptiles	insects	cars	trains	bells	sirens	other
		caw							*boing*
									thud

Write your sound words (onomatopoeia) next to their consonant or digraph.

B   R
C   S
D   T
F   V
G   W
H   X and Y
J   Z
K
L   CH
M   SH
N   TH
P   WG
Qu   NG

Let's Feel the Consonant Sounds

□ **NOW:** As you say each sound, touch your Adam's apple and feel your breath vibrating (It's movin across your vocal chords). Also feel your lips, tongue, mouth, and teeth forming the sounds. Have fun!

B	(ball, boy)	Feel how you bump your LIPS together. Then blow them apart with your VOICE.
C	(cat, city)	C's a *total* Copy Cat with *no sound of its own*. It copies k (coin) and s (city).
D	(door, dad)	Feel your TONGUE behind your upper TEETH. Now blow your TONGUE down.
F	(fish, farm)	Feel your top TEETH over your lower LIP. Now, blow out AIR with no VOICE.
G	(goose, go)	Bring your LIPS together in a circle. Blow out AIR with VOICE. G also copies J (gem).
H	(horse, hat)	Say, "Ha, Ha." and feel AIR come out through your MOUTH. H is formed by AIR.
J	(jazz, jet)	Feel your TEETH together and use VOICE to push the sound out of your MOUTH.
K	(kite, kick)	Say *Kick* and feel the K sound at the back of your THROAT. Now push it out.
L	(lion, lamb)	Feel your TONGUE behind your TEETH. Now hum out an L sound from your throat.
M	(mouse, mom)	Say *mom* and feel a HUM come out your NOSE as your LIPS open and close.
N	(nest, nun)	Feel your TONGUE touch the roof of your mouth and the HUM of the N sound as it comes out your NOSE, like you did for M, but with your MOUTH opened.
P	(pine, pep)	Feel your LIPS together, and then just blow them apart with a kind of POP sound.
Qu	(queen, quilt)	Copies K and W together (KW in queen, quilt).
R	(rain, roar)	Feel your TONGUE pulled back and raised against the roof of your MOUTH as you make a kind of ERRR… sound at the back of your mouth.
S	(sun, sis)	Feel your TONGUE and TEETH together. HISS the S sound out. S also copies Z.
T	(tiger, tent)	Say *Tut* and feel your TONGUE behind your TEETH and blow it down.
V	(vine, vest)	Feel your TEETH over your lower LIP and make a HUM. Compare this to B.
W	(window, wow)	Feel your LIPS pursed together and let a little AIR out. W is also a vowel (low).
X	(x-ray, ox)	X is a *total* Copy Cat without its own sound. X copies KS (x-ray, ox) and Z (xylophone).
Y	(yo yo, yell)	Feel your LIPS apart as the Y sound comes from the back of your THROAT. Remember that Y is also a vowel (toy, play).
Z	(zipper, zoo)	Feel your LIPS and TEETH clenched as you create a buzzz…sound with AIR.

ONOMATOPOEIA: baa, bang, bark, batter, beep, bop, boing, bonk, boo, boom, bow wow, bump, burp * caw, coo * ding, dizzy, dong, drip, drop, drum * fizz * giggle, gong * heehaw, hiccup, hiss, honk, hoot, howl, huff 'n puff, humm, hurrah, hush * jabber, jangle, jingle, jump * kerchoo * largo * meow, moan, moo, murmur * neigh * ping, pitter patter, pop, pow, purr * quack, queasy * rat a tat rattle, ring, rip, roar, rumble, rustle * sigh, sizzle, sob * tick tock, tinkle, toot * varoom * woof * yahoo, yikes * zap, zing, zip, zoom.

The Many Ways that Consonant Sounds Are Spelled

Now that you've felt the sounds of single consonants, let's look at the ways these consonant sounds are spelled. Most of these sounds are spelled according to *Phonics Rules*, but there are also a number of exceptions (in parentheses). Although it's challenging for spellers, this variety shows that many languages have added to the rich vocabulary of English.

❑ **NOW**: As you read these words, notice the different ways the same consonant sound can be spelled. Then add at least two words for each consonant. You might want to rhyme some words.

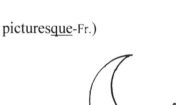

B   **b**alloon, bu**bb**les

C   copies **K** in **c**aterpillar, ac**c**ount   (<u>ch</u>orus-Gr.)   **C** copies **S** in **c**ent, **c**ity

D   **d**ance, la**dd**er, rolle**d**   (col<u>d</u>)

F   **f**ish, co**ff**ee   (so<u>f</u>ten, lau<u>gh</u>, ha<u>lf</u>)

G   own sound: **g**oose, e**gg**   (<u>gh</u>ost, <u>gu</u>ard)   **G** copies **J** in coura**g**e, **g**iant   (fu<u>dg</u>e)

H   **h**orse   (<u>wh</u>o)

J   **j**azz and **j**ustice   (gra<u>d</u>uate, sol<u>di</u>er, ju<u>dg</u>ment)

K   **k**ite   (<u>c</u>at, ac<u>c</u>ept, <u>ch</u>aos-Gr., bla<u>ck</u>, <u>kh</u>aki-Persian, wa<u>lk</u>, bou<u>qu</u>et-Fr., pictures<u>que</u>-Fr.)

L   **l**ion and ba**ll**

M   **m**ouse, su**mm**er   (pal<u>m</u>, clim<u>b</u>, autum<u>n</u>)

N   **n**est, spi**nn**er   (<u>gn</u>ome, <u>kn</u>ot, <u>pn</u>eumonia-Gr.)

P   **p**ine and pe**pp**er   (she<u>ph</u>erd)

Qu   copies **KW** in **qu**it, s**qu**eeze   **Qu** copies **K** in pictures**qu**e, uni**qu**e

R   **r**ain, e**rr**or   (<u>rh</u>ythm, <u>rh</u>yme, <u>wr</u>ite)

S   own sound: **s**unset, glo**ss**y   (<u>c</u>ent, <u>p</u>sychology-Gr., <u>sc</u>ent, fa<u>s</u>ten)   **S** copies **Z** in **s**ci**ss**ors

T   **t**iger, ki**tt**en   (de<u>b</u>t, dou<u>b</u>t, jump<u>ed</u>, ni<u>gh</u>t, recei<u>p</u>t)

V   **v**ine, ha**v**e, sa**vv**y

W   **w**ind   (<u>o</u>ne)

X   copies **KS** in **x**-ray and bo**x**   **X** copies **Z** in **x**ylophone

Y   **y**oyo, **y**outh   (on<u>i</u>on, b<u>eau</u>tiful-Fr., fe<u>w</u>, ew<u>e</u>, hallelu**j**ah, pavil<u>i</u>on (Gr. building), C<u>u</u>pid)

Z   **z**ipper, ja**zz**, fu**zz**y   (cho<u>s</u>e, choo<u>s</u>e, sci<u>ss</u>ors, and <u>x</u>ylophone)

❑ **NOW**: Write each word next to its consonant sound: **b**eep, **b**u**bb**le, **b**u**zz**ing, **c**a**ct**us, **c**ertain, **d**i**zz**y, **f**inger, **g**em, **g**old, **h**eart, **j**uice, **k**ic**kb**all, **l**ove**l**y, **m**ur**m**ur, **n**a**nn**y, **p**o**pp**ing, **qu**ack, **r**inging, **r**ive**r**, **r**ose, **t**oo**t**, **v**alentine, **v**anished, **w**onder, **X**ero**x**, **y**oung, and **z**ooming.

LESSON 8
Feeling the Power of the Beat

The ***POWER OF THE BEAT*** is the accent or emphasis that is given to one syllable in a word; and sometimes to more than one syllable in a long word. It is important to learn about this beat, because when you can FEEL this special emphasis in a word, it helps you to pronounce the word and to divide it into syllables. No matter how long it is, once you have divided a word into syllables, it is so much easier to spell. Now each syllable seems like a friendly, short word.

Have you ever read the story *Tikki Tikki Tembo* about a firstborn son whose true Chinese name was so long that it was nearly impossible for his younger brother to get someone to help pull him out of a well? Every time his brother tried telling someone, "*Tikki tikki tembo-no sa rembo-chari bari ruchi-pip peri pembo* has fallen into the well," the person would become impatient and stop listening. After the younger brother finally got his brother rescued from the well, Tikki tikki tembo… changed his name to a little short name, *Chang*. Unfortunately, we cannot shorten spelling words, but FEELING the beat and dividing the word into syllables will give you a lot of short little syllables that are easier to say and spell.

Another way you can FEEL the ***POWER OF THE BEAT*** in spelling is to spell out the letters of a word, as in the familiar rhyme:

> Mike and Molly
> Sitting in a tree,
> K-I-S-S-I-N-G.

You can simply spell the letters to a beat like R-H-Y-T-H-M, or you can try even a longer word, like E-N-C-Y-C-L-O-P-E-D-I-A. Let's learn more about KISSING, ENCYCLOPEDIA, and RHYTHM later. For now, let's just concentrate on FEELING the beat in some words.

It's Time to Start Feeling the Beat

The beat is a kind of special rhythm inside of you, an accent that you can FEEL when you say words like – RHY-THM, MU-SIC, HAR-MON-I-CA, GUI-TAR, DRUM-MER, SAX-O-PHONE, KEY-BOARD, and PI-A-NO. It's also there in – CON-CERT, VI-O-LIN, CLAR-I-NET, TRUM-PET, TROM-BONE, CYM-BALS… AP-PLAUSE…and EN-CORE… ENCORE! You can hear it in other words, too, because every word in every sentence has a beat!!! All words in all languages have a beat!!!!!

62

Let's Feel and Mark That Beat

Say each word, and tap it out so you can feel the beat. Draw an accent mark above the syllable where you feel the strongest beat. If you ever need extra help, you can always check a dictionary where all words are divided into syllables and the accent is always marked.

al – bum	mu – si – cian
au – di – ence	or – ches – tra
cel – lo	or – gan
cho – rus	per – cus – sion (drums, cymbals, xylophone…)
clar – i – net	pi – a – no
com – po – ser	quar – tet
con – cert	sym – pho – ny
con – duc – tor	trom – bone
cym – bals	trum – pet
gui – tar	vi – o – la
key – board	vi – o – lin
lis – ten	wood – winds (flutes, clarinets, oboes, bassoons)

Let's Use Crazy POWER Clues and Other Tools

❑ **TRY THIS:** For the words below, fill in the blanks or follow other directions. Have fun!

album: Write a *Clue* using a name and word in *album*.

audience: The _ _ _ _ _ _ _ _ sat on a f _ _ _ _ for the concert. *Roots*: <u>audi</u> (L. to hear) + <u>ence</u>.

cello: Can you play a _ _ _ _ _ while eating J _ _ _ _ ? *Phonics*: C = ch sound.

composer: Can you _ _ _ _ _ _ _ a song about a _ _ _ _ ?

concert: He was <u>certain</u> to go to the _ _ _ _ _ _ _ : con + _ _ _ _ = _ _ _ _ _ _ _ .

conductor: *Clue-in-a-Row*: A _ _ _ _ _ _ _ _ _ can _ _ _ _ _ _ _ _ _ watch an orchestra play.

drummer: *Rule*: <u>2</u> _ 's keep the _ _ short in _ _ _ _ _ _ _ . Put <u>drummer</u> to a *Beat*:

musician: *Special Phonics Pronunciation*: Say: <u>mu – si – ci – an</u> to hear each letter in _ _ _ _ _ _ _ _ .

orchestra: In my heart _ _ _ _ _ _ _ , I *feel* the music of the _ _ _ _ _ _ _ _ _ : <u>or + chest + ra</u>.

symphony: Don't be a _ _ _ _ _ at a <u>symphony</u>. *Roots*: <u>sym</u> (G. harmonious) + <u>phon</u> (G. sound) + <u>y</u>.

woodwinds: _ _ _ _ _ _ _ _ _ are instruments made of _ _ _ _ that you blow your _ _ _ _ through.

staccato: Cats jump quickly like _ _ _ _ _ _ _ _ notes. Find 2 cats back to back: s + _ _ _ _ + _ _ _ _ + o.

❑ **MARK THAT BEAT**: Until Shakespeare's time (1564-1616), all of these words all had the beat on the second syllable. Then some words like *outlaw, rebel,* and *record* began moving the beat to the first syllable when words were NOUNS and leaving the beat on the second syllable for VERBS. By 1900, about 150 words had two beats. There are still many with one: *bother, mistake, practice…*

NOUNS	VERBS		NOUNS	VERBSS
1. com - bine	com - bine		11. in - sult	in - sult
2. con - duct	con - duct		12. pro - ceed	pro - ceeds
3. con - fine	con - fine		13. pro - duce	pro - duce
4. con - flict	con - flict		14. pro - gress	prog - ress
5. con - tract	con - tract		15. pro - ject	proj - ect
6. de - sert	des - ert		16. pro - test	pro - test
7. dis - card	dis - card		17. re - bel	reb - el
8. ex - port	ex - port		18. re - cord	rec - ord
9. ex - tract	ex - tract		19. re - ject	re - ject
10. im - port	im - port		20. sub - ject	sub - ject

Let's Spell Some Letters to a Beat

Now, back to **K-I-S-S-I-N-G** and **E-N-C-Y-C-L-O-P-E-D-I-A**. As mentioned, a great way to use the ***POWER OF THE BEAT*** is to put the letters of a word to a beat or rhythm that's easy to say and remember. Each time you repeat the beat, it gets more inside your memory:

MIKE AND MOLLY,   SITTING IN A TREE,   K – I – S – S – I – N – G.

Notice that "kissing" is very easy to remember because it goes to a beat that you know and have said. It's easy to spell words to a beat, particularly if the word ends in -ing, has double letters, or the same number of letters in each syllable. Look at the beats and rhythms for *accommodate, encyclopedia,* and *Mississippi.* Then put *fluff, performance, running,* and *tickle* to a beat.

a-c-c - o-m-m- o-d-a-t- e

M-i-s-s - i-s-s-i-p-p-i !

e-n-c-y- c-l-o- p-ed-i- a !

- **NOW**: Write down two of each of the following kinds of words. Pick words where you feel a beat.

  Words that end in -ing: *dancing*

  Double-Letter Words: *balloon*

  Two-Syllable Words (same number of letters in each syllable): *ballet, rhythm*

Put three or more of these words to a beat by using dashes and spaces. Add musical notes if you'd like. Also, divide *arithmetic* and *mathematics* into 4 syllables and put these to a beat.

Finally, put the letters of some of these words to a beat: *bubble, drumming, music, rhythm, Mickey Mouse.* If you'd like, put Chan's long name to a syllable beat: "*Tik-ki – tik-ki – tem-bo – no-sa – rem-bo – char-i – bar-i – ru-chi – pip – pe-ri – pem -bo*" (which means: *the most wonderful thing in the whole wide world!*), and try some of *your* words. You'll probably need more paper. Have fun!

LESSON 9

Divide and Conquer: Dividing Words into Syllables

A powerful way to conquer a spelling word is to divide it into syllables. Then, you can see and hear each little part, rather than trying to spell the *whole, monstrous word*. Once you've divided the word, you have "little words" that are manageable. In a way, this process is like taking a puzzle apart to see how each piece works. It's also like climbing a mountain, one step at a time. When you divide a word, you simply pronounce, learn and spell each small syllable, one by one, until you have learned to spell them all. Then you can see how all the syllables fit back together. By using this powerful tool, you can divide and conquer words like a *POWER SPELLER!*

One of the longest words in English is "antidisestablishmentarianism." Whew! As one word, it can look overwhelming; but, if you divide it into syllables, you can see the little parts: prefixes + the root word: <u>establish</u> + suffixes that make it up. If you carefully pronounce each syllable, and look for common prefixes: <u>anti-</u>, <u>dis-</u>; common suffixes: <u>-ism</u>; and smaller words: <u>anti</u>, <u>establish</u>, <u>men</u>, <u>tar</u>, <u>I</u>, <u>an</u>, you might be able to spell it right now: an – ti – dis – <u>es – tab – lish</u> – men – tar – i – an – ism.

The Beat Goes On...

Both music and words are languages that can work together. As you have learned, feeling the beat of a word helps you hear the syllable divisions. When words are put to the beat and rhythm of a poem or song, each syllable goes with a note and beat, so it's very easy to feel and hear each syllable.
❑ **NOW TRY THIS**: For the poems and songs below, tap out the beat as you feel, hear, and see where the syllables divide. Also, for each word, mark where the strongest accent falls.

The fog comes in on lit-tle cat feet.
It sits look-ing o-ver har-bor and ci-ty on si-lent haunch-es
And then, moves on. *
Fog by Carl Sandburg (1878-1967)

O beau-ti-ful, for spa-cious skies, for am-ber waves of grain,
For pur-ple moun-tains ma-jes-ty, a-bove the fruit-ed plains.
A-mer-i-ca, A-mer-i-ca, God shed His grace on thee.
And crown thy good with broth-er-hood from sea to shin-ing sea.
From *America, the Beautiful,* words by Katherine Bates and music by Samuel Ward, 1893

❑ **YOUR SONGS AND POEMS**: Now, write out some words from songs or poems you like or have written. Divide the words into syllables and mark the accents. Check a dictionary if you need help.

66

Eight Helpful Rules for Dividing Words into Syllables

❏ **WHAT DO YOU THINK?** As you've seen, heard, and felt the words in poems and songs, you've probably learned more than you might realize about syllable division. Write down one or more points about syllable division that you've learned:

Now, as you read the 8 rules below, put a star by any that you already know or have figured out on your own. If you *ever* have any questions about dividing syllables, a good dictionary can show you: where the syllables are divided, which syllable gets the strongest beat, how the letters in each syllable are pronounced… Use a dictionary whenever you need help with this lesson or any lesson!!!

❏ **NOW:** Read each rule and examples. Then divide the words under the examples into syllables. You can simply draw lines between the syllables or write the words with dashes between syllables. Remember: <u>Don't divide qu or digraphs: ch, sh, th wh and ng</u>. Any questions? Check a dictionary.

RULE 1-COMPOUNDS: Compound words are simply two complete words joined together, so you always divide between the two words. English also has Latin and Greek compound words: <u>astronaut</u> (star sailor), <u>photograph</u> (light map). *Divide compound words, plus any syllables in the individual words.*

    camp – fire   sun – rise   dew – drop   pus – sy wil – low

❏   breakfast   pancake   granddad   cattails   wheelbarrow   phonograph

RULE 2-PREFIXES: When a prefix (syllable that's <u>added before</u> a word to change its meaning) is added to a word, you always divide between the prefix and the word. The prefix always keeps its own separate syllable. *Underline each prefix and divide the word into syllables.*

    <u>un</u> – der – line   <u>re</u> – build   <u>trans</u> – port   <u>mis</u> – spell – ing

❏   disagree   mistake   accept   except   unaware   unicycle

RULE 3-SUFFIXES: When a suffix (syllable that's <u>added after</u> a word to change it to another part of speech, to change it to past or present, or to make it plural) is added to a word, you usually divide between the suffix and the word. When a suffix is added to a verb ending in *d* or *t* or to other parts of speech, it adds its own syllable. A suffix usually joins the syllable for verbs ending in other letters and for plurals. *Underline the suffix and divide the words into syllables.*

    guard – <u>ed</u>   sur – pri<u>sed</u> (suffix joined syllables)   shin – <u>ing</u>   hop<u>ped</u> (joined)

    cool – <u>ly</u>   po – ta – to<u>es</u> (joined)   hap – pi – <u>ness</u>   a – part – <u>ment</u>

❏   dancing   accidentally   carefully   hushed   establishment   haunches-hind part

RULE 4-TWO CONSONANTS: When two consonants come together or the same consonant is doubled in a word, the word is usually divided between the consonants; but, never divide digraphs. You can usually hear the division between syllables. *Mark the short vowels and divide the words.*

cer – tain   dif – fer – ent   sum – ma – ry   pic – ture

☐ mountains   harbor   summer   letters   pumpkin   Harry Potter

RULE 5-SHORT VOWEL ENDING IN A CONSONANT: When the first single vowel is short and accented, you usually divide the word right after the consonant, digraph or consonant blend that closes the word (a closed syllable). Listen carefully to hear the break. *Mark the vowel and accent and divide the word into syllables.*

am – ber   sep – a – rate   ben – e – fit   val – u – a – ble

☐ parachute   helicopter   limit   phonics   manageable (keep e after g)

(Note: When you have a syllable with a single short vowel, followed by one or more consonants, like—am, Sam, push, plush…it is called a CLOSED SYLLABLE. You'll learn about these later.)

RULE 6-VOWEL SHORT AND UNACCENTED: When a vowel in a word is a short *a* or *i* and it is unaccented, you usually divide the word right after the vowel. You can usually hear this vowel clearly. *Mark the short vowels and divide these words.*

cha – rade   a – bove   di – vine   a – mong   in – di – vi – du – al

☐ America   majesty   multiplication   division   city

RULE 7 FIRST VOWEL LONG: When the first vowel in a word is long, you divide the word right after the vowel. Again, you can usually hear this open syllable. *Mark the long vowels and divide words in syllables.*

ha – zy   be – lieve   fi – nal   o – boe   cu – cum –ber

☐ apex   defense   silent   usual   quiet   remember

(Note: When you have a syllable that is a single vowel or ends in a single vowel, short or long, like—a, be, go, to, de, fi, cha… this syllable is called an OPEN SYLLABLE.)

RULE 8 FINAL LE: A word with a final le picks up the preceding consonant to form a syllable.

pud – dle   rat – tle   syl – la – ble   tur – tle   noo – dle

☐ fable   pebble   squiggle   cuddle   poodle   rumble

8

Summary of Rules for Dividing Words into Syllables

❑ **LET'S REVIEW:** As you review the rules below, think of and add three words that fit each rule, and divide them into syllables

RULE 1 COMPOUNDS: You always divide between the two complete words.
but – ter – fly   snow – flake   cat – tails   grand – dad   wheel-bar-row

RULE 2 PREFIXES: You always divide between the prefix and the word.
<u>ac</u> – cept   <u>dis</u> – agree   <u>ex</u> – cept   <u>mis</u> – take   <u>trans</u> – port   <u>un</u> – a – ware

RULE 3 SUFFIXES: You usually divide between the suffix and the word.
care – <u>ful</u> – <u>ly</u>   danc-<u>ing</u>   es – tab – lish – <u>ment</u>   haunch – <u>es</u>   hush<u>ed</u>

RULE 4 TWO CONSONANTS OR DOUBLED CONSONANTS: The word is usually divided between the consonants, except for digraphs: ch, sh, th, wh and ng.
ha<u>r</u> – <u>b</u>or   moun – <u>t</u>ains   su<u>m</u> – <u>m</u>ar – y   Ha<u>r</u> – <u>r</u>y Pot – ter

RULE 5 SHORT VOWEL ENDING IN A CONSONANT: You usually divide the word right after the consonant, digraph or consonant blend that follows the vowel.
<u>par</u> – a – chute   <u>phon</u> – ics   <u>man</u> - age – a – ble   <u>hel</u> – i – cop – ter

RULE 6 VOWEL SHORT AND UNACCENTED: You usually divide right after the vowel.
<u>A</u> – mer – i – ca   <u>ma</u> – jes – ty   mul – ti – pli – ca – tion   <u>di</u> – vi – sion

RULE 7 FIRST VOWEL LONG: You divide the word right after the vowel.
<u>a</u> – pex (peak)   <u>de</u> – fense   <u>si</u> – lent   <u>re</u> – mem – ber   <u>u</u> – su – al

RULE 8 FINAL LE: The le picks up the preceding consonant to form a syllable.
peb – <u>ble</u>   rum – <u>ble</u>   fa – <u>ble</u>   poo – <u>dle</u>   squig – <u>gle</u>

REMEMBER: Dividing a word into syllables gives you a lot of *SPELLING POWER*. You can CLEARLY FEEL and SEE THE WORD and CLEARLY SAY and HEAR THE WORD. Then you can CLEARLY SPELL THE WORD!

LESSON 10

Let's Pronounce That Word Correctly Now!

If you were living a thousand years ago (900-1485), back when people still spoke Old and Middle English, pronunciation and spelling would not have been a problem. Back then, words were simply spelled like they were pronounced. Each letter had one sound, and all consonants and vowels were pronounced (even silent e's): *ber-ern* (barn), *gras* (grass), *hors* (horse), *e-or-the* (earth), *tre-o* (tree), *fre-ond* (friend), *na-ma* (name). Alas, by 1500, this clear spelling was never seen or heard again.

Today, although 15% of the words in English are not spelled like they're pronounced, the remaining 85% are. If you learn NOW to correctly pronounce these words, you will be able to hear all the letters, spell them correctly, and remember them!! This lesson presents 7 **POWER** Pronunciation **Keys** that will help you correctly pronounce words and defeat the **Mispronunciation Monsters**.

Then you'll learn about **Special Phonics Pronunciations** (*SPP's*), a great **POWER** *Spelling Tool* that you can use for the 15% of words that aren't spelled like they're pronounced!

7 Power Pronunciation Keys

Since you've probably heard words rushed and mispronounced, you could be repeating some

Mispronunciation Monsters without even knowing it. *You'd be suprised, but jus like ervrybody, yer probaly hurring, and you accidently misprinounce werds and sylables.*

Are you leaving out letters or making other mispronunciation errors? The 7 **POWER** Pronunciation **Keys** show you what to watch out for. For example, <u>athlete</u> gets misspelled because people add an extra <u>e</u> (athelete). ***PP Key 3*** warns: *Don't add extra vowels or create syllables that aren't in the word.* A *Clue* helps: The <u>athlete</u> did a <u>high leap</u> (Keep <u>hl</u> together.). ***PP Key 4*** helps with <u>surprise</u> by saying: *Pronounce all consonants.* Again, a *Clue* helps: To see a whale <u>surface</u> and <u>rise</u> is quite a <u>surprise</u>.

❑ **NOW**: Star each word you think is correct. Read *POWER Pronunciation Keys* and cross out *Mispronunciation Monsters*. Read *Special Phonics Pronunciations* and cross out Silent Letter errors.

Antartica	Antarctica	hospital	hospitol	preform	perform
arctic	artic	intresting	interesting	privilege	privlege
arithmetic	arithemetic	jewelry	jewelery	probaly	probably
athelete	athlete	literature	litrature	sanwich	sandwich
dimond	diamond	mathmatics	mathematics	strickly	strictly
every	ervry	marrige	marriage	temprature	temperature
exacly	exactly	miniature	minature	tragedy	tradegy

0

Using POWER Pronunciation Keys

Read these **Keys** to learn how to pronounce words correctly. After each **Key**, mark any words *you* mispronounce. Then underline the **PP** for the words and use *Clues* or other *Tools* to remember them. (The *POWER Pronunciation* for each word is the same pronunciation you'll find in the dictionary.) !!SO, learn these words NOW! Stop mistaking *Mispronunciation Monsters* for the true words!!

❑ **KEY 1:** Pronounce letters in their proper order. Don't confuse and change letters around. Correctly pronounce and underline each **PP**. Create *Clues* for perform and tragedy.

SPELLING WORD	*MISPRONUNCIATION MONSTER*	*POWER PRONUNCIATION*	*CLUES* and *TOOLS* for REMEMBERING WORDS
perspire	*prespire*	pers-pire:	A person climbing the spire began to _ _ _ _ _ _ _.
perform	*preform*	per-form:	
tragedy	*tradegy*	tra-ge-dy:	

❑ **KEY 2:** Pronounce all the vowels in all of the syllables. Underline each **PP** and create *Clues*.

environment	*envirement*	en-vir-on-ment:	
interesting	*intresting*	in-ter-est-ing:	The intern is an _ _ - _ _ _ - _ _ _ - _ _ _ person.
mathematics	*mathmatics*	math-e-ma-tics:	_ _ _ _ - _ - _ _ - _ _ _ _ (like arithmetic) has 4 beats.
miniature	*minature*	min-i-a-ture:	I saw a _ _ _ _ dog _ _ a _ _ _ _ _ _ _ _ show.
privilege	*privlege*	pri-vi-lege:	Don't give a _ _ _ _ _ _ _ _ to a vile person.
sophomore	*sophmore*	soph-o-more:	Ho! Did the _ _ _ _ _ _ _ _ like chocolate?
temperature	*temprature*	tem-per-a-ture:	
withdrawal	*withdrawl*	with-draw-al:	

❑ **KEY 3:** Don't add extra vowels and create syllables that aren't in a word. Also, don't pronounce vowels incorrectly. Underline each **PP** and write *Clues* for athlete, familiar, and separate.

arithmetic	*arithemetic*	a-rith-me-tic:	A tutor worked with me on _ _ _ _ _ _ _ _ _ _. _ - _ _ _ _ - _ _ - _ _ _ has. 4 beats (like mathematics).
athlete	*athelete*	ath-lete:	
disastrous	*disasterous*	di-sas-trous:	_ _ _ _ _ _ _ _ _ _ winds are as troublesome as waves.
familiar	*fermiliar*	fa-mil-iar:	
hindrance	*hinderance*	hin-drance:	The hind (female deer) ran into a _ _ _ _ _ _ _ _ _.
jewelry	*jewelery*	jewel-ry:	I looked in my _ _ _ _ _ _ _ for the lost ring.
separate	*seperate*	sep-a-rate:	

❏ **KEY 4:** <u>Pronounce each syllable as it's pronounced in the dictionary</u>. Fill in blanks and create clues.

SPELLING WORD	MISPRONUNCIATION MONSTER	POWER PRONUNCIATION	CLUES and TOOLS for REMEMBERING WORDS
arctic	*artic*	ar<u>c</u>-tic:	The _ _ _ _ _ Ocean forms an <u>arc</u> over the N. Pole (*Arktos* is Greek for *Bear*: the most northern constellation)
Antarctica	*Antartica*	Ant-arc-ti-ca:	_ _ _ _ _ _ _ _ _ _ forms an <u>arc</u> at the S. Pole (anti + Arktos)
congratulate	*congradulate*	con-grat-u-late:	<u>Con</u>-with + <u>grat</u>-thanks + <u>ulate</u> = _ _ _ _ _ _ _ _ _ _ _
exactly	*exatly*	ex-ac<u>t</u>-ly:	
government	*goverment*	gov-er<u>n</u>-ment:	
instinct	*instink*	in-stin<u>ct</u>:	There's lots of <u>instinct</u> in <u>cat</u>s: _ _ _ _ _ _ _ _ .
sandwich	*sanwich*	san<u>d</u>-wich:	No <u>sand</u> or <u>T</u> (tea) with my _ _ _ _ _ _ _ _ .
strict	*strick*	stric<u>t</u>:	We had to be _ _ _ _ _ _ to win a baseball <u>vict</u>ory.
surprise	*suprise*	su<u>r</u>-prise:	

❏ **KEY 5:** <u>Compound Words: If the 1st word ends with the same letter with which the 2nd word begins, be sure to keep the double letters</u>. <u>Write</u> each word twice.

book + keeper = bookkeeper _____

news + stand = newsstand _____

team + mate = teammate _____

❏ **KEY 6:** <u>Prefixes: Simply add the entire prefix to the entire base without changing either word</u>. <u>Write</u> each word and <u>learn</u> the clue to remember it.

dis + appoint = _____ (Did that <u>apple</u> <u>disappoint</u> you?)

dis + similar = _____ (Rule: <u>dis</u> + <u>similar</u>. Also, <u>3 i's</u>.)

un + healthy = _____ (Can a doctor <u>heal</u> my <u>unhealthy heart</u>?)

un + naturally = _____ (<u>Nat, U rally</u> our team well: un + <u>natu</u>rally)

❏ **KEY 7:** <u>Suffixes: When the adverb suffix is *-ally* (for adjectives that end in -al and -ic)</u>, pronounce it correctly and learn a *Clue* to remember it.

accidental + ly = _____ (I <u>accidentally</u> made a wrong <u>tally</u>.)

occasional + ly = _____ (<u>O, C Casi on all</u> [+ y] <u>occasions</u>.)

tragic + al + ly = _____ (He's my <u>ally</u> if I <u>tragically fall</u>.)
(artisti<u>cally</u>, magi<u>cally</u>, romanti<u>cally</u>...)

usual + ly = _____ (<u>Usually</u>, we <u>all</u> pitch in.)

❏ **NOW:** Go back to the first page and cross out those **Mispronunciation Monsters!!!**

Using Special Phonics Pronunciations

A **Special Phonics Pronunciation** (**SPP**) is a great *POWER Spelling Tool* for words that aren't spelled like they're pronounced: *business, guard, meant, Wednesday...* For **Special Phonics Pronunciations**, you *say every consonant and vowel* just like people did when they spoke Old English: *bus-i-ness, gu-ard; Wed-nes-day; me-ant*. Then spell these words just like you're pronouncing them.

❑ **NOW**: Fill in the blanks. Create *Clues* for words that do not have one. Star words you need to learn.

SPELLING WORD	COMMON PRONUNCIATION	SPECIAL PHONICS PRONUNCIATION	CLUES and TOOLS for REMEMBERING WORDS
asked	*ast, axt*	as<u>k</u>-<u>e</u>d:	
brilliant	*brilyant*	bril-<u>li</u>-ant:	*See* 4 _ _ _ _ _ _ _ _ candles <u>illi</u>, plus an a _ _. br*i*ll*i*ant
business	*bizness*	b<u>us</u>-<u>i</u>-ness:	
calendar	*calender*	cal-<u>en</u>-d<u>ar</u>:	A _ _ _ _ _ _ _ has <u>days</u> and <u>dates</u>.
conscience	*conshunts*	con-<u>sci</u>-<u>en</u>-<u>ce</u>:	
courageous	*curagejus*	c<u>our</u>-a-<u>ge</u>-<u>ous</u>:	In <u>our age</u>, you need to be _ _ _ _ _ _ _ _ _.
diamond	*dimond*	di-<u>a</u>-mond:	Measure the <u>diamond</u>'s <u>diameter</u>. *Amo* means *I love* in French: <u>I amo</u> you: diamond.
everybody	*ervrybuddy*	ev-<u>er</u>-y-bo-dy:	Will I see _ _ _ _ _ _ _ _ for _ _ _?
February	*Febuary*	Feb-<u>ru</u>-ar-y:	<u>R U</u> and M<u>ary</u> making Valentines in _ _ _ _ _ _ _?
guard	*gard*	<u>gu</u>-ard:	<u>G, U</u> are a great _ _ _ _ _ s. (Gee, you are a great <u>guard</u>.)
guess	*gess*	<u>gu</u>-ess:	<u>G, U</u> (and) <u>Bess</u> made a great _ _ _ _ _: G + U + ~~Bess~~.
handkerchief	*hankerchief*	han<u>d</u>-ker-ch<u>ie</u>f:	I hold a _ _ _ _ _ _ _ _ _ _ _ in my _ _ _ _.
hospital	*hospitul*	hos-pi-t<u>a</u>l:	The _ mbulance raced to the _ _ _ _ _ _ _ _.
knowledge	*knol-lege*	<u>k</u>-no<u>w</u>-led-<u>ge</u>:	I sat on a <u>ledge</u> and read to <u>know</u> _ _ _ _ _ _ _ _.
laboratory	*labratory*	la-b<u>or</u>-<u>a</u>-tor-y:	Scientists often <u>labor</u> in a _ _ _ _ _ _ _ _ _.
language	*languij*	lan-<u>gu</u>-<u>a</u>-<u>ge</u>:	A <u>guard</u> my <u>age</u> and spoke in my _ _ _ _ _ _ _.
limb	*lim*	lim-<u>b</u> (limber):	
marriage	*marrige*	mar-ri-<u>a</u>-<u>ge</u>:	Change *y* in <u>marry</u> to <u>i</u> + <u>age</u> = _ _ _ _ _ _ _.
meant	*ment*	me-<u>ant</u>:	They saw <u>me</u> and <u>ant</u>, friends _ _ _ _ _ forever.
often	*offen*	of-<u>t</u>en:	
special	*speshul*	spe-<u>ci</u>-al:	Look, a _ _ _ _ _ _ _ <u>speci</u>es of fish. (facial, racial)
vacuum	*vacume*	vac-<u>u</u>-um:	My _ _ _ _ _ _ goes <u>uum</u>, _ _ _.

❑ **FINALLY**: Check those *Confusing* and *Silent Letter Words* on the first page.

LESSON 11

The Power of Ancient Roots
Latin and Greek –Our Origin for Over 60,000 English Words

You are truly becoming a **POWER SPELLER** when you can discover ANCIENT ROOTS in words. Also, since these ROOTS are spelled like they sound, as you keep learning them, you will find hundreds of words that will be easier for you to spell. What is also exciting is that roots not only build spelling *POWER*, but they also build vocabulary. Most of these ancient roots, with their prefixes and suffixes, have come from Latin and Greek, languages that are over 2,000 years old.

If you use a *dictionary* or a *magnifying* glass; go to the *library*; have seen an *aquarium*, watch *videos*; or have heard that *gravity* holds you to the Earth, you are using Latin – the language of the vast and ancient Roman Empire - the language that has most enriched the vocabulary of English. This Latin was used during Rome's Golden Age of Literature (106 B.C. – A.D. 14) to write great masterpieces still read today: Cicero's powerful speeches; Julius Caesar's histories of war, Virgil's *Aeneid* about the Trojan War and the founding of Rome. Perhaps you, or someone you know, has a Latin name: *Anthony* (deserving praise); *Felix* (happy); *Laura* or *Laurence* (crowned with a laurel wreath); *Lucy* (light); *Patricia* (noble); *Rex* or *Roy* (king). You just might be speaking more Latin than you thought!

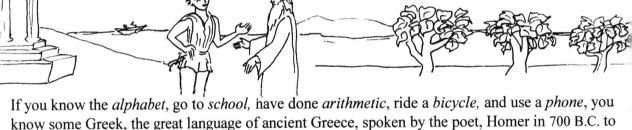

If you know the *alphabet*, go to *school,* have done *arithmetic*, ride a *bicycle,* and use a *phone*, you know some Greek, the great language of ancient Greece, spoken by the poet, Homer in 700 B.C. to tell about the Trojan War, and by the great philosophers Plato and Aristotle (384 – 322 B.C.). Greek, the language of Athens and its Golden Age of drama (427 – 347 B.C.), was used to write great tragedies and comedies. Then, 2,000 years later, many medical and scientific words were added to English from Greek. Maybe you have also heard some Greek names: *Dora* (gift); *Eugene* (eu + gen: well born); *George* (man of the earth; farmer); *Helen* (sunlight); *Irene* or *Renee* (peaceful); *Philip* (loving horses).

❑ **NOW**: Find these Latin and Greek words in this lesson. Then underline the roots and next to the root, write its meaning. A few word are made of two roots: *astronaut, manuscript, philosophy*.

animation	labor	astronaut
aquarium	magnify	science
captain	manual	inspect
creed (one's beliefs)	manuscript	thermos
dictionary	origin	interrupt
erupt	pedal	verdict
fragile	video	philosophy

NOTE: Roots do not usually make a word on their own. They live in a kind of *word sandwich*. The *root* is the *meat*, and sometimes a *prefix* comes before the root, and usually a *suffix* comes after it.

74

Discovering and Learning Some Latin Roots

❑ **TRY THIS**: As you look at these Latin roots and the examples of words where they are found, underline the root in each example. Since a prefix or suffix is often added to a root, try to detect these.

LATIN ROOT	MEANING(S)	EXAMPLES
anim	*life, spirit*	animal (alive), animated, animation, inanimate (not + alive)
aqua, aque	*water*	aquarium, aquatic, aqueduct, aqueous (watery)
audi, aur	*hear*	audible, audience, auditor, auditorium, aural (re: hearing)
cap, cep, cept	*take, hold*	captivate (to hold attention), captive, capture, accept (to take)
card, cord	*heart*	cardiology, cord, cordial (heart felt), accord, discord
cred, creed	*believe*	credential, credible (believable), creed (belief), discredit (not + believe), incredible (not + believable)
dic, dict	*speak, declare*	dictionary, predict (say in advance), verdict (speak judgment)
feli	*happy*	felicity (happiness), Felix
fract, frag	*break*	fraction, fracture, fragile, fragment (broken-off part)
grav	*heavy*	grave (heavy, solemn), gravitational, gravity
imag	*likeness*	image, imagery, imagination, imagine
jud, jur, jus	*right, law*	judgment, judicious (able to judge well), jurist, justice
labor	*work, toil*	labor, laboratory, laborious, elaborate (requiring work)
lib, libr	*book*	librarian, library
liter	*letter*	literate (able to read letters), literature, illiterate (not...letters)
luc, lum	*light*	luminous (full of light), Lucy, translucent (light comes across)
magn	*great*	magnificent, magnification, magnify, magnitude
man, manu	*hand*	manicure, manual, manually, manufacture, manuscript
ped	*foot*	pedal, pedestal (base upon which foot rests), pedestrian
port	*to carry*	portable, porter, export, import, transport
rex, roy	*king*	Rex, Roy, royal, royalty
rupt	*break*	rupture, abrupt (break off), eruption, interrupt (break into)
scrib, script	*write*	scribble, scribe, scripture, circumscribe (write around), describe, inscribe, prescribe (write before), prescription
spec, spic	*see*	specimen (sample to see), spectacles, spectacular (something you need to see), spectator, specter (ghost), inspect
vid, vis	*see*	video, visible, vision, visual, evidence

Discovering and Learning Some Greek Roots

❏ **TRY THIS:** Read each root and its meaning. Then underline the root in each example.

GREEK ROOT	MEANING(S)	EXAMPLES
Alpha + Beta	*A and B*	alphabet, alphabetical, alphanumeric (letters and numbers)
arche	*ancient, origin*	archaic (ancient), archaeology (study of ancient civilizations)
astr, aster	*star*	asterisk, asteroid, astronaut, astrology, astronomy
auto	*self*	autobiography, autograph, automatic, automobile
bio	*life*	biography, biology, antibiotic (against + life of a bad organism)
cycl	*wheel, circle*	cycle, cyclone, bicycle, motorcycle, recycle
gen	*begin, birth*	genesis (beginning), gender, generation, genius (born this way), Eugene (eu-well + born), origin
geo	*earth*	geography (Earth map), geology (study of Earth's history), George (man of the earth)
gram, graph	*picture, writing*	graph, autograph, photograph (light picture), telegraph
helio	*sun*	Helen (sunlight), helium (gas of the sun), heliotrope (flower that faces s
hippo	*horse*	hippo, hippopotamus, Philip
mens, meter, metre	*measure*	meter, metrical, perimeter (measure around) speedometer
min	*small, less*	mini, miniature, minimize, minimum, minor
ped	*child*	pediatrician, pediatrics, encyclopedia (well-rounded for childre
phil	*love*	philosophy, philanthropist, philharmonic
phob, phobia	*fear*	phobia, phobic, agoraphobia (market place, open places + fear)
phon, phone	*sound*	phone, phonics, phonograph, symphony, microphone, telephone
psych, psyche	*mind, soul*	psyche, psychiatrist (physician who treats mind), psychologist
rene	*peaceful*	Renee ((peace), Irene (peaceful), serene (peaceful), serenity (peace)
scho, school	*leisure*	scholastic, school (School was loved in Greece. *Scholē* was lei time spent by Plato, Socrates, and students, walking and sharing dia in the grove of Academeus which was protected by the gods.)
sci, scio	*know*	science, conscience, conscious (able to know), omniscient
scop, scope	*see*	microscope, periscope (around + see), telescope (far + see)
therm	*heat*	thermal, thermometer, thermos, thermostat
zo	*animal*	zoo, zoology

All Kinds of Greek Phobias and Philos

As you have learned, *phobia* is a root meaning *fear*, and *Philos* is a Greek root meaning *love*. Both of these roots can be added to other roots to create some pretty amazing words. For the *phobia words*, *phobia* is added after each root. For the *philos-words*, *philos* can come before or after the root.

eeqik... Phobias ...yipes...

Now, you can decide which phobias you and your friends might have – and say the phobia in style!

acrophobia	fear of heights
androphobia	fear of men
agoraphobia	fear of open spaces (agora-market place)
ailurophobia	fear of cats
Anglophobia	fear or dislike of Englishmen
arachnophobia	fear of spiders
aquaphobia	fear of water
arachibutyrophobia	fear of peanut butter sticking to the roof of your mouth
astraphobia	fear of lightning
claustraphobia	fear of closed spaces
cynophobia	fear of dogs
hemophobia	fear of blood
necrophobia	fear of death
ophidiophobia	fear of snakes
phonophobia	fear of speaking aloud
pyrophobia	fear of fires
triskaidekaphobia	fear of the number thirteen
xenophobia	fear of strangers

Yipes, I have acrophobia...

Philos

And, you can decide which loves you and your friends have by reading these *philos* and *philes*: *Ailurophile* (lover of cats), *Anglophile* (admirer of Englishmen). You can also take some of the roots above and add them before or after *philo* to create some other loves: *acrophile* (lover of heights); *aquaphile* (lover of water).

ailurophile, ailurophilia	lover of cats (*ailur*)
Anglophile, Anglophilism	lover of Englishmen (*Anglo*)
philosopher, philosophy	lover of knowledge (*soph*)
philogynist, philogyny	lover of women (*gyn*)
philatelist, philately	lover of stamps (*atelia*)
philanthropist, philanthropy	lover of mankind (*anthro*)
philologist, philology	lover of words (*logy*)

"pvrrrrrr..."

77

LESSON 12

Focusing on Visual Power

For many people, **VISUAL POWER** is the sense they most naturally use or the skill they have *developed* the most for learning and remember spelling. Some people even have what is called a *Photographic Memory*, or they have developed the ability to picture a word in their mind. Others know if a word is correct – if they can just see the word written out. They have their own "Mental Spell Check" or they have developed a strong proof-reading ability by *READING, Reading, reading...*

Another skill people enjoy is detecting *Visual Pictures* or *Patterns* in the way words look. They find *Letter Pictures*: 2 balls and 2 sticks in balloon; 3 parallel lines in parallel. They discover *Patterns* and *Word Play*: *Palindromes* (level, racecar); *Reversals* (deer – reed; drawer – reward); *Echo Words* (eraser, onion); and *Bookends* (senses, decided). *VISUAL Memory* and the ability to see *Patterns* in words can be learned, so let's have some fun and develop your **VISUAL POWER**!

Photographic Memory or Picturing Words in Your Mind

Perhaps you have a *Photographic Memory* or would like to develop this special *VISUAL Skill*. You can learn to picture words by following these easy steps. Let's do it for the word mountain.

- First, write the word very clearly and carefully look at the whole word: *mountain*.

- Then carefully look at the word letter by letter, and look for smaller words: mo-u-n-t + a + in. Also, see if there's a clue in how the letters look: *Mountain* goes up and down like its shape.

- Next, mark difficult parts: letters that don't follow phonics, copy cats, or silent letters: mountain.

- Now, close your eyes and picture the word. If you have trouble picturing the word, see the word being written on a blackboard: mountain   *mountain*   .

- As you picture the word, spell it out letter by letter in your mind and go over the difficult parts.

- Then, open your eyes and clearly write the word again: *mountain*.

- Finally, carefully look at the word again, and then write it out one more time: *mountain*.
    !!!For extra reinforcement, repeat the process!!!

- **TRY THIS**: Keep developing your *VISUAL* skill by following these steps for each word below.

    visual

    amazement

    brilliant

    climbed

    initiate

Try Out Your Own Spell Check on the Written Word

Most people who seem to have a *natural* ability to spot spelling mistakes are *people who read a lot.* Day after day, they see correctly spelled words and develop their own *Visual Spell Checker*. Also, people who edit books or other writing have developed this ability by proofreading again and again.

❑ **WHICH WORD LOOKS RIGHT?**: Test *your Visual Spell Checker* by underlining the correct word in each group. If you read a lot, it helps to follow your first intuition since reading *stores* correct words in your mind. Once you're finished, check your words in a dictionary. Cross out the wrong ones.

beautiful	beautifull	buetiful
hankerchief	handkerchief	hankercheif
arguement	argument	arguedment
brilyant	brillent	brilliant
scissors	scizzers	sciszors
conschients	conscience	consciounce
pairalel	parrallel	parallel
girrafe	giraffe	giraffe
liesure	leisure	leizure
freind	friend	frend
inishiate	initiate	innitiate
superintendant	superentendant	superintendent
autumm	autumn	awtum
disappeer	dissapear	disappear
suprise	surprise	suprize
committee	commitee	comittee

The best way to build your **VISUAL POWER** and keep it growing day after day is truly through READING, *READING*, Reading…T he more that you read, the more you can keep storing correctly spelled words in your brain. Treat yourself to the gift of ALWAYS keeping a good book handy!

❑ **NOW**: Test your visual skill on *Homophones*. On the next page, read "The Morning News." Underline all the incorrect homophones and <u>write</u> the <u>right</u> word above each error. Even though there are many *Mixed-Up Homophones* "The Morning News" *made it through computer spell check without any correction*!! The reason is that none of the words are misspelled! Check your answers with the list of Mixed-Up Homophones on page 5 of this lesson.

The Morning News with Anchorman I. C. Daily

Good Morning too you:

This is I. C. Daily, reporting on the gnus—everything that's fit to be said and red! Excuse me, but I'm a little horse today. My sun came to visit me for the weak end, and it got chili out. It seams we both caught coals. My voice should be a little boulder bye tomorrow.

Know, for the World Gnus from Around the Glob: The raining Prince of Wails, and his Princess, are planning there bridle party, where, of coarse, the hand sum Prince will merry his bride   and give her a wring. The Princess will wok down the isle with her bouquet. The kind of flour she has chosen has still been kept a surprise. We do no that she will ware a gown maid from tears of lace, and her hare will be filled with her beaus. After the wedding, everyone will whine and dine and then dance at the Royal Bawl.

From the desserts of Arabia: Kernel Cornwall has finely gotten a suite piece treaty. We all hop this will bring a chord to the aria and solve the mane problems. (Excuse my voice. I'm still a little horse.)

From the North Pole: The rain deer report that Rudolph's read nose blue a fuse too day. Accordion to Santa Claws, Rudolph's nose will be heeled and back to read reel soon.

And know for the Local Gnus: Wells Go Far was robed today. The robber just picked up the lute and ran. I believe that those who wood steel and lye should leave hour city. We have know use for lyres hear.

Fryer Roost has been trying a knew roll bye writing a him for Sunday. Were hopping the choir won't fowl up, or chicken out, as they wok down the isle, so that well awl prophet from his mew sick.

Lightening struck a mail whale at see two day. He's resting on a beech on a dessert aisle. We hop he will have enough to eat—too meat his kneads—wile he's their.

And, finely, the Whether Report: Clouds blue in too day, so expect more rein. Just be sure to ware warm close, so you won't become a little horse, like me.

This is I. C. Daily, singing off until tomorrow.

Visual Patterns That Repeat or Reverse

Sometimes letters in a word or entire words have a special pattern because they repeat or reverse their letters like echoes and bookends. As you discover words that have these patterns, this can add a spark to your spelling. So let's get to know *Echoes, Bookends, Palindromes*, and *Reversals*!

❏ **TRY THIS**: Take a good look at the words below and see if you can discover anything unique about the entire word or the way some letters repeat or reverse. For each word, <u>underline</u> letters that repeat or reverse. Then <u>deci</u>de if the word should be called a *Palindrome, Reversal, Echo,* or *Bookend* (a few words may be more than one of these.) Write the name by the word. Since the mind easily connects with these *Visual Patterns*, you'll easily remember these tools!

decide	**museum**
deer	**racecar**
drawer	**sense**
level	**swallows**

| Echo Word |: The letters that begin the word are *echoed* at the end: <u>deci</u>de and <u>sen</u>se.

| Bookend |: Letters at the beginning and end look like *bookends*: <u>lev</u>el, <u>mus</u>eum, <u>race</u>car, <u>swall</u>ows.

| Palindrome |: The word reads the same forwards and backwards: <u>level</u>, <u>racecar</u>.

| Reversal |: The word is one word forward and a different word reversed: <u>deer</u> – <u>reed</u>; <u>drawer</u> – <u>reward</u>.

❏ **NOW**: Fill in the blanks and enjoy figuring out these *Echoes, Bookends, Palindromes*, and *Reversals*.

1. o n _ o n   *Echo*: vegetable with strong odor

2. c h _ _ c h   *Echo*: place for worship

3. e r _ _ e r   *Echo*: used to rub out writing

4. h e _ _ _ _ h e   *Echo*: pain in the head

5. u n d _ _ _ _ _ u n d   *Echo*: below the Earth's surface

6. e n _ _ n e   *Bookend*: part of a car or train that runs it

7. r e _ _ e r   *Bookend*: one who loves books

8. s e _ _ e s   *Bookend*: You have 5: hearing, seeing, feeling, tasting, smelling.

9. s t _ _ t s   *Bookend*: long poles with raised foot rests used for walking

10. n e _ _ _ e n   *Bookend*: males who report the news

11. k a _ a k   *Palindrome*: watertight, Eskimo canoe

12. s a _ a s   *Palindrome*: ancient stories; tales

13. s o _ o s   *Palindrome*: music, song, or flight performed by one person

14. l _ _ _ – p _ _ _   *Reversal*: I swam the _____ around the _____.

15. d _ _ _ – l _ _ _   *Reversal*: I went to _____ the phone, and then _____ it down.

Detecting Visual Pictures in Words and Letters

A great way to use your *Visual POWER* is to look for words where you see something you can draw in the whole word or in the letters. For example: In <u>brilliant</u>, you might see *4 candles*; in <u>eye</u>: *2 eyes and a nose*. Try *yo-yo* or *sleep*. Discovering and drawing pictures will help you remember words and letters because your mind can connect the pictures you've draw with the word's spelling

❑ **NOW**: LOOK at these words:

shampoo	twinkle	repetition
yo-yo	luggage	merry-go-round
giraffe	ooze	kickball
squirrel	look	cycle
brilliant	high	castle
balloon	giggling	pool
hiccup	parallel	eye
mountain	monotonous (boring)	wavy

Pick eight of these words where you can see shapes or pictures *in the whole word, or in the letters, that you can draw* and use as *Memory Tools*. (See examples. You can draw these too, if you'd like). Also, discover a few words of your own and draw these. Have fun!!!

Mixed-Up Homophones

Visual: Seeing Words in Words

ANAGRAMS: Have you ever been spelling a word and found you could make another word out of the same letters: <u>eat</u> – <u>tea</u> and <u>ate</u> ; <u>heart</u> – <u>earth</u>..? If yes, you have an idea of how *Anagrams* probably began. An *Anagram* is like unscrambling a word. You simply look in the word for another word or phrase that uses all the letters and connects to the word in some way: <u>surgeon</u> – <u>Go nurse</u>…

❑ **NOW**: Find an anagram for each word below, and also create one of your own anagrams.

kids: _ _ _ _; float: <u>a</u> _ _ _ _ ; rescue: <u>s</u> _ _ _ _ _ ; measured: m_ _ _ s _ _ _.

WORD SEARCH: This game truly sharpens your visual skills by challenging you to look at words and find all the different words where the letters are in a row. *Example*: <u>argument</u>: <u>gum</u>, <u>men</u>, <u>me</u>…; <u>separated</u>: <u>a</u>, <u>ate</u>, <u>rat</u>, <u>rate</u>, <u>rated</u>…; and <u>heartbeat</u> contains 11 words. Can you find them?

(3) begin with <u>a</u>:   (3) begin with <u>b</u> (3-One is a name.):

(2) begin with <u>e</u>:   (3) begin with <u>h</u>:

❑ **NOW**: Play *Word Search* for these words. It helps to *alphabetically* list the words you find.

1. important: 10 words: (3) begin with <u>a</u>:

(4) begin with <u>i</u>:

(1) begins with <u>o</u>:   (1) with <u>p</u>:   (1) with <u>t</u>:

2. knowledge: 10 words:

3. operated: 12 words:

4. separated: 11 words:

5. throwing: 9 words:

Choose 2 of your own words:

How about <u>experimentally</u> (15 words)?

WORD FUN: Finally, it's just fun to look at words to *see what you can see*. The great <u>Sequoia</u> has all 5 vowels: <u>e</u>, <u>u</u>, <u>o</u>, <u>i</u>, <u>a</u>. Also, if you take <u>a</u> out of <u>loaves</u>, you get <u>love</u>. What do you see in the musical word <u>staccato</u> (quick)? Also, write down some of the things *you have noticed* in words.

Introducing the Copy Cat Kids

In the English language, there are *four single letters* – **C, G, S,** and **X** – and *four pairs of letters* – **CH, GH, PH,** and **Qu** – that like to *copy other sounds*. We call these *imitators* the **Copy Cat Kids**, and once you get to know them, you'll find that they really are quite friendly and easy to understand. In this lesson, we'll be taking a look at some of the words that the Copy Cat Kids appear in. They show their faces in really quite a lot of places. They appear not only at the beginning of words, but also in the middle, and sometimes at the end. So, let's meet and get to know these Copy Cat Kids!

Introducing the One-Letter Copy Cat Kids – C, G, S, and Z

Francisco is a total **COPY CAT KID**. He copies **K** (**c**at) and **S** (**c**ity).
Gidget makes her own **G** sound (**g**um) and also copies **J** (**g**ym).
Susannah makes her own **S** sound (**s**ong) and also copies **Z** (mu**s**ic), **SH** (**s**ure), and **ZH** (trea**s**ure).
Alexi, like Cisco, is a total **COPY CAT KID**. He copies **KS** (bo**x**) and **Z** (**x**ylophone).

Here's Cisco Cat Who Cycles in the City

C IS A TOTAL COPY CAT AND COPIES K AND S

C copies **K** (**c**at)			**C** copies **S** (**c**ity)		
INITIAL	MIDDLE	FINAL	INITIAL	MIDDLE	FINAL
came	across	black	cent	accent	dance
coat	American	clock	certain	concert	fancy
cookies	because	electric	cereal	decide	ice
country	cycle	music	circle	decision	mice
crocodile	echo	Pacific	circus	Pacific	peace
curl	nickel	picnic	cycle	pencil	piece
crowd	record	tragic	cyclone	percent	since

❑ **OBSERVING COPY CAT C:** When **C** copies **K**, what vowels follow it? _____ When **C** copies **S**, what vowels follow it? _____ Underline the **COPY CATS**: corny, crocodile, nickel, cyclone, percent.

Greet Gidget Girl Who Goes to the Gym

G MAKES ITS OWN SOUND AND ALSO COPIES J

G makes its own sound (girl)

INITIAL	MIDDLE	FINAL
garden	again	big
ghost	angle	chug
give	began	egg
gold	energy	frog
guest	sugar	hug
gum	wagon	twig

G copies J (gym)

INITIAL	MIDDLE	FINAL
gem	angel	age
gentle	badger	bridge
germ	danger	college
giant	legend	garage
ginger	magic	huge
gym	vegetables	village

❑ **OBSERVING COPY CAT G:** When **G** makes its own sound; what vowels follow it? _____
When **G** copies **J**, what vowels follow it? _____ Underline the **COPY CATS**: angle, angel, engine, huge.
How do you think the word <u>margarine</u> should really be spelled? _____

Starring Susannah – She Sure Sings Songs

S MAKES ITS OWN SOUND AND COPIES SH AND Z
S copies Z

S makes its own sound (sun)

INITIAL	MIDDLE	FINAL
sand	answer	cats
sea	castle	guess
sentence	herself	hopes
soared	listen	hops
super	person	its
sword	question	this

S copies SH (sure)

INITIAL/MIDDLE
sure
assure
S copies ZH (leisure)
division
measure
pleasure

S copies Z (as)

MIDDLE	FINAL
casual	eyes
desert	clothes
dessert	does
music	goes
roses	horses
scissors	says

❑ **OBSERVING COPY CAT S:** When **S** makes its own sound, what vowels follow it? _____
When **S** copies **SH** or **ZH** what vowels follow it? _____ Underline the **COPY CATS**: answer, listen,
leisure, measures, pleasure, questions, scissors, seasons.

Exuberant Alexi Excels on Xylophones

X IS A TOTAL COPY CAT KID AND COPIES KS AND Z

X copies KS (box)

INITIAL	MIDDLE	FINAL
axis	galaxy	box
exact	mixes	fox
excel	sixteen	index
x-ray	sixty	reflex

X copies Z (Xerox)

INITIAL
Xerox
xylophone

❑ **COPY CAT X:** When X copies KS, it's at the (beginning, end) of the syllable.
Underline these **COPY CATS**: axis, excellent, explain, extra, toxic, xylophone.

Getting to Know the Two-Letter Copy Cat Kids – *Ch, Gh, Ph, and Qu*

Christy sometimes copies **K** as in **ch**ord and **SH** as in **ch**ef.
Rou**gh**y copies **F** at the end of words, like cou**gh**, enou**gh**, and lau**gh**.
Kristo**ph** copies **F** in some words, like **ph**one, nephew, paragra**ph**, and **Ph**iladel**ph**ia.
Racquel makes a **KW** or **K** sound as in **qu**ack, **qu**een, uni**que**, and pictures**que**.

☐ Circle these **COPY CATS**: ached, pit**ch**er, **ch**ord, cou**gh**, ele**ph**ant, ne**ph**ew, **qu**art, uni**que**.

Christy Teaches Children's Orchestras

CH makes its **own** digraph sound			CH copies K	CH copies SH
INITIAL	MIDDLE	FINAL	INITIAL/MIDDLE	INITIAL
chance	a**ch**ed	chur**ch**	**ch**aracter	**ch**ef
chest	in**ch**es	lun**ch**	**ch**ord	**ch**ord
child	mer**ch**ant	mu**ch**	**ch**orus	**ch**apeau (French cap)
choose	pit**ch**er	pea**ch**	or**ch**estra	
chug	rea**ch**ed	tea**ch**		

Roughy's Rough and Tough

GH copies **F** at the end of a few words

cou**gh**	enou**gh**	lau**gh**	rou**gh**	tou**gh**

Kristoph Is Phenomenal at Phonics

PH copies **F**

INITIAL	MIDDLE		FINAL
phenomenon	al**ph**abet	ne**ph**ew	autogra**ph**
photograph	ele**ph**ant	ne**ph**ew	hum**ph**
phrase	geogra**ph**ic	or**ph**an	paragra**ph**
physical	go**ph**er	telep**h**one	triump**h**

Racquel Quotes Quite Eloquently

Qu copies **KW**

INITIAL		MIDDLE		Qu copies K
				FINAL
quack	**qu**een	ac**qu**aint	fre**qu**ent	pictures**que**
quail	**qu**estion	e**qu**al	li**qu**id	techni**que**
quake	**qu**iet	e**qu**ator	s**qu**irrel	uni**que**
quart	**qu**ite	e**qu**ip	s**qu**are	

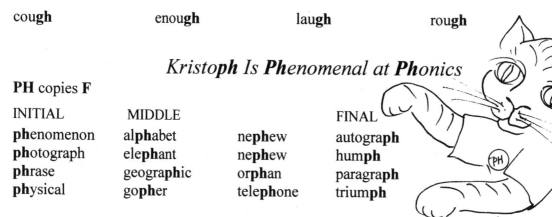

Creating Copy Cat Clues

❑ **NOW**: Fill in the letter that each *Copy Cat* copies and complete the *Copy Cat Clues*.
Where it says *Clue* or *Clue-in-a-Row*, have fun creating *Copy Cat Clues* that truly work
for you! *Helpful Hint*: Look for lots of *small words* inside of these *Copy Cat* words.

QU   PH   CH   CH

1. **angel**: __ copies __. *Clue*: They made an _ _ _ _ _-shaped dessert out of <u>gelatin</u>.

2. **angle**: __ has its __ sound. *Clue*: You can put the <u>e</u> in the <u>angle</u>: angl_.

3. **asphalt**: __ has its __ sound. <u>Ph</u> copies __ (Greek). *Clue-in-a-Row*:

4. **axis**: __ copies __. __ makes its __ sound. *Clue-in-a-Row*:

5. **challenge**: __ has its __ sound. __ copies __. *Clue*:
    Clue: The Little <u>Engine</u> faced a _ _ the _ _ _ _ _ _ _ _ and said *I think I can*...

6. **chorus**: __ copies __. __ copies __. *Clue*: A _ _ _ _ _ _ sang <u>for us</u>.

7. **college**: __ copies __. __ copies __. *Clue*: They need to <u>collect</u> their _ _ _ _ _ _ _ tuition.

8. **courage**: __ copies __ and __ copies __. *Almost-Clue-in-a-Row*:

9. **cough**: __ copies __ and __ copies __ sound. *Clue*:   *Pattern*:

10. **crocodile**: Both __'s copy __. *Clue*: <u>Croco</u> my _ _ _ _ _ _ _ _ _ swims on the <u>Nile</u>.

11. **cyclone**: __ copies __ and __ copies __. *Clue*: We want no cl _ _ _ of that _ _ _ _ _ _ _.

12. **elephant**: __ copies __ (Greek). *Clue*: The huge _ _ _ _ _ _ _ _ had a tiny _ _ _ on its back.

13. **pigeon**: __ copies __. *Clue-in-a-Row*:

14. **pleasure**: __ copies __. *Clue-in-a-Row*:

15. **nephew**: __ copies __ in Greek. *Clue*: I see a <u>few</u> (Gk. phew) people who know my _ _ _ _ _ _.

16. **pitcher** (plays ball): __ has its __ sound. *Clue*: Can a _ _ _ _ _ _ _ <u>pitch</u> a <u>cherry</u> _ _ _?

17. **quaint**: __ copies __. *Clue*: That p _ _ _ _ has a _ _ _ _ _ _ color.

18. **question**: __ copies __. __ has its __ sound. *Clue*: The _ _ _ _ _ _ _ _ is what quest am I on.

19. **scissors**: __ has one __ sound. 3 s's copy __. *Clue*: My pair of _ _ _ _ _ _ _ _ <u>is</u> the <u>sort</u> I use.

20. **village**: __ copies __. *Clue*: At what <u>age</u> did you build that <u>villa</u> in your _ _ _ _ _ _ _?

➢ **decision**: __ copies __ and __ copies <u>ZH</u>. *SPP*: de-ci-<u>si</u>-on. *Clue*: The _ _ _ _ _ _ _ _ was:
   <u>Dec. is in on</u> calendars as the 12th month: <u>Dec-is-in-on</u>. (Roman calendars: Dec. is 10th.)

Let's Grasp and Learn Those Consonant Blends

In addition to Single Consonants, Copy Cats, and Digraphs (two consonants = one sound: CH, SH, TH, WH, plus NG and special ZH), English also has CONSONANT BLENDS, and that's it for consonants!!!

CONSONANT BLENDS are the sounds that happen when each letter in a word *keeps its own sound, and also blends* with one or more other letters to make the sounds you hear in: *grasp, learn, consonant, blends, crown, sprint, stars, stripes.* Consonant Blends are usually found at the beginning of words, but are sometimes found in the middle and at the end: *stop, tasty,* and *west.* As you say and spell Consonant Blends, hear and feel the sounds working together.

Introducing the Initial Consonant Blends

❑ **NOW**: Write 1-2 words for each Initial Blend and <u>underline</u> the blends: <u>fl</u>uff, <u>cl</u>own. Say each word. Try to *hear the single sound of each letter* in the Initial Blend, plus *all the sounds blending together*

INITIAL CONSONANT BLENDS

L FAMILY	R FAMILY	S FAMILY	3-LETTER S	OTHER
BL *blossom*	BR	SC	SCH	DW
CL	CR	SK	SCR	TW
FL	DR	SM	SHR	THR
GL	FR	SN	SPL	
PL	GR	SP	SPR	
SL	PR	ST	SQU	
	TR	SW	STR	
			WR	

Introducing the Final Consonant Blends

❑ **NOW**: Write 1-2 words for each *Final Consonant Blend.* <u>Underline</u> all the <u>blends</u>: <u>elf</u>, <u>brunch</u>. Pronounce the words and try to *hear and feel the single sound of each letter*, plus *all the sounds blending together*. If you use the same vowel and same *Final Blend*, your words will rhyme.

FINAL CONSONANT BLENDS

L FAMILY	N FAMILY	R/M FAMILY	S FAMILY	T FAMILY
bold LD	NC(e)	RD	SK	CT
LF	NCH (n + ch)	RK	SP	FT
LM	ND	RT	ST	*kept* PT
help LP	NK			
LT	NT	MP		

Don't forget ~LF

Creating More Initial Consonant 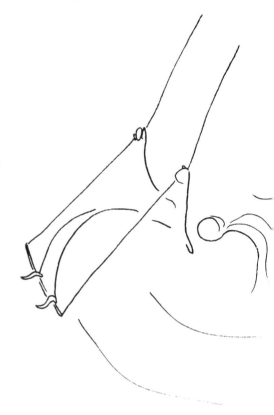 *ends*

❑ **NOW**: Write each word next to its *Initial Blend*: blanket, bleachers, bread, close, clothes, drawer, from, glacier, group, pleasant, practice, score, skater, sleek, smile, snack, splash, splendor, sports, spring, square, strange, stretch, tragic, trophy and twirl Also add 10 or more words. *Note*: In dictionaries, words with the same *Initial Blend* are listed together alphabetically.

L/M FAMILY
BL: blend, blossom

CL: clam, cyclone, eclipse

FL: fly, snowflakes

GL: glass, burglar

PL: plant, pleasure, multiply

SL: sled, slippers

R FAMILY
BR: brush, celebrate

CR: cross, democracy

DR: dress, raindrop

FR: fruit, fragile

GR: grape, fragrant

PR: prize, privilege, program, surprise

TR: train, trampoline, trapeze, attract

WR: wren, wreckage, wring, wrote

S FAMILY
SC: scarf, scared, science

SK: skate, skis, skunk, sky

SM: smile, smooth, smush

SN: snail, sneeze, sniff, snorkel, snow

SP: spaceship, spell, special

SQU (Qu works as one letter): squirrel, squeak

ST: story, statue, stayed, steal, steel, stone

SW: swallow, swan, swimming

3-LETTER and 4-LETTER BLENDS
SCH: school, scheme, schedule

SCR: screw, scribe, screech, describe

SHR: shrub, shrink

SPL: splash, splendor

SPR: sprig, spring, sprain

STR: straw, strange, strength

[SCHLep (Hebrew, carry), SCHMooze (H. talk), SCHMuck (H. pest), SCHNauzer (Ger. dog), SCHWA (H. vowel sound)]

OTHER
DW: dwarf (dwarfs, dwarves)

TW: twelfth, twine, twig

THR: three, thrill, thrive

Detecting More Final Consonant Ble

❑ **NOW**: Write each word next to its matching *Final Blend*. <u>Underline</u> all <u>blend(s)</u>: against, blend, built, bulb, burnt, desk, ditch, drift, elf, extinct, instinct, field, fifth, film, grasp, growl, lamp, legends, lunch, most, ninth, scent, shark, since, stitches, strength, thirst, toward, twelfth, twirl, want, watch, yield. Now add 10 or more words that rhyme with words below. You can build rhyming words like: calm, palm; chomp, stomp; stump jump; skunk, stunk, etc.

L/M FAMILY

LD: ho<u>ld</u>

LM: ba<u>lm</u>

LP: he<u>lp</u>

LT: me<u>lt</u>

WL: gro<u>wl</u>

MP: ca<u>mp</u>

N FAMILY

NC(e) si<u>nce</u>

NCH: mu<u>nch</u>

ND: ba<u>nd</u>

NK: wi<u>nk</u>

NT: ce<u>nt</u>, sce<u>nt</u>

R FAMILY

RD: wo<u>rd</u>

RK: ba<u>rk</u>

RT: fo<u>rt</u>

RNT: a<u>rn't</u>

S FAMILY

SK: ma<u>sk</u>

SP: cri<u>sp</u>

ST: ho<u>st</u>

T FAMILY

CT: fa<u>ct</u>

FT: so<u>ft</u>

PT: ke<u>pt</u>

TCH (T connected to digraph, ch): ca<u>tch</u>, la<u>tch</u>

90

Creating Tongue Twisters and Rhymes with Consonant Blends

A great way to hear and feel the sounds of *Initial Consonant Blends* is to create and say tongue twisters because then the blend get repeated again and again… and again.

The best way to hear and feel the sounds of *Final Consonant Blends*, is to create and say rhymes. These blends are easy to rhyme if you add the <u>same vowel</u> before the <u>same blend</u> (On this ca<u>lm</u>, ba<u>lmy</u> day, I watched the pa<u>lms</u> sway.). Did you know that there are *Rhyming Dictionaries* that are organized by the end-sounds of words? These are a great help for rhyming words.

Tongue Twisters with Initial Blends

❑   **NOW**: To create an tongue twister, follow the steps below:

First, choose an *Initial Blend* _____.

Then write down as many words as you can think of that begin with this blend.
(Remember: *Initial Blends* are alphabetically together in the dictionary.)

Keep putting your words together until you create a tongue twister you like. Write it here:

Now, choose another Initial Blend _____ .

Then, again, write down as many words as you can think of that begin with this blend.

Keep putting your words together until you create a tongue twister you like. Write it here.

Creating Rhymes with Ending Blends

❑   **NOW**: To create a rhyme, choose an *Ending Blend* that's easy to rhyme: _____ .

Then write down as many words as you can think of that rhyme with this blend. For example, you could choose the word *cold* and have the words *bold, fold, gold, hold, mold, sold, told…* that rhyme with it.

Keep putting your words together until you create a rhyme or poem you like, and write it below.

Focusing on Silent Letters

There once was a time (449 – 1400), when *English had no Silent Letters* Anglo-Saxon (Old English) was spoken, and every consonant and vowel was pronounced (even silent e's): *climban, cealf, cnotta, dette, gnawen, iland, rime, neahgebur...* From 1400-1600, *letters* became *silent* for 4 main reasons:

| climban | calf | ballet | love | gnaw | knot | thought | neighbor | psychology |

1st: From 1400-1600, immigrants poured into London, and for some reason, the way long vowels were pronounced changed to a higher sound. This *Great Vowel Shift* spread throughout England.

2nd: Printed books and spelling dictionaries established the way words were spelled at the same time that letters once pronounced: *b, e, g, h, k, l, t, w*...became silent: *climb, gnaw, calf, love, knot*. (From 1476 [printing press] to 1640, 20,000 different books had been printed. People wanted the familiar spelling.)

3rd: In the 1600s, people in England became passionate about ancient Latin and Greek. They even changed simple words into Latin spelling: dette became *debt*; dout – *doubt*; iland – *island*; rime – *rhyme*; sissors – *scissors*... Greek words were added too: *phantom, pneumonia, psychology*.

4th: English often keeps the spelling of other languages, which adds more *silent letters*: *chocolate, bomb*... from Spanish; *ballet, champagne*...from France; *gnu* from South Africa; and the list goes on...

Special Phonics Pronunciations are great for *silent letters*. For *SPP's,* you say all the letters like people once did in Old English: *g-na-w, sig-n... Other Word Forms* and *Same Patterns* also help.

Try *thumb*. You can use an *SPP:* thum-b. Try an *OWF and Clue*: Thumbelina was no bigger than a thumb. *Same Patterns* help too: crumb, dumb, numb, thumb.

❑ **NOW**: For each *SPP* write the word so *you can say all the letters*. Do this in *your own way*.

b   bom**b** *SPP: bom-b*   de**b**t *OWF: debit; SPP:*   lim**b** *OWF: limber; SPP: lim-b*

     clim**b** *SPP:*   dou**b**t *SPP: do-ub-t*   num**b** *OWF: number; SPP:*

     com**b** *SPP:*   dum**b** *OWF: Dumbo; SPP:*   plum**b**er *SPP: plum-ber*

     crum**b** *OWF: crumble; SPP:*   lam**b** *SPP:*   thum**b** *OWF: Thumbelina; SPP:*

g   desi**g**nation *SPP: de-sig-n*   **g**narled *SPP: g-nar-led*   **g**naw *SPP: g-na-w*

     resi**g**n *SPP:*   **g**nashed *SPP: g-nash-ed*   **g**nome *SPP: g-no-me*

     si**g**n *OWF: signal; SPP:*   **g**nat *SPP:*   **g**nu *SPP:*

gh   cau**gh**t *SPP: ca-ugh-t*   dou**gh** *SPP:*   brou**gh**t *SPP: bro-ugh-t*

     dau**gh**ter *SPP:*   thou**gh** *SPP:*   ou**gh**t *SPP:*

     strai**gh**t *SPP: stra-ig-h-t*   toni**gh**t *SPP: to-nig-h-t*   thou**gh**t *SPP:*

h ex**h**aust *SPP: ex-ha̲-ust*

ex**h**ibit *SPP: ex-hi̲-bit*

g**h**ost *SPP: g-ho̲st*

heir *SPP: he̲-ir*

herb *SPP: h̲-erb*

honesty *SPP: h-on-es-ty*

☆ **h**onor *SPP:*

hour *SPP: ho̲-ur*

r**h**yme *SPP: r-hy̲-me*

r**h**ythm *SPP: r-hy̲-th-m*

she**ph**erd *SPP: shep-he̲rd*

w**h**arf *SPP:*

---

k **k**nack *SPP: k-nac-k̲*

knapsack *SPP: k-nap-sac-k*

knave *SPP: k-na-ve̲*

knead *SPP: k-ne-a̲d*

knee *SPP:*

knelt *SPP:*

knew *SPP: k-ne-w*

knife *SPP: k-ni-fe*

knight *SPP: k-nig-h̲-t*

knit *SPP:*

knob *SPP:*

knock *SPP:*

knot *SPP:*

know *SPP:*

☆ **k**nuckle *SPP: k-nuc-kle̲*

These **kn** words are written so that each letter can be said: I **k-noc-ked** my **k-ne-e** on a **k-ni-fe** in my **k-nap-sac-k**.

☆

---

l a**l**mond *SPP: al̲-mond*

ba**l**my (mild) *SPP: bal̲-my*

ca**l**f *SPP: cal̲-f*

cou**l**d *SPP: co-ul̲d*

fo**l**k *SPP: fol̲-k*

ha**l**f *SPP:*

pa**l**m *SPP: pal̲-m*

psa**l**m *SPP: p-sal̲-m*

yo**l**k *SPP:*

---

n autum**n** *SPP: a-u-tum-n̲*

colum**n**ist *SPP:*

condem**n**ation *SPP: con-dem-n̲*

hym**n**al *SPP:*

solem**n**ity *SPP:*

---

p cu**p**board *SPP: cup̲-bo-ard* **r** ras**p**berry *SPP: rasp̲-ber-ry* **r** recei**p**t *SPP: re-ce-ip̲-t*

---

s ai**s**le *SPP: a-is̲-le* I i**s**land *SPP:* I i**s**le *SPP: is̲-le*

---

t cas**t**le *SPP: cast̲-le*

chris**t**en *SPP: chris-te̲n*

depo**t** *SPP: de-po̲t*

fas**t**en *SPP:*

has**t**en (to hurry) *SPP: has-te̲n*

lis**t**en *SPP:*

mis**t**letoe *SPP: mist̲-le-toe:*

nes**t**le *SPP:*

of**t**en *SPP:*

rus**t**le (soft sound) *SPP: rust̲-le*

sof**t**en *SPP:*

whis**t**le *SPP: whist̲-le*

w /ans**w**ered *SPP: ans-wer-ed*   **w**ren *SPP:*   **w**rist *SPP:*

s**w**ord *SPP: s-word*   **w**rench *SPP: w-rench*   **w**rite *SPP: w-ri-te*

whole *SPP: w-ho-le*   **w**restle *SPP: w-rest-le*   **w**ritten *SPP: w-rit-ten*

wrap *SPP:*   **w**ring *SPP:*   **w**rong *SPP:*

wreath *SPP: w-re-ath*   **w**rinkle *SPP: w-rink-le*   **w**rote *SPP: w-ro-te*

❑ **NOW**: Fill in the blanks and review how *Special Phonics Pronunciations* can help you hear, see, and remember all the consonants and vowels in these words, including Silent Letters.

clim**b**: *SPP:* _ _ _ _ - _

thum**b**: *SPP:* _ _ _ _ - _

desi**g**n: *SPP:* _ _ - _ _ _ - _

gnaw: *SPP:* _ - _ _ - _

brou**gh**t: *SPP:* _ _ _ - _ _ _ - _

cau**gh**t: *SPP:* _ _ - _ _ _ - _

ghost: *SPP:* _ - _ _ _ _

honest: *SPP:* _ - _ _ - _ _ _

wharf: *SPP:* _ - _ _ _ _

knead: *SPP:* _ - _ _ - _ _

kni**gh**t: *SPP:* _ - _ _ _ - _ - _

know: *SPP:* _ - _ _ - _

cal**f**: *SPP:* _ _ _ - _

coul**d**: *SPP:* _ _ - _ _ _

pal**m**: *SPP:* _ _ _ - _

autum**n**: *SPP:* _ _ - _ _ _ - _

colum**n**: *SPP:* _ _ _ - _ _ - _

ras**p**berry: *SPP:* _ _ _ _ - _ _ _ - _ _

cas**t**le: *SPP:* _ _ _ _ - _ _

lis**t**en: *SPP:* _ _ _ - _ _ _

s**w**ord: *SPP:* _ - _ _ _ - _

soa**r**ed: SPP: _ _ - _ _ - _ _

wreath: *SPP:* _ - _ _ - _ _ _

wrench: *SPP:* _ - _ _ _ _ _

94

Mnemonics for Silent-Letter Words

<u>Mnemonics</u> (ne-mon-ics) is a Silent-Letter Word which means *ways of remembering or improving memory*. It comes from *Mnemosyne* (Ne-mos-o-ne), the ancient Greek Goddess of Memory. *Clues, SPPs, OWFs,* and *Same Patterns* are *Mnemonics* because they are tools for remembering spelling.

❑ **NOW**: See how these Mnemonics can help you remember these Silent-Letter Words. Note that *Clues* often include *Other Word Forms* (*OWFs*) and *Same Patterns*.

1. clim**b**: *Clue*: I can _ _ _ _ _ on that <u>limb</u> to stay <u>limb</u>er.

2. dum**b**: *Clue/OWF*: <u>Dumb</u>o was not _ _ _ _ . He could fly!

3. sub**t**le: *Clue*: Help me write a _ _ _ _ _ _ <u>subtit</u>le.

4. thum**b**: *Clue/OWF*: <u>Thumb</u>elina was no bigger than a _ _ _ _ _ _ .

5. de**s**ign: *Clue/OWF*: I wanted to _ _ _ _ _ _ _ a <u>sign</u> and <u>sign</u>al.

6. **g**naw: *Clue/Pattern*: A <u>gn</u>at tried to _ _ _ _ on my <u>saw</u> with his <u>jaw</u>.

7. brou**gh**t: *Clue/ Pattern*: I <u>ought</u> to have _ _ _ _ _ _ _ the **gh**ost book I <u>bought</u>.

8. cau**gh**t: *Clue*: When they _ _ _ _ _ _ me, I yelled, " <u>Ugh</u>!"

9. **gh**ost: *Clue/Pattern*: A _ _ _ _ _ was my <u>host</u>. *Same Pattern*: <u>host</u>, <u>most</u>.

10. **h**onest: *Clue*: Our bees make <u>h</u> _ _ _ _ _ <u>honey</u>.

11. **w**harf: *Clue*: You can find a _ _ _ _ _ for boats at a <u>harbor</u>.

12. **k**nead: *Clue/Pattern*: I need to <u>read</u> about how to _ _ _ _ _ b<u>read</u>.

13. **k**night: *Clue/Pattern*: Can a _ _ _ _ _ _ in black armor be seen at <u>night</u>?

14. **k**now: *Clue*: I think I _ _ _ _ you <u>now</u>.

15. cal**f**: *Clue/Pattern*: My _ _ _ _ , <u>Alf</u>ie, grew <u>half</u> a foot this week.

16. coul**d**: *Clue/Pattern*: I w<u>ould</u> if I _ _ _ _ _ , and I know that I sh _ _ _ _ .

17. pal**m**: *Visual*: A _ _ _ _ ' s tall like <u>l</u>. *Clue/Pattern*: _ _ _ _ s sway in c<u>alm</u>, b<u>alm</u>y breezes.

18. autum**n**: *Clue*: The last month of _ _ _ _ _ _ is **N**ovember.

19. colum**n**: *Clue/OWF*: The <u>column</u>ist wrote a *Spelling* _ _ _ _ _ _ .

20. ra**s**pberry: *Clue/OWF*: _ _ _ _ _ _ _ _ _ vines are <u>rasp</u>y.

21. cas**t**le: *Clue/OWF*: The _ _ _ _ _ _ <u>cast lengt</u>hs of light across the moat.

22. lis**t**en: *Clue*: <u>Is ten</u> the number who are here to _ _ _ _ _ _ to your concert?

23. s**w**ord: *Clue*: He bet his <u>word</u> on his skill with a _ _ _ _ _ .

24. soared: *Clue-in-a-Row*: <u>So a red</u> bird _ _ _ _ _ _ by my window.

25. **w**reath: *Clue*: We kissed ben<u>eath</u> a _ _ _ _ _ _ of mistletoe.

26. **w**rench: *Clue*: A <u>wren</u> sat on the _ _ _ _ _ _ on the b<u>ench</u>.

Pronounce All the Letters Like People Did in Old English

NOW: For each of these sets of Silent-Letter Words, write a sentence using as many words as you can. Add any extra words you need for your sentence and underline the Silent Letters. Then write your sentence using *SPP's* so that *you say and hear all the consonants and vowels*. Read some sentences aloud. They'll sound a bit like the way words were spoken in Old English.

| SILENT B | crum<u>b</u>, dum<u>b</u>, num<u>b</u>, plum<u>b</u> (measure, depth), plum<u>b</u>er, succum<u>b</u> (give in), thum<u>b</u>.

YOUR SENTENCE:

SPP SENTENCE:

| SILENT K | <u>k</u>nack, <u>k</u>napsack, <u>k</u>nave, <u>k</u>nead, <u>k</u>nee, <u>k</u>nelt, <u>k</u>new, <u>k</u>nife, <u>k</u>night , <u>k</u>nit, <u>k</u>nob, <u>k</u>nock, <u>k</u>not, <u>k</u>now, <u>k</u>nuckle…<u>Your SENTENCE</u>: He <u>k</u>new he <u>k</u>nocked his <u>k</u>nee on a <u>k</u>nife in his <u>k</u>napsack.
     SPP SENTENCE: He <u>k</u>-ne-w he <u>k</u>-noc-<u>k</u>ed his <u>k</u>-nee on a <u>k</u>-ni-f<u>e</u> in his <u>k</u>-nap-sac-<u>k.</u>

YOUR SENTENCE:

SPP SENTENCE:

| SILENT L | (L's almost silent): a<u>l</u>ms (money for poor), ba<u>l</u>m, ba<u>l</u>my, ca<u>l</u>m, pa<u>l</u>m, <u>p</u>sa<u>l</u>m, qua<u>l</u>m (uneasy feeling).

YOUR SENTENCE:

SPP SENTENCE:

| SILENT T | cas<u>t</u>le, chris<u>t</u>en, depo<u>t</u>, fas<u>t</u>en, has<u>t</u>en (hurry), lis<u>t</u>en, mis<u>t</u>letoe, nes<u>t</u>le, of<u>t</u>en, rus<u>t</u>le, sof<u>t</u>en, whis<u>t</u>le.

YOUR SENTENCE:

SPP SENTENCE:

| SILENT W | <u>w</u>hole, <u>w</u>rap, <u>w</u>ren, <u>w</u>rench, <u>w</u>restle, <u>w</u>ring, wrung, <u>w</u>rinkle, <u>w</u>rist, <u>w</u>reath, <u>w</u>rite, <u>w</u>ritten, <u>w</u>rong, <u>w</u>rote.

YOUR SENTENCE:

SPP SENTENCE:

ESSON 16

I've Got Those Syllables! Got That Power Beat!

If someone asked you to spell pneumonoultramicroscopicsilicovolcanoconiosis (longest word in English: lung disease from inhaling ultra-microscopic silica dust) and then that person gave you the word supercalifragilisticexpialidocious, you just might give these words right back! HOWEVER, if you knew how to hear the beat, and how to divide these words into syllables, it might not be so bad. It might even be *good,* which is what *supercalifragilisticexpialidocious* means, at least to Mary Poppins, but more about that later. For now let's learn about syllables and beats!

Knowing about syllables and beats truly helps you spell. Hearing where the beat falls helps you feel the rhythm of the word – which helps you pronounce the word – which helps you divide it into syllables – which makes it easier to spell – because now you can spell the word, syllable by syllable. If you still have questions, check the dictionary. It has all the answers about syllables and beats, even about the word: pneu-mo-no-ul-tra-mi-cro-scop-ic-sil-i-co-vol-ca-no-co-ni-o-sis.

Syllables are built with consonants and vowels – and words are built from syllables. A word can be as simple as a one-syllable word, NO, or you can add more syllables and have VOL-CA-NO. To build words, you just add prefixes and suffixes to roots to get words like UL-TRA-MI-CRO-SCOP-IC and SU-PER-MAG-NI-FI-CA-TION. You're simply adding one syllable to another to make words – words that you can then break back down into syllables so you can spell them.

Introducing the Six Kinds of Syllables

Since there only six kinds of syllables that build the entire English language, it's very helpful to learn these. These six syllables help you detect where one syllable ends and the next begins – so that you can spell words one syllable at a time!

OPEN SYLLABLES *always stay o-pen* by ending in a vowel. They can be a single vowel (**a**, **a**-like, **e**-qual, **I**, **o**-pen, **u**-nit) or be a syllable that ends with a single vowel (**ta**-ble, **me**, **ti**-ger, **no**, **mu**-sic, **di**-vide, **my**).

CLOSED SYLLABLES *are always closed* by a consonant that has one short vowel before it (**ant**, **cat**, **egg**, **pin**, **on**, **frog**, **up**, **sun**, **cat**-a-**log**, **book**-**end**). *Most short vowel words* are closed syllables.

VOWEL-CONSONANT-E SYLLABLES *always end in final e* with a vowel plus a consonant before the final e (**ace**, **face**, **these**, **kite**, **rose**, **flute**). Final e usually makes the vowel before it long.

TWO VOWELS TOGETHER SYLLABLES *always have 2 vowels that make one sound* (**rain**, **bee**, **sea**, **pie**, **coat**, **book**, **moo**, **fruit**, **show**-**boat**). They can end with vowels or with one or more consonants.

R-CONTROLLED SYLLABLES *always have a letter R right after the vowel(s)*. The letter R controls and changes the vowel sound (**star**, **fern**, **bird**, **fork**, **turn**, **hair**, **care**, **tear**, **cheer**).

CONSONANT + LE SYLLABLES *always have a consonant + le*, and are always connected to another syllable. They are usually found at the end of a word (pic-**kle**, pur-**ple**, squig-**gle**).

Let's Try Out the Six Kinds of Syllables

OPEN SYLLABLES *are always kept o̲-pen by ending in a single vowel.* An open syllable can simply be a single vowel or a syllable that ends with a single vowel. *All the long vowels* have open syllables. Only *short a* and *short i* have open syllables, and only *when they don't get a beat.* Since an Open Syllable always ends in one vowel, its formula could be written ...V .

❑ **NOW:** Add one or more Open Syllables to each vowel sound. Just follow the pattern.

LONG AND ACCENTED (all vowels)

1. **a**, **ma**, **ta**-ble:
2. **me**, **e**-qual:
3. **I**, **ti**-ger:
4. **do**-nut, **o**-pen:
5. **mu**-sic, **u-ni-cy**-cle, **u-ni**-corn:
6. **my**, mys-ter-**y**:

SHORT and UNACCENTED (short a and i)

a-mong, **a**-like (*uh sound*):

at-**ti**-tude, **di**-vide (*short i*):

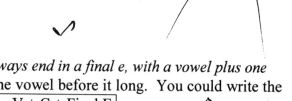

CLOSED SYLLABLES *always close with one or more consonants preceded by just one short vowel.* Closed syllables can start with a consonant(s) or a vowel. The rule is that at least one consonant must follow the short vowel. The consonant is like a DOOR that CLOSES the syllable. A Closed Syllable's formula could be written ...Short V + C(s) .

❑ **NOW:** Add at least 2 Closed Syllable words for each vowel sound. Try rhyming your words.

1. **ant**, **cat**, **cat**-a-**log**:
2. **egg**, **stretch**, book-**ends**:
3. **in**, **pin**, **fish**:
4. **on**, **frog**, **gob**-let:
5. **up**, **sun**, **hum**-bug:

VOWEL-CONSONANT-FINAL E SYLLABLES *always end in a final e, with a vowel plus one consonant directly before it.* Usually Final E makes the vowel before it long. You could write the formula for a Vowel-Consonant-Final E Syllable as ...V + C + Final E .

❑ **NOW:** Add 2 or more Final E Syllables for each vowel sound. It's easy if you rhyme them.

1. **ace**, or-**ange** (exception), **blaze**:
2. **these**, pre-**cede**:
3. **ice**, **kite**, **fire**:
4. **rose**, **dome**, wish-**bone**:
5. **cube**, **cure**, **flute**:

| TWO-VOWELS TOGETHER SYLLABLES | *always have 2 vowels that make one sound*, and the
2nd vowel usually makes the 1st vowel long. These are called *Vowel Digraphs* (G. <u>di</u>-two + <u>graphs</u>-letters).
Two-Vowel Syllables can begin or end in vowels or consonants. The formula is | …V + V (one sound)… |.

- ❑ **NOW**: Add some <u>Two Vowels Together Syllables</u> for each vowel sound. Try rhyming them.
1. **hay**, **rain**, **rain**-ing:
2. **tree**, **peach**, **peach**-y:
3. **pie**, pot-**pie**, **tried**:
4. **bow**, **boat**, **show-boat** (w is a vowel):
5. **fruit**, **fruit**-less:

(Also, there are 2 <u>Final Two-Vowel Together Syllables</u>: -sion and -tion. They always comes at the
end of words: vi-**sion**, mo-**tion**…and are always pronounced /shun/ or /zhun/.)

| R-CONTROLLED SYLLABLES | *always have a vowel followed by <u>R</u>*. This <u>R</u> is so powerful that it
controls the sound of the vowels it follows(except long <u>i</u> and long <u>u</u>): *gar*-den, *her*, *fir*, *storm*, *pur*-ple,
hair, *dear*, *deer* (animal). The formula for an R-Controlled Syllable can be written: | …V + R… |.

❑ **NOW**: Add 2 <u>R-Controlled Syllables</u> for each vowel sound. It's easy if you rhyme them.
Note: There are five different R-Controlled vowel sounds (<u>ar</u>, <u>er</u>, <u>or</u>, <u>air</u>, <u>ear</u>):
1. **ar**   as in st**ar**:   **ar**-tist:
2. **er**   as in f**er**n: pan-**ther**:
    er   as in b**ir**d: **cir**-cle:
    er   as in t**ur**n: **urn**, **tur**-tle:
3. **or**   as in h**or**n, **ore**:   a-**corn**, be-**fore**
4. **air**   as in h**air**, squ**are**:   **pair**-ing, **care**:
5. **ear**   as in d**ear**, deer: **tear**, **cheer**

| CONSONANT + LE SYLLABLES | *always have a C + LE that follows another syllable*. They're
found at the end of words, and B, D, G, K, and P often come before -LE: (peb-*ble*, noo-*dle*, gig-*gle*,
tic-*kle*, rip-*ple*…). The formula for this syllable can be written | C + LE |.

- ❑ **NOW**: Add some <u>C + LE Syllables</u> below . Try some of the different endings: *ble, dle, gle…*
1. bab-**ble**, rat-**tle**
2. met-**tle** (courage),   peb-**ble**:
3. gig-**gle**, pic-**kle**, tic-**kle**:
4. oo-**dles**, poo-**dle**:
5. pur-**ple**, snug-**gle**:

IN SUMMARY: Remember: There are six main kinds of syllables in the English language:

1. <u>Open Syllable ...V</u> $\boxed{...V}$ ma, pa, hi-fi, cha-cha-cha

2. <u>Closed Syllable V-C</u> $\boxed{...\text{Short V} + C(s)...}$ pond, splash, wet, swim, fun

3. <u>Vowel-Consonant-Silent-e V-C-E</u> $\boxed{...V + C + \text{Silent E}}$ ig-nite, fuse, flame, fire, shone

4. <u>Two Vowels Together Syllable V - V</u> $\boxed{...V + V \text{ (one sound)}...}$ look, bee, pain, oint-ment

5. <u>R-Controlled Syllable V - R</u> $\boxed{...\text{Short V} + R...}$ North, first, star, turn, burn

6. <u>Consonant-le Syllable C - le</u> $\boxed{... - C + LE}$ cud-dle, tic-kle, gig-gle, tum-ble

❑ **NOW**: Let's label syllables. First, write <u>C</u> above the *Closed Syllables*. Then write <u>E</u> above *Final E Syllables*. Write <u>VV</u> above *2-Vowel Syllables* and an <u>R</u> above *R-Controlled Syllables*. Write <u>CLE</u> above the *Consonant + LE Syllables*. Finally, hear and mark the beat!

red   (Danish <u>rood</u>, O. E. <u>red</u>: color of blood)

yel - low   (O.E. geolu: deep yellow of egg yolk).

blue   (O. E. <u>blewe</u>: angry or discolored).

green   (O. E. grene: grass color)

pur - ple   (O.E. purpure: shellfish for purple dye)

or-ange   (O.Fr. orenge: fruit; Sp. naranja)

white   (L. albus: white):

mis - use

he - ro - ic

home - work

phe - no - men - on

su - per - mag - ni - fi - ca - tion

mis - un - der - stand - ing - ly

floc - ci - nau - ci - ni - hil - i - pil - i - fi - ca - tion   (measuring as worthless, 2nd longest English word)

su - per - cal - i - fra - gi - lis - tic - ex - pi - al - i - do - cious   (Mary Poppins's word for *good*)

pneu - mo - noul - tra - mi - cro - scop - ic - si - li - co - vol - ca - no - co - ni - o - sis

Tik -ki - tik - ki - tem -bo -no -sa - rem -bo - char -i - bar -i - ru -chi- pip - per-i- pem- bo

100

Discovering How the Short Vowels Work

SHORT vowels make SHORT, quick sounds, and are usually found in SHORT words and syllables that end in a consonant: CLAM, SWAM, RED SLED, SHIP, RIP, FROG, DOG, BUG, RUG. Also, except for *you*, the other words below have short vowels: *on, and, felt, the, a, that, in.*

SCRAM, CLAM, you SWAM on PAM.

RED SLED on FRED and TED.

The SHIP felt the TIP and a RIP on that TRIP.
(What ship was it?)

FROG on DOG in FOG on a LOG.

HUG a BUG in a RUG.

Discovering How the Short Vowel Sounds Are Made and Feel

❑ **NOW**: Short vowels FORM their sound by vibrating inside your throat and releasing air over your tongue and out your mouth. If you FEEL your throat as you make each sound, you can probably detect where the sound vibrates the most for each short vowel. Also, you can feel the shape of your tongue and your breath as you release each sound.

Short a makes the sound you hear in **a**nt and c**a**t. It is the sound you make when you feel like you are gagging and say, "**Gaa**...g." Make this sound, and try to feel the vibration, back under your jawbone. Notice what happens with your tongue and feel your breath.

Short e makes the sound you hear in **e**gg and **E**d. It is the sound you might make when you move your ear to hear what someone said, and you say, "**Eh**...eh?" As you make this sound, feel the vibration halfway between your chin and neck. Where is your tongue?

Short i makes the sound you hear in **i**gloo p**i**n. It is the sound you might make when you don't like the taste of something, and say, "This tastes **i**cky...icky" Try to feel the sound vibration near the front of your chin. Be aware of the position of your tongue.

Short o makes the sound you hear in cl**o**ck and **o**n. It is the sound you make if your doctor says, "Say **ah**..."or when you sing, "**Aaa**h..." or say, "Ha, ha." Try this sound and feel the vibration go through your throat. What happens to your tongue and breath?

Short u makes the sound in s**u**n and **u**p. It is the deep sound you make when you say, "**Ugh**...ugh..." like a caveman, from the base of your throat and beat your chest. See if you can feel the throat vibration. Notice your tongue and breath as you say, "**Ugh**..."

101

□ **SUN GAME**: To learn more about how short vowels work, try the *Sun Game*. Pick any consonant,
digraph (2-consonant Together Team) or blend on the sun. Then choose a vowel from the center. Finally, choose any consonant(s) to end your word. If you'd like, you can also begin in the middle of the sun with a short vowel and then pick a consonant to end your word. List your words under their vowel sound.

a (ant, apple)	**e** (egg, elephant)	**i** (igloo, pin)	**o** (frog, octopus)	**u** (sun, umbrella)
at	*set*	*trip*	*mop*	*cut*

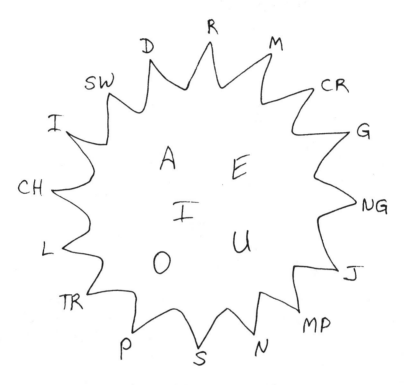

Discovering a Short Vowel Rule

□ **YOUR THOUGHTS**: Now, read the words you have just made and put a short vowel mark over all the short vowels. Then carefully look at your words, and explain how you think the consonants and a short vowel work together to keep the vowel short.

□ Does a consonant need to come before the vowel to keep it short?

□ **NOTICE**: The words below begin or end with digraphs (ch, sh, th, wh, ng) or consonant blends. Write three or more words under each vowel that begin or end with a digraph or consonant blend.

a	e	i	o	u
lamp	*check*	*sing*	*sock*	*cluck*

□ **NOW**: Find the 5 words that have long vowels and circle them (you can hear the <u>name</u> of the vowel). Then, above each short vowel word, make a short vowel mark or draw a tiny picture (Choose what you want to draw: ant, egg, pin, etc.) Note: All the words with a short vowel close with one or more consonants.

a (ant, ap-ple)   **e** (egg, el-e-phant)   **i** (ig-loo, pin)   **o** (clock, oc-to-pus)   **u** (up, um-brel-la)

a	e	i	o	u
am	egg	in	odd	us
asks	jet	imp	globe	hush
name	sled	time	hop	clue
hat	treat	swim	frog	just
ad, add	wren	limb	broth	crunch

Based on the information you have read so far, we could write a short vowel rule that says—

> **A SINGLE VOWEL STAYS SHORT WHEN IT IS FOLLOWED BY AT LEAST ONE CONSONANT WITH NO VOWEL COMING RIGHT AFTER THE CONSONANT.**

□ **TRY THIS:** Write a short vowel rule in any way that makes sense to you.

Changing a Short Vowel into a Long Vowel

□ **NOW TRY THIS**: Take the short vowel words below and form any new words you can by putting a silent <u>e</u> at the end of the word, or by putting another vowel next to the short vowel.

at *ate*	bet *beat*	pin *pine, pain*	mop *mope*	cub *cube*
hat	met	fin	cot	cut
man	net	kit	hop	sup *soup*
rat	set	prim	rob	plum
wag	ten	strip	slop	tub

□ **OBSERVATIONS**: What happens when you put a silent <u>e</u> after a single consonant that follows a short vowel as in *rate* and *kite*?

□ What happens when you put another vowel next to a short vowel as in *main* and *teen*?

Short Vowels and Closed Syllables

CLOSED SYLLABLES are easy to understand. Syllables with a single short vowel that end in a consonant are CLOSED SYLLABLES. (The *consonant* is like a little *door* that *closes* the syllable.) Also, if you use **V** for vowel and **C** for consonant, you can say: A closed syllable must have a **V + C**. You can add consonants before or after the short vowel, so a closed syllable also = **C(s) + V + C(s)**.

A VOWEL IN A CLOSED SYLLABLE IS SHORT. CLOSED SYLLABLES must have a **V + C**.

❑ **NOW**: Find and circle the 6 syllables hidden in this list that have long vowels (You can hear their long vowel name). Then put a short vowel mark above all the short vowels.

cat – nip	hel – met	lim – <u>it</u>	home – run	fun – gus
fan – tas – tic	den – tist	pic – nic	pom – pom	blue – bell
man – age	mag – net	vic – tim	ton – sils	pump – kin
hat – band	gob– let	pine – cone	frog – man	hum – drum
can – did	en – gage	lis – ten	op – tic (visual)	sub – ject

NOTE: All the vowels in the syllables that are not circled are short and should have short vowel marks. Also, since each short vowel is followed (*closed*) by a consonant, these syllables are *closed syllables*.

FOR SUMMARY: From your experiments and observations, you have discovered that:

1. A single vowel always remains short when a single consonant follows it without another vowel coming right after the consonant. (…V + C = short vowel): A CLOSED SYLLABLE.

   at   set   pin   mop   cut

2. A single vowel remains short when it is followed by more than one consonant (except for a few long *i* and *o* words like *night*, and *both*). (… + V + CC…= usually short) CLOSED SYLLABLE

   lamp   chick   sing   moth   luck

3. A vowel becomes long when it's followed by a single consonant plus <u>e</u> (V + C + V-e = long) or when another vowel is added to it (…V + V + C…= long vowel).

   ate   seat   pine, pain   mope   cute

Taking all of this information, you can write a **SHORT VOWEL RULE**:

A SINGLE VOWEL STAYS SHORT WHEN IT IS FOLLOWED BY ONE CONSONANT WITHOUT A VOWEL COMING RIGHT AFTER THE CONSONANT.

A SINGLE VOWEL USUALLY STAYS SHORT WHEN IT IS FOLLOWED BY MORE THAN ONE CONSONANT.

You could also write: (…V + C = short)   and   (…V + CC = usually short)

(Words like *pint, flight, both,* and *cold* look like Closed Syllables but they aren't because *their vowel is long*.)

Long Vowel Sounds and the Powerful Silent E

LONG vowels make a LONG, full sound, where you can hear the name of the vowel, as in the words: *jade* (green gemstone), *glade* (open place in a forest), *Crete, thrive, hope, flute...* Silent E makes vowels long.

❏ **NOW:** As you read the words below, listen for how Silent E makes all the vowels before it long.

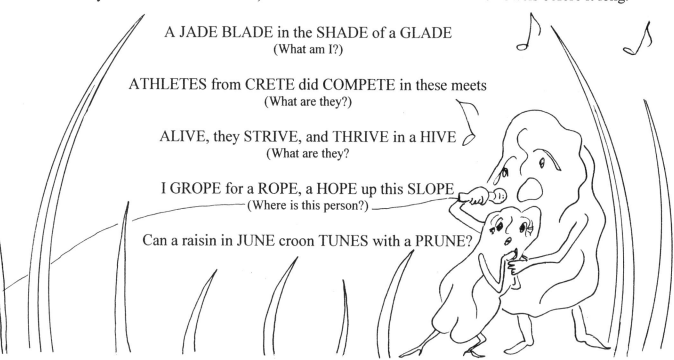

A JADE BLADE in the SHADE of a GLADE
(What am I?)

ATHLETES from CRETE did COMPETE in these meets
(What are they?)

ALIVE, they STRIVE, and THRIVE in a HIVE
(What are they?

I GROPE for a ROPE, a HOPE up this SLOPE
(Where is this person?)

Can a raisin in JUNE croon TUNES with a PRUNE?

❏ **TRY THIS:** Let's learn more about long vowels by discovering how these sounds are made. The long sounds are made in your throat, as your tongue, teeth and mouth help shape the sounds. For long vowels, you can feel the shape of your mouth more, and your breath and voice make the sound fuller and last longer.

Long a makes the sound you hear in **jade** and **face**. This sound vibrates from the middle front of your throat. As you make this sound, feel your tongue rise to a medium height, as it rests in front by your teeth. Your lips are opened and relaxed.

Long e makes the sound you hear in **eek** and **meet** (event where athletes compete). This sound vibrates from the high front of your throat. You can feel your tongue high and in the front by your teeth. Your lips are spread wider than for any other sound.

Long i makes the sound you hear in **ice** and **hive**. This sound vibrates from the low back of your throat, and as you make it, your tongue is low, and you can feel it moves from the back of your mouth to the front.

vocal chords

Long o makes the sound you hear in **oak** and **hope**. You can feel this sound vibrate from the middle back of your throat. As you make it, your tongue is raised in the back of your mouth and your lips are rounded to help form the sound.

Long u is the sound heard in **use** and **tune**. This sound vibrates from the high back of your throat, and you can feel your tongue high in the back of your mouth. The lips help form the sound, but are less rounded and opened than for the o sound.

❏ **NOW:** Write down anything you learned from your making these long vowel sounds.

Discovering the Powerful Silent E

❑ **TO LEARN MORE:** Take one of the short vowel words below: *glad, met, stag...* and add a Silent E to change it into a long vowel word: *glade, mete* (measure), *stage*. Write your words below.

a		e		i		o		u	
Short	**Long**	**Short**	**Long**	**Short**	**Long**	**Short**	**Long**	**Short**	**Long**
glad	*glade*	met	*mete*	kit		glob		cub	
mat		pet		quit		hop		cut	
pan		them		Tim		mop		hug	
stag				slid		rob		us	

❑ **WHAT DO YOU THINK?** What can *silent e* do that makes it so powerful?

❑ **STAR GAME:** To discover more about *final e*, let's play the Star Game. Choose a consonant. Then, pick a vowel from the center, and then choose another consonant. Then add a *final e* to your word. Write it under the vowel sound. Note: All your words follow the Final E Pattern: (...V + C + e).

A (tale, whale)   **E (Crete, metes)**   **I (kite, pine)**   **O (lone, tone)**   **U (cube, flute)**

place, jade

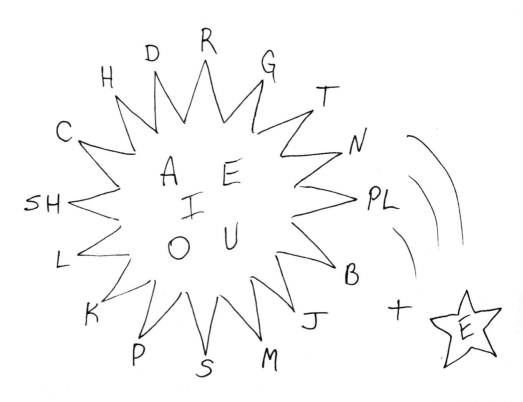

❑ **NOW:** Write down what you learned as you did this exercise. Also, write your own Silent E Rule.

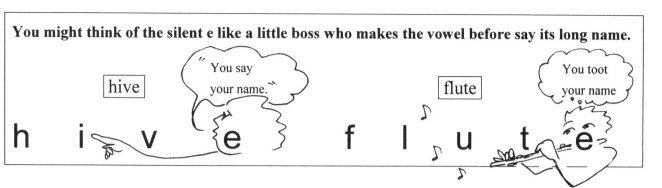

You might think of the silent e like a little boss who makes the vowel before say its long name.

hive — "You say your name."

h i v e

flute — "You toot your name"

f l u t e

❑ **NOW TRY THIS:** Take two or three long-vowel words that end with a silent e and draw a person telling the vowel before the silent e to say its name.

Creating a Silent E Rule

On the last page, you played a Silent E Game and then took a try at creating a Silent E Rule. Now, let's look at a Silent E Rule. You'll probably find that it's very easy to understand and remember.

WHEN YOU PUT A SILENT E AFTER A SINGLE CONSONANT, IT MAKES THE VOWEL THAT COMES BEFORE THE CONSONANT LONG.

Also, you could say… **Vowel + Consonant + V (silent e) = makes V before C long**, or
(… V + C + V (final e)… = **Long Vowel**)

… V + C + V(silent e)… = Long Vowel.

❑ **TESTING THE SILENT E RULE**: For these, mark all the long vowels with the long vowel mark. Also, underline all the silent e (final e) syllables (every syllable with …V + C + silent-e…). See examples.

blade	ath-lete	ad-vice	broke	ac-cuse
es-cape	ēve-ning	bag-pipes	dome	a-stute
flame	com-pete	camp-fire	globe	cos-tume
frus-trate	mete	hive	mi-cro-phone	huge
glade	re-cede	nine-ty	roses	im-mune
jade	scene	strive	slope	prune
trans-late	theme	thrive	whole	tunes

Exceptions to the Final Silent E Rule

You have learned that when *final e* follows a single consonant, it makes the vowel before that consonant long; however, some words end in a single consonant and *final e*, but the vowel before the *e* is not long (1st group below). There are also some words where *silent e* follows two consonants (2nd group). Before 1500, *final e* was always pronounced, but since this is not true today, these words are challenging to spell.

-me, -ne	-re	-ve		-ce	-dge (j sound)	-se
(These words have a vowel, a consonant and a silent e, but the silent e does not make the vowel before it long.)				(These words have 2 consonants after the vowel. Silent e does not make vowel long, and it is not pronounced)		
come	are	have		chance	large	else
some	here	give		dance	edge	tense
done	there	live		glance	hedge	rinse
gone	where	dove-bird		prince	ledge	horse
none	core	glove		since	bridge	Norse
one	more	love		once	ridge	worse
become	shore	move		trance	dodge	course
overcome	store	prove		force	lodge	house
redone	sure	shove		entrance	fudge	mouse…
undone	measure	above			judge	purse

Unaccented -ice syllables: *cowardice, licorice, notice, office, precipice-cliff, prejudice, surface* (and *police*).

Unaccented -ate syllables: *accurate, chocolate, considerate, delicate, desperate, fortunate, separate…*

Two-Syllable -re words: *adore, ashore, before, explore…* NOTE: R is the most powerful vowel. It can take words where *final e* has made the vowel long, and take the long sound away: *thee-there*; *foe-fore…*

Notice for -ve words: Since no English words end in -v, *final e* completes these words. There are also -ve words with a long vowel: *gave, alive, dive, five, hive, jive, strive. thrive, arrive…*

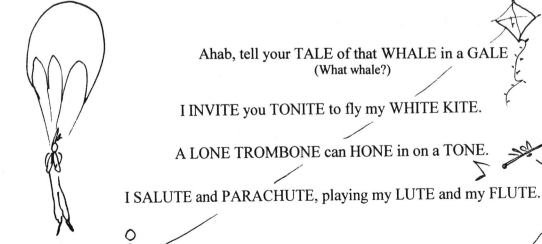

Ahab, tell your TALE of that WHALE in a GALE
(What whale?)

I INVITE you TONITE to fly my WHITE KITE.

A LONE TROMBONE can HONE in on a TONE.

I SALUTE and PARACHUTE, playing my LUTE and my FLUTE.

"blah, blah, blah ~

When Two Vowels Go Walking, the First One Does the Talking

Now that you know the *Silent E Rule*, let's discover another **POWER SPELLING RULE**. Here's your challenge: Discover and write down 3 points that the vowels in the capital letter words have in common.

A DEAL for a SEAL is REAL tricks for REAL MEALS.

Do BEES have KNEES?

1. If you wrote, "<u>Two vowels</u>, *you have one point*! (2 Vowels = *Long Vowel Digraph*: <u>di</u>: two + <u>graph</u>: letters).
2. If you added, "<u>The first vowel is long and the second vowel is silent</u>," *you've detected two points*!!
3. Finally, if you wrote, "<u>The second vowel makes the first vowel long</u>," *you've found all three points*!!!

Seal and **boat** show how this *Rule* works.

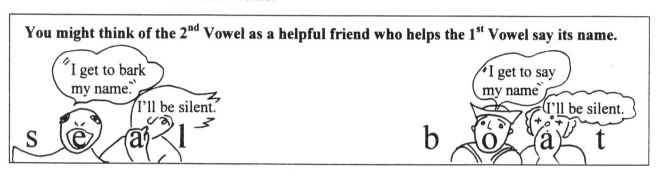

□ **BEAT TOAD**: GOAL: B<u>ea</u>t T<u>oa</u>d by making all the 2-vowel words you can. TO PLAY: First, jump to a *Consonant* tile (*Single, Digraph,* or *Blend*). Then jump to a *Long Vowel Digraph* tile. You can end your word with the *Vowel Digraph* or leap back and get another *Consonant* tile. Finally, write each word under its <u>VV</u>. (NOTE: Try starting a words with a VV tile.)

SINGLE CONSONANTS: d   k   l   m   n   p   r   t

CONSONANT DIGRAPHS: ch   sh

CONSONANT BLENDS: fl   pl   sn   sp   st

LONG VOWEL DIGRAPHS
ai   ay   ea   ee   oa   oe   ow   ue   ui
maid   *hay*   *seal*   *deep*   *boat*

□ **NOW**: Read your words and *circle* any words where the first vowel is *not long*. (NOTE: When <u>w's</u> a consonant, <u>ow</u> words aren't long. Write down anything you learned from playing this game.)

Long Vowel Digraphs Words "...The First Vowel Does the Talking"

❏ **TRY THIS**: Rhymes like - *The **rain** in **Spain** falls **mainly** on the **plains*** - help you hear *Long Vowel Digraphs*. For each set of words below, write a: 2-word rhyme (*Rays Play*); a sentence (*Rays play each day in our bay*); or a question (Do b<u>ee</u>s have kn<u>ee</u>s?) Write more of these if you wish. Have fun!

AI as in braid: laid, maid, mermaid, paid, raid * bail, fail, hail, jail, mail, nail, pail, quail, rail, sail, snail, tail, trail, wail (cry) * acquaint, faint, gait (walking style), paint, quaint, saint, trait, taint (trace), wait *

AY as in ray: bay, clay, day, gay, gray, hay, jay, lay, May, nay, pay, play, pray, say, slay, spray, stray, sway, tray, way * away, betray, castaway, essay, holiday, today *

EA as in sea: flea, pea, plea, tea * beach, bleach, leach, peach, preach, reach * beak, bleak (gloomy), creak, leak, peak, sneak, speak, squeak, streak, teak (wood), weak * deal, heal, meal, peal, real, reveal, seal, squeal, teal (blue-green), veal, zeal * ease, cease, lease, please, tease *

EE as in bee: cheese, fee, free, glee, knee, see, tee-hee, tree * deed, feed, heed, reed (flute; grass), seed, weed, bleed, breed, creed, freed, greed, speed, steed * beep, cheep, creep, deep, Jeep, keep, seep (ooze), sheep, sleep, steep, sweep, weep * beet (veg.), feet, fleet, greet, meet, sheet, sleet, street, sweet. tweet *

IE as in pie: die, fie, lie, tie, vie (compete) * died, dried, fried, lied, tied * dies, cries, dries, flies, fries, lies, pies, skies, ties, tries, vies *

OA as in coach: broach (bring up), poach (cook w/steam), roach (cockroach: insect) * load, road, toad * loaf, oaf * coal, foal (young horse), goal, shoal (sand bank) * foam, loam (rich soil), roam * loan, moan, groan * boast, coast, roast, toast * boat, coat, float, gloat (brag), goat, moat (water surrounding a castle), oat, throat *

OE as in does: foe, hoe, Joe, roe (fish eggs), toe, woe * cargoes, echoes, goes, heroes, tomatoes, potatoes, zeroes *

OW as in blow: crow, elbow, flow, glow, grow, know, low, mow, row, show, sow (female pig), throw, tow * blown, flown, grown, known, mown, shown, sown, thrown *

UE as in glue: blue, cue, clue, cruel, duel, fuel * flue, hue (color tone), rescue, Sue, true, ensue (happen) *

UI as in fruit: suit * bruise, cruise * (2 sounds): bruin (bear), ruin * nuisance

❏ **NOW**: Put a ⬜box around the following words in the lists above and <u>underline</u> the 2 vowels: braid, laid, main, quaint, clay, spray, creak, creek, reach, speak, street, tied, tries, foal, loaf, groan, grown, cruel, statue, fruit, unbeaten. See if you can write the *Rule* for these words in one sentence:

110

Summary of the Long Vowel Digraph Rule
"When Two Vowels Go Walking, the First Vowel Does the Talking."

**WHEN 2 VOWELS ARE TOGETHER IN THE SAME SYLLABLE,
THE 2nd VOWEL MAKES THE 1st VOWEL LONG.**

V + V = 1st Vowel long + 2nd Vowel silent.   Long Vowel Digraphs = V + V Syllable Pattern.

The OW Words

□ **NOW**: *Say* and *hear the difference in the 2 OW sounds.* Underline just the vowels in each set of words.

OW	W is a VOWEL O in OW is LONG.

bow (for hair)	row (line)
grow	show
grown	stow
know	sown (planted)
known	throw
low	thrown (tossed)
mow	below
mown	elbow

OW	W is a CONSONANT, O in OW is SHORT.

bow (curtsy)	drown	owl
brow	fowl	pow
brown	frown	prowl
clown	gown	row (fight)
cow	growl	scowl
crowd	how	SOW (female pig)
crown	howl	vow
down	now	wow

How Now, Brown Cow?

UI Words that Follow the Long V + V Rule and UI Exceptions

□ **NOW**: Say and hear the difference in the UI sounds. Then, underline the vowels and learn the *Clues*.

UI : LONG U SOUND;	UI : LONG U + SHORT I

bruise	fruit	bruin (bear)
nuisance	suit	ruin

UI : LONG I SOUND;	UI : SHORT I SOUND

guidance	guide	built	liquid	squid
guise (disguise)		guilt	quit	squint

bruise: I see a bruise: br + u + I see = bruise.

fruit: The fruit U and I got isn't ruined: fr + UI + t.

nuisance: Ants are a nuisance. *SPP*: nu-i-san-ce.

ruin (and bruin): *SPP*: Say: ru-in and hear ui.

suit: U and I have the same suit: s + UI + t.

built: *See* a sack (u) for nails (ilt); I built a bug house.

guidance: G, U (and) I dance well without guidance.

guise: G, U (and) I seemed fooled by his guise.

quit: Quit it. *Rule*: Qu works like a consonant.

squid: Squids squirt liquid. *SPP*: s-qu-id.

Exceptions Where the Second Vowel Speaks Up

❑ **TRY THIS**: You've learned the Rule: *When Two Vowels Go Walking, the First Vowel Does the Talking.* Let's look now at some *Exceptions* where *the Second Vowel Speaks Up.* The sound of the *second vowel* can be long, short, silent, a y sound...   Now, underline the 2 vowels in each word, and for 6 or more sets, write a sentence, question, or rhyme using as many words as possible.

| AI | *ONE SYLLABLE* (-tn) *SOUND*: Britain, certain, curtain, fountain, mountain, villain *

| IA | *Y SOUND*: civilian (yen), Peruvian, reptilian (yen) * familiar, peculiar (yer; 2 words; For spelling, say i-ar.)

| IA | *TWO SYLLABLES*: median (middle: di-en), guardian (di-en) * social (ci-el or shel), special *

| EA | *LONG A SOUND*: break, steak, great * (Other *EA Exceptions* are on the next page.)

| EU | *LONG U SOUND*: eucalyptus (tree), eulogy (tribute to one who has died), euphoria (great happiness), eureka (triumph), Europe * (Many of these *EU Words* are names or Greek words. Look under <u>eu</u> in the dictionary.)

| IE | *LONG E SOUND*: chief, grief, relief, thief * grieves, relieves, thieves * (See Lesson 20: IE/EI words)

| OU | *SHORT U SOUND*: courteous, dangerous, famous, glorious... (The -ous suffix is added to *many* words.

| OU | *LONG U SOUND*: you * through

| UI | *LONG I SOUND*: guide, guile (trickery; deceit); guise (disguise); disguise, guidance...

| UI | *SHORT I SOUND*: built, guilt, quilt * squid, liquid * quit, squint * guitar

| UY | *LONG I SOUND*: buy, guy

EA Exceptions to "When Two Vowels Go Walking" Rule

❑ **TRY THIS**: *EA Words* have the most exceptions to the *When Two Vowels Go Walking... Rule.*
To learn more about these challenging words, fill in the blanks for the *Clues* below. For *Same Pattern,*
write down 2 or more words with the same letter pattern. (Words with same sound are together.)

1. **bear**:   Can a b_ _ _ w_ _ _ a b_ _ _ suit? *Same Pattern:*
2. **pear**:   A p_ _ _ and a p_ _ ch are both fruits.
3. **tear** (rip): I'll w_ _ _ my new shirt that doesn't have a t_ _ _ .
4. **swear**:   S_ _ _ _ word sounds bad to my e_ _ s. *Same Pattern:*
5. **wear**:   There's a saying: "Some people w_ _ _ their h_ _ _ t on their sleeve."

6. **dear**:   You are very n_ _ _ and d_ _ _ to me. (*Homophone*: deer. *Reversal*: deer – reed.)
7. **hear**:   You h_ _ _ with your _ _ _ . *Same Pattern:*
8. **tear** (liquid): A t_ _ _ rolled down n_ _ _ my e_ _ .

9. **bread**:   She r_ _ _ a recipe for making b_ _ _ _ . *Same Pattern:*
10. **dead**:   When people are d_ _ _ , they have no br_ _ th.
11. **head**:   He stored what he r_ _ _ inside of his h_ _ _ .
12. **instead**:   He r_ _ _ i_ _ _ _ _ _ of watching TV.
13. **read**:   R_ _ _ is the past tense of to r_ _ _ (same spelling).
14. **thread**:   She r_ _ _ about how to t_ _ _ _ _ a needle.
15. **deaf**:   When you are d_ _ _ , your _ _ rs have a problem h_ _ ring.
16. **sweat**:   I s_ _ _ _ from the h_ _ _ of the sun in hot w_ _ _ her
17. **threat**:   The t_ _ _ _ _ made him sw_ _ _ . *Same Pattern:*
18. **breadth**:   B_ _ _ _ _ _ is a m_ _ surement of something's wi_ _ _ .
19. **breath**:   Can you take a b_ _ _ _ _ and e_ _ at the same time?

20. **dealt**:   D_ _ _ _ is the past tense of the verb, to d_ _ _ .
21. **health**:   The noun, h_ _ _ _ _ comes from the verb, to h_ _ _ .
22. **jealousy**: J_ _ _ _ _ _ _ is a l_ _ _ _ emotion.
23. **stealth**:   Zorro could s_ _ _ _ through the night with s_ _ _ _ _ _ (act of going about silently).
24. **wealth**:   W_ _ a_ l wanted to earn w_ _ _ _ _ . *Same Pattern:*

25. **break**:   There is an expression: "Let us b_ _ _ _ b_ _ d together."
26. **steak**:   Please don't s_ _ _ m my s_ _ _ _ in hot water. *Same Pattern:*

27. **earth**:   He put his e_ _ to the e_ _ _ _ to h_ _ _ its h_ _ _ _ beat (*Anagrams*: earth – heart).
28. **hearse**:   I h_ _ _ d him say that a h_ _ _ _ _ carries bodies to be buried in the _ _ _ th.
29. **rehearse**: He came to see and h_ _ _ them r_ _ _ _ _ _ _ . *SPP*: r_-_ _ _ _ _-_ _ .

30. **heart**:   Can you h_ _ _ your h_ _ _ _ beat? H_ _ _ _ has h_ _ and a_ _ _ in it.
31. **hearth**:   The bricks on the h_ _ _ _ _ were made from e_ _ _ _ _ .

32. **ocean**:   An o_ _ _ _ is also called a s_ _ _ . *OWF*: Oceanic refers to the o_ _ _ _

Rules and Patterns for the IE, EI Words

To help with these words, you might remember the famous jingle. But what does this really mean?

> I before E
> Except after C (C sounds like S),
> Or when sounded as A
> As in neighbor, their or weigh (A sound <u>always</u> spelled EI).

❑ **WINNING WITH IE AND EI:** First, write each word below. Then get ready for your first question: *How Are These Words Alike?* Complete the sentence that follows these words.

1. **believe** _____
2. **chief** _____
3. **field** _____
4. **friend** _____

5. **niece** _____
6. **piece** _____
7. **shield** _____
8. **shriek** _____

The way all these words are alike is:

If you wrote something like: All these words are spelled I before E... **YOU ARE RIGHT!!!**

❑ **ARE YOU READY** for your second question? Do I hear a "Yes?" Then: *How Are These 8 Words Alike?* Notice what they have in common as you write them, and complete the sentence.

1. **ceiling** _____
2. **conceit** _____
3. **conceive** _____
4. **deceit** _____

5. **deceive** _____
6. **perceive** _____
7. **receipt** _____
8. **receive** _____

The way all these words are alike is:

If you wrote something like: The spelling is CEI, and C = s sound... **YOU ARE RIGHT AGAIN!!!**

❑ **NOW:** for your final question! *How Are These Words Alike?* Write them and answer the question.

1. **eight** _____
2. **freight** _____
3. **heir** _____
4. **vein** _____

5. **neighbor** _____
6. **reign** _____
7. **sleigh** _____
8. **weight**

The way all these words are alike is:

If your answer was: The spelling is EI, and EI = A sound... **YOU ARE TOTALLY RIGHT!!!**
Now, with ***POWER CLUES, PATTERNS,*** and ***PRONUNCIATION,*** you can conquer these words.

Exceptions for Lines One and Two

Let's try that jingle again and learn the exceptions for lines one and two. Lines 3-4 have no exception.

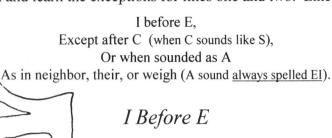

I before E,
Except after C (when C sounds like S),
Or when sounded as A
As in neighbor, their, or weigh (A sound <u>always spelled EI</u>).

I Before E

believe, belief	fiery	pierce
brief	friend	priest
cashier	grieve, grief	relieve, relief
chief	niece	shield
field	piece	shriek
fierce	pier	thief, thieves

EXCEPTIONS: There are a few words that don't follow the rule, and here are some of them. They can be learned with ***POWER CLUES*** like the ones on the next page.

either	height	seismic (quake, shake)
foreign	leisure	seize, seizure
forfeit	neither	weird

Except After C (EI when C copies S)

When **C = S sound**, the spelling is **CEI** and **E** is long. Also, **conceive** is related to **conception**, **deceive** to **deception**, **perceive** to **perception, receive** to **reception**. You can <u>hear E follow C</u>.

ceiling	deceit	receipt
conceit	deceive	receive
conceive	perceive	reception

EXCEPTIONS: When **C = SH sound**, the spelling is **IE**. You can hear the **SH** if you say each syllable: slowly: <u>an-ci-ent</u>; <u>ef-fi-ci-ent</u>; <u>con-sci-ence</u>. Also, when you say <u>science, you can hear i in sci-</u>.

ancient	efficient	sufficient	conscience	science

When Sounded as A in Neighbor, Their and Weigh (EI <u>always</u>)

When the **sound is A**, the spelling is <u>ALWAYS</u> **EI** – *NO EXCEPTIONS*.

eight	neighbor	sleigh
freight	reign	weight
heir, their	rein	veil
lei	skein (yarn wound on a coil: hair wound in a coil; a flock of geese in flight is also a skein.)	vein

Some Extra Challenging Words

Fill in the blanks. **CLUES, SPECIAL PHONICS PRONUNCIATION,** and **PATTERNS** help a lot.

♦ The I usually comes before the E after all letters, except C.

1. **achievement**: I said hi (on the) eve of my achievement to my chief assistants.

2. **alien** (an E.T. or foreign person): Ali met an a _ _ _ _ by his rocket. *Say*: a-li-en.

3. **cashier**: The c _ _ _ _ _ _ said, "H _," while cashing my check.

4. **diesel** (engines; fuel): Without d _ _ _ _ _ fuel, a d _ _ _ _ _ engine dies.

5. **fiery**: The fire was fierce and f _ _ _ _. *SPP*: fi-er-y

6. **hieroglyphics** (hier: sacred + o + glyphics: carvings): Reach high for the h _ _ _ _ _ _ _ _ _ _ _ _.

7. **priest**: The p _ _ _ _ _ established a church. *SPP*: pri-est

8. **retriever, retrieve**: I tried to get my r _ _ _ _ _ _ _ _ to r _ _ _ _ _ _ _ a ball.

9. **sieve**: Each eve, Eve used her s _ _ _ _ to clean vegetables in her sink.

10. **wield** (actively use): The eldest got to w _ _ _ _ the largest sword. *SPP*: wi-eld

11. **yield**: I always try to y _ _ _ _ to elders out of respect for age. *SPP*: yi-eld

---

EXCEPTIONS – where the E comes before the I.

1. **caffeine**: Coffee has c _ _ _ _ _ _ _ in it. *SPP*: caf-fe-in-e.

2. **counterfeit**: Some people c _ _ _ _ _ _ _ _ _ _ anything if people pay the fee for it.

3. **Fahrenheit**: My F _ _ _ _ _ _ _ _ _ thermometer is at a height of eighty-eight degrees.

4. **feisty** (full of energy; spirited): Einstein was _ _ _ _ _ _ and drank from a stein.

5. **heinous** (hein: evil + ous): He (acts) in h _ _ _ _ _ _, hellish ways.

6. **heist** (robbery; hold-up): He is the robber who held the h _ _ _ _ at the bank.

7. **seismic** (Gr. seismos; re: shakes, quakes): S _ _ _ _ _ _ jolts separate the land.

8. **sovereign** (supreme ruler, n., adj.): S _ _ _ _ _ _ _ _ _s have sole reign (Put v in for l.).

9. **stein** (Ger. beer mug): Einstein puts. his beer in ein stein: s _ _ _ _ (G., ein = one).

♦ When C = S sound, spelling is always CIE… *EXCEPTIONS*: When C = SH sound, spelling is CIE

1. **omniscient** (omni-all + scient-knowing): *SPP* om-ni-sci-ent. *SAME PATTERN*: science, conscience.

2. **sufficient**: *SPP*: suf-fi-ci-ent. *SAME PATTERN*: ancient, efficient, quotient, patient…

♦ EI when sounded as A. This part of the rule has NO EXCEPTIONS. You can totally trust it.

When you hear an A sound, the spelling is ALWAYS EI: beige, eight, freight, heir, lei, chow mein, neighbor, reign, rein, reindeer, skein, sleigh, their, weigh, veil, vein, inveigle (lure by flattery).

❑ **TRY THIS:** Fill in the blanks, and learn **Crazy *POWER CLUES*** to remember these words.

◆ I usually comes before E after all letters, except c.

1. **believe, belief**: Don't b _ _ _ _ _ _ a l _ _ _.

2. **brief**: Even b _ _ _ _ effort brings rel*ief*.

3. **chief**: The c _ _ _ _ said, "H _."

4. **field**: The elder farmer planted the f _ _ _ _.

5. **fierce**: The f _ _ _ _ _ giant yelled, "Fie…"

6. **friend**: Fri.(the) end of week, I see my f _ _ _ _ _.

7. **grieve**: After I g _ _ _ _ _, I get a grip on _ _ _ _ _.

8. **niece**: My n _ _ _ _ is n _ _ _.

9. **piece**: We ate a p _ _ _ _ of p _ _.

10. **pier**: We sat on the p _ _ _ and ate p _ _.

11. **relief**: Telling a l _ _ gave no r _ _ _ _ _.

12. **shield**: An elder in the tribe carried a s _ _ _ _ _.

13. **shriek**: They gave a shrill _ _ _ _ _ _, "Ek!"

14. **thieves**: Th _ _ _ _ _ often steal in the eves.

EXCEPTIONS – There are a few exceptions when E comes before I.

1. **either**: _ _ _ _ _ _ = m _ + _ _ + _ _ _.

2. **foreign**: I was f _ _ _ _ _ _ before.

3. **forfeit**: I had to f _ _ _ _ _ _ i _.

4. **height**: His h _ _ _ _ _ is e _ _ _ _ feet.

5. **leisure**: A Hawaii lei sure is for l _ _ _ _ _ _.

6. **protein**: Lots of p _ _ _ _ _ _ is in ten steaks.

7. **seize, seizure**: S _ e them s _ _ _ _ it.

8. **weird**: W _ are w _ _ _ _.

◆ When C = S + Long E Sound, the spelling is CEI.

1. **ceiling**: You face a ceiling when you look up.

2. **conceited**: C _ _ _ _ _ ed means self-centered.

3. **conceive**: Hear ce in c _ _ _ _ _ _ _ in conception.

4. **deceive**: Hear ce in d _ _ _ _ _ _ in deception.

5. **perceive**: Hear ce in _ _ _ _ in perception.

6. **receipt**: Hear ce in r _ _ _ _ _ _ in reception.

EXCEPTIONS – For science and when C = SH Sound, spelling is CIE or TIE: ancient, patient…

CLUES and **SPECIAL PHONICS PRONUNCIATIONS** (*SPP's*) truly help with these words.

1. **ancient**: The A _ _ _ _ _ _ One entered the tent.

2. **efficient**: *SPP*: e _ – _ _ – _ _ – _ _ _.

3. **patient**: *SPP*: p _ – _ _ – _ _ _.

4. **science**: *Say*: sci – ence, and hear i before e.

5. **conscience**: *SPP*: c _ _ – _ _ _ – _ _ _ _.

6. **quotient** (division answer): *SPP*: qu – o– ti – ent.

◆ Spelled EI – When sounded as A as in neighbor, their, and weigh.   *NO EXCEPTIONS*!

If you hear an A sound, the spelling is ALWAYS: EI: eight, rein, reign, veil, vein, heir, their, weight.
Write fun lines you'll remember: Our **neighbor's eight reindeer** pull **their sleigh** without **reins**.

EA Exceptions to "When Two Vowels Go Walking" Rule

❑ **TRY THIS:** _EA Words_ have the most exceptions to the _When Two Vowels Go Walking... Rule_. To learn more about these challenging words, fill in the blanks for the _Clues_ below. For _Same Pattern_, write down 2 or more words with the same letter pattern. (Words with same sound are together.)

1. **bear:** Can a <u>b</u> _ _ _ w _ _ _ a <u>b</u> _ _ _ suit? _Same Pattern:_
2. **pear:** A <u>p</u> _ _ _ and a p _ _ ch are both fruits.
3. **tear** (rip): I'll w _ _ _ my new shirt that doesn't have a <u>t</u> _ _ _.
4. **swear:** <u>S</u> _ _ _ _ word sounds bad to my <u>e</u> _ _ s. _Same Pattern:_
5. **wear:** There's a saying: "Some people <u>w</u> _ _ _ their h _ _ _ t on their sleeve."

6. **dear:** You are very n _ _ _ and <u>d</u> _ _ _ to me. (_Homophone:_ <u>deer</u>. _Reversal:_ <u>deer</u> – <u>reed</u>.)
7. **hear:** You <u>h</u> _ _ _ with your _ _ _. _Same Pattern:_
8. **tear** (liquid): A <u>t</u> _ _ _ rolled down n _ _ _ my <u>e</u> _ _.

9. **bread:** She <u>r</u> _ _ _ a recipe for making <u>b</u> _ _ _ _. _Same Pattern:_
10. **dead:** When people are <u>d</u> _ _ _, they have no br _ _ th.
11. **head:** He stored what he r _ _ _ inside of his <u>h</u> _ _ _.
12. **instead:** He r _ _ _ i _ _ _ _ _ _ of watching TV.
13. **read:** <u>R</u> _ _ _ is the past tense of to <u>r</u> _ _ _ (same spelling).
14. **thread:** She <u>r</u> _ _ _ about how to <u>t</u> _ _ _ _ _ a needle.
15. **deaf :** When you are <u>d</u> _ _ _, your _ _ rs have a problem h _ _ ring.
16. **sweat:** I <u>s</u> _ _ _ _ from the h _ _ _ of the sun in hot <u>w</u> _ _ _ her
17. **threat:** The <u>t</u> _ _ _ _ _ made him sw _ _ _. _Same Pattern:_
18. **breadth:** <u>B</u> _ _ _ _ _ _ _ is a m _ _ surement of something's wi _ _ _.
19. **breath:** Can you take a <u>b</u> _ _ _ _ _ and <u>e</u> _ _ at the same time?

20. **dealt:** <u>D</u> _ _ _ _ is the past tense of the verb, to <u>d</u> _ _ _.
21. **health:** The noun, <u>h</u> _ _ _ _ _ _ comes from the verb, to <u>h</u> _ _ _.
22. **jealousy:** <u>J</u> _ _ _ _ _ _ _ _ is a l _ _ _ _ emotion.
23. **stealth:** Zorro could <u>s</u> _ _ _ _ through the night with <u>s</u> _ _ _ _ _ _ (act of going about silently).
24. **wealth:** <u>W</u> _ a _ l wanted to earn <u>w</u> _ _ _ _ _. _Same Pattern:_

25. **break:** There is an expression: "Let us <u>b</u> _ _ _ _ b _ _ d together."
26. **steak:** Please don't <u>s</u> _ _ _ m my <u>s</u> _ _ _ _ in hot water. _Same Pattern:_

27. **earth:** He put his <u>e</u> _ _ to the <u>e</u> _ _ _ _ to h _ _ _ its h _ _ _ _ beat (_Anagrams:_ earth – heart).
28. **hearse:** I <u>h</u> _ _ _ d him say that a <u>h</u> _ _ _ _ _ carries bodies to be buried in the _ _ _ th.
29. **rehearse:** He came to see and <u>h</u> _ _ _ them <u>r</u> _ _ _ _ _ _ _. _SPP:_ r _ - _ _ _ _ - _ _.

30. **heart:** Can you <u>h</u> _ _ _ your <u>h</u> _ _ _ _ beat? <u>H</u> _ _ _ _ has <u>h</u> _ and <u>a</u> _ _ in it.
31. **hearth:** The bricks on the <u>h</u> _ _ _ _ _ were made from <u>e</u> _ _ _ _.

32. **ocean:** An <u>o</u> _ _ _ _ is also called a s _ _. _OWF:_ <u>Ocean</u>ic refers to the <u>o</u> _ _ _ _

Special Two-Vowel Combinations and Sounds

☆ *au, aw and al; ✦oi and oy, ★ou and ow,✦ and ew;✦and oo and oo* ✿

❑ **NOW**: Let's discover how the sounds of the *Special Two-Vowel Combinations* work. They don't fit the rule: *When Two Vowels Go Walking, the First One Does the Talking* or the *IE, EI Rule*. Look at these two-vowel combinations words, detect the patterns they share, and write these below:

AU and **AW**	**OI** and **OY**	**OU** and **OW**	**EW**	**OO** and **OO**
auto saw	coil joy	cloud owl	mew	moon book
launch fawn	oink toy	house crown	blew	zoom look

If you wrote, "<u>The VV combinations don't make a long sound in any word</u>," *you have one point*!
If you added, "<u>Both vowels are needed to make the special sound or sounds in each word</u>,"*you have both!*

✦ **AU, AW** – *Short Vowel Digraphs* (G. two letters) Two vowels make one *short sound called a Broad O.*
✦ **OI, OY, OU, OW, EW** – *Diphthongs* (G. two sounds). Two vowels *blend so you hear two sounds.*
✦ **OO, OO** – are *Double-O Vowels*. Two vowels *stretch out the O sound* in <u>oo</u> and <u>oo</u>.

Let's Play: Launch into the Vowel Pool

❑ **VOWEL POOL**: To get to know these *Special 2-Vowel Combos*, let's play *Vowel Pool* and create words. TO PLAY: First, pick out a BALL<u>OO</u>N T<u>OY</u>. Then L<u>AU</u>NCH into the V<u>OWEL</u> P<u>OOL</u> and CH<u>OO</u>SE 2 V<u>OWELS</u>. Next, pick up a T<u>OWEL</u>. (One towel is blank, so you can choose the letter.) Finally, write the letters on the BALLOON TOY + the 2-VOWELS + the TOWEL letters under the VOWEL sound.

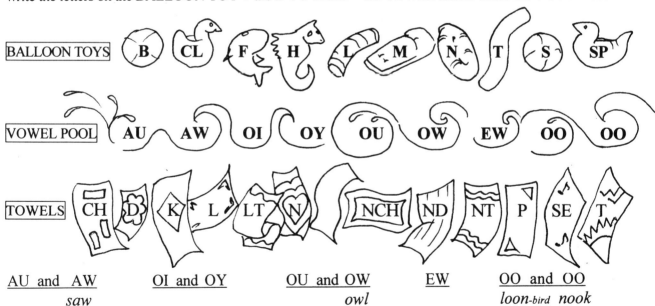

AU and AW	OI and OY	OU and OW	EW	OO and OO
saw		*owl*		*loon*-bird *nook*

AU, AW, and AL: Broad O Sound (Short Vowel Digraphs)

On our LAWN at DAWN, we saw a FAWN YAWN.

❏ **NOW**: Choose rhyming words in each set and write at least one: 2-Word Rhyme, Sentence, or Question.

AU as in auto: caught, fraught (bothered), naught (nothing), taught; fault, vault, assault * daunt, haunt, jaunt (short walk), taunt (tight) * because, cause, clause, pause; author, caution, saucer

AW as in saw: caw, claw, draw, flaw, gnaw, jaw, law, paw, raw, saw, slaw, straw * bawl, brawl, crawl, drawl, scrawl, shawl, trawl; brawn, dawn, drawn, fawn, lawn, pawn, prawn, spawn, yawn

AL as in ball, also: balk (refuse), chalk, stalk, talk, walk; all, ball, call, fall, hall, mall, pall (sadness), small, squall (storm), stall, tall, wall; halt, malt, salt; balmy, calm, psalm, qualm (a worry)

***POWER* POINTS**: Spelling is <u>AU</u> when the word ends in *2 or more consonants* (*caught*) or in a consonant + <u>e</u> (*pause*). It's <u>AW</u> when the word ends in <u>aw</u> or when *one consonant* follows <u>aw</u> (*dawn*).

OI and OY; OU and OW; and EW: Diphthong Sounds

Oh BOY, what JOY, an OYSTER with SOY!

❏ **NOW**: Say each word above. Hear the *Diphthong*: a special 2-vowel sound the vowels make together. Use rhyming words in each group to write one or more: 2-Word Rhymes, Sentences, or Questions.

OI as in coil: boil, broil, foil, soil, spoil, toil * coin, groin, join, loin * foist, hoist, joist (support beam), moist * choice, noise, poise, rejoice, voice * doily, ointment, point, poison, recoil, turmoil, turquoise

OY as in boy: ahoy, coy (shy), joy, ploy, soy, toy * enjoy, decoy, oyster, royalty, voyage

❏ ***POWER* POINTS**: The spelling is <u>OI</u> when the words end in –
The spelling is <u>OY</u> when the word ends in –

Please, MR. GROUCH, don't SLOUCH on my COUCH!

OU as in cloud: loud, proud * couch, crouch, grouch, ouch, pouch, slouch, vouch; * bound, found, ground hound (dog), mound, pound, round, sound, wound-like a clock * count, encounter, mount * bout, clout, gout, grout, out, pout, scout, shout, snout, spout, sprout, stout, trout

OW as in owl: fowl, growl, howl, jowl, prowl, scowl *: bow, brow, chow, cow, how, now, plow, row (fight), sow, vow * brown, clown, crown, down, drown, frown, gown, town

POWER **POINTS**: Spelling is OU when d, t, or 2 consonants end the word (*loud, trout, ouch, mount*). Spelling is OW when l, n, or ow ends the word (*bow, owl, gown, own*).

An OU CHALLENGE: Some OU WORDS have the *short o* sound in *frog*:   ought, bought, brought. Other OU WORDS have the *short u* sound you hear in *sun*:   enough, rough, tough (gh = f). Finally, some OU WORDS have the *oo* sound in *book*:   could, should, would.

While the wind BLEW, We watched the NEW morning DEW.

EW as in blew: brew, crew, dew, ewe, few, flew, hew, knew, mew, new, pew, phew * crewel (sewing)

The Double O Sounds: OO and OO

❑ **NOW**: Say *moon* and *book*. Hear the difference between the oo and oo sounds. For each set of double-o words, choose rhyming words and write one or more: 2-Word Rhymes, Questions or Sentences.

OO as in moon, coon, croon, loon, noon, soon, spoon, swoon *: boo, coo, moo, shoo, too, woo, zoo * cool, fool, pool, tool, school, spool, stool * bloom, boom, broom, doom, gloom, groom, loom (for weaving; tower over), room, zoom * coop, droop, hoop, loop, scoop, sloop (sailboat), snoop, stoop, swoop, troop * goose, loose, moose, noose * boot, hoot, loot-rob, moot, root, toot, scoot, shoot *   (EXCEPTIONS: through, threw)

OO as in book, brook, cook, crook, hook, look, nook, rook (shepherd's staff), shook, took, cookies * good, hood, stood, wood, driftwood * hoof, hooves, scrapbooks, wool, woolen * Bigfoot * (EXCEPTIONS: could, would, should: same pronunciation, different spelling)

In my POOL staying COOL, I play my KAZOO.

Special Vowel Sounds: AU, AW; OI, OY; OU, OW; and OO, OO

☐ **NOW**: As you read this list, star the nouns (The ____) and put a dash by verbs (I ____; We ____).

OI(coil)	OY (boy)	OU(cloud)	OW(owl)	AU(launch)	AW(saw)	OO (book)	OO (moon)
boil	boy	bound	bow	assault	bawl	book	bloom
broil	coy	bough	brow	author	brawl	brook	broom
coil	joy	bounce	brown	caught	brawn	cook	croon
coin	ploy	bout	browse	daunt	craw	crook	cool
foil	Roy	cloud	clown	fault	caw	foot	food
foist	soy	clout	cow	flaunt	dawn	good	hoop
groin	Troy	couch	crown	fraught	drawl	goods	loom
hoist	toy	crouch	down	gaunt	drawn	hood	mood
join	ahoy	douse	drown	haul	fawn	hoof	moon
joist	boyfriend	gout	fowl	haunch	gnaw	hook	pool
loin	decoy	grouch	frown	haunt	jaw	hooves	proof
moist	deploy	grout	gown	jaunt	law	look	roof
noise	employ	found	how	launch	lawn	nook	room
poi	enjoy	ground	now	maul	paw	rook	root
poise	joyful	house	prowl	naught	pawn	shook	school
poised	joyride	hound	row	Paul	raw	soot	scoop
soil	royal	loud	scowl	paunch	saw	stood	shoot
toil	royalty	mound	sow	quality	claw	took	spoon
spoil	soybean	mouth	vow	quantity	draw	wood	swoon
voice	soymilk	mouse	wow	Saul	flaw	wool	too
voiced	toying	pounce		taught	scrawl	Bigfoot	tooth
adjoin		pound		taunt	shawl	bookcase	zoo
doily		pout		vault	slaw	bookend	zoom
embroil		proud			spawn	cookie	balloon
enjoined		round				cooking	bamboo
foisted		route		straw	dogwood	foolish
hoisted		scout		trawl	driftwood	igloo
moisten		shout		yawn	firewood	kazoo
moisture		snout			football	monsoon
noisy		sound			foothold	moonbeam
recoil		spouse			footprint	mushroom
topsoil		spout			rookie	raccoon
		stout			rosewood	roommate
		trout			scrapbook	seafood
		trounce			textbook	shampoo
		vouch			woodpile	tattoo
		fountain			woolen	tycoon
		mountain				voodoo

22

The Powerful R Can Control Any Vowel

<u>R</u> Rules! Whenever <u>R</u> comes after a vowel, it not only makes its own sound, but its rrr…sound is so powerful that it changes the sound of the vowels it follows. Just like a Tyrannosaurus-Rex could master any dinosaur, the Powerful <u>R</u>-Rex masters vowels. When <u>R</u> is added to a vowel, it makes the vowel vibrate over a raised tongue in the back of the mouth. This rrr… changes the sound of the word that comes out. W*hee* becomes *where*; *bid* changes to *bird*; and even a *gem* can become a *germ*.

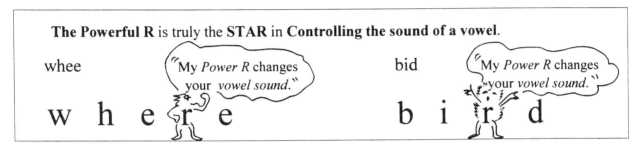

The Powerful R is truly the **STAR** in **Controlling the sound of a vowel**.

whee — "My *Power R* changes your *vowel sound*." — w h e r e

bid — "My *Power R* changes your *vowel sound*." — b i r d

When <u>R</u> follows vowels, it only makes <u>3 different short vowel sounds</u> and <u>2 different long vowel sounds</u>. Since these <u>R sounds can be spelled in a number of ways</u>, R's words can be very challenging. Now, look at these sounds.

R has 3 Short Vowel Sounds: <u>ar</u>-star and <u>or</u>-horn.	R has 2 Long Vowel Sounds: <u>ar</u>-hair and <u>er</u>-tear.
Er, ir, and ur all make the <u>same sound</u>.	Ur and ir keep their long sound. <u>Ore</u> has the same sound as <u>or</u>.
ar: st**ar**: <u>ar</u>mor, d<u>ar</u>kness, famili<u>ar</u>, l<u>ar</u>gest	**air**: h**air**, h**eir**, squ**are**: wh<u>ere</u>, t<u>er</u>rible, th<u>ere</u>
er: f**er**n: hib<u>er</u>nate, liz<u>ar</u>d, sev<u>er</u>al, <u>ear</u>th, w<u>ere</u>	**ear**: d**ear**, d**eer**: <u>year</u>s, app<u>ear</u>, fi<u>er</u>ce, n<u>ear</u>ly
(**ir**: b**ir**d same as <u>er</u>): f<u>ir</u>, f<u>ir</u>st, th<u>ir</u>st	(**ire**: f**ire** same as <u>long i</u>): de-s<u>ire</u>, l<u>yre</u>
or: h**or**n: <u>ar</u>m<u>or</u>, f<u>or</u>med, en<u>or</u>mous, <u>or</u>	(**ore**: c**ore** same as <u>or</u>): dinosa<u>ur</u>, <u>ore</u>, m<u>ore</u>
(**ur**: t**ur**tle same as <u>er</u>): p<u>ur</u>pose, s<u>ur</u>rounded, s<u>ur</u>vive	(**ure**: p**ure** same as <u>long u</u>): d<u>ur</u>ing, J<u>ur</u>assic, temperat<u>ure</u>

❑ **NOW:** In this R-Article: <u>Dinosaurs</u>, underline each R plus the vowel or vowels that come before it.

Dinosaurs: They Ruled the Earth and Then Disappeared

Nearly 200 million years ago, during the time when our continents probably formed one land mass surrounded by an enormous sea, the dinosaurs appeared – the dinosaurs whose name in Greek meant "terrible lizards." Some were very terrifying, especially the fierce meat-eater, Tyrannosaurus Rex, measuring 40 feet long with an enormous head and a mouth of sharp, piercing incisors (teeth). The largest dinosaurs, however, were the plant eaters, the Diplodocus and Brontosaurus who stood like towers seven stories high, and the Brachiosaurus who grew to be 85 tons. These dinosaurs, plus others whose names are familiar, lived during the Jurassic Periods: the Stegosaurus with plates of armor, the horned Triceratops, and the Pterodactyl who flew through the air with wings that measured 40 feet. Dinosaurs ruled the earth until 65 million years ago when they suddenly disappeared. Scientists have several theories for why. Some say a nearby star exploded or a large asteroid hit the earth, causing darkness and freezing temperatures. Without fur for warmth or places to hibernate, the dinosaurs could not survive. The Age of Great Reptiles was over.

"RRRRRr.

(Asteroids are like small planets and can be as large as 480 miles across.)

❑ **LET'S PLAY ELEVATOR LOADER:** To learn more about what *Powerful R* does when it's added right after a vowel, let's play Elevator Loader. TO PLAY: First, pick up a CONSONANT PACKAGE from the *4TH FLOOR*. Then pick up a VOWEL PACKAGE from the *3RD FLOOR*. Next, get a POWERFUL R BOX on the *2ND FLOOR*. Finally, if you need a FINAL SILENT E, you can pick that up on the *1ST FLOOR*. Skip this floor if you'd like. Deliver your completed words by writing then under their vowel sounds below. Notice the soft growling sound you hear as you deliver your words – *rrr* …

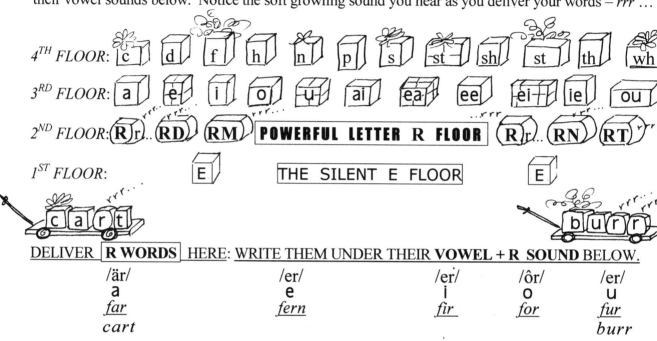

4TH FLOOR: c d f h n p s st sh st th wh

3RD FLOOR: a e i o u ai ea ee ei ie ou

2ND FLOOR: Rr … RD RM **POWERFUL LETTER R FLOOR** Rr … RN RT

1ST FLOOR: E THE SILENT E FLOOR E

DELIVER R WORDS HERE: WRITE THEM UNDER THEIR **VOWEL + R SOUND** BELOW.

/är/	/er/	/er/	/ôr/	/er/
a	e	i	o	u
far	*fern*	*fir*	*for*	*fur*
cart				burr

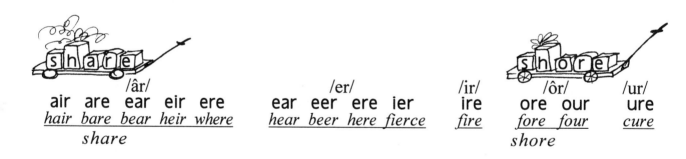

/âr/					/er/				/ir/	/ôr/		/ur/
air	are	ear	eir	ere	ear	eer	ere	ier	ire	ore	our	ure
hair	*bare*	*bear*	*heir*	*where*	*hear*	*beer*	*here*	*fierce*	*fire*	*fore*	*four*	*cure*
		share								shore		

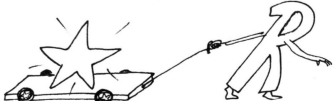

❑ **NOW:** Write each word under its <u>vowel + R sound</u>: air, appear, bird, birthday, darkness, desire, dinosaur (or), during, earth (er), enormous, germ, hibernate, horned, horse, important, lizard, pear (air), pure, purpose, several, sport, star, surround, survive, terrible (air), water, where (air), world (er), and years (er).

What Does Powerful <u>R</u> Do When It's Added to Vowels?

Short Vowels

❏ **NOW**: Let's look at what *Powerful R* does when it's added to SHORT VOWELS that end in a consonant. First, pronounce the words below without the *R*. Then add an *R* after the vowel in each word. What happens to the vowel once the *Powerful R* is in the word?

| am | <u>a m</u> | bet | <u>Be t</u> | bid | <u>bi d</u> | con | <u>co n</u> | bun | <u>bu n</u> |
| ham | <u>ha m</u> | gem | <u>ge m</u> | skit | <u>ski t</u> | spot | <u>spo t</u> | spun | <u>spu n</u> |

Also add an *R* to the two-letter words below. What happens to the vowel sounds when R's in control?

| fa | <u>fa____</u> | ma | <u>ma____</u> | pa | <u>pa____</u> |

Long Vowels

❏ **NOW**: *Powerful R* can take on LONG VOWELS that end in *Silent E*: First, pronounce these words just the way they are. Notice that all the vowels are long. Put an *R* in the blank after the vowel for each word. Now, notice what happens to the words once *Powerful R* is in control. Star all the words where *R* has changed the vowel sound.

| bake | <u>ba e</u> | fine | <u>fi e</u> | mole | <u>mo e</u> | cute | <u>cu e</u> | Luke | <u>lu e</u> |
| made | <u>ma e</u> | site | <u>si e</u> | hose | <u>ho se</u> | tone | <u>to e</u> | shone | <u>sho e</u> |

Powerful R can take on LONG VOWEL sounds made by *2 Vowels*. First, pronounce these words just the way they are. Notice that all the words have *2 vowels* that make a *long sound*. Put an *R* in the blank for each of the words. Notice what happens to the words once the *Powerful R* has been added. Star all the words where *R* has changed the vowel sound.

fail	<u>fai____</u>	pea	<u>pea____</u>	hee	<u>he e</u>	foe	<u>fo e</u>	sou	<u>sou .</u>
hail	<u>hai____</u>	peal	<u>pea l</u>	thee	<u>the e</u>	Moe	<u>mo e</u>	cue	<u>cu e</u>
pail	<u>pai____</u>	tea	<u>tea____</u>	whee	<u>whe e</u>	toe	<u>to e</u>	Sue	<u>su e</u>

NOTE: *Powerful R* is so strong that in some words, even *Silent E* cannot overcome its power. *For* and *fore,* and *or* and *ore* sound alike, even with *Silent E*. Also, for the words that became *fore, more, tore,* and *sure,* when *R* was added, *Silent E* lost its power to make the vowels long. In the arm wrestling match between *Silent E* and *R,* the *R* won!!!

spurn (to reject); sou (an ancient bronze French coin)

❏ **NOW**: Circle three words in the top row with the same *Vowel + R* sound. Now, add *R* after the vowel in the 2nd row. Now, circle the *W Words* with the same sound. How many did you find?

arm	her	bird	sport	burn
wa m	we e	whi l	wo d	liverwu st

NOTE: When you place <u>w</u> directly before <u>or</u>, w usually changes the *or sound* to an *er sound*:

word   **wor**k   **wor**ld   **wor**m   **wor**n

worry   **wor**se   **wor**ship   **wor**th   **wor**thy

❏ **LET'S PLAY CATEGORIES**: Read these VOWEL + R WORDS. Put a dash by all the animal, bird, fish and insect words. Put a box around all the people words or words that refer to people. Star anything people eat or drink from food to spice. Finally, write the words under their category.

<u>ANIMALS, BIRDS and FISH</u>   <u>INSECTS</u>   <u>PEOPLE and OCCUPATIONS</u>   <u>FOOD and SPICES</u>

VOWEL + R WORDS: **SHORT VOWELS**: <u>ar, er, ir, or, ur</u>; **LONG VOWELS**: <u>air, eer, ire, ure</u>

<u>AR SOUND</u>	shark	ranger	shirt	porch	<u>AIR SOUND</u>
aardvark	sugar	reader	skirt	porcupine	bear
archer	<u>ER SOUND</u>	rooster	squirrel	pork	berries
artist	berries	serve	thirteen	porpoise	carrots
asparagus	butter	silver	uniform	professor	chair
blizzard	carpenter	speaker	<u>OR WORDS</u>	record	parrot
burglar	cherry	spider	actor	sculptor	pears
custard	chowder	sweater	alligator	shorts	sparrow
garden	composer	teacher	aviator	stork	<u>EER SOUND</u>
garlic	entertainer	termite	conductor	<u>UR SOUND</u>	auctioneer
guard	ginger	thunder	corn	burro	beer
jaguar	hamster	tiger	doctor	church	deer
lark	juggler	water	forest	hamburger	dreary
margarine	lantern	watermelon	gorilla	hour	engineer
marlin	lawyer	wrestler	horse	nurse	<u>IRE SOUND</u>
marshmellow	manager	<u>IR WORDS</u>	hornet	purple	Fireman
mustard	otter	bird	memory	purse	tire
partridge	panther	birthday	oarsman	surfer	<u>URE SOUND</u>
sardine	pepper	category	oranges	turkey	cure
scarlet	persimmon	circle	orator	turnips	measure
scholar	otter	girl	orbit	turtle	pure

Discovering How Open Syllables Work
and What's a Schwa?

Knowing that **OPEN SYLLABLES** *always end in a vowel* gives you spelling *POWER*. It helps you know when a syllable ends in a vowel so you won't double consonants at the wrong time. Knowing about **SCHWAS** helps with spelling too, especially once you know the kind of syllables where you find them. Also, just open a dictionary, and you'll find schwas in half of the words.

Discovering Open Syllables

Open Syllables can be a *single vowel* (<u>*I*</u>, <u>*a*</u>) or a syllable that *ends in a single vowel* (<u>*by*</u>, <u>*me*</u>, <u>*to*</u>). Understanding this helps you know that there won't be a double letter in words with short vowels, like *cri-sis* and *di-vide*, because the *Open Syllable* ends in a vowel.

❑ **NOW**: <u>Underline</u> the Open Syllables in these words. Notice what Open Syllables are like.

a	e – go	I	go	my
a – mong	e – qual	cri – sis	ho – tel	ac – tu – al
ma – trix	he – ro	di – vide	o – pen	Cu – pid
sa – ga	re – a – lize	li – a – ble	po – em	men – u

Remember: An *Open Syllable* is one vowel or it ends in a vowel. <u>O</u>-PEN begins with an *Open Syllable*.

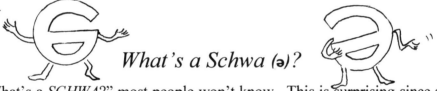

What's a Schwa (ə)?

If you ask, "What's a *SCHWA*?" most people won't know. This is surprising since schwas occur in about half of English words. Schwas are simply unaccented vowels with very little sound. Most unaccented *Open <u>A</u> Syllables* are *schwas* that makes an *uh* sound (<u>*aglow, along*</u>). *<u>E</u>, <u>I</u>, <u>O</u>*, and <u>*U*</u> can also be schwas that sound a little like *short vowels*. If you aren't sure if a vowel's a schwa, check a dictionary. If you see an upside down <u>*e*</u>, the vowel's a schwa. Now, say and hear these schwas.

a /ə/: <u>*A*</u> is a schwa in most unaccented <u>*Open A Syllables*</u>. <u>*A*</u> has an *uh* sound: *a-like, a-gen-da, a*-mong, *a*-mount, c*a*-nal, ca-su-*a*l, ch*a*-rade, g*a*-rage, h*a*-rass, m*a*-jes-tic, mar-*a*-thon .

e /ə/: <u>*E*</u> is a schwa in most <u>-*el*</u>, <u>-*em*</u>, <u>-*en*</u>, <u>-*er*</u>, and <u>-*ment*</u> syllables: bro-th*er*, el-*e*-ph*a*nt, el-*e*-va-tor, i-t*em*, la-b*e*l, lis-t*en*, o-p*en*, pay-m*en*t, po-*em*, se-v*en*, sys-t*em*, the-*a*-t*er*.

i /ə/: <u>*I*</u> is usually a schwa before the suffixes <u>-*ment*</u> and <u>-*ly*</u>: com-pl*i*-ment, ea-s*i*-ly, hap-p*i*-ly, sen-t*i*-ment. Also, in-d*i*-vi-du-*a*l, med-*i*-cine, pen-c*i*l.

o /ə/: <u>*O*</u> is a schwa in <u>com</u>, <u>-*ion*</u> (and -*yon*), <u>-*on*</u>, <u>-*or*</u>, <u>-*sion*</u>, and <u>-*tion*</u>: can-y*on*, c*o*m-plete, em-per-*or*, i-r*on*, le-m*on*, mir-r*or*, o-pin-*ion*, so-lu-ti*on*, p*a*-vil-i*on* (open building for concerts).

u /ə/: <u>*U*</u> is a schwa in most <u>-*ful*</u>, <u>-*ular*</u>, <u>-*um*</u>, and <u>-*us*</u> syllables: aw-f*u*l, cir-c*u*s, cir-c*u*-lar, col-*u*mn, mi-n*u*s, ra-di-*u*m, reg-*u*-lar, u-k*u*-le-le, u-ra-ni-*u*m, vol-*u*n-teer.

Observing Open Syllables A and I

Open Syllable A

Open Syllables with vowels <u>A</u> and <u>I</u> have something in common that Open Syllables with vowels: <u>E</u>, <u>O</u>, and <u>U</u> don't have. Try to discover this as you read and learn about these Open Syllables.

❑ **TRY THIS**: <u>Underline the Open A Syllables</u> below. Put a long vowel mark above any long a's. Then pronounce each word and put an accent mark to the right of the strongest syllable. Notice: The *accented a's* have a *long vowel sound*. The *unaccented a's* make a *schwa /ə/ sound*, which has very little sound. Now, answer the questions that go with this set of words.

a – gent

a – pex

la – bel

ta – ble

a – gen – da (- gen - da)

a – pol – o – gy (- pol - o - ge)

re – a – lize (re - - lize)

ul – tra (ul – tr)

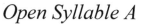

These Open Syllable *a's* are (long, not long).

These Open Syllables are (accented, unaccented).

These Open Syllable *a's* have a schwa sound: T F.

These Open Syllables are (accented, unaccented).

Open Syllable I

❑ **NOW TRY THIS**: For the words below, <u>underline the Open I Syllables</u>. Put a long vowel mark above the long i's. Then pronounce each word and put an accent mark to the right of the strongest syllable. Notice: The *accented i's* have a *long vowel sound*. The *unaccented i's* make a *schwa   sound*. Finally, answer the questions that go with this set of words.

i - tem

cri – sis

gi – ant

mi – nus

an – ti – dote (an - t - dote)

di – vide (d - vide)

im – i – tate (im - - tate)

med – i – cine (med - - sin)

These Open Syllable *i's* are (long, not long).

These Open Syllables are (accented, unaccented).

These Open Syllables have a schwa sound: T F.

These Open Syllables are (accented, unaccented).

❑ **A RULE FOR OPEN SYLLABLES A and I**: From what you have observed, write a rule for Open Syllables <u>A</u> and <u>I</u> telling when the vowel is long and when the vowel is a schwa.

Observing Open Syllables E, O, and U

□ **NOW**: Observe Open Syllables <u>E</u>, <u>O</u>, and <u>U</u> in the words below. Then <u>underline</u> Open Syllables <u>E</u>, <u>O</u>, and <u>U</u>, and put a long vowel mark above the long vowels. Next, pronounce each word, and put an accent mark to the right of the syllable with the strongest beat. Finally, answer the questions for Open Syllables <u>E</u>, <u>O</u>, and <u>U</u>.

Open Syllable E

be – have	de – fine
fre – quent	e – lope
he – ro	re – fresh
se – cret	ze – ro

Open Syllable O

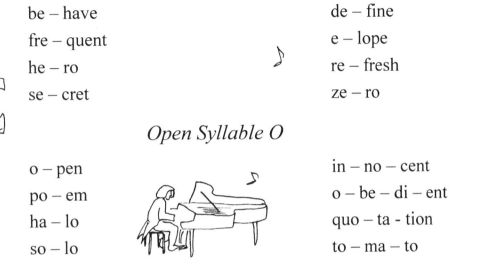

o – pen	in – no – cent
po – em	o – be – di – ent
ha – lo	quo – ta - tion
so – lo	to – ma – to

Open Syllable U

ac – tu – al	cal – cu – late
Cu – pid	imp – u – dent
mu – sic	pen – in – su – la
u – nite	en – thu – si – as – tic

The vowels in *Open Syllables <u>E</u>, <u>O</u>* and <u>U</u> are (short, long).

For *Open Syllables <u>E</u>, <u>O</u>* and <u>U</u>,* the syllable must be accented to make the vowel long (yes, no).

What is one way that *Open Syllables <u>E</u>, <u>O</u>,* and <u>U</u> are different from *Open Syllables A* and *I*?

Writing A Rule for All Open Syllables

From what you've observed about Open Syllables <u>A</u> and <u>I</u>, and <u>E</u>, <u>O</u>, and <u>U</u>, write a rule for *Open Syllables*. Tell when the vowels are long and also explain which 2 vowels make a *Schwa Sound*.

If what you wrote was like this: "The vowel is always long in Open Syllables <u>E</u>, <u>O</u>, and <u>U</u>. To be long for <u>A</u> and <u>I</u>, the syllable with the vowel needs to be accented. When Open Syllables <u>A</u> or <u>I</u> are unaccented, they make a *Schwa Sound*," then **YOU ARE RIGHT!!**

Clues and Tools for Remembering Open Syllable Words

Fill in the blanks and add answers. Also, try other *Tools* like the *Beat*, *Phonics*, *Rules*, and *Roots*.

1. **a-lone**: *Clue-in-a-Row*: <u>A lone a</u> is all _ _ _ _ _. *Rule*: Silent <u>e</u> makes <u>o</u> in _ _ _ _ long.

2. **sa-gas** (ancient legends): *Visual*: _ _ _ _ _ is a palindrome which means:

3. **ta-ble**: A <u>tablet</u> is like a _ _ _ _ _ for writing. In <u>tablet</u>, you can hear the <u>ble</u> in _ _ _ _ _.

4. **cer-e-al**: *Phonics*: <u>c</u> = __ sound. *Roots*: The Roman Goddess of <u>cereal</u> was <u>Ceres</u>.

5. **el-e-va-tors**: I can fit <u>eleven gators</u> on the _ _ _ _ _ _ _ _: <u>eleven</u> + <u>gators</u>.

6. **e-ra-ser**: *Visual*: Letters _ _ echo in _ _ _ _ _ _. *Clue*: An _ _ _ _ _ _ <u>serves</u> for <u>erasing</u>.

7. **me-te-or**: Can you <u>mete or</u> figure out the size of this _ _ _ _ _ _?

8. **me-ter**: Can you <u>measure eternity</u> in _ _ _ _ _ s? _ _ _ _ (meter = approx 3 feet: 2.9 yards.)

9. **mi-nus**: *Phonics*: One <u>n</u> keeps the __ long in _ _ _ _ _. *Clue*: The party will be _ _ _ _ _ <u>us</u>.

10. **min-ute** (60 seconds): *Exception*: _ _ _ _ _ _ is pronounced *mi-nut*, but spelled like <u>minute</u> (tiny).

11. **o-be-di-ent**: <u>To bed I went</u> to be _ _ _ _ _ _ _ _: <u>to</u> + <u>bed</u> + <u>I</u> + <del>went</del>!

12. **ro-bot**: <u>Robo</u>, our _ _ _ _ _, does lots of housework.

13. **tor-na-do**: *Phonics*: One __ keeps <u>a</u> long. *Clue*: The _ _ _ _ _ _ _ had <u>torn a door</u>: <u>torn</u> + <u>a</u> + <u>door</u>.

14. **pu-pil**: *Phonics*: One __ keeps __ long in _ _ _ _ _. *Clue*: That <u>pup</u> is not my _ _ _ _ _.

15. **stu-dent**: <u>Stan</u> asked the _ _ _ _ _ _ _, "Did <u>U dent</u> my car?"

16. **can-yon**: *Phonics*: <u>c</u> =__ sound. *Visual*: <u>Y</u> looks like a _ _ _ _ _ _. I <u>can yonder</u> see a _ _ _ _ _ _.

17. **cit-i-zen**: <u>C</u> = __ sound. *Rule*: Change <u>y</u> to <u>i</u> before consonant suffix: city + i + zen = _ _ _ _ _ _ _.

18. **e-le-ven**: *Visual*: See 3 __'s in _ _ _ _ _ _. *Clue*: _ _ _ _ _ _ is not an <u>even</u> number.

19. **gal-ax-y** (star system): *Phonics*: <u>x</u> = _ _ sound. *Clue*: I want a <u>gala</u> (showy) party in the _ _ _ _ _ _.

20. **man-a-ger**: *Clue*: That <u>man (has the) age</u> and skills to be a _ _ _ _ _ _ _: <u>man</u> + <u>age</u> + <u>r</u>.

21. **civ-i-li-za-tion**: 4 __'s in _ _ _ _ _ _ _ _ _ _ _. *Roots*: <u>civil</u> (L. citizen) + <u>ize</u> (v. suf.) + <u>ation</u> (n. suf.-organization) = <u>civilization</u> (organization of citizens).

22. **en-cy-clo-pe-di-a**: <u>en</u> (pre. in) + <u>cyclo</u> (G. well-rounded) + <u>ped</u> (G. teaching) + <u>ia</u> (n. suf.) = <u>encyclopedia</u>

23. **u-ni-verse**: I wrote <u>uni (one) verse</u> about the _ _ _ _ _ _ _ _.
    Latin Compound Word: <u>uni</u> (one) + <u>verse</u> = _ _ _ _ _ _ _ _.

24. **u-ra-ni-um**: <u>U ran</u> over to see the _ _ _ _ _ _ _. *Roots*: <u>uran</u> (Uranus: most powerful Greek god) + <u>ium</u> (n. suf.) = <u>uranium</u> (radioactive element used for nuclear power).

Beat: e-n-c-y-c-l-o-p-e-d-i-a

Let's Try All the Vowel Sounds
The Many Different Ways the English Language Spells Its Sounds

WHEW! Just look at the many different ways that sounds in the English Language are spelled today – *far more spellings than in any other language*! Although this is challenging for spellers, this variety shows that many languages are part of the rich vocabulary of English: German, Latin, French, Greek, Spanish, etc. (The sounds that follow phonics spelling are in bold letters. Exceptions are in parentheses.)

Aa
Short Vowel: **ant**, **cat**, **baa** (pl**ai**d, c**al**ves, l**au**gh)
Long Vowel: **ace**, **rain**, **hay**, **table** (g**au**ge, br**ea**k, n**eigh**, th**ey**, ball**et**-Fr., bouqu**et**-Fr.)
Short Vowel + R: **star**, **garden** (h**ear**t, s**er**geant-Fr., baz**aar**-market-Fr., biz**arre**-strange-Per.)
Long Vowel + R: **hair**, squ**are** (pr**ayer**, p**ear**, th**eir**, th**ere**, th**ey're**, v**ery**)
Broad O: **vault**, **saw**, **ball** (c**au**ght, br**oa**d, s**ou**ght)
Schwa Sound: **alike**

Ee
Short Vowel: **egg**, **elephant** (fr**ie**nd, m**a**ny, s**ai**d, s**ay**s, r**ea**d-past, l**eo**pard)
Long Vowel: **mete**, **tree**, **each**, rec**ei**ve, **me** (p**eo**ple, k**ey**, f**ie**ld, na**ï**ve-Fr., sk**i**, qu**ay**-Sp., coyot**e**-Sp., am**oe**ba)
Short Vowel + R: **mer**maid (er) (l**ear**n)
Long Vowel + R: **hear**, **deer** (h**ere**, p**ier**, f**ier**ce)
EW Sound: **few**
Silent E in lov**e** (*The e completes v without making o long.*)
Schwa Sound: **eleven** LE Sound: cand**le**

Ii
Short Vowel: **pin**, **igloo** (g**y**m, s**ie**ve, for**ei**gn, mount**ai**n, w**o**men, b**ui**ld, b**u**siness, b**ee**n)
Long Sound: **kite**, **pie**, **tiger** (l**igh**t, **ai**sle, st**ei**n-mug, h**eigh**t, k**i**nd, sk**y**, b**uy**)
Short Vowel + R (same as er): **bird**, **circle**
Long Vowel + R (long i): **fire** (ch**oir**)
Schwa Sound: **divide** IL Sound: penc**il**

Oo
Short Vowel: **clock**, **octopus** (c**ou**gh, br**oa**d, **au**thor, w**a**tch, y**a**cht-Dan., **ah**, s**aw**)
Long Sound: **rose**, **boat**, **bow**, **open** (g**oe**s, s**ew**, **oh**, y**o**lk, b**eau**-Fr., br**oo**ch-Fr.)
Vowel + R: **horn**, bef**ore** (din**o**saur, d**oo**r, qu**ar**ter) Long and Short Vowel + R = Same
OU Sound: **cloud**, **owl**, **flower** (b**ou**gh, s**au**erkraut)
OI Sound: **coil**, **boy** (Iroqu**oi**s, b**uoy**)
Double O: **moon** (tr**u**th, gl**ue**, m**o**ve, gr**ew**, can**oe**)
Double O: **book** (w**o**lf, c**ou**ld, p**u**t)
Schwa Sound: **canyon**

Uu
Short Vowel: **sun**, **umbrella** (fl**oo**d, tr**ou**ble, s**o**n, s**o**me, d**oe**s, w**a**s)
Long Vowel: **flute**, **fruit**, **music** (b**eau**ty, f**ew**, h**u**ge, v**ie**w, y**ou**, c**ue**, **yu**le, thr**ou**gh)
Short Vowel + R (er): **turn**, **turtle** (l**ear**n, t**er**m, **err**, th**ir**sty, w**or**k, p**urr**)
Long Vowel + R (same as long u): **lure**
Schwa Sound: **circus** UL Sound: aw**ful**

Ww Sound: **bow** (same as long o) **ewe** (same as long u)
Yy Sound: **eye**, **sky**, **lyre** (same as long i) bunny (same as long e) (s**a**yonara-Japanese)

What Can You Find Inside and Outside This Room?

TRY THIS: Now that you've reviewed all the vowel sounds, try this game to test your ear. Look at the picture of the room and notice all the things you see inside and outside: person, hair, sky, rug… Write these things next to their correct vowel sound and <u>underline the sound</u>. You can write words with more than one syllable next to more than one sound. Feel free to draw extra things in the room.

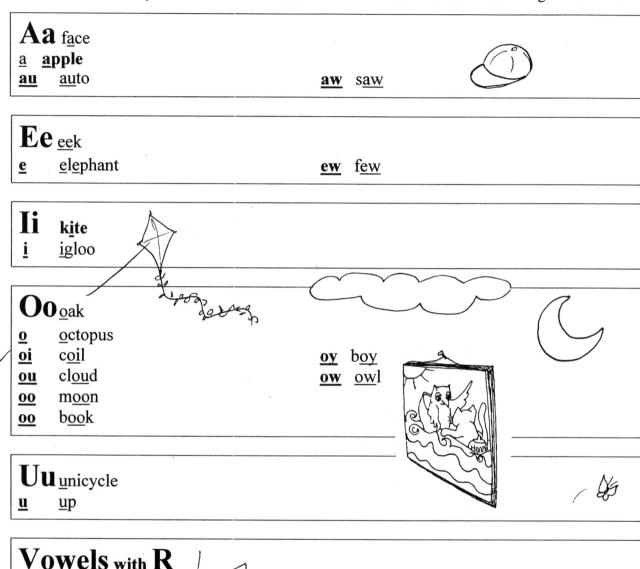

Aa f<u>a</u>ce
<u>a</u>   **apple**
<u>au</u>   <u>au</u>to   <u>aw</u>   s<u>aw</u>

Ee <u>ee</u>k
<u>e</u>   <u>e</u>lephant   <u>ew</u>   f<u>ew</u>

Ii   k<u>i</u>te
<u>i</u>   <u>i</u>gloo

Oo <u>oa</u>k
<u>o</u>   <u>o</u>ctopus
<u>oi</u>   c<u>oi</u>l   <u>oy</u>   b<u>oy</u>
<u>ou</u>   cl<u>ou</u>d   <u>ow</u>   <u>ow</u>l
<u>oo</u>   m<u>oo</u>n
<u>oo</u>   b<u>oo</u>k

Uu <u>u</u>nicycle
<u>u</u>   <u>u</u>p

Vowels with **R**

<u>ar</u>	st<u>ar</u>		<u>ar</u>	h<u>air</u>, squ<u>are</u>
<u>er</u>	f<u>er</u>n		<u>ear</u>	t<u>ear</u>, d<u>eer</u>
<u>ir</u>	b<u>ir</u>d		<u>ire</u>	f<u>ire</u>
<u>or</u>	h<u>or</u>n		<u>ore</u>	<u>ore</u>
<u>ur</u>	t<u>ur</u>n		<u>ure</u>	l<u>ure</u>

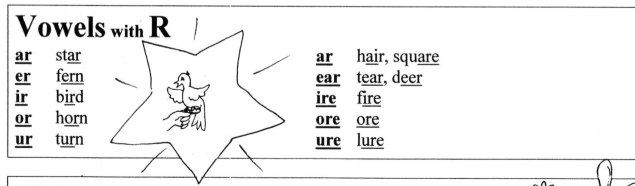

W bl<u>ow</u> and <u>ew</u>e

Y sk<u>y</u>, <u>eye</u>, l<u>yre</u>, bunn<u>y</u>

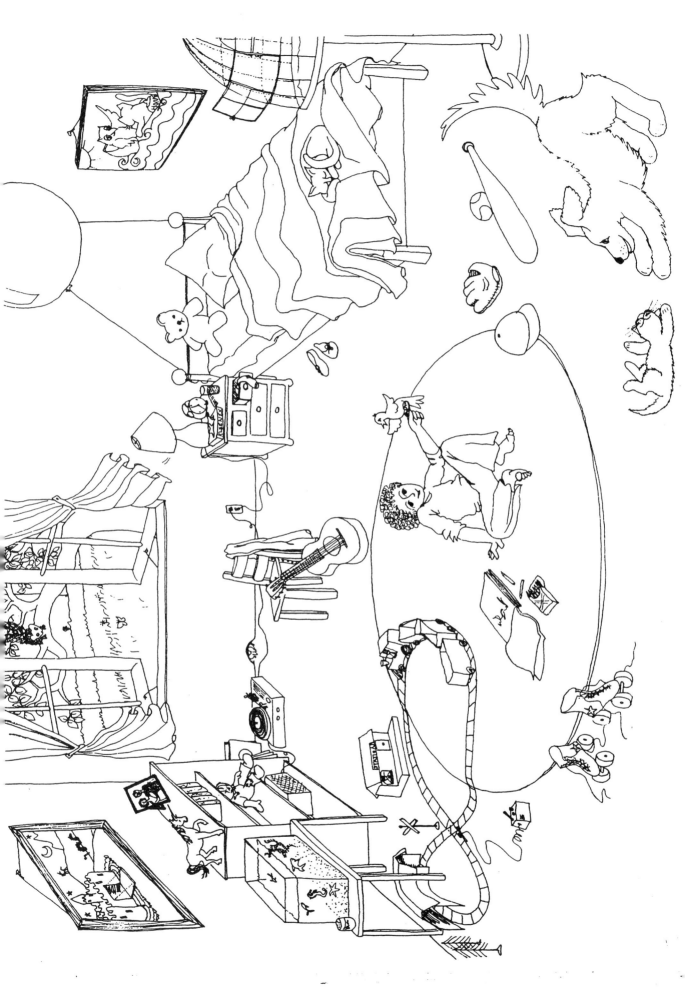

Matching Words with Their Vowel Sound

❑ **NOW**: Write each word by the vowel sound it matches. <u>Underline</u> the vowel sound: **co**lor, **ea**sy, **fl**uff, **fe**ather, **hai**r-on head, **ha**lf, **ho**nest, **hou**se, **la**ter, **la**tter, **oy**ster, **pee**r-equal, **pie**r-dock, **poi**se, **pow**er, **ro**de-ride, **row**ed-oars, **sea**ring, **se**nse, **snoo**py, **swi**rl, **qui**t, **qui**te, **the**rmometer, **tu**rn, **tru**th. <u>Underline</u> these *exceptions* (words not spelled like they sound): **hea**rt, **bea**uty, **ligh**t, **ma**ny, **peo**ple, **qua**rter, **yo**lk, **wo**rds.

Aa Short Vowel: **an**t, **c**at, **b**aa
Long Vowel: **ace**, **rai**n, **hay**, **ta**ble
Short Vowel + R: **sta**r, **gar**den   (*Exception*: **hea**rt)
Long Vowel + R: **hai**r, **squa**re
Broad O: **au** in v**au**lt, **aw** in s**aw**, **al** in b**al**l

---

Ee Short Vowel: **e**gg, **e**lephant   (*Exception*: m**a**ny)
Long Vowel: m**e**te, tr**ee**, p**ea**ch, rec**ei**ve, m**e**   (*Exception*: p**eo**ple)
Short Vowel + R: f**er**n, m**er**maid   (*Exception*: w**or**d)
Long Vowel + R: h**ea**r, d**ee**r
EW Sound: f**ew**
Silent E in lov**e**   LE Sound: cand**le**

Ii Short Vowel: **pi**n, **i**gloo
Long Sound: k**i**te, p**ie**, t**i**ger   (*Exception*: l**igh**t)
Short Vowel + R (same as **er**): b**ir**d, c**ir**cle
Long Vowel + R(same as long **i**): **fi**re   IL Sound: penc**il**

Oo Short Vowel: cl**o**ck, **o**ctopus
Long Sound: r**o**se, b**oa**t, b**ow**, **o**pen   (*Exception*: y**o**lk)
Vowel + R (short, long = same): h**or**n, bef**ore** (*Exception*: qu**ar**ter)
OU Sound: cl**ou**d, **ow** in fl**ow**er   (*Exception*: b**ou**gh)
OI Sound: c**oi**l, **oy** in b**oy**
Double O: m**oo**n
Double O: b**oo**k

Uu Short Vowel: s**u**n, **u**mbrella
Long Vowel: fl**u**te, fr**ui**t, m**u**sic   (*Exception*: b**ea**uty)
Short Vowel + R(same as **er**): t**ur**n, t**ur**tle
Long Vowel + R (same as long **u**): l**u**re   UL Sound: awf**ul**

Ww Sound: b**ow** (same as long **o**)   **ew**e (same as long **u**)
Yy Sound: **eye**, sk**y**, l**y**re (same as long **i**)   bunn**y** (same as long **e**)

34

Hear the Vowel Sounds in "Jazz Fantasia"*

Jazz Fantasias has rhythm, jazzy onomatopoeia, and most of the vowel sounds (except those squared).

❑ **NOW**: Write words from this jazz piece next to their vowel sound (Don't worry about schwas).

Drum on your drums, batter on your banjoes
sob on the long cool winding saxophone, Go to it, O jazzmen

Sling your knuckles on the bottoms of the happy tin pans,
let your trombones ooze, and go husha-husha-hush with the slippery sand-paper.

Moan like an autumn wind high in the lonesome treetops, moan soft like
you wanted somebody terrible, cry like a racing car slipping away
from a motorcycle cop, bang-bang! You jazzmen, bang altogether drums,
traps, banjoes, horns, tin can...

Can the rough stuff . . . now a Mississippi steamboat pushes up the night
River with a hoo-hoo-hoo-oo . . . and the green lanterns calling to the high
Soft stars . . . a red moon rides on the humps of the low river hills . . .
Go to it, O jazzmen.

by Carl Sandburg

Aa	a	in cat, apple *batter*	
	a	in ace, rain, hay, table *racing*	
	a	in star, garden	
	ar	in hair	**are** in square (Exception: terror)
	au	in auto	**aw** in saw **al** in ball.
Ee	e	in egg, elephant	
	e	in tree, peach, equal	
	e	in fern, mermaid	
	er	in tear, deer	
Ii	i	in pin, igloo	
	i	in kite, pie, tiger, child (Exceptions: k<u>i</u>nd, l<u>i</u>ght)	
	ir	in bird	
	ire	in fire	
Oo	o	in clock, octopus	
	o	in rose, boat, toe, bow, open	
	or	in horn	
	ou	in cloud	**ow** in owl
	oi	coil	**oy** in boy
	oo	moon	
	oo	book (Ex: tough, wolf)	
Uu	u	in sun, umbrella	
	u	in flute, fruit, cue, music	
	ur	in turn, turtle	
	ure	in lure	
Yy	y	in sky, eye lyre bunny	**Ww** in bow, ewe

(SCHWA SOUNDS /ə/: alike (*a, away*); eleven (*th<u>e</u>*); divide (*terr<u>i</u>ble*); canyon (*lones<u>o</u>me*); circus: (*aut<u>u</u>mn*)

*"Jazz Fantasia" from SMOKE AND STEEL by Carl Sandburg, copyright 1920 by Harcourt, Inc. and renewed 1948 by
Carl Sandburg, reprinted by permission of the publisher.   **135**

The Solid Compound Word Rule

THE SOLID COMPOUND WORD RULE gives lots of spelling *POWER* because there are hundreds of solid compound words (compound words that are one word) and only a few exceptions. To create these, simply add 2 words together without making any changes: kick + ball = <u>kickball</u>; straw + berry = <u>strawberry</u>; sun + flower = <u>sunflower</u>; lamp + lighter = <u>lamplighter</u>

❑ **NOW**: Add these pairs of nouns together to create Compound Words. Be very careful with words like new<u>ss</u>tand and ea<u>rr</u>ing where the same letters come together.

fire + works	=	*fireworks*	pin + wheels	=	
air + plane	=		space + ship	=	
basket + ball	=		horse + back	=	
cup + board	=		news + stand	=	
bean + stalk	=		grape + fruit	=	
cup + cake	=		dough + nut	=	
post + man	=		lamp + lighter	=	
team + mate	=		scrap + book	=	
ear + ring	=		hand + kerchief	=	
wrist + watch	=		sun + dial	=	
snow + flake	=		rain + bow	=	
body + guard	=		wind + surfer	=	

❑ **TRY THIS**: You can build more Compound Words by adding other parts of speech together: <u>blacksmith</u> (adj. + noun); <u>scarecrow</u> (verb + noun); <u>together</u> (prep. + verb + pronoun); <u>sunrise</u> (noun + verb):

grand + parent	=	gentle + man	=	
earth + quake	=	head + ache	=	
sun + set	=	water + fall	=	
break + fast	=	kick + ball	=	
some + one	=	hand + some	=	
every + body	=	no + thing	=	
to + get + her	=	never + the + less	=	
inter + net	=	on + line	=	

❑ **EXCEPTIONS**: These words lose a letter when you join them to make Compound Words.

alphabet	alph~~a~~	+	bet~~a~~	=	
awful	aw~~e~~	+	ful	=	
pastime	pas~~s~~	+	time	=	*pastime* (activity)
shepherd	she~~e~~p	+	herd	=	
until	un	+	til~~l~~	=	
welcome	wel~~l~~	+	come	=	
wherever	wher~~e~~	+	ever	=	

136

Open Compound Words

For **OPEN COMPOUND WORDS**, it's important to note that while words like <u>airport</u>, <u>postman</u>, <u>someone</u>, and <u>grapefruit</u> form one word, *Open Compound Words* are written as separate words.

roller skates   roller coaster   photo album   post office   fairy tale   Roman candles

no one   ice hockey   polar bear   fire engine   French fries   in spite of   grape juice

Hyphenated Compound Words

HYPHENATED COMPOUNDS are simply single words that are connected with a hyphen. They fit into these helpful categories. If you have questions, *always* check a dictionary.

COMPOUND NUMBERS: (numbers from twenty-one to ninety-nine and words with fractions)
forty-four   two-thirds   one-fifth   half-an-hour   quarter-after-four   two-year-old

COMPOUNDS with IN-LAW or GREAT:
father-in-law   great-grandmother   son-in-law   daughter-in-law   great-great-aunt

COMPOUND DESCRIPTIVE WORDS (before nouns): first-rate movie   wide-eyed child
soft-spoken man   old-fashioned dress   fast-moving train   make-believe toy
middle-aged lady   kind-hearted gentleman   sad-looking eyes   city-wide search

TITLES of PEOPLE: runner-up   sergeant-at-arms   president-elect   (ex: Vice President)

OTHER WORDS: jack-o-lantern   jack-in-the-box   ice-skating   horse-back riding
hand-me-downs   forget-me-not   hide-and-seek   e-mail   rough-and-ready   T-shirt

❑ **MORE SOLID COMPOUNDS**: List any *Solid Compound Words* you can think of that fit these categories. Then read *A List of Compound Words* on the next page and find other words to add.

<u>CANDY</u>   <u>CLOTHING</u>   <u>JEWELRY</u>   <u>FOOD</u>   <u>OCCUPATIONS</u>   <u>PLACES</u>   <u>SPORTS</u>
                                    earrings

(*Be Careful*: Directions are *Solid Compounds*: northwest, southeast, northeastern, southwestern.)

The Al, Ful, and Wel Words: Three Special Groups that Drop One L

The "Al Words"

AL : Words that begin with <u>al</u>: <u>almost</u>, <u>always</u>, etc. ALWAYS drop <u>one l</u>. There are no exceptions. Also, all of these words with <u>one l</u>, are always *adverbs*.

Almighty	(al~~l~~ + mighty)	=	
almost	(al~~l~~ + most)	=	
already	(al~~l~~ + ready)	=	
altogether	(al~~l~~ + together)	=	
always	(al~~l~~ + ways)	=	*always*

ALL : When <u>two ll's</u> occur as in <u>all ready</u> and <u>all right</u>, there is ALWAYS a space in between the two words, and <u>all</u> is a *pronoun*.

all ready: When you are <u>all</u> <u>ready</u> (all of you), you can all read.

all right: Your answers are <u>all</u> (all of them) <u>right</u>.

The "Ful Words"

Words that end in <u>ful</u> and mean <u>full of</u>: <u>careful</u>, <u>useful</u>, etc., ALWAYS drop <u>one l</u>: <u>ful</u>. No exceptions.

awful	(aw~~e~~ + full)	=	*awful*	(Notice for *awful* that both the <u>e</u> and an <u>l</u> are dropped.)
careful	(care + ful~~l~~)	=	*careful*	
helpful	(help + ful~~l~~)	=		
mouthful	(mouth + ful~~l~~)	=		
spoonful	(spoon + ful~~l~~)	=		

The "Wel Words"

The 2 words that start with "wel" have just <u>one l</u>: wel + come =   wel + fare =

Compound Word Fun

Sometimes *Compound Words*, like *carpool* and *doughnut*, are created; but, if you really think about them, they don't make sense. Try drawing these words. Then think of other ones and draw these too.

hotdog   doughnut   firecracker   brainstorm   carpool

A List Of Common Solid Compound Words

English has more compound words than any other language because of its incredible ability to join different parts of speech (*Note*: Many of these words were added to English after 1800 A.D.)
❑ **NOW**: Star the words that refer to people. Put a dash by the words that are a food or drink.

afternoon	cowboy	headline	peppermint	stepfather
afterthought	cupcake	headset	pinball	stepmother
airplane	daydream	heartwarming	pinwheel	strawberry
anybody	dogcatcher	herself	playground	suitcase
anyone	doorbell	highway	playmate	sundial
anything	downstairs	himself	ponytail	sundown
anywhere	driveway	homesick	popcorn	sunflower
applesauce	earring	homework	postcard	sunlight
armchair	egghead	horseback	quarterback	sunrise
ballpark	everybody	hotdog	railroad	sunset
ballroom	everyone	indoor	rainbow	sunshine
barefoot	everything	Internet	raspberry	suntan
bartender	everywhere	jellybean	sailboat	sweatshirt
baseball	fairytale	jellyfish	salesperson	swimsuit
basketball	farmhand	keyboard	seafood	takeoff
bathrobe	fingerprint	kickball	seagull	teammate
beanbag	firefighter	leftover	seahorse	themselves
bedroom	fireplace	lemonade	seashell	timeout
bellhop	fireworks	lifeguard	seashore	today
billfold	flamethrower	lighthouse	seesaw	toenails
birdhouse	flashlight	lipstick	semicolon	together
birthday	football	loudspeaker	shortstop	tomcat
blackberry	forever	maybe	showoff	toothbrush
blackboard	frankfurter	meatball	sidewalk	touchdown
blacksmith	girlfriend	moonlight	silverware	trailblazer
blueberries	glassblower	motorcycle	skateboard	tugboat
bobcat	glowworm	necklace	skyscraper	turtleneck
bodyguard	goldfish	newscast	snowball	underground
bookcase	goodbye	newspaper	snowfall	upstairs
bookkeeper	grandchildren	nightgown	snowflakes	wastebasket
boyfriend	grandfather	notebook	snowman	watercolor
breakfast	grandmother	oatmeal	softball	waterfall
campfire	grandparents	online	somebody	waterfront
carhop	grapefruit	ourselves	someone	watermelon
carpool	grasshopper	outcome	someplace	weekend
catnap	groundhog	outfield	something	weeknights
cheeseburger	gumdrop	outside	sometimes	wheelbarrow
cheesecake	haircut	outstanding	somewhere	wheelchair
classmate	hamburger	overalls	spaceship	whenever
coffeecake	handkerchief	overcoat	spotlight	windbreaker
coleslaw	handsome	pancake	stardust	wingspan
cornbread	headache	paperback	starfish	woodpecker
countdown	headdress	peanut	starlight	wristwatch

139

Learning About Prefixes-Just Fasten Them in Front

Prefix comes from Latin and means *to fasten in front* (*pre: in front* + *fix: fasten*). This is exactly what you do with a prefix. You simply fasten it in front of a root word. You don't take out letters or add letters. You just *add the prefix on*! This makes words with prefixes quite easy to spell. You spell the prefix and then the root.

sub + marine

EXAMPLES: pre + historic = prehistoric   sub + marine = submarine

Small, but powerful, prefixes like **mis-**, **under-**, **sub-**, and **super-** are fastened before words to add to their meaning of a word or to change it. This way, words like: take, stand, marine, and man can become **mistake**, **understand**, **submarine**, and **Superman**!!! As you learn the meaning of prefixes, plus the meaning of the words they're added to, you'll be adding hundreds of new words to your vocabulary. So, let's meet some prefixes and create some words!!!

❑ **NOW**: Try the prefix **dis-** which means *not*. Simply add this prefix to form new words.

dis + appear	=	*disappear*
dis + cover	=	
dis + ease	=	
dis + honest	=	

POP!

❑ **JUST ADD**: It's as easy as that. Just as you did for compound words, you add the prefix to the word and there you are. It is simply 1 + 1 = 2! Be very careful, though, when the prefix ends with the same letter with which the root word begins, as in *misspell* and *underrate*. When you add these words together, make sure you keep both consonants.

mis (wrong)
mis + spell   =
mis + take   =
mis + treat   =

un (not)
un + fair   =
un + known   =
un + beaten   =

over (too much)
over + do   =
over + due   =
over + run   =

under (below, less than)
under + rate   =
under + stand =
under + take   =

dis (not)
dis + cuss   =
dis + service =
dis + solve   =

non (not)
non + fiction =
non + human   =
non + sense   =

□ **TRY THIS:** Look at these roots and prefixes. Then take a prefix and see which roots you can put it before and have words that make sense. Remember: <u>Just add the entire prefix to the entire root</u>. Write your words under their prefix. To see if a word exists or for fun, look up some of these common prefixes in a dictionary. You'll find *amazingly* long lists of words where these prefixes are added to root words. For fun, count one of these lists and put the number of words by the prefix.

active	cover	order, ordered	sell
aged	cut	paid	set
appear	date	paint	solve, solved
armed	dress	pay, paid	study
bid	educated	price	take
bite	handed	rate	treat
card	heat	run	use
claimed	mark	scribe	wash
clean	move, moved	script	write

<u>dis (apart, not)</u>

<u>mis (not)</u>

mistook

<u>un (not)</u>

unarmed

<u>re (again, over)</u>

<u>pre (before)</u>

predate

<u>post (after)</u>

postscript (abbrev: P.S.)

<u>over (too much)</u>

<u>under (less than, not enough)</u>

underbid

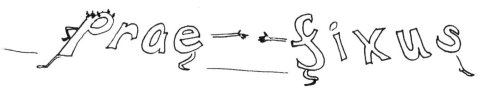

141

Let's Learn Some Common Prefixes and See What They Do

Most of the prefixes used in English have come from Latin (pre-, post-) and Greek (auto-, hemi-), and there are still some prefixes that were used in Old English (over-, un-, with-). When you spell these prefixes and their roots, what is most important to remember is: <u>Simply add the entire prefix to the entire root word!</u>

When you add a prefix to a root, the prefix does not change the spelling, but it does change or add to the meaning. The ways that prefixes describe or change the meaning of words fit into these categories:

<u>AGAINST or BAD</u>: anti- (against); counter-, contra- (against); mal (bad)

<u>FOR or GOOD</u>: bene- (good); pro- (for); super-, supra- (more, above)

<u>NOT</u>: dis-; in-; mis-; non-; un-

<u>NUMBERS, FRACTIONS</u>: uni- (one); bi- (two); tri- (three); hemi (half); milti-, poly- (many)

<u>RELATIONSHIP</u>: ad- (together); com (with, for); dis- (apart)

<u>WHEN</u>: fore-; pre- (before); post- (after)

<u>WHERE</u>: circum- (around); in-, intro- (into); inter (between); intra (within); over-, super- (over or above); re- (go back, do again); sub-, under- (under); trans- (across)

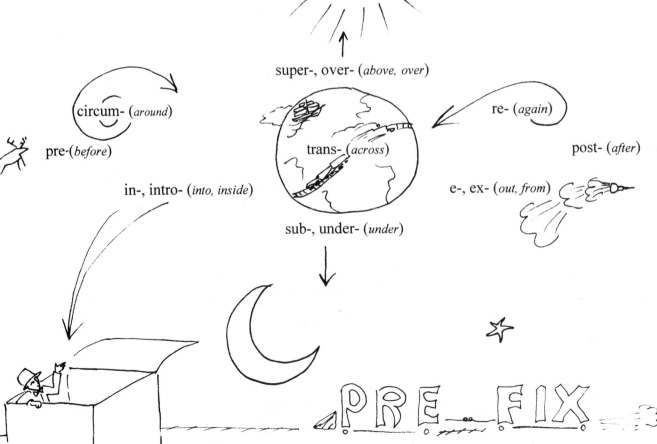

super-, over- (*above, over*)

circum- (*around*)

re- (*again*)

pre-(*before*)

trans-(*across*)

post- (*after*)

in-, intro- (*into, inside*)

e-, ex- (*out, from*)

sub-, under- (*under*)

PRE FIX

Ten Common Prefixes

❑ **NOW:** Add two or more words to each of these common prefixes. For fun, check a dictionary.

dis-   *apart, away from, not*   disagree (not agree), discontinue

mis-   *badly, wrongly*   mistake (take wrongly), mishandle

non-   *not, no*   nonsense (no sense), nonprofit

over-   *again, too much*   overspend (spend too much), overreact

post-   *after*   postscript P.S. (after the letter), postdate

pre-   *before*   prejudge (judge before), prefix, prepaid, prepare

re-   *again, back, repeat*   replay (play again), return, recess, rearrange

super-, sur-   *above, greater*   surface (above the face of), supernatural

un-   *not, opposite of*   uncommon (not common), unable

under-   *under, below, less than*   underground (below ground), underage

Greek and Latin Numbers

❑ **TRY THIS:** As you read through these number prefixes, you'll probably see a lot of words you're familiar with. Check any words you don't know in the dictionary and write the meaning by the word. Also, use the dictionary to find additional words and write these by each prefix.

hemi-   *half*   hemisphere

semi-   *half*   semicircle, semicolon

mono-, uni-   *one*   monarch, monk, monogamy (one wife), monogram

bi-   *two*   bicycle, bimonthly, binoculars

di-   *two*   digraph

tri-   *three*   triad, triangle, tricycle, trio

quadra-, tetra-   *four*   quadrangle, quadruplets, quartet

pent-, quint-   *five*   pentagon, quintuplets

hex-, sex-   *six*   hexagon, sextuplets

hept-, sept-   *seven*   September, septuagenarian (70-80 years old)

oct-   *eight*   octagon, October, octopus, octogenarian (80-90 years old)

non, nove-   *nine*   November, nonagenarian (90-100 years old)

deca-, dec-   *ten*   decade, decathlon, December

cent-, centi-   *hundred*   centimeter, century   *centipede*

milli-   *thousand*   million (in the metric system *milli-* means thousandth)

multi-, poly-   *many*   multitude, polygamous (having more than one wife)

Note: Before Augustus Caesar added July and August around 40 B.C., the months matched their numbers: September was the 7th month; October the 8th; November the 9th; and December, the 10th.

Three Prefixes that Have Different Forms
In-, Ad-, and Com-

For prefixes, REMEMBER the rule that ALWAYS works: When you connect a prefix and a root, you simply add them together. Now, let's learn about three prefixes: **in-**, **ad-**, and **com-**, that have different forms they add, depending on the letter with which the root begins. For example *in-* adds the form *il-* for *illogical and im-* for *immobile*; *ad-* uses *ac-* for *accept*; *com* adds *con-* for *connect*. The form is added that's easiest to pronounce with the roots. This often create a double-letter.

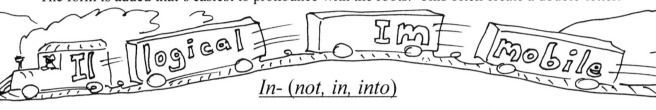

In- (not, in, into)

In- has 3 forms (*il-, im-, ir-*) that match roots that begin with *l, m,* and *r*. This means the completed word is spelled with a double letter: *il + legal = illegal*. This gives you a great SPELLING RULE, the *One Plus One Rule*: When the last letter of a prefix (il-) matches the first letter of the root (-legal), this creates a double letter: *one* letter + *matching letter = a double letter*.

In- uses the form *il-* before *l*

il + legal	=	*illegal*
il + legible	=	(not clear)
il + literate	=	(not reading)
il + logical	=	(not making sense)

In- uses the form *im-* before *m*

im + mature	=	*immature*
im + mediate	=	
im + mobile	=	(not moving)
im + mortal	=	(not dying)

In- uses the form *ir-* before *r*

ir + rational	=	*irrational* (not reasonable)
ir + regular	=	
ir + religious	=	
ir + removable	=	

For pronunciation, *in-* uses *im-* before *p*

im + patient	=	*impatient*
im + polite	=	
im + portant	=	(carries weight)
im + possible	=	

In-, which usually means *not*, means *in* or *into* for a few words: *important* and *immigrant*.
Ex- (and form *e-*) means *out or away from*. See how each prefix changes the root *migrate* (*move*).

in (*in; into*) + migrate (*move*) = immigrate
immigrate means *move into* a country.
Note: 2 m's: *immigrating, immigrants*

e (*out; away from*) + migrate (*move*) = emigrate
emigrate means *move out* of country.
Note: one m: *emigrating, emigrants*

(REMEMBER: *Emigrant* has just one *m*, because its prefix is a single *e-*.)

"I'm off to the New"

Im-migrant   WELCOME!   = migrant

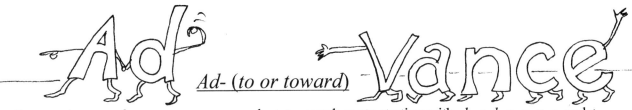

Ad- (to or toward)

Ad- has forms *ab-, ac-, al-, an-, ap-, ar- as-,* and *at-* to match roots starting with *b, c, l, n, p, r, s,* and *t.* For the rest of roots that begin with other letters, *ad-* simply uses ad-: addition, adjust, advance, adverb.

ac + cident	=	*accident*	
ac + cept	=		
ac + curate	=		
ac + cuse	=		
ac + custom	=		
al + low	=		
an + nounce	=	*(to divide)*	
an + nual	=	*(yearly)*	

ap + pear	=	*appear*	
ap + point	=		
ap + preciate	=		
ap + proach	=		
ar + range	=		
ar + rest	=		
as + sistant	=		
at + tend	=		

<u>Ad-</u> uses the form *ac-:* acquaint...before roots beginning with *k* and *qu*.

ac + quire	=	*acquire*
ac + knowledge	=	

<u>Ad-</u> uses the form *a-:* ascribe, aspect...before roots beginning with blends *sc, sp* and *st*.

a + spect	=	*aspect*	*(viewpoint)*
a + scend	=		*(to go up)*

<u>Ad-</u> and <u>com-</u> also follow the *One Plus One Rule*. When the last letter of the prefix (<u>ar-</u>, <u>con-</u>) matches the first letter of the root (-<u>r</u>ange, -<u>n</u>ect), you always get a double letter: a<u>rr</u>ange, co<u>nn</u>ect.

Com- (*together* or *with*)

Com- has forms *col-, con-, cor-* to match roots starting with *l, n,* and *r*. *Con-* also connects to *c roots.*

col + lect	=	*collect*	
col + lege	=		
con + nect	=		

con + note	=	*connote*	
cor + rect	=		
con + cert	=		

Com- keeps the form *com-* before roots beginning with *p* and for the rest of the *com-* words.

com + bine	=	
com + fort	=	
com + mand	=	
com + mercial	=	

com + pare	=	
com + pete	=	
com + pose	=	
com + puter	=	

Getting to Know Some Common Prefixes

Keep learning about prefixes, and you'll build both your spelling and vocabulary. Sometimes it's easy to understand the meaning of words formed by a prefix and root: *dislike* and *immature*. However, there are times when the meaning of a word is difficult to understand. When this happens, it's very helpful to look in a dictionary. Here you can find the meaning of the prefix and root and the history of the word. Also, you can discover which prefixes connect to the most words.

❑ **NOW:** As you read through this list, underline the prefix in each word. Add an extra line under double letters, which happen when the prefix ends with the same letter with which the root begins.

PREFIX	MEANING	EXAMPLES
ad- (ac-, ad-, an-, ap-, as-)	*to, toward*	accept, addition, admit, annual, approach
after-	*after, following*	aftermath, afternoon, aftertaste, aftershock, afterwards
ambi-	*both*	ambidextrous, ambiguous, ambivalent
amphi-	*around*	amphibian, amphitheatre
ante-	*before, prior*	anteroom (a room before), antemeridian (before noon)
anti-	*against*	antibiotic, antidote, antifreeze, antiseptic (against infection)
auto-	*self*	autobiography, autograph, automatic, automobile
be-	*make*	become, befriend, belittle, beloved, below
bene-	*good*	benefactor, benefit, beneficial, benevolent
bi-, bin-	*two*	biannual, bicycle, bifocals, bimonthly, binoculars
cent-, centi-	*hundred*	centennial, centigrade, centimeter, century
cir-, circum-	*around*	circle, circumscribe, circumference
com- (col-, con-, cor-)	*with*	college, combat, combine, command, concert, correct
contra-	*against, opposite*	contradict, contrary, contrast
counter-	*against, opposite*	counteract, counterproposal
de-, des-	*down, away*	decide, decision, depart, descend, describe, destroy
dec-, deci-	*ten, tenth*	decade, decathlon, December, decimal
dis-	*not*	disappear, disarm, dishonest, dissimilar
e-, ex-	*away from, out*	eject, emigrate, erupt, evict, excited, exercise
equi-, equa-	*equal*	equation, equator, equidistant, equilibrium, equinox
extra-	*beyond*	extracurricular, extraordinary, extraterrestrial

for-	*not, against, away*	forbid, forsake, forswear, forward
fore-	*before*	foreshadow, foreword
hemi-	*half*	hemisphere, hemicycle (semi-circle)
hyper-	*excessive*	hyperactive, hypercritical, hypersensitive
hypo-	*under*	hypodermic, hypothermia
in- (il-, im-, ir-)	*not*	independence, illegal, immigration, impossible
inter-	*between*	interfere, international, interrupt, interstate (btw. states)
intra-	*inside, within*	intramurals, intrastate, intravenous (within veins)
magni-	*great, large*	magnanimous, magnificent, magnify
meta-	*change*	metamorphosis, metaphor
micro-	*small, short*	microbe, microfilm, microphone, microscope
mid-	*middle*	middle, midnight, midsummer, midway
mis-	*not, wrong*	misbehave, misfortune, mishandle, mistake
mon-, mono-	*one*	monarch, monk, monogamy, monorail
multi-	*many, much*	multicolored, multicultural, multiply
non-	*not*	nonfat, nonfiction, nonsense, nonstop, nonviolent
over-	*too much*	overactive, overbearing, overdo, overdue, overpriced
post-	*after*	postcard, postdate, postpone, postscript (P.S.)
pre-	*before*	preamble, precaution, precede, prefix, prejudge
pro-	*forward*	process, program, progress, promotion, prophet
re-	*again*	reappear, redo, reheat, relive, rewrite
sub-	*below, under*	subhuman, submarine, submerge
super-	*above, beyond*	superior, supernatural, Superman
tele-	*distant*	telegram, telephone, telescope, television
trans-	*across*	transfer, translate, transportation,
un-	*not*	unable, unbeatable, uncomfortable, unnatural
under-	*below, less than*	underage, undercover, underground, underneath

❑ **NOW:** Underline the prefixes in these words. Then add them to the prefix list, or underline them if they're already there: accuse, annual, appear, arrange, assistant, because, become, below, collect, compete, connect, correct, describe, destroy, excited, exercise, foreword, forward, illegal, impact, impolite, important, impossible, infinite, ascend, descend, emigrate, immigrate.

Magical Suffixes – Just Add Them at the End

SUFFIXES have the *POWER* to turn words into different parts of speech! When a suffix is *added to the end of a word*, it not only changes the meaning of the word, but it can also turn the word into a noun, verb, adjective, or adverb.

$$cloud + less$$

NOUN: Her *cheerfulness*; The *playfulness*   **VERB:** I *cheered* for my friend. My puppy *played*.
ADJEC.: *Cheerful* birds; A *playful* puppy.   **ADV.:** Birds sang *cheerfully*. A pup jumped *playfully*.

□ **NOW:** Add suffixes to the words below. Simply <u>add</u> <u>the</u> <u>entire</u> <u>suffix</u> AFTER the <u>entire</u> <u>root</u>. (The only time changes are made is when a word ends in <u>silent e</u> or <u>y</u> and for words where you must <u>double the final consonant</u> to keep a vowel short. You'll learn about these in the other suffix lessons.)

-ful (turns word into adjective: *full of*)

care	+ ful	= *careful*	(Keep e)
cheer	+ ful	=	
faith	+ ful	=	
grate	+ ful	=	(Keep e)
thank	+ ful	=	
thought	+ ful	=	
wonder	+ ful	=	

-ly (turns word into adverb: *in that way*)

brave	+ ly	= *bravely*	(Keep e)
final	+ ly	=	
happy	+ ly	=	(Change y to i)
final	+ ly	=	
near	+ ly	=	
natural	+ ly	=	
usual	+ ly	=	

-less (turns word into adjective: *without*)

cloud	+ less	=
harm	+ less	=

-ness (turns word into adjective: *state of being*)

happy	+ ness	=	(Change y to)
like	+ ness	=	(Keep e)

-al (turns word into adjective: *like*)

accidental	+ al	=	
nature	+ al	=	(Keep the e.)
origin	+ al	=	
profession	+ al	=	

-ment (turns word into noun: *action or process*)

achieve	+ ment	= *achievement*
arrange	+ ment	=
entertain	+ ment	=
wonder	+ ment	=

-er, -est (turns words into adjectives: *more, most*)

close	+ er, est	= *closer, closest*
large	+ er, est	=
mean	+ er, est	=
strong	+ er, est	=

-ship (turns word into noun: *state or quality of*)

citizen	+ ship	=
court	+ ship	=
friend	+ ship	=
scholar	+ ship	=

Turning Words into Nouns, Verbs, Adjectives, and Adverbs

❑ **NOW:** Try out some suffix magic with the words below. Try out these words with suffixes, until you find ones that can be added and make sense. Then, simply <u>add</u> <u>the</u> <u>entire suffix</u> to the <u>entire base</u> word, and write the new word under the suffix it matches. Some words can connect to more than one suffix. How many nouns, verbs, adjectives, and adverbs can you create?

actual (real)	fresh	loose	ship
base	glad	mad	skill
clever	great	pave	soft
doubt	heart	play	state
enchant	help	region	stress
end	ill	rest	swift
engage	job	rot	tire
enrich (add to)	like	rude	will
fast	large	sad	wish

-ful (adjective suffix: *full of*)
joyful

-ly (adverb suffix: *like*)
joyfully

-less (adjective suffix: *without*)
joyless

-ness (noun suffix: *state of being*)
happiness

-al (adjective suffix: *resembling or like*)
unusual

-ment (noun suffix: *action or process*)
enjoyment

-er and **-est** (adjectives suffixes: *more, most*)
happier   happiest

-ed and **-ing** (verb suffixes: past, present)
enjoyed   enjoying

Suffix Magic: Some Words Can Turn into Many Parts of Speech

Let's review four parts of speech, and learn how suffix magic can change words into nouns, verbs, adjectives, and adverbs. Then, let's discover how some roots can be all four parts of speech.

NOUN : A noun names a person, place, object, or state of being. You can put *the* or *a* before any common noun and it will always make sense (A common noun names ordinary things and is not capitalized: *a president*. A proper noun names specific things and is capitalized: *President Lincoln*.)

 PERSONS: the *children*, a *dancer*, the *artist*, a *musician*, a *writer*, the *juggler*
 PLACES: the *park*, the *theatres*, a *beach*, the *mountains*
 THINGS: a *star*, the *harmonica*, the *skis*, the *entertainment*, the *clouds*
 STATES OF BEING or EMOTION, ACTION: the *happiness*, the *freedom*, *friendship*, the *comfort*

VERB : A verb shows action or it means equals. Verbs also show time: present, past, future.

 ACTIONS: I *juggle*; He *dances*; We *write*; We are *comforting*; I *played* music.
 STATES OF BEING: I *am*; We *are*.
 PAST, PRESENT, FUTURE: I *spell*; I *am spelling*; I *spelled*; I *will spell* well.

ADJECTIVE : An adjective is added to a noun to describe it. (Perhaps they should be called *adnouns*). Adjectives also describe pronouns, but to do this the adjective must follow a verb that means equals.

 ADJECTIVES DESCRIBE NOUNS: the *amazing* juggler; the *wonderful* dancer; a *windy* beach; the *glittery* star; a *skilled* musician; the *closest* friendship; a *comforting* friend
 ADJECTIVES DESCRIBE PRONOUNS: She is *lively*. They were *grateful*. He is *taller*.

ADVERB : An adverb is added to a verb to describe it. Most adverbs end in -ly and tell how an action is done; others tell how, when, and where.

 ADVERBS DESCRIBE VERBS: He juggled *amazingly*. She sang *wonderfully*.
 A musician plays *skillfully*. I fly *monthly*. We dance *well*. A star *always* glitters.

❏ **NOW:** Choose 2 or more of these words: *cheer, hope, love, power*. Add suffixes and turn them into a noun, verb, adjective, and adverb. Some roots like *wonder* can be turned into 4 parts of speech.

NOUN: I find *wonder* in natural things: snowflakes, flowers, and animals.

VERB: I *wonder* what mysteries ancient civilizations discovered?

ADJECTIVE: You are my truly *wonderful* friend.

ADVERB: I slept *wonderfully* out under the stars..

Memory Tools for Suffixes

USING MEMORY TOOLS: Create and write down ways to remember these words by using *POWER SPELLING MEMORY TOOLS (Clues, Same Patterns Rules, Pronunciations...).* For example, you can create a *Clue-in-a Row* for <u>abandoned</u>. <u>Careless</u> and <u>grateful</u> follow the *E Rule*. <u>Happily</u> follows the *Y Rule*. Then, keep using these *Tools* and your mind will remember them. Ideas for *Tools* are below, but take the challenge of thinking of your own ideas first.

1. abandoned: *Clue-in-a-Row*:

2. careless:

3. cheerful:

4. early:

5. finally:

6. grateful:

7. greatly:

8. happiness

9. heartfelt:

10. luckily:

11. nearly

12. scholarship:

13. sincerely:

14. wonderment

"...if I only had a heart."

---

1. abandoned: *Clue in a Row*: Ed was not <u>abandoned</u>; there was <u>a band on Ed</u>.
2. careless: Careless follows *Long E Rule* and *Suffix Rule*: <u>care</u> + <u>less</u>; *Same Pattern*: bare, dare, fare, hare, share…
3. cheerful: They raised their b<u>eer</u> to give a <u>cheer</u>; *Same Pattern*: beer, deer, peer,
4. early: I knew it was <u>early</u> when my <u>ear</u> heard the rooster crow.
5. finally: *Long Vowel Rule*: <u>One n</u> keeps the <u>i</u> long; *Suffix Rule*: Add entire suffix: final + ly = <u>finally</u>.
6. grateful: He was <u>grateful</u> that they <u>rated</u> him so high.
7. greatly: When your stomach is growling <u>greatly</u>, you're ready to <u>eat</u>.
8. happiness: *Y Rule*: When *y* follows consonant, *change y to i* before adding consonant suffix: <u>happy + i + ly</u>.
9. heartfelt: I put my <u>heart</u> close to the <u>earth</u> and <u>felt</u> its <u>heartfelt</u>: <u>h + earth + felt =heartfelt.</u>
10. luckily: *Y Rule*: When *y* follows consonant, *change y to i* before adding consonant suffix: <u>lucky + i + ly</u>
11. nearly: <u>Clearly</u>, she was <u>nearly</u> and d<u>early</u> loved
12. scholarship: His <u>scholarship</u> let him go <u>far</u> in <u>school</u>: <u>school + far + ship</u> = scholarship.
13. sincerely: <u>Since</u> you're <u>here</u>, I can <u>sincerely</u> <u>rely</u> on you:
14. wonderment: When I <u>won</u>, I felt <u>wonderment</u>. *Suffix Rule*: <u>wonder</u> + <u>ment</u>.

The Rule for Adding Suffixes after Silent E

You truly gain SPELLING *POWER* when you learn the SILENT E RULE because this rule covers more words than any other spelling rule. Hundreds of English words end in a Silent E, and hundreds more are built from Silent E words plus suffixes.

love: lovable, loving… safe: safer, safest, safely… hope: hoped, hoping, hopeful…
free: freer, freeing… canoe: canoeing… shoe: shoeing

!!!So…Let's learn this most-important rule!!!

THE RULES FOR ADDING SUFFIXES AFTER SILENT E

When a **CONSONANT** comes before Silent E
 Keep Silent E before a <u>suffix that begins with a consonant</u>: *hopeful, excitement, likeness…*
 Drop Silent E before a <u>suffix that begins with a vowel</u>: *lovable, excited, using, pleasure…*
 (<u>Exception</u>: For Pronunciation, keep Silent E after <u>C</u> and <u>G</u> to keep them <u>soft</u> before -able and -ous)

When a **VOWEL** comes before Silent E
 Keep Silent E before <u>all suffixes</u>: *freer, seeing, canoeing, hoeing, shoeing…*
 (<u>Exceptions</u>: For Pronunciation, change IE to Y: tie – tying ; and drop E from UE: rescuing, cuing…)

When a Consonant Comes Before Silent E

Before consonant suffixes, I'm <u>useful</u> and <u>likely</u> to stay for <u>encouragement</u>…

Before vowel suffixes, I'm <u>desiring</u> to stay, but <u>deciding</u> I must be <u>leaving</u>…

❑ **TRY THIS**: Keep Silent E if suffix begins with a consonant: useful, likely… Drop Silent E if the suffix begins with a vowel: *coming, leaving,* Add the Silent E Words to the suffixes below:

amuse	*amused*	*amusing*	*amusement* *amuses*
come	*came*	ing	s
decide	ed	ing	sion (Exception: Decide drops

-de to make *decision*. Also: *incision* and *revision*)

desire	ed	ing	able s
encourage	ed	ing	ment s
excite	ed	ing	able ment
hope	ed	ing	ful
like	ed	ing	able ly
love	ed	ing	able ly

°to e, or not to e? *That is the question…*

make	_made_	_____ing	_____er	_____able
please	_____ed	_____ing	_____ure	
sense	_____ed	_____ing	_____ible	
write	_wrote_	_____ing	_____er	_____en

(*T* is doubled to keep *i* short)

Exceptions to the Rule When Silent E Follows a Consonant

EXCEPTIONS: Soft C (s sound) and Soft G (j sound) keep Silent E Before -able and -ous

C and G keep Silent E so C can keep its soft s sound, and g can keep its soft j sound.

advantage	_advantageous_	notice	_____able
change	_____able	manage	_____able
courage	_____ous	service	_____able
outrage	_____ous	trace	_____able
enforce	_____able	marriage	_____able
hinge	_____ing-hooking on door	dungeon	
singe	_____ing-slightly burning	gorgeous	
tinge	_____ing-add hint of color...	pigeon	

(Finding words that follow the Same Pattern before suffixes is very helpful for Silent E Words)

EXCEPTIONS: WORDS THAT DROP SILENT E BEFORE A CONSONANT SUFFIX

awe	+	ful	=		nine	+	th	=	
double	+	ly	=		possible	+	ly	=	
decide	+	sion	=		twelve	+	fth	=	
divide	+	sion	=		whole	+	ly	=	
judge	+	ment	=		wise	+	dom	=	

EXCEPTIONS: WORDS THAT KEEP SILENT E BEFORE A VOWEL SUFFIX

acre	+	age	=	_acreage_	here	+	in	=	
line	+	age	=		there	+	in	=	
mile	+	age	=		where	+	as	=	

153

When a Vowel Comes before Silent E

Remember: When a Vowel comes before Silent E, keep Silent E for all suffixes; or, you could say:
<u>Keep Silent E before all suffixes when it's preceded by a vowel</u>: **freeing, seeing, canoeing**…

❏ **NOW TRY THIS**: All of these words keep e before all suffixes because e is preceded by a vowel.

canoe _____*canoed*_____ *canoeing*

hoe _____ed_____ing_____down

shoe _____d_____ing_____less_____maker_____string

toe _____ed_____ing_____less

agree_____ed_____ing_____ment

free _____ed_____ing_____er_____est_____ly_____dom

EXCEPTIONS: IE CHANGES TO Y BEFORE -ING (THEN: Y+ING stay together)

d~~ie~~ y + ing = *dying*   t~~ie~~ y + ing = tying (or tieing)

l~~ie~~ y + ing =   v~~ie~~ y-compete + ing =

EXCEPTIONS: UE WORDS ALWAYS DROP FINAL E BEFORE SUFFIXES
Words, <u>ending in a silent e preceded by u</u> drop the <u>final e</u> before ALL suffixes.

argue _____ed_____ing _____*argument* (Exc: Leave off "e")

cue _____ed_____ing (cue, cued, cuing: giving lines for a play; signaling)

value _____ed_____ing _____able

rescue _____ed_____ing_____able_____er

blu~~e~~ + ish =   tru~~e~~ + ly =

du~~e~~ + ly =   unruly is also spelled like truly.

!!A final salute to the **FINAL SILENT E RULE** that affects more words than any other rule!!

"at your service!"

154

Clues and Other Tools for Challenging Silent E Words

SUMMARY of RULES for ADDING SUFFIXES after SILENT E WORDS

When a **CONSONANT** comes before Silent E:
 Keep Silent E before a <u>suffix that begins with a consonant</u>: hopeful, excitement, likeness
 Drop Silent E before a <u>suffix that begins with a vowel</u>: lovable, excited, using, pleasure
Ex.: <u>Soft C and G words keep Silent E</u> to <u>keep their soft sound</u>: noticeable: soft s; courageous: soft j
Ex.: Drop E before vowel suffix: awful, decision, judgment, ninth, possibly, twelfth, wholly
Ex.: Keep Silent E before vowel suffix: acreage, mileage, herein, therein

When a **VOWEL** comes before Silent E:
 Keep Silent E before <u>all suffixes</u>: freer, seeing, canoeing, hoeing, shoeing
Ex.: <u>IE changes to y before -ing</u> (Then: y + ing stay together.): dying, lying, tying
Ex.: <u>UE words drop Silent E before all suffixes</u>: cuing, rescuing, valuing, valuable, truly…

❑ **NOW**: Fill in the blanks. Use *Clues* and *Phonics* to learn these Silent E Words.

noticeable: *Clue-in-a-Row*: Is it _ _ _ _ _ _ _ _ _ _ that my soda is _ _ _ _ _ _ _ _ _ _?

courageous: In <u>our age</u> you need to be _ _ _ _ _ _ _ _ _: <u>c + our + age + ous</u>.

outrageous: Traffic is such an <u>out rage</u>, I think it's _ _ _ _ _ _ _ _ _ _: <u>out + rage + ous</u>.

singeing (slightly burning): *Phonics*: Keep _ _ in <u>singeing</u> so the _ _ stays soft (keeps j sound).

dyeing (changing color): *Phonics*: _ _ _ _ _ _ keeps an <u>e</u> so it won't be confused with *dying*.

awful: Can something _ _ _ _ _ still be <u>lawful</u>?

judgment: You can trust the _ _ _ _ _ _ _ _ of a good <u>man</u>.

ninth: This book is the _ _ _ _ _ one <u>in the</u> series: <u>n + in + the</u> = _ _ _ _ _.

wholly: We decorated our house _ _ _ _ _ _ with <u>holly</u>: <u>w + holly</u>.

argument: It's hard to have an _ _ _ _ _ _ _ _ with _ _ _ in your mouths.

rescuing: I'll be _ _ _ _ _ _ _ _ _ U <u>in</u> a minute. (Drop <u>e</u> before a suffix for all <u>UE</u> words.)

truly: He was _ _ _ _ _ acting un<u>ruly</u>. (Drop <u>e</u> for all <u>ue</u> words; <u>e</u> is not needed for pronunciation)

valuable: <u>Val</u>, are <u>U able</u> to help me search for my _ _ _ _ _ _ _ _ ring? <u>val + U + able</u>.

canoeing: Can you go _ _ _ _ _ _ _ _ through <u>volcanoes</u>?

hoeing: When I was _ _ _ _ _ _ _, I caught my <u>toe in</u> a hole: <u>h + toe + in + g</u>.

ta da! *ta da!*

155

LESSON 30

The Rule for Adding Suffixes After a Final Y

The FINAL Y RULE gives you a lot of SPELLING *POWER* because hundreds of words end in a Final Y, and hundred more are built by adding suffixes to words ending with Final Y.

carry: carried, carrying... merry: merrier, merriest... study: studied, studying...

play: played, playing... enjoy: enjoyed, enjoyment, enjoying... buy: buying, buyer...

!!!Just like Silent E, Final Y has a very important Rule!!!

THE FINAL Y RULE FOR ADDING SUFFIXES

When a **CONSONANT** comes before y, <u>change y to i before all suffixes except -ing</u>: tries, tried, trying; empties, emptied, emptying; happier, happiest, happily, happiness...

When a **VOWEL** comes before y, <u>keep y before all suffixes</u>: buying, enjoyed, enjoying, plays, playing, stayed, staying...

<u>TRY ends in Y.</u> <u>A CONSONANT – R comes before Y</u>
<u>Change the y to i</u> = tri – before all suffixes: tries, tried, except for the suffix – ing: trying   (<u>Y</u> + <u>-ING</u> together =

<u>BUSY ends in Y.</u> <u>A CONSONANT – S comes before Y.</u>
<u>Change y to i</u> = busi – before all suffixes: busier, busiest, business. except for the suffix – ing: busying (<u>Y</u> + <u>-ING</u> together = <u>YING</u>.)

<u>STAY ends in Y.</u> <u>A vowel – A comes before Y</u>:
<u>Keep the Y</u> = stay – before all suffixes: stay, staying
HEY... BUY... TOY... PLAY... STAY...

When a Consonant Comes before Y

☐ **NOW**: Complete the words below. REMEMBER: When a CONSONANT comes before y, <u>change y to i before all suffixes except -ing</u>: readies, readied, readying, readily, readiness...

carry   *carries*   *carried*   *carrying*   *carrier*   *carriage*

busy_____es_____ed_____ing_____er_____est_____ness

cry_____es_____ed_____ing_____er

empty_____es_____ed_____ing____er_____est_____ness

easy _____er_____est _____ly

"*I stay for -ing!*"   "*I go u the*"

156

happy_____er_____est_____ness_____ly

hurry_____es_____ed_____ing

lazy_____er_____est_____ness_____ly

like_____s_____d_____ing_____ly_____ness

lonely_____er_____est_____ness

marry_____es_____ed_____ing_____age

pretty_____er_____est_____ing_____ly

ready_____es_____ed_____ing_____er_____est_____ly_____ness

worry_____es_____ed_____ing_____er_____some

EXCEPTIONS: Words like: crybaby, ladybug, shyly, wryly…

When a Vowel Comes before Final Y

"When a VOWEL comes before me   Y   I'm STAYING and PLAYING…"

❏ **TRY THIS:** Complete the words below. Follow the second part of the rule: <u>When a VOWEL comes before y, keep the y before all suffixes</u>: stayed, staying; buyer, buying; playing…

betray_____s_____ed_____ing_____er_____al

buy_____s_____ing_____er

enjoy_____s_____ed_____ing_____able_____ment

parley_____s_____ed_____ing_____iament (exception)

play_____s_____ed_____ing_____ful

pray_____s_____ed_____ing_____ers

prey_____s_____ed_____ing_____er

stay_____s_____ed_____ing

Exceptions to Rule for Words Where a Vowel Comes before Y

A few words <u>change Y to I before -D and -N, but keep Y before all other suffixes</u>: laid, lain, laying, layer; said, saying… Finally, <u>day</u> changes Y to I for the word <u>daily</u>.

lay:	laid	have lain	laying	layer
pay:	paid	have paid	paying	payer	payment
say:	said,	have said	saying	
slay:	(slew)	have slain	slaying	slayer

"Bye!"   O "I'll take over! (day: daily)   "Y," I think I'll stay

☐ **NOW:** Add suffixes to these words where a vowel comes before Y. Three words follow the Rule, and keep the Y before all suffixes. The rest are exceptions: <u>Y changes to I before -d and -n, and Y stays for all other suffixes.</u>

employ_____ed_____ing_____er_____ment

lay_____d_____ing_____er_____n

pay_____d_____ing   er   ment

pray_____ed_____ing_____ers

slay   (slew)_____ing_____er_____n

stay_____ed_____ing

day_____ly

158

Clues and Other Tools for Final Y Words

SUMMARY of RULES and EXCEPTIONS for FINAL Y WORDS

When a **CONSONANT** comes before FINAL Y, <u>change y to i before all suffixes except -ing</u>.
(Y + -ing stay together: <u>Ying</u>): *cried, crying; studied, studying...*

When a **VOWEL** comes before FINAL Y, <u>keep y before all suffixes</u>:
<u>play</u>: played, playing; <u>lay</u>: laying, layer...

NOTE: For both **CONSONANTS** and **VOWELS**, <u>keep Y before -ING</u>: <u>Y</u> + <u>I</u> = <u>YING</u>.

EXCEPTIONS: A few words change <u>y</u> to <u>i</u> before -<u>d</u> and -<u>n</u> and keep <u>y</u> before all other suffixes:
<u>laid</u>, <u>lain</u>, laying; <u>paid</u>, paying; <u>said</u>, saying; <u>slain</u>. Also, <u>day</u> changes to <u>daily</u>.

□ **NOW**: Use *Clues, Rules* and *Same Patterns* to learn these Final Y Words.

1. **carriage**: <u>Carri</u> is the right <u>age</u> to ride in a _ _ _ _ _ _ _ _ : <u>Carri</u> + <u>age</u> = _ _ _ _ _ _ _ _ .

2. **crying**: <u>Ying</u> sees that you are _ _ _ _ _ _ . *Rule*: <u>Y</u> stays before -ing: <u>cry</u> + -ing = _ _ _ _ _ _

3. **emptiness**: The <u>emp</u>eror wore a <u>tin</u> crown: <u>emp</u> + <u>tin</u> + <u>ess</u> = _ _ _ _ _ _ _ _ _ .
   Rule: After a consonant, change <u>y</u> to <u>i</u> before consonant suffix: empt<s>y</s> + i + ness = _ _ _ _ _ _ _ _ _ .

4. **laziness**: I feel <u>lazy in</u> the sun. *Rule*: Change y to I and add ness: laz<s>y</s> + i + ness = _ _ _ _ _ _ _ _ .

5. **worrying**: I'm <u>sorry</u> you're _ _ _ _ _ _ _ _ . *Rule*: <u>Y</u> stays before -<u>ing</u>: <u>worry</u> + -ing = _ _ _ _ _ _ .

6. **enjoyed**: <u>Joy</u> and <u>Ed</u> enjoyed the game. *Rule*: <u>Y</u> stays after a vowel: <u>enjoy</u> + ed = _ _ _ _ _ _ _ .

7. **paid**: I _ _ _ _ for <u>aid</u>. *Rule*: A few words change __ to __ before <u>d</u> and <u>n</u>: pa<s>y</s> + i + d = _ _ _ _ .
   Same Pattern: aid, l _ _ _, m _ _ _, r _ _ _, s _ _ _.

8. **praying**: <u>Ying</u> sees you are _ _ _ _ _ _ _ _ . *Rule*: <u>Y</u> stays before -<u>ing</u>: <u>pray</u> + -ing = _ _ _ _ _ _ .
   preyed: Before the fox _ _ _ _ _ _ on his <u>prey</u>, he first <u>eyed</u> it: pr + eyed = _ _ _ _ _ _ .

9. **said**: *Rule*: A few words change <u>y</u> to <u>i</u> before <u>d</u> and <u>n</u>: sa<s>y</s> + i + d = _ _ _ _ (Also: laid, paid).

10. **saying**: <u>Ying</u> hears what you are _ _ _ _ _ _ _ . *Rule*: <u>Y</u> stays before -ing: <u>say</u> + -ing = _ _ _ _ _ _ .

11. **allies** (people on your side): *Clue-in-a-Row*: I don't understand why <u>Al lies</u> to his _ _ _ _ _ _ .

12. **tragedies** (sad plays; disasters): I feel <u>rage</u> when heroes _ _ _ _ in _ _ _ _ _ _ _ _ _ : t + rage + dies.

FINAL Y PLURALS : Add -s: *alleys, valleys, volleys.* Change y to i and add -es: *allies, batteries, tragedies.*

!!!Look for words with the *Same Pattern* because they'll be spelled the same way!!!

159

The Power of Suffixes to Create Nouns

It's fun to discover – *SUFFIX MAGIC* – that, with just a few letters, suffixes can change words into NOUNS, ADJECTIVES, VERBS, and ADVERBS. Knowing how to use and spell suffixes gives *you* lots of freedom – because then *you* can choose the way you'd like to use a word in a sentence. Look at these sentences and notice the different ways that suffixes can change the words *act* and *care*.

NOUN: The puppy's <u>activ*ity*</u> and <u>act*s*</u> were funny. (Noun suffixes *-ity, -s* create *activity, acts.*)
VERB: The puppy <u>act*ed*</u> like a curious child. Now the pup *is* act*ing* silly. (V. suffixes *-ed, -ing*)
ADJECTIVE: The puppy is <u>act*ive*</u>. Her pup is <u>happ*ier*</u>. His is the <u>happ*iest*</u>. (*-Er, -est* don't go with *act.*)
ADVERB:  The puppy played <u>active*ly*</u>. (Adverb suffix *-ly,* is added to create the adverb *actively.*)

NOUN: We had many <u>cares</u>. (Plural noun suffix *-s,* is added to create *cares.*)
VERB: She <u>care*s*</u> for you. I <u>car*ed*</u> for you. He <u>is car*ing*</u> for you. (Verb suffixes *-s, -ed, -ing*)
ADJECTIVE: He is <u>care*ful*</u>. I was <u>care*less*</u>. He is a <u>car*ing*</u> man. (Adjective suffixes *-ful, -less, -ing*)
ADVERB: We worked <u>carefu*lly*</u>. (Adverb suffix *-ly*, added to adjective suffix *-ful* creates <u>carefu*lly*</u>.)
NOUN: Our <u>careful*ness*</u> was helpful, but <u>careless*ness*</u> was not helpful (Noun suffixes *-ness* and *-less* are added to adj. suffix *-ful* to turn <u>careful</u> into a noun again: <u>careful*ness;*</u> <u>careless*ness*</u>).

> If your native language is English, using suffixes comes naturally to you. Without even knowing it, you have been adding suffixes to words all your life – in a natural, intuitive kind of way!

❑ **NOW TRY THIS**: See how many suffixes you can add to the words below. Also, try adding a suffix to another suffix, as in the words: *carefulness* and *carelessness*. Write your new words under: NOUN, VERB, ADJECTIVE, or ADVERB. The *pattern each part of speech follows* and *some suffixes* for each part of speech are written under NOUN SUFFIXES, VERB SUFFIXES…below.

NOUN SUFFIXES	VERB SUFFIXES	ADJECTIVE SUFFIXES	ADVERB SUFFIXES
The_____	I ___… We___…	The _____ person	I worked _____.
(*-dom, ness, -er, -or, -s*)	(*-ed, -ing*)	(*-ful, -less, -ive*)	(*-ly*)

thought
The *thought, thoughtfulness* I *think, thought*   *thoughtful, thoughtless*   I worked *thoughtfully*

brave

free

play

rest

quiet

Look at the Many Ways Suffixes Turn Words into Nouns

❑ **LEARN MORE**: <u>Underline</u> the roots and fill in the blanks for each group of noun suffixes. Feel free to add words you think of to the suffix groups. (Adjective, adverb and verb suffixes are in the next lesson.)

SUFFIX	MEANING	EXAMPLES
-ade	*action, thing*	blockade, lemon_____, marmelade, par_____
-age	*action or process*	carriage, marriage, pack_____, voy_____
-al	*action or process*	arrive_____, retrieval, survive_____
-ance, -ancy	*state or quality of*	ambul_____, bal_____, inst_____, instant, tru____
-ant	*one who*	assist_____, emigrant, immigrant, serv_____
-ar, ard, -arian	*one who; study of*	begg____, gram____, liar, school____, wiz____
-arium, -ary	*place for*	aqua____, aviary (for birds), diction____, libr____, planetarium
-ation	*state or quality of*	determination, imagine_____, inform_____, inspiration
-cle, -cule	*small*	cubicle, ici____, miniscule, mole_____, parti_____
-dom	*state or quality of*	boredom, free_____, king_____, wisdom
-ectomy	*surgical removal of*	adenoidectomy, append_____, tonsill_____
-ence, -ency, -ent	*state or quality of*	absence, differ_____, experience, intellig_____
-ent	*one who*	incident, presid_____, resident, superintend_____
-ense	*state, an item*	def____, expense, license, presents, susp____, tense
-er	*one who*	bak___, commander, charact__, teach__, painter, writ__
-ery, -ry	*occupation, trade*	archery, dentist_____, surg_____, brav_____
-ery	*establishment*	bak____, groc____, fishery, hatch_____
-ery, -ry	*goods,*	cutl____, jewelry, pott____ (2 t's keep vowel short)
-ery, -ry	*place or state of*	brave____, cemetery, dentist____, station____
-ess, -ress	*one who (female)*	act_____, hostess, princ_____, wait_____

More Noun Suffixes

-et, -t (m), **-ette** (f) *small*   bagette, eagle____, major____, midg____, owl<u>et</u>

-hood   *state, quality of*   adult<u>hood</u>, child____, false____, state____

-ian   *one who*   histor____, libr____, nonagenar<u>ian</u> (90-100 years)

-ics   *kind of system*   econom<u>ics</u>, phys____, polit____

-ier, -yer   *one who*   cash____, gondol<u>ier</u>, law____, sold____

-ine, -ide   *substance*   caffe____ (Keep <u>e</u>.), chlor<u>ine</u>, medic____, iod____

-ing   *material*   bedd<u>ing</u> (sheets, etc.), frost____, roof<u>ing</u>, stuff____

-ion   *state, quality of*   ambit<u>ion</u>, compan____, champ<u>ion</u>, suspic____

-ity   *state of*   curios____, divin<u>ity</u>, infin____, opportune____

-ization   *state, quality of*   civil____, standard<u>ization</u>, organ____

-let, -ling,   *small*   duck____, gos<u>ling</u>, leaf<u>let</u>, pamph<u>let</u>, year____

-ment   *action, quality of*   amuse____, govern____, predica<u>ment</u>, tourna____

-ment   *product or thing*   frag<u>ment</u>, instru____, orna~~te~~____, parlia____

-mony   *process or product*   cere____, matri____, testi<u>mony</u>

-ness   *state, quality of*   good<u>ness</u>, happi____, kind<u>ness</u>, quiet____, still____

-ology   *study of*   biol____, theol<u>ogy</u>, psych____, zoology

-or   *one who, state of*   act____, doct____, edit____, err<u>or</u>, sculpt____, splend<u>or</u>

-orium, -ory   *place for*   audit____, emp<u>orium</u>, conservat<u>ory</u>, laborat____

-phobia (Greek)   *fear of*   agora____, claustra____, arachno<u>phobia</u> (fear of spiders)

-s, -es, -ies   *makes plural*   heart__, cook<u>ies</u>, box__, dance__, parenthes<u>es</u>

-ship   *skill, art, quality of*   citizen____, horseman____, penman<u>ship</u>, friend____

-sion, -ion   *state, quality of*   inci<u>sion</u>, suspens~~e~~____, tens~~e~~____, televis~~e~~____

-tion   *state, quality of*   atten____, caution, imagina____, invent____

-tude   *state, quality of*   atti____, forti<u>tude</u> (strength; character), grati____

-t, -ty, -y   *state, quality of*   compan__, honest__, integri__, loyal__

-ure   *action, process, thing*   creat~~e~~____, expos<u>ure</u>, measure, pleas~~e~~____, treas____

Challenging Suffixes (-ar, -er -or)

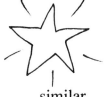

ar

altar	cellar	hangar (planes)	nectar	similar
beggar	circular	liar	particular	spectacular
burglar	collar	lunar	peculiar	sugar
calendar	dollar	molar	regular	vinegar
caterpillar	familiar	muscular	scholar	vulgar

er

alter	bolder	disaster	messenger	prisoner
announcer	boulder	employer	minister	singer
baker	carrier	hanger (clothes)	observer	soldier
beginner	debater	jeweler	officer	teacher
believer	defender	lawyer	partner	traveler
border	diameter	manager	passenger	writer

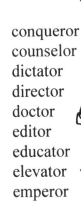

or

actor	conqueror	escalator	legislator	sailor
alligator	counselor	factor	major	sculptor
anchor	dictator	governor	minor	senator
author	director	harbor	motor	suitor
aviator (pilot)	doctor	humor	neighbor	superior
bachelor	editor	inferior	odor	supervisor
behavior	educator	inventor	pastor	tenor
collector	elevator	investigator	professor	traitor
competitor	emperor	janitor	protector	visitor

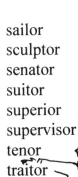

One More Challenging Set of Suffixes (-sion and –tion)

Words like *tension, caution, cushion,* and *fashion* all sound alike, but there are just too many to list. Here are a few that you can visually reinforce. Make up clues for the ones that are the most challenging.

sion

admission	extension	pretension	session
compulsion	incision	remission	suspension
expulsion	inclusion	revulsion	tension

tion

addiction	conviction	examination	initiation	nutrition
addition	coordination	explanation	inspiration	relaxation
caution	creation	fascination	intention	salvation
completion	desperation	imagination	nation	starvation

163

Two Sets of Challenging Suffixes (-ance, -ence, -ense, and -ar, -er, -or)

These words are challenging because they are pronounced the same way. Since they're used so often it's important to look at them very carefully so that you can store the correct spelling in your mind. Underline any ones that may seem difficult, and try to create clues for these.

-ance, -ant, -iance, -iant

abundance	appearance	elegance	insurance	remembrance
acceptance	attendance	endurance	maintenance	repentance
acquaintance	balance	entrance	nuisance	resistance
allegiance	brilliance	entrant	observance	significance
allowance	brilliant	guidance	performance	significant
ambulance	distance	instance	radiance	substance
annoyance	distant	instant	reliance	tolerance

-ence, -ent, -ience, -ient

The words with the pattern of cur**rent** or con**ference** are ALWAYS spelled **-ent** and **-ence**. Mark them

absent	conscience	excellent	interference	reference
audience	convenience	existence	obedience	residence
circumference	convenient	experience	occurrence	reverence
coincidence	correspondence	fence	patience	sentence
competent	dependent	incident	permanent	silence
completion	difference	influence	present	silent
conference	different	innocent	prudent (wise)	violence
confidence	evidence	insistence	recent	violent

-ense (There are only a few -ense words. Write down a *Power Spelling Tool* for each of these.)

defense	incense	offense	suspense
expense	intense	pretense	tense
immense	license	sense	

Suffixes Can Create Adjectives, Verbs and Adverbs

Now that you have learned that suffixes have the POWER to create nouns by adding endings to words like you see in *happiness* and *free*_dom_, let's learn more about the *POWER* that suffixes have to create adjectives, verbs, and adverbs. Let's take the words, *help* and *free* and see how suffixes create adjectives, verbs, and adverbs with these words.

NOUN: The child needed some *help* with her balloon. (Noun: some *help*)
ADJECTIVE: When the balloon escaped, he made a *helpless* cry. (Suffix-*less* creates adj. *helpless* cry)
VERB: We were *helping* him get the balloon out of the tree. (Suffix -*ing* creates verb: were *helping*)
ADVERB: He cried *helplessly* until we found the balloon in a tree. (Suffix-ly creates an adverb: cried helplessly)

NOUN: A bird has the *free*_dom_ to fly above everything. (Suffix -*dom* create a noun: the *freedom*.)
ADJ: This *free* bird was not caged. (free is an adjective added to bird: *free* bird)
VERB: She *freed, is freeing* the bird from the cage. (-*d*, -*ing* create verbs: She *freed, is freeing*)
ADVERB: The bird flew *freely*. (-*ly* creates an adverb added to the verb: flew *freely*.)

❏ **LET'S BUILD SOME WORDS:** Try the nouns below, and see how many adjectives, verbs and adverbs you can build with each word. Add any endings that will work. Notice that you can sometimes create additional adjective endings by adding -*er* or -*est*. Also, you can build additional verb endings by adding -*s*, -*ed*, -*ing* because the suffixes change the tense (present, past, future). Some of the words below can only be made into three parts of speech.

NOUN	ADJECTIVE	VERB	ADVERB
(person, place, thing, emotion…)	(Describes a noun, pronoun)	(Action or state of being)	(Describes action of verb)
The _____	The _____ person	I _____. You _____.	We worked _____.
care	*careful*	*cares, cared*, is *caring*	*carefully*
beauty			
description			
happiness			
life			
play			
treat			
wisdom			

Adjective Suffixes

❑ **NOW**: Complete the adjectives below. An adjective will always make sense when it's <u>added</u> to a noun or pronoun to describe it: A <u>*comfortable*</u> couch. The <u>*free*</u> bird. A <u>*helpful*</u> person.

SUFFIXES	MEANING	EXAMPLES
-able	*is, can be*	comfort_____, depend<u>able</u>, imagin_____, lov_____
-al, -an	*relating to*	Americ<u>an</u>, natur___, matern<u>al</u>, roy___, urban (city)
-ant	*inclined to*	buoy_____, pleas<u>ant</u>, significant, vac_____.
-ate	*state or quality of*	desper_____, fortun<u>ate</u>, passion_____
-en, -ent	*relating to*	differ_____, earthen, excell_____, gold___, wooden
-er	*more (comparative)*	mean<u>er</u>, pretti____, simpl____, smart<u>er</u>, wis____
-ern	*direction*	east_____, northern, south_____, western
-ese	*nationality or quality*	Chin_____, Japan<u>ese</u>, Vietnam_____
-esque	*relating to*	pictur<u>esque</u>, statue_____
-est	*most (superlative)*	mean____, pretti____, simpl____, smart<u>est</u>, wis___
-ful	*full of*	care____, grace<u>ful</u>, joy____, plenti<u>ful</u>, thought____
-ial, -ian	*relating to*	commerc<u>ial</u>, financ_____, spec_____
-ible	*is, can be*	digest_____, eligible, sens_____, vis<u>ible</u>
-ic, -ical	*relating to*	com<u>ic</u>, histor_____, ident<u>ical</u>, med_____, poet___
-id	*state or quality of*	cand<u>id</u>, rig____, splend____
-ile	*state or quality of*	ag<u>ile</u> (moves easily), docile (gentle), frag_____
-ine	*relating to*	fel_____, femin<u>ine</u>, mascul_____, marine (re: ocean)
-ious	*state or quality of*	ambit<u>ious</u>, consc____, grac___, myster___, precious
-ish	*relating to*	child_____, imp<u>ish</u>, Ir<u>ish</u>, Scott_____
-ive	*inclined to be*	act_____, affirmat<u>ive</u>, negat_____, pass<u>ive</u>
-less	*without*	age<u>less</u>, care_____, rest<u>less</u>, thought_____
-ly	*resembling*	brother__, father<u>ly</u>, mother__, scholar<u>ly</u>
-like	*resembling*	child_____, life_____,
-ly	*every*	annual____, dai<u>ly</u>, month____, week<u>ly</u>, year____
-ous	*full of*	joy<u>ous</u>, virtu_____, wondr_____
-some	*inclined to*	awe<u>some</u>, gruesome, lone_____, tire_____
-th, -eth	*numbers*	four<u>th</u>, nin___ (9th), twenti_____, sixti_____

-ular	relating to	cellular, circ_____, pop_____
-ulent	full of	turbulent (stirred up: turbulent sea), fraud_____ (dishonest)
-uous	state or quality of	sens_____, tempestuous (wild like a tempest)
-ward, -wards	direction	backwards, for_____, east_____, toward, upward
-y	state or quality of	happy, fun___, rain___, sunny, thirst__

Verb Suffixes

The *verb* is the *action* that the noun or pronoun in the sentence does: We *freed* the bird. Dad *helped*.

SUFFIX	MEANING	EXAMPLES
-ade, -age	action or process	block_____, parade, pill_____, ravage
-ate	to do or make	activ_____, fascinate, hesitate, illustr_____
-ed, -d	past tense	beautified, dance__, discovered, shelter__, walk___
-en, -n	completed action	eaten, giv____, prov____, seen, tak____
-er	action or process	conquer, deliv____, discov____, rememb____
-fy	to do or make	beauty____, electrify, quali____, satisfy, terri____
-ine	to do or make	determine, imag_____
-ing	continuous action	ask_____, dancing, jump____, playing, sing_____
-ish	action or process	fin_____, nourish, pun_____, refurnish
-ise	to do or make	advertise, adv_____, arise, exerc____, surpr_____
-ize	to do or make	computerize, energ_____, final_____, visual_____
-ure	action or process	endure, meas_____, pleas_____, treas_____

Adverb Suffixes

An adverb is a word that is added to a verb to tell the manner or way something is done. He *always* worked. The bird flew *freely*. He cried *helplessly* until they got his balloon out of a tree.

SUFFIXES	MEANING	EXAMPLES
-ly	how something is done	beautiful___, comfortab___, gently, gracious___
	(changes adj. to adv)	ordinarily, quiet___, unusually, weak___, week___
-ways	manner or way	al_____, crossways, side_____
-wise	manner, direction	clockwise, length_____, time_____

Some Challenging Adjective Suffixes (-able and -ible)

Since these adjectives are so commonly used, take a good look at them and keep storing them visually. You may already know a lot of them. Underline any words that seem difficult, and try to create clues for these. Sometimes other word forms can give you the best clue to the spelling.

acceptable	dependable	laughable	profitable
available	desirable	likable	readable
avoidable	drinkable	lovable	reliable
believable	eatable-table	noticeable-notation	seasonable
breakable	fashionable	perishable	transportable-transportation
capable-capacity	favorable	pleasurable	usable
changeable (soft g)	imaginable-imagination	predictable	valuable-valuation
comfortable	irritable-irritation	presentable-presentation	workable

ible If you are not left with a complete word when you drop the suffix, the spelling is usually -ible. Also, if -ion could be added to the base and make sense, as in *collection*, the spelling is -ible. Also, after c or g, the i keeps these letters soft.

collectible-collection	divisible-division	invisible-vision	responsible-responsive
convertible-conversion	eligible	legible	reversible-reversion
destructible-destruction	horrible-horrific	negligible	sensible
digestible-digestion	impossible	permissible-permission	terrible-terrific
dirigible (blimp, n)	intelligible	possible	visible-vision

Some Challenging Verb Suffixes (-ise, -ize, and -yze)

There is a small group of *-ise* words, only two *-yze* words, and then several hundred *-ize* words.

-ise

cise: circumcise, exercise
prise: enterprise, surprise
rise: arise, moonrise, rise, sunrise
mise: compromise, promise
tise: advertise, chastise,
vise: advise, advertise, supervise-supervision

-yze There are only four words: analyze, catalyze, electrolyze, and paralyze.

-ize Most of the several hundred remaining words are *-ize*

computerize	characterize-characterization	finalize-finality	realize-realization,
authorize-authorization	energize	popularize-popularity	visualize-visualization...

Let's Connect Nouns, Verbs, Adjectives, and Adverbs

LET'S CONNECT GAME: You've learned that suffixes can *turn* a root into all four parts of speech: *free, freedom, frees, freely.* Since all you need for a sentence is a noun and a verb, see what kinds of crazy sentences you can make: *Play, plays; Thoughts think.* Then you can add adjectives to nouns and adverbs to verbs (and also put a determiner before the noun): *The playful play plays playfully; The thoughtful thought thinks thoughtfully.* Suffixes give you *freedom* to use a word in many ways!

❑   **TO PLAY**: Choose a word from each list. Then connect your words to make sentences. Use the same root for all the words *or choose different roots.* Have fun connecting words you've never tried before. Write ten or more sentences.

Determiners and Possessive Words	Adjectives	Nouns	Verbs	Adverbs
the	playful	play, players	plays, played	playfully
a	beautiful	beauty	beautifies	beautifully
an	careful	care	cares	carefully
my	active	act, action, actors	acts	actively
our	restful	rest	rests	restfully
your	free	freedom	frees	freely
his	quiet	quietness	quiets, quieted	quietly
her	lively	life	live, lived	lively
their	brave	brave, bravery	braves, braved	bravely
	thoughtful	thought, thinkers	thinks, thought	thoughtfully
	icy	icicle	ices, iced	icily
	imaginative	imagination	imagines	imaginatively
	joyful	joy	enjoys	joyfully
	lovely, loving	love, lovers	loves	lovingly
	mysterious	mystery	mystifies	mysteriously
	powerful	power	empowers	powerfully
	descriptive	description	describes	descriptively
	sleepy	sleep, sleepers	sleeps, slept	sleepily
	timely	time, timers	times, timed	timely
	gentle	gentleness	(holds, held)	gently
	kind	kindness	(rocks, rocked)	kindly
	happy	happiness	happens	happily
	patient	patience	(gives)	patiently
	peaceful	peace	(hopes)	peacefully
	starry	star	stars, starred	(brightly)
	wise	wisdom	(wishes, wished)	wisely

The Doubling Final Consonants Rule
for One-Syllable Words and for Words with More Than One Syllable

The DOUBLING FINAL CONSONANTS RULE is a great spelling rule that ALWAYS works (except for *excellent* and *excellence*). This rule tells you when to double the final consonant before a suffix that begins with a vowel (-ed, -en, -er, -est, -ing...) Two parts of the rule work for all words. A third point about the accent (the beat) is added for words with more than one syllable.

Even though this rule's a little challenging, get to know it, because it gives you true spelling POWE Let's look first at one-syllable words, and then look at two-syllable words.

The Doubling Final Consonants Rule
for One-Syllable Words

---

1. If a one-syllable word **ends with a single consonant**; and
2. If the **consonant has a single short vowel before it**; then:
   Double the final consonant before adding a suffix that begins with a vowel (-ed, -en, -er, -est, -ing..

Double the final consonant for the words: hop-hopped   star-starred;   swim-swimming;
Do not double consonant for the words: hope-hoped   stare-stared;   play-playing;

The word **hop** is a one-syllable word.
   that ends with a single consonant: **p**.
It's preceded by a single short vowel: **o**, so
Double the consonant: **hopped, hopping**.

The word **swim** is a one-syllable word.
   that ends with a single consonant: **m**.
It's preceded by a single short vowel: **i**, so
Double the consonant: **swimming, swimmer**.

"We're m and m!"

"Let's d...dou!

❑ **TRY THIS:** Follow the Doubling Rule to add suffixes to these words:

drum	_____ ed	_____ ing	_____ er
red	_____ er	_____ est	_____ en
stop	_____ ed	_____ ing	_____ er

NOTE: Double the consonant after a single vowel (before adding a vowel suffix) to keep the vowel short

❑ **TRY THIS:** Now that you know the two parts of the *Doubling Final Consonant Rule*, write one reason why each of the words below *does not* double the consonant before adding suffixes -ed and -ing.

dance	danced	dancing:	*Dance ends in a silent e, not a consonant.*
live	lived	living:	
play	played	playing:	
rain	rained	raining:	

170

□ **TO LEARN MORE:** Use the *Doubling Final Consonants Rule* to decide whether or not you should double the final consonant (before adding vowel suffixes) for these one-syllable words.

bar _____ed _____ing

bare _____ed _____ing

bug _____ed _____ing

chase _____ed _____ing

cool _____ed _____ing _____er _____est

hop _____ed _____ing

hope _____ed _____ing

hug _____ed _____ing

like _____ed _____ing

live _____ed _____ing _____er

low (w = vowel) _____er _____est

rob _____ed _____ing _____er

robe _____ed _____ing

scar _____ed _____ing

scare _____ed _____ing

slam _____ed _____ing

sled _____ed _____ing _____er

star _____ed _____ing

stare _____ed _____ing

toast _____ed _____ing _____er

trot _____ed _____ing

win _____(*won*) _____ing _____er

write_____(*wrote*) _____ing _____er (have)_____en

NOTE: **Write** ends in <u>silent e</u>, so follow the *Silent E Rule* to add suffixes: **writing, writer**. After **have**, the word **write** changes to **written**. Since **written** has a short **i**, the consonant needs to be doubled.

The Doubling Final Consonants Rule
for Words with More than One Syllable

The first two parts of *The Doubling Final Consonants Rule for One-Syllable Words* are the same as the *Rule for Words with More than One-Syllables*. Just add a third point about the accent (strongest beat).

---

1. If a word with more than one syllable **ends in a single consonant**; and
2. If **the consonant has a single short vowel before it**; and
3. If, when the word is completed, **the accent falls on the last syllable of the original word**, then: **Double the final consonant** before a suffix that begins with a vowel (-ed, -en, -er, -est, -ing…)

The word **be-gin** has more than one syllable.
   and ends with a single consonant: **n**
It's preceded by a single short vowel: **i**.
When the word is completed, the accent falls
   on the last syllable of **be-gin**; so
Double the final consonant: **beginning, beginner**

The word **oc-cur** has more than one syllable
   and ends with a single consonant: **r**
It's preceded by a single short vowel: **u**.
When the word is completed, the accent falls
   on the last syllable of **oc-cur**; so
Double the final consonant: **occurred, occurrin**

"We're just beginning!"   "WE'RE... and"

❑ **CHECK THAT ACCENT**: For each word, ask: When the suffix has been added, will the accent (strongest beat) fall on the last syllable of the original word? If it will, then double the final consonant before adding a suffix that begins with a vowel.

ad – mit	_____ ed	_____ ing	_____ *admittance* (Accent fall on mit-.)
dif – fer	_____ ed	_____ ing	_____ *difference* (Accent falls on dif-.)
e – quip	_____ ed	_____ ing	_____ *equipment* (Suffix starts w/consona)
oc – cur	_____ ed	_____ ing	_____ *occurrence* (Accent falls on cur-.)

❑ **NOW**: Mark the accent for each word and explain why you <u>did not double the final consonant</u>. REMEMBER: If the accent falls on the last syllable of the original word, double the final consonant before adding a vowel suffix. If it doesn't, don't double the final consonant.

level	leveled	leveling	*The accent falls on <u>le</u>, not <u>vel</u>.*
gallop	galloped	galloping	
excite	excited	exciting	
travel	traveled	traveling	

□ **LET'S REVIEW:** Complete this rule in your own words: You double the final consonant for words with more than one syllable when –

---

1. If a word with more than one syllable **ends in a single consonant**; and
2. If **the consonant has a single short vowel before it**; and
3. If, when the word is completed, **the beat falls on the last syllable of the original word**, then:
   Double the final consonant before a suffix that begins with a vowel (-ed, -en, -er, -est, -ing…)

REMEMBER: Double the final consonant before adding a suffix ONLY if the accent falls on the last syllable of the original word,

" ♯ for two and two for ♯

□ **NOW:** Use the *Doubling Final Consonants Rule* to add suffixes.

admit _____ ed _____ ing

blossom _____ ed _____ ing

commit _____ ed _____ ing

control _____ ed _____ ing

differ _____ ed _____ ing

enter _____ ed _____ ing

happen _____ ed _____ ing

forget ____*forgotten*____ ing _____ er

occur _____ ed _____ ing _____ ence

propel _____ ed _____ ing _____ er

patrol _____ ed _____ ing

travel _____ ed _____ ing _____ er

(For travel, both the American and British spellings are in the dictionary. The American spelling is: traveled, traveling. The British spelling is: *travelled, travelling*. In America, it's best to learn and use the American spelling.)

excel _____ ed _____ ing _____ ence _____ ent

(*Excellence* and *excellent* are the only two exceptions. *Clue*: We showed excellence on our cell report and rated excellent!)

Excellent

EXCEPTION!

Words that Change the Beat

☐ **TRY THIS CHALLENGE:** Three of these *-fer words* and *excel-* change their accent (strongest beat) depending on the suffix that's added. Complete these words and then mark the beat. Only double the consonant if the accent falls on the last syllable of the original word. (See answers below.)

confer _____ ed   _____ ing   _____ ence

differ _____ ed   _____ ing   _____ ence   _____ en

prefer _____ ed   _____ ing   _____ enc

refer _____ ed   _____ ing   _____ ence   _____ al

excel _____ ed   _____ · ing   _____ ence / _____ en

Doubling the Final Consonant
Short Vowel Words that Double and Silent E Words that Don't

These pairs of words help you see when you double the final consonant and when you don't. When one-syllable word ends in a single consonant, preceded by a single short vowel, ALWAYS double the final consonant. If a word ends in silent e, NEVER double the consonant. (For some reason, there are lots of pairs of <u>a</u>, <u>i</u>, and <u>o</u> words; but it's not the same for <u>e</u> and <u>u</u>.) Add any extra words you wish.

<u>a</u>	<u>e</u>	<u>i</u>	<u>o</u>	<u>u</u>
bar-barred	her	fin-finned	cop-copped	cub
bare-bared	here	fine-fined	cope-coped	cube-cubed
scrap-scrapped	met	grip-gripped	dot-dotted	cut
scrape-scraped	mete-meted	gripe-griped	dote-doted	cute
star-starred	them	pin-pinned	hop-hopped	hug-hugged
stare-stared	theme	pine-pined	hope-hoped	huge
tap-tapped		slim- slimmed	rob-robbed	lube-lubed
tape-taped		slime-slimed	robe-robed	rub-rubbed
wag-wagged		strip-stripped	slop-slopped	tub-tubbed
wage-waged		stripe-striped	slope-sloped	tube-tubed

ANSWERS for *Words that Change the Beat*: confer: conferred, conferring, conference; differ: differed, differing, difference; prefer: preferred, preferring, preference; refer: referred, referring, reference, referral; excel: excelled, excelling (*Excellence* and *excellent* = only two exceptions. They keep <u>*ll*</u>.)

174

Suffixes Make Nouns Plural in Many Ways

To learn about the ways suffixes make nouns plural, let's journey back in time to before 900 A.D. where you'll find basic Old English plurals: *men, women, children, calves, dwarfs, elves, halves.* Then let's move forward to French and Latin plurals (1100-1350): *democracies, families, libraries*; and on to the Renaissance (1500s) when Latin and Greek plurals were added by writers and scientists: *media, nuclei...* Along the way, you'll meet Norse words: *shirts, skies*; Algonquian Indian plurals: *buffaloes, canoes...*; Spanish words: *mosquitoes, rodeos...*; some Italian musical plurals: *pianos, solos...*, and even an Arabic plural: *zeroes* or *zeros...* A whole mixing pot of plurals!

<u>Most words, though, form their plural by simply adding good old -s.</u>

Since some plurals can be challenging, they're divided into eight groups below. *Clues* are included to help you remember these. Have fun discovering these plurals from many different times and places.

(1) PLURALS FOR NOUNS ENDING IN O

Most Spanish/Indian nouns with <u>no vowel before the -o, add -es</u>		When a vowel comes before <u>the final -o, simply add -s</u>		Italian musical nouns add -s. <u>Add s for auto, banjo and hello</u>	
buffalo	buffaloes (Ind)	patio	patios (Sp)	alto	pianos (Ita.)
mosquito	mosquitoes (Sp)	rodeo	rodeos (Sp.)	piano	pianos (Ita.)
potato	potatoes (Ind, Sp)	cameo	cameos (Fr)	solo	solos (Ita.)
tomato	tomatoes (Sp)	radio	radios (Fr)	soprano	sopranos (Ita.)
tornado	tornadoes (Ind, Sp)	studio	studios (L)	banjo	banjos (Jamaican)
volcano	volcanoes (Sp)	video	videos (L)	auto	autos (L.)

(MORE O PLURALS: <u>Greek/Latin</u>: echo: echoes; hero: heroes; torpedo: torpedoes * <u>Arabic</u>: zero: zeroes, zeros * <u>British</u>: hello: hellos * <u>Spanish</u> (os endings): bronco: broncos, avocado: avocados, poncho: ponchos * <u>Eskimo</u>: Eskimos. NOTE: Cameos are French carvings made on stone and used for jewelry.)

❑ **LET'S TRY SOME *POWER CLUES***: Since <u>nouns that end in *-oes*</u> get misspelled so often, let's create clues for *-oes* words. Some ideas are below, but try your own clues first.

1. canoes   

2. echoes

3. heroes

4. mosquitoes

5. potatoes

6. tomatoes

7. tornadoes

8. volcanoes

Also: Create a sentence that uses the Italian musical words: <u>altos</u>, <u>pianos</u>, <u>solos</u> and <u>sopranos</u>.

(Are there any hol<u>es</u> in the <u>canoes</u>? My <u>echo</u> <u>goes</u> away; then <u>echoes</u> back; <u>Heroes</u> play many <u>roles</u>; <u>Mosquitoes</u> keep biting my <u>toes</u>; <u>Potatoes</u> have ey<u>es</u> and <u>toes</u>; do <u>tomatoes</u> too; The wind power of <u>tornadoes</u> <u>does</u> damage; The lava from <u>volcanoes</u> <u>goes</u> out the vent at the top.)

(2) PLURALS FOR NOUNS ENDING IN F OR FE: Most of these words are Old English. These Old English words that end in *-f* or *-fe* form the plural by adding *-s*.

| cliff | cliffs | belief | beliefs | roof | roofs |
| dwarf | dwarfs | grief | grief (same form) | hoof | hoofs (or hooves) |

(Verbs are spelled <u>believe</u> and <u>believes</u>; <u>grieve</u> and <u>grieves</u>.)

The words below that end in *-f* or *-fe* change the *-f* to *-v* and then add *-es* to form the plural.

calf	calves	life	lives	wife	wives
elf	elves	loaf	loaves	wolf	wolves
half	halves	self	selves (ourselves)	knife	knives
leaf	leaves	thief	thieves	shelf	shelves

❑ **MORE *POWER CLUES***: Let's create *Clues* for words that change from *-f* to *-fe* and *-f* to *-ves*.

1. beliefs
2. calves
3. dwarfs
4. elves, shelves
5. halves
6. knives

7. leaves
8. lives
9. loaves
10. thieves
11. wives
12. wolves

(3) PLURALS FOR NOUNS ENDING IN Y: Most of these words are French and Latin. Form the plural for a noun ending in *-y* preceded by a consonant by changing the *y* to *i* and adding *-es*.

baby	babies	country	countries	library	libraries
candy	candies	democracy	democracies	pony	ponies
city	cities	family	families	sky	skies (Norse)

Form the plural for a noun ending in *-y* preceded by a vowel by simply adding *-s*.

| key | keys | chimney | chimneys | turkey | turkeys |
| play | plays | journey | journeys | valley | valleys |

(Don't have <u>beliefs</u> in <u>lies</u>; <u>Calvin</u> has se<u>ven</u> <u>calves</u>; Old <u>dwarfs</u> were at <u>war</u> for <u>silver</u>; <u>Elves</u> were hiding on my <u>shelves</u>; Cut the ol<u>ives</u> into <u>halves</u>; <u>Knives</u> can take <u>lives</u>; There are <u>leaves</u> in my <u>eaves</u>; He <u>lives</u> to <u>give</u> kindness; Put <u>a</u> in the middle of <u>love</u> for <u>loaves</u>; <u>Thieves</u> come out on dark <u>eves</u>; As I...St. <u>Ives</u>, I...seven <u>wives</u>; Two <u>wolves</u> can <u>love</u> for life

176

(4) PLURALS FOR NOUNS ENDING IN CH, S, X, OR SH

Nouns that end in *-ch, -s, -sh -x,* or *-z* form their plural by adding *-es*. Simply adding *s* would create a pronunciation problem where you couldn't even say the word.

bench	benches	buzz	buzzes	loss	losses
bush	bushes	dish	dishes	pass	passes
box	boxes	fox	foxes	watch	watches

(5) NOUNS THAT HAVE IRREGULAR PLURALS

The plurals of some nouns are formed in irregular ways. Here, *Ancient Roots* come in since some of these nouns are basic Old English words before 900 A.D. Others were borrowed from ancient Greek and Latin (with their plurals) during the Renaissance (1500 +) and used for philosophy, writing, and science.

NOUNS FROM OLD ENGLISH (before 900 A.D.)   NOUNS FROM GREEK and LATIN ROOTS (1500 +)

brother	brethren	man	men	alumnus	alumni	medium	media
child	children	mouse	mice	axis	axes	oasis	oases
foot	feet	ox	oxen	basis	bases	nucleus	nuclei
goose	geese	tooth	teeth	crisis	crises	radius	radii
louse	lice	woman	women	hypothesis	hypotheses	stimulus	stimuli

(6) THE PLURALS OF COMPOUND NOUNS

For solid (one word) compound words, just add an *-s* at the end. For open or hyphenated compound words, make the base word (coasters, brother, mother...) plural.

buttercup	buttercups	roller coaster	roller coasters
grandfather	grandfathers	brother-in-law	brothers-in-law
snowflake	snowflakes	mother-in-law	mothers-in-law
jukebox	jukeboxes	runner-up	runners-up

(7) THE PLURAL OF NUMBERS, LETTERS, SIGNS, ETC.

The plural of numbers, letters, signs, etc., is formed by adding an apostrophe and *-s*.

12's	12's	+	+'s	ABC	ABC's
100	100's	7	7's	j	j's

(8) NOUNS THAT STAY THE SAME IN BOTH THE SINGULAR AND PLURAL

Some basic Old English words (before 900 A.D.) for animals, fish, and grain stay the same in the plural. Also, some nouns for measurement, groups, races and nationalities stay the same.

ANIMALS or FISH		GRAIN	MEASURES or GROUPS		RACES
fish	deer	barley	bunch	group	British
salmon	moose	rye	dozen	party	Chinese
cattle	sheep	wheat	gross	series	French
chicken	swine (pigs)	milk	ton	traffic	Japanese

(Other nouns that stay the same in the plural, are <u>underlined</u> in the *Collective Nouns* below.)

Collective Nouns

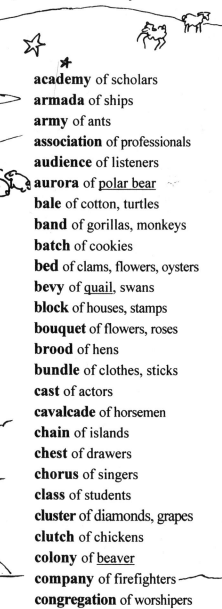

academy of scholars
armada of ships
army of ants
association of professionals
audience of listeners
aurora of <u>polar bear</u>
bale of cotton, turtles
band of gorillas, monkeys
batch of cookies
bed of clams, flowers, oysters
bevy of <u>quail</u>, swans
block of houses, stamps
bouquet of flowers, roses
brood of hens
bundle of clothes, sticks
cast of actors
cavalcade of horsemen
chain of islands
chest of drawers
chorus of singers
class of students
cluster of diamonds, grapes
clutch of chickens
colony of <u>beaver</u>
company of firefighters
congregation of worshipers
constellation of stars

convocation of eagles
cord of wood
corps of marines
council of advisors
covey of doves
crew of sailors
deck of cards
drove of <u>cattle</u> (also herd)
exultation of larks
faculty of teachers
fleet of cars, ships
flight of planes
flock of birds, seagulls <u>sheep</u>
flush of ducks
gaggle of geese
galaxy of stars
grove of trees
herd of <u>buffalo</u>, cows, <u>deer</u>, <u>moose</u>
herd of pigs, <u>reindeer</u>, seals, <u>sheep</u>
hive of bees
host of angels
litter of kittens, puppies
mob of kangaroo(s)
nest of mice, snakes, spiders
network of computers
orchestra of instruments
pack of <u>bear</u>, dogs, lies, mules

pack of gum, matches, wolves
panel of experts
parliament of owls
plague of locusts
pod of whales
pride of lions
range of mountains
rookery of penguins
school of <u>bass</u>, <u>fish</u>, <u>porpoise</u>, <u>salm</u>
set of dishes, glasses
shelf of books
shock of hair
slew of homework
sloth of <u>bear</u>
snarl of traffic
stack of pancakes
staff of employees
stash of nuts, coins
string of pearls
swarm of bees, reporters
team of athletes, horses, oxen
town of prairie dogs
tribe of Indians
troop of kangaroo(s), scouts
troupe of performer
wave of emotions
wealth of information

Challenging L Endings: -al, -el, -le, -il, -ol

Do I spell it *-al, -el, -le,* or *-il?* It's easy to spell "it," but the Challenging **L** Endings cause lots of confusion because they all sound alike. Fortunately, *POWER Spelling Tools* can help you hear and remember which suffix a word has. *Other Word Forms* help you *hear* L Endings (royal-royally; crumble-crumbly) and *Clues* and *Roots* help you remember and understand which L Ending to spell.

-AL Can Turn Nouns and Roots into Adjectives that Mean "Concerning"

bridal: concerning brides (bride + al)

global: concerning global things (globe + al).

tidal: concerning tides (tide + al).

educational: concerning education (education + al)

medical: concerning medicine (medicine + al)

royal: concerning royalty: kings, queens (roy + al)

OTHER WORD FORMS: You can also *turn* each adjective above (except bridal) into an adverb by adding the adverb suffix -<u>ly</u>: *globally, tidally, medically, educationally, royally.*

❑ **TRY THIS**: Add suffix -<u>al</u> to *turn* these nouns and roots into adjectives that mean *concerning.* Then, add adverb suffix -<u>ly</u> to *turn* the adjectives into adverbs. The spelling is always -<u>al</u> and -<u>ally</u>.

addition + al = *additional, additionally*

magic + al =

origin + al =

tribal: + al =

leg- (*L. law*) + al =

manu- (*L. hand*) + al =

nautic-: (*L. ships*) + al =

species- (*L. species*) + al =

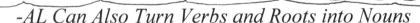

-AL Can Also Turn Verbs and Roots into Nouns

❑ **NOW**: Fill in the blanks and see how *Clues, Rules,* and *OWF's* help you remember -<u>AL</u> Words.

arrival: I awaited <u>Val</u>'s _ _ _ _ _ _ _ _ . *Rule*: Drop Silent <u>e</u> before -al: arriv<del>e</del> + al = _ _ _ _ _ _ _ _ .

capital (city): The _ _ _ _ _ _ _ _ , <u>Tallahassee</u>, is in Florida. **capital** (lette)r: A _ _ _ _ _ _ _ letter is <u>tall</u>.
Capitol (building): The _ _ _ _ _ _ _ building has a d<u>o</u>me (shaped like <u>o</u>) on top.

hospital: An <u>a</u>mbulance raced to the _ _ _ _ _ _ _ _ . *OWF*: In <u>hospitality</u>, hear the _ in _ _ _ _ _ _ _ _ .

medal: Ed and Al each wore a _ _ _ _ _ . *OWF*: A <u>medal</u>lion is a large _ _ _ _ _ .

metal: *OWF*: Something _ _ _ _ _ is <u>metal</u>lic.

pedal: *OWF*: I'm not dallying, I'm <u>pedal</u>ing the _ _ _ _ _ fast.

petal: My <u>pet al</u>ways eats a _ _ _ _ _ or two.

recital: I saw <u>tal</u>ent at the _ _ _ _ _ _ _ . *Rule*: Drop silent <u>e</u> before -<u>al</u>: recit<del>e</del> + al = _ _ _ _ _ _ _ .

signal: The stop sign <u>always</u> helps _ _ _ _ _ _ us. *Rule*: Just dd -<u>al</u> to the root: <u>sign</u> + <u>al</u> = _ _ _ _ _ _ .

total: *OWF*: The final _ _ _ _ _ of <u>al</u>l the toys is the <u>total</u>ity we have to give away.

The -LE Ending Forms Consonant + LE Syllables: -ble, -ple, -tle

❑ **NOW**: Add some C + LE words to this list. You can try rhyming words with other words below: *crumble, jumble...* (Be careful: Some rhyming words are spelled with other l endings: *label, mental...*)

BLE	CLE	DLE	FLE	GLE	KLE	PLE	TLE	ZLE
humble	article	bridle	baffle	eagle	ankle	apple	gentle	dazzle
marble	circle	candle	muffle	mingle	freckle	maple	kettle	drizzle
pebble	cuticle	cradle	raffle	mingle	tickle	people	shuttle	sizzle
scribble	particle	ladle	sniffle	single	twinkle	ripple	throttle	nuzzle
stable	vehicle	saddle	trifle	tangle	wrinkle	simple	whittle	puzzle

❑ **TRY THIS**: Fill in the blanks and try these *Clues, OWF's* and *SPP's* for -LE Words.

article: I wrote a clear _ _ _ _ _ _ _ on art: art + I + cle. *SPP*: _ _ - _ _ - _ _ _ .

bridled (for horse): I _ _ _ _ _ _ _ and led my horse with a _ _ _ _ _ _ . *OWF*: bridling.

disciple: The kick boxer helped his _ _ _ _ _ _ _ _ learn discipline. *OWF*: discipline, discipling.

fable: The _ _ _ _ _ blessed us all with truth. *SPP*: _ _ - _ _ _ . *OWF*: fabling (to write fables).

kettle: Let Polly put the _ _ _ _ _ _ on. *SPP*: _ _ _ - _ - _ _ .

mantle (cloak): The man had a _ _ _ _ _ _ of leather. *SPP*: _ _ _ - _ _ _ .

muscle: Uncle Clem cleverly clenches each _ _ _ _ _ _ ? *SPP*: _ _ _ - _ _ _ . *OWF*: muscling

trouble: I got hit during the _ _ _ _ _ _ _ and bleds. *SPP*: _ _ _ - _ _ _ . *OWF*: troubling.

uncle: _ _ _ _ _ Clem is clever. *SPP*: _ _ - _ _ _ .

The -IL Ending is Found in Only Five Words

❑ **NOW**: Two -IL Words concern writing: *stencil, pencil*; 2 involve citizens: *civil, council*; and the last says: *Live* not by *evil*: (*Reversal*: evil – live). Fill in the blanks and learn -*IL Clues* and *OWF's*.

civil: Civilized people act in _ _ _ _ _ ways. Civic, a palindrome, has the same *Roots* as _ _ _ _ _ _ .

council: The _ _ _ _ _ _ _ member was ill. (The *Homophone* counsel means to see and help people.)

evil: Do not live life in an _ _ _ _ way. Live is _ _ _ _ spelled in reverse.

pencil: I use a _ _ _ _ _ _ to illustrate. *OWF*: She is penciling in a _ _ _ _ _ _ drawing.

stencil: I _ _ _ _ _ _ _ and illustrate with my pen _ _ _ . *OWF*: I am stenciling a _ _ _ _ _ _ _ .

The -EL Suffix Once Meant Small

English gained these -EL words from French. Two suffixes (-elle, -ella) once made words mean *small.*

chapel (capella): small church; part of a church

hovel (hovelle): small, very humble dwelling

quarrel (quarrella): a small fight

model (modelle): small copy of something

morsel (morselle): small amount; tidbit

novel (novella): short or small novel

panel (panelle): individual pane of (wood, glass…)

parcel (parcelle): a small package

satchel (satchelle): a small bag; small suitcase

towel (towella): small cloth for drying

trowel (truella): small tool for plaster or gardening

tunnel (tunnelle): small underground passage

It's fun to think of an **ELF** using these *small things.*

Kernel (*corn*) and nickel (Old English) are *small* things too, plus vessel (*Latin, small tube: vein, artery…*).

-EL Suffixes: -Del, -Mel, -Nel, -Vel, -Wel… Make Great Clues

❏ **NOW**: Fill in the blanks to see how *SPP's*, *Clues*, and *OWF's* help you hear and remember EL.

camel: The _ _ _ _ _ came to his knees for M_ _ : came + l = _ _ _ _ _ . *SPP:* _ _ – _ _ _ .

cancel: Please _ _ _ _ _ _ my celery order. *SPP:* _ _ _ – _ _ _ . *OWF:* cancellation

channel: Ch _ _ and N_ _ swam the _ _ _ _ _ _ _ : Chan + Nel = _ _ _ _ _ _ _ . *SPP:* _ _ _ _ – _ _ _ .

counsel: We selected our _ _ _ _ _ _ _ carefully. *SPP:* _ _ _ _ – _ _ _ . *OWF:* counselor

kennel: K _ _ and N _ _ run a _ _ _ _ _ _ : Ken + Nel = _ _ _ _ _ _ . *SPP:* _ _ _ – _ _ _ .

jewel: My prize ewe (female sheep) wears a _ _ _ _ _ around her neck. *SPP:* _ _ _ – _ _ .

level: Eve wants it _ _ _ _ _ . *Visual:* _ _ _ _ _ is a palindrome (same both ways). *SPP:* _ _ – _ _ _ .

mantel: Can a man tell if he wants his _ _ _ _ _ _ above the fireplace? *SPP:* _ _ _ – _ _ _ .

model: D _ _ is a _ _ _ _ _ . *SPP:* _ _ – _ _ _ . *OWF:* Del _ _ _ _ _ s a nice mode (style) of dress.

sentinel: I sent Nel a sign from the _ _ _ _ _ _ _ _: sent + I + Nel. *SPP:* _ _ _ _ – _ – _ _ _ .

shovel: Shove that _ _ _ _ _ _ and _ _ _ _ _ _ the snow for V _ _ da. *SPP:* _ _ _ – _ _ _ .

towel: To welcome them, we put out a fresh guest _ _ _ _ _ : to + welcome. *SPP:* _ _ – _ _ _ .

travel: Velda likes to _ _ _ _ _ _ down the _ _ _ nue. *SPP:* _ _ _ – _ _ _ . *OWF:* traveling.

vessel: Which _ _ _ _ _ _ hold less: a vein or artery? (4 letters reversed = less.) *SPP:* _ _ _ – _ _ _ .

Summary of Memory Tools for L Suffixes -al, -el, -le, -il, and -ol

-AL *turns* some nouns and roots into adjectives that mean *concerning*: *tidal, accidental, tribal*...
-Al is the only suffix that *can turn* verbs and roots into other nouns: *proposal, medal, petal*.
CLUES: Use -AL words: *I see talent at recitals; Capital letters are tall; Tallahassee's a capital city.*
OTHER WORD FORMS: Suffix -ly helps you hear -al: *accidentally, magically*.
Suffixes -ty and -ture help you hear -al: *originality, personality, signature*.

-EL *turns* some roots into nouns and verbs ending in: -del, -nel, -wel...: *model, panel, towel, jewel*.
Say these words slowly: *mo-del, pa-nel, to-wel*... and you can hear the -EL sound.
Suffixes -elle and -ella were added to words to mean *small*: *parcelle* (small package); *morselle* (small bite).
CLUES: Use: *Del, Mel, Nel*... for *Clues*: *Del's a model; Chan and Nel ran a news channel*.
NOTE: The -EL word *level* is a palindrome (the same backwards and forwards).
OTHER WORD FORMS: Suffix -ing helps you hear -el: *shoveling, traveling*.

-LE is the *L suffix with the most words*. It has a special Consonant + LE Syllable which is made from -LE + the Consonant before it: *cir-cle, crum-ble, ket-tle, peb-ble, sin-gle, puz-zle*...
Also, suffix -able *turns* some nouns and verbs into nouns and adjectives: *miser-able, not-able*.
CLUES: Use words with -LE: *Clench your muscle; Clever Uncle Clem; That fable blessed me*.
OTHER WORD FORMS: Suffixes -ing and -ly help you hear l right after a consonant: *crumbly, bridling, miserably, notably, simply, singly, troubling, twinkling*...

-IL is found in *only* 5 words: Two concern writing; *pencil* and *stencil*; two involve citizens: *civil* and *council*; and one reminds you: *Live* not by *evil*.
CLUES: Use words with -IL: *A pencil and stencil illustrate things; a council member was ill*.
OTHER WORD FORMS: Suffix -ing helps you hear -IL: *penciling, stenciling*...
Add suffix -ize to *civil*, and you can hear -il: *civilization, civilizing* (Note: 4 i's).

-OL is a suffix for: *gambol* (play), *idol, symbol, Capitol* (bldg.): *A Capitol has a dome on top*.

Choose the Correct L Suffix: -al, -el, -le, -il, -ol

□ **NOW**: Draw on *Memory Tools* and underline the correct word in each set. Cross out wrong words.

artical	article	hospitol	hospital	shovel	shoval	traval	travel
chaple	chapel	single	singel	pedal	pedel	panel	panal
channel	channal	pensil	pencil	kettel	kettle	petal	petel
wrinkel	wrinkle	frugal	frugle	civil	cival	bridel	bridle
Capital-bldg	Capitol-bldg	nickle	nickel	totel	total	kennel	kennal

182

Power Clues, OWF's SPP's for -al, - el, -le, -il, -ol Words

-Al Suffixes   (-AL *turns* nouns and roots into adjectives, and verbs and roots into nouns.)

1. capital: A capital letter is tall. Tallahassee is the capital city of Florida.
2. cymbals: Don't bang cymbals bang; play them.
3. medal: Ed and Al won medals. *OWF*: Large medal is a medallion. (*Homophone*: Meddle: interfere)
4. metal: I met Al in his metal shop. *OWF*: Metal's metallic. (Homophone: Mettle: courage; fortitude).
5. petal   My pet always eats a petal or two.
6. total: To total means to tally up all the items. *OWF*: The totality is the total…
7. special: Al specializes in special food. *SPP*: spe-ci-al. *OWF*: He has a special speciality.
8. tidal: Don't dally when a tidal wave's coming.
9. total: To total means to tally up all the items. *OWF*: The totality is the total.

-El Suffixes   (Emphasize the *-del, -gel, -mel, -nel, -pel, -vel, -wel* endings in the -EL words.)

10. angel: She created an angel out of gelatin: an + gel~~atin~~ = angel.
11. channel: Chan and Nel hosted the news channel.
12. nickel: An elf gave Nick an elf green nickel. *OWF*: nickeling
13. shovel: Shovel that snow away from the hovel.   *OWF*: shoveling
14. towel: We put a fresh welcome towel out to welcome guests.
15. travel: She loved to travel in velvet gowns. *OWF*: traveling

-LE Suffixes   (*Other Word Forms* with the suffixes -ing or -ly truly help you hear the Consonant + L.)

16. angle: The e fits in the angle of the L.
17. able: *OWF*: Hear the bl in able in enabing,
18. castle: The castle cast lengths of reflection across the lake.
19. example: Please give an example.
20. handled: They handled us so well, we felt hand led.
21. possible: Is living with siblings (brothers and sisters) impossible? OWF: impossibly
22. little: The Littlest Angel was a little less sad once he had his wonderful box.
23. muscle: We like to clench our muscles.
24. title: Let the title be *POWER Spelling*. *OWF*: Hear the tl in title in titling,
25. uncle: Uncle Clem cleverly clenches his muscle.
26. troubled: I felt troubled when my cut bled.

-IL Suffixes   (5 -IL Words: 2 about government: civil, council; 2 about writing: pencil, stencil; and evil.)

27. council: The council member was ill.   (Counsel means to see and help people.)
28. pencil: He liked to illustrate with a pencil. OWF penciling

-OL Suffixes

29. Capitol: A Capitol building has dome – o – on the top.
30. symbol: A good symbol bolsters (builds) a company's image.

Words with Roots *sede, ceed, cede, plus old seed*

Words with the roots *sede, ceed,* and *cede* are often confusing, in contrast to *good old SEED*, a basic Old English Word from before 900 A.D., which still means *seed* today! For the other words, **POWER SPELLING TOOLS** can help you master them.. *POWER Rules, POWER Clues, Visual POWER, and the POWER of Ancient Roots* can help you learn and remember these words forever!!

POWER RULES The Rule for the Roots: <u>sede</u>, <u>ceed</u>, and <u>cede</u> ALWAYS works. Just learn this simple rule, and you'll be on your way to having these words down for life.

1. One word has the root   **<u>sede</u>** (to sit):   **super<u>sede</u>** (super and <u>sede</u> start with <u>s</u>.)

2. Three words have the root **<u>ceed</u>** (go, move):   **ex<u>ceed</u>, pro<u>ceed</u>, suc<u>ceed</u>**

3. Eight words have the root **<u>cede</u>** (go, move):   **ac<u>cede</u>, ante<u>cede</u>, <u>cede</u>, con<u>cede</u>, inter<u>cede</u>, pre<u>cede</u>, re<u>cede</u>, and se<u>cede</u>**

POWER CLUES: The biggest challenge with these words is to remember if the root is spelled *-sede, -ceed,* or *-cede*. For this, you can create your own *Clues* or learn one of the *Clues* below.

❑ **NOW**: For <u>supersede</u>, remember that *super, sede,* and *sit* start with <u>s</u>: supersede (sit above).

Then for the <u>3 ceed words</u>, learn one of these Clues to say, and the <u>8 cede words</u> will be easy.

<u>PROCEED</u> (Continue moving forward.)   As you <u>proceed</u> through life
<u>SUCCEED</u> (Move to your goal.)   And seek to <u>succeed</u>,
<u>EXCEED</u> (Go beyond your goal.)   Don't let wealth <u>exceed</u> your goodness.

These sayings are easy to remember because one step follows the other:
You *pro<u>ceed</u>,* You *suc<u>ceed</u>,* and then you *ex<u>ceed</u>*...

VISUAL POWER: First, notice that the *sede, ceed* and *cede* words are all action verbs, ending in a syllable with either: **-ede** (<u>vowel + consonant + silent e</u>) or **-eed** (<u>vowel + vowel + consonant</u>).

sede: Again see that <u>s</u>uper<u>s</u>ede has an <u>s</u> for the prefix *super* and an <u>s</u> for the root *sede*.

ceed: Also visually picture pro<u>ceed</u>, suc<u>ceed</u>, and ex<u>ceed</u>. See all three words ending in *<u>ceed</u>*.

cede: Finally, the other eight are *cede*.

...and then there's good old SEED, a simple, basic word.

The POWER of Ancient Roots

Since these prefixes and roots come from Latin, knowing their meaning helps with the spelling. The root **sede** means _sit_ and begins with _s_. The root spelled: **ceed**, and **cede** mean _go, move,_ or _yield._

❑ **NOW:** For each word, draw a line under the root and circle the prefix. Then, under each word, write a sentence showing that you understand the meaning. Two examples are given below.

* **supersede** (super: _above_ + sede: _sit_): Sit above in power; take the place of the person or rule that was there before so that it no longer has power.

                    The rules of our new principal supersede the old ones.

1. **proceed:** (pro: _forward_ + ceed: _go, move_) Move forward; go onward, especially after stopping; to continue on a journey.

2. **succeed:** (suc-form of sub: _under_ + ceed: _go_) Go from under and achieve the desired goal or result.

3. **exceed:** (ex: _beyond_ + ceed: _go, move_) Go beyond what was expected; to surpass; to _exceed_ to a school or work requirements.

1. **accede:** (ac: _to, toward_ + cede: _go move_) Move toward; accept or agree to an idea or plan like to _accede_ to a dress code.

                    They were willing to accede to a new dress code.

2. **antecede:** (ante: _before_ + cede: _go_) To have gone before like your ancestors or events in history that came before you.

3. **cede:** (cede: _to yield; give up_) Give up or formally surrender something like territory or land. (_Cede_ involves _giving something physical._)

4. **concede:** (con: _with_ + cede: _go; yield to_) To yield to someone's point of view or yield a victory. (_Concede_ involves yielding a view or victory _to another person._)

5. **intercede:** (inter: _between; among_ + cede: _go_) Go between; _intercede_ with a teacher for a student. (You _intercede_ on behalf of someone or a cause.)

6. **precede:** (pre: _before_ + cede: _go_) Go before in time, rank or importance. A precedent (a ruling that comes before) can set the policy for decisions by judges, etc.

7. **recede:** (re: _back, over_ + cede: _go; move_) Return or go back like waves or a receding hairline.

8. **secede:** (se: _apart_ + cede: _go, move_) Formally withdraw from a nation or group, as states did during the Civil War.

SEDE (_L. Root: sit_); **CEED** and **CEDE** (**CEDERE**: _Latin Root: to go; move; yield_)

supersede   succeed   proceed   exceed   recede   antecede   concede   intercede   accede   precede   secede

Ancient Latin Roots

cede "I'm leaving!" -ed -ing ~

Let's Add Some Verb Suffixes

❏ **TRY THIS:** Add the verb suffixes -ed and -ing to all the words below. For words ending in -de, drop -e, and add -ed. For words ending in -eed, just add -ed.

*	supersede:	(replace in power or authority)	_____ed	_____ing
1.	proceed:	(go onward or forward)	_____ed	_____ing
2.	succeed:	(achieve the desired result)	_____ed	_____ing
3.	exceed:	(go beyond in degree, quality)	_____ed	_____ing
1.	accede:	(move toward; agree to; accept)	_____ed	_____ing
2.	antecede:	(have gone before, like ancestors)	_____ed	_____ing
3.	cede:	(yield or surrender, like land)	_____ed	_____ing
4.	concede:	(yield to a person's point or view)	_____ed	_____ing
5.	intercede:	(go between on behalf of someone)	_____ed	_____ing
6.	precede:	(go before in order, rank…)	_____ed	_____ing
7.	recede:	(go back, as waves; to retreat)	_____ed	_____ing
8.	secede	(withdraw from a nation, group)	_____ed	_____ing

Let's Change the Verbs Into Nouns

❏ **NOW:** Add noun suffixes to change these verbs into nouns. These words are tough, but see how many you can figure out. Questions? A dictionary will show you all the Other Word Forms for each word.

proceed: _*process*_   _*processor*_   _*procession*_   _*procedure*_ (e long)

succeed: _____ss   _____or   _____ion

exceed: _____ss   _____er

concede: _____ion

accede: _____ss   _____or

antecede: _____or (person who comes before you)

intercede: _____or   _____ion (acting on someone behalf)

precede: _*precedent*_ (comes befor

recede: _____ss   _*recession*_

"I accede."   Procession   "Procee forwa

186

Let's Add Some Verb Suffixes

❑ **VERB SUFFIXES** You can add the verb suffixes -ed and -ing to all of these words. Notice that when you add these, the vowel -e in the last syllable stays long. Remember to follow the Silent-e Rule before adding suffixes. For the words ending in -d, just add -d.

*	supersede:	(replace in power or authority)	_____ ed	_____ ing
1.	proceed:	(go onward or forward)	_____ ed	_____ ing
2.	succeed:	(achieve the desired result)	_____ ed	_____ ing
3.	exceed:	(go beyond in degree, quality)	_____ ed	_____ ing
1.	accede:	(move toward; agree to; accept)	_____ ed	_____ ing
2.	antecede:	(have gone before, like ancestors)	_____ ed	_____ ing
3.	cede:	(yield or surrender, like land)	_____ ed	_____ ing
4.	concede:	(yield to a person's point or view)	_____ ed	_____ ing
5.	intercede:	(go between on behalf of someone)	_____ ed	_____ ing
6.	precede:	(go before in order, rank…)	_____ ed	_____ ing
7.	recede:	(go back, as waves; to retreat)	_____ ed	_____ ing
8.	secede	(withdraw from a nation, group)	_____ ed	_____ ing

Let's Change the Verbs into Nouns

❑ **NOUN SUFFIXES** Add noun suffixes to the verbs on the left to change them into nouns that are things or people. Questions? A dictionary will show you all the Other Word Forms for each of these words. These words are tough, but see how many you can figure out or look up.

proceed: _*process*_ _*processor*_ _*procession*_ _*procedure*_ (e long)

succeed: _____ ss _____ or _____ ion

exceed: _____ ss _____ er

concede: _____ ion

accede: _____ ss _____ or

antecede: _____ or (person who comes before you)

intercede: _____ or _____ ion (acting on someone behalf)

precede: _*precedent*_ (comes before)

recede: _____ ss _*recession*_

187

Let's Change the Nouns Into Adjectives and Adverbs

❑ **ADJECTIVE and ADVERB SUFFIXES**: You can turn the three nouns into adjectives simply by adding adjective suffixes: *-ful*, *-ive*, and *-ible*.

Then, you can turn the adjectives into adverbs by adding the adverb suffix *-ly*.

1. success: _____ful _____ly

   We were _ _ _ _ _ _ _ _ _ _ in school. We did our work _ _ _ _ _ _ _ _ _ _ _ _ .

2. excess: _____ive _____ly

   Our homework was _ _ _ _ _ _ _ _ _ . I worked _ _ _ _ _ _ _ _ _ _ _ hard.

3. access: _____ible

   The home is _ _ _ _ _ _ _ _ _ _ through the basement.

NOTE: It is interesting to note that you can even take some adjectives and turn them back into nouns again by adding the noun suffix *-ness*: successiveness, excessiveness, and accessibility.

REMEMBER: In ending this lesson on the *-sede, -ceed*, and *-cede* words, remember the *Rule*:

1. Only one word ends in <u>sede</u>:	supersede
2. Only three words end in <u>ceed</u>:	exceed, proceed, succeed
3. All the other words end in <u>ede</u>:	accede, antecede, cede, concede, intercede, precede, recede, secede

❑ **FINALLY:** In the box above, underline all the roots.

...and a final salute to SEED for being such a simple basic word.

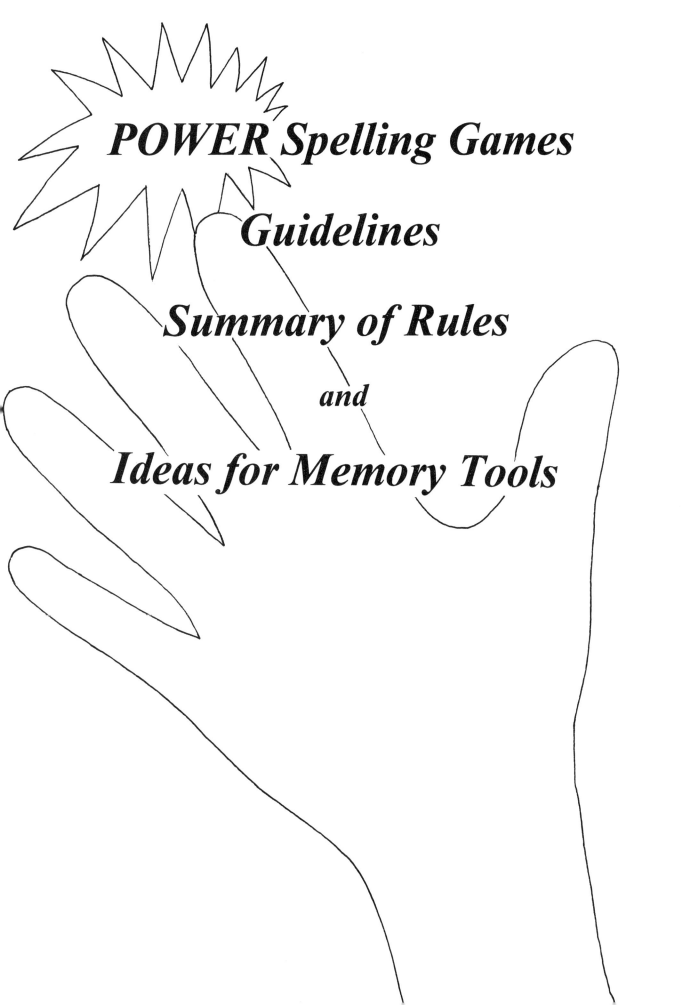

POWER *Spelling Games*

Guidelines

Summary of Rules

and

Ideas for Memory Tools

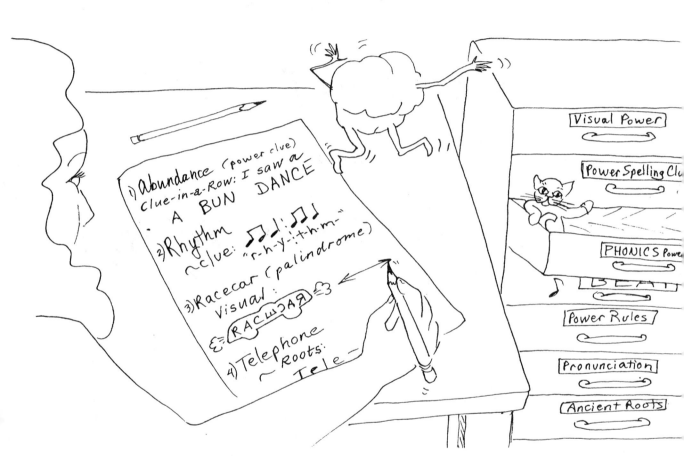

Guidelines for Playing the POWER Spelling Games

The GOAL for each *POWER Spelling Game* is for YOU to use the *POWER Spelling Tools* to detect and find ways to remember every word in the game (Suggestions of *Tools* that work are included next to each word.). Then write your ideas by the words. The only RULE for the Game is: Use each one of the seven *POWER* Spelling Tools at least once in each Game.

This is easy, though, because each game is put together so that all the Tools can be used at least once. Also, each game includes at least one: *Clue-in-a-Row, Word Search Word, Set of Homophones...* You get to be a Spelling Detective who searches and tries out different tools until you find the ones that work best for you! The reason for using all seven tools in each game is that getting weekly practice in the different ways to learn and remember words reinforces: the ways you are TRAINING YOUR BRAIN to RETAIN spelling.

Key Ways You Can Use Each POWER Spelling Tool

POWER Spelling Clues: You can create *Clues* in at least 5 ways. Look for:
1. *Words in the Word*: (*juice*: I want *ice* in my *juice*;   *great*: We can cook and *eat great* food).
2. *Clues-in-a-Row*: (*at-ten-dance*: *At ten, dance*; *cat-a-log*: See *cat* (and) a *log* in a *catalog*).
3. *Letter Clues*: (*dessert*: My *dessert* was *s*trawberry *s*hortcake; *athlete*: The *athlete* did a *high* *l*eap; *creek*: I took my rod and *reel* to the *creek*).
4. *Other Word Forms* (*OWF's*) to hear letters: (*crumbs*: If your cookie *crumbl*es, you eat *crumb*s).
5. *Same Pattern Clues*: (*prom*: We rode home *from* the *prom*; *each*: We can *reach each* peach.)

Clues truly help for *Homophones* and *Confusing Words* because they give you ways to remember differences (*their*: *Their* son is his *heir*; *there*: I went *here* and *there*; *they're*: Hey, *they're* home.)

Phonics POWER: Since almost 85% of the words in English follow the sounds of *Phonics*, knowing the sounds consonants and vowels make and how to spell them is a very powerful tool. For *CONSONANTS*, look for:
   One-Letter Copy Cats: *C* copies *K* and *S-city*; *G* – *J-gem*; *S* – *Z-trys*; and *X* = KS-*box* and Z.
   Two-Letter Copy Cats: *CH* copies K-*chord*; *GH* – F-*tough*; *PH* – F-*phone*; *Qu* – KW-*quilt*.
   Digraphs (2 letters-1sound): *CH*-chug; *SH*-ship; *TH*-thud, then; *WH*-wheat; *NG*- sing(sometimes)
   Beginning and *Ending Blends* (sounds of individual letters blend): *crown*, *elf*, *glide*, *swamp*, *train*.

For *VOWELS*, look for all the sounds vowels make: *Short, Long, Special Sounds, R-Controlled*.
   Short Vowel Sound (no vowel after V + C): *ant*, *apple*, *egg*, *igloo*, *octopus*, *sun*, *a*-long, *me*-tal.
   Long Vowel Sound (Silent E; 2 Vowels Together; Open Syllables): *ace*, *eek*, *ice*, *oak*, *cube*, *a*-ble.

EXCEPTIONS (examples): *eigh* = *long a*: *eight*; *ps* = *s*: *psyche*; *pn* = *n*: *pneumonia*; *zh*: *treasure*.

Feeling the POWER of the Beat and Syllables: Look for words with a *Rhythm* you can put to a *Beat* you can remember. *Double-letter* and *-ing* words often work: *p-o-s-s – e-s-s*, *r-h-y t-h-m*, *d-a-n-c-i-n-g*. Also, say words and *divide them into syllables*: *a-rith-me-tic*, *math-e-ma-tics*, so you can spell one syllable at a time. Finally, write each word 2-3 times so you can feel your *Motor Memory* (feeling memory from *writing* words correctly).

"s-k-a-t-i-n-g"

POWER Rules that Work: *Rules* help with thousands of words, and some rules always work or have very few exceptions: *Contraction Rule; Short Vowel Rule; Final E Rule; Compound Word Rule; Prefix Rule; Doubling Final Consonants Rule.*
Also, look for words that follow the *Same Pattern* and *Rule*: *file, mile, smile, tile; gain, main, train*
The *Summary of Rules that Work* (next page) will help you understand and use rules for the games.

Pronunciation POWER: Look for words that need *Pronunciation POWER*: words misspelled because they're incorrectly pronounced: *every, library*. Use *Special Phonics Pronunciations* (*SPP's*) for other words so you can hear all the consonants and vowels: *clim-b, Feb-ru-a-ry, res-ta-u-rant, Wed-nes-day*. Finally, *Pronouncing Other Word Forms* (OWF's) can help you better hear the letters in some words: a<u>th</u>letic – a<u>th</u>letically; med<u>al</u> – med<u>al</u>lion; met<u>al</u> – met<u>al</u>lic.

The POWER of Ancient Prefixes, Roots, and Suffixes: Learn to detect Latin, Greek, and other word parts: <u>Prefixes</u>: (*dis*: not; *re*: again; *trans*: across; *un*: not); <u>Roots</u>: (*ease*-comfort; *port*-carry; friend); and <u>Suffixes</u>: (*-ed, -ly,- ship*). Prefixes and Suffixes add to the meaning of words; plus suffixes can change a word into a noun, verb, adjective, or adverb. These word parts are usually spelled the same way: *disease, friendship, transported*. A great way to learn about a word's *Prefixes, Roots,* and *Suffixes* and their meaning is to look up words in an *Unabridged Dictionary*.

Visual POWER and Patterns: You can make amazing *Visual Discoveries* in words. Look for words where you can *Draw the Letters*: <u>Bicycle</u> (2 wheels and a pedal). <u>Wavy</u> (looks like the motion of waves). Look for *Palindromes*: <u>racecar</u>, b<u>anana</u>; *Reversals*: *deer-reed*; *drawer-reward*; *Echoes*: <u>decide, sense</u>; *Bookends*: <u>museum, onion</u>.   Find *Repeated Letters*: <u>murmur, picnic</u>,…or *All 5 Vowels* in <u>sequoia</u>.   Look for words with the *Same Spelling Pattern*, even though their pronunciation may be different: *does, goes, hoes*. Also, try the *Word Search Challenge*: Look for 6 words in <u>heart</u> and 9 in <u>important</u>. With *Visual Power*, it's fun to see what you can see!!!

POWER Spelling Summary of Rules That Work

Apostrophe-Contraction Rule – When you have a set of *Homophones* with a contraction (pronoun + verb) *and* a possessive pronoun: *it's – its*; *they're – their*; *you're – your*; *who's – whose*; the contraction ALWAYS gets the apostrophe. The possessive NEVER does. This rule ALWAYS works.

Qu Rule – Q is ALWAYS followed by u, except at the end of a word: quail, queen, quit, quote, Iraq.

Short Vowel Rule – A single vowel stays short when it's followed by one consonant without a vowel coming right after the consonant: *cat, apple, net, pin, top, octopus, up, umbrella...* Also, it usually stays short when it's followed by more than one consonant: *band, list, end, cloth, bunt...*

Silent E Rule – When Silent E comes right after a single consonant, it usually makes the vowel before that consonant long: *face, these, kite, rose, flute, graceful...* Exceptions: *come, have, love...*

When Two Vowels Go Walking Rule – When two vowels go walking, the first vowel does the talking, and says its own name. The second vowel makes the first vowel long: *rain, boat, fruit...*

I Before E Rule – I before E (*believe, friend, grief, niece, piece*), except after C (when c sounds like s: *ceiling, deceive, receive*), or when sounded as A, as in *neighbor* and *weigh*: (*vein, sleigh*).

Solid Compound Word Rule – To create solid compound words, add two words together without making any changes to make a new word: fire + works = *fireworks*; race + car = *racecar*.

Prefix Rule – When you add a prefix to a word, simply fasten it in front of the word. Don't take out letters and don't add letters. Just spell the prefix and then the word: *disease, enjoy, submarine...*

Suffix Rule – When a suffix is added to the end of a word, it changes not only the meaning, but it can also turn the word into a noun, verb, adjective, or adverb: *darkness, enjoyment, runs, fastest, slowly, snowing...* The rest of the rules explain how you add suffixes to words.

Silent E Rule Before Suffixes – When a consonant comes before Silent E, keep Silent E before a suffix that begins with a consonant: *hopeful, likeness.* Drop Silent E before a suffix that begin with a vowel: *exciting.* When a vowel precedes Silent E, keep Silent E before all suffixes: *hoeing, freeing.*

Rule for Final Y before a Suffix – Words ending in y preceded by a consonant change the y to i before all suffixes except -ing: *carried, carrying; tried, trying.* Most words ending in y preceded by a vowel do not drop the y: *enjoyment, enjoying; canoed, canoeing.* Exceptions: *rescuing, truly...*

Inserted K Rule – Words that end in hard c (k sound) insert k before suffixes that begins with e, i, or y to keep the k sound: *frolic-frolicked; panic-panicky; picnic-picnicking...*

Doubling Final Consonants Rule for One-Syllable Words.
1.   If a word has one syllable, and
2.   If a word ends with a consonant, and
3.   If the consonant has a single vowel before it: *run, swim...*, then:
Double the final consonant before a suffix that begins with a vowel (-ed, -er, -ing): *running, swimming...*

Doubling Final Consonants Rule for Words with More than One Syllable.
1.   If a word has more than one syllable, and
2.   If a word ends in a single consonant, and
3.   If a single short vowel comes before the consonant: *admit, occur, travel...*, and
4.   If, in the completed word, the accent falls on the last syllable of the original word, then:
Double the final consonant before a suffix that begins with a vowel: *admitted, occurred...*

Getting to Know Your POWER SPELLING Tools

1. attendance (*Find 9 Words; Clue*)

2. island (*Phonics; SPP; Clue*)

3. together (*Clue*)

4. tomorrow (*Clue; Same Pattern*)

5. hear-v., listen (*Clue; Same Pattern*)

6. here-adv., his place (*Clue; Same Pattern*)

7. hangar-storage for airplanes (*Clue*)

8. hanger-for hanging clothes (*Clue*)

9. earring (*Visual; Compound Rule*)

10. racecar (*Phonics; visual; Compound Rule; Silent E Rule*)

11. disagree (*Prefix Rule; 2 Vowel Rule*)

12. misspell (*Clue; Short Vowel Rule; Prefix Rule*)

13. reread (*Prefix Rule; 2 Vowel Rule*)

14. February (*Pronunciation; Clue*)

15. meant (*SPP; Clue*)

16. library (*Clue; OWF*)

17. geography (*Phonics; 2 Roots*)

18. telephone (*Phonics; Rule; 2 Roots*)

19. transport (*Find 6 Words; Prefix Rule; Roots*)

20. balloon (*Visual; Clue*)

➤ biology (*Rule; 2 Roots*)

➤ disease (*Clue; 2 Vowel Rule; Prefix Rule*)

➤ noticed (*Find 7 Words, Phonics; Clue*)

➤ parallel (*Visual; Clue*)

➤ rhythm (*Visual; Beat*)

OTHER WORD FORMS

agree: agrees, agreed, agreeing, disagree
attend: attending, attended, attendance
hear: hears, heard, hearing, hearer
library: libraries, librarian
mean: meant, meaning, meaner, meanest

notice: noticed, noticing, noticeable
read: reads, reading, reader, reread
spell: spelling, speller, misspell, misspelled
telephone: telephones, telephoned, telephoning
transport: transported, transporting, transportation

Discovering the History of the English Language

1. altar-n. in a church (*Visual*)
2. alter-v. to change (*Clue*)
3. bagel (*Phonics; Clue*)
4. banana (*Visual; Beat*)
5. candle (*Phonics; Clue*)
6. candy (*Phonics; Clue; Same Pattern*)
7. chocolate (*Phonics; SPP; Roots*)
8. computer (*Phonics; Rule; Roots*)
9. father (*SPP; Clue; Roots*)
10. friend (*Clue*)
11. hamburger (*Rule; Roots*)
12. liberty (*Clue; Roots*)
13. mother (*Clue; Roots*)
14. neighbor (*Phonics; Clue*)
15. photograph (*Find 6 Words; Phonics; Rule; Roots*)
16. rodeo (*Visual; Clue*)
17. scribe (*Silent E Rule; Same Root*)
18. skate (*Clue; Silent E Rule*)
19. spaghetti (*Phonics; SPP; Roots*)
20. volcano (*Clue*)
- antiseptic (*Find 8 Words; Clue; Roots*)
- chili-n. pepper; Mexican dish (*Visual*)
- chilly-adj. cold (*Clue; Same Pattern*)
- phantom (*Phonics; Clue*)
- restaurant (*SPP; Clue; Roots*)

OTHER WORD FORMS

alter: alters, altered, altering
chill: chilled, chilling, chilly, chillier, chilliest
compute: computed, computing, computer
father: fathers, fatherhood; fatherly
friend: friendly, friendlier, friendliest, befriend

mother: mothers, motherly; motherhood
neighbor: neighbors, neighborly; neighborhood
photograph: photographed, photographing
skate: skates, skated, skating, skater
volcano: volcanoes, volcanic, volcanically

Let's Create Some POWER Spelling Clues

1. ache (*Phonics; SPP: Clue*)

2. address (*Clue; Short Vowel Rule*)

3. again (*SPP; Clue*)

4. argument (*Clue; Rule Ex.*)

5. beautiful (*Clue; Y Rule*)

6. bicycle (*Visual; Clue; Rule; Roots*)

7. business (*Phonics; Clue; Y Rule*)

8. calendar (*Phonics; Clue*)

9. certain (*Phonics; Clue; Beat*)

10. desert-a dry place (*Phonics; Clue*)

11. desert-to abandon, leave alone (*Phonics; Clue*)

12. dessert-treat after meal (*Phonics; Clue; Beat*)

13. does (*Phonics; Clue; Same Pattern*)

14. goes (*Phonics; Clue; Same Pattern*)

15. horse (*SPP: Clue*)

16. often (*Phonics; SPP; Clue*)

17. separate (*Find 6 Words; Clue; Silent E Rule*)

18. stairs-steps (*Clue; Same Pattern*)

19. stares-gazes intensely (*Find 6 Words; Clue; Same Pattern*)

20. straight (*Phonics; Clue; 2 Vowel Rule*)

➢ familiar (*Clue; Y Rule; Roots*)

➢ threw-tossed (*Clue; Same Pattern*)

➢ through-finished; to pass through (*Phonics; Clue*)

➢ tired (*Clue; Rule*)

➢ tried (*Clue; Rule*)

OTHER WORD FORMS

ache: aches, ached, aching, headache
address: addresses, addressed, addressing
argue: argues, argued, arguing, argument
beauty: beauties, beautiful, beautify, beautified
bicycle: bicycles, bicycled, bicycling

desert: deserted, deserting
separate: separated, separating, separation
throw: throws, threw, throwing, thrown
stare: stares, stared, staring
try: tries, tried, trying, trial

Conquering Contractions and Possessives
Learning How the Tiny, Powerful Apostrophe Works

(Write out each contraction. Words 1-9 are *Homophones*: contractions (pron. + verb) and possessive pronouns)

1. they're (*Clue*)
2. their (*Find 4 Words; Clue*)
3. there (*Find 4 Words; Clue*)
4. it's (*Clue; Rule*)
5. its (*Clue; Same Pattern*)
6. you're (*Clue; Same Pattern*)
7. your (*Visual; Clue*)
8. who's (*SPP; Clue*)
9. whose (*SPP; Clue; Roots*)
10. I'm (*Clue; Same Pattern*)
11. he'd (*Clue; Same Pattern*)
12. she'll (*Clue; Same Pattern*)
13. we're (*Rule*)
14. let's (*Clue; Same Pattern*)
15. aren't (*Clue; Beat*)
16. doesn't (*Phonics; Clue; Same Pattern*)
17. haven't (*Clue; Rule*)
18. isn't (*Phonics; Clue; Same Pattern*)
19. wasn't (*Phonics; Clue*)
20. o'clock (*Clue; Same Pattern*)

➤ couldn't (*SPP; Same Pattern; Roots*)
➤ should've (*SPP; Same Pattern*)
➤ friends' (*Clue*)
➤ horse's (*Clue*)
➤ penguin's (*SPP; Clue*)
➤ EXTRA: nightingale's (*Clue*)

OTHER WORD FORMS

am: are, is, aren't, isn't
can: can't, could, couldn't, could've
do: did, does, doesn't, doing, don't
horse: horse's, horses, horses'
friend: friend's, friends, friends'

might: mightn't, might've
shall: should, shouldn't, should've
was: wasn't, were, weren't
will: would, wouldn't, would've
penguin: penguin's, penguins, penguins'

Tackling Homophones and Words that Get Confused

1. bear-animal (*Clue; Same Pattern*)

2. bare-naked (*Clue; Same Pattern*)

3. buy-purchase (*Phonics; Clue*)

4. by-near; good-by (*Visual; Rule*)

5. bye-bye or good-bye (*SPP*)

6. capital-city; letter (*Find 5 Words; Clue*)

7. Capitol-building (*Visual; Clue*)

8. dear-greeting; loved one (*Clue*)

9. deer-animal (*Visual; Clue*)

10. flours-grain (*Clue*)

11. flowers-bloom (*Clue; Beat*)

12. hour-sixty minutes (*SPP; Clue; Roots*)

13. our-poss. pron. (*Clue*)

14. principal-person in charge…(*Find 6 Words; Clue*)

15. principle-rule (*Phonics; Clue*)

16. stationary-fixed; stable (*Clue*)

17. stationery-paper for letters (*Clue*)

18. to-prep. toward (*Visual; Pronunciation*)

19. too-adv. also (*Visual; Pronunciation*)

20. two-number 2 (*Phonics; Clue*)

➤ though-in spite of (*Clue*)

➤ thought-idea (*Visual; Clue; Same Pattern*)

➤ ought-should (*Clue; Same Pattern*)

➤ weather (*Find 7 Words; Clue*)

➤ whether (*Visual; SPP; Clue*)

OTHER WORD FORMS
bare: bared, baring, barer, barest, barely
buy: buys, bought, buying, buyer
dear: dears, dearer, dearest, dearly
flower: flowers, flowered, flowering

hour: hours, hours, hourly
ride: rides, rode, riding, ridden, rider
think: thinks, thought, thinking, thinker
weather: weathers, weathered, weathered

Phonics: The Building Blocks of Spelling

1. ant-insect (*Clue; Same Pattern*)   aunt-relative (*Clue; Same Pattern*)
2. seven (*Phonics; Clue*)
3. igloo (*Visual; Clue*)
4. octopus (*Phonics; Roots*)
5. umpire (*Clue; Rule; Roots*)
6. amaze (*SPP; Clue; Rule*)
7. these (*Phonics; Rule*)
8. idea (*Visual; Clue*)
9. opened (*SPP; Clue*)
10. fuel (*SPP; Clue; Same Pattern*)
11. party (*Clue; Roots*)
12. very (*Clue; Roots*)
13. birthday (*Rule; Same Pattern*)
14. store (*SPP; Clue; Same Pattern*)
15. turtle (*Clue; Beat*)
16. airplane (*Find 7 words; Clue; Rules*)
17. tear-from crying (*Clue; Same Pattern*)   tear-rip (*Clue; Same Pattern*)
18. sure (*Phonics; Clue; Same Pattern*)
19. looked (*SPP; Same Pattern*)
20. mouth (*SPP; Clue*)
- loose-not tight (*Phonics; Clue; Same Pattern*)   lose-can't find (*Phonics; Clue*)
- ointment (*Phonics; Clue*)
- pause-brief stop (*Clue; Same Pattern*)   paws-animal feet (*Clue; Same Pattern*)
- remember (*Visual; Clue; Same Pattern*)
- voyage (*Phonics; Clue*)

OTHER WORD FORMS
born: birth, birthday
look: looks, looked, looking, onlooker
loose: loosed, loosen, loosely
lose: loses, lost, losing
open: opens, opened, opening, openly
pause: pauses, paused, pausing

remember: remembered, remembrance
store: stores, stored, storing, storehouse
tear: tears, tearful, tearfully
tear: tears, tore, tearing, torn
verify: verifies, verified, verifying, very, every
voyage: voyages, voyaged, voyaging, voyager

Feeling the Sounds of Single Consonants and Digraph

1. bubble (*Visual; Clue*)
2. buzzing (*Clue; Rule; Beat*)
3. choose-pick out (*Clue; Same Pattern*)
4. chose-past of choose (*Phonics; Clue; Rule*)
5. church (*Visual*)
6. dizzy (*Clue; Same Pattern; Beat*)
7. gong (*Clue; Roots; Same Pattern*)
8. hush (*Clue; Same Pattern*)
9. kickball (*Find 6 Words; Visual; Rule; Same Pattern*)
10. laugh (*Phonics; SPP; Clue; Roots*)
11. murmur (*Visual; Beat*)
12. popping (*Rule; Beat*)
13. ringing (*Clue; Roots*)
14. shadow (*SPP; Clue; Roots*)
15. shape (*Clue; Rule; Same Pattern*)
16. tough (*Phonics; SPP; Clue; Same Pattern*)
17. treasure (*SPP; Clue; Same Pattern*)
18. when (*SPP; Clue; Root*)
19. which (*SPP; Clue; Beat*)
20. zooming (*Visual; Same Pattern*)
   ➤ enough (*Phonics; SPP; Clue*)
   ➤ phonics (*Phonics; Roots*)
   ➤ vanished (*Clue; Suffix Rule*)
   ➤ whistle (*SPP; OWF; Same Pattern*)
   ➤ young (*Clue; Same Pattern*)

OTHER WORD FORMS

bubble: bubbled, bubbling, bubbler
buzz: buzzes, buzzed, buzzing, buzzer
choose: chose, choosing, chosen, choice
kick: kicked, kicking, kicker, kickball
laugh: laughs, laughed, laughing, laughter
murmur: murmurs, murmured, murmuring
pop: popped, popping, popcorn

ring: rings, rang, rung, ringing, ringer
tough: toughen; tougher, toughest, toughly
treasure: treasures, treasured, treasuring, treasurer
vanish: vanishes, vanished, vanishing, vanisher
whistle: whistles, whistled, whistling, whistler
young: younger, youngest, youngster, youth
zoom: zooms, zoomed, zooming

Feeling the Power of the Beat

1. album (*Clue; Roots*)
2. brass (*Phonics; Clue*)
3. cello (*Phonics; Clue; Rules*)
4. composer (*OWF, Rule; Roots*)
5. concert (*Phonics; Clue*)
6. conductor (*Clue; Rule; Roots*)
7. drummer (*Clue; Rule; Beat*)
8. flute (*Clue; Rule; Same Pattern*)
9. guitar (*SPP; Clue*)
10. harmonica (*Find 7 Words; Phonics; Y Rule*)
11. harp (*Clue; Same Pattern*)
12. keyboard (*Find 6 Words; Clue; Rule*)
13. musician (*Phonics; SPP; Clue*)
14. orchestra (*Phonics; Clue*)
15. piano (*Pronunciation; Clue; Roots*)
16. strings (*Clue; Same Pattern*)
17. symphony (*Phonics; Clue; Roots*)
18. trumpet (*Clue; Beat*)
19. violin (*Pronunciation; Clue*)
20. woodwinds (*Clue; Compound Rule*)
➤ audience (*Clue; Roots*)
➤ choir (*Phonics; Clue; Roots*)
➤ chord-3 or more combined tones (*SPP; Clue*)
➤ cord-rope; measure of wood (*Clue; Same Pattern*)
➤ percussion (*Clue; Roots*)

OTHER WORD FORMS
audience: audiences, audio, auditorium
chord: chords, chording, chorus, choruses
conduct: conducted, conducting, conductor
compose: composed, composing, composer
drum: drums, drummed, drumming, drummer
keyboard: keyboards, keyboarded, keyboarding
music: musician, musical, musically
orchestra: orchestra, orchestrate, orchestrating
symphony: symphonies, symphonic
trumpet: trumpets, trumpeted, trumpeting

Divide and Conquer: Dividing Words into Syllables

1. cattails (*Rule; Same Pattern*)

2. glassblower (*Find 12 Words; Rule*)

3. granddad (*Rule; Same Pattern*)

4. phonograph (*Phonics; Roots; Rules*)

5. wheelbarrow (*Clue; Rule; Roots*)

6. accept-v. to take; to receive (*Roots*)

7. except-prep. to exclude (*Roots*)

8. mistake (*Clue; Roots*)

9. unaware (*Clue; Rule; Roots*)

10. fundamentally (*Find 15 Words; Clue*)

11. harbors (*Phonics; Clue*)

12. mountains (*SPP: Clue*)

13. letters (*Clue; Rule; Same Pattern*)

14. summer (*Clue; Rule*)

15. benefits (*Clue; Roots*)

16. majesty (*Clue; Roots*)

17. silent (*Clue; Rule*)

18. fable (*Clue; OWF*)

19. hurdle (*Visual; OWF*)

20. middle (*Visual; OWF*)

➢ amiable-friendly (*Clue; Roots*)

➢ establishment (*Clue; Rule*)

➢ helicopter (*Clue; Roots*)

➢ occasion (*Phonics; SPP; Clues*)

➢ parachute (*Clue; Roots*)

OTHER WORD FORMS

accept: accepts, accepted, accepting, acceptance
aware: awareness, unaware, warily
benefit: benefits, benefited, benefiting
blow: blows, blew, blowing, blower, glassblower
establish: establishes, established, establishment
except: exception, exceptionally

fable: fables, fabled, fabling, fabler
hurdle: hurdles, hurdled, hurdling
mistake: mistook, mistaking, mistaken
occasion: occasions, occasional, occasionally
parachute: parachuted, parachuting, parachutist
usual: usually, unusual, unusually

Let's Pronounce That Word Correctly Now!

1. perform (*Clue; Rule*)

2. tragedy (*Phonics; Clue; Roots*)

3. interest (*Pronounce 3 Syllables; Clue; Roots*)

4. temperature (*Pronounce 4 Syllables; Clue*)

5. arithmetic (*Pronounce 3 Syllables; Clue; Beat*)

6. athlete (*Pronounce 2 Syllables; Clue; Rule*)

7. jewelry (*Pronounce 2 Syllables; Clue*)

8. Arctic-at North Pole (*SPP; Clue; Roots*)

9. Antarctica-opposite North Pole (*Roots*)

10. asked (*SPP; Rule*)

11. exactly (*Clue; Rule*)

12. sandwich (*Clue; Roots*)

13. surprise (*Phonics; Clue*)

14. diamond (*Visual; SPP; Clue*)

15. every (*SPP; Clue; Beat*)

16. guard (*SPP; Clue*)

17. guessed (*SPP; Clue*)

18. hospital (*Clue; OWF*)

19. marriage (*SPP; Rule*)

20. government (*Find 6 Words; SPP; Clue*)

➢ literature (*Clue; Roots*)

➢ mathematics (*Pronounce 4 Syllables; Visual; Clue*)

➢ miniature (*Pronounce 4 Syllables; Clue*)

➢ privilege (*SPP; Clue*)

➢ probably (*Pronounce 3 Syllables; SPP; Clue*)

OTHER WORD FORMS

ask: asks, asked, asking
athlete: athletic, athletically
govern: governed, government, governor
guard: guards, guarded, guarding
guess: guesses, guessed, guessing
hospital: hospitalize, hospitalized, hospitalizing

interest: interested, interesting, interestingly
jewel: jewels, jeweled, jewelry
marry: married, marrying, marriage
perform: performed, performing, performance
surprise: surprised, surprising, surprisingly
tragic: tragically, tragedy, tragedies

203

The Power of Ancient Roots
Latin and Greek –Our Origin for Over 60,000 English Words

1. animal (*Clue; Roots*)

2. aquarium (*Rule; Roots*)

3. captain (*Clue; Roots*)

4. creed (*Clue; Same Pattern*)

5. dictionary (*Phonics; Roots*)

6. erupt (*SPP; OWF*)

7. fragile (*Phonics; Roots*)

8. labor (*Clue; Root*)

9. magnify (*Phonics; Roots*)

10. manual (*Clue; Roots*)

11. manuscript (*Phonics; Roots*)

12. origin (*Clue; Roots; Beat*)

13. pedal-n. v. foot lever; to ride (*Clue; Roots*)

14. peddle-v. to travel about selling (*Clue; Roots; Same Pattern*)

15. video (*Clue; Roots*)

16. astronaut (*Clue; 2 Roots*)

17. science (*Clue; Roots*)

18. inspect (*Clue; OWF*)

19. thermos (*Clue; Roots*)

20. verdict (*Clue; Roots*)

➢ agoraphobia (*Visual; Phonics; Rule; Roots*)

➢ animation (*Clue; Rule; Roots*)

➢ interrupt (*SPP; Roots*)

➢ philharmonic (*Phonics; Find 8 Words; Clue; Beat*)

➢ philosophy (*Phonics; 2 Roots*)

➢ EXTRA: claustrophobia (*Rule; Clue; Roots*)

OTHER WORD FORMS

<u>anim</u>ate: animated, animation, animal, inanimate
<u>erupt</u>: erupted, eruption, interrupt, interruption
<u>in</u>spe<u>ct</u>: inspected, inspecting, spectator
<u>labor</u>: labors, labored, laboring, laboratory
<u>magnify</u>: magnified, magnification, magnificent

<u>manual</u>: manually, manufacture, manuscript
<u>origin</u>: originated, original, originally
<u>science</u>: scientific, conscience, conscious
<u>table</u>: tables, tabled, tabling, tablet
<u>thermos</u>: thermoses, thermal, thermometer

Focusing on Visual Power and Patterns

1. visual (*Phonics; SPP; Clue*)

2. brilliant (*SPP; Visual*)

3. autumn (*SPP; Clue; OWF*)

4. benefit (*Clue; Roots*)

5. committee (*Phonics; Visual; Beat*)

6. disappear (*Clue; Roots*)

7. giraffe (*Visual; Clue; Roots*)

8. handkerchief (*SPP; Clue; Rule*)

9. heard (*Phonics; Clue*)

10. superintendent (*Find 9 Words; Clue*)

11. rain-precipitation (*Clue; Rule; Same Pattern*)

12. reign-time one rules (*Phonics; SPP; Clue*)

13. rein-harness (*Phonics; SPP; Clue*)

14. profit-benefit (*Clue*)

15. prophet-seer; wise man (*Phonics; Clue; Roots*)

16. four-number-4 (*Visual; Clue*)

17. before-fore-toward front (*Clue; Silent E Rule*)

18. giggling (*Visual; Rule; OWF*)

19. hiccup (*Visual; Clue; Rule*)

20. merry-go-round (*Visual; Same Pattern*)

➢ twinkle (*Visual; Clue; OWF*)

➢ decided (*Phonics; Visual; Clue; Silent E Rule)*)

➢ engine (*Visual; Clue*)

➢ museum (*Phonics; Visual; Clue*)

➢ onion (*Phonics; Visual; Clue*)

➢ EXTRA: staccato-short, quick notes (*Phonics; Visual*)

OTHER WORD FORMS

commit: committed, committing, committee
decide: decides, decided, deciding, decision
disappeared: disappearing, disappearance
giggle: giggles, giggled, giggling
hiccup: hiccups, hiccupped, hiccupping
hear: hears, heard, hearing, hearer

profit: profits, profited; profiting, profiteer
prophet: prophetic, prophecy, prophecies
rain: rains, rained, raining, raindrops
reign: reigns, reigned, reigning; rein: reined
twinkle: twinkles, twinkled, twinkling
visual: visuals, visualized, visualizing, vision

Introducing the Copy Cat Kids

Underline 10 or more letters that are Copy Cat Kids and next to them write the letter they copy.

1. crocodile (*Phonics; Clue; Rule*)

2. cyclone (*Phonics; Clue*)

3. angel-heavenly being (*Phonics; SPP; Clue*)

4. angle-as in triangle (*Visual; Same Pattern*)

5. college (*Phonics; Visual; Clue*)

6. courage (*Find 5 Words; Phonics; Clue*)

7. pigeons (*Clue; Roots*)

8. village (*Phonics; Clue*)

9. cousin (*Phonics; Clue*)

10. pleasure (*Phonics; Same Pattern*)

11. scissors (*Visual; Phonics; Beat*)

12. axis-center balancing line (*Phonics; Clue; Root*)

13. Xerox (*Visual; Phonics; Clue*)

14. champion (*Find 7 Words; SPP; Clue*)

15. chorus (*Phonics; Clue; Roots*)

16. cough (*Phonics; Same Pattern*)

17. elephant (*Phonics; Clue*)

18. nephew (*Phonics; Clue*)

19. quaint (*Phonics; SPP; Clue*)

20. question (*Phonics; Clue; Rule*)

➢ asphalt (*Phonics; Clue*)

➢ challenge (*SPP; Clue*)

➢ decision (*SPP; Clue*)

➢ pitcher-ball thrower (*Clue*)

➢ unique (*Phonics; SPP*)

➢ EXTRA: triumphant (*Phonics; Visual; Clue*)

OTHER WORD FORMS

angle: angles, angled, angling, angler
challenge: challenged, challenging, challenger
cough: coughs, coughed, coughing
courage: courageous, courageously
decide: decides, decided, deciding, decision

pitch: pitches, pitched; pitching, pitcher
please: pleased, pleasant, pleasure (measure, treasure)
question: questioned, questioning, questionnaire
unique: uniquely, uniqueness
Xerox: Xeroxes, Xeroxed, Xeroxing

Let's Grasp and Learn Final Consonant Blends

1. drift (*Clue; Same Pattern*)

2. bulb (*SPP; Visual*)

3. yield (*Clue*)

4. film (*SPP; OWF*)

5. built (*SPP; Clue*)

6. stamp (*Clue; Same Pattern*)

7. since (*SPP; Clue*)

8. legends (*Clue*

9. want (*Phonics; Clue*)

10. toward (*Find 6 Words; SPP; Clue; Rule*)

11. shark (*Clue; Same Pattern*)

12. twirl (*Clue; Same Pattern*)

13. grasp (*Clue; Rule*)

14. most (*Clue; Same Pattern*)

15. growl (*Clue; Same Pattern*)

16. fifth (*SPP; Clue; Beat*)

17. lunch (*Clue; Same Pattern*)

18. against (*Phonics; Clue*)

19. thirst (*Clue; Roots*)

20. watch (*SPP; Clue; Same Pattern*)

➤ extinct (*OWF; Roots*)

➤ instinct (*Clue; Roots*)

➤ ninth (*SPP; Clue; Beat*)

➤ strength (*Visual; Phonics; Clue*)

➤ twelfth (*Visual; Phonics; Clue*)

OTHER WORD FORMS

build: builds, built, building, builder
drift: drifts, drifted, drifting, drifter
extinct: extinguished, extinguishing, extinguisher
film: films, filmed, filming, filmy
grasp: grasps, grasped, grasping
instinct: instincts, instinctual, instinctually

legend: legends, legendary
nine: ninth, nineteen, ninety, ninetieth
thirst: thirsts, thirsted, thirsting, thirsty
want: wants, wanted, wanting
watch: watches, watching, watcher, watchman
yield: yields, yielded, yielding, yielder

Focusing on Silent Letters

1. clim**b** (*SPP; Clue*)

2. thum**b** (*SPP; OWF*)

3. desig**n** (*Phonics; SPP; Clue; OWF*)

4. **g**naw (*SPP; Clue; Same Pattern*)

5. brou**gh**t (*SPP; Clue*)

6. cau**gh**t (*Phonics; SPP; Clue*)

7. **g**host (*SPP; Clue; Beat*)

8. **k**ni**gh**t-medieval soldier (*SPP; Clue*)

9. ni**gh**t-evening (*Phonics; SPP; Clue*)

10. **h**onest (*Find 6 Words, Clue;*)

11. **w**harf (*SPP; Clue*)

12. **k**nead-for bread dough (*SPP; Clue; Homophone: need*)

13. coul**d** (*Phonics, SPP; Same Pattern*)

14. hal**f** (*SPP; Clue*)

15. pa**l**m (*SPP; Visual; Clue*)

16. lis**t**en (*SPP; Clue; Roots*)

17. s**w**ord-weapon (*SPP; Clue*)

18. soared-flew upward (*Find 7 Words; Clue*)

19. **w**reath (*Clue; 2 Vowel Rule*)

20. **w**rong (*SPP; Clue*)

➤ ans**w**ered (*SPP; Clue*)

➤ cas**t**le (*SPP; Clue*)

➤ colum**n** (*Visual; SPP; OWF; Beat*)

➤ ras**p**berry (*SPP; Clue*)

➤ sub**t**le (*SPP; Clue, Beat*)

OTHER WORD FORMS

answer: answers, answered, answering
cast-cast a play, make: casts, casting, castle
climb: climbs, climbed, climbing, climber
column: columns, columnar, columnist
design, designing, designation, signature
gnaw: gnaws, gnawed, gnawing

honest: honesty, honestly
knead: kneads, kneaded, kneading
listen: listens, listened, listening, listener
soar: soars, soared, soaring
subtle: subtler, subtlest, subtly, subtlety
wrong: wrongs, wronged, wronging

I've Got Those Syllables! Got That Power Beat!

1. catalog (*Clue; Beat*)

2. goblet (*Clue; Short Vowel Rule*)

3. blaze (*Clue; Silent E Rule*)

4. peach (*Clue; 2 Vowel Rule*)

5. showboat (*Find 8 Words; Compound Rule; 2 Vowel Rule*)

6. acorn (*Clue; Roots*)

7. among (*Same Pattern*)

8. divide (*Visual; Silent E Rule*)

9. unicorn (*Roots; Same Pattern*)

10. starlight (*Phonics; Rule; Same Pattern*)

11. super (*Clue; Silent E Rule*)

12. purple (*Clue; OWF*)

13. squiggle (*Visual; Clue; OWF*)

14. splash (*Phonics; Clue; Same Pattern*)

15. blew-past of to blow (*Clue; 2 Vowel Rule*)

16. blue-color of the sky (*Clue; 2 Vowel Rule*)

17. yellow (*Clue; Same Pattern*)

18. white (*Clue; Silent E Rule*)

19. green (*Clue; Roots*)

20. homework (*Phonics; Compound Rule*)

➢ understand (*Rules; Root*)

➢ igniting (*Visual; Rule*)

➢ magnification (*Phonics; Visual; Y Rule; Roots*)

➢ orange (*SPP; Clue*)

➢ syllables (*3 Syllables; Visual; Clue*)

➢ EXTRA: phenomenon (*Find 8 Words; Clue*)

OTHER WORD FORMS

blaze: blazes, blazed, blazing, blazer
blow: blows, blew, blowing, blown
blue: blues, bluer, bluest, blueness, bluish
divide: divides, divided, division, dividend
ignite: ignites, ignited, igniting, igniter
light: lights, lit, lighted, lighting, starlight

magnify: magnified, magnifying, magnification
show: shows, shone, showing, showboat
splash: splashes, splashed, splashing, splashdown
squiggle: squiggles, squiggled, squiggling
understand: understands, understood, understanding
work: works, worked, working, homework

209

Discovering How the Short Vowels Work

1. **ad-**advertisement (*Clue; Same Pattern*)

2. **add-**join together (*Visual; Clue*)

3. **catnap** (*Phonics; Rule; Same Pattern*)

4. **fantastic** (*Phonics; Clue*)

5. **hatband** (*Find 8 Words; Rule*)

6. **cent** (*Phonics; Clue*)

7. **scent** (*Phonics; Clue*)

8. **desk** (*Clue; Rule*)

9. **kitten** (*Clue; Same Pattern*)

10. **limit** (*Visual; Clue*)

11. **picnic** (*Phonics; Visual*)

12. **victim** (*Phonics; Clue*)

13. **frogman** (*Rule; Same Pattern*)

14. **optic-**re: eyes (*Visual; Clue*)

15. **robin** (*Clue; Roots*)

16. **pumpkin** (*SPP; Clue; Rule*)

17. **summit** (*Clue; Rule; Roots*)

18. **umbrella** (*Clue; Roots*)

19. **plum** (*Clue; Same Pattern*)

20. **plume** (*Clue; Rule*)

➤ **cold** (*Phonics; Clue; Same Pattern*)

➤ **both** (*Phonics; Clue; Same Pattern*)

➤ **pint** (*Phonics; Clue; Same Pattern*)

➤ **hundred** (*Phonics; Clue; Beat*)

➤ **magnet** (*Phonics; Clue; Rule*)

OTHER WORD FORMS

add: adds, added, adding, addition

cold: colds, colder, coldest, coldly

hundred: hundreds, hundredth

limit: limits, limited, limiting, limitless, unlimited

picnic: picnics, picnicked, picnicking, picnicker frolicked, panicking, mimicked (*Inserted K Rule*)

magnet: magnetize, magnetic, magnetically

nap: naps, napped, napping, catnaps

optic: optics, optical, optician

victim: victims, victimize, victimizes, victimizing

Long Vowel Sounds and the Powerful Silent E

1. escape (*Clue; Roots*)

2. glade (*Clue; Rule*)

3. translate (*Find 7 Words; Rule; Roots*)

4. whale (*Clue; Same Pattern*)

5. meters (*Clue; Roots*)

6. scene (*Phonics; SPP; Clue*)

7. theme (*Visual; Find 5 Words; Clue; Roots*)

8. chime (*Clue, Same Pattern*)

9. ninety (*SPP; Rule; Beat*)

10. strike (*SPP; Clue*)

11. while (*SPP; Clue*)

12. write-v. to write (*SPP; Rule*)   right-adj. correct (*Phonics; Clue*)

13. roses (*Phonics; Clue; Roots*)

14. whole-adj. total (*SPP; Clue; Rule*)

15. hole-n. opening (*Clue; Same Pattern*)

16. costume (*Phonics; Clue; Rule*)

17. huge (*Phonics; Clue; Same Pattern*)

18. picture (*SPP; Clue; Roots*)

19. give (*Phonics; Clue; Same Pattern*)

20. love (*Clue; Same Pattern; Roots*)

➤ fudge (*Phonics; SPP; Clue*)

➤ more (*Clue; Same Pattern*)

➤ none (*Clue; Same Pattern*)

➤ some (*SPP; Clue; Same Pattern*)

➤ were (*Clue; Roots*)

OTHER WORD FORMS: (Words 1-17 follow the *Silent E Rule*. The rest of the words are exceptions.)

chime: chimes, chimed, chiming
escape: escapes, escaped, escaping
give: gives, gave, giving, giver
love: loving, lovable, lovely, lovelier, loveliest
mete: metes, meted, meting, meter, meters
nine: nineteen, ninety, ninetieth, ninth

picture: pictures, pictured, picturing, picturesque
scene: scenes, scenic, scenically
strike: strikes, struck, striking, striker, strikingly
translate: translated, translating, translation
whole: wholly (exception), wholeness
write: writes, wrote, writing, written, writer

When Two Vowels Go Walking, the First One Does the Talking

1. braid (*Clue; Same Pattern*)

2. laid (*Clue; Same Pattern*)

3. spray (*Clue; Same Pattern*)

4. creak-squeaking sound (*Clue; Same Pattern*)

5. creek-stream (*Clue; Same Pattern*)

6. reach (*Clue; Same Pattern*)

7. speak (*Clue; Same Pattern*)

8. unbeaten (*Find 10 Words; Clue; Same Pattern*)

9. street (*Clue; Same Pattern*)

10. tied (*Clue; Same Pattern*)

11. foal (*SPP; Clue*)

12. groan-moan (*Clue; Same Pattern*)

13. grown-mature (*Clue; Same Pattern*)

14. cruel (*SPP; Clue*)

15. statue (*Clue; Rule; Same Pattern*)

16. fruit (*Clue; Rule; Same Pattern*)

17. breath (*Clue; Rule Ex.*)

18. breathe (*Find 6 Words; Clue*)

19. heart (*Find 5 Words; Clue; Rule Ex.*)

20. read-to read (*Clue; Same Pattern*)   read-past of to read (*Clue; Same Pattern*)

➤ been (*Clue; Rule Ex.*)

➤ brake-to stop (*E Rule; Same Pattern*)

➤ break-to break; dissolve (*Clue; Rule Ex.*)

➤ instead (*Clue; Rule Ex.; Same Pattern*)

➤ ocean (*Phonics; SPP; Clue*)

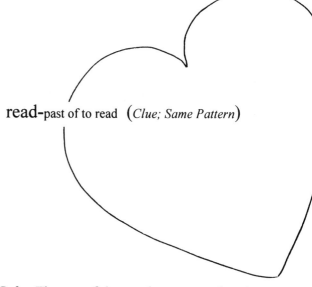

OTHER WORD FORMS (Words 1-16 follow *VV Rule*. The rest of the words are exceptions.)

braid: braids, braided, braiding	lay: lays, laid, laying, lain
brake: brakes, braked, braking	reach: reaches, reached, reaching
break: broke, breaking, broken	read: reads, read (past) reading, reader
breathe: breathes, breathed, breathing, breath	speak: speaks, spoke, speaking, speaker
groan: groans, groaned, groaning	spray: sprays, sprayed, spraying, sprayer
grow: grows, grew, growing, grown, grown-up	tie: ties, tied, tying, retie, retied

The Rules and Patterns for the IE, EI Words

1. believe (*Find 5 Words; Clue; Same Pattern*)
2. chief (*Clue; Same Pattern*)
3. grief (*SPP; Clue; Same Pattern*)
4. field (*Clue; Same Pattern*)
5. fierce (*Phonics; Clue; Same Pattern*)
6. niece (*Phonics; Clue*)
7. piece-n. individual amount, a work (*Phonics; Clue;*)
8. peace-stillness, no war (*Phonics; Clue*)
9. shield (*SPP; Clue*)
10. shriek (*SPP; Clue*)
11. foreign (*Find 6 Words; Clue*)
12. either (*Clue; Same Pattern*)
13. height (*Clue*)
14. seize (*Clue; Beat*)
15. ceiling (*Phonics; Clue*)
16. receive (*OWF; Same Pattern*)
17. leisure (*Phonics; Clue*)
18. sleigh (*Phonics; Rule; Clue*)
19. weight (*Clue; Rule*)
20. vein-blood vessel to the heart (*Phonics; Rule; Clue*)
➤ ancient (*Phonics; SPP; Clue*)
➤ efficient (*Phonics; SPP; Same Pattern*)
➤ fiery (*SPP; Clue*)
➤ retriever (*SPP; Clue*)
➤ quotient-answer in division (*Phonics; SPP; Same Pattern*)
➤ EXTRA: hieroglyphics (*Phonics; Clue; Roots*)

OTHER WORD FORMS

believe: believes, believed, believing, belief
efficient: efficiently, efficiency
fierce: fiercer, fiercest, fiercely
fire: fires, fiery, firefly, firelight, fireman
grieve: grieves, grieved, grieving, grief
leisure: leisurely, leisured, leisureliness

receive: received, receiving, reception, receipt
retrieve: retrieves, retrieved, retrieving, retriever
seize: seizes, seized, seizing, seizure
shield: shields, shielded, shielding
shriek: shrieks, shrieked, shrieking
weigh: weighs, weighed, weighing, weight

Special Two-Vowel Combinations and Sounds

au and aw, oi and oy, ou and ow, oo and oo, and ew

1. authored (*Find 6 Words; SPP; Clue*)
2. haunt (*Clue; Same Pattern*)
3. taught (*Phonics; Clue*)
4. fawn (*Clue; Same Pattern*)
5. also (*Rule; Same Pattern*)
6. coil (*Phonics; Clue; Same Pattern*)
7. loyalty (*Rule; Roots*)
8. about (*Clue; Same Pattern*)
9. aloud (*Clue; Same Pattern*)
10. allowed (*Clue; SPP*)
11. fountain (*Clue; Same Pattern*)
12. ground (*Clue; Same Pattern*)
13. outside (*Rule; Same Pattern*)
14. crowd (*SPP; Clue; Roots*)
15. downtown (*Clue; Same Pattern*)
16. knew-v. past of know (*SPP; Same Pattern*)
17. new-fresh (*Clue; Same Pattern*)
18. moonlight (*Phonics; Rule; Same Pattern*)
19. soon (*Clue; Same Pattern*)
20. cookbook (*Visual; Rule; Same Pattern*)
    - ➤ noise (*SPP; Clue; Same Pattern*)
    - ➤ poise (*Clue; Same Pattern*)
    - ➤ root-n. part of plant; v. cheer (*Clue; Same Pattern*)
    - ➤ route-n. way (*SPP; Clue*)
    - ➤ typhoon (*Phonics; Clue; Beat; Roots*)
    - ➤ EXTRA: porpoise (*Clue; Roots*)

OTHER WORD FORMS

allow: allows, allowed, allowing, allowance
author: authors, authored, authoring
coil: coils, coiled, coiling, recoil
crowd: crowds, crowded, crowding
ground: grounds, grounded, grounding

haunt: haunts, haunted, haunting, hauntingly
loyal: loyally, loyalty, loyalties, loyalist
noise: noisy, noisier, noisiest, noisily, noiseless (poise)
root: roots, rooted, rooting, rooter
route: routes, routed, routing

Powerful R Can Control Any Vowel

1. star (*Clue; Same Pattern*)

2. germ (*Phonics; Clue*)

3. bird (*Clue*)

4. horned (*Clue; Roots*)

5. survive (*Clue; Roots*)

6. desire (*Phonics; Same Pattern*)

7. pure (*Clue; Same Pattern*)

8. air-n. what you breathe (*Clue; Same Pattern*)

9. heir-n. one who inherits (*SPP; Clue*)

10. where (*Clue; Same Pattern*)

11. appeared (*Find 8 Words; SPP; Clue*)

12. years (*Clue; Same Pattern*)

13. darkness (*Rule; Same Pattern*)

14. dinosaur (*SPP; Roots*)

15. during (*E Rule; Roots; SPP*)

16. earth (*Visual; Clue*)

17. lizard (*Phonics; Clue; Roots*)

18. several (*Clue; Beat*)

19. enormous (*Clue; Roots*)

20. world (*Visual; Phonics; SPP*)

➢ important (*Find 10 Words; Clue*)

➢ purpose (*Clue; Same Pattern*)

➢ surround (*Clue; Roots*)

➢ terrible (*Clue; Beat*)

➢ water (*Clue; Rule Ex.; Roots*)

➢ EXTRA: tyrannosaurus rex (*Clue*)

OTHER WORD FORMS

appear: appears, appeared, appearing, appearance
dark: darker, darkest, darken, darkening, darkness
desire: desires, desired, desiring
import: importance, important, importantly
pure: purer, purest, purely, purify, purity

purpose: purposes, purposed, purposely, purposeful
star: stars, starred, starring, starlight
surround: surrounds, surrounded, surrounding
survive: survives, survived, surviving, survivor
terror: terrorizes, terrorized, terrorizing, terrible

Discovering How Open Syllables Work
and What's a Schwa?

1. aglow (*Phonics; Clue; Roots*)

2. alone (*Find 5 Words; Clue; Silent E Rule*)

3. sagas-legends, tales (*Visual; Phonics; Clue*)

4. table (*Clue; OWF*)

5. cereal (*SPP; Clue; Roots*)

6. elevator (*Clue; Silent E Rule*)

7. eraser (*Open Syllables; Clue; Silent E Rule*)

8. meteor (*Open Syllables; Roots*)

9. minus (*Phonics; Clue*)

10. minute-tiny (*Pronunciation*)   minute-60 seconds (*Rule Exception*)

11. obedient (*Open Syllables; Clue*)

12. robot (*Visual; Clue; Beat*)

13. tornado (*Clue; Open Syllable.*)

14. pupils (*Open Syllables; Clue*)

15. student (*Clue; Open Syllable.*)

16. canyon (*Phonics; Visual*)

17. citizen (*Phonics; Clue; Y Rule*)

18. eleven (*Visual; Clue*)

19. galaxy-n. system of stars (*Clue*)

20. manager (*Clue*)

   ➢ civilization (*Visual; Roots; Beat*)

   ➢ encyclopedia (*Visual; Roots; Beat*)

   ➢ intimidated-v. made afraid (*Find 15 Words; Clue*)

   ➢ universe (*SPP; Roots*)

   ➢ uranium (*Clue; Roots*)

OTHER WORD FORMS   (All the words below have open syllable. The schwas are underlined.)

civilized: civilizes, civilized, civilization, civic
elevate: elevates, elevated, elevating, elevator
erase: erases, erased, erasing, eraser, erasure
galaxy: galaxies, galactic, intergalactic
intimidate: intimidates, intimidating, intimidator
lone: lonely, lonelier, loneliest, loner, alone

manage: manages, managed, managing, manager
mete: metes, meted, meting, meter, thermometer
obedient: obey, obeying, obediently, obedience
study: studies, studied, studying, student
table: tables, tabled, tabling, tablet, roundtable
universe: university, universal, universally

Let's Try All the Vowel Sounds

1. later (*Clue; Rule*)

2. latter (*Rule; Same Pattern*)

3. hair-on head (*Clue; Same Pattern*)   hare-rabbit (*Clue; Same Pattern*)

4. sense (*Phonics; Clue*)

5. easy (*Clue; Rule*)

6. feather (*Phonics; Visual; Clue*)

7. thermometer (*Find 8 Words; Clue; Roots*)

8. peer-equal (*Clue; Same Pattern*)   pier-dock (*Clue; Same Pattern*)

9. quit (*Clue; Qu Rule; Short Vowel Rule*)

10. quite (*Silent E Rule; Same Pattern*)

11. swirl (*Clue; Roots*)

12. honorable (*SPP; Clue*)

13. road-path (*Clue; 2 V. Rule*)   rode-did ride (*Clue; E Rule*)   rowed-oared (*2 V. Rule; Same Pat.*)

14. colorful (*Visual; Roots*)

15. quarter (*Clue; Roots*)

16. word (*Phonics; Clue; Roots; Same Pattern*)

17. truth (*Clue; Roots; S Vowel Ex.*)

18. snoopy (*Clue; Same Pattern; Roots*)

19. house (*Clue; Same Pattern; Roots*)

20. power (*Phonics; Same Pattern*)

➤ many (*Find 5 Words; Clue; Roots*)

➤ oyster (*Phonics; Clue*)

➤ people (*SPP; Clue; Visual; Beat*)

➤ searing-burning (*Clue*)

➤ yolk (*SPP; Clue; Roots*)

OTHER WORD FORMS

ease: eases, eased, easier, easiest, easily
honor: honors, honoring, honorable, honest
late: later, lately, latter
peer: peers, peered, peering, peerless
power: powers, powered, powerful, powerfully
quit: quits, quitting, quitter

row: rows, rowed, rowing, rower
sear: sears, seared, searing
sense: senses, sensed, sensing, sensible, sensation
snoop: snoops, snooped, snooping, snoopy
swirl: swirls, swirled, swirling
true: truth, truths, truly, truthful

The Solid Compound Word Rule

1. beanstalk (*Find 8 Words; Clue*)

2. breakfast (*Clue; Roots*)

3. cupboard (*Phonics; Clue*)

4. fireworks (*Clue; Silent E Rule*)

5. handsome (*SPP; Clue*)

6. horseback (*SPP; Same Pattern*)

7. lamplighter (*Clue; Same Pattern*)

8. lifeguard (*Clue; SPP; E Rule*)

9. newsstand (*Phonics; Visual; Beat*)

10. spaceship (*Phonics; Clue; Rule*)

11. teammate (*9 Words; Visual; Clue; 2 Vowel*)

12. weeknights (*Phonics; Clue; 2 Vowel Rule*)

13. everybody (*SPP; Clue*)

14. Internet (*Roots; Same Pattern*)

15. nothing (*Clue; Roots*)

16. nevertheless (*Visual; Clue*)

17. jack-o-lantern (*Find 7 Words, Clue, Roots*)

18. roller coaster (*Rules; Same Pattern*)

19. alphabet (*Phonics; Comp. Rule Ex.*)

20. shepherd (*Clue; Comp. Rule Ex.*)

➢ although (*Phonics; Clue; Comp. Rule Ex.*)

➢ passed-v. went by; succeeded (*Rule; Same Pattern*)   past-n. time before (*Clue; Same Pattern*)

➢ pastime-n. interest; hobby (*Clue; Comp. Rule Ex.*)

➢ until (*Compound Rule Ex.*)

➢ welcome (*SPP; Rule Exception; Roots*)

OTHER WORD FORMS (<u>Well</u>, <u>till</u>, <u>all</u>, <u>pass</u> drop a letter. Sheepherd and alphabeta also drop a letter.)

alphabet: alphabetize, alphabetical, alphabetically
break: breaks, broke, breaking, broken, breakfast
coast: coasts, coasted, coasting, roller coaster
fast: fasts, fasted, fasting, breakfast
guard: guards, guarded, guarding, lifeguard

light, lights, lighting, lighter, lightest, lamplighter
pass: passes, passed, passing, past, pastime
shepherd: shepherds, shepherded, shepherding
team: teams, teamed, teaming, teammate
welcome: welcomes, welcomed, welcoming

Learning About Prefixes-Just Fasten Them in Front

1. discovery (*Find 7 Words; Clue; Roots*)

2. discuss (*Phonics; Clue; Roots*)

3. mistreat (*Clue; Prefix Rule*)

4. multiply (*Rule; Roots*)

5. nonfiction (*SPP; Clue; Roots*)

6. nonsense (*Phonics; Visual; OWF*)

7. underrate (*Rules; Beat*)

8. unknown (*SPP; Clue*)

9. prehistoric (*Clue; Roots*)

10. prejudge (*SPP; Same Pattern*)

11. prefix (*Clue; Prefix Rule*)

12. prepare (*Clue; Roots*)

13. prescribe (*Rule; Roots*)

14. postdate (*Clue; Beat; Same Pattern*)

15. postscript (*Clue; Roots*)

16. recount (*Clue; Same Pattern*)

17. repaid (*Clue; 2 Vowel Rule*)

18. replay (*Clue; 2 Vowel Rule*)

19. return (*Clue; Prefix Rule; Same Pattern*)

20. surface (*SPP; Clue; Roots*)

➤ overdo-do too much (*Clue*)

➤ overdue-late (*Clue: 2 Vowel Rule*)

➤ overreact (*Visual; Roots*)

➤ rearrange (*Find 7 Words; Clue; Same Pattern*)

➤ submarine (*Rule; Roots*)

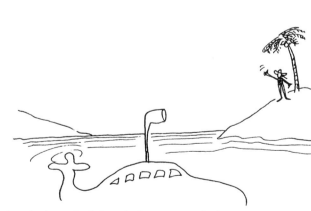

OTHER WORD FORMS

arrange: arranges, arranged, arranging, rearrange
discover: discovered, discovering, discovery
discuss: discussed, discussing, discussion
fair: fairs, fairer, fairest, fairly, unfair
handle: handles, handled, handling, mishandle
history: historic, historically, prehistoric

judge: judges, judging, judgment, prejudge
multiply: multiplies, multiplied, multiplying
prepare: prepares, prepared, preparation
react: reacts, reacted, reacting, reaction, reactor
recount: recounts, recounted, recounting; encounter
repay: repays, repaid, repaying, repayment (replay)

Three Prefixes That Have Different Forms

1. accuse (*Phonics; Same Pattern; Beat*)

2. annual (*Clue; Beat*)

3. assistant (*Visual; Find 12 Words; Clue*)

4. because (*Phonics*)

5. become (*Clue; Roots*)

6. collect (*Clue; Roots*)

7. compete (*Clue; Root*)

8. connect (*Visual; Rule*)

9. correct (*Clue; Rule*)

10. describe (*Rule; Roots*)

11. destroy (*Clue; Roots*)

12. excited (*Clue; Rule; Roots*)

13. exercise (*Phonics; Clue; Beat*)

14. foreword-word before the book (*Clue; Rule*)

15. forward-to move toward (*Clue; Rule*)

16. illegal (*Clue; Roots*)

17. impact (*Phonics; Clue*)

18. impolite (*Clue; Rule; Roots*)

19. infinite (*Visual; Clue*)

20. inherit (*Clue*)

➤ ascend-go up (*Clue; Roots*)

➤ descend-go down (*Clue; Roots*)

➤ emigrate (*Roots*)

➤ immigrate (*Clue; Roots; Rule*)

➤ impossible (*SPP; Clue; OWF; Roots*)

OTHER WORD FORMS (<u>In</u>-, <u>ad</u>-, <u>com</u>- create double-letters by matching 1st letter of root they're added to.)

ascend: ascended, ascending, ascent, ascension

assist: assists, assisting, assistants, assistance

collect: collected, collecting, collection, collector

compete: competed, competing, competition

connect: connected, connection, connector

correct: corrected, correcting, correction, correctly

descend: descended, descending, descent

describe: described, description, descriptive

destroy: destroyed, destroying, destroyer

emigrate: emigrated, emigrating, emigrant

excite: excited, exciting, excitement, excitedly

immigrate: immigrated, immigrating, immigrant

Magical Suffixes: Just Add Them at the End

1. cheerful (*2 Vowel Rule; Rule Ex., Same Pattern*)

2. faithful (*2 Vowel Rule; Clue*)

3. harmful (*Clue; Same Pattern*)

4. careless (*Silent E Rule; Suffix Rule*)

5. helpless (*Clue; Suffix Rule*)

6. thoughtless (*Visual; Phonics; Suffix Rule*)

7. early (*Clue; Roots*)

8. finally (*Find 7 Words; Clue; Beat*)

9. monthly (*Phonics; Clue*)

10. naturally (*Clue; Rule*)

11. sincerely (*Phonics; Clue; Roots*)

12. smoothly (*Phonics; Clue*)

13. surely (*Phonics; Clue; Silent E Rule*)

14. happiness (*Y Rule; Short Vowel Rule*)

15. kindness (*Clue; Rule*)

16. stillness (*Clue; Rule*)

17. lemonade (*Clue; Roots*)

18. highest (*Phonics; Visual*)

19. largest (*Phonics; Clue*)

20. nearer (*Clue; Rule, Roots*)

➢ abandoned (*Find 10 Words; Clue*)

➢ grateful-thankful (*Clue; Roots*)

➢ greatly-highly (*Clue; Roots*)

➢ scholarship (*Roots*)

➢ wonderment (*Visual; Clue*)

OTHER WORD FORMS

abandon: abandoned, abandoning, abandonment
care: cares, caring, careful, carefully, careless
great: greater, greatest, greatly, greatness
happy: happier, happiest, happily, happiness
harm: harmed, harming, harmful, harmfully

school: schools, schooling, scholar, scholarship
smooth: soother, smoothest; smoothed, smoothing
sure: surer, surest, surely, sureness, assurance
thought: thoughtfully, thoughtfulness, thoughtlessly
wonder: wondering, wonderfully, wonderment

The Rule for Adding Suffixes after Silent E

1. achievement (*Clue; Silent E Rule*)
2. excitement (*Prefix Rule; Silent E Rule*)
3. likely (*Silent E Rule*)
4. making (*E Rule; Roots*)
5. notable (*Find 6 Words; Clue*)
6. pleasing (*Clue; E Rule*)
7. unusual (*Clue; E Rule*)
8. writing (*E Rule; Suffix Rule; Same Pattern*)
9. coming (*Phonics; Rule*)
10. giving (*Rule; Same Pattern*)
11. having (*Rule; Same Pattern*)
12. lovable (*Silent E Rule; Beat*)
13. changeable (*SPP; E Rule for Soft G.*)
14. noticeable (*Clue; E Rule for Soft C*)
15. courageous (*Clue; E Rule for Soft G*)
16. outrageous (*SPP; Clue; E Rule for Soft G*)
17. canoeing (*Phonics; Clue; E Rule*)
18. shoeing (*E Rule; Same Pattern*)
19. dying (*E Rule Exception; Same Pattern*)
20. dyeing (*Clue; Rule*)

➢ awful (*E Rule Exception; Same Pattern*)
➢ rescuing (*Clue; Rule Exception*)
➢ truly (*Clue; Rule Exception*)
➢ valuable (*Clue; Rule Exception*)
➢ wholly (*Clue; Rule Exception*)

OTHER WORD FORMS (When <u>e</u> follows consonants, keep <u>e</u> before consonant suffixes. Drop <u>e</u> before vowel suffixes, except for Soft C-s sound and Soft G-j sound. When <u>e</u> follows a vowel: keep the <u>e</u>. *Exceptions*: lying, rescuing, truly..

canoe: canoes, canoed, canoeing
change: changes, changed, changing, changeable
die: dies, died, dying
dye: dyes, dyed, dyeing, redyeing
excite: excited, exciting, excitable, excitement
like: likes, liked, liking, likable, likely, likeliness

love: loved, loving, lovable, lovely, loveliness
notice: notices, noticed, noticing, noticeable
please: pleased, pleasing, pleaser, pleasant, pleasure
rescue: rescues, rescued, rescuing, rescuer
shoe: shoes, shoed, shoeing
true: truer, truest, truly; whole: wholly

The Rule for Adding Suffixes after Final Y

1. busily (*Phonics; Clue; Rule*)

2. carriage (*Phonics; SPP; Clue; Y Rule*)

3. crying (*Clue; Y Rule; Same Pattern*)

4. easily (*Phonics; Y Rule; 2 Vowel Rule*)

5. emptiness (*Clue; Y Rule*)

6. emptying (*Clue; Y Rule*)

7. hurrying (*Y Rule; S V Rule; Beat*)

8. laziness (*Clue; Y Rule*)

9. prettier (*Short Vowel Rule; Y Rule; Same Pattern*)

10. readying (*Find 6 Words; Y Rule*)

11. tried (*SPP; Y Rule; Same Pattern*)

12. worrying (*Clue; Y Rule; S V Rule*)

13. buyer (*Visual, Clue; Y Rule*)

14. buying (*Y Rule; Beat*)

15. enjoyed (*Y Rule; Same Pattern*)

16. enjoyment (*Y Rule; Same Pattern*)

17. playing (*Find 6 Words; Clue; Same Pattern*)

18. prayed-v. said prayers (*Clue; Same Pattern*)

19. preyed-v. hunted (*Clue; Y Rule*)

20. stayed (*SPP; Clue; Beat*)

➤ daily (*SPP; Clue; Y Rule Ex.; Beat*)

➤ lying (*Rule; Same Pattern*)

➤ paid (*Clue; Y Rule Ex.; 2 V Rule; Same Pattern*)

➤ said (*Phonics; SPP; Clue; Y Rule Ex.; Same Pattern*)

➤ parliament-parley-to talk (*SPP; Y Rule Ex.*)

OTHER WORD FORMS (Words 1-20 follow *Y Rule*: When y follows a consonant, change y to i, before all suffixes except -ing. When y follows a vowel, keep y before all suffixes. Exceptions: *paid, said, parliament.*)

buy: buys, bought, buying, buyer
carry: carries, carried, carrying, carrier, carriage
cry: cries, cried, crying (lie: lied, lying)
ease: eases, eased, easing, easily
enjoy: enjoys, enjoyed, enjoying, enjoyment
hurry: hurries, hurried, hurrying

pay: pays, paid, paying, payment
pray: prays, prayed, praying, prayer (play-played)
prey: preys, preyed, preying
ready: readies, readied, readying, readily
say: says, said, saying, sayings
try: tries, tried, trying, trial

The Power of Suffixes to Create Nouns

1. abundance (*Phonics; Clue*)

2. ambulance (*Clue; Roots*)

3. balance (*SPP; Roots; Beat*)

4. instance-an occurrence (*SPP; Clue*)

5. instant-moment (*Find 7 Words; Rule*)

6. beggar (*Short Vowel Rule; Clue*)

7. dollar (*Clue; Rule*)

8. sugar (*Phonics; Clue*)

9. character (*Phonics; SPP; Clue*)

10. teacher (*Phonics; Clue*)

11. actor (*Phonics; Clue*)

12. alligator (*Clue; S V Rule*)

13. doctor (*Phonics; Clue*)

14. inventor (*Clue; Short Vowel Rule*)

15. exploration (*Clue, Rule; Roots*)

16. imagination (*Clue; E Rule*)

17. information (*Find 10 Words; Roots*)

18. vacation (*Phonics; E Rule*)

19. surgeon (*Phonics; Clue*)

20. company (*Phonics; Roots*)

➤ experience (*Visual; Beat*)

➤ initiation (*7 Words; Clue; Rule*)

➤ intelligence (*Phonics; Visual*)

➤ license (*SPP; Clue; OWF; Same Pattern*)

➤ remembrance (*3 syllables; SPP; Clue*)

OTHER WORD FORMS

act: acts, acted, acting, action, actor
balance: balances, balancing, balancer
experience: experiences, experiencing, experiment
explore: explores, exploring, exploration, explorer
imagine: imagined, imagining, imagination
inform: informed, information, informer

initiate: initiated, initiating, initiation, initiator
invent: invented, inventing, invention, inventor
license: licenses, licensed, licensing, licensure
remember: remembers, remembering, remembrance
teach: teaches, taught, teaching, teacher
vacation: vacationed, vacationing, vacant

POWER SPELLING GAME 32

Suffixes Can Create Adjectives, Verbs and Adverbs

1. comfortable (*Phonics; Find 8 Words; Roots*)

2. fourth (*Clue; Suffix Rule*)

3. medical (*Phonics; Root*)

4. mysterious (*Clue; Y Rule*)

5. simplest (*Suffix Rule*)

6. splendid (*Clue; S V Rule*)

7. vacant (*Phonics; Clue*)

8. celebrated (*Phonics; Clue; E Rule*)

9. danced (*Phonics; SPP; Clue; Rule*)

10. energize (*Phonics; OWF; Beat*)

11. finished (*Clue*)

12. isolate (*Clue*)

13. always (*Rule Ex. for <u>all</u>; Same Pattern*)

14. accidentally (*Find 12 Words; Phonics; Clue*)

15. fortunately (*Clue; Rule*)

16. gently (*Phonics; Clue; Same Root*)

17. slowly (*Clue; 2 Vowels Rule; Same Pattern*)

18. usually (*Phonics; Clue*)

19. weakly-adv. with little strength (*Clue; 2 Vowels Rule*)

20. weekly-adv. every seven days (*Clue; 2 Vowel Rule*

➤ exorbitant (*Find 9 Words; Clue*)

➤ judicial (*SPP; Clue; Roots*)

➤ sensible (*Phonics; Clue*)

➤ significant (*Phonics; Clue*)

➤ visible (*Clue; Roots*)

OTHER WORD FORMS (All these words follow the *Suffix Rule*.)

celebrate: celebrates, celebrating, celebration

dance: dances, danced, dancing, dancer

energy: energize, energized, energetically

finish: finished, finishing, finisher

hear: hears, heard, hearing, hearer

medicine (medic + in + e): medical, medically

sense: sensed, sensible, sensibility, sensibly

sign: signify, signified, significant, significantly

simple: simpler, simplest, simply, simplification

weak: weaker, weakest, weakly, weaknesses

225

The Doubling Final Consonants Rule
(for One-and Two-Syllable Words)

1. currant-small red berry (*Phonics; Clue; Rule*)

2. current-Flow of water, electricity. (*Phonics; Clue; Rule*)

3. hugged (*SPP; Phonics; Rule*)

4. planned (*SPP; Clue; Rule*)

5. quitting (*Qu and S V Rule; Same Pattern*)

6. scared (*Clue; E Rule; Same Pattern*)

7. scarred (*Clue; S V Rule; Same Pattern*)

8. skipping (*Rule; Same Pattern; Beat*)

9. slammed (*SPP; Clue; Rule*)

10. sledding (*Find 6 Words; Clue*)

11. staring (*E Rule; Same Pattern*)

12. starring (*Clue; Rule*)

13. swimming (*Clue; Roots*)

14. trotting (*Visual; Rule; Beat*)

15. beginning (*Find 7 Words; Clue; Rule*)

16. controlled (*Phonics; Clue; Rule*)

17. forgetting (*Rules*)

18. happening (*Clue; Rule*)

19. limiting (*Visual; Rule*)

20. traveling (*Clue; Rule; Same Pattern*)

➢ excellent (*Visual; Clue; Rule Exception*)

➢ picnicking (*Phonics; Visual; Inserted K Rule*)

➢ preferred (*Visual; SPP; Clue; Same Pattern*)

➢ reveled (*Clue; Same Pattern*)

➢ oc-cur-rence (*Phonics; Clue; Rule*)

OTHER WORD FORMS   {All words, except *excellent*, follow the Doubling Final Consonants Rule.}

begin: began, beginning, beginner

control: controlled, controlling, controller

excel: excelled, excelling, excellent, excellence

forget: forgot, forgetting, forgotten forgetful

happen, happens, happened, happening

limit: limits, limited, limiting, limitless

occur: occurred, occurring: occurrence (concur, prefer)

picnic: picnicked, picnicking (frolicked, panicked, trafficked)

scar: scars, scarred, scarring, scarless

scare: scares, scared, scaring, scary

star: stars, starred, starring, starry, starlight

travel: travels, traveled, traveling, traveler

Suffixes Make Nouns Plural in Many Ways

1. buffaloes (*Clue; Roots: Indian Plural*)

2. echoes (*Phonics; SPP*)

3. heroes (*Clue; 2 Vowels Rule*)

4. mosquitoes (*Clue; Roots: Sp.-Indian Plural*)

5. potatoes (*Clue; Roots*)

6. torpedoes (*Find 6 Words; Clue*)

7. altos (*Clue; Roots*)

8. pianos (*Clue; Rule for Ital. Musical Words*)

9. radios (*Clue*)

10. sopranos (*Clue; Roots*)

11. stereos (*Clue; Roots*)

12. studios (*Clue; Roots*)

13. videos (*Roots; Roots*)

14. halves (*SPP; Clue; OE Pattern*)

15. loaves (*Clue; Same Pattern*)

16. beliefs (*Clue; Roots' Beat; OE Pattern*)

17. countries (*SPP; Clue; Y Rule*)

18. families (*Clue; Y Rule; Roots*)

19. valleys (*Clue; Rule; Roots*)

20. children (*Clue; Roots; Roots*)

21. moose (*Clue; Rule; Roots*)

22. gnus-African antelopes (*Phonics; SPP; Clue*)

23. news-report of events (*Phonics; Clue*)

24. women-woman (*SPP; Roots; Same Pattern*)

25. lunches (*Phonics; Same Pattern*)

➤ princesses (*Clue; Rule*)

➤ feat-festive achievement (*Clue; Same Pattern*)

➤ feet-body part (*Clue; Roots; Same Pattern*)

➤ parentheses (*Find 14 Words; Same Pattern; Roots*)

➤ alumna, alumnae; alumnus, alumni (*Roots*)

227

The Challenging L Endings: al, el, le, il, and ol

1. bridal-re: wedding (*Clue; E Rule; Same Pattern*)

2. bridle-re: horse (*Visual; Clue*)

3. medal (*Clue; OWF; Homophone*)

4. metal (*Clue; OWF; Homophone*)

5. petal (*Clue; Same Pattern; Roots*)

6. tidal (*Clue; Rule; Roots*)

7. total (*SPP; Clue*)

8. channel (*Clue; Beat*)

9. nickel (*Phonics; Clue; Roots*)

10. shovel (*Clue; Beat*)

11. towel (*SPP; Clue; Rule*)

12. tunnel (*Clue; OWF; Rule*)

13. able (*Clue; OWF*)

14. example (*Phonics; Clue*)

15. handled (*Find 7 Words; SPP; Clue*)

16. little (*OWF; Clue; S V Rule*)

17. muscles (*Phonics; SPP; Clue*)

18. title-name of book, poem... (*Clue; OWF*)

19. trouble (*Clue; OWF*)

20. pencil (*Phonics; Clue*)

> council-like city council (*Phonics; Clue*)

> counsel-advice; advise (*Clue*)

> cymbals (*Clue; Roots*)

> symbols (*Clue; Roots*)

> special (*Phonics; SPP; Roots*)

OTHER WORD FORMS

able: abler, ablest, ably, enable, enabler
bridle: bridles, bridled, bridling
counsel: counseled, counseling, counselor
handle: handle, handling, handler
little: littler, littlest
muscle: muscled, muscular (Homophone: mussels)

shovel: shovels, shoveled, shoveling
special: specially, specialty, especially
title: titles, titled, titling, entitled
towel: towels, toweled, toweling
trouble: troubles, troubled, troubling
tunnel: tunnels, tunneled, tunneling

Words with Roots: sede, ceed, cede, plus Old Seed

1. seed (*Clue; Root; Same Patterns*)

2. seedling (*Visual; Rule; Roots*)

3. supersede-replace in power (*Rule; Roots*)

4. proceed-go onward (*Clue; 2 V Rule*)

5. process (*Clue; Roots*)

6. succeed-achieve the result (*Clue; 2 V Rule*)

7. success (*Phonics; Clue; Rule; Roots*)

8. exceed-go beyond (*Clue; Rule*)

9. exceeding (*Clue; 2 V Rule*)

10. antecede (*Visual; Roots*)

11. cede-yield land (*Clue; Roots*)

12. concede-yield to someone's view (*Clue; E Rule; Roots*)

13. intercede-go between for someone (*E Rule; Roots*)

14. interceding (*Clue; Same Pattern*)

15. precedent-went before (*Phonics; Roots*)

16. recede-move back like waves or hairline (*Clue; Roots*)

17. receding (*Phonics; Clue*)

18. reseeding (*Find 9 Words; Clue, Rules*)

19. recess (*Clue; Roots; Same Pattern*)

20. secede-withdraw from, like a nation (*Phonics; Roots*)

➢ ancestors (*Phonics; Clue; Roots*)

➢ concession-act of yielding (*SPP; Beat*)

➢ intercession (*SPP; Beat*)

➢ procedure (*SPP; Clue*)

➢ successor (*Clue*)

OTHER WORD FORMS

seed: seeds, seeded, seeding, seedling
supersede: supersedes, superseded, superseding
proceed: proceeded, process, processor, procedure
succeed: succeeded, successfully, successor
exceed: exceeded, exceeding, excess, excessively
antecede: anteceding, antecedent, ancestors

cede: cedes, ceded, ceding
concede: conceded, conceding, concession
intercede: interceded, intercession, intercessor
precede: precedes, preceding, precedent
recede: recedes, receded, receding, recess
secede: secedes, seceded, seceding

Getting to Know Your POWER Spelling Tools

1. **at-ten-dance**: *Find 9 Words*: <u>a</u>, <u>an</u>, <u>at</u>, <u>attend</u>, <u>Dan</u>, <u>dance</u>, <u>end</u>, <u>ten</u>, <u>tend</u>.
   Clue-in-a-Row: After <u>attendance</u>, they said, "<u>At ten, dance</u>."

2. **is-land**: *Phonics*: <u>c</u> = <u>k</u>; <u>s</u> = <u>silent</u>. *Clue-in-a-Row*: There <u>is land</u> on an <u>island</u>.

3. **to-get-her**: *Clue-in-a-Row*: We all went <u>together</u> <u>to get her</u>: <u>to</u> + <u>get</u> + <u>her</u>.

4. **to-mor-row**: *Clue*: <u>Tom or (I will) row</u> the boat <u>tomorrow</u>: <u>Tom</u> + <u>or</u> + <u>row</u>.

5. **hear** (v., listen): *Clue*: I can <u>hear</u> with my <u>ear</u>. *Same Pattern*: dear, fear, gear, near, sear, tear.

6. **here** (adv., this place): *Clue*: <u>Here</u> is w<u>here</u> the place is. *Same Pattern*: here, there, w<u>here</u>.

7. **hang-ar** (n., storage for airplanes): *Clue*: The <u>hangar</u> with an <u>a</u> is an <u>airplane</u> <u>hangar</u>.

8. **hang-er** (n., for hanging clothes): *Clue*: The <u>hanger</u> with an <u>e</u> is a clothe<u>s</u> <u>hanger</u>.

9. **ear-ring**: *Visual*: See <u>2 r's</u> in <u>earring</u>. *Compound Rule*: Add: <u>ear</u> + <u>ring</u> = <u>earring</u>.

10. **race-car**: *Phonics*: <u>c</u> = <u>s</u>; <u>c</u> = <u>k</u>. *Visual*: <u>Racecar</u> is a palindrome (same backwards and forwards).
    Compound Rule: <u>race</u> + <u>car</u> = <u>racecar</u>. *Rule*: <u>Silent e</u> makes <u>a</u> in <u>race</u> long

11. **dis-a-gree**: *Prefix Rule*: <u>dis</u> (pre.:not) + <u>agree</u> = <u>disagree</u> (not agree). *Rule*: The <u>e</u> makes <u>e</u> long.

12. **mis-spell**: *Clue-in-a-Row*: <u>Miss Pell</u> said, "Please don't <u>misspell</u>."
    Rule: <u>2 s's</u> make <u>i short</u>; <u>2 l's</u> makes <u>e short</u>. *Prefix Rule*: <u>mis</u> (G. pre: wrong) + <u>spell</u> = <u>misspell</u>.

13. **re-read**: *Rule*: Add prefix: <u>re</u> (L. pre: again) + <u>read</u> = <u>reread</u>. *2 Vowel Rule*: <u>A</u> makes <u>e</u> long.

14. **Feb-ru-ary**: *Pronounce*: <u>2 r's</u>: Feb-<u>ru</u>-ary. *Clue*: <u>R U</u> making <u>February</u> Valentines?

15. **meant**: *SPP*: me-ant. *Clue*: I saw that me and my <u>ant</u> were <u>meant</u> to be friends: <u>me</u> + <u>ant</u> = <u>meant</u>.

16. **li-brar-y**: *Clue*: <u>R</u>are books are in our <u>library</u>. *OWF*: Our libr<u>ar</u>ian (Hear 2 r's) runs the <u>library</u>.

17. **ge-og-ra-phy**: *Phonics*: <u>g's</u> = <u>g sound</u>. *Roots*: <u>geo</u> (G. earth) + <u>graphy</u> (G. map) = <u>geography</u>

18. **tel-e-phone**: *Phonics*: Gk. <u>ph</u> = <u>f</u>. *Rule*: <u>Silent e</u> at the end of <u>phone</u> makes the <u>o long</u>.
    Roots: <u>tele</u> (G. far) + <u>phone</u> (G. sound) = <u>telephone</u>.

19. **trans-port**: *6 Words*: <u>a</u>, <u>an</u>, <u>or</u>, <u>port</u>, <u>ran</u>, <u>sport</u>. *Roots* : <u>trans</u> (L. across) + <u>port</u> (L. carry) = <u>transport</u>

20. **bal-loon**: *Clue*: <u>Ball</u>'s in <u>balloon</u>. *Visual*: 2 sticks <u>l l</u> and 2 balloons <u>o o</u> in <u>balloon</u>.

➤ **bi-ol-o-gy**: *Rule* and *Roots*: <u>bio</u> (G. life) + <u>logy</u> (G. study of) = <u>biology</u> (study of life).

➤ **dis-ease**: *Clue*: <u>Disease</u> means your body is not (<u>dis</u>) at <u>ease</u>.
   Prefix Rule: Add: <u>dis</u> (L. prefix: not) + <u>ease</u> (M.Eng. comfort) = <u>disease</u>.

➤ **no-ticed**: *7 Words*: <u>Ed</u>, <u>I</u>, <u>ice</u>, <u>iced</u>, <u>no</u>, <u>not</u>, <u>notice</u>.
   Phonics: <u>c</u> = <u>s sound</u>. *Clue in a Row*: I <u>noticed</u> my juice was <u>not iced</u>.

➤ **par-al-lel**: *Visual*: 3 parallel <u>l's</u>. *Clue*: <u>All</u> 3 <u>l's</u> are <u>parallel</u> – on a <u>par</u>: <u>par</u> + <u>all</u> + <u>el</u>.

➤ **rhy-thm**: *Visual*: rhy – <u>thm</u> (no vowel in *thm*). *Beat*:

Discovering the History of the English Language

1. **al-tar** (n. in church): *Visual*: In some churches the altar area rises like an A (L. altaria).

2. **al-ter** (v. to change): *Clue*: He wanted to alter the president's term (L. alter: change).

3. **ba-gel**: *Phonics*: g = g. *Clue*: A bagel in my bag is for my elephant: bag + el (Yid: begyl).

4. **ba-na-na**: *Visual*: See the palindrome: anana inside banana. *Beat*: b-a n-a n-a (Afr.).

5. **can-dle**: *Phonics*: c = k. *Clue*: Please let me light the candle (L. candera: to shine).

6. **can-dy**: *Phonics*: c = k. *Clue*: They sent me candy in a can. *Same Pattern*: dandy, handy, sandy.

7. **choc-o-late**: *Phonics*: c = k. *SPP*: cho-co-la-te. *Roots*: cho-co-la-te (Sp. Pronunciation.).

8. **com-pu-ter**: *Phonics*: c = k. *Rule*: E makes u long. *Roots*: com(pre: with) + put (L. puta: counting; thinking) + er (noun suf.) = computer (with thinking).

9. **fa-ther**: *SPP*: fa-the-r. *Clue*: Her father works at her home: f + at + her (O.E. faeder).

10. **friend**: *Clue*: On Fri., (the) end of the week, I see my friend (M.E. friend).

11. **ham-bur-ger**: *Rule*: All syllables follow *Short Vowel Rule*. *Roots*: Hamburger is a German word from the German city, Hamburg (+ er).

12. **li-ber-ty**: *Clue*: Bert values life and liberty: li + Bert + y. *Roots*: liber (Fr./L. liber: free) + ty (n. suf.).

13. **moth-er**: *Clue*: We wanted no other mother. *Roots*: mother (O. E. modor).

14. **neigh-bor**: *Phonics*: eigh = long a. *Clue*: Eight neighbors were born in 2001: n + eight + born. *Roots*: neighbor: (Old English, *nigh-ge-bur* means *near by farm* or *barn*.)

15. **pho-to-graph**: *6 Words*: graph, ho, hot, photo, rap, to. *Phonics*: Gk., ph = f. *Rule and Roots*: *Gk. Compound Word*: photo (G. light) + graph (G. writing) = photograph (light writing).

16. **ro-de-o**: *Visual*: rode + o = rodeo. *Clue*: He rode his horse in the rodeo (Sp. rodeo).

17. **scribe**: *Rule*: Silent e makes i long. *Same Root*: describe, prescribe, scribble.

18. **skate**: *Clue*: Kate loved to skate. *Rule*: Silent e makes a in skate long (Norse/Dutch: skati).

19. **spa-ghet-ti**: *Phonics*: H = silent. *SPP*: spag-het-ti. *Roots*: spaghetti (Ital. long thin ropes).

20. **vol-ca-no**: *Clue*: How much lava vol(ume) can there be in a volcano: volume + can + o (Ital.).

➤ **an-ti-sep-tic**: *8 Words*: a, an, ant, anti, I, Sept., septic, tis *Clue*: I used antiseptic in Sept. *Roots*: anti (pre: against) + sept (Gk. septos: rotted) + ic (n. suf.) = anti + sept + ic (against what's rotted).

➤ **chil-i** (Sp./Mex. pepper; hot dish): *Visual*: Turn ili (palindrome) into 3 chili peppers: (ili) (also: chile).

➤ **chilly** (adj. cold): *Clue*: We've had our fill of chilly weather. *Same Pattern*: Billy, hilly, silly

➤ **phan-tom**: *Phonics*: In Gk., ph = f. *Clue*: Tom was a phantom for Halloween: phan + Tom.

➤ **res-tau-rant**: *SPP*: res-ta-u-rant. *Clue*: I saw an ant rest at a restaurant (Fr. restaurare: to restore).

Let's Create Some POWER Spelling Clues

1.   **ache**: *Clue*: I had <u>a ch</u>est ache. *Phonics*: <u>ch</u> = <u>k</u>. *SPP*: ac-<u>he</u>. *Roots*: <u>ache</u> (O.E. acan).

2.   **ad-dress**: *Clue*: <u>Add</u> my <u>address</u> to your <u>address</u> book.. *Rule*: <u>2d's</u> keep <u>a</u> short; <u>2s's</u> keeps <u>e</u> short.

3.   **a-gain**: *SPP*: a-ga-in. *Clue-in-a-Row*: Practice <u>again</u> and <u>again</u> to make <u>a gain</u> in skill.

4.   **ar-gu-ment**: *Clue*: It's hard to have an <u>argument</u> with <u>gum</u> in your mouth. *E Rule Ex.*

5.   **beau-ti-ful**: *Clue*: <u>Be a</u> <u>b…utiful</u> person. *Rule*: <u>Y</u> changes to <u>i</u> except before -ing: beaut<u>y</u> + i + ful.

6.   **bi-cy-cle**: *Visual*: 2 wheels and a pedal: cyc. *Clue*: Don't ride a b<u>icy</u>cle on <u>icy</u> streets. *Roots* and *Prefix Rule*: <u>bi</u> (G. two) + <u>cycle</u> (G. wheel) = <u>bicycle</u>.

7.   **busi-ness**: *Clue*: I need a bus in my business. *Y Rule*: bus<u>y</u> + i + ness.

8.   **cal-en-dar**: *Phonics*: <u>c</u> = <u>k</u>. *Clue*: A <u>calendar</u> has a list of <u>dates</u>.

9.   **cer-tain**: *Phonics*: <u>c</u> = <u>k</u> sound. *Clue*: It's cert<u>ain</u> to r<u>ain</u>. *Beat*: c - e - r - t - a - i -n.

10. **des-ert** (n., dry place): *Phonics*: <u>s</u> = <u>z</u>. *Clue*: A <u>desert</u> can feel silent and alone: <u>one s</u>.

11. **de-sert** (v., abandon): *Phonics*: <u>s</u> = <u>z</u>. *Clue*: The <u>s</u> in <u>desert</u> is <u>one s</u> alone and abandoned.

12. **des-sert** (n., after-meal treat): *Phonics*: <u>s</u> = silent; <u>s</u> = <u>z</u>. *Clue*: For <u>ss</u>, think of <u>s</u>trawberry <u>s</u>hortcake; <u>s</u>omething <u>s</u>weet; or: I want <u>s</u>econd<u>s</u> on de<u>ss</u>ert. *Beat*: d - e - s - s - e - r - t .

13. **does** (v., past of do): *Phonics*: <u>s</u> = <u>z</u>. *Clue*: <u>Does</u> has 2 <u>does</u> (deer) in it. *Pattern*: goes, hoes, toes.

14. **goes**: *Phonics*: <u>s</u> = <u>z</u>. *Clue*: While he <u>goes</u> driving, I <u>go</u> escape to a beach. *Same Pattern*: toes, woes

15. **horse**: *SPP*: hor-<u>se</u>. *Clue*: She cooled down her <u>horse</u> with a <u>hose</u>.

16. **of-ten**: *Phonics*: <u>t</u> = silent. *SPP*: of-<u>ten</u>. *Clue-in-a-Row*: I'm of<u>ten</u> one <u>of ten</u> kids who run.

17. **sep-a-rate**: *Visual*: *6 Words*: <u>a</u>, <u>at</u>, <u>ate</u>, <u>par</u>, <u>rat</u>, <u>rate</u>. *Clue*: As I tried to sep<u>a rat</u>e the oranges and apples, <u>a rat</u> jumped out. *Rule*: <u>Silent e</u> makes <u>a</u> long in <u>rate</u>.

18. **stairs** (n., steps): *Clue*: Sometimes I jump the <u>stairs</u> in p<u>airs</u>. *Same Pattern*: chairs, fair.

19. **stares** (n., v., gaze): *6 Words*: <u>a</u>, <u>are</u>, <u>star</u>, <u>tat</u>, <u>tare</u>, <u>tares</u>. *Clue*: She <u>stares</u> at <u>stars</u> with c<u>are</u>.

20. **straight**: *Phonics*: <u>aigh</u> = long <u>a</u>. *Clue*: A <u>straw</u> is <u>right</u> if it's <u>straight</u>: stra~~w~~ + ~~r~~ight. *Rule*: <u>I</u> makes <u>a</u> long.

➤   **fa-mil-iar**: *Clue*: It's not good to be <u>familiar</u> with a <u>liar</u>. *Y Rule*: Change <u>y</u> to <u>i</u> except before <u>-ing</u>: fam<u>ily</u> + i + ar = <u>familiar</u> (M.E. familie).

➤   **threw** (v., tossed): *Clue*: We <u>threw</u> out the b<u>rew</u>. *Same Pattern*: brew, crew, drew, flew, stew.

➤   **through** (done; go through): *SPP*: thro-<u>ugh</u>. *Phonics*: <u>ough</u> = oo. *Clue*: It's <u>rough</u> walking <u>through</u> doo

➤   **tired**: *Clue*: When I get t<u>ired</u>, my eyes are <u>red</u>. *Rule*: <u>Silent e</u> makes <u>i</u> long in t<u>ired</u>.

➤   **tried**: *Clue*: <u>Ed</u> and <u>I tried</u> hard: <u>tr</u> + <u>I</u> + <u>Ed</u>. *Rule*: Change <u>y</u> to <u>i</u> except before -ing: tr<u>y</u> + i + ed.

Conquering Contractions and Possessives

1. **they're** (they are): *Clue*: <u>Hey</u>, <u>they're</u> at school. (*Note* – <u>the</u>y're, <u>the</u>ir, <u>the</u>re begin with <u>the</u>.)

2. **their** (poss. pron.): *4 Words*: <u>he</u>, <u>heir</u>, <u>I</u>, <u>the</u>. *Clue*: <u>He</u> is the<u>i</u>r <u>heir</u> (one who inherits).

3. **there** (adv., tells where): *4 Words*: <u>ere</u>, <u>he</u>, <u>here</u>, <u>the</u>. *Clue*: We went <u>here</u>, <u>there</u>, and every<u>where</u>.

4. **it's** (it is): *Clue*: <u>It's</u> a b<u>it</u> early for leaves to change color. *Rule*: <u>It</u> follows *Short Vowel Rule*.

5. **its** (poss. pron.): *Clue*: We <u>sit</u> and watch our tree shed <u>its</u> leaves. *Same Pattern*: fit, lit, knit.

6. **you're** (you are): *Clue*: <u>You're</u> my friend, <u>Lou</u> who shows c<u>are</u>. *Same Pattern*: Lou, you.

7. **your** (poss. pronoun): *Visual* and *Clue*: See the *possessive pronoun* <u>our</u> in y<u>our</u>.

8. **who's** (who is): *SPP*: <u>w</u>-ho's. *Clue*: <u>Who's</u> playing kickball with <u>whom</u>?

9. **whose** (poss. pron.): *SPP*: <u>w</u>-hose. *Clue*: <u>Whose</u> <u>hose</u> is this? *Roots*: <u>whose</u> (O. E. hwaes).

10. **I'm** (I am): *Clue*: <u>I'm</u> riding a horse named S<u>am</u>. *Same Pattern*: am, ham, Pam, ram, wham.

11. **he'd** (He would): Clue: I knew <u>he'd</u> come with T<u>ed</u> because he said <u>he</u> <u>would</u>.

12. **she'll** (She will): <u>She'll</u> help you find a <u>shell</u>. *Pattern*: I'll, he'll, they'll, you'll, we'll.

13. **we're** (we are): *Rule*: <u>We're</u> is a contraction (We are). <u>Were</u> is a verb (We <u>were</u> h<u>ere</u>).

14. **let's** (let us): *Clue*: <u>Let's</u> get a <u>net</u> to catch pollywogs. *Same Pattern*: bet, met, set, wet.

15. **aren't** (are not): *Clue*: <u>Aren't</u> you going to take c<u>are</u> of your horse? *Beat*: a-r-e-n-(apostrophe)-t.

16. **doesn't** (does not): *Phonics*: s = z. *Clue*: <u>Does</u> has <u>does</u> (deer) in it. *Same Pattern*: goes, toes…

17. **haven't** (have not): *Clue*: <u>Haven't</u> you ridden to the c<u>ave</u> before? *Rule*: Contraction <u>n't</u> = <u>not</u>.
Exception: <u>Silent e</u> does not make <u>a</u> in <u>have</u> long (<u>E</u> just completes <u>have</u>: also true for *give, love…*)

18. **isn't** (is not): *Phonics*: s = z. *Clue*: <u>Isn't</u> that h<u>is</u> home? *Same Pattern*: his, tis.

19. **wasn't** (was not): *Phonics*: <u>was</u> = <u>wuz</u> sound. *Clue*: <u>Wasn't</u> (was not) the road just ahead?

20. **o'clock** (of the clock). *Clue*: The <u>clock</u> was made of r<u>ock</u>. *Same Pattern*: block, dock, flock.

➤ **couldn't** (could not): *SPP*: <u>co-uld-n't</u>. *Same Pattern*: should, would (O. E. colde, sholde, wolde).

➤ **should've** (should have): *SPP*: sho-ul-d. *Same Pattern*: I <u>should've</u>, and I w<u>ould've</u> if I c<u>ould've</u>.

➤ **friends'** (poss. plur. noun): *Clue*: On <u>Fri. (the) end</u> of the week, I see my <u>friends'</u> puppies.

➤ **horses'** (poss. plur. noun): *Clue*: My <u>horses'</u> legs weren't <u>worse</u> after their run: <u>h</u> + ~~worses~~.

➤ **pen-guin's**: *SPP*: pen-gu-in. *Clue*: <u>G, U in</u> the <u>penguin's</u> suit, here's your <u>pen</u>: <u>pen</u> + G U in.

➤ EXTRA: **nightingale's**: *Clue-in-a-Row*: Even at <u>night, in gales</u> of wind, a <u>nightingale's</u> mate sings.

Tackling Homophones and Other Confusing Words

1. **bear** (animal; carry): *Clue*: The <u>bear</u> listened with his <u>ears</u>. *Same Pattern*: bear, pear, tear (rip).

2. **bare** (adj., naked): *Clue*: If you're <u>bare</u>, someone might st<u>are</u>. *Same Pattern*: bare, care, dare.

3. **buy** (v., pay for): *Visual* and *Clue*: Put the gift y<u>ou</u> <u>buy</u> in a sack (<u>u</u>). *Phonics*: <u>uy</u> = long <u>i</u>.

4. **by**: (prep. adv.): *Visual* and *Rule*: I raced <u>by</u> the park. (Prepositions are usually short: at, by, in, of, to.)

5. **bye**: (farewell) *SPP*: Some people say, "<u>by-e</u>." *Same Pattern*: dye, lye, rye.

6. **cap-i-tal** (n. city): *5 Words*: <u>a</u>, <u>Al</u>, <u>cap</u>, <u>I</u>, <u>pit</u>. *Clue*: <u>Tallahassee</u> is the <u>capital</u> of Florida.
   cap-i-tal (adj. letters): *Clue*: <u>Capital</u> letters are t<u>all</u>er than lower case letters.

7. **Cap-i-tol** (n. building): *Visual* and *Clue*: Most <u>Capitol</u>s have a d<u>o</u>me on t<u>o</u>p: <u>O</u>.

8. **dear** (adj., treasured): *Clue*: My children are <u>near</u> and <u>dear</u> to me. *Same Pattern*: fear, hear.

9. **deer** (n., animal): *Visual*: *Reversal*: <u>deer</u> – <u>reed</u>. *Clue*: The <u>deer</u> nibbled on a <u>reed</u>.

10. **flo-urs** (n., grain): *Clue*: We need <u>our</u> <u>flours</u> to make <u>our</u> cake.

11. **flow-ers** (n., a bloom): *Clue*: April sh<u>owers</u> bring May <u>flowers</u>. *Beat*: f-l-o w-e-r.

12. **hour** (n. time): *SPP*: <u>h</u>-our. *Clue*: Half an <u>hour</u> is 30 minutes. *Roots*: <u>hour</u> (L., G. <u>hora</u>: time).

13. **our** (poss. pron: belonging to us): *Clue*: <u>Our</u> pickles are s<u>our</u>. *Same Pattern*: hour, our, sour.

14. **prin-ci-pal** (n., person in charge): *6 Words*: <u>a</u>, <u>Al</u>, <u>I</u>, <u>in</u>, <u>pa</u>, <u>pal</u>. *Clue*: Is the <u>principal</u> your <u>pal</u>?

15. **prin-ci-ple** (n., rule): *Clue*: The <u>principle</u> that's a <u>rule</u> has <u>le</u> at the end: <u>principle</u>.

16. **sta-tion-ary** (adj., stable; in one place): *Clue*: Something <u>stationary</u> st<u>ay</u>s in one place.

17. **sta-tion-ery** (n., for writing letters): *Clue*: You use <u>stationery</u> for lett<u>er</u>s.

18. **to** (prep. <u>to</u> a place): *Visual*: <u>To</u> is short. *Pronunciation*: *Say* <u>to</u> quickly like *ta*: <u>to</u> school, <u>to</u> work…

19. **too** (adv. also; in addition): *Visual*: <u>Too</u> stretches out. *Say*: I ate *too*… much. I want to go *toooo*…

20. **two** (n., adj. number): *Phonics*: silent <u>w</u>. *Clue*: The <u>two</u> (2) of us have <u>two</u> (2) great kids.

➤ **though** (in spite of): *Clue*: Even <u>though</u> it's <u>rough</u>, I'll see it thr<u>ough</u>.

➤ **thought** (n., idea): *Visual*: *Bookend Word*: <u>thought</u>. *Beat*: t - h - o - u - g - h - t.
   Clue: I <u>ought</u> to have <u>thought</u> first. *Same Pattern*: bought, brought.

➤ **ought** (v. should): *Clue*: I <u>ought</u> to have br<u>ought</u> the book I b<u>ought</u>. *Same Pattern*: fought, thought.

➤ **wea-ther**: *7 Words*: <u>a</u>, <u>at</u>, <u>eat</u>, <u>he</u>, <u>her</u>, <u>the</u>, <u>we</u>. *Clue-in-a-Row*: Why are <u>we at her</u> over the <u>weather</u>?

➤ **whe-ther**: *Clue-in-a-Row*: He aimed to <u>whet her</u> interest in <u>whether</u> or not ETs existed.
   Clue: My surgeon decides <u>whether</u> or not to use <u>ether</u>. *See* <u>whet</u> (sharpen; make eager) + <u>her</u>.

Phonics: The Building Blocks of Spelling

1. **ant** (n., insect): *Clue*: An <u>ant</u> <u>can't</u> move a rubber tree pl<u>ant</u>. *Pattern*: pant, Santa.
   aunt (n., relative): *Clue*: My <u>aunt</u> went on a <u>jaunt</u> (short journey). *Pattern*: gaunt (thin), haunt.

2. **se-ven**: *Phonics*: <u>s</u> = <u>s</u> sound. *Clue*: <u>Seven</u> is not an <u>even</u> number.

3. **ig-loo**: *Visual*: <u>Igloo</u> is shaped like an <u>igloo</u>. *Clue*: A white m<u>oon</u> l<u>oom</u>ed above the <u>igloo</u>.

4. **oc-to-pus**: *Phonics*: <u>c</u> = <u>k</u>; <u>c</u> = <u>s</u>. *Roots*: <u>octo</u> (G. okto: 8) + <u>pus</u> (G. pous: feet) = <u>octopus</u> (8 feet).

5. **um-pire**: *Clue*: Don't f<u>ire</u> the <u>umpire</u>. *Rule*: <u>Silent e</u> makes <u>i</u> long. *Roots*: <u>um</u> (pre: not) + <u>pire</u> (O. Fr. peer) = <u>umpire</u> (not a peer: An <u>umpire</u> is above peers in making decisions).

6. **a-maze**: *SPP*: a-ma-ze. *Clue-in-a-Row*: Does a challenge of <u>a maze</u> <u>amaze</u> you? *Rule*: <u>E</u> makes <u>a</u> long.

7. **these**: *Visual*: <u>S</u> turn <u>thee</u> into <u>these</u>. *Phonics*: <u>s</u> = <u>z</u>. *Rule*: <u>Silent e</u> makes <u>e</u> before it long.

8. **i-de-a**: *Visual*: 3 *Open Syllables*: <u>i</u> – <u>de</u> – <u>a</u> (a vowel or end in a vowel). *Clue*: <u>I deal</u> with new <u>ideas</u>.

9. **o-pened**: *SPP*: o-pen-ed. *Clue-in-a-Row*: Please leave an <u>opened</u> door <u>open, Ed</u>: <u>open + Ed</u>.

10. **fuel**: *SPP*: fu-el. *Clue*: It's cr<u>uel</u> to not share <u>fuel</u>. *Same Pattern*: cruel, duel, fuel.

11. **par-ty**: *Clue*: I did my <u>part</u> to create <u>art</u> at the <u>party</u>. *Roots*: party (O. Fr. <u>parti</u>: share).

12. **ve-ry** (adv., much): *Clue*: E<u>very</u> time I run I'm <u>very</u> free. *Roots*: <u>ver</u> (L. verus: truth) + <u>y</u> (suf.).

13. **birth-day**: *Compound Rule*: Add <u>birth</u> + <u>day</u>. *Same Pattern*: girth (holds saddle on), mirth (joy).

14. **store**: *SPP*: sto-re. *Clue*: She <u>tore</u> through the <u>store</u> to buy m<u>ore</u>. *Same Pattern*: bore, core, fore.

15. **tur-tle**: *Clue*: <u>Let</u> me feed B<u>urt</u>, my <u>turtle</u>, some <u>lettuce</u>: <u>t + Burt + le</u>. *Beat*: t-u-r   t-l-e.

16. **air-plane**: *7 Words*: <u>a</u>, <u>air</u>, <u>an</u>, <u>I</u>, <u>lane</u>, <u>plan</u>, <u>plane</u>. *Clue*: The <u>airplane</u> ran down a runway <u>lane</u>. *Compound Rule*: Add: <u>air + plane</u>. *Rule*: <u>Silent e</u> makes <u>a</u> in <u>plane</u> long. (Homophone: plane-plain).

17. **tear** (n., fluid from eyes): *Clue*: A <u>tear</u> flowed n<u>ear</u> my <u>ear</u>. *Same Pattern*: fear, gear, hear, near.
    tear (v., rip): *Clue*: The b<u>ear</u> began to <u>tear</u> open the food. *Same Pattern*: pear, wear.

18. **sure**: *Phonics*: <u>S</u> = <u>sh</u> sound. *Clue*: This water <u>sure</u> is p<u>ure</u>. *Same Pattern*: cure, lure, pure.

19. **looked**: *Visual*: He <u>looked</u> with 2 eyes: <u>l-o o-ked</u>. *SPP*: look-ed. *Pattern*: booked, looked.

20. **mouth**: *SPP*: mo-u<u>th</u>. *Clue*: His <u>mouth</u> yelled out, "<u>south</u>."

➤ **loose** (adj. not tight): *Phonics*: <u>s</u> = <u>s</u>. *Clue*: The <u>goose</u> got <u>loose</u>. *Same Pattern*: moose, papoose.
  lose (v., can't find): *Phonics*: <u>s</u> = <u>z</u>. *Clue*: Don't <u>lose</u> your n<u>ose</u>?

➤ **oint-ment**: *Phonics*: <u>oi</u> = diphthong. *Clue*: They gave me <u>ointment</u> at my <u>appointment</u>.

➤ **pause**: *Clue-in-a-Row*: I often hear <u>pa use</u> a <u>pause</u>. *Same Pattern*: clause.
  paws: *Clue*: <u>Paws</u> often have cl<u>aws</u>. *Same Pattern*: flaws, saws.

➤ **re-mem-ber**: *Visual*: <u>3 e's</u>. *Clue*: <u>Remember</u> December. *Same Pattern*: member, September…

➤ **voy-age**: *Phonics*: <u>g</u> = <u>j</u>; <u>oy</u> = <u>oi</u>. *Clue*: The b<u>oy</u> is <u>age</u> for a <u>voyage</u> to sea: v + ~~boy~~ + age.

Feeling the Sounds of Single Consonants and Digraph

1. **bub-ble**: *Visual*: 3 b's look like <u>bubble</u> <u>bl</u>owers. *Clue*: They <u>bl</u>ew <u>bubbles</u>. · *TOOT!*

2. **buz-zing**: *Clue*: Do you hear that <u>fuzzy buzzing</u>? *Beat*: b-u-z-z-i-n-g.
   Rule: When a word ends in a consonant, just add the suffix: <u>buzz</u> + <u>ing</u> = <u>buzzing</u>.

3. **choose**: *Clue*: I <u>choose</u> that <u>goose</u>. *Same Pattern*: caboose, goose, loose, moose.

4. **chose**: *Phonics*: <u>s</u> = <u>z</u>. *Clue*: I <u>chose</u> a <u>hose</u> to water the <u>rose</u>. *Rule*: <u>Silent e</u> makes <u>o</u> long.

5. **church**: *Visual*: *Echo Word*: See and hear <u>ch</u> at the beginning and end: <u>ch</u>-ur-<u>ch</u>.

6. **diz-zy**: *Clue*: <u>Lizzy</u> felt <u>dizzy</u> (O. E. ysig: foolish). *Same Pattern*: fizzy, tizzy. *Beat*: d-i-z-z-y.

7. **gong**: *Clue*: A <u>gong</u> makes a d<u>ong</u> sound (Malay language, Java). *Same Pattern*: bong, song.

8. **hush**: *Clue*: <u>Shh</u>…<u>hush</u> little baby. *Same Pattern*: bush, gush, hush, mush, push.

9. **kick-ball**: *6 Words*: <u>a</u>, <u>Al</u>, <u>all</u>, <u>ball</u>, <u>I</u>, <u>kick</u>. *Visual*: See 2 <u>kick</u>ers: <u>k</u> <u>k</u>.
   Compound Rule: Add: <u>kick</u> + <u>ball</u> = kickball. *Same Pattern*: Nick, Rick, pick; call, fall, tall.

10. **laugh**: *Phonics*: <u>ugh</u> = <u>f</u>. *SPP*: la-ugh. *Clue*: <u>Laurel's</u> <u>laugh</u> went "<u>la-ugh</u>." (M.E., *laughen*)

11. **mur-mur**: *Visual*: 3 letters repeat: mur + mur = <u>murmur</u>. *Beat*: m-u-r   m-u-r.

12. **pop-ping**: *Rule*: 2 p's keep <u>o</u> short: popping. *Beat*: p-o-pp-i-n-g. *POP POP*

13. **ring-ing**: *Clue*: I'm <u>ringing</u> bells and <u>singing</u>. *Roots*: <u>ring</u> (O. E. h<u>ringan</u>) + <u>ing</u> (v. suf.) = <u>ringing</u>.

14. **sha-dow**: *SPP*: sha-do-w. *Clue*: Out of the <u>shade</u>, you'll have a <u>shadow</u> (Old Saxon: skadowan).

15. **shape**: *Clue*: What's the <u>shape</u> of Superman's <u>cape</u>? *Rule*: <u>Silent e</u> makes <u>a</u> long. *Pattern*: ape, tape

16. **tough**: *Phonics*: <u>gh</u> = <u>f</u> *SPP*: to-ugh. *Clue* and *Pattern*: <u>R</u>oughy's <u>rough</u> and <u>tough</u> en<u>ough</u>.

17. **trea-sure**: *Phonics*: <u>s</u> = <u>zh</u>. *Clue*: A <u>treasure</u> is a <u>trea(t for) sure</u>: <u>treat</u> + <u>sure</u> (measure, pleasure).

18. **when**: *SPP*: w-hen. *Clue*: <u>When</u> did the <u>hen</u> lay the egg? *Roots*: <u>when</u> (O.E., *hwenne*: <u>when</u>).

19. **which**: *SPP*: w-hich. *Clue*: <u>Which</u> color is truly <u>rich</u>? *Beat*: w – h – i – c – h.

20. **zoom-ing**: *Visual*: See the wheels of a <u>zooming</u> racecar: <u>o o</u>. *Same Pattern*: booming, rooming.

➤ **e-nough**: *Phonics*: <u>gh</u> = <u>f</u>. *SPP*: e-no-ugh. *Clue*: That sandpaper's <u>rough</u> <u>enough</u>.

➤ **pho-nics**: *Phonics*: Gk. <u>ph</u> = <u>f</u>. *Roots*: <u>phon</u> (Gk. sound) + <u>ics</u> (n. suf.) = <u>phonics</u>.

➤ **van-ished**: *Clue-in-a-Row*: My <u>van I shed</u> when I <u>vanished</u>. *Suffix Rule*: Add: <u>vanish</u> + <u>ed</u>.

➤ **whis-tle**: *SPP*: whis-t-le. *OWF*: I'm <u>whistling</u> with my <u>whistle</u>. *Same Pattern*: bristle, thistle.

➤ **young**: *Clue*: <u>You</u> are <u>young</u>: <u>you</u> + <u>ng</u> (digraph). *Same Pattern*: you, yours, youth

Feeling the Power of the Beat

1. **al-bum**: *Clue*: <u>Al</u> did not make an <u>album</u> for a <u>bum</u>: <u>Al + bum</u>. *Roots*: <u>album</u> (L. <u>albus</u>: white).

2. **brass**: *Phonics*: <u>2 s's</u> = <u>s</u>. *Clue*: The <u>brass</u> section practiced in cl<u>ass</u> (metal instruments in orchestra).

3. **cel-lo**: *Phonics*: <u>c</u> = <u>ch</u>. *Clue*: She played a <u>cello</u> while eating J<u>ello</u>. *Rule*: <u>2 l's</u> make <u>o</u> short.

4. **com-pos-er**: *OWF*: <u>Compose</u> ends in <u>e</u>, so add <u>r</u> for <u>composer</u> *Rule*: <u>Silent e</u> makes <u>o</u> long.
   Roots: <u>com</u> (pre: together; with) + <u>pose</u> (L. put) + <u>r</u> (n. suf: one who) = <u>composer</u> (one who puts together).

5. **con-cert**: *Phonics*: <u>c</u> = <u>k</u>; <u>c</u> = <u>s</u>. *Clue*: He was <u>cert</u>ain to go to the <u>concert</u>: <u>con + cert</u>.

6. **con-duc-tor**: *Clue-in-a-Row*: You can <u>conduct or</u> watch the <u>orchestra for</u> this <u>concert</u>.
   Rule and *Roots*: <u>con</u> (L. pre: with) + <u>duct</u> (L. lead) + <u>or</u> (n. suf: one who) = <u>conductor</u> (one who leads).

7. **drum-mer**: *Clue*: I love the summer drummer. *Rule*: <u>2 m's</u> keep <u>u</u> short. *Beat*: d-r-u-m-m-e-r.

8. **flute**: *Clue*: I play a <u>lute</u> and a <u>flute</u>. *Rule*: <u>Silent e</u> makes <u>u</u> long. *Pattern*: mute, cute.

9. **gui-tar**: *SPP*: gu-i-tar. *Clue*: <u>G, U</u> (and) <u>I</u> (got) tar on my <u>guitar</u>: <u>G + U + I + tar</u>.

10. **har-mon-i-ca**: *8 Words*: <u>a</u>, <u>arm</u>, <u>ha</u>, <u>harm</u>, <u>I</u>, <u>Mon.</u>, <u>Monica</u>, <u>on</u>. *Phonics*: <u>c</u> = <u>k</u>.
    Rule: Change <u>y</u> to <u>i</u> except before -<u>ing</u>: harmon~~y~~ + i + ca = harmonica.

11. **harp**: *Clue*: I play <u>sharps</u> on my <u>harp</u>. *Same Pattern*: harp, sharp tarp.

12. **key-board**: *6 Words*: <u>a</u>, <u>boa</u>, <u>boar</u>, <u>board</u>, <u>oar</u>, <u>key</u>. *Clue*: A <u>boar</u> (pig) ate my <u>keyboard</u>.
    Compound Rule: Add: <u>key</u> + <u>board</u> + <u>keyboard</u>.

13. **mu-si-cian**: *Phonics*: <u>s</u> = <u>z</u>; <u>ci</u> = <u>sh</u>. *SPP*: mu-<u>si</u>-<u>ci</u>-<u>an</u>. *Clue*: <u>Musicians</u> play <u>music</u>.

14. **or-ches-tra**: *Phonics*: <u>ch</u> = <u>k</u>. *Clue*: An <u>orchestra</u> is a pit <u>or chest</u> of instruments: <u>or + chest + ra</u>.

15. **pi-a-no**: *Pronounce 3 Open Syllables*: <u>pi-a-no</u>. *Clue*: <u>Pia</u> played the <u>piano</u>: <u>Pia + no</u> = <u>piano</u>.

16. **strings**: *Clue*: The <u>strings</u> of violins seem to s<u>ing</u>. *Same Pattern*: ding, ring, sing, wings.

17. **sym-pho-ny**: *Phonics*: Gk. <u>ph</u> = <u>f</u>. *Clue*: The <u>symphony</u> was not <u>phony</u>; it was great.
    Roots: <u>sym</u> (Gk. same) + <u>phon</u> (Gk. phonus: sound) + <u>y</u> (n. suf.) = <u>symphony</u> (same sound; harmonious).

18. **trum-pet**: *Clue*: I <u>strum</u> a guitar while my <u>pet</u> blows a <u>trumpet</u>: ~~strum~~ + pet. *Beat*: t-r-u-m-p-e-t.

19. **vi-o-lin**: *Pronounce 2 Open Syllables*: <u>vi-o</u>-lin. *Clue*: <u>Linda</u> studies <u>violin</u>: <u>vio + Lin</u>~~da~~.

20. **wood-winds**: *Clue*: <u>Woodwinds</u> are <u>wooden</u> instrument you blow <u>wind</u> through.
    Compound Rule: wood + winds = <u>woodwinds</u>.

➤ **au-di-ence**: *Roots*: <u>audi</u> (L. hear) + <u>ence</u> (n. suf.) = <u>audience</u>.
   Clue: The <u>audience</u> heard <u>audio</u> sound through a <u>fence</u>: audi~~e~~ + ~~f~~ence.

➤ **choir**: *Phonics*: <u>choir</u> = <u>kwir</u>. *Clue*: This <u>choir</u> is my choice choi~~ce~~ + r (O.E. choir).

➤ **chord** (n., 3 or more notes together): *Phonics*: <u>ch</u> = <u>k</u>. *SPP*: <u>c</u>-hord. *Clue*: A <u>chorus</u> sang <u>chords</u> for us.

➤ **cord** (n., rope; measure of wood): *Clue*: I <u>ord</u>ered a <u>cord</u> of wood tied with a <u>cord</u>. *Pattern*: Ford, lord.

➤ **per-cus-sion**: *SPP*: per-cus-si-on. *Clue*: Can each <u>person</u> dis<u>cuss</u> their <u>percussion</u> solo with me?
   <u>per</u> + <u>cuss</u> + <u>ion</u>. *Roots*: <u>percuss</u> (L., strike) + <u>ion</u> (n. suf) = <u>percussion</u>. *Beat*: p-e-r-c-u-ss-ion.

Divide and Conquer: Dividing Words into Syllables

1. **cat-tails**: *Compound Rule*: Add <u>cat</u> + <u>tails</u> = <u>cattails</u>. *Same Pattern*: hat, pat; hails, pails.

2. **glass-blow-er**: *12 Words*: <u>a</u>, <u>as</u>, <u>ass</u>, <u>glass</u>, <u>blow</u>, <u>blower</u>, <u>lass</u>, <u>low</u>, <u>lower</u>, <u>ow</u>, <u>owe</u>, <u>we</u>. *Compound Rule*: Add: <u>glass</u> + <u>blower</u> = <u>glassblower</u>.

3. **grand-dad**: *Compound Rule*: Add: <u>grand</u> + <u>dad</u> = <u>granddad</u>. *Pattern*s: hand, land; had, lad.

4. **pho-no-graph**: *Phonics*: Gk. <u>ph</u> = <u>f</u>. *2 Roots*: <u>phono</u> (G. sound) + <u>graph</u> (G. writing) = <u>phonograph</u>.

5. **wheel-bar-row**: *Clue*: He had an <u>arrow</u> in the <u>wheelbarrow</u>. *Compound Rule*: <u>wheel</u> + <u>barrow</u> = <u>wheelbarrow</u> (O. E. <u>barrow</u>: cart with handles).

6. **ac-cept**: *Roots*: <u>ac</u> (L. toward; to) + <u>cept</u> (L. ceptus: take; receive) = <u>accept</u> (to take; receive).

7. **ex-cept**: *Roots*: <u>ex</u> (L. not) + <u>cept</u> (L. ceptus: take; receive) = <u>except</u> (not take; exclude).

8. **mis-take**: *Clue*: Don't m<u>ake</u> the same <u>mistake</u>. *Roots*: <u>mis</u> (L. incorrectly; wrongly) + <u>take</u> (O.E. tacan: grasp; handle) = <u>mistake</u> (incorrectly handle).

9. **un-a-ware**: *Clue*: Is a baby's <u>unaware</u> of c<u>ares</u>? *Roots*: <u>un</u> (not) + <u>aware</u> (O. E. watchful) = <u>unaware</u>.

10. **fund-a-men-tal-ly**: *15 Words*: <u>a</u>, <u>Al</u>, <u>all</u>, <u>ally</u>, <u>am</u>, <u>amen</u>, <u>dam</u>, <u>dame</u>, <u>fun</u>, <u>fund</u>, <u>fundamental</u>, <u>men</u>, <u>mental</u>, <u>tall</u>, <u>tally</u>. *Clue-in-a-Row*: <u>Fundamentally</u>, we need to <u>fund a men tally</u> for the census.

11. **har-bors**: *Phonics*: <u>s</u> = <u>z</u>. *Clue*: The <u>boats</u> <u>bordered</u> the <u>harbors</u>.

12. **moun-tains**: *SPP*: mo-un-ta-ins. *Clue*: <u>Mountains</u> <u>mount</u> up to where it r<u>ains</u>: <u>mount</u> + <u>rains</u>.

13. **let-ters**: *Clue*: I write <u>letters</u> b<u>etter</u> now. *Rule*: <u>2 t's</u> keep <u>e</u> short. *Same Pattern*: better, wetter.

14. **sum-mer**: *Clue*: I was a dr<u>ummer</u> this <u>summer</u>. *Rule*: <u>2 m's</u> keep <u>u</u> short.

15. **ben-e-fits**: *Clue*: Mr. <u>Ben E. Fits</u> does <u>benefits</u>. *Roots*: <u>bene</u> (L. good) + <u>fits</u> (L. deed) = <u>benefits</u>.

16. **maj-es-ty**: *Clue*: <u>Ma</u> and a <u>jester</u> did tricks for his <u>Majesty</u>: <u>ma</u> + <u>jest</u> + <u>y</u> (M.E. majeste: dignity).

17. **si-lent**: *Clue*: Be <u>silent</u> when you <u>enter</u>. *Rule*: <u>Silent e</u> makes the <u>i</u> in <u>silent</u> long.

18. **fa-ble**: *Clue*: The truth in a <u>fable</u> can <u>bless</u> you. *OWF*: You can hear <u>bl</u> in <u>fabling</u>.

19. **hur-dle**: Clue: Don't get hurt when you hurdle. *OWF*: You can hear -<u>dl</u> in <u>hurdling</u>.

20. **mid-dle**: *See*: <u>2 d's</u> in the <u>middle</u>. *OWF*: Hear <u>dl</u> in, "I'm feeling fair to <u>middling</u>."

➤   **a-mi-a-ble** (adj. friendly): *Clue-in-a-Row*: <u>Am I able</u> to be <u>amiable</u>? (Fr. <u>ami</u>: friend + <u>able</u> = friendly).

➤   **es-tab-lish-ment**: *Rule*: All the syllables follow the short vowel rule. *Clue*: I paid my <u>tab</u> to the <u>men</u> in the <u>establishment</u>: <u>es</u> + <u>tab</u> + <u>lish</u> + <u>men</u> + <u>t</u>.

➤   **hel-i-cop-ter**: *Clue*: The blade of a <u>helicopter</u> turns like a <u>helix</u> (G. spiral): <u>helix</u> + <u>copter</u>. *Roots*: <u>heli</u> (G. helix: to turn; spiral) + <u>copter</u> (G. with wings) = <u>helicopter</u>.

➤   **oc-ca-sion**: *Phonics*: <u>c's</u> = <u>k</u>; <u>sion</u> = <u>zhun</u>. *SPP*: oc-ca-si-on. *Clue*: <u>O, C Casi on</u> this <u>occasion</u>.

➤   **par-a-chutes**: *Roots*: <u>para</u> (pre.: prepare against) + <u>chute</u> (Fr. chute: falling) = <u>parachute</u>. *Clue*: We were on <u>a par</u> (same level) in the sky when our <u>chutes</u> opened: <u>par</u> + <u>a</u> + <u>chutes</u>.

238

Let's Pronounce That Word Correctly Now!

1. **per- form**: *Clue*: Each <u>per</u>son can <u>perform</u> with <u>form</u>. *Rule*: Add <u>per</u> + <u>form</u> = <u>perform</u>.

2. **tra-ge-dy**: *Phonics*: g = j. *Clue*: I feel <u>rage</u> at a villain in a <u>tragedy</u>.
   Roots: <u>trag</u> (L. trag: goat) + <u>edy</u> (L. edie; ode: song) = <u>tragedy</u> (goat song).

3. **in-ter-est** (3 syllables): *Clue*: If you feel <u>intense</u>, take <u>interest</u> in <u>restful</u> things: <u>intense</u> + <u>rest</u>.
   Roots: <u>inter</u>(L. prefix: between; among) + est (L. esse: be) = <u>interest</u> (be among; involved in)

4. **tem-per-a-ture** (4 syllables): *Clue*: Control your <u>temper</u> <u>at</u> kids for <u>sure</u>: <u>temper</u> + <u>at</u> + <u>sure</u>.

5. **a-rith-me-tic**(4 syllables): *Clue*: Please work <u>with</u> <u>me</u> on <u>arithmetic</u>: <u>a – r + with + me + tic</u>.
   Beat: Both <u>arithmetic</u> and mathematics have 4 syllables. (Don't add <u>e</u> after <u>th</u> in <u>arithmetic</u>.)

6. **ath-lete** (2 syllables): *Clue*:The <u>athlete</u> did a <u>high</u> leap. *Rule*: <u>Silent e</u> make <u>e</u> long.

7. **jewel-ry** (2 syllables): *Clue*: She looked in her <u>jewelry</u> for the lost <u>r</u>ing.

8. **Arc-tic**: *SPP*: Ar<u>c</u>-tic. *Clue*: The Arctic Ocean forms an <u>arc</u> at the North pole.
   Roots: <u>Arctic</u> (G. Arktos: Bear. The Bear is the most northern constellation).

9. **Ant-arc-ti-ca**: *Roots*: <u>Ant</u> (Gk. pre: <u>anti</u>: opposite) + <u>arctic</u> (Gk. arktos: bear): <u>Anti</u> + <u>arctic</u> + a.

10. **asked**: *Clue-in-a*-Row: When I <u>asked</u> how to help, they said, "<u>Ask + Ed</u>." *SPP*: ask-ed.

11. **ex-act-ly**: *Clue*: The first <u>act</u> began <u>exactly</u> on time. *Rule*: Add: <u>ex + act + ly</u> = <u>exactly</u>.

12. **sand-wich**: *Clue*: No <u>t</u> in my <u>sandwich</u>! I want a <u>sandwich</u>, not a <u>sand</u> witch! (Earl of Sandwich)

13. **sur-prise**: *Phonics*: <u>s</u> = <u>s</u>; <u>s</u> = <u>z</u>. *Clue*: It's a <u>surprise</u> to see a whale <u>surface</u> and <u>rise</u>: <u>sur</u> + <u>p</u> + <u>rise</u>.

14. **dia-mond**: *Visual*: <u>Diamond</u> has an <u>o</u> like a ring. *SPP*: di-a-mond (For spelling, say the a.)
    Clue: Measure the <u>diameter</u> of the <u>diamond</u>.

15. **eve-ry**: *SPP*: e-ver-y. *Clue*: I know <u>every</u> person here <u>very</u> well: <u>e</u> + <u>very</u>. *Beat*: e-v-e-r-y.

16. **guard**: *SPP*: gu-ard. *Clue*: G, U (work h)ard as a <u>guard</u>: G. U. + <del>h</del>ard.

17. **guessed**: *SPP*: gu-ess-ed. *Clue*: G, U <u>guessed</u> <u>less</u> than the number: G + U + <del>l</del>ess + ed.

18. **hos-pi-tal**: *Clue*: The <u>a</u>mbulance raced to the <u>hospital</u>.
    OWF: The <u>hospital</u> had true <u>hospitality</u>.

19. **mar-riage**: *SPP*: mar-<u>ri</u>-age. *Rule*: Change <u>y</u> to <u>i</u> except before -ing: marr<del>y</del> + i + age.

20. **gov-ern-ment**: *6 Words*: go, govern, over, me, men, Vern. *SPP*: gov-er<u>n</u>-ment
    Clue: A <u>government</u> exists to <u>govern men</u> + <u>t</u>.

➤ **lit-er-a-ture**: *Clue*: There's lots of great <u>literature</u> in our <u>era</u>. *Roots*: (L. literatus: learned).

➤ **math-e-ma-tics**: *Visual*: <u>ma-the-ma</u>. *Clue*: <u>Ma, the (good) ma</u>, helped with <u>mathematics</u>.

➤ **min-i-a-ture** (4 syl.): *Clue*: I'll find a <u>mini</u> horse <u>at</u> a <u>miniature</u> store for <u>sure</u>: <u>mini</u> + <u>at</u> + <del>sure</del>.

➤ **priv-i-lege** (also, privi-lege): *SPP*: priv-i-lege. *Clue*: Don't give a <u>privilege</u> to a <u>vile</u> (bad) person.

➤ **pro-bab-ly**: *SPP*: pro-b<u>a</u>b-ly. *Clue*: My pet will <u>probably</u> act like a <u>baby</u>: <u>pro</u> + <u>bab</u> + <u>ly</u>.

The Power of Ancient Roots
Latin and Greek: Our Origin for Over 60,000 English Words

1. **an-i-mal**: *Clue*: An animal is a mammal. *Roots*: anim (L. alive; spirit) + al (n. suf.) = animal. *Same Root*: animation (making things come alive), inanimate (not alive.)

2. **a-quar-i-um**: *Rule*: Qu = one letter. *Roots*: aqua (L. water) + rium (n. suf.) = aquarium.

3. **cap-tain**: *Clue*: Can I be captain and wear the cap again?: cap + t + again (M.E. capitain: head).

4. **creed**: *Clue*: We need a creed to live by (L. creed: belief). *Same Pattern*: deed, feed, heed.

5. **dic-tion-ary**: *Phonics*: c = k. *Roots*: diction (L. spoken word) + ary (n. suf. place for) = dictionary.

6. **e-rupt**: *SPP*: e-rup-t. *OWF*: In eruption and rupture, you hear t in erupt. *Beat*: e-r-u-p-t.

7. **fra-gile**: *Phonics*: g = j. *SPP*: fra-gi-le. *Roots*: frag (L. fragilus: break) + ile (adj suf.) = fragile.

8. **la-bor**: *Clue-in-a-Row*: I labor on work at my lab or home. *Roots*: lab (L. work) + or (n. suf.) = labor.

9. **mag-ni-fy**: *Roots*: magni (Lat. great) + fy (verb suf.) = magnify.

10. **man-u-al**: *Clue*: Manual work is by hand. *Roots*: manu (L. manus: hand) + al = manual (by hand).

11. **ma-nu-script**: *Clue-in-a-Row*: I said to the scribe writing the manuscript, "Man U script well." *Root*: manu (L. manus: hand) + script (L. writing) = manuscript (writing done by hand).

12. **o-rig-in**: *Phonics*: g = j. *Clue*: Tell the origin of that o(ld) rig in the sea: old rig in = origin. *Roots*: origin (L origin: source something comes from). (rig: mast and sails of a ship).

13. **ped-al**: *Clue*: Al liked to pedal on his bike. *Roots*: ped (L. foot) + al (n. suf.) = pedal.

14. **ped-dle**: *Visual*: 2 d's. *OWF Clue*: When peddling, he liked to peddle fiddles. (L. ped: foot)

15. **vid-e-o**: *Clue*: My video screen is wide. *Roots*: vide (L. vide: see) + o (L. audio: hear) = video.

16. **as-tro-naut**: *Clue*: An astronaut needs to be a strong person. *2 Roots*: astro (L. astro: star) + naut (G. naute: sailor) = astronaut (star sailor).

17. **sci-ence**: *Clue*: I built a fence in science. *Roots*: scien (G. knowledge) + ce (n. suf.).

18. **in-spect**: *Clue*: I put spectacles on to inspect the project. *OWF*: spectator.

19. **ther-mos**: *Clue*: Her most loved drink is in her thermos: t + her + most. (thermos: G. heat).

20. **ver-dict**: *Clue*: He got a very good verdict. *Roots*: ver (L. ver: truth) + dict (L. dict: spoken word).

➤ **ag-o-ra-pho-bi-a**: *Roots*: agora (G. agora: market place) + phobia (fear) = agoraphobia (fear of open places).

➤ **a-ni-ma-tion**: *Clue*: Animation makes animals come alive. *E Rule*: animate + ion = animation. *Roots*: anim (L. anim: alive; spirit) + ation (n. suf.) = animal.

➤ **in-ter-rupt**: *SPP*: in-ter-rup-t. *Roots*: inter (Lat. to) + rupt (Lat. break apart) + ed (v. suf.).

➤ **phil-har-mon-ic**: *8 Words*: a, arm, harm, harmonic, hi, I, on, Phil. *Phonics*: Gk. ph = f. *Roots*: phil (Gk. love) + harmonic (Gk. harmony) = philharmonic.

➤ **phi-los-o-phy**: *Roots*: philo (G. philos: love) + soph (G. sophie: wisdom) + y = philosophy (love of wisdom).

➤ EXTRA: **claus-tro-pho-bi-a**: *Clue*: He got a trophy when he got over claustrophobia. *Roots*: claustro (Gk. enclosed like a clause) + phobia (Gk. fear) = fear of enclosed places.

Focusing on Visual Power and Patterns

1. **vi-su-al**: *Phonics*: <u>su</u> = <u>zhoo</u>. *SPP*: vi-su-al. *Clue*: <u>Vi, U</u> always learn <u>visual</u> skills.

2. **brilliant**: *SPP*: bril-<u>li-ant</u>. *Visual*: See 4 candles (<u>illi</u>) and an <u>ant</u>: <u>br + illi + ant</u>.

3. **au-tumn**: *SPP*: au-tum-<u>n</u>. *Clue*: <u>N</u>ovember is last month of <u>autumn</u>. *OWF*: Hear <u>n</u> in <u>autumn</u>al.

4. **ben-e-fit**: *Clue-in-Row*: Mr. <u>Ben E. Fit</u> helps <u>benefit</u> people. *Roots*: <u>bene</u> (Fr. good) + <u>fit</u> (deed)

5. **com-mit-tee**: *Phonics*: <u>c</u> = <u>k</u>. *Visual*: 3 double letters: <u>*mm*</u>, <u>*tt*</u>, <u>*ee*</u>. *Beat*: c-o-mm-i-tt-ee.

6. **dis-ap-pear**: *Clue*: There's part of <u>apple</u> and a <u>pear</u> in <u>disappear</u>: <u>dis + ap + pear</u>.
    Roots: <u>dis</u> (pre: not) + <u>ap</u> (pre: to) + <u>pear</u> (L. parare: be visible) = <u>disappear</u> (not be visible).

7. **gi-raffe**: *See* 2 giraffes = ff. *Clue*: She's a <u>girl</u> <u>giraffe</u> (Ital: giraffa; Arab: zirafah).

8. **hand-ker-chief**: *Clue*: Wave *<u>Hi Chief</u>* with a <u>handkerchief</u>. *Rule*: <u>hand + kerchief</u> (ME scarf).

9. **heard**: *Phonics*: <u>hear + d</u> = <u>heard</u>. *Clue*: I <u>hear</u> you <u>heard</u> I was n<u>ear</u>.

10. **su-per-in-ten-dent**: *9 Words*: <u>super</u>, <u>in</u>, <u>ten</u>, <u>dent</u> + <u>den</u>, <u>I</u>, <u>intend</u>, <u>sup</u>, <u>tend</u>.
    Clue: The <u>superintendents</u> saw <u>ten</u> <u>super</u> <u>dents</u> <u>in</u> the bus.

11. **rain**: *Clue*: The <u>rain</u> in Sp<u>ai</u>n falls m<u>ai</u>nly on the pl<u>ai</u>n. *VV Rule*: <u>A</u> makes <u>i</u> long.

12. **reign**: *Phonics*: <u>eig</u> = <u>a</u> sound (spelling <u>ei</u>). *SPP*: rei-g-n. *Clue*: <u>Eight</u> rulers <u>reign</u>ed.

13. **rein**: *Phonics*: <u>ei</u> = sounds like <u>a</u>. *SPP*: re-in. *Clue*: She held the horse's <u>rein</u> <u>in</u> her hand.

14. **pro-fit**: *Clue-in-a-Row*: Is this <u>pro fit</u> to <u>profit</u> from experience.

15. **pro-phet**: *Phonics*: Gk. <u>ph</u> = <u>f</u>. *Clue*: A <u>prophet</u> <u>let</u>s people know truth.
    Roots: pro (prefix: for) + phet (Gk. phetes: to speak) = <u>prophet</u> (to speak for God or another).

16. **four** (number 4): *Visual*: <u>Four</u> has 4 letters. *Clue*: <u>Four</u> is <u>our</u> favorite number.

17. **be-fore**: *Clue*: Can you eat the c<u>ore</u> <u>before</u> the apple? (O. E. beforen). *Rule*: be + fore = <u>before</u>.

18. **gig-gling**: *Visual*: <u>4 giggling g's</u>. *Rule*: Drop <u>silent e</u> before vowel suffix: giggl<s>e</s> + ing = <u>giggling</u>.

19. **hic-cup**: *Visual*: See <u>hic-cup</u>. *Clue*: A hic s I drank from my <u>cup</u>. *Rule*: <u>2 c's</u> keep <u>i</u> short.

20. **merry-go-round**: *Visual*: <u>Merry-go-round</u> can <u>go</u> <u>round</u> with <u>go</u> in the center.
    Same Pattern: berry, cherry, merry; ground, mound, round.

➢   **twin-kle**: *Visual and Clue*: There's a <u>wink</u> and <u>in</u> twinkle and also a <u>twin</u>.
    OWF: In <u>twinkl</u>ing, you can hear the <u>kl</u> in <u>twinkle</u> (O. E. twinklan: brief interval).

➢   **de-cid-ed**: *Phonics*: <u>c</u> = <u>s</u>. *Visual*: *Echo Word*: See same letters <u>echo</u> at end: <u>decided</u>.
    Clue: <u>Cid</u> (and) <u>Ed</u> finally de<u>cided</u>: de + Cid +Ed. *Rule*: <u>Silent e</u> make <u>i</u> long in de<u>cid</u>ed.

➢   **en-gine**: *Visual*: *Bookend*: <u>engine</u>. *Clue*: <u>GI</u> Joe ran the <u>engine</u>: <u>en + GI + ne</u> (M.E. engin).

➢   **mu-se-um**: *Phonics*: <u>s</u> = <u>z</u>. *Visual*: *Bookend Word*: <u>mu</u>-se-<u>um</u>. *Clue*: <u>Use</u> the <u>museum</u>.

➢   **on-ion**: *Visual*: *Echo Word*: <u>onion</u>. *Phonics*: <u>ion</u> = <u>yun</u>. *Clue*: <u>On I</u> (go) on cutting <u>onion</u>.

➢   EXTRA: **stac-ca to**: *Phonics*: <u>c</u> = <u>silent</u>; <u>c</u> = <u>k</u>. *See*: 2 cats back to back in: <u>staccato</u>.

Introducing the Copy Cat Kids

1. **croc-o-dile**: *Phonics*: <u>c</u>'s copy <u>k</u>. *Clue*: <u>Croco</u> (my <u>crocodile</u>) swam on the Nile: <u>croco + dile</u>. *Rule*: <u>Silent e</u> makes <u>i</u> long in -<u>dile</u>.

2. **cy-clone**: *Phonics*: <u>c</u> copies <u>k</u>. *Clue*: We want no <u>clone</u> (copy) of that <u>cyclone</u>: <u>cy + clone</u>.

3. **an-gel**: *Phonics*: <u>g</u> = <u>j</u>. *SPP*: an-gel. *Clue*: I made a <u>gelatin angel</u> (G. angelos: messenger).

4. **an-gle**: *Visual*: See <u>e</u> in the <u>angle</u> of the L. *Same Pattern*: angle, bangle, jangle.

5. **col-lege**: *Phonics*: <u>c</u> copies <u>k</u>; <u>g</u> copies <u>j</u>. *Visual*: See <u>ll</u> as 2 pi<u>ll</u>ars of <u>college</u> learning. *Clue*: They need to <u>collect</u> her <u>college</u> tuition.

6. **cour-age**: *5 Words*: <u>a</u>, <u>age</u>, <u>our</u>, <u>rag</u>, <u>rage</u>. *Phonics*: <u>c</u> = <u>k</u>; <u>g</u> = <u>j</u>. *Almost-Clue-in-Row*: It takes courage to live in <u>our age</u>: <u>c + our + age</u>.

7. **pig-eon**. *Phonics*: <u>g</u> = <u>j</u>. *Clue*: My <u>pigeon</u> has loved my <u>pig (for an) eon</u> (long time): <u>pig + eon</u>.

8. **vil-lage**: *Phonics*: <u>g</u> copies <u>j</u>. *Clue*: There's a <u>villa</u> (house) in the <u>village</u>: <u>villa + ge</u>.

9. **cous-in**: *Phonics*: <u>s</u> copies <u>z</u>. *Clue*: Our <u>cousin</u> is with <u>us in</u> the <u>Co.</u>: <u>co + us + in</u>.

10. **pleas-ure**: *Phonics*: <u>s</u> = <u>zh</u>. *Clue*: When his <u>plea</u> was heard, he <u>sure</u> felt <u>pleasure</u>: <u>plea + sure</u>. *Same Pattern*: measure, treasure.

11. **scis-sors**: *Phonics* and *Visual*: 4 s's in scissors: <u>1 s</u> = <u>s</u>; <u>3 s's</u> = <u>z</u>. *Beat*: s-c-i-ss-o-r-s.

12. **ax-is**: *Phonics*: <u>x</u> = <u>ks</u>; s = s. *Clue*: An <u>ax is</u> resting on an axis (center line things rotate around): <u>ax + is</u>.

13. **Xe-rox**: *Phonics*: <u>x</u> = <u>z</u>; <u>x</u> = <u>ks</u>. *Clue*: I have <u>zero</u> to <u>Xerox</u> now that I've copied the <u>ox</u>,

14. **champ-i-on**: *7 Words*: <u>a</u>, <u>am</u>, <u>amp</u>, <u>champ</u>, <u>ham</u>, <u>I</u>, <u>on</u>. *SPP*: cham-pi-on. *Clue*: The <u>champ</u> and <u>I</u> are <u>on</u> a <u>champion</u> team: <u>champ + i + on</u>. *Beat*: c-h-a-m p-i-o-n.

15. **chor-us**: *Phonics*: <u>ch</u> = <u>k</u>. *Clue*: A <u>chorus</u> sang <u>for us</u>: <u>ch + for + us</u> (G. choros: group of singers).

16. **cough**: *Phonics*: <u>c</u> = <u>k</u>; <u>gh</u> = <u>f</u>. *Clue*: I have a <u>rough cough</u>. *Same Pattern*: enough, tough.

17. **el-e-phant**: *Phonics*: <u>ph</u> copies <u>f</u>. *Clue*: That huge <u>elephant</u> has a tiny <u>ant</u> friend. (Gk. elephas)

18. **neph-ew**: *Phonics*: <u>ph</u> copies <u>f</u>. *Clue*: <u>Phew</u>! I have quite a <u>few nephews</u>: <u>ne + phew + s</u>.

19. **quaint**: *Phonics*: <u>qu</u> copies <u>kw</u>. *SPP*: qu-aint. *Clue*: That <u>paint</u> is a <u>quaint</u> color.

20. **ques-tion**: *Phonics*: <u>qu</u> = <u>kw</u>. *Clue*: The <u>question</u> is what <u>quest I</u> ('m) <u>on</u>. *Rule*: <u>qu</u> = one letter.

➤   **as-phalt**: *Phonics*: <u>ph</u> copies <u>f</u>. *Clue-in-a-Row*: Look on the <u>asphalt</u>, an <u>asp, halt</u>.

➤   **chal-lenge**: *SPP*: chal-len-<u>ge</u>. *Clue*: <u>All</u> the Little <u>Engine</u> could do was face the <u>challenge</u>.

➤   **de-ci-sions**: *SPP*: de-ci-<u>si</u>-ons. *Clue*: <u>Dec. is</u> when I make gift <u>decisions</u>: <u>dec + is + ions</u>.

➤   **pit-cher** (ball player; container): *Clue*: Can a <u>pitcher</u> pitch the <u>pit (of a) che~~rry~~</u>: <u>pit + cher~~ry~~</u>?

➤   **u-nique**: *Phonics*: <u>qu</u> = <u>kw</u>. *SPP*: u-ni-que. *Clue*: I own a <u>unique antique</u> (L. unique: one of a kind).

➤   EXTRA: **tri-um-phant**: *Clue*: A <u>triumphant ant</u> said, "<u>Umph</u>! Work to do!" <u>tri-umph + ant</u> (ph = f).

Let's Grasp and Learn Initial Consonant Blends

1. **blank-et**: *Clue*: An E.T. was drawn in the blank space on her blanket: blank + E.T.

2. **blend-ing**: *7 Words*: blend, end, ending, I, in, lend, lending. *Rule*: Just add a suffix to a word ending in a consonant: blend + ing = blending. *Pattern*: ending, sending.

3. **close** (near): *Phonics*: s = s sound in dose. *Rule*: Silent e makes o long. *Clue*: It's close to the time for a dose of cough syrup.

   close (shut a door): *Phonics*: s = z sound like rose. *Clue*: I'll close the gate by the rose garden. *Rule*: Silent e makes o long. *Same Pattern*: chose, hose, nose, pose.

4. **clothes**: *Phonics*: s = z. *OWF*: In cloth, hear th in clothes: cloth + es. *Rule*: E makes o long.

5. **pleas-ant**: *7 Words*: a, an, ant, as, Lea, plea, pleas. *Clue*: Hear my pleasant pleas, ant: "Please leave our picnic alone. *Rule*: Drop silent e : please + ant = pleasant. *Same Root*: please, pleasure.

6. **sleek** (smooth): *Reversal*: sleek = keels. *Clue*: The keels of boats cut sleek lines through water.

7. **bread**: *Clue*: She read about making bread. *Same Pattern*: dread, head, stead, tread.

8. **draw-er**: *Visual*: *Reversal*: Drawer backwards is reward. *Clue*: I put my reward in my drawer.

9. **from**: *Clue*: We walked from the prom at midnight.

10. **group**: *SPP*: gro-up. *Clue*: I groped up a hill to join the group for soup: groped + up = group.

11. **score**: *Clue*: You earned more points for your score. *Same Pattern*: bore, core, lore.

12. **ice-skat-er**: *Phonics*: c = s. *Clue*: Nate is an ice-skater. *Rule*: E makes i and a long.

13. **smile**: *Clue*: I'd walk a mile for your smile. *Rule*: Silent e makes i long.

14. **snack**: *Phonics*: c = silent. *Clue*: He put a snack in his pack. *Same Pattern*: back, pack, snack.

15. **sports**: *Clue*: He enjoyed all sorts of sports. *Same Pattern*: ports, snorts, sports.

16. **square**: *Clue*: The sides of a square are equal: s + qu + are. *Pattern*: glare, stare. *Beat*: s-q-u a-r-e.

17. **trag-ic**: *Phonics*: G = j. *Clue*: Their attempt at magic was tragic.

18. **twist**: *Clue*: I want to do the twist like I did last summer. *Same Pattern*: mist, twist, wrist.

19. **splendor**: *Clue*: Can you lend or borrow splendor? sp + lend + or.

20. **spring**: *Visual*: The g in spring looks like a spring. *Clue*: He gave her a ring in the spring.

➤ **gla-cier**: *Phonics*: cier = shur. *SPP*: gla-ci-er. *Root and Rule*: glace (Fr. glace: ice) + i + er = glacier.

➤ **prac-tice**: *Phonics*: c = s; c = k. *Clue*: Practice your act: pr + act + ice. *OWF*: Hear 2 c's in practical.

➤ **strange**: *Clue*: Ghosts stories fit into the range of *strange*: st + range. *Pattern*: change, danger.

➤ **stretch**: *SPP*: Say *Blend*-str and *Digraph*-ch: s-t-r-e-t-ch. *Same Pattern*: etch, sketch, stretch.

➤ **tro-phy**: *Phonics*: Gk. ph = f. *Clue*: She won a trophy for tropical survival. *Beat*: T-R-O P-H-Y.

Let's Grasp and Learn Final Consonant Blends

1. **drift**: *Clue*: A large snow <u>drift</u> blocks a <u>driveway</u>. *Same Pattern*: gift, lift, sift (division).

2. **bulb**: *SPP*: bul-b. *Visual*: The <u>b</u>'s look like <u>bulbs</u> growing up; <u>u</u> and <u>l</u> lines are like stems.

3. **yi-eld**: *Clue*: When I plant the <u>field</u>, I <u>yield</u> to the <u>elder</u> who has done it for years.

4. **film**: *SPP*: <u>fil-m</u>. *OWF*: In <u>filming</u>, you can better hear the <u>l</u> and <u>m</u> in <u>film</u>.

5. **built**: *SPP*: <u>bu</u>-ilt. *Visual*: <u>U</u> is a bag in which to put nails (<u>ilt</u>). *Clue*: They <u>bu-ilt</u> a <u>bug</u> house.

6. **stamp**: *Clue*: I read the st<u>amp</u> under a lamp. *Same Pattern*: camp, damp, ramp.

7. **since**: *SPP*: sin-<u>ce</u>. *Clue*: <u>Since</u> the <u>prince</u> win<u>ce</u>s at m<u>ince</u>, we'll make a cherry pie.

8. **legends**: *Clue-in-a-Row*: Tell the <u>legend</u> where the brave's <u>leg ends</u> up holding him to a cliff.

9. **want**: *Phonics*: <u>ant</u> in <u>want</u> = <u>ahnt</u> sound. *Clue*: I w<u>ant</u> <u>an</u> <u>ant</u> for a pet.

10. **toward**: *6 Words*: <u>a</u>, <u>ow</u>, <u>to</u>, <u>tow</u>, <u>war</u>, <u>ward</u>. *SPP*: to-ward. *Clue*: Don't move <u>to war</u>; move <u>toward</u> peace: <u>to + war + d</u> (O. E. toward). *Rule*: Simply add prefix: <u>to + war + d</u>.

11. **shark**: *Clue*: <u>Hark</u>, a <u>shark</u> is in the <u>park</u> lake. *Same Pattern*: bark, dark, lark, mark.

12. **twirl**: *Clue*: The little <u>girl</u> loved to wh<u>irl</u> and <u>twirl</u>. *Same Pattern*: swirl, whirl.

13. **grasp**: *Clue*: I'd never gr<u>asp</u> a <u>wasp</u> or an <u>asp</u> (poisonous snake). *Rule*: <u>A</u> follows short vowel rule.

14. **most**: *Clue*: Do <u>most</u> people believe in gh<u>osts</u>? *Same Pattern*: ghost, host, lost, post.

15. **growl**: *Clue*: We heard zoo animals h<u>owl</u> and <u>growl</u>. *Pattern*: fowl, owl, prowl, scowl.

16. **fifth**: *Phonics*: fif + th <u>fifth</u>. *Clue*: How old are you on your <u>fifty-fifth</u> birthday? *Beat*: f-i-f-t-h.

17. **lunch**: *Clue*: I cr<u>unch</u> and m<u>unch</u> a b<u>unch</u> for <u>lunch</u>. *Same Pattern*: bunch, hunch, lunch.

18. **a-gainst**: *Phonics*: <u>again</u> + <u>st</u> = <u>against</u>. *Clue*: I want to box <u>against</u> the bag <u>again</u>.

19. **thirst**: *Clue*: The b<u>ird</u> had <u>thirst</u>. *Roots*: <u>thirst</u> (L. thyrstan: thirst). *Pattern*: f<u>irst</u>, w<u>orst</u>, bu<u>rst</u>.

20. **watch**: *Phonics*: -t + ch. *SPP*: wa-t-ch. *Clue*: <u>Watch</u> me c<u>atch</u> the ball. *Pattern*: catch, match.

➤ **ex-tinct**: *OWF*: Hear <u>ex + tin</u> in <u>extinct</u> in <u>extinguish</u>. *SPP*: ex-tin-c-t.
   Roots: <u>ex</u> (beyond) + <u>tinct</u> (M.E. <u>tinctus</u>: putting out) = <u>extinct</u> (beyond putting out – making extinct).

➤ **in-stinct**: *Clue*: You react to <u>stings</u> by <u>instinct</u>.
   Roots: <u>in</u> (pre: to) + <u>sinct</u> (M. E. sting: sting) = <u>instinct</u> (to react instantly as if stung or pricked).

➤ **ninth**: *SPP*: nin-th. *Clue*: We wo<u>n in the</u> <u>ninth</u> inning.

➤ **strength**: *Visual*: <u>7 consonants</u>, <u>1</u> vowel. *Phonics*: (blend) <u>str</u> + <u>e</u> + <u>ng</u> + <u>th</u> (digraphs).

➤ **twelfth**: *Phonics*: <u>tw</u>, <u>elf</u> (blends) + <u>th</u> (digraph). *Clue*: <u>TW</u> is the <u>twelfth</u> elf.

Focusing on Silent Letters

1. **climb**: *SPP*: clim-b. *Clue*: I want to climb on that limb and be limber.

2. **thumb**: *SPP*: thum-b. *OWF Clue*: Thumbelina was no bigger than a thumb.

3. **de-sign**: *Phonics*: S = z. *SPP*: de-sig-n. *Clue*: I'll design a sign. *OWF*: Hear n in designation.

4. **g-naw**: *SPP*: g-naw. *Clue*: Gnus were gnawing on my saw. *Same Pattern*: gnaw, gnat, gnus.

5. **brought**: *SPP*: bro-ugh-t. *Clue*: I ought to have brought that ghost book I bought.

6. **caught**: *Phonics*: augh = ah. *SPP*: ca-ugh-t. *Same Pattern*: caught, daughter, fraught.
   Clue: The kids caught on and didn't say *ugh* about spelling: ca + ugh + t.

7. **ghost**: *SPP*: g-host. *Clue*: A ghost was our host. *Beat*: g-h-o-s-t.

8. **knight**: *SPP*: k-nig-ht. *Clue*: Can a knight be seen in the dark of night? k + night.

9. **night**: *Phonics*: igh= long i. *SPP*: nig-ht. *Clue*: I watch the city lights at night.

10. **hon-es-t**: *6 Words*: ho, hon, hone, nest, on, one. *Clue*: Our bees make honest honey.

11. **wharf**: *SPP*: w-harf. *Clue*: A wharf and a harbor are both places for boats.

12. **knead**: *SPP*: k-ne-ad. *Clue*: He read about how to knead bread. *Homophone*: need (feed, steed).

13. **could**: *Phonics*: could= kod. *SPP*: coul-d. *Same Pattern*: I could if I would, and I should!

14. **half** (halves): *SPP*: hal-f. *Clue*: This half is all yours, and the rest is for my calf, Alfie.

15. **palm** (tree; palm of hand): *SPP*: pal-m. *Visual*: The l's tall like a palm.
    Clue: The palm sways in a calm, balmy breeze.

16. **lis-ten**: *SPP* lis-ten. *Clue*: Is ten the number who came to listen to his concert: l + is + ten.

17. **sword** (n., armor): *SPP*: s-word. *Clue*: He bet his word on his skill with a sword.

18. **soared** (v., flew): *7 Words*: a, are, Ed, oar, oared, red, so, soar.
    SPP: so-ar-ed. *Clue-in-Row*: So a red bird soared by my window this morning.

19. **wreath**: *SPP*: w-reath. *Clue*: We eat beneath a wreath. *Rule*: A makes e long. *Pattern*: heath.

20. **wrong**: *SPP*: w-rong. *Clue*: I hurt my wrist ringing the wrong gong?

➤ **an-swered**: *SPP*: an-s-wer-ed. *Clue*: Were your questions answered? (O.E. andswerian: state).

➤ **cas-tle**: *SPP*: cast-le. *Clue*: The castle cast lengths of reflection across the lake (O.E. castel).

➤ **col-umn**: *SPP*: col-um-n. *Visual*: In column, find 1 tall and 7 small columns.
    OWF: In columnist, you can hear the n in column. *Beat*: c-o-l u-m-n.

➤ **rasp-berry**: *SPP*: rasp-berry. *Clue*: The raspberry vines were raspy (rough like a saw).

➤ **sub-tle**: *SPP*: sub-tle. *Clue*: A subtitle explains the subtle title (O. Fr. subtile). *Beat*: s-u-b t-l-e

I've Got Those Syllables! Got That Power Beat!

1.   **cat-a-log**: *Clue*: Let's order a <u>cat, a log</u> and a star from the <u>catalog</u>. *Beat*: c-a-t-a-l-o-g.

2.   **gob-let**: *Clue*: <u>Let</u> me put a <u>gob</u> of chocolate in a <u>goblet</u>. *Rule*: <u>O</u> and <u>e</u> follow *Short Vowel Rule*.

3.   **blaze**: *Clue*: We like to <u>gaze</u> a campfire <u>blaze</u>. *Rule*: <u>Silent e</u> makes <u>a</u> long.

4.   **peach**: *Clue*: <u>Each peach</u> and <u>pear</u> are <u>easy</u> to <u>reach</u>. *2 Vowels Rule*: <u>A</u> makes <u>e</u> long.

5.   **show-boat**: *8 Words*: <u>a</u>, <u>at</u>, <u>boa</u>, <u>boat</u>, <u>ho</u>, <u>how</u>, <u>oat</u>, <u>show</u>. *Compound Rule*: Add <u>show</u> + <u>boat</u> <u>showboat</u>. *Rule*: <u>W</u> makes <u>o</u> long in <u>show</u>; <u>a</u> makes <u>o</u> long in <u>boat</u>.

6.   **a-corn**: *Open Syllable*: <u>a</u> (vowel or ends in vowel). *Clue*: An <u>acorn</u> is like <u>a corn</u> kernel (M. E. <u>acorne</u>).

7.   **a-mong**: *Clue*: <u>Among</u> my pets is <u>a monkey</u>: <u>a monkey</u> + g. *Same Pattern*: dong, gong, long, song.

8.   **di-vide**: *Palindrome*: <u>divid</u> in <u>divide</u>. *Clue*: I <u>divide</u> the time when I <u>ride</u> and walk. *Rule*: First <u>i</u> in <u>divide</u> = *Open Syllable*. <u>Silent e</u> make the second <u>i</u> long: <u>divid</u> + <u>e</u> = <u>divide</u>.

9.   **u-ni-corn**: *Roots*: <u>uni</u> (L. one) and <u>corn</u> (L. cornu: horn). *Pattern*: born, horn, morn.

10.   **star-light**: *Phonics*: <u>igh</u> = <u>long i</u>. *Rule*: <u>star</u> + <u>light</u> = <u>starlight</u>. *Pattern*: car, far; night.

11.   **su-per**: *Clue*: That was a <u>super</u> <u>duper</u> <u>supper</u>. *Rule*: <u>Silent e</u> makes <u>u</u> long.

12.   **pur-ple**: *Clue*: I know some <u>purple</u> <u>fur</u> <u>people</u>: p + <del>fur</del> + -ple. *OWF*: Hear <u>pl</u> in <u>purplish</u>. *Roots*: <u>purple</u> (O.E. purpure, kind of shellfish used for purple dye.)

13.   **squig-gle**: *Visual*: The <u>gg's</u> = <u>squiggles</u>. *OWF Clue*: I drew <u>squiggles</u> squiggling with <u>glee</u>.

14.   **splash**: *Pronunciation*: Say all consonants: <u>s-p-l a sh</u>. *Clue*: <u>Dash</u> and make a <u>flash</u> <u>splash</u>.

15.   **blew**: *Clue*: I <u>blew</u> <u>dew</u> off a <u>few</u> blades of grass. *2 Vowels Rule*: <u>W</u> makes <u>e</u> long.

16.   **blue**: *Clue*: There is a <u>blue</u> <u>hue</u> in my paint. *Rule*: <u>E</u> makes <u>u</u> long (Scottish, blae + hue: = <u>blue</u>).

17.   **yel-low**: *Clue*: <u>Yell</u> for the <u>mellow</u> <u>yellow</u> team (M.E. geolu: yellow). *Same Pattern*: bellow, fellow.

18.   **white**: *Clue*: I fly my <u>white</u> <u>kite</u> - an awesome <u>site</u>. *Rule*: <u>Silent e</u> makes <u>i</u> long. (M.E. white like wheat)

19.   **green**: *Clue*: The moon has a <u>green</u> <u>sheen</u>. *Roots*: <u>green</u> (O.E. grene: like growing things).

20.   **homework**: *Phonics*: <u>ork</u> = <u>erk</u> sound. *Compound Rule*: Add <u>home</u> + <u>work</u> = <u>homework</u>. *Same Patterns*: gnome, Rome; cork, stork (-have same spelling, but not same sound as <u>work</u>).

➢   **un-der-stand**: *Rules* and *Roots*: <u>under</u> (L. pre: beneath) + <u>stand</u> (L. standan: support) = <u>understand</u>.

➢   **ig-nit-ing**: *Visual*: See a 7-letter palindrome in <u>igniting</u>. *Rule*: <u>Silent e</u> makes <u>i</u> in <u>nite</u> long.

➢   **mag-ni-fi-ca-tion**: *Visual*: See 3 *Open Syllables* (end in vowel): mag-<u>ni</u>-<u>fi</u>-<u>ca</u>-tion *Rule* and *Roots*: Change <u>y</u> to <u>i</u>: magni (L. magni: increase) + f<del>y</del>-i + cation = <u>magnification</u> (increasing)

➢   **orange**: *Clue*: <u>Orange</u> is in the <u>range</u> of bright colors: <u>o</u> + <u>range</u>. (O.Fr. orenge; Sp. naranja).

➢   **syl-la-ble**: *Pronounce* 3 syllables. *Clue*: Say each <u>syllable</u>, and you wi<u>ll</u> be <u>able</u> to hear the letters for spelling: <u>sy</u> + <del>will</del> + <u>able</u> = <u>syllable</u>.

➢   EXTRA: **phe-no-me-non**: 2 *Open Syllables* (end in vowel). *Phonics*: G. <u>ph</u> = <u>f</u>. *9 Words*: <u>he</u>, <u>hen</u>, <u>me</u>, <u>men</u>, <u>no</u>, <u>non</u>, <u>Nome</u> (Alaska), <u>omen</u>, <u>phenom</u> (slang). *Clue*: A <u>phenomenon</u>: He (left) no men on base.

Discovering How the Short Vowels Work

1. **ad** (advertisement): *Clue*: That <u>ad</u> is b<u>ad</u>. <u>Ad</u> is simply short for <u>ad</u>vertisement.

2. **add** (add together): *Visual*: <u>Add</u>: <u>ad</u> + <u>d</u> = <u>add</u>. *Clue*: <u>Add</u> my <u>add</u>ress to your book.

3. **cat-nap**: *Phonics*: <u>C</u> = <u>k</u>. *Compound Rule*: Add: cat + nap = <u>catnap</u>. *Pattern*: bat; lap, tap.

4. **fan-tas-tic**: *Phonics*: <u>s</u> = <u>s</u>; <u>c</u> = <u>k</u>. *Clue*: What a <u>fantastic</u> pl<u>astic</u> <u>fan</u>: <u>fan</u> + <u>t</u> + ~~plastic~~.

5. **hat-band**: *8 Words*: <u>a</u>, <u>an</u>, <u>and</u>, <u>at</u>, <u>bad</u>, <u>band</u>, <u>ha</u>, <u>hat</u>. *Compound Rule*: <u>hat</u> + <u>band</u> = <u>hatband</u>.

6. **cent**: *Phonics*: <u>c</u> = <u>s</u>. *Clue*: Even a b<u>ent</u> <u>cent</u> is <u>c</u>ash. *Pattern*: bent, dent, sent, tent, went.

7. **scent**: *Phonics*: silent c. *Clue*: The <u>scent</u> at the <u>scene</u> was roses. (*Homophone*: sent: past of to send).

8. **desk**: *Clue*: I <u>d</u>evelop <u>sk</u>ills at my <u>desk</u>. *Rule*: <u>E</u> in <u>desk</u> follows *Short Vowel Rule*.

9. **kit-ten**: *Clue-in-a-Row*: In her <u>kit, ten</u> <u>kittens</u> were curled up like mittens: <u>kit-ten</u>.

10. **li-mit**: *Visual*: 2 straight letters set a <u>limit</u>: <u>l</u>imi<u>t</u>. Also, <u>imi</u> is a palindrome in <u>limit</u>.
    Clue: I had to <u>limit it</u> on <u>limes</u>: <u>lime</u> + <u>it</u>.

11. **pic-nic**: *Visual*: 2 syllables that are alike: <u>pic</u> + <u>nic</u>. *Phonics*: Both <u>c's</u> = <u>k</u> sound.

12. **vic-tim**: *Phonics*: <u>c</u> = <u>k</u>. *Clue*: Neither <u>Vic</u> (or) <u>Tim</u> has ever been a <u>victim</u>.

13. **frog-man**: *Compound Rule*: <u>frog</u> + <u>man</u> = <u>frogman</u>. *Same Pattern*: dog, hog, log; can, fan, pan.

14. **op-tic**: *Phonics*: <u>c</u> = <u>k</u>. *Clue*: He was a t<u>op</u> <u>optic</u> specialist (L. opticos; G. optikos: concerns seeing).

15. **rob-in**: *Clue-in-a-Row*: A <u>robin</u> saw <u>Rob in</u> our yard. *Roots*: <u>robin</u> (Robin Redbreast, 1540).

16. **pump-kin**: *SPP*: pump-kin. *Clue*: Our <u>kin</u> (relatives) help carve <u>pumpkins</u>: <u>pump</u> + <u>kins</u>.

17. **sum-mit**: *Clue*: That <u>summ</u>er we climbed <u>It</u> (Mount Everest) to the <u>summit</u>: <u>summ</u>~~er~~ + <u>it</u>.
    Rule: <u>2 s's</u> keep u short. *Roots*: <u>summit</u> (L. summus: highest).

18. **um-brel-la**: *Clue*: Did Cinder<u>ella</u> lose an <u>umbrella</u>? <u>um-b</u> + <u>rella</u>.
    Roots: <u>umbra</u> (L. shade) + <u>umbel</u> (L. flower with stalks sticking out from center) = <u>umbrella</u> (shade flower).

19. **plum**: *Clue*: She chewed pl<u>um</u> g<u>um</u>. *Same Pattern*: bum, glum, hum, rum.

20. **plume**: *Clue*: She held a <u>plum</u>-colored <u>plume</u> (M.E. plume, 1350). *Rule*: <u>Silent e</u> makes <u>u</u> long.

➤ **cold**: *Phonics*: <u>c</u> = <u>k</u>. *Rule Ex*: <u>o</u> is long. *Clue*: In that <u>cold</u>, I felt b<u>old</u>. *Pattern*: gold, old, told.

➤ **both**: *Phonics Rule Ex*: <u>both</u> = <u>long o</u> (moth, cloth = short o). *Clue*: <u>Both</u> m<u>oths</u> have velvet cl<u>oth</u> wings.

➤ **pint**: *Phonics Rule Ex*: <u>pint</u> = <u>long i</u>. (<u>pint</u>o = short i). *Clue*: My <u>pinto</u> drank a <u>pint</u> of water (O. Fr. pinte).

➤ **hun-dred**: *Phonics*: <u>dred</u> = <u>drud</u> sound.
  Clue: I held a <u>hundred</u> <u>red</u> balloons: <u>hund</u> + <u>red</u> = <u>hundred</u> (Ger. hundert). *Beat*: h-u-n-d-r-e-d.

➤ **mag-net**: *Phonics*: <u>mag</u> = <u>short a</u>; <u>net</u> = <u>nit</u> sound. *Clue*: A <u>magnet</u> can hold a metal <u>net</u>.

Long Vowel Sounds and the Powerful Silent E

Silent e makes the vowel before it long (words 1-17). The rest of the words are exceptions to the Rule.

1. **es-cape**: *Clue*: Superman escaped in his S cape. *Roots*: es (ex: away from) + cape (hooded cloak).

2. **glade**: *Clue*: Each blade of grass in the glade was jade. *Rule*: Silent e makes a in glade long.

3. **trans-late**: *Visual*: 8 Words: a, an, at, ate, late, ran, slat, slate.
   Rule and *Roots*: trans (across) + late (L. bear) = translate (bear across from one language to another).

4. **whale**: *Clue*: Tell the tale of that whale in the gale. *Same Pattern*: male, pale, sale

5. **me-ters** (n., measure): *Clue*: I mete things with meters (.9 yards) *Roots*: meter (O.E. meter).

6. **scene** (n. plan): *Phonics*: Silent c. *PP*: s-ce-ne. Clue: We worked on scenic scenes for the play.

7. **theme**: *Visual*: Final e turns them into theme. *5 Words*: he, hem, me, the, them.
   Clue: The theme was fun for me to write: the + me (L., Gk. thema: to put down).

8. **chime**: *Clue*: It's time for the bells to chime. *Same Pattern*: dime, lime, mime.

9. **nine-ty**: *SPP*: ni-ne-ty. *Rule*: Keep silent e before vowel suffix. *Beat*: n-i-n-e-t-y.

10. **strike**: *SPP*: stri-ke. *Clue*: He did not mean to strike Mike with his bike.

11. **while**: *SPP*: w-hile. *Clue*: Please say hi while I cook dinner. *Roots*: while (O. E. hwil: away).

12. **write** (v., to pen): *SPP*: w-ri-te. *Clue*: I write at a quiet site. *Rule*: Silent e makes i long.
    right (adj., correct): *Phonics*: Igh = long i. *Clue*: I can rig my sail right at night without light.

13. **ro-ses**: *Phonics*: s's = z. *Clue*: I smell roses with my nose. *Roots*: rose (O. E. rose; Fr. rose: pink).

14. **whole** (adj. total): *SPP*: w-hole. *Clue*: Who did the whole lesson? *Rule*: Silent e makes o long.

15. **hole** (n., opening): *Clue*: A mole went down a hole. *Same Pattern*: pole, role, sole (fish).

16. **cos-tume**: *Phonics*: c = k. *Clue*: What was the cost of the plume for your costume?

17. **huge**: *Phonics*: g = j. *Clue*: I want a huge hug. *Rule*: Silent e turns hug into huge.

18. **pic-ture**: *Phonics*: c = k. *Clue*: Pick a picture and he'll sign his signature: pick ture (L. pictura).

19. **give**: *Clue*: They live to give. *Phonics*: No English word ends in v, so silent e is added to complete *give, have, love*, and other *v-words* without making the vowel long.

20. **love**: *Phonics*: love = luv. *Same Pattern*: above, dove. *Roots*: love (O.E. lufu; O. Fr. luve).

➤ **fudge**: *Phonics*: g = j. *SPP*: fud-ge. *Clue*: D in fudge is for *delicious*. *Pattern*: grudge, smudge.

➤ **more**: *Clue*: The more I wore it, the more it tore. *Same Pattern*: core, lore (literature).

➤ **none**: *Clue-in-a-Row*: None means not one: not + one. *Same Pattern*: done, one.

➤ **some**: *SPP*: so-me. *Clue*: Will someone come with me? *Same Pattern*: come.

➤ **were**: *Clue*: Where were you, here or there? : w + ere = were. *Roots*: were (O.E. were).

When Two Vowels Go Walking, the First One Does the Talking

(Words 1-16, the 2nd vowel makes the 1st vowel long. The other words are exceptions.)

1. **braid**: *Clue*: I p<u>ai</u>d for her to <u>braid</u> my hair (O.E. bregdan: weave). *Same Pattern*: laid, maid.

2. **laid**: *Clue*: The m<u>ai</u>d came to my <u>aid</u>. *Same Pattern*: laid, raid, paid, said.

3. **spray**: *Clue*: We <u>spray</u> water when we pl<u>ay</u> in the sp<u>ri</u>ng. *Same Pattern*: bay, play, tray.

4. **creak** (sound): *Phonics*: <u>c</u> = <u>k</u>. *Clue*: Don't speak or make a <u>creak</u>. *Pattern*: beak, teak.

5. **creek** (stream): *Clue*: <u>Eek</u>, I fell in the <u>creek</u>. *Same Pattern*: meek (humble), peek, seek.

6. **reach**: *Clue*: <u>Each</u> child could to <u>reach</u> for a p<u>each</u>. *Same Pattern*: each, beach, teach.

7. **speak**: *Clue*: <u>Speak</u> up for those who are w<u>eak</u>. *Same Pattern*: beak, creak, peak, speak.

8. **un-beat-en**: *9 Words*: <u>a</u>, <u>at</u>, <u>ate</u>, <u>be</u>, <u>Bea</u>, <u>beat</u>, <u>beaten</u>, <u>eat</u>, <u>eaten</u>, <u>ten</u>.
   Clue-in-a-Row: Don't be <u>beaten</u>, <u>be a ten</u> in facing challenges. *Same Pattern*: feat, seat.

9. **street**: *Clue*: He liked to <u>greet</u> people on his <u>street</u>. *Same Pattern*: beet, feet, meet, sleet.

10. **tied**: *Clue*: He tr<u>ied</u> and <u>tied</u> his <u>tie</u>. *Same Pattern*: die-died, lie-lied (*Homophone*: tide).

11. **foal**: *Anagram*: foal – loaf. *SPP*: <u>fo-al</u>. *Clue*: The little <u>foal</u> was the color of c<u>oal</u>.

12. **groan** (moan): *Clue*: A <u>groan</u> is like a m<u>oan</u>. *Same Pattern*: groan, loan, moan.

13. **grown** (matured): *Clue*: My bird has <u>grown</u> and fl<u>own</u> away. *Same Pattern*: blown, shown.

14. **cruel**: *SPP*: cru-el. *Clue*: Can you be tr<u>ue</u> to someone who's <u>cruel</u>?

15. **sta-tue**: *Clue*: I'm looking <u>at</u> a tr<u>ue</u> <u>statue</u>. *Rule*: <u>Silent e</u> makes <u>u</u> long. *Pattern*: due, true.

16. **fruit**: *Clue*: We fed the br<u>ui</u>ns (bears) <u>fruit</u>. *Rule*: <u>I</u> makes <u>u</u> long. *Pattern*: suit, pursuit, recruit.

17. **breath**: *Clue*: Her <u>breath</u> on my arm felt like a f<u>eath</u>er. *Rule Exceptions*: breath, feather, death.

18. **breathe**: *6 Words*: <u>a</u>, <u>at</u>, <u>breath</u>, <u>eat</u>, <u>he</u>, <u>the</u>. *Phonics*: Blend-<u>br</u>; Digraph-<u>th</u>: <u>b-r-ea-th-e</u>.
   SPP: bre-<u>at</u>-<u>he</u>. *Clue*: Can he <u>breathe</u> and <u>eat</u> at the same time? : <u>br + eat + he</u>.

19. **heart**: *5 Words*: <u>a</u>, <u>art</u>, <u>ear</u>, he, <u>hear</u>. *Anagram Clue* My <u>heart</u> lay close to the <u>earth</u>: <u>heart</u> – <u>earth</u>.

20. **read** (to read): *Clue*: I like to <u>read</u> about b<u>ead</u>s. *Same Pattern*: knead, lead (show way).
    read (past of read): *Clue*: I <u>read</u> about b<u>read</u>. *Same Pattern*: head, instead, lead (for pencil).

➢ **been**: *Clue*: I have <u>been</u> there and have <u>seen</u> the sights. *Rule Exception*: been.

➢ **brake** (to stop): *Rule*: Silent <u>e</u> makes the <u>a</u> long in <u>brake</u>. *Same Pattern*: cake, fake, lake, make.

➢ **break** (v. damage; take part off): *Clue*: Let's <u>break</u> b<u>read</u> together (share a meal). *Rule Ex*: break, steak

➢ **in-stead**: *Clue*: He r<u>ead</u> <u>instead</u>. *Same Pattern*: bread, lead (pencil), tread (walk).

➢ **o-cean**: *Phonics*: <u>c</u> = <u>sh</u>. *SPP*: o-<u>ce</u>-an. *Clue*: <u>Ocean</u> and <u>sea</u> are synonyms (mean same thing).

Rules and Patterns for IE, EI Words

1. **be-lieve**: *5 Words*: <u>be</u>, <u>eve</u>, <u>belie</u>, <u>I</u>, <u>lie</u>. *Clue*: Don't <u>believe</u> a <u>lie</u>. *Pattern*: grieve retrieve.

2. **chief**: *Clue*: The <u>chief</u> said, "<u>Hi</u>." *Same Pattern*: chief, mischief.

3. **grief**: *SPP*: gri-ef. *Clue*: I be<u>lieve</u> you feel <u>grief</u>. *Same Pattern*: chief, relief.

4. **field**: *Clue*: The <u>elder</u> farmer planted the <u>field</u>. *Same Pattern*: field, shield, wield, yield.

5. **fierce**: *Phonics*: <u>c</u> = <u>s</u>. *Clue*: The <u>fierce</u> giant yelled, "<u>Fie</u>!" *Same Pattern*: fierce, pierce.

6. **niece**: *Phonics*: <u>c</u> = <u>s</u>. *Clue*: My <u>niece</u>, All<u>ie</u>, is <u>nice</u>.

7. **piece** (amount; a work): *Phonics*: <u>c</u> = <u>s</u>. *Clue*: He ate a <u>piece</u> of <u>pie</u>.

8. **peace** (no war): *Phonics*: <u>c</u> = <u>s</u>. *Clue*: <u>Each</u> country wanted <u>peace</u>.

9. **shield**: *SPP*: shi-eld. *Clue*: The <u>elder</u> carried a <u>shield</u>.

10. **shriek**: *SPP*: shri-ek. *Clue*: I heard a <u>shrill</u> <u>shriek</u>, "<u>Eeek</u>!"

11. **for-eign**: *6 Words*: <u>for</u>, <u>fore</u>, <u>I</u>, <u>or</u>, <u>ore</u>, <u>reign</u>. *Clue*: Be<u>fore</u> here, he lived in a <u>foreign</u> country.

12. **ei-ther**: *Clue*: It's <u>either me, it (or) her</u>: <u>e + it + her</u>. *Same Pattern*: either, neither.

13. **height**: *Clue*: He has a <u>height</u> of <u>eight</u> feet: <u>h + eight</u>.

14. **seize**: *Clue*: <u>See</u> him <u>seize</u> it. *Beat*: s – e – i – z – e.

15. **ceil-ing**: *Phonics*: <u>c</u> = <u>s</u> sound. *Clue*: You fa<u>ce</u> the <u>ceiling</u> when you look up.

16. **re-ceive**: *OWF*: Hear <u>ce</u> in re<u>ception</u>. *Same Pattern*: conceive-conception; deceive-deception.

17. **lei-sure**: *Phonics*: <u>s</u> = <u>zh</u>. *Clue-in-a-Row*: My <u>lei sure</u> smelled sweet during my <u>leisure</u> trip.

18. **sleigh**: *Phonics and Rule*: <u>eigh</u> = <u>a</u> sound; <u>spelling is ei</u>. *Clue*: <u>Eight</u> reindeer pull Santa's <u>sleigh</u>.

19. **weight**: *Clue*: He has a <u>weight</u> of <u>eight</u> pounds. *Rule*: Sounds like <u>a</u>; spelling is <u>ei</u>. *Same Pattern*: neigh, neighbor, sleigh, weigh.

20. **vein**: *Phonics* and *Rule*: <u>ei</u> = <u>a</u> sound: <u>spelling is ei</u>. *Clue*: <u>Veins</u> <u>veer</u> <u>into</u> the heart.

➤ **an-cient**: *Phonics*: <u>cient</u> = <u>shunt</u> *SPP*: an-<u>ci</u>-ent. *Clue*: <u>An</u> <u>ancient</u> <u>c</u>itizen <u>entered</u> the <u>tent</u>.

➤ **ef-fi-cient**: *Phonics*: <u>cient</u> = <u>shunt</u>. *SPP*: ef-<u>fi</u>-<u>ci</u>-ent. *Pattern*: quotient, patient, sufficient.

➤ **fier-y**: *SPP*: fi-er-y. *Clue*: The giant yelled, "<u>Fie</u>," to the <u>fiery</u> dragon.

➤ **quo-tient**: *Clue*: <u>Enter</u> the numbers to get a <u>quotient</u>. *SPP*: quo-<u>ti</u>-<u>ent</u>. *Pattern*: efficient, patient.

➤ **re-triev-er**: *SPP*: re-tri-<u>ever</u>. *Clue*: My Golden <u>Retriever</u> <u>tries</u> to <u>retrieve</u> for<u>ever</u>: <u>re + tri + ever</u>.

➤ EXTRA: **hie-ro-gly-phics**: *Phonics*: Gk. <u>ph</u> = <u>f</u>. *Clue*: Reach <u>high</u> to touch <u>hieroglyphics</u>.
Roots: <u>hiero</u> (G. sacred) + <u>glyphics</u> (G. carvings;) = <u>hieroglyphics</u> (sacred Greek carvings).

Special Two-Vowel Combinations and Sounds

✦ au and aw ✦ oi and oy ✦ ou and ow ✦ oo and oo ✦ and ew ✦

1. **au-thored**: *Visual*: *7 Words*: <u>a</u>, <u>author</u>, <u>Ed</u>, <u>or</u>, <u>ore</u>, <u>red</u>, <u>Thor</u>. *SPP*: au-thor-ed
   Clue: She <u>authored</u> a book on <u>Thor</u>, the Scandinavian Thunder God. (M.E. autor: self.

2. **haunt**: *Clue*: Did her <u>aunt</u> <u>haunt</u> the house? *Same Patterns*: undaunted (brave); gaunt (thin).

3. **taught**: *Phonics*: <u>augh</u> = <u>ah</u>. *Clue*: When I <u>taught</u> kids, they didn't say, "<u>Ugh</u>": <u>ta + ugh + t</u>.

4. **fawn**: *Clue*: A <u>fawn</u> was on our <u>lawn</u> at <u>dawn</u>. *Same Pattern*: pawn, tawny (tan).

5. **al-so**: *Rule*: When <u>all</u> is added to words, it has <u>just one l</u>. *Pattern*: <u>almost</u>, <u>also</u>, <u>always</u>…

6. **coil**: *Clue*: The snake saw <u>oil</u> and started to <u>coil</u>. *Same Pattern*: boil, foil, recoil, soil.

7. **loy-al-ty**: *Rule and Roots*: Add: <u>loy</u> (L. loy-legally faithful) + <u>al</u> (adj. suf.) + ty (n. suf.) = <u>loyalty</u>.

8. **a-bout**: *Phonics*: ab<u>out</u> (ou sound). *Clue*: M cat was <u>about</u> to go <u>out</u>. *Pattern*: <u>aloud</u>; gout, shout.

9. **a-loud**: *Clue-in-a-Row*: When he spoke <u>aloud</u>, he said things in <u>a loud</u> voice. *Pattern*: loud, proud.

10. **al-lowed**: *Clue-in-a-Row*: <u>All owed</u> ticket money to be <u>allowed</u> into the show. *SPP*: al-low-ed.

11. **foun-tain**: *Clue*: I <u>found</u> a <u>fountain</u> where water fell like <u>rain</u>. *Same Pattern*: count; mountain.

12. **ground**: *Clue*: She drew a very <u>round</u> circle on the <u>ground</u>. *Same Pattern*: found, sound.

13. **out-side**: *Compound Rule*: Add: <u>out + side</u> = <u>outside</u>. *Same Pattern*: about, pout; abide, hide.

14. **crowd**: *SPP*: cro<u>w</u>-d. *Clue*: My <u>crow</u> was in a <u>crowd</u> of <u>crows</u>: <u>crow + d</u>. (O.E. crowdan)

15. **down-town**: *Clue*: She walked <u>downtown</u> in a velvet <u>gown</u>. *Same Pattern*: clown, frown.

16. **knew** (past of to know): *SPP*: <u>k</u>-new. *Clue*: I <u>knew</u> I had <u>new</u> books. *Pattern*: <u>knew</u>, know, new.

17. **new** (fresh): *Clue*: I looked at the <u>new</u> morning <u>dew</u>. *Same Pattern*: dew, few, <u>new</u>, mew…

18. **moon-light**: *Phonics*: <u>igh</u> = long <u>i</u> sound. *Compound Rule*: Add <u>moon</u> + <u>light</u> = <u>moonlight</u>.
    Same Pattern: coon, loon, moon, noon; flight, light, might, right, tight.

19. **soon**: *Clue*: <u>Soon</u> the m<u>oo</u>n will rise. *Same Pattern*: croon, loon, noon.

20. **cook-book**: *Visual*: Same, except first letter: <u>cook</u>, <u>book</u>. *Rule*: <u>cook + book = cookbook</u>.

➤ **noise**: *SPP*: n<u>oi</u>-<u>se</u>. *Clue*: Eat with <u>poise</u>, not with <u>noise</u>. *Same Pattern*: noise, poise.

➤ **poise**: *SPP*: p<u>oi</u>-<u>se</u>. *Clue*: We ate <u>poi</u> (Hawaiian dish from tarot root) with <u>poise</u>: <u>poi + se</u>.

➤ **root** (v., cheer; n., part of plant). *Clue and Pattern*: <u>Root</u>, and <u>toot</u> and watch the <u>roots</u> grow.

➤ **route** (way, n.): *SPP*: rou-t<u>e</u>. *Clue*: They had to go <u>out</u> of their way to find a <u>route</u>.

➤ **ty-phoon**: *Phonics*: Gk. ph = f . *Clue*: A <u>typhoon</u> is due at n<u>oon</u>. *Beat*: t-y-p-h-o-o-n.
   Roots: (Gk. typhon: violent wind).

➤ EXTRA: **por-poise**: *Clue*: A <u>porpoise</u> jumps with <u>poise</u> and makes a clicking n<u>oise</u> (M. E. porpoys).

Powerful R Can Control Any Vowel

1. **star**: *Clue*: The <u>star</u> twinkled in the d<u>ar</u>k. *Same Pattern*: car, far, jar, par.

2. **germ**: *Phonics*: <u>g</u> = <u>j</u>. *Clue*: What's the t<u>erm</u> (of time) for a <u>germ</u> to <u>get</u> in and cause illness?

3. **bird**: *Clue*: A golden <u>bird</u> was ch<u>ir</u>ping in a f<u>ir</u> tree.

4. **horned**: *Clue*: The unic<u>orn</u> has one <u>horn</u>. Roots: horn (L. cornus-horn) + ed (verb suffix) = <u>horned</u>.

5. **sur-vive**: *Clue*: Those who <u>sur</u>faced al<u>ive</u> will <u>survive</u>. *Roots*: <u>sur</u> (beyond, above) + <u>vive</u> (live) = <u>survive</u>: (live beyond; keep living). *Same Root*: re<u>vive</u> (again live); <u>survive</u>or.

6. **de-sire**: *Phonics*: <u>s</u> = <u>z</u>. *Clue*: Prometheus' <u>desire</u> was to bring f<u>ire</u> to mankind. *Pattern*: tire, wire.

7. **pure**: *Rule*: <u>Silent e</u> makes <u>u</u> in p<u>ure</u> long. *Same Pattern*: cure, endure, lure, pure…

8. **air** (what you breathe, n.): *Clue*: The <u>air</u> was f<u>air</u> today. *Same Pattern*: fair, lair, pair, stairs…

9. **heir** (one who inherits, n.): *Visual*: See <u>he</u> in <u>heir</u>. *SPP*: he-ir. *Clue*: <u>He</u> is the <u>heir</u>.

10. **where**: *Clue*: Where were you? Just add h: <u>w + h + ere</u>. *Same Pattern*: here, there, everywhere

11. **ap-peared**: *8 Words*: <u>a</u>, <u>appear</u>, <u>are</u>, <u>ear</u>, <u>Ed</u>, <u>pea</u>, <u>pear</u>, <u>red</u>.
    SPP: ap-pear-ed: *Clue*: A magician made an <u>apple</u> and <u>pear</u> <u>appear</u>: <u>ap</u> + <u>pear</u> + <u>Ed</u>.

12. **years**: *Clue*: <u>Fears</u> can hurt you for <u>years</u>. *Same Pattern*: dears, hears, nears.

13. **dark-ness**: *Rule*: Add suffix, <u>ness</u>: <u>dark</u> + ness = darkness. *Same Pattern*: lark, mark; less.

14. **di-no-saur**: *SPP*: di-no-<u>sa</u>-<u>ur</u>. *Roots*: <u>dino</u> (G. deinos: monstrous) + <u>saur</u> (G. saurus: lizard) = <u>dinosaur</u>.

15. **dur-ing**: *E Rule* and *Roots*: <u>dure</u> (M.E. last) + <u>ing</u> = <u>during</u>. *Same Pattern*: curing, enduring, insuring.

16. **earth**: *Visual*: *Anagram*: earth – heart. *Clue*: I put my <u>ear</u> close to the <u>earth</u> to h<u>ear</u> its h<u>eart</u>

17. **li-zard**: *Clue*: Many a <u>lizard</u> has a h<u>ard</u> shell: <u>liz</u> + <u>hard</u>. *Roots*: lizard (G. saurus-as in dinosaur).

18. **sev-er-al**: *Clue*: If <u>several</u> things are bad, can you <u>sever (break) all</u> ties. ? *Beat*: s-e-v-e-r-a-l.

19. **e-nor-mous**: *Clue*: The T-Rex has an <u>enormous</u> <u>mouth</u>.
    Roots: <u>e</u> (pre: beyond) + <u>norm</u> (L. norm: standard) + ous (adj. suf.) = <u>enormous</u> (beyond the norm).

20. **world**: *Phonics*: <u>wor</u> = <u>wer</u>. *SPP*: wor-l-d. *Visual*: The <u>o</u> in <u>world</u> is round like a globe: <u>O</u>.

➢ **im-por-tant**: *10 Words*: <u>a</u>, <u>an</u>, <u>ant</u>, <u>I</u>, <u>I'm</u>, <u>imp</u>, <u>import</u>, <u>or</u>, <u>port</u>, <u>tan</u> (ort: food scrap). *Roots*: <u>im</u> (pre: to) + <u>port</u> (L. carry) + <u>ant</u> (adj. suf.). *Clue-in-a-Row*: It's <u>important</u> not to <u>import ants</u> in picnic baskets.

➢ **pur-pose**: *Phonics*: ose = <u>us</u>. *SPP*: pur-po-<u>se</u>
    Clue: I pro<u>pose</u> a grand <u>purpose</u> for this <u>purple rose</u>: <u>purple</u> + <u>rose</u> = <u>purpose</u>. (O. Fr. purposer).

➢ **sur-round**: *Phonics*: <u>s</u> = <u>s</u>. *Clue*: <u>Surround</u> us on the <u>ground</u>. *Roots*: <u>sur</u> (above) + <u>round</u> (L. rotund)

➢ **ter-ri-ble**: *Clue*: Where did the <u>terrible</u> pterodactyl crush your <u>rib</u>? *Beat*: t-e-rr i-b-l-e.

➢ **wa-ter**: *Clue*: Do you say: I ate water? : <u>w + ate + r</u>. *Long Vowel Rul Exceptione*. (O.E. waeter).

➢ EXTRA: **tyrannosaurus rex**: *Clue*: <u>tyran</u>(t) (harsh ruler) + <u>no</u> + <u>saurus</u> (lizard): <u>tyrant</u> + <u>no</u> + <u>saurus</u>. Then add <u>rex</u> (L. king).= <u>tyrannosaurus rex</u> (Lat. Ruling Lizard King).

Discovering How Open Syllables Work
and What's a Schwa?

(*Open Syllable* = single vowel or ends in a vowel. *Schwa* = <u>underlined</u> below: unaccented vowel w/little sound.)

1. **a-glow**: *Phonics:* <u>ow</u> = long <u>o</u>. *Clue-in-a-Row:* My <u>glow</u>worm has <u>a glow</u> when she's <u>aglow</u> (OE, glowan).

2. **a-lone**: *5 Words:* <u>a</u>, <u>Al</u>, <u>on</u>, <u>one</u>, <u>lone</u>. *Clue:* A lone a is all <u>alone</u>. *Rule:* <u>Silent e</u> makes <u>o</u> long.

3. **sa-gas**: *Visual:* <u>sagas</u> = palindrome. *Phonics:* s = s; s = z. *Clue:* We listened while <u>sages</u> told <u>sagas</u>.

4. **ta-ble**: *Clue:* A <u>tablet</u> is like a <u>table</u> you write on. *OWF:* In <u>tablet</u>, you can hear <u>ble</u> in <u>table</u>.

5. **ce-re-al**: *SPP:* ce-<u>re</u>-al. *Clue:* I want <u>real cereal</u>. *Roots:* Roman Goddess of <u>cereal</u> was <u>Ceres</u>.

6. **el-e-va-tor**: *Clue:* Put the <u>elephant</u> or <u>gator</u> on the <u>elevator</u>: ele + v-ator. *E Rule:* <u>elevate</u> + or.

7. **e-ra-ser**: *Open Syllables:* <u>e</u>-<u>ra</u>-ser. *Clue:* An <u>eraser</u> <u>serves</u> for <u>erasing</u> boards: e + ra + ser~~ve~~.

8. **me-te-or**: *2 Open Syllables:* <u>me</u>-<u>te</u>-or. *Clue:* Can you <u>mete or</u> measure a <u>meteor</u>? (G. raised in air).

9. **mi-nus**: *Phonics: Open Syllable* <u>mi</u> = <u>long i</u>. *Clue:* The party will be <u>minus us</u>: mi + n + us.

10. **min-ute** (60 seconds): *Pronounce:* <u>Minute</u> (time) like (mi-nut), but it spelled like <u>minute</u> (tiny).
    mi-nute (tiny): *SPP:* mi-<u>nu</u>-te. *Open Syllable* <u>mi</u> = <u>long i</u>. *Rule:* <u>Silent e</u> makes <u>u</u> long.

11. **o-be-di-ent**: *Open Syllables* <u>o-be-di</u>. *Clue:* T<u>o</u> <u>bed</u> <u>I</u> w<u>ent</u>-to be <u>obedient</u>: ~~to~~ + be-di + ~~went~~.

12. **ro-bot**: *Palindrome* inside <u>robot</u>: <u>obo</u>. *Clue:* <u>Robo</u>, our <u>robot</u> does a lot. *Beat:* r-o b-o-t.

13. **tor-na-do**: *2 Open Syllables* in tor-<u>na</u>-<u>do</u> = <u>long a and o</u> *Clue:* A <u>tornado</u> has <u>torn a do</u>~~or~~ off the barn.

14. **pu-pils**: *Open Syllable* in <u>pu</u>-pil = <u>long u</u>. *Clue:* That <u>pup</u> is not one of my <u>pupils</u>:

15. **stu-dent**: *Open Syllable* <u>stu</u> = <u>long u</u>. *Clue:* Ask the <u>student</u>, "Did <u>U</u> <u>dent</u> my car?" st + U + dent.

16. **can-yon**: *Visual:* <u>Y</u> goes down like a <u>canyon</u>. *Clue:* I <u>can yonder</u> see a <u>canyon</u>: can yon~~der~~.

17. **cit-i-zen**: *Clue:* A <u>citizen</u> teaches <u>Zen</u>. *Rule:* Change y to i before consonant suffix: cit~~y~~ + i + zen.

18. **e-le-ven**: *Visual:* See <u>2</u> *Open Syllables* and <u>3 e's</u>. *Clue:* <u>Eleven</u> is not an <u>even</u> number.

19. **gal-ax-y** (n., system of stars): *Clue:* They wanted to have a <u>gala</u> (showy) party in the <u>galaxy</u>.

20. **man-a-ger**: *Clue:* That <u>man</u> has the <u>age</u> and skills to be a <u>manager</u>: man + age + r.

➤ **civ-i-li-za-tion**: *Visual:* <u>4 i's</u>; <u>3 *Open Syllables*</u>. *Beat:* c-i v-i l-i za tion.
   Roots: <u>civil</u> (citizen) + <u>ize</u> (v. suf) + <u>ation</u> (n. suf. organization) = civilization (organization of citizens).

➤ **en-cy-clo-pe-di-a**: *Visual:* 5 *Open Syllables*. *Roots:* <u>en</u> + <u>cyclo</u> (Gk. circle; well-rounded) + ped (Gk. teaching) + ia (n. suf.) = encyclopedia (well-rounded teaching). *Beat:* e-n-c-y-c-l-o-p-e-d-i-a.

➤ **in-tim-i-da-ted**: *15 Words:* <u>a</u>, <u>at</u>, <u>ate</u>, <u>date</u>, <u>dated</u>, <u>Ed</u>, <u>I</u>, <u>id</u>, <u>I'm</u>, <u>in</u>, <u>intimidate</u>, <u>mid</u>, <u>Ted</u>, <u>Tim</u>, <u>timid</u>.
   Clue-in-Row: <u>In Tim I dated</u> a guy who never <u>intimidated</u> me: in + Tim + I + dated.

➤ **u-ni-verse**: *Roots:* <u>uni</u> (pre.: one; united) + <u>verse</u> (L. versus: turned) = <u>universe</u> (turned into one; entire).

➤ **u-ra-ni-um**: *Clue:* <u>U</u> ran to see the <u>uranium</u>: <u>U</u> + ran + ium. *Roots:* <u>uran</u> (from Uranus, most powerful Gk. god) + <u>ium</u> = <u>uranium</u> (white radioactive element used to power nuclear fuel).

Let's Try All the Vowel Sounds

1. **la-ter** (after a time, adj.; adv.): *Clue*: We <u>ate</u> <u>later</u>. *Phonics and Rules*: Silent <u>e</u> makes <u>a</u> long: <u>late</u>.

2. **lat-ter** (second, near end. adj.): *Rule*: <u>2 t's</u> keep <u>a</u> short. *Same Pattern*: batter, matter, patter.

3. **hair** (on head): *Clue*: The <u>air</u> is blowing through my <u>hair</u>. *Same Pattern*: fair, pair.
   hare (rabbit): *Clue*: I <u>care</u> for my <u>hare</u>. *Same Pattern*: bare, dare, fare, mare, rare, share.

4. **sense**: *Phonics*: 2s's = s. *Visual Echo Word*: <u>se</u>-n-<u>se</u>. *Clue*: We had an int<u>ense</u> <u>sense</u> of joy.

5. **ea-sy**: *Clue*: You're <u>easy</u> to t<u>ease</u>. *Rule*: Drop <u>silent e</u> before a vowel suffix: eas<s>e</s> + y = <u>easy</u>.

6. **feath-er**: *Clue*: For the eagle, it was a true <u>feat (for) her</u> to keep each <u>feather</u>: <u>feat + her</u>.

7. **ther-mom-e-ter**: *8 Words*: <u>he</u>, <u>her</u>, <u>me</u>, <u>met</u>, <u>mete</u>, <u>meter</u>, <u>mom</u>, <u>the</u>.
   Roots: <u>thermo</u> (G. heat) + <u>meter</u> (G. metron: measure) = <u>thermometer</u>.

8. **peer** (equal; look searchingly): *Clue*: I want to p<u>eer</u> at the <u>deer</u>. *Same Pattern*: beer, cheer, jeer, seer
   pier (dock): *Clue*: They ate <u>pie</u> by the <u>pier</u>. *Same Pattern*: pier, tier (layer).

9. **quit**: *Clue*: <u>Quit</u> <u>it</u>. *Rule*: <u>Qu</u> = one letter, except at end of a word. *Same Pattern*: lit, quit, sit.

10. **quite**: *Rules*: <u>Qu</u> = one letter. Silent <u>e</u> turns <u>quit</u> into <u>quite</u>. *Same Pattern*: bite, quite, site.

11. **swirl**: *Phonics*: *Blends*-<u>sw</u> and <u>rl</u>: <u>s-w-i-r-l</u>. *Clue*: S<u>wirl</u> and tw<u>irl</u>. *Roots*: <u>swirl</u> (Scand. *svirla*).

12. **ho-nor-a-ble**: *8 Words*: <u>a</u>, <u>able</u>, <u>ho</u>, <u>hon</u>, <u>honor</u>, <u>nor</u>, <u>on</u>, <u>or</u>. *SPP*: <u>h</u>-on-est.
    Clue-in-a-Row: Your <u>honor, able</u> am I to be <u>honorable</u>.

13. **road** (path): *Clue*: I saw a t<u>oad</u> jumping on the r<u>oad</u>. *2 Vowel Rule*: <u>A</u> makes <u>o</u> long.
    rode (past of ride): *Clue*: He r<u>ode</u> to his ab<u>ode</u>. *Rule*: <u>Silent e</u> makes <u>o</u> long. *Pattern*: mode, rode.
    rowed (used oars): *2 V Rule*: <u>W</u> makes <u>o</u> long. *SPP*: row-ed. *Same Pattern*: glowed, showed.

14. **col-or-ful**: *Visual*: See <u>o l o</u> as 2 paint jars with an easel: <u>o l o</u> (L. color or hue).

15. **quar-ter**: *Clue*: Can I b<u>arter</u> (bargain) with a <u>quarter</u>? qu + <s>b</s>arter. *Roots* <u>quarter</u>: (L. quartus: fourth.)

16. **word**: *Phonics*: <u>or</u> = er. *Clue*: I stake my <u>word</u> on my <u>sword</u> (O. E. word). *Same Pattern*: ford, lord.

17. **truth**: *Clue*: <u>R</u>uth spoke <u>truth</u>. *Roots*: <u>truth</u> (O. E. treowth: truth). *Short Vowel Rule Ex.*

18. **snoop-y** (prying; good old Snoopy): *Clue*: <u>Snoopy</u> rolled into a l<u>oop</u>.
    Roots: <u>snoopy</u> (Danish: snoepen: take and eat food on the side). *Same Pattern*: hoop, loop.

19. **house**: *Clue*: Come see a m<u>ouse</u> at our <u>house</u> (O.E. hus; M.E. housen). *Pattern*: louse.

20. **pow-er**: *Phonics*: <u>w</u> = consonant. *Clue*: Do they <u>owe</u> <u>power</u>? *Pattern*: bower (high castle room)

➤ **ma-ny**: *5 Words*: <u>a</u>, <u>an</u>, <u>any</u>, <u>ma</u>, <u>man</u>. *Clue*: <u>Many</u> a <u>man</u> hasn't <u>any</u> (O. E. manig: many).

➤ **oy-sters**: *Phonics*: <u>oy</u> = diphthong. *Clue*: The b<u>oys</u> and their sist<u>ers</u> found some <u>oysters</u>.

➤ **peo-ple**: *SPP*: pe-o-ple. *Clue*: <u>People</u>, <u>O</u> please come help: <u>pe-o + ple</u>. *Beat*: p-e-o p-l-e.
   Visual: See the 5 rounded letters (<u>people</u>) as people's faces.

➤ **sear-ing** (burning): *Clue-in-a-Row*: The <u>searing</u> sun made a <u>sea ring</u> around the island (O.E. sear).

➤ **yolk**: *SPP*: yol-k. *Clue*: My f<u>olks</u> eat the egg <u>yolks</u>. *Roots*: <u>yolk</u> (O. E. geolu: yellow for yolk).

The Solid Compound Word Rule

(Add 2 words together. *Exceptions*: <u>alphabet</u>, <u>shepherd</u>, <u>welcome</u>, <u>almost</u>, <u>although</u>, <u>pastime</u>.)

1. **bean-stalk**: *8 Words*: <u>a</u>, <u>an</u>, <u>be</u>, <u>Bea</u>, <u>bean</u>, <u>beans</u>, <u>stalk</u>, <u>talk</u>.
   Clue-in-a-Row: Do <u>beans talk</u> on a <u>beanstalk</u>? *Same Pattern*: deans, means; chalk, walk.

2. **break-fast**: *SPP*: <u>bre</u>-ak-fast. *Clue*: I had <u>tea</u> with <u>breakfast</u>. *Roots*: <u>breakfast</u> (ME, <u>break</u> a <u>fast</u>).

3. **cup-board**: *Phonics*: <u>c</u> = <u>k</u>. *SPP*: cup-b<u>o</u>-ard. *Clue*: A <u>cupboard</u> is a <u>board</u> where <u>cup</u> are set.

4. **fire-works**: *Clue*: I des<u>ire</u> to see <u>fireworks</u> overhead. *Rule*: <u>Silent e</u> makes <u>i</u> long.

5. **hand-some**: *SPP*: hand-so-<u>me</u>. *Clue*-in-a-Row: <u>Hand some</u> of those <u>handsome</u> guys sodas.

6. **horse-back**: *SPP*: hor-<u>se</u>-bac-<u>k</u>. *Same Pattern*: horse, Norse; black, Jack, lack, tack…

7. **lamp-lighter**: *Clue*: Even in the d<u>amp</u> of n<u>ight</u>, the <u>lamplighter</u> must <u>light</u> each <u>lamp</u> (1740).

8. **life-guard**: *SPP*: li-<u>fe</u> gu-<u>ard</u>. *Clue*: <u>G, U</u> work h<u>ard</u>, <u>guard</u>: <u>G, U</u> + h̶a̶r̶d̶. *Rule*: <u>E</u> makes <u>i</u> long.

9. **news-stand**: *Visual*: Add <u>news</u> + <u>stand</u> and *see* <u>2 s's</u>: <u>newsstand</u>. *Beat*: n-e-w-s s-t-a-n-d.

10. **space-ship**: *Phonics*: <u>s</u> = <u>s</u>. *Clue*: Do ET's <u>race</u> in <u>spaceships</u>? *Rule*: <u>E</u> makes <u>a</u> long.

11. **team-mate**: *Visual*: <u>2 m's</u>. *9 Words*: <u>a</u>, <u>am</u>, <u>at</u>, <u>ate</u>, <u>ma</u>, <u>mat</u>, <u>mate</u>, <u>tea</u>, <u>team</u>. *Clue*: When <u>teammates</u> hit homers, our <u>team</u> b<u>eams</u>. *Rules*: <u>A</u> makes <u>e</u> long (<u>team</u>); <u>E</u> makes <u>a</u> long (<u>mate</u>).

12. **week-nights**: *Clue*-in-a-Row: On <u>weeknights</u>, <u>wee knights</u> spar with miniature swords.

13. **ev-ery-bo-dy**: *SPP*: e-<u>ver</u>-y-bo-dy. *Clue*: <u>Everybody</u> came for New Year's, so <u>every</u> <u>body</u> was here.

14. **In-ter-net**: *Clue*: <u>Internet</u> = <u>inter</u> (between) networks. *Roots*: Modern word: <u>inter</u> (between) + <u>net</u> (O.E., netten: to get) = <u>Internet</u>. *Same Pattern*: Internet, Interstate (btw. states).

15. **noth-ing**: *Clue*: <u>Nothing</u> means <u>no</u> <u>thing</u>. *Roots*: <u>nothing</u> (OE, nanthing: <u>nothing</u>).

16. **nev-er-the-less**: *Visual*: <u>4 e's</u>. *Clue*: <u>Nevertheless</u> <u>never</u> has any vowel but <u>eeee</u>.

17. **jack-o-lan-tern**: *7 Words*: <u>a</u>, <u>an</u>, <u>ant</u>, <u>ante</u>, <u>Jack</u>, <u>tern</u> (bird), <u>lantern</u>. *Clue*: Jack put a <u>lantern</u> by a <u>tern</u>.

18. **rol-ler coas-ter**: *Rule*: <u>A</u> makes <u>o</u> in <u>coaster</u> long. *Same Pattern*: knoll, poll; roaster, toaster.

19. **al-pha-bet**: *Phonics*: Gk. <u>ph</u> = <u>f</u>. <u>Alpha</u> + <u>Beta</u> = first letters of Gk. <u>alphabet</u>: <u>Alpha</u> +<u>Bet</u>a̶.

20. **shep-herd**: *Clue*: I watched a <u>shepherd</u> <u>herd</u> <u>sheep</u>. *Rule Ex*: <u>shee</u>p + <u>herd</u> (Sheep drops <u>e</u>.).

➤ **although**: *Phonics*: <u>ough</u> = long <u>o</u>. *Rule Ex.*: <u>All</u> <u>al</u>ways drops an <u>l</u> : <u>almost</u>, <u>although</u>.

➤ **passed**: (v., went by; didn't fail): *Rule*: <u>2s's</u> keeps <u>a</u> short. *Same Pattern*: harassed, sassed.
   past: (n., adj., prep. time in past): *Clue*: <u>Last</u> year is in the <u>past</u>. *Same Pattern*: cast, fast, mast.

➤ **pas-time** (interest, hobby, n): *Clue*-in-a-Row: <u>Pa's time</u> is spent doing <u>pastimes</u>.
   Rule Exception: One <u>s</u> is dropped: <u>pass̶</u> + <u>time</u> = <u>pastime</u>.

➤ **un-til**: *Rule Ex.*: <u>Till</u> has one <u>l</u> when added to a word: un + till̶.

➤ **wel-come**: *SPP*: wel-co-<u>me</u>. *Rule Ex.*: <u>Well</u> has one <u>l</u> when added to <u>welcome</u>:
   wel<u>l̶</u> + <u>come</u> = <u>welcome</u> (also, <u>welfare</u>). *Roots*: <u>welcome</u> (O. E., wilcuma).

Learning about Prefixes: Just Fasten Them in Front

1. **dis-co-ver-y**: *7 Words*: <u>cove</u>, <u>cover</u>, <u>disco</u>, <u>discover</u>, <u>I</u>, <u>is</u>, <u>very</u>. *Clue-in-Row*: <u>Dscovery</u>: <u>Disco</u> <u>Very</u> Noisy! *Roots*: <u>dis</u> (apart from) + <u>cover</u> (M.E. <u>coveren</u>: cover) + y (n. suf.) = <u>discovery</u>.

2. **dis-cuss**: *Clue*: <u>Discuss</u> it with <u>Russ</u>. *Roots*: <u>dis</u> (not) + <u>cuss</u> (L. strike) = <u>discuss</u> (not strike: *talk*).

3. **mis-treat**: *Clue*: Don't <u>mistreat</u> your body – <u>eat</u> good food! *Prefix Rule*: <u>mis</u> + <u>treat</u> = <u>mistreat</u>.

4. **mul-ti-ply**: *Rule* and *Roots*: <u>multi</u> (many times) + <u>ply</u> (L. fold) = <u>multiply</u> (fold many times).

5. **non-fiction** (not made-up): *SPP*: non-fic-ti-on. *Clue*: In <u>nonfiction</u> books, I see <u>pi</u>ctures of the real people. *Roots*: <u>non</u> (prefix: not) + <u>fiction</u> (untrue; made-up) = <u>nonfiction</u>.

6. **non-sense**: *Phonics*: S's = s. *Visual*: *Echo Syllables*: <u>non</u> and <u>sense</u>. The beginning letter(s) are echoed at the end. *Clue*: <u>Nonsense</u> means <u>non</u> (no) <u>sense</u>: <u>non</u> + <u>sense</u>.

7. **un-der-rate**: *Rule*: Add the prefix + root: <u>under</u> + <u>rate</u> = <u>underrate</u>. *Beat*: u-n d-e r-r-a-t-e.

8. **un-known**: *SPP*: un-k-now-n. *Clue*: They are still <u>unknown</u> <u>now</u>.

9. **pre-his-tor-ic**: *Clue-in-a-Row*: <u>Hi, story</u> time for <u>history</u>: <u>pre</u> + <u>hi</u> + <u>story</u>.
    Rule and *Roots* : <u>pre</u> (before) + <u>history</u> (G. historia: knowing) <u>i</u> + <u>c</u> (adj. suf.) = <u>prehistoric</u>.

10. **pre-judge**: *SPP*: pre-jud-ge. *Roots*: <u>pre</u> (before) + <u>judge</u>. *Same Pattern*: budge, fudge, grudge.

11. **pre-fix**: *Clue* and *Rule*: You add or <u>fix</u> a <u>prefix</u> right before (pre) a word. You <u>pre</u>-fix it.

12. **pre-pare**: *Clue*: Do you c<u>are</u> if we <u>prepare</u> dinner?. *Roots*: <u>pre</u> (before) + <u>pare</u> (make ready: trim).

13. **pre-scribe**: *Rule*: <u>Silent e</u> makes <u>i</u> in <u>scribe</u> long. *Roots*: <u>pre</u> (before) + <u>scribe</u> (write) = <u>prescribe</u> (write before you get it-like a prescription).

14. **post-date**: *Clue*: If they <u>postdate</u> a package, do I get a better r<u>ate</u>? *Same Patterns*: most; late.

15. **post-script**: *Blends*-<u>st</u>, <u>scr</u>, <u>pt</u>: po-s-t s-c-r-i-p-t. *Roots*: <u>post</u> (L. after) + <u>script</u> (L. writing) = postscript (P.S. (<u>postscript</u>) is written after the written letter.).

16. **re-count**: *Clue*: Please <u>record</u> the <u>recount</u>. *SPP*: re-co-unt. *Same Pattern*: count, fount, mount.

17. **re-paid**: *Clue*: With <u>aid</u> and savings, we <u>repaid</u> our college loans. *2 Vowel Rule*: <u>I</u> makes <u>a</u> long.

18. **re-play**: *Clue*: Please <u>replay</u> that part. *2 V Rule*: <u>Y</u> makes <u>a</u> long. *Roots*: <u>re</u> (again) + <u>play</u>.

19. **re-turn**: *Clue*: <u>Return</u> the <u>urn</u> (large vase). *Same Pattern*: burn, churn, refurnish.

20. **sur-face**: *SPP*: sur-fa-ce. *Clue*: The <u>surface</u> is over (<u>sur</u>) the <u>face</u> of the water: <u>sur</u> + <u>face</u>. *Roots*: <u>sur</u> (pre: over; above) + <u>face</u> (M. E. facen: face) = <u>surface</u>.

➤ **ov-er-do** (do too much): *Clue*: <u>Do</u> you <u>overdo</u> if you look all day for 4-leaf cl<u>over</u>s?

➤ **ov-er-due** (past due): *Clue*: My book was <u>due</u> on Tues. *VV Rule*: <u>E</u> makes <u>u</u> long: <u>due</u>.

➤ **ov-er-re-act**: *Roots*: <u>over</u> (above) + <u>re</u> (again) + <u>act</u> (M.E. <u>acte</u>) = <u>overreact</u> (react above normal).

➤ **re-ar-range**: *7 Words*: <u>a</u>, <u>an</u>, <u>arrange</u>, <u>ear</u>, <u>ran</u>, <u>range</u>, <u>rear</u>. *SPP*: re- ar-<u>ran</u>-ge. *Clue-in-a-Row*: I want to <u>rearrange</u> the <u>rear</u> <u>range</u>.

➤ **sub-ma-rine**: *Rules* and *Roots*: Add <u>sub</u> (under) + <u>marine</u> (Fr. <u>marine</u>: sea) = <u>submarine</u> (under sea).

Three Prefixes That Have Different Forms

(Ad-, com-, and in- have forms that match the first letter of some roots and create double-letters.)

1. **ac-cuse**: *Phonics*: 2 c's = k; s = z. *Roots*: ac (pre: to) + *cuse* (L. call to account).
    Same Pattern: excused (ex: above + cuse: call to account). *Beat*: a-c-c u-s-e.

2. **an-nu-al**: *Clue*: Come to our annual picnic, Ann, U (and) Al: Ann + U + al. *Beat*: a-n-n u-a-l.

3. **as-sis-tants**: *Visual*: 4 s's. *12 Words*: a, an, ant, ants, as, ass, assist, assistant, I, is, sis, tan.
    Clue-in-Row: I assist ants who are assistants to the queen. *Roots*: as (to) + sist (L. stand by) + ants.

4. **because**: *Phonics*: c = k. *Clue*: I need it because I use it: be + ca-use (ME, by cause became: because).

5. **be-come**: *SPP*: be-co-me. *Clue*: How did I become me? *Roots*: become (Danish: bekomen).

6. **col-lect**: *SPP*: col-lect: *Clue*: Colleen collects art for her collection. *Rules*: 2 l's keep o short.

7. **com-pete**: *Clue*: Pete got to compete. *Same Root*: competition, competitor. *Beat*: c-o-m p-e-t-e.

8. **con-nect**: *Visual*: Connect 2n's (nn) = m. *Roots*: con (with) + nect (L. tie) = connect (with tying).

9. **cor-rect**: *Clue*: Rectify means to correct something. *Same Pattern*: The words: collect, connect,
    correct all have double letters that keep o short. (Also, all 3 words end in ect.)

10. **de-scribe**: *Rule and Roots*: de (pre: not) + scribe (L. write) = describe (not to write; to tell).

11. **de-stroy**: *Clue*: Rome was destroyed by Troy. *Roots*: de (not) + stroy (L. build) = destroy (not build).

12. **ex-ci-ted**: *Clue*: They were excited about the city. *Rule*: Silent e makes the i in excite long.
    Roots: ex (above) + cite (L. set in motion) + d (v. suf.). = excited (above just set in motion).

13. **ex-er-cise**: *Phonics*: c = s; x = ks. *Clue*: It's wise to exercise. *Beat*: e-x-e-r c-i-s-e.

14. **fore-word**: *Clue*: The foreword comes before the word in books. *Rule*: fore + word = foreword.

15. **for-ward** (L. toward): *Clue*: Let's go forward toward the goal. *Rule*: for + ward = forward.

16. **il-le-gal**: *Clue*: For a gal to get ill isn't illegal. *Roots*: il (pre: not) + legal (L. law) = illegal (not the law).

17. **im-pact**: *Phonics*: c = k. *Clue-in-a-Row*: The way that imp acts has an impact: imp + act.

18. **im-po-lite**: *Clue*: Impolite means not polished in manners, like an imp.
    Roots: im (pre: not) + polite (L. politus: polished) = impolite (not polished).   "NYAH, NYAH!"

19. **in-fi-nite**: *Visual*: 3 i's. *Clue-in-a-Row*: In finite, you can hear the 3 i's in infinite.

20. **in-her-it**: *Clue-in-a-Row*: In her it is clear that we inherit features from our parents.

➤   **a-scend**: *Clue*: I could smell the scent ascend. *Roots*: a (to) + scend (climb) = ascend (to climb).

➤   **de-scend**: *Clue*: I'll descend from my scenic view. *Roots*: de (from) + scend (climb) = descend.

➤   **e-mi-grate**: *Roots and Rule*: e (out; away from) + migrate (L. move) = emigrate (move *out of* a country).

➤   **im-mi-grate**: *Rule and Roots*: im (in; into) + migrate (L. move) = immigrate (move *into* a country).

➤   **im-pos-si-ble**: *SPP*: Say: im-pos-sib-le (Fr. pronunciation). *OWF*: Impossibly lets you hear bl.
    Clue: Is it impossible for siblings to get along? *Roots*: im (pre: not) + possible (L. possibilis).

Magical Suffixes: Just Add Them at the End

1. **cheer-ful**: *Rule*: When you add <u>full</u> to a word, always drop an <u>l</u>: <u>cheer</u> + <u>full</u> = <u>cheerful</u>. *Same Pattern*: cheerful, joyful, playful.

2. **faith-ful**: *Clue*: <u>B</u>ait your hook and have <u>faith</u>: <u>f</u> + <del>bait</del>-h (M.E. feith). *Rule*: <u>I</u> make <u>a</u> long.

3. **harm-ful**: *Clue*: Sound an al<u>arm</u> if something <u>harmful</u> is near. *Same Pattern*: charm, farm, harm.

4. **care-less**: *E Rule*: Keep <u>e</u> before consonant suffix. *Suffix Rule*: <u>care + less</u> = <u>careless</u>.

5. **help-less**: *Clue*: I felt <u>helpless</u> swimming in k<u>elp</u>: <u>h</u> + <del>kelp</del> + less. *Rule*: <u>help + less</u> = <u>helpless</u>.

6. **thought-less**: *Clue*: We <u>ought</u> not to be <u>thoughtless</u>. *Rule*: <u>thought + less</u> = thoughtless.

7. **ear-ly**: *Clue*: He got up <u>early</u> to h<u>ear</u> the birds: <del>hear</del> + ly = <u>early</u>. *Roots*: <u>early</u> (O. E. aerlic: early)

8. **fi-nal-ly**: *7 Words*: <u>a</u>, <u>Al</u>, <u>all</u>, <u>fin</u>, <u>final</u>, <u>I</u>, <u>in</u>. *Clue*: <u>Finally</u>, we're <u>all</u> here. *Beat*: f-i-n-a-ll-y.

9. **month-ly**: *Phonics*: <u>th</u> = digraph. *Clue*: There are usually 4 Mondays monthly: <u>Mon. + th + ly</u>

10. **nat-u-ral-ly**: *Clue-in-a-Row*: <u>Nat, U rally</u> our team so <u>naturally</u>.
    Rule: Drop <u>silent e</u> before vowel suffix: <u>nature</u> + <u>al</u> (adj. suf.) + <u>ly</u> (adv. suf.) = <u>naturally</u>.

11. **sin-cere-ly**: *Phonics*: <u>s</u> = s; <u>c</u> = s. *Clue*: <u>Since (I) rely</u> on you, I <u>sincerely</u> trust you: <u>since + rely</u>.
    Rule: Just add a suffix that begins with a consonant to the root: sincerely, closely, nearly.

12. **smooth-ly**: *Phonics*: <u>sm</u> = blend; <u>th</u> = digraph. *Clue*: Your t<u>ooth</u> came out <u>smoothly</u>.

13. **sure-ly**: *Phonics*: <u>s</u> = <u>sh</u>. *Clue*: I s<u>urely</u> <u>rely</u> on you. *Rule*: <u>S</u>ilent e stays before consonant: <u>sure + ly</u>.

14. **hap-pi-ness**: *Rule*: <u>Y</u> becomes <u>i</u> before all suffixes except <u>-ing</u>: <u>happ</u><del>y</del> + i + ness. <u>2 p's</u> keep <u>a</u> short.

15. **kind-ness**: *Clue*: <u>Kindness</u> <u>binds</u> our friendship. *Rule*: Add: <u>kind + ness</u>. *Beat*: k-i-n-d n-e-s-s.

16. **still-ness**: *Clue*: I took my f<u>ill</u> of the <u>stillness</u> at the lake. *Rule*: <u>still + ness</u> = <u>stillness</u>.

17. **le-mon-ade**: *Clue*: On <u>Mon</u>. I m<u>ade</u> <u>lemonade</u>: <u>le + Mon + </u><del>m</del>ade = <u>lemonade</u>.
    Roots: <u>lemon</u> (Lat. lemonium: lemon) + <u>ade</u> (noun suffix: drink) = <u>lemonade</u>.

18. **high-est**: *Phonics*: <u>igh</u> = long <u>i</u>. *Visual*: Climb on chairs (<u>h h</u>) to be the <u>highest</u> up.

19. **lar-gest**: *Phonics*: g = <u>j</u>. *Clue*: That's the <u>largest</u> b<u>arge</u> I've ever seen.

20. **near-er**: *Clue*: Each y<u>ear</u> you grow <u>nearer</u> and d<u>ear</u>er. *Rule*: Add <u>near + er</u>. (O. E. near: nigh).

➢ **a-ban-doned**: *Visual*: *9 Words*: <u>a</u>, <u>an</u>, <u>and</u>, <u>abandon</u>, <u>ban</u>, <u>band</u>, <u>Don</u>, <u>Ed</u>, <u>on</u>, <u>one</u>.
    Clue-in-a-Row: Ed did not feel <u>abandoned</u>; there was <u>a band on Ed</u>.

➢ **grate-ful** (thankful): *Clue*: She gave them the best <u>rate</u> because she was <u>grateful</u>.
    Roots: <u>grate</u> (L. pleasing) + <u>ful</u> (adj. suf.) = <u>grateful</u>.

➢ **great-ly**: *Clue*: When I <u>eat</u>, I enjoy it <u>greatly</u>: <u>gr-eat</u> + <u>ly</u>. *Roots*: greatly (O. E. great).

➢ **scho-lar-ship**: *Roots*: <u>scho</u><del>o</del>l (L. school) + <u>ar</u> (n. suf) + <u>ship</u>. (n. suf: to help) = <u>scholarship</u>.

➢ **won-der-ment**: *Visual*: <u>wonder</u> reversed = <u>red now</u>. *Clue*: After they <u>won</u> the race,
    the <u>men</u> felt <u>wonderment</u>: <u>won + der + men-t</u> (O. E., Danish: wonder).

The Rule for Adding Suffixes after Silent E

Consonant precedes silent e: Keep e before consonant suffixes. Drop e before vowel suffixes(*Ex: ce, ge*).
Vowel precedes silent e, keep e before all suffixes (*Ex: rescuing, truly, wholly*).

1.   **a-chieve-ment**: *Clue*: I waved hi on the eve of the men's achievement: ac-hi-eve + ment.
     Rule: When consonant precedes silent e, keep e before a consonant suffix: achieve + ment.

2.   **ex-cite-ment**: *Rules*: Silent e makes i long. Keep silent e before consonant suffix: excite + ment.

3.   **like-ly**: *Rule*: Keep silent e before a consonant suffix: like + ly. *Same Root*: likable, likeness.

4.   **mak-ing**: *Rule*: Drop silent e before vowel suffix. *Roots*: make (M.E.maken) + ing (v. suf) = making.

5.   **no-ta-ble**: *Visual*: 6 Words: a, able, no, not, tab, table.
     Clue-in-a-Row: Is it notable that since we have no table we're not able to eat on a table?

6.   **pleas-ing**: *Clue*: I'm leasing a pleasing car. *Same Root*: pleased, pleasure.

7.   **u-su-al**: *Phonics*: s = z. *Pronounce*: 3 syllables. *Clue*: Come with us, U all, for our usual pizza
     outing: us + U + all. *Rule*: Drop silent e before vowel suffix: use + ual. *Same Root*: using, useful.

8.   **writ-ing**: *Rule*: Drop silent e before vowel suffix: write + ing. *Same Pattern*: biting, igniting.

9.   **com-ing**: *Phonics*: c = k. *Rule*: Drop silent e before vowel suffix: come + ing = coming.
     Silent e does not make the vowel before it long for some words like come, give, have, love…

10. **giv-ing**: *Rule*: Drop silent e before vowel suffix: give + ing = giving. *Same Pattern*: living.

11. **hav-ing**: *Rule*: Drop silent e before vowel suffix: have + ing = having (Silent e doesn't make o long.).

12. **lov-a-ble**: *Rule*: Drop silent e before vowel suffix: love + able = lovable. *Beat*: l-o-v-a-b-l-e.

13. **change-a-ble**: *Rule Ex*: E stays to keeps g soft before -able: change + able = changeable

14. **no-tice-a-ble**: *Clue-in-a-Row*: It is noticeable that my soda is not ice able. (E keeps c soft before -a.)

15. **cour-a-geous**: *Clue*: He's courageous to live in our age: c + our age +ous. (E keeps g soft before -o.)

16. **out-ra-geous**: *SPP*: out-ra-ge-ous. *Roots*: out (beyond) + rage + ous (adj. suf.) = outrageous.

17. **ca-noe-ing**: *Phonics*: c = k. *Clue*: He rested his toes on the canoe.
     Rule: Vowel precedes silent e: Keep e before suffix: canoe + ing = canoeing.

18. **shoe-ing** (for horse): *Rule*: Vowel precedes silent e: Keep e before suffix: shoe + ing = shoeing.

19. **dy-ing**: *Rule Ex*: Change die to dy. Then keep y for -ing. *Same Pattern*: die-dying, tie tying.

20. **dye-ing** (v., coloring): *Clue*: I'm dyeing sheets a rye color. *Rule*: Dyeing = e. Dying (to die) = no e.

➢   **aw-ful**: *Rule Ex*: Awe drops e and full drops l: awe + full = awful. *Same Pattern*: lawful.

➢   **res-cu-ing**: *Clue*: They were cuing him on rescuing. *Exception*: E's not needed to keep u long.

➢   **tru-ly**: *Rule Ex*: True drops e: true + ly = truly (duly). *Clue*: They were truly unruly.

➢   **val-u-a-ble**: *Clue*: Val, U (are) able to care for this valuable crown. *Exception*: E's not needed.

➢   **whol-ly**: *Clue*: Our wreath is wholly holly. *Rule Ex*: Whole drops e: whole +ly = wholly.

259

Rule for Adding Suffixes after Final Y

Words 1-20 follow the *Y Rule*: When y follows a consonant, change y to i for all suffixes except -ing.
When y follows a vowel, keep y before all suffixes (Exception after # 20)

1. **bus-i-ly**: *Phonics*: <u>bus</u> = <u>biz</u>. *Clue*: I'm <u>busily</u> working on a <u>business</u>.
   Y Rule: Change <u>y</u> to <u>i</u> except before -ing: bus~~y~~ + i + <u>ly</u> = <u>busily</u>.

2. **car-riage**: *Phonics*: <u>c</u> = <u>k</u>; <u>g</u> = <u>j</u>. *SPP*: car-ri-age. *Clue*: <u>Carri</u> is the <u>age</u> for a <u>carriage</u> ride.
   Rule: Change <u>y</u> to <u>i</u> except before -ing: carr~~y~~ + i + <u>age</u> = <u>carriage</u>. *Same Pattern*: marriage.

3. **cry-ing**: *Clue*: She was <u>crying</u> while <u>frying</u> onions. *Rule*: Keep <u>y</u> before <u>ing</u>: <u>crying</u> (drying trying).

4. **eas-ily**: *Phonics*: <u>s</u> = <u>z</u>. *Y Rule*: eas~~y~~ + i + <u>ly</u> = <u>easily</u>. *2 V Rule*: <u>A</u> makes <u>e</u> long in <u>ease</u>.

5. **emp-ti-ness**: *Rule*: Change <u>y</u> to <u>i</u> except before -ing: empt~~y~~ + i + <u>ness</u> (Only keep y before -ing).

6. **emp-ty-ing**: *Rule*: Keep <u>y</u> before <u>ing</u>: empty + ing = <u>emptying</u>.

7. **hur-ry-ing**: *Rule*: 2 r's keeps <u>u</u> short. *Rule*: Keep <u>y</u> before -ing. *Beat*: h-u-r-r-y-i-n-g.

8. **laz-i-ness**: *Rule*: Change y to i before all suffixes except -ing: laz~~y~~ + i + <u>ness</u> = <u>laziness</u>.

9. **pret-ti-er**: *Rule*: Change y to i except before -ing: prett~~y~~ + i + er = <u>prettier</u>. *Pattern*: easier, readier.

10. **read-y-ing**: *6 Words*: <u>a</u>, <u>ad</u>, <u>dying</u>, <u>I</u>, <u>in</u>, <u>read</u>, <u>ready</u>. *Rule*: Keep <u>y</u> before -ing: <u>readying</u>.

11. **tried**: *SPP*: tri-<u>ed</u>. *Y Rule*: Change y to i except before -ing: tr~~y~~ + i + ed. *Pattern*: cried, died.

12. **wor-ry-ing**: *Y Rule*: Keep <u>y</u> before -ing: worry + ing = <u>worrying</u>. *Rule*: 2 r's keep o short.

13. **buy-er**: *Clue*: That <u>guy</u> is the <u>buyer</u>. *Rule*: <u>Y</u> stays when it follows a vowel: <u>buy</u> + <u>er</u> = <u>buyer</u>.

14. **buy-ing**: *Rule*: <u>Y</u> stays when it follows a vowel : <u>buy</u> + <u>ing</u> = <u>buying</u>. *Same Pattern*: praying.

15. **en-joyed**: *Rule*: <u>Y</u> stays when it follows a vowel : <u>enjoy</u> + <u>ed</u>. *Same Pattern*: employed, toyed…

16. **enjoyment**: *Rule*: <u>Y</u> stays when it follows a vowel : en + joy + ment (n. suf.) = <u>enjoyment</u>.

17. **play-ing**: *6 Words*: <u>a</u>, <u>I</u>, <u>in</u>, <u>lay</u>, <u>laying</u>, <u>play</u>. *Y Rule*: <u>Y</u> stays before -ing: <u>play</u> + <u>ing</u>.

18. **prayed** (said prayers): *SPP*: pra-yed. *Clue*: I p<u>layed</u> during the day and <u>prayed</u> at night.

19. **preyed** (hunted): *Clue*: The eagle <u>eyed</u> its <u>prey</u>: <u>pr</u> + <u>eyed</u>. *Rule*: <u>Y</u> stays after vowel: <u>prey</u> + <u>ed</u>.

20. **stayed**: *SPP*: stay-ed. *Clue*: She <u>stayed</u> and p<u>layed</u> with her grandson. *Beat*: s-t-a y-e-d.

➤ **dai-ly**: *SPP*: da-i-ly. *Clue*: She got <u>daily</u> mail. *Rule Ex.*: da~~y~~ + i + <u>ly</u> = <u>daily</u> (O. E. daeg).

➤ **ly-ing**: *Rule Ex*: <u>Lie</u> changes to ly- before -ing: li~~e~~ + y + ing. *Same Pattern*: die-dying; tie-tying.

➤ **paid**: *5 Words*: <u>a</u>, <u>aid</u>, <u>I</u>, <u>id</u>, <u>pa</u>. *Clue*: He <u>paid</u> for first <u>aid</u>. *2 Vowel Rule*: <u>I</u> makes <u>a</u> long.
   Rule Ex. Pattern: laying-laid; paying-paid; saying-said. The rest use -ed: played, stayed.

➤ **said**: *SPP*: sa-id. *Phonics*: said = sed sound *Clue*: He <u>said</u> he <u>paid</u> her. *Same Pattern*: aid, afraid.

➤ **par-li-a-ment**: *SPP*: par-<u>li</u>-<u>a</u>-ment.
   Rule Ex. <u>parley</u> (Change <u>ey</u> to <u>ia</u>) + <u>ia</u> + ment = <u>parliament</u> (place to parley).

The Power of Suffixes to Create Nouns

1. **a-bun-dance**: *Phonics*: c = s. *Clue-n-Row*: With our abundance of food, we even saw a bun dance.

2. **am-bu-lance**: *Clue*: Like a lance (sword), the ambulance raced to the hospital (chance, dance). *Roots*: ambul (L. ambul: walking) ance (hospital) = ambulance (L. walking hospital).

3. **bal-ance**: *Clue*: Keep your balance when you spar with a lance: b + a + lance. *Beat*: b-a-l a-n-c-e. *Roots*: ba (M.E. two; pair of) + lance (M.E. scales; metal dishes) = balance (pair of metal dishes; scale)

4. **in-stance** (occurrence): *SPP*: in-stan-ce. *Rule*: Change t to ce: instant-instance (resistant-resistance)

5. **in-stants** (moments): *SPP*: in-stan-t. *Clue*: In instants the ants were gone: in + st + ants.

6. **beg-gar**: *Rule*: 2 g's keep e short. *Clue*: The beggar looked in garbage: beg + gar.

7. **dol-lar**: *Clue*: A doll artist painted eyes on my doll. *Rule*: 2 l's keep o short.

8. **sug-ar**: *Phonics*: s = sh. *Clue*: For a sugar garnish, put powdered sugar on top of a doily: su + gar.

9. **cha-rac-ter**: *Phonics*: ch = k. *SPP*: c-har-ac-ter. As a pirate, he was a terrifying character.

10. **teach-er**: *Phonics*: ch = digraph ch. *Clue*: I had tea (with) Cher's teacher: tea + cher.

11. **ac-tor**: *Phonics*: c = k. *Clue-in-a-Row*: Act or come to the play and see each actor: act + or.

12. **al-li-ga-tor**: *Clue*: Alli, the gator is my alligator friend: Alli + gator. *Rule*: 2 l's keep a short.

13. **doc-tor**: *Phonics*: c = k. *Clue*: A doctor works to heal the torment of disease: doc + torment.

14. **in-ven-tor**: *Clue-in-a-Row*: An inventor can invent or make exciting discoveries: invent + or.

15. **ex-plor-a-tions**: *Clue*: We took rations (measured food) on explorations: ex + plo + rations. *Roots and Rule*: ex (beyond) + plore (L. hunting cries) + ation (n. suf.) = exploration (beyond hunting cries).

16. **im-ag-i-na-tion**: *Clue*: Think of an Imagi-Nation. *E Rule*: imagine + ation = imagination.

17. **in-for-ma-tion**: *10 Words*: a, at, for, form, formation, I, in, inform, ma, mat. *Rule and Roots*: inform (L. ideas formed in mind) + ation (n. suf.) = information.

18. **va-ca-tion**: *Phonics*: c = k. *E Rule*: Drop e before vowel suffix: vacate + ion = vacation.

19. **sur-geon**: *Phonics*: s = s; geon = jun. *Clue-in-a-Row*: Surge on through the surgery, surgeon.

20. **com-pa-ny**: *Phonics*: c = k. *Roots*: com (pre: with) + pan (L. bread) + y (n. suf.) = company (You share bread: pan with company).

➤ **ex-per-i-ence**: *Visual*: 4 e's; 1i. *Clue*: Peri had an experience. *Beat*: e-x p-e-r i-e-n-c-e.

➤ **i-ni-ti-a-tion**: *7 Words*: a, at, ate, I, in, it, on. *Rule*: 4 Open Syllables (end in a vowel). *Clue*: After initiation, we went to a pizza parlor and in it I ate a lot: in-it-I-ate + ion = initiation.

➤ **in-tel-li-gence**: *Visual*: 4 words: in + tell + i + gent = intelligent (Change t to ce.) = intelligence.

➤ **li-cense**: *SPP*: li-cen-se. *OWF*: You can hear the s in license in licensing. *Same Pattern*: 6 common words end in -ense: defense incense, license, sense, suspense, tense.

➤ **re-mem-brance**: *SPP*: re-mem-bran-ce. *Clue*: What brand of remembrance cards do you like?

Suffixes Can Create Adjectives, Verbs and Adverbs

1. **com-for-ta-ble**: *Visual*: *8 Words*: <u>a</u>, <u>able</u>, <u>comfort</u>, <u>for</u>, <u>fort</u>, <u>or</u>, <u>tab</u>, <u>table</u>.
   Roots: <u>com</u> (pre: with) + <u>fort</u> (L. fortis: strength) + <u>able</u> (adj. suf.) = <u>comfortable</u> (<u>able</u> with strength).

2. **fourth**: *Clue*: When we were <u>four</u>, <u>our</u> friends came to <u>our</u> <u>fourth</u> birthday party.

3. **med-i-cal**: *Roots*: <u>medic</u> (L. medicus: heal) + <u>al</u> (adj. suf. regarding) = <u>medical</u> (regarding healing).

4. **mys-ter-i-ous**: *Clue*: It's <u>mysterious</u> – <u>my stereo</u> is gone. *Y Rule*: <u>mystery</u> + i + ous = <u>mysterious</u>.

5. **sim-plest**: <u>simple</u> + <u>er</u> (comparative suf.) = <u>simpler</u>; <u>simple</u> + <u>est</u> (superlative suf.) = <u>simplest</u>.

6. **splen-did**: *Clue*: Will you <u>lend</u> me that <u>splendid</u> dress? <u>sp</u> + <u>lend</u> + <u>id</u>.

7. **va-cant**: *Phonics*: <u>c</u> = <u>k</u>; *Clue*: <u>Can't</u> an <u>ant</u> live in a <u>vacant</u> house? <u>va</u> - <u>c</u> + <u>ant</u>.

8. **ce-le-bra-ted**: *Phonics*: <u>c</u> = <u>s</u>. *Clue-in-a-Row*: We <u>celebrated</u> with a <u>celeb rated</u> high at the theatre. *E Rule*: Drop <u>Silent e</u> before a vowel suffix: <u>celebrate</u> + <u>ion</u> = <u>celebration</u>.

9. **danced**: *Phonics*: <u>c</u> = <u>s</u>. *SPP*: dan-ced. *Clue*: <u>Dan</u> <u>danced</u> with me. *Rule*: <u>dance</u> + <u>d</u>.

10. **en-er-gize**: *Phonics*: <u>g</u> = <u>j</u>. *OWF*: In <u>Energizer</u>, you hear <u>z</u> in <u>energize</u>: <u>energy</u> + <u>i</u> + <u>ze</u>.

11. **fin-ished**: *Clue-in-a-Row*: The Little Mermaid <u>finished</u> life at sea and said "My <u>fin I shed</u> forever."

12. **i-so-late**: *Clue*: <u>I (was) so late</u> recovering, they <u>isolated</u> me from well friends: <u>i</u> + <u>so</u> + <u>late</u>.

13. **al-ways**: *Exception*: <u>All</u> <u>always</u> drops an <u>l</u>: <u>all</u>: + <u>ways</u> = <u>always</u>. *Same Pattern*: also, almost.

14. **ac-ci-den-tal-ly**: *12 Words*: <u>a</u>, <u>accident</u>, <u>accidental</u>, <u>Al</u>, <u>all</u>, <u>ally</u>, <u>den</u>, <u>dent</u>, <u>dental</u>, <u>I</u>, <u>tall</u>, <u>tally</u>.
    Phonics: <u>c</u> = <u>k</u>; <u>c</u> = <u>s</u>. *Clue*: <u>Accidentally</u> <u>I</u> got a <u>dent</u> driving with my <u>ally</u>: <u>ac-ci</u> + <u>dent</u> + <u>ally</u>.

15. **for-tu-nate-ly**: *Clue-in-a-Row*: <u>Fortunately</u>, the <u>fort U (and) Nate</u> built is still standing.
    Rule: After <u>silent e</u>, just add a consonant suffix: <u>fortunate</u> + <u>ly</u>.

16. **gent-ly**: *Phonics*: <u>g</u> = <u>j</u>. *Clue*: The <u>gentle</u> father rocked his baby <u>gently</u>. *Same Root*: gentleness

17. **slow-ly**: *Clue*: I <u>blow</u> big bubbles <u>slowly</u>. *Same Pattern*: flow, glow, lowly, mow, slowly.

18. **u-su-al-ly** (4 beats): *Phonics*: <u>su</u> = <u>zhoo</u>. *Clue*: He <u>usually</u> invites <u>us, U (and) Ally</u>: <u>us</u> + <u>U</u> + <u>Ally</u>
    E Rule and Suffix Rule: <u>use</u> (M.E. <u>usen</u>) + <u>ual</u> (adj. suf.) + <u>ly</u> (adv. suf.).

19. **weak-ly** (adv., with little strength): *Clue*: The bird with the broken <u>beak</u> walked <u>weakly</u>

20. **week-ly** (adj., adv. every 7 days): *Clue*: I pay a <u>wee</u> <u>weekly</u> <u>fee</u> for fresh flowers.

➤ **ex-or-bi-tant** (adj. out of this orbit): <u>a</u>, <u>an</u>, <u>ant</u>, <u>bit</u>, <u>I</u>, <u>it</u>, <u>or</u>, <u>orbit</u>, <u>tan</u>.
  Clue-in-a-Row: <u>Ex</u>it from our <u>orbit, ant</u>, your appetite is <u>exorbitant</u>.

➤ **ju-di-cial** (re: justice): *Clue-in-Row*: <u>Judi (worked for the) CIA</u> and the Justice Dept.: <u>judi + CIA +</u>

➤ **sen-si-ble**: *Clue*: It was <u>sensible</u> for my <u>siblings</u> (brothers, sisters) to have a reunion: <u>sen+ sibl + in</u>

➤ **sig-ni-fi-cant**: *7 Words*: <u>an</u>, <u>ant</u>, <u>can</u>, <u>can't</u>, <u>I</u>, <u>if</u>, <u>sign</u>. *Beat*: s-i-g n-i f-i c-a-n-t.
  Clue-in-a-Row: This is so <u>significant</u>, please <u>sign if I can't</u>.

➤ **vi-si-ble**: *Clue*: My <u>siblings</u> are <u>visible</u> in a photo: <u>vi</u> + <u>sibl</u> + <u>ing</u>. *Roots*: <u>visi</u> (L. vision) + <u>ble</u> (adj. suf).

The Doubling Final Consonants Rule
for One-Syllable Words and for Words with More Than One Syllable

1.   **cur-rant** (n. small red berry) *Clue*: An <u>ant</u> ate a curr<u>ant</u>. *Rule*: <u>2 r's</u> keep <u>u</u> short.

2.   **cur-rent** (adj. now; n. flow of water, electricity, etc.): *Clue*: <u>Current rent</u> is due. *Rule*: <u>2 r's</u> keep <u>u</u> short.

3.   **hugged**: *SPP*: hug-<u>ged</u>. *Phonics*: <u>g's</u> = g sound. *Rule*: <u>2 g's</u> keep <u>u</u> short (<u>Huge</u>: g = j; long <u>u</u>).

4.   **planned**: *SPP*: plan-<u>ned</u>. *Clue*: <u>Ned</u> <u>planned</u> a <u>plan</u>. *Rule*: <u>2 n's</u> keeps <u>a</u> short.

5.   **quit-ting**: *Rules*: <u>Qu</u> = one letter. <u>2 t's</u> keep <u>i</u> short. *Same Pattern*: knitting, sitting.

6.   **scared**: *Clue*: He <u>cared</u> and got <u>scared</u> when I was lost. *Same Pattern*: bared, dared.

7.   **scarred**: *Clue*: When he got <u>scarred</u>, the <u>scar</u> turned <u>red</u>: <u>scar + red</u>. *Pattern*: barred, starred.

8.   **skip-ping**: *Rule*: <u>2 p's</u> keep <u>i</u> short. *Same Pattern*: dipping, flipping. *Beat*: s-k-i-p-p-i-n-g.

9.   **slammed**: *SPP*: slam-<u>med</u>. *Clue*: <u>Sammy</u> <u>slammed</u> the door. *Rule*: <u>2 m's</u> keep <u>a</u> short.

10. **sled-ding**: *6 Words*: <u>din</u>, <u>ding</u>, Ed, <u>in</u>, <u>led</u>, <u>sled</u>. *Clue*: I got a <u>sled ding</u> from <u>sledding</u> into a rock.

11. **star-ing**: *Rule*: Drop <u>silent e</u> before vowel suffix: star~~e~~ + ing = <u>staring</u>.

12. **star-ring**: *Clue-in-a-Row*: The <u>starring</u> actor wore a <u>star ring</u>. *Rule*: <u>2 r's</u> keep the <u>a</u> short.

13. **swim-ming**: *Clue*: The sky was <u>dimming</u> when we went <u>swimming</u> (O.E. swimman).

14. **trot-ting**: *Visual*: <u>3 t's</u>. *Rule*: <u>2 t's</u> keep <u>o</u> short. *Beat*: t-r-o-t-t-i-n-g.

15. **be-gin-ning**: *Visual*: *7 Words*: <u>be</u>, <u>beg</u>, <u>begin</u>, <u>gin</u>, <u>in</u>, <u>inn</u>, <u>inning</u> (ginning) *Clue*: We stayed at an <u>inn</u> at the <u>beginning</u> of our trip. *Rule*: Accent on <u>gin</u>, double <u>n</u> to keep <u>i</u> short: <u>beginning</u>.

16. **con-trolled**: *Clue*: The <u>troll</u> <u>controlled</u> the bridge. *Rule*: Beat's on <u>trol</u>, double <u>l</u> to keep <u>o</u> short.

17. **for-get-ting**: *Rule*: Beat is on <u>get</u>, double <u>t</u> to keep <u>e</u> short: <u>forgetting</u>.

18. **hap-pe-ning**: *Clue*: What's <u>happening</u>? <u>Hap</u> found my <u>pen</u>: <u>Hap + pen +ing</u>. *Rule*: Accent's on <u>hap</u>, don't double <u>n</u>: <u>happening</u>.

19. **lim-it-ing**: *Visual*: See <u>3 i's</u>. *Rule*: Accent on first syllable: <u>lim</u>, don't double <u>t</u>: <u>limiting</u>.

20. **tra-veled**: *Clue*: We <u>traveled</u> where the <u>Ave led</u>: <u>tr + Ave. + led</u>. *Rule*: Accent on first syllable, don't double <u>l</u>: <u>traveling</u>. *Same Pattern*: leveled, reveled.

➢   **ex-cel-lent**: *See*: <u>3 e's</u>. *Clue*: I found an <u>excellent cell</u>. *Exception*: Beat's on <u>ex</u>, but <u>l</u> is doubled.

➢   **pic-nick-ing**: *Visual*: pic + nic. *Phonics* and *Inserted K Rule*: Most words ending in <u>c</u>, insert <u>k</u> after <u>c</u> before adding suffixes (<u>ed</u>, <u>ing</u>, or <u>y</u>) to keep the soft <u>k</u> sound: <u>picnicking</u>.

➢   **pre-ferred**: *Visual*: <u>3 e's</u>. *SPP*: pre-fer-red. *Clue-in-a-Row*: When asked what color I <u>preferred</u>, I said, "I <u>prefer red</u>." *Same Pattern*: occurred-occurrence; preferred-preference…

➢   **re-veled**: *Clue*: We <u>reveled</u> when <u>Eve led</u> us out of the tunnel: <u>r + Eve + led</u>. *Pattern*: leveled.

➢   **oc-cur-rence**: *Phonics*: <u>2c's</u> = <u>k</u>; <u>c</u> = <u>s</u>. *Clue*: <u>O, C</u> the <u>current</u> on this <u>occurrence</u>: <u>O + C + curren~~t~~ + ce</u>.

Excellent
EXCEPTION **263**

Suffixes Make Nouns Plural in Many Ways

(Italian Musical Words end in -os. Most *Spanish-Indian* plurals end in -oes.)
*(Most irregular plurals are *Old English* words: children, dwarves, men, loaves.)

1. **buf-fa-loes** (or buffalos): *Clue-in-a-Row*: Do buffaloes buff aloes (cacti) on the prairie?

2. **ech-oes**: *SPP*: e-cho-es. *Visual*: E goes out and e echoes back. *Beat*: e-c-h o-e-s

3. **her-oes**: *Clue*: The heroes went out to find the roes (deer): he + roes = heroes.

4. **mos-qui-toes**: *Clue*: Mosquitoes even bit his toes. *Roots*: (Spanish-Indian)

5. **po-ta-toes**: *Clue*: Potatoes have toes and eyes. Roots: (Spanish-Indian).

6. **tor-pe-does**: *6 Words*: do, doe, does, or, to, torpedo. When a ship's hit by torpedoes, does it sink?

7. **al-tos**: *Clue*: Halt the altos. *Musical words* end in -os: sopranos, pianos, solos (They're Italian).

8. **pi-a-nos**: *Clue*: Pia plays piano. *Rule*: Open syllables: pi-a-no.

9. **ra-di-os**: *Clue*: Disc jockeys play stereos on radios (Include radios in *musical words ending in -os*.)

10. **so-pra-nos**: *Clue*: So practice, sopranos. *Rule*: 3 Open syllables: so-pra-no.

11. **ster-e-os**: *Clue*: Steve plays stereos in the stern of his boat. Add stereos (Gk.) to *musical words*.

12. **stu-di-os**: *Y Rule*: Change y to i except before -ing: study + i + os = studios (Ital. musical word)

13. **vi-de-os**: *Roots*: vide (L. videre: see) + o (L. audio: hear) = video (see/hear): Add to *-os musical words*.

14. **halves** (half): *Clue*: Hal's vest has 2 halves. *Pattern*: calf-calves; half-halves.

15. **loaves** (loaf): *Clue*: Put a in the middle of loves to get lo-a-ves.
    Pattern: Change f to v and add es: loaf-loaves; dwarf-dwarves; hoof-hooves.

16. **be-liefs** (belief): *Clue*: We do not have a lie in our beliefs. *Beat*: b-e l-i e-f-s.

17. **coun-tries**: *SPP*: coun-tries. *Clue*: Can you count all the countries. *Y Rule*: country + ies.

18. **fam-i-lies**: *Clue*: These families tell no lies. *Y Rule*: family + i + es = families (M. E. families).

19. **val-leys**: *Clue*: Are there keys to special valleys (O. E. vale)? *Rule*: 2 l's keep a short.

20. **chil-dren**: *Clue*: They have ten children. *Roots*: child (O. E. cild: child).

21. **moose**: *Clue*: The moose got loose. *Rule*: moose (Algonquain), deer, salmon = same plural.

22. **gnus** (n., Afr. antelope): *Phonics*: silent g. *SPP*: g-nu. Clue: Gnats sat on gnus (gnu: sing. of gnus).

23. **news** (n., recent events report): *Phonics*: s = z. *Clue*: The news (noun) is always new. (adj. is new).

24. **wo-men** (woman): *SPP*: wo-men. *Plurals*: man, men = woman, women (Basic Old. Eng. words).

25. **lun-ches**: Phonics: s = z sound. *Same Pattern*: bunch-bunches; ranch-ranches.

➢ **prin-ces-ses**: *Clue*: The princes and princesses saw our successes. *Rule*: Add -es for plural.

➢ **feats** (achievements): *Clue*: Are Great Eating Feats eating 100 pizzas or pies? (heat, seat).

➢ **feet**: *Clue*: My feet meet the ground with each step. *Roots*: feet (O. E. feet = plural).

➢ **parentheses**: *14 Words*: a, are, aren't, he, he's, pa, par, parent, rent, the, these, theses, he, he's.
    Same Pattern: Gk. words ending in -is: oasis-oases; parenthesis-parentheses; thesis-theses.

➢ **alumna, alumnae**: (L Roots: sing. and plural: girl graduates); **alumnus, alumni** (L. guy graduates).

The Challenging L Endings—al, el, il and le

(*Special Phonics Pronunciations, Clues*, and *Other Word Forms* help a lot with these words.)

1. **bri-dal** (for a wedding): *Clue:* A <u>bridal</u> shower is <u>all</u> for the <u>bride</u>. *Rule:* Drop <u>silent e</u> before vowel suffix: <u>bride</u> + <u>al</u> = <u>bridal</u>. *Roots:* <u>bride</u> (O. E. bryd). *Same Pattern:* causal, tidal…

2. **bri-dle** (n., for a horse): *Visual:* <u>Bridle</u> ends in <u>e</u> like hors<u>e</u>. *Clue:* <u>Let</u>'s put a <u>bridle</u> on my horse.

3. **me-dal** (n., award): *Clue* and *OWF:* A <u>medallion</u> is a large <u>medal</u> (*Homophone:* meddle: fortitude).

4. **me-tal**: *Clue:* I <u>met Al</u> in a <u>metal</u> shop. *OWF:* <u>Metal</u> is <u>metallic</u> (*Homophone:* mettle: interfere).

5. **pe-tal**: *Clue:* My <u>pet</u> always eats a <u>petal</u> or two. *Same Pattern:* metal.

6. **ti-dal**: Clue: Don't <u>dally</u> when a <u>tidal</u> wave's coming. *E Rule:* <u>tide</u> + <u>al</u> = <u>tidal</u>. (O.E. tid: time).

7. **to-tal**: *Clue:* You can hear <u>al</u> in <u>total</u> in <u>totality</u>. *Roots:* <u>total</u> (L. totalis: entire).

8. **chan-nel**: *Clue:* <u>Chan (and) Nel</u> swam the English <u>Channel</u>. *Beat:* c-h-a n-n e-l.

9. **nick-el**: *Phonics:* <u>c</u> = <u>k</u>. *Clue:* I won't <u>nick</u> my <u>elf</u>-green <u>nickel</u> I found: <u>nick</u> + <u>elf</u>.

10. **sho-vel**: *Clue:* We're <u>shoveling</u> snow with our <u>shovel</u> for <u>Velda</u>. *Beat:* s-h-o v-e-l.

11. **towel**: *SPP:* <u>to</u>-<u>wel</u>. *Clue:* <u>To welcome</u> people we put out <u>welcome</u> <u>towels</u>: to wel~~come~~.

12. **tun-nel**: *SPP:* tun-<u>nel</u>. *Clue:* <u>Nel</u> likes the <u>fun</u> of a <u>tunnel</u>. *Rule:* <u>2 n's</u> keeps <u>u</u> short.

13. **a-ble**: *Clue:* I am <u>able</u> to set the <u>table</u>. *OWF:* In <u>ably</u>, you can hear <u>bl</u> in <u>able</u>.

14. **ex-am-ple**: *Phonics:* <u>x</u> = <u>ks</u>. *Clue:* My <u>exam</u>'s complete, once I give <u>examples</u>: exam + ~~complete~~.

15. **han-dled**: *7 Words:* <u>a</u>, <u>an</u>, <u>and</u>, <u>Ed</u>, <u>hand</u>, <u>handle</u>, <u>led</u>. *SPP:* hand-led
    Clue-in-a-Row: They <u>handled</u> us so well, we felt <u>hand-led</u>. *Same Pattern:* candle, handle.

16. **little**: *OWF Clue: The <u>Littlest</u> Angel* is about a <u>little</u> boy angel. *Rule:* <u>2 t's</u> keep <u>i</u> short.

17. **mus-cles**: *Phonics:* <u>c</u> = <u>s</u>. *SPP:* mus-<u>cles</u>. *Clue:* I can <u>clench</u> my <u>muscle</u> (L. musculus: little mouse).

18. **ti-tle**: *Clue:* <u>Let</u> the <u>title</u> be *POWER Spelling*. *OWF:* Can you hear the <u>tl</u> in <u>title</u> in <u>titling</u>,

19. **trou-ble**: *Clue:* <u>Let</u>'s not have <u>double</u> <u>trouble</u>. *OWF:* In <u>troubling</u>, you hear <u>bl</u> in <u>trouble</u>.

20. **pen-cil**: *Phonics:* <u>c</u> = <u>s</u>. *Visual:* Think of <u>il</u> as a short and a long <u>pencil</u> (<u>il</u>)
    Clue: I <u>pencil</u> <u>illustrations</u>, and with my <u>pen</u> I st<u>encil</u>.

➤ **coun-cil** (n. group): *Phonics:* <u>c</u>= <u>k</u>; <u>c</u> = <u>s</u>. *Clue:* There's a <u>City Council</u> in our <u>city</u>: <u>coun</u> + ci~~ty~~ + l.

➤ **coun-sel** (v. advise): *Clue:* I <u>select</u> my own <u>counsel</u>: <u>coun</u> + sele~~ct~~ (roles = last 5 letters reversed: counselor).

➤ **cym-bals**: *Clue:* Keep your <u>cymbals</u> <u>balanced</u> as you <u>clash</u> them (L. cymbalums: hollow objects).

➤ **symbols**: *Clue:* Great <u>old</u> <u>symbols</u> <u>bolster</u> (build-up) a company's image (L., G., symbolums: signs).

➤ **spe-cial**: *Phonics:* c= sh. *SPP:* spe-ci-<u>al</u>. *Roots:* <u>speci</u> (L. speci: species) + <u>al</u> (adj. suf) = <u>special</u>.

Words with Roots: sede, ceed, cede, plus Old Seed

All of these words are Latin except *good old seed* (Old Eng. 900 A.D.) For all words (except supersede: sede = sit), prefixes and suffixes are added to the root: ceed, which is also spelled cede (go; move; yield).

1. **seed**: *Clue*: Plant a seed, not a weed. *Roots*: seed (O. E. sed). *Same Pattern*: deed, need, feed.

2. **seed-ling**: *Visual*: Letters li look like seedlings. *Rule*: 2 e's create long e (seedling: young plant).

3. **su-per-sede**: *Rule*: One English word ends in sede. *Roots*: super (above) + sede (sit) = supersede.

4. **pro-ceed**: *Clue*: Proceed through life. Seek to succeed. Don't let your wealth exceed your goodness. *Rule*: 2 e's create long e: proceed.

5. **pro-cess**: *Clue*: Create a process for success; not for excess. (Also: Please process this mess.) *Roots*: pro (forward) + cess (moving) = process (act of moving forward to do something).

6. **suc-ceed**: *Clue*: Seek to succeed. *2 Vowels Rule*: 2 e's create long e. *Pattern*: proceed, exceed.

7. **suc-cess**: *Phonics*: 3 s's = s; c = k, s. *Clue*: I confess, I love success. *Rule*: 2 c's keep u short. *Roots*: suc (under) + cess (move out; prosper) = success. *Same Pattern*: excess, process, recess.

8. **ex-ceed**: *Clue*: Don't let your wealth exceed your goodness. *Rule*: 2 e's create long e: exceed.

9. **ex-ceed-ing**: *Clue*: The gifts are exceeding what I'm needing. *2 Vowels Rule*: 2 e's create long e.

10. **an-te-ce-dent**: *Visual*: 4 e's. *Roots*: ante (before) + cedent (L. come) = antecedent (It comes before).

11. **cede**: *Clue*: He ceded the land where his. cedar trees grew. *Roots*: cede: (L. cede: to yield *territory*).

12. **con-cede**: *Clue*: Connie conceded to Cedric. *Roots*: con (with) + cede (yield) concede (yield-to...).

13. **in-ter-cede**: *Roots*: inter (between) + cede (go) = intercede (go between to help).

14. **in-ter-ced-ing**: *Clue*: Both Ed's interceded. *Same Pattern*: conceded, preceded, receded (ed + ed).

15. **pre-ce-dent**: *Roots*: pre (before) + cedent (go) = precedent (Courts follow a precedent: what's gone before)

16. **re-cede**: *Clue*: The tide recently receded. *Roots*: re (back; again) + cede (go; move) = recede (move back)

17. **re-ce-ding**: *Clue*: Our line of cedar trees is recently receding. My hairline is recently receding.

18. **re-seed-ing**: *9 Words*: din, ding, Ed, I, in, reseed, see, seed, seeding *Clue-in-a-Row*: As. I do reseeding, I resee dings on my pots. *Rules*: re (pre.) + seed + ing.

19. **re-cess**: *Clue*: I love my success playing ball at recess. *Roots*: re (back) + cess (go) = recess. recess (You recede: withdraw, pull back for a time). *Same Pattern*: process, success, excess.

20. **se-cede**: *Phonics*: s, c = s. *Roots*: se (apart) + cede (to move) = secede (States seceded from the U.S.).

➤ **an-ces-tors**: *Phonics*: C = s. *Clue*: Some of your ancestors lived in ancient times. *Roots*:

➤ **con-ces-sion** (act of yielding; business): I concede; I'll stand in the procession to the concession stand.

➤ **in-ter-ces-sion** (help by going between people): *SPP*: in-ter-ces-si-on. *Pattern*: procession, succession.

➤ **pro-ce-dure**: *Clue*: Be sure to follow the correct procedure.

➤ **suc-cess-or**: *Clue*: A successor to a throne can have success or failure. *Beat*: s-u-c-c-e-s-s-o-r.

POWER Spelling Special Lessons

Teacher's Guide

Games

and

Ideas for Memory Tools

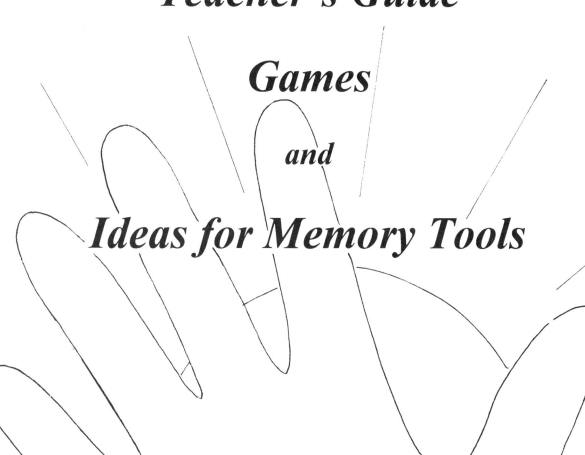

Special Lessons
Inspiration and Ideas for Teachers

The *Special Lessons* have been written to add an extra sparkle, fun and a unique stimulus for your students in spelling. These lessons can be used to intrigue students at any time, or they can be used to supplement particular lessons. Below are some fun ideas for introducing these lessons:

Special Lesson 1: Do Geese See God ?
and other Palindromes plus Reversals, Anagrams, and More Word Play (*See BL: Tool 7: Visual*)
Objectives: Students will be intrigued by *Palindromes, Reversals, Anagrams, Acronyms, Echoes* and *Bookends*. They'll learn and create this *Word Play* and find these make great *Visual Memory Tools*.

To involve students, write, DO GEESE SEE GOD? on the board. Then, ask, "Does anyone notice something special about this sentence. If someone does, acknowledge them and say, "I'm going to add some more sentences and words. (Keep adding sentences and words until more students notice.)

Palindromes (same backwards and forwards)	
DO GEESE SEE GOD?	RACECAR
STEP ON NO PETS.	LEVEL
MADAM, I AM ADAM	DAD

Then, ask students who first put their hands up, to tell what they sees. Write *Palindrome* on the board, and challenge students to think of some, particularly 3-letter ones: mom, pop, sos...toot, kayak...

After you've discussed Palindromes, write a *Reversal* on the board: *drawer - reward*. Again ask, "Do you notice anything special about these. Go through the same process you did for *Palindromes*.

Reversals
DRAWER – REWARD
REED – DEER
STEP – PETS

Also, briefly show students *Echo Words* (letters repeated: <u>on</u>i<u>on</u>, <u>sen</u>se) and *Bookends* (letters reversed at end: <u>mus</u>e<u>um</u>). Finally, hand out *Special Lesson 1* and enjoy it with your students.

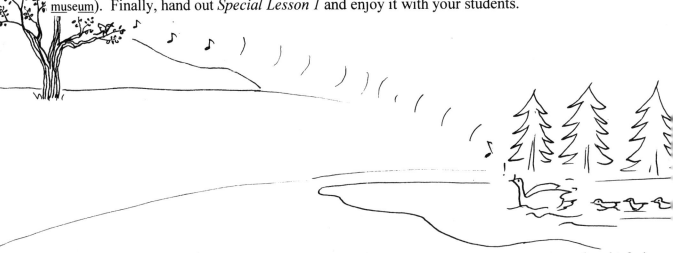

ANSWERS: *Echo and Bookend Words*: salsa, decade, decode, orator, sense, tomato, museum, stunts, thought, foolproo receiver, seashores. *More Palindromes*: civic, kayak, level, racecar, sagas, solos. *Palindromes Inside of Words*: ban<u></u> <u>divide, garage, igniting, synony</u>m.

Special Lesson 2: Aardvarks, Llamas, and Other Double Letter Words.
Objectives: Students will have fun seeing *double, and double-double letter words*. They will learn about six *Patterns for Double Letter Words* and be able to sort words under each of these patterns.

Write the bold words on the boards. Then begin by asking your students to think of *double, and double-double letter words*. If they have trouble, write the categories at the bottom of the page: *animals, insects, names, people, food/d rink, flowers/trees*.

Then say, "As I read through the 6 lists on the board, try to discover what each group has in common." As students discover a common point, write this above the group's list. (See below.) Then ask, "Who can add a word to one of these groups?" (Tell them it's okay to use names.) Add the words your students share. Finally, pass out *Special Lesson 2*. Point out that as they read this lesson, they're to write the words on the first page in the blanks. Later, review the different groups.

Double Consonants	Double Vowels	Compound Words	Prefixes (one + one)	Suffixes (doubling)	C + LE Words
rabbit	aardvark	bookkeeper	accept	drummer	bubble
coffee	green	cattails	appear	hopping	giggle
kitten	skiing	lamppost	illogical	sitting	pebble
squirrel	moon	newsstand	misspell	beginning	riddle
tennis	vacuum	taillight	unnatural	occurring	snuggle

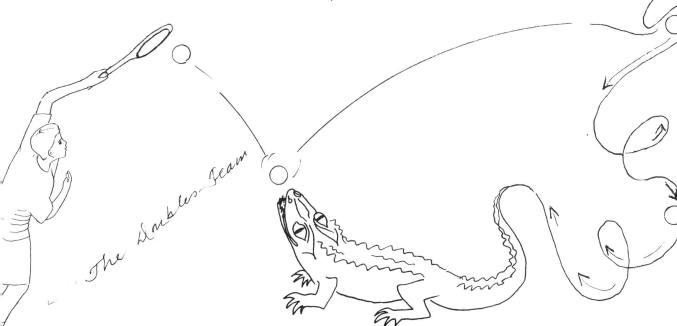

The Doubles-Team

DOUBLE-DOUBLE LETTER WORDS: accidentally, accommodate, annulled, appaloosa, assassin, cappuccino, committee, embarrass, grasshopper, illogically, Mississippi, occasionally, occurred, possession, raccoon, unnecessary *
ANIMALS: aardvark (anteater), alligator, appaloosa, armadillo, baboon, buffalo, bull, bunny, burro, chimpanzee, deer, gazelle, giraffe, goose, gorilla, hippopotamus, kangaroo, kitten, mandrill (baboon w/blue and scarlet face), opossum, otter, piggy, poodle, rabbit, raccoon, sheep, squirrel *
INSECTS: bee, beetle, boll weevil, butterfly, daddy longlegs, grasshopper, yellow jacket *
NAMES: Aaron, Annie, Barrie, Betty, Billy, Bobby, Carrie, Chrissy, Colleen, Danielle, Harry Potter *
PEOPLE: daddy, granddad, granddaughter, granny, mommy, nanny, engineer *
FOOD/DRINKS: apples, beef, beets, berries, broccoli, butter, carrots, cabbage, cheese, cherries, croissant, currants, green beans, lettuce, peppers, persimmons, spaghetti, waffle, zucchini * beer, cappuccino, coffee, latte, root beer *
FLOWERS/TREES: bluebells, dogwood, narcissus, poinsettia, poppy, sweet pea, zinnia * beech, holly, pussy willow *

Special Lesson 3: Looking at Nouns, Adjectives, Verbs and Adverbs

Objectives: Students will use their visual skills to understand and identify four parts of speech: nouns, verbs, adjectives and adverbs. Students will retain an understanding of how these four parts of speech function. This knowledge will help students with understanding suffixes since suffixes change words into nouns, verbs, adjectives, and adverbs.

Write the bold words on the board. To introduce <u>Nouns</u>, have students take the *Rainbow Scene* and name things: *the boy, a giraffe*... Then ask, "What do nouns do?" and write answers on the board. For <u>Adjectives</u>, also use this scene. Have students *see, feel,* and *imagine* some of the adjective: *prickly, cold, red, green, blue, violet, tall*... Then have them add adjectives to nouns and define what adjectives do. Next, use the *Castle Scene* to introduce <u>Pronouns</u>. Have students name nouns and substitute a pronoun: *princess (she), king and queen (they), dragon (it).* Also mention linking verbs (=).

For <u>Verbs</u>, use the Mountain/Ocean scene and ask, "What actions do you see going on in this picture?" Have students pick out a noun, and *say* and *feel* the action, the <u>verb</u>, that the noun is doing: *A balloon <u>rises</u>. A boat <u>sails</u>. The girl <u>rides</u>.* Then, for <u>Adverbs</u>, point out that in the same way an <u>adjective</u> is <u>added</u> to a noun to describe it, an <u>adverb</u> is <u>added</u> to a verb. (Add: Most adverbs end in -ly.) Then have students choose a noun and a verb, from this scene and add an adverb to each verb: *The balloon rises high (rapidly, higher), A boat sailed <u>smoothly</u>; The girl <u>rides</u> joyfully*...

Nouns, Verbs, Adjectives, and Adverbs

NOUNS: *the <u>boy</u>, a <u>giraffe</u>, a <u>rainbow</u>, the <u>ocean</u>*... <u>Nouns</u> name persons, places, things, and qualities. You can put <u>a</u> or <u>the</u> before all common nouns.

PRONOUNS: I, you, he...: *princess* (she), *king and queen* (they), *dragon* (it). <u>Pronouns</u> replace nouns.

ADJECTIVES: *a <u>prickly</u> porcupine, the <u>cold</u> ocean*... Adjective are <u>added</u> to nouns to describe them.

VERBS: *A balloon <u>rises</u>, The girl <u>climbs</u>*... <u>Verbs</u> show action a noun is doing (also show state of being).

ADVERBS: *A balloon rises <u>high</u>. The girl rides <u>joyfully</u>*...<u>Adverbs</u> are <u>added</u> to verbs to describe them.

Finally, these four parts of speech are all brought together in the game: *Adding Nouns, Verbs, Adjectives, and Adverbs.* Here, students have a column of words for each speech part (plus determiners) and they experiment with putting words together from each column to see the kinds of crazy and wonderful sentences they can get. For added fun, have 5 students each be a speech part and choose a word. Then put their words together, and see the sentences you get. You can also have students draw words out of a container, and add their own words too.)

(*Note*: For this lesson, you can interchange the pictures. Also, for grammar lessons you teach, you can use these pictures to introduce state of being verbs, direct objects, objects of the preposition, etc.)

Special Lesson 4: Discovering What's Inside the Amazing Dictionary

Objectives: Students will discover the many kinds of unique information and pictures they can find in the dictionary. They will learn about the history and amazing writers of the English and American dictionaries. Students will be able to identify the main kinds of information you can find for words in the dictionary: *Spelling, Syllables, Accent, Pronunciation, Part Of Speech, Other Word Forms, Prefixes, Roots, Suffixes, Definition, Etymology* (History and Origin), *Synonym*.

To introduce this lesson, write the bold words in the *Learning Box* below on the board. Then, briefly discuss these 6 main writers of dictionaries. For <u>Samuel Johnson,</u> point out that he was blind in one eye and spent 8 years working in an attic room, creating his masterpiece – in which he defined 43,000 words – using quotations from the works of the best English writers. Note that <u>Noah Webster</u> richly drew on Johnson's dictionary to write *The American Spelling Book* which has sold more copies than any book in America, except for the Bible. Share that A. H. Murray spent 36 years, working with his assistants and 11 children, to spell and define all the words in English since 1150.

Who Wrote the First Dictionaries?

Richard Mulcaster: 1st English Spelling Dictionary; written for scholars; contained 8,000 words.
Edmunde Coote: 1st English Spelling Dictionary for common people; extremely popular; used in schools.
Robert Cawdrey: 1st English Dictionary with both Spelling and Definitions; contained 3,000 words.
Samuel Johnson: 1755: Established Spelling and Usage for 43,000 English words; used quotes of great writers.
Noah Webster: 1788: *The American Spelling Book* (Spelling and Definitions); a *Best Seller* in America.
James Augustus Henry Murray: Spent 36 years; spelled and defined all English words (414,825) since 1150.

What Amazing Discoveries are Inside the Dictionary?

astronaut: What do the 2 Greek Roots mean?   **Morse Code**: Write your name in Morse Code.
basketball: What's the diameter of the basket?   **muscles**: What does Latin Root for *muscle* mean?
Heimlich maneuver: How do you do this maneuver?   **nightingale**: Which nightingale sings at night? Why?
manta ray: How many feet across? How long?   **Portuguese man-of-war**: How long are tentacles?

AMAZING DICTIONARY DISCOVERIES: gauntlet; little star; 18 inches, 84 or 94 feet; *cent*-hundred, *ped*-feet; Latin, com-with + pain-bread; 8 inches, *dach*-dog + *hund*-hound; HEIMLICH MANEUVER: To save someone from choking, you put a fist on lower abdomen below ribs, and with both hands, thrust inward and upward with force to eject the object; *hippo*-horse + *patamos*-river; girth; 10 feet; equals 18 feet across, 20 feet long; insect, 2 inches; *manus*-hand; *multi*-many + *plier*-folds; male nightingale; *paene*-almost + *insula*-island; 16 syllables; 8 inches, 40 to 165 feet; un; *sehors*-walrus, 3-4 inches; 28 inches; Washington, 1990; Old English *geolu*-yellow.

MAGIC			SQUARE
10	3	8	
5	7	9	
6	11	4	

Do Geese See God?

and Other Palindromes, plus Anagrams and Acronyms

If you carefully look at the question – *Do Geese See God?* – letter by letter, backwards and forwards, you will be able, in time, to figure out the wonder and challenge of palindromes. Palindromes are truly amazing visual and verbal creations that can, at times, fill you with awe.

Palindromes

Palindromes are ancient creations that go back over 2,000 years – to the third century B.C. when they were first recorded by the Greek poet Sotades of Maroneia. Since writing palindromes is like playing a complex game, they were often referred to as *literary chess*.

A palindrome is a word, phrase, sentence, song, or any other kind of writing that reads the same way backwards and forwards, letter by letter. They're fun to discover and an amazing challenge to write. Since they're spelled the same both ways, they're truly helpful to spelling.

❑ **NOW**: Read these word and name palindromes, plus the phrases and sentence palindromes that follow. Add any palindromes you can think of or would like to create. Have fun!

Single, Compound-Word, and Name Palindromes

civic	peep	Anna
dad	racecar	Aviva
deed	reviver (restorer to life)	Bob
kayak	rotator (It rotates.)	Eve
level	sagas (old Norse tales)	Hannah
madam	sees	Otto
mom	solos	Yenney (artist for book)

Sentence and Phrase Palindromes

Do geese see God?

Don't nod.

Was it a rat I saw?

Step on no pets.

I'm. alas, a salami.

Niagara, O roar again.

We sew.

Name no one man.

A man, a plan, a canal—Panama.
(Leigh Mercer of London created this famous line.)

Never a foot too far, even.

Too hot to hoot.

I did, did I.

Net ten.

Draw, O coward.

Red rum, sir, is murder.

No lemons, no melon.

No word, no bond, row on.

Cigar, toss it in a can. It is so tragic.

In a regal age ran I.   Are we not drawn onward…we few, drawn onward to new era.

Palindromes with Names in the Phrases

Here are some palindromes for those of you with the names below, or for your friends with these names.

Madam, I'm Adam.

Able was I, ere I saw Elba.

Ned, go gag Ogden.

Evade me, Dave.

Harass selfless Sarah.

I saw wonder. Fred now was I.

Ned, I am a maiden.

Pat and Edna tap.

Poor Dan is in a droop.

Sit on a potato Pan, Otis.

Sue, dice do, to decide us.

Bob, did Anna peep? Anna, did Bob?

Sir, I soon saw Bob was no Osiris (Egyptian king of the dead).

Palindromes Inside of Words

Discover and <u>underline</u> palindromes inside of these words. Finding these is helpful to spelling.

banana	garage	monotonous
divide	igniting	motto
dresser	minimum	synonym

Reversals Remain a Word Forwards and Backwards

Reversal words are fun to find, and they provide great spelling clues. Also, these words are very helpful when you are creating a palindrome. Can you think of more reversals?

deer – reed (music pipe; grass)   net – ten   reward – drawer

deliver – reviled (put down)   now – won   sleek – keels (bottom structure of ships)

desserts – stressed   peek – keep   sleep – peels

dial – laid   Leon – Noel   stop – pots

pools – sloop (sailboat)   revel – lever   time – emit (send forth)

regal – lager (aged beer)   snoops – spoons   wonder – red now

Anagrams

Anagram is a Greek word that means *again written* (ana-again + gram-written; drawn) which is exactly what an anagram does. To create an anagram, just *rearrange* the letters of the word or phrase and write them again in a new way to form another word or phrase that connects to the first.

Anagrams, like palindromes, are also ancient, and go back to 260 B.C. – when they were first recorded by the Greek poet Lycophron. Over a thousand years later in France, during the 7th century, anagrams became the *literary passion of the day*, and in the 1600s, King Louis XIII even appointed a *Royal Anagrammist* to entertain his court. Anagrams are still fun today and can help with spelling when you use them to make sure you've included all the letters in the word.

Aloft – Float

Anagrams – Ars Magna (Latin for *Great Art*)

An aisle – Is a Lane

Auction – Caution

Astronomers – Moon Starers

Committees – Cost Me Time

Considerate – Care Is Needed

Conversations – Voices Rant On

Destination – It Is to an End

Dormitory – Dirty Room

Endearment – Tender Name

Measured – Made Sure

Moonlight – Thin Gloom

Morse Code – Here Come Dots

Palindromes – I am Splendor

Rescue – Secure

Separation – One is Apart

Slot Machines – Cash Lost in 'em

Statue of Liberty – Built to Stay Free

Snoozed – Dozes On

Surgeon – Go Nurse

Sword – Words

The Eyes – They See

Valentine Poem – Pen Mate in Love

Acronyms

Acronyms are words made from the first letters of the words they stand for. You may know some because many acronyms have become part of our English language. See how many you've heard.

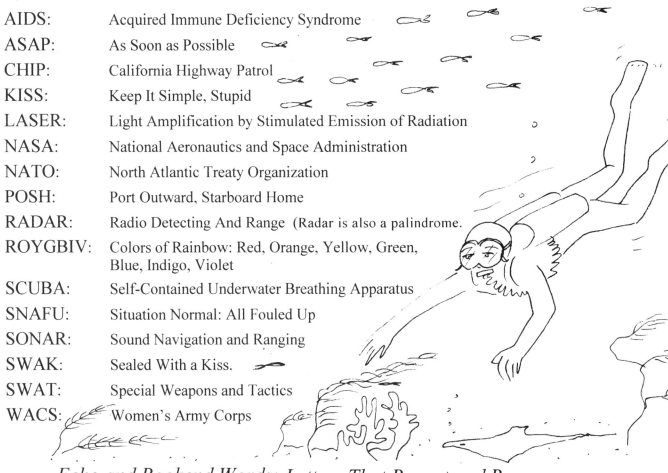

AIDS: Acquired Immune Deficiency Syndrome

ASAP: As Soon as Possible

CHIP: California Highway Patrol

KISS: Keep It Simple, Stupid

LASER: Light Amplification by Stimulated Emission of Radiation

NASA: National Aeronautics and Space Administration

NATO: North Atlantic Treaty Organization

POSH: Port Outward, Starboard Home

RADAR: Radio Detecting And Range (Radar is also a palindrome.

ROYGBIV: Colors of Rainbow: Red, Orange, Yellow, Green, Blue, Indigo, Violet

SCUBA: Self-Contained Underwater Breathing Apparatus

SNAFU: Situation Normal: All Fouled Up

SONAR: Sound Navigation and Ranging

SWAK: Sealed With a Kiss.

SWAT: Special Weapons and Tactics

WACS: Women's Army Corps

Echo and Bookend Words: Letters That Repeat and Reverse

Echoes and *Bookends* repeat and *reverse letters*. For *Echoes*, the *letters* that begin the word *echo* at the end: <u>onion</u>. For *Bookends*, the letters at each end *reverse* and match like bookends: <u>senses</u>.

1.   s a _ s a   Mexican sauce with tomatoes and onions; n. (*Echo*)

2.   d e _ _ d e   ten-year period; n. (*Echo*)

3.   d e _ _ d e   decipher (discover; figure out); v. You _ _ _ _ _ _ a message (*Echo*)

4.   o r _ _ o r   skilled speaker; n. (*Echo*)

5.   s e _ s e   way of knowing: hearing, seeing, touching; n. feel; understand; v. (*Echo*)

6.   t o _ _ t o   round and red and used in salads; n. (*Echo*)

7.   m u _ _ u m   place where objects of value are kept and displayed; n. (*Bookend*)

8.   s t _ _ t s   training is needed to do these daring feats; n. (*Bookend*)

9.   t h _ _ _ h t   something you think; idea; n. (*Bookend*)

10.   f o _ _ _ _ _ o f   never failing; can't be broken into; adj. His safe is _ _ _ _ _ _ _ _ . (*Bookend*)

11.   r e _ _ _ _ _ e r   answer in subtraction; amount that is left in division; n. (*Bookend*)

12.   s e _ _ _ _ _ e s   beaches; areas of land by the ocean; n. (*Bookend*)

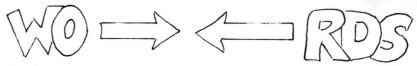

Word Play with Palindromes, Reversals, and Anagrams

Fill in the missing letters below.

1. palindromes: *Clue*: My <u>pal</u> <u>in</u> <u>Rome</u> loves a good p _ _ _ _ _ _ _ _ : <u>pal + in + d + Rome</u>.

2. auction: <u>Caution</u> is an *anagram* for _ _ _ _ _ _ _ . Use c _ _ _ _ _ _ when you bid at an a _ _ _ _ _

3. reviver (*Palindrome*): A r _ _ _ _ _ _ helps you feel r _ _ _ _ _ _ and come al _ _ _ again.

4. anagram: *Clue*: C<u>an a g</u> _ _ _ be measured? <u>ean</u> + a +<u>gram</u> = _ _ _ _ _ _ _ .

5. surgeon: <u>Go, nurse</u> is an *anagram* for _ _ _ _ _ _ _ . *Clue*: <u>Surge on</u>, Oh _ _ _ _ _ _ _ !

6. measure: A *Clue* and *Anagram* for <u>measure</u> is: Please give m _ _ _ s _ _ _ m _ _ _ _ _ _ .

7. emit (send forth heat, light): *Reversal*: _ _ _ _ . *Clue*: It took t _ _ _ to e _ _ _ heat into the room.

8. keels (backbone structures under ships): *Reversal*: _ _ _ _ _ . *Clue*: The k _ _ _ _ of ships feel s _ _ _ _ .

9. reviled (put down): *Reversal*: _ _ _ _ _ _ _ . *Clue*: I felt r _ _ _ _ _ _ by words he had to d _ _ _ _ _ _ .

10. reward: *Reversal*: _ _ _ _ _ _ . *Clue*: I put my r _ _ _ _ _ into my d _ _ _ _ _ .

More Palindromes

1. _ _ v _ _   refers to a city and citizens
2. _ _ y _ _   Eskimo canoe
3. _ _ v _ _   flat and even; used to make a surface even
4. _ _ _ e _ _ _   A person drives this auto fast.
5. _ _ g _ _   ancient stories
6. _ _ l _ _   songs, flights, etc. performed by one-person

Palindromes Inside of Words

Palindromes that are found inside of words can be very helpful to spelling. As you remember and use these palindromes, your mind will remember them and draw on them for spelling.

1. b _ _ _ _ _   fruit wrapped in yellow skin
2. _ _ _ _ _ e   opposite of multiply
3. _ _ _ _ _ e   place where a car is usually kept.
4. i _ _ _ _ _ _ _   lighting paper, charcoal, or wood on fire
5. s _ _ _ _ _ m   another word that has the same meaning

Do Geese See God?

and Other Palindromes; plus Reversals, Echoes, Anagrams and Acronyms

1. palindromes (*Clue; Rule; Roots*)

2. kayak (*Palindrome; Clue; Roots*)

3. level (*Palindrome; Visual*)

4. madam (*Palindrome; Find 8 Words; Clue*)

5. racecar (*Palindrome; Phonics; Rule*)

6. solos (*Palindrome; Rule; Roots*)

7. backwards (*Phonics; Clue; Same Pattern*)

8. forward (*Clue; Roots*)

9. emit-send out from (*Reversal; Clue; Roots*)

10. keels-bottom part that guides boat (*Reversal; Clue*)

11. reviled-put down (*Reversal; Clue; Rules*)

12. reward (*Reversal; Clue; Rule*)

13. wonder (*Reversal; Clue*)

14. orator-speaker (*Echo Word; Visual; Roots*)

15. senses (*Bookend Word; Visual; Phonics*)

16. anagrams (*Visual; Clue; Roots*)

17. caution (*Anagram; Clue*)

18. conversation (*Anagram; Phonics; Rule; Roots*)

19. measured (*Anagram; Clue*)

20. surgeon (*SPP; Clue*)

➢ reviver-who or what brings alive (*Palindrome; Clue; Rule, Beat*)

➢ acronyms (*Anagram, Clue; Roots*)

➢ laser (*Acronym; Phonics; Clue*)

➢ radar (*Palindrome; Acronym; Clue*)

➢ sonar (*Acronym; Clue*)

OTHER WORD FORMS

caution: cautioned, cautioning, precaution
converse: converses, conversing, conversation
emit: emits, emitted, emitting, emission
kayak: kayaks, kayaked, kayaking
laser: lasers, lased, lasing, laserscope
level: levels, leveled, leveling, leveler

measure: measuring, measurement, remeasure
orate: orates, orated, orating, orator
revile: reviles, reviled, reviling, reviler (revive)
reward: rewards, rewarded, rewarding, rewarder
solo: solos, soloed, soloing
wonder: wonders, wondered, wondering, wonderful

Do Geese See God?

and Other Palindromes; plus Reversals, Anagrams, and Acronyms

1. **pal-in-drome**: *Clue*: My pal in Rome loves a good pa;indrome: <u>pal</u> + <u>in</u> + <u>d</u> + <u>Rome</u>. *Rule*: Silent <u>e</u> makes <u>o</u> long. *Roots*: <u>palin</u> (back again) + <u>drome</u> (running) = <u>palindrome</u> (running back again).

2. **ka-yak** (*Palindrome*): *Clue*: <u>Kay</u> was rowing a <u>kayak</u>. *Roots*: <u>kayak</u> (Eskimo, qayaq: a palindrome).

3. **lev-el** (*Palindrome*): *Visual*: It's <u>level</u> between the <u>l</u>'s. Also, <u>eve</u> (palindrome) is in <u>level</u>.

4. **ma-dam** (*Palindrome*): *Visual*: *8 Words*: <u>a</u>, <u>ad</u>, <u>Ada</u>, <u>Adam</u>, <u>am</u>, <u>dam</u>, <u>mad</u>, <u>ma</u>. *Clue*: Madam, <u>I'm Adam</u> (*Sentence Palindrome*). *madA m'I madai*

5. **race-car** (*Palindrome*): *Phonics*: <u>c</u> = <u>s</u>. *Compound Rule*: Add: <u>race</u> + <u>car</u> = <u>racecar</u>.

6. **re-viv-er** (*Palindrome*): *Clue*: A <u>reviver</u> helps you feel al<u>ive</u>. *Beat*: r-e-v-i-v-e-r. *Rule*: <u>Silent e</u> makes <u>i</u> long. *Prefix Rule*: Add <u>re</u> (prefix: again) + <u>vive</u> (to live) + <u>r</u> (n. suf.) = <u>reviver</u>.

7. **so-los** (*Palindrome*): *Rule* and *Roots*: Italian music plurals have a single <u>s</u>: <u>solos</u> (L. solis: alone).

8. **back-wards**: *Phonics*: See and say *Blend*: <u>ba</u> + <u>ck</u> + <u>wa</u> + <u>r-d-s</u>. *Clue*: My <u>pack's</u> on <u>backwards</u>. *Roots*: <u>back</u> (L. behind) + <u>wards</u> (L. ward-direction). *Same Pattern*: forwards, towards.

9. **for-ward**: *Clue*: Do we go <u>forward</u> by being <u>for war</u>? *Roots*: <u>for</u> (L. ahead) + <u>ward</u>(L. ward: direction)

10. **e-mit** (*Reversal* = **time**): *Clue*: Clocks <u>emit</u> <u>time</u>. *Roots*: <u>e</u> (pre: out from) + <u>mit</u> (L. send) = <u>emit</u> (send out

11. **re-viled**-put down (*Reversal* = **deliver**): *Clue*: Why did they <u>deliver</u> words that <u>reviled</u> her? *Rule*: Silent <u>e</u> makes <u>i</u> long. *Roots*: <u>re</u> (pre: again) + <u>vile</u> (L. of little worth) + <u>ed</u> = <u>reviled</u>;

12. **re-ward** (*Reversal* = **drawer**): *Clue*: My <u>reward</u> is in my <u>drawer</u>. *Prefix Rule*: <u>re</u> + <u>ward</u> = <u>reward</u>.

13. **won-der** (*Reversal* = **red now**): *Clue*: I <u>wonder</u> if the sky's <u>red now</u>? When I <u>won</u>, I felt <u>wonder</u>.

14. **or-a-tor** (*Echo*): *Visual*: <u>Or</u> in <u>orator</u> echoes at end. *Roots*: <u>orator</u> (M.E. oratour: plead with mouth).

15. **sen-ses** (*Bookend*): *Visual*: <u>3 s's</u>. See <u>senses</u> start and close like bookends. *Phonics*: 2 s's = s; s = z.

an-a-grams: *Visual*: <u>3 a's</u>. *Clue*: <u>Can a gram</u> be an <u>anagram</u>? <u>ean</u> + <u>a</u> + <u>gram</u> *Roots*: <u>ana</u> (pre: again) + <u>grams</u> (Gk. letters; maps) = <u>anagrams</u> (again write letters of a word in new way).

16. **cau-tion** (*Anagram* = **auction**): *Clue*: Use <u>caution</u> when you bid at an <u>auction</u>?

17. **con-ver-sa-tion** (*Anagram* = **Voices rant on**): *Phonics*: c = <u>k</u> sound. *Silent-E Rule*: <u>converse</u> + <u>ation</u> = <u>conversation</u>. *Roots*: <u>con</u> (prc: with) + <u>versa</u> (L. verse) + <u>tion</u> (n. suf.) = <u>conversation</u>.

18. **meas-ured** (*Anagram* = **made sure**): *Clue*: Please give <u>me a sure</u> measure: <u>me</u> + <u>a</u> + <u>sure</u>.

19. **sur-geon** (*Anagram* = **Go Nurse**): *SPP*: sur-ge-on. *Clue-in-a-Row*: <u>Surge on</u>, Oh s<u>urgeon</u>.

➤ **a-cro-nym** (*Anagram* = **am corny**): *Clue*: I sent <u>acronyms</u> to <u>a crony</u> (buddy) of mine: <u>a</u> + <u>crony</u> + <u>m</u>. *Roots*: <u>acr</u> (G. tall; capital) + <u>onym</u> (G. word; letter) = <u>acronym</u> (capital letters of words): WAC-<u>W</u>omen's <u>A</u>ir <u>C</u>orps.

➤ **la-ser** (*Acronym*): <u>L</u>ight <u>A</u>mplification by <u>S</u>timulated <u>E</u>mission and <u>R</u>adiation. *Phonics*: <u>s</u> = <u>z</u>. *Clue*: He built a <u>laser</u> on the base: <u>l</u> + base + <u>r</u>.

➤ **ra-dar** (*Palindrome*; *Acronym*): <u>Ra</u>dio <u>D</u>etecting and <u>R</u>ange. *Clue*: <u>Radar</u> is <u>a darn</u> good invention.

➤ **so-nar**-echolocation (*Acronym*): <u>S</u>ound <u>N</u>avigation <u>R</u>anging (locating by sound waves). *Phonics*: <u>s</u> = <u>s</u>. *Clue*: <u>So navy</u> subs (and dolphins) use <u>sonar</u> to locate things: <u>so</u> + navy + <u>r</u>.

Aardvarks, Llamas and Other Double-Letter Words

To begin this Doubles Challenge, write down any double-letter or double-double letter words you know.

If you need ideas, try thinking of double-letter words in the categories below. Also, don't feel baffled, but struggle to remember some Consonant + LE Words, like puzzle and squiggle…

ANIMALS/INSECTS	FOOD/DRINKS	FLOWERS/TREES	NAMES/PEOPLE	C + LE
llama / boll weevil	*apple / root beer*	*sweet pea / beech*	*Harry / nanny*	*juggle*

Seeing, Hearing and Feeling the 6 Double-Letter Patterns

Double-Letter Words can either double your spelling trouble or double your fun, depending on how well you do at seeing, hearing and remembering them. One thing that can help is to know that you can organize Double-Letter Words into six ***POWER SPELLING PATTERNS***. Once you have learned these patterns, you can conquer Double-Letter Words like a *brilliant, witty, terrific, better-equipped, enthralling, exceedingly successful, dazzling* ***POWER SPELLER!!***

❏ **TRY THIS:** As you read the 6 Double-Letter Patterns, write each of the words below under the pattern where it fits. Also, for each pattern, add any of your own words that come to mind.

aardvark-anteater	committee	illogically	puppet
accord-agreement	cooperate	llama	scissors
applause-to clap in praise	forgetting	mirror	skiing
beginning	gaggle-group of geese	occasion	squiggle
career	heartthrob	patrolling	vacuum

PATTERN 1: DOUBLE CONSONANTS: Double consonants usually occur when two syllables meet in the middle of a word. They can also occur at the beginning and at the end of words.

BEGINNING: Just two words and one name *begin* with a double letter. They all begin with l:

_____ (Sp. wooly pack animal)   llano (Sp. vast, grassy plains in South America)   Lloyd

MIDDLE: Many words have a double letter in the middle. This happens when a syllable ends in the same consonant with which the next syllable begins:

BB: bub-ble, hob-by, rab-bit, tab-by-cat with colored streaks
CC: hic-cup, _____, oc-cupy, oc-cur…
FF: chauf-feur, cof-fee, saf-fron (spice made from crocus), taffy…

279

GG: bag - gage, luggage, rag-ged, foggy...

LL: bril-liant, cel-lo, wil-low, yel-low, constel-lation

MM: com-ment, ham-mer, plum- met (to dive; drop, v)...

NN: ban-ner, bun-ny, cin-namon, man-ners, run-ner, ten-nis...

PP: cap-puc-ci-no, hip-po, pep-per, _____, whop-per...

RR: ar-row, er-ror, Har-ry, hur-ry, _____, squir-rel...

SS: des-serts, glos-sy, Mis-sis-sip-pi, per-cus-sion, _____

TT: bat-ter, bet-ter, but-ton, cot-ton, kit-ten, mit-ten, ...

ZZ: bliz-zard, buz-zard, diz-zy, fiz-zy, fuz-zy...

<u>END</u>: F, L, and S are the most common double-letters at the end of words. Also a few words end in -<u>rr</u>: burr, purr... and -<u>zz</u>: buzz, jazz... Add words that you can rhyme with the words below.

FF: staff, Jeff, cliff, off, huff, fluff, puff...

LL: ball, bell, bill, doll, bull, eggshell...

SS: class, Bess, kiss, across, moss, fuss...

PATTERN 2: DOUBLE VOWELS (vowel digraphs): Although most of the double-letter vowels are created by OO and EE, there are also a few AA words and at least one II and one UU word.

AA: _____, laager (South African camp protected by a circle of wagons)

EE: bee, _____, eek, free, green, hee hee, tree...

II: _____: only word with <u>II</u>-like 2 ski poles. Why are both <u>i's</u> needed?

OO (as in moon): appaloosa, marooned-washed up on a shore, ooze, tool, zoom...

OO (as in book): forsook-past of forsake, abandoned, look...

UU: _____: only English word with <u>UU</u>.

PATTERN 3: COMPOUND WORDS: Since you just glue the two words together, double-letters happen for compounds when the last letter of the 1st word is the same as the first letter of the 2nd word.

can + not	grand + dad	news + stand
cat-tails	head + dress	step + parent
flat-top	_____	tail + light
grab-bag	lamp + post	team + mate

PATTERN 4: PREFIXES: When the last letter of a prefix is the same as the first letter of a root, you get a Double-Letter when you join the prefix and root: mis<u>s</u>pell, il<u>l</u>ustrate (like Compound Words).

DIS (not)	dis-sent-disagree w/majority	dis-similar	dis-solve
MIS (not):	mis-sized	mis-step	mis-spell
UN (not):	un-natural	un-necessary	un-needed

PREFIXES: **-AD**, **-COM**, and **-IN** have special forms they add to match the letter they precede.

AC: ac-cept (to take)   _____ (toward the heart)

AF: af-firm (to make firm)   af-fix (to fasten)

AL: al-leviate (to lighten)   al-li-ance (to bind to)

AN: an-nex (to tie to)   an-nounce (to send a messenger)

AP: ap-pear (to become visible)   _____ (to clap hands)

AR: ar-rest (to stop)   ar-rive (to come to the riverbank)

AS: as-semble (to bring together)   as-so-ci-ate (to join to)

AT: at-tract (to draw others)   at-tune (to bring in harmony)

COM: com-mand (to order)   com-mute (to change)

CO: _____ (to work with)   co-ordinate (with order)

IL: il-luminate (to light-up)   _____ (not logical)

IN: in-nate (to be born)   in-nocent (not harmful)   in-numerable (can't be numbered)

illustration

PATTERN 5: SUFFIXES: Adding a suffix can double the final letter for one-syllable-words and also for words with more than one syllable.

   UNDERLINE ONE-SYLLABLE WORDS: Double the final consonant when the word ends in a single consonant preceded by a single vowel. Add the suffix -ing to these words.

   drum   drum-med   _____   *drummer.*

   hop   hop-ped   _____

   set   set   _____   *setter*

   star   star-red   _____   *starry*

   MORE THAN ONE SYLLABLE: Double final consonant when word ends in a single consonant preceded by a single vowel, and the accent falls on the last syllable. Add -ing to these words.

   begin   began   _____   *beginner*

   forget   forgot   _____

   patrol   patrol-led   _____

   occur   occur-red   _____   *occurrence*

PATTERN 6: DOUBLE CONSONANT WITH A FINAL C+LE: Double letters occur when the syllable before C+LE ends with the same consonant with which C+LE begins.

   cud-dle   dap-pled (spotted...dappled horse)   _____ (of geese)

   ket-tle   set-tle   peb-ble

   gig-gle   rid-dle   _____ (curvy drawing)

   bub-ble   cop-per   wob-ble

DOUBLE-DOUBLE WORDS: Finally, list any Double-Double Words that have come to mind: appaloosa-a horse, accidentally, illogically…, and the TRIPLE-LETTER WORD: _____.

An Extra Double-Letter Challenge

❏ **TRY THIS**: Ten of the words below present an extra challenge. They all have a short vowel that should be followed by a double consonant, but it's not (See underlined letters). Since these words do not follow phonics rules, you need *Clues*…to remember them. Fill in the blanks, and learn these clues.

1. **applause**: My prize <u>apple</u> won lots of _ _ _ _ _ _ _ (like c<u>lause</u>): ap-to + <u>plause</u>.

2. **attitude**: It takes a good _ _ _ _ _ _ _ _ to clean out an _ _ _ _ c : <u>atti</u>e + tude.

3. **alleviate**: <u>Al (and) Levi</u> ate papayas to _ _ _ _ _ _ _ _ all indigestion: Al + Levi + ate.

4. **career**: Take _ _ _ _ when you choose a _ _ _ _ _ _ : <u>care + er</u> = _ _ _ _ _ _ .

5. **cinnamon**: At our <u>inn, a Mon</u>. morning treat is fresh _ _ _ _ _ _ _ _ rolls: c + inn + a + Mon.

6. **gorilla** (ape): When our _ _ _ _ _ _ _ runs, we cheer, "<u>Go Rilla</u>!": Go + Rilla.

7. **guerrilla** (Sp. soldier: guerra-war): A _ _ _ _ _ _ _ _ _ can not <u>err (or be) ill</u> prepared: gu + err + ill + a.

8. **innocent**: <u>In no</u> way, not for a <u>cent</u>, would I harm an _ _ _ _ _ _ _ _ person: in + no + cent.

9. **necessary**: <u>Recess</u> is _ _ _ _ _ _ _ _ _ for Ma<u>ry</u> at school: n + ̶recess + M̶ary.

10. **occasion**: <u>O C Casi on</u> this _ _ _ _ _ _ _ _ : O + C + Casi + on = _ _ _ _ _ _ _ _ .

11. **patrolling**: <u>Pa, Troll</u> is _ _ _ _ _ _ _ _ _ _ the bridge: <u>pa + troll + ing</u> = _ _ _ _ _ _ _ _ _ _ .

12. **terrific**: Will I <u>err if I</u> say you're simply _ _ _ _ _ _ _ _ : <u>t + err + if + I +c</u>? *Y Rule*: terrif̶y + ic.

13. **illogically**: My <u>logic ally</u> helps me to not think _ _ _ _ _ _ _ _ _ _ _ : <u>il + logic +ally</u>.

14. **vacuum**: My _ _ _ _ _ _ goes, "Uum, _ _ _ ," as I _ _ _ _ _ _ my room: <u>vac + uum</u>.

DOUBLE-DOUBLE-LETTER WORDS: accidentally, accommodate, annulled, appaloosa, assassin, cappuccino, committee, embarrass, grasshopper, illogically, Mississippi, occasionally, occurred, possession, raccoon, unnecessary…
ANIMALS: aardvark (anteater), appaloosa, armadillo, buffalo, bull, bunny, burro, chimpanzee, deer, gazelle, giraffe, goose, gorilla, hippopotamus, kangaroo, kitten, mandrill (baboon w/blue and scarlet face), opossum, otter, piggy, poodle, rabbit, raccoon, sheep, squirrel… INSECTS: bee, beetle, boll weevil, butterfly, daddy longlegs, grasshopper, yellow jacket…
NAMES: Aaron, Annie, Barrie, Betty, Billy, Bobby, Carrie, Chrissy, Colleen, Danielle, Harry Potter… PEOPLE: daddy, granddad, granddaughter, granny, mommy, nanny, engineer… FOOD/DRINKS: apples, beef, beets, berries, broccoli, butter, carrots, cabbage, cheese, cherries, croissant, currants, green beans, lettuce, peppers, persimmons, spaghetti, waffle, zucchini…/ beer, cappuccino, coffee, latte, root beer… FLOWERS/TREES: bluebells, dogwood, narcissus, poinsettia, poppy, sweet pea, zinnia… /beech, holly, pussy willow…

Aardvarks, Llamas, and Other Double-Letter Words

1. aardvark (*Visual; Roots*)

2. llama (*Clue; Rule*)

3. cinnamon (*Phonics; Roots*)

4. luggage (*Visual; Clue; Rule*)

5. mirror (*Rules; Beat*)

6. puppet (*Clue; Rules; Visual*)

7. terrific (*Clue; Rules*)

8. career (*Clue; Open Syllable Rule*)

9. skiing (*Visual; Pronunciation*)

10. vacuum (*Phonics; Pronunciation; Clue*)

11. heartthrob (*Clue; Rule*)

12. alleviate (*Clue; Roots*)

13. applause (*Clue; Same Pattern; Roots*)

14. attitude (*Rule; Beat*)

15. committee (*Visual; Clue; Beat*)

16. cooperate (*Find 12 Words; Clue; Roots*)

17. innocent (*Phonics; Clue*)

18. forgetting (*Clue; Rules*)

19. patrolling (*Clue; Same Pattern*)

20. gaggle (*Visual; OWF Clue; Rule*)

➢ gorilla (*Clue; Beat*)

➢ guerrilla (*Clue; SPP; Roots*)

➢ illogically (*Clue; Phonics; Roots*)

➢ occasion (*Phonics; Clue*)

➢ unnecessary (*Phonics; Clue*)

OTHER WORD FORMS

alleviate: alleviates, alleviated, alleviating
applaud: applauded, applauding, applause
commit: committed, committing, committee
coordinate: coordinated, coordination, coordinator
equip: equipped, equipping, equipment

forget: forgetting, forgetfully, forget-me-nots
logic: logical, logicize, logically, illogically
mirror: mirrors, mirrored, mirroring
ski: skis, skied, skiing, skier
vacuum: vacuums, vacuumed, vacuuming

Aardvarks, Llamas, and Other Double-Letter Words

1. **aard-varks**: *Visual*: 3 a's. *Clue*: It's hard to get aardvarks on arks: a + hard + v + arks = aardvarks. *Roots*: aard (Danish, aarde: earth) + varks (varkens: pig) = aardvarks (earth pigs).

2. **lla-ma**: *Clue*: We saw a mama llama. *Rule*: *2 Open Syllables*: lla-ma (Sp. llama).

3. **cin-na-mon**: *Clue*: At our inn, a Mon. treat is cinnamon rolls: c + inn + a + Mon (Gk. kinnamomon).

4. **lug-gage**: *Visual*: 3 bags (ggg); 1 sack (u). *Clue*: I age lugging luggage. *Rule*: 2 g's keep u short.

5. **mir-ror**: *SPP*: mir-ror. *Rule*: 2 r's keep i short. *Beat*: m-i-r-r-o-r. *Visual*: 3 mirrors (r r r).

6. **pup-pet**: *Clue*: My pup (has a) pet cat puppet. *Rule*: 2 p's keep u short. *Visual*: 3 puppets (p p p)

7. **ter-ri-fic**: *Clue*: Will I err if I say you're terrific: t + err + if + I +c? *Rule*: 2 r's keep e short. *Y Rule*: Change y to i except before -ing: terrify + i + c = terrific.

8. **ca-reer**: *Clue*: I care about my career: care + er. *Rule*: *Open Syllable* = ca (ends in vowel).

9. **ski-ing**: *Visual*: See ii as 2 skiing poles. *Pronunciation*: 2 syllables: ski-ing.

10. **vac-u-um**: *Phonics*: c = k. *Pronunciation*: 3 syllables: vac-u-um. *Clue*: My vacuum goes uum.

11. **heart-throb**: *Clue*: Can you hear my heartthrob. *Compound Rule*: heart + throb = heartthrob.

12. **al-le-vi-ate**: *Clue*: Al (and) Levi ate papaya to alleviate all indigestion: Al + Levi + ate. *Roots*: al (to) + levi (L. levi: lighten) + ate (v. suf.) = alleviate (to lighten).

13. **ap-plause**: *Clue*: My prize apple won applause for a good cause: apple + cause. *Same Pattern*: clause, pause. *Roots*: ap (pre: to) + plause (L., plaudels: praise) = applause (to praise).

14. **at-ti-tude**: *Clue*: It takes a good attitude to clean an attic. *Beat*: a-t-t-i-t-u-d-e. *Rules*: Silent e makes u long; 2 t's keep a short.

15. **com-mit-tee**: *Visual*: mm, tt, ee. *Clue*: I commit tees to our golf committee. *Beat*: c-o-m-m i-t-t-e-e.

16. **co-op-er-ate**: *Clue*: In a co-op era, teams cooperate. *12 Words*: a, at, ate, Co., coo, coop, era, operate, opera, per, rate, rat. *Roots*: co (pre: with) + oper (L. work) + ate (v. suf.) = cooperate.

17. **in-no-cent**: *Phonics*: c = s. *Clue*: In no way, not for a cent, could I harm an innocent person: in + no + cent

18. **for-get-ting**: *Clue-in-a-Row*: Thanks for getting my book and not forgetting it. *Rule*: 2 t's = e short.

19. **pa-trol-ling**: *Clue*: Pa, (a) troll is patrolling the bridge: pa + troll + ing. *Same Pattern*: knoll, roll, to

20. **gag-gle** (geese): *Visual*: 3 g's. *OWF Clue*: My gaggle was gaggling with glee. *Rule*: 2 g's make a short.

➤ **go-ril-la** (ape): *Clue*: When our gorilla runs, we cheer, "Go, Rilla!" *Beat*: g-o-r-i-l-l-a.

➤ **guer-ril-la** (soldier): *Clue*: Guerrilla, G. U. can not err or be ill-prepared: G.U. + err + ill + a. *SPP*: gu-er-ril-la. *Roots*: guerr (Sp. guerra: war) + illa (those who) = guerrilla (other spelling: guerilla).

➤ **il-log-i-cal-ly**: *Clue*: If I think illogically, my logic ally helps me: il + logic +ally. *Phonics*: g = j; c = k. *Roots*: il (not) + logic (G. logicos: reason) + al (adj. suf) + ly (adv. suf) = illogically.

➤ **oc-ca-si-on**: *Phonics*: c = k; s = zh. *Clue*: O C Casi on this occasion: O + C + Casi + on

➤ **un-ne-ces-sary**: *Phonics*: c = s; s's = s. *Clue*: Is recess unnecessary?: un + n + recess + ary.

Looking at Nouns, Adjectives, Verbs and Adverbs

Understanding how the parts of speech, like NOUNS, ADJECTIVES, VERBS, and ADVERBS, work can seem very challenging. It's really easy, though, once you understand what each part of speech does, and how you can use these four kinds of words to share what's going on in your world – to tell about the people, animals and things you see and the actions they do. So, let's learn these parts of speech by using some wonderful pictures. Let's learn how you can use NOUNS and ADJECTIVES, plus VERBS and ADVERBS to describe many interesting things you see going on in the world.

Understanding Nouns

You use NOUNS to name the people and animals, places, and objects in the world: a *boy*, the *bunnies*, a *rainbow*... Nouns also name feelings and states of being: the *love*, the *sadness*, the *joy*... There's an easy way to determine if a word is a noun, and that's to use a DETERMINER (Some books call these articles). Determiners are little words, like: *a, an, the*... that can come before all common nouns and ALWAYS make sense (Common nouns are not capitalized: *a bell, the president*... Proper nouns are capitalized and name specific things: *the Liberty Bell, President Lincoln*...)

REMEMBER: A noun is the only part of speech that can stand alone with a determiner and make sense.

❑ **NOW:** Look at the Rainbow Picture. Touch some of the animals and people, and the places, and objects. Then, list some of these nouns with a determiner: *a, an, the*. Also, try to think of some emotions or states of being: the *beauty*, the *peacefulness*. Very soon, you'll be adding adjectives to these nouns.

NOUN	ADJECTIVES	NOUN with ADJECTIVE(S)
the box	*magical, open, white, hand-made*	*a magical hand-made box*
the beauty	*natural, gentle, tranquil, sweetest,*	*the natural beauty*

285

Understanding Adjectives

You can also use ADJECTIVES to tell about the world. <u>A</u>djectives are single words you <u>add</u> to nouns to describe them: a *sandy* beach, the *joyful* dolphin, a *tiny* mouse… Adjectives can also show comparison: a <u>*small*</u> friend, a <u>*smaller*</u> friend; a <u>*bright*</u> sun, the <u>*brightest*</u> sun… Adjectives can also come after a verb that mean *equals*: The beach <u>was</u> *sandy*. A dolphin is <u>*joyful*</u>… When adjectives follow these verbs, they can also be added to pronouns (words like *he, she, it, they*… that replace nouns): <u>It</u> is *sandy*. <u>She</u> is *joyful*. Finally, since <u>a</u>djectives <u>add</u> description to nouns and pronouns, perhaps they should be called "<u>ad</u>nouns". What do *you* think?

REMEMBER: Adjectives describe nouns. They can come before nouns or follow a verb that means equals. Adjective can also describe pronouns when they follow a verb that means equals.

ADJECTIVES DESCRIBING NOUNS: a <u>*curious*</u> boy, the <u>*magical*</u> boxes and triangle; a <u>*dancing*</u> star; the <u>*deepest*</u> ocean. The girl was <u>*sleepy*</u>. The friendship is <u>*precious*</u>…

ADJECTIVES DESCRIBING PRONOUNS: He was <u>*curious*</u>. They are <u>*magical*</u>. She is <u>*sleepier*</u>…

❑ **NOW**: Read over your nouns on the first page. Then observe the Rainbow Picture again and *see* the size, shape, color…of these nouns; or *imagine* how they might *feel* if you could *touch* them; or *sound* if you could *hear* them Choose some special adjectives, and write these under ADJECTIVES Finally, <u>add</u> one or more <u>adjectives</u> to each noun and write these under NOUN with ADJECTIVES.

Time Out for Pronouns

As mentioned above, PRONOUNS are special little words that replace nouns. An easy way to remember what a pronoun does is to know that the word *pronoun* has the word *pro* in it which means *for*, and the word *noun*. A *pronoun* can be substituted *for a noun*. For example, you can substitute the pronoun *he* for the noun *jester*. The *princess* can be replaced by the pronoun *she*.

❑ **TRY THIS**: There are drawings of many nouns in the Castle Scene: people, animals and objects. List at least 8 nouns below. Then, write some pronouns you could substitute for the nouns Finally, write a sentence or two where you use a pronoun in place of a noun.

NOUN	PRONOUNS	SENTENCE(S) WITH PRONOUN SUBSTITUTED FOR NOUN
the fish	*they, them*	*They were swimming in the moat. I watched them.*

287

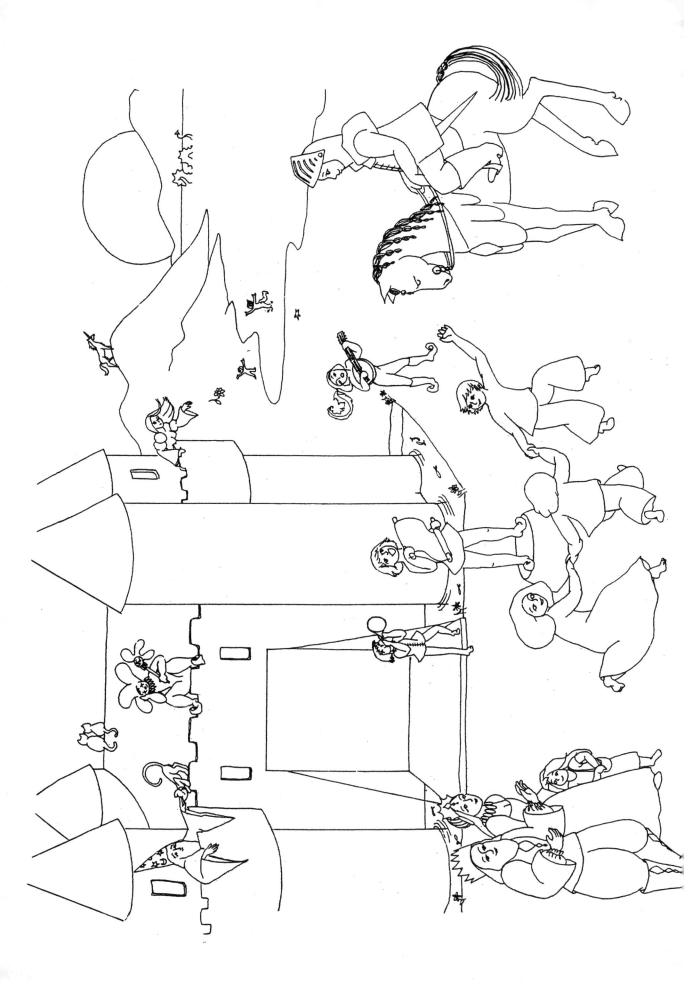

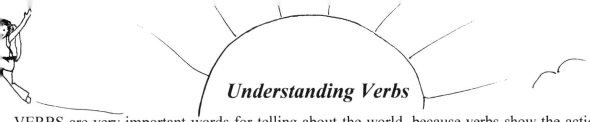

Understanding Verbs

VERBS are very important words for telling about the world, because verbs show the action that nouns and pronouns in the world are doing: A girl _climbs_. Birds are _flying_. The sun _is beaming_... Another kind of verb, called a _verb of being_, means equals: The girl _is_ brave (girl = brave). The sun _was_ grand and golden (sun = grand, golden). Also verbs show _time_: past, present, and future. Finally, there's an easy way to know if a word is a verb: A verb always make sense directly after a noun because a verbs follows a noun to show the action that the noun is doing.

ACTION: A clown _juggled_. Three musicians _are playing_ wooden instruments.
STATE OF BEING (verb means =): A swimmer _is_ swift. The snowflakes _are_ wondrous.
PAST, PRESENT, FUTURE: We _spell!_ We _spelled!_ We _will spell!_

NOW: Look at the actions that people, animals, and objects are doing in the Mountain/Ocean Picture. List some of these nouns, and after each noun, write a verb that shows the action that the noun is doing: A bird _flew_. The snowflakes _glitter_. Soon you'll be adding adverbs to the verbs.

NOUNS with VERBS	ADVERBS	NOUN WITH VERB PLUS ADVERB
A bird flew.	_gracefully, above, now_	_A bird flew gracefully above._
The snowflakes glitter.	_happily, overhead, always_	_The snowflakes always glitter happily._

Understanding Adverbs

Like adjectives add description to nouns, ADVERBS are single words that add description to verbs. Most adverbs end in -ly and tell _how_ the verb's action is done: He fished _joyfully_. The students _skillfully_ sail. She swims _swiftly_. Other adverbs tell _when_ and _where_ the verb's action is done: The islands rise _upward_. She balances _perfectly_. The snowflakes _always_ glittered _above_...

❑ **NOW:** Observe the action of the verbs in the picture are doing. Notice _how, where_ or _when_ these actions are being done: _swiftly, slowly, well; now, later; above, below_... In the space above, list some adverbs that you could add to each verb. Then, write a sentence with the noun and verb, plus one or more adverbs added before or after the verb. You can even add adjectives to the noun if you'd like. Then you'll be using NOUNS, ADJECTIVE, VERBS and ADVERBS – all working together, as you tell about what's happening in the world!

Adding Nouns, Verbs, Adjectives and Adverbs Game

❑ **TRY THIS**: All you need for a sentence is a noun plus a verb. Then you can add adjectives to the noun and adverbs to the verb. For this game, choose a word from each list. Then add them together and see what kind of sentence you create. Have fun experimenting, and write at least 10 sentences below. (For added fun, have 5 students each pick a word from a different list. Then put the 5 different kinds of words together, and see what kinds of crazy sentences you get. You can also draw words out of a can or box.)

Determiners and Possessive Words	Adjectives	Nouns	Actions Verbs Verbs that mean =	Adverbs-go before or after Verbs
the	beautiful	baby	am, is, are (=)	always
a	bold	bicycle	ate, eats	away
an	careful	bird	balanced	boldly
my	courageous	butterfly	blew, blows	carefully
our	dizzy	fawn	climbed, climbs	cheerfully
your	dreamy	frog	cooed, coos	dangerously
his	excited	heart	danced, dances	dizzily
her	fluffy	horse	flew, flies	dreamily
their	friendly	icicle	galloped	elegantly
	furry	imagination	imagines	fiercely
	gentle	kite	juggled	forever
	happy	kitten	lasted, lasts	freely
	hearty	knight	laughed	gently
	joyful	musician	leaped, leaps	happily
	loving	pilot	loved, loves	heartily
	magnificent	pitcher	padded, pads	joyfully
	mysterious	prince	played, plays	mischievously
	orange	princess	pounced	mysteriously
	peaceful	principal	rocketed	playfully
	playful	puppy	rode, rides	rapidly
	powerful	racecar	seems (=)	shyly
	purple	runner	sings, sang	skillfully
	shy	scooter	skates, skated	slowly
	skillful	skater	spun, spins	softly
	sleepy	spaceship	sleeps, slept	steadily
	sweet	surfer	speaks, spoke	stealthily
	tiny	tiger	speeded, sped	surprisingly
	wise	time	swam, swims	victoriously
	wild	train	was, were (=)	wildly
	young	wind	will be (=)	wisely

291

Discovering What's Inside the Amazing Dictionary

Good spellers use a dictionary…, but did you know that some people actually *love to read* a *Dictionary*, especially an *Unabridged Dictionary* (2000+ pages; include all the words in English).   They say things like:

When I meet a new word, the <u>Unabridged Dictionary</u> *helps me find everything I can use to learn and remember the spelling. I see how syllables are divided; how the word is pronounced; look at the prefixes, roots, and suffixes, find out the origin…and more.* (Linda Skerbec, Educator)

My <u>Unabridged Dictionary</u> *is the first resource book I go to when I'm trying to understand the meaning and history of a word. I also like the drawings of the eye and ear, the maps and flags, and the drawings of all the animals, flowers, leaves, shells…* (Winfield Huppuch, Publisher)

For casual reading… I still find the Dictionary the most interesting book in our language. (A. J. Nock, 1943)

YOU might enjoy the *Dictionary*, too, especially once you see the amazing information and drawings you can discover. Explore what's under: *armor, bagpipes, clipper…*

ARMOR: See the drawing of 16th century armor with all the parts labeled.

ASTRONAUT: Learn 2 Gk. roots: <u>astro</u> (*star*) + <u>naut</u> (*sailor*) = <u>astronaut</u>: *star sailor; one who sails the stars.*

AUSTRALIA: See a map of Australia, plus all the other continents, states, and countries. There's also information on the depth of oceans, the height of mountains.

BAGPIPES: See a bagpiper in kilts, playing the bagpipes. *All the instruments* have drawings.

BASKETBALL: See the *basketball court* (*hockey rink, football field*) with its measurements.

CLIPPER: The details of a *clipper ship* are drawn, along with *planes, trucks, motorcycles…*

EAR: All the parts of the *ear* are drawn and labeled. Look up *eye, heart*, and other organs.

HEIMLICH MANEUVER: Good dictionaries show how to do this to stop a person from choking.

HORSE: All the parts of a *horse* are drawn and labeled. Look for drawings of other *animals*.

HIEROGLYPHICS: This word is from 2 Greek roots: <u>hiero</u> (*sacred*) and <u>glyphics</u> (*writings*).

MUSCLES: The muscle you clench comes from a Latin root: *musculus-little mouse.*

NEIGHBOR: This is an Old Eng. word from before 900 A.D., <u>neahbur</u>: *neah* (near by) + *bur* (farm or farmer). Back then, your closest neighbor was the *farmer* at the *near-by farm.*

PNEUMONOULTRAMICROSCOPICSILICOVOLCANOCONIOSIS: the longest word in English, is in an unabridged dictionary, along with *antidisestablishmentarianism* and other monstrous words.

(Most dictionaries have lists of presidents, volcanoes with dates of eruption, drawings of cubes and other shapes, nails, tools, architecture, bridges, and even drawings of the ways knots are tied.)

A Little History of the English and American Dictionaries

So, just how did we get the dictionaries you can read and use today? Who wrote the first dictionaries? What great masterpiece did Samuel Johnson write? Who's Noah Webster? Who is A. H. Murray, and how did the *Oxford English Dictionary*, that now has 615,000 words, get its first 414,825 words?

The history of the English and American dictionaries goes from 1582 when Richard Mulcaster, an English schoolmaster, published *The Elementarie* (1st dictionary with English words) to 1788 in America when Noah Webster published *The American Spelling Book* (1st dictionary with American words). It's amazing to think about the power of the brain. These dictionaries, plus later masterpieces, were put together without the use of any of the computers we have today, *computers programmed by the brain!*

Before the first English dictionary was published in 1582 (Elizabeth I was ruling and Shakespeare was writing plays.), scholars and writers in England had been using Latin dictionaries. Also, the way English words were spelled was not consistent. These educated people now wanted a dictionary for English words. To meet this need, in 1582, Richard Mulcaster collected and organized the English words of his day. Then he chose 8,000 of these words for a book and recommended how they should be spelled. Instead of deciding to spell each word like it sounded, Mulcaster chose to use the common spelling, printed in books, that was already familiar to scholars and writers.

Fourteen years later (1596), Edmunde Coote, another English schoolmaster, published *The Englishe Schoole-maister*. Like Mulcaster, Coote wrote a spelling dictionary with familiar spelling, but he wrote his for the common people of England. Coote's dictionary was so popular that it set spelling standards for people from all walks of life – for shopkeepers, farmers and kings, and for schools in England. This dictionary (which also had synonyms) remained in print for over 200 years.

Then in 1604, Robert Cawdrey published *A Table Alphabetical*. Although it was less than a hundred pages and had only 3,000 words, this book has often been called *the first true dictionary* because Cawdrey not only spelled these words, but he also defined them.

Over the next hundred years, *the way words should be spelled* became more and more established. One reason was that Coote's spelling continued to be taught in schools. Also, by 1640, over 20,000 different books had been published in English and spelling was becoming consistent. There was now a demand in England for a dictionary that would define words and set permanent spelling standards.

In 1747, Samuel Johnson, a struggling writer, who was blind in one eye, was the one hired to write this great English dictionary. For eight years, he worked in an attic room, defining the meaning and establishing the spelling for **43,000** English words. To show the meaning of words and the way they were used, Johnson chose thousands of quotations from books by the best English writers.

Finally, in June 1755, Johnson's *Dictionary of the English Language* was published. His grand masterpiece captured the majesty of the English language and set permanent standards for the use and spelling of English words. The spellings and definitions established by Johnson were so excellent that they crossed the ocean to America where Noah Webster used them to write his dictionaries.

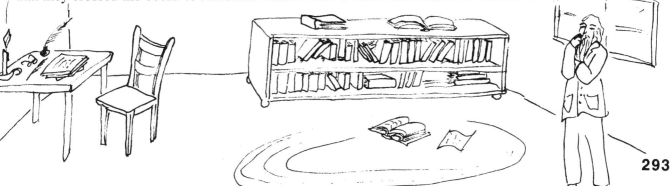

Meanwhile in America, Noah Webster wasn't even born when Johnson published his dictionary in 1775. By 1788, though, at age 30, Webster had completed his first dictionary, *The American Spelling Book*, a small school-dictionary that had familiar spelling and also some simplified words. Webster spelled and defined *American words* for two main reasons. One, he was a patriotic American. Encouraged by Benjamin Franklin and other leaders, he wanted to set a standard for American English to show that it was as good as British English. Also, Webster was a teacher who wanted his students to have better textbooks, so he wrote his own for spelling, grammar and reading.

The spelling section, *The American Spelling Book*, was published separately, and soon became a household book. Except for the *Bible*, it was the top selling book in American history. Webster then worked 40 more years to complete his *American Dictionary of the English Language* (1828) with **70,000** clearly defined words. Today, *Webster's Third International Dictionary* has **450,000** words.

A true hero in the history of the dictionary is James Augustus Henry Murray. Chosen in 1879 *to spell and define every English word since 1150*, A. H. Murray worked non-stop 36 years (until death, 1915) to collect, spell, and define **414,825** words. He even walked the docks to hear and find words.

Just try to imagine A. H. Murray, and his eleven children and assistants, collecting, defining and alphabetizing all these words on thousands of pieces of paper. With such incredible effort, Murray produced *The Oxford English Dictionary*, the dictionary considered to be *the greatest dictionary of all time*! Today it contains over **615,000** words and, *it is now organized by computers*!

With all these great dictionaries and their spelling, one question still remains: *Should spelling be reformed so that all words are spelled like they're pronounced*? Benjamin Franklin, Mark Twain, Noah Webster, and others worked very hard to try to simplify English spelling. Webster *even asked Congress to write a law to simplify spelling*. Also, in England, A. H. Murray and others pushed for spelling reform. Over time, though, the spelling already familiar to people has remained, even though about 15% of the words are not spelled like they're pronounced. This is the spelling you use today.

❑ **WHAT DO YOU THINK?** Should words with confusing spelling or silent letters be changed so all words are spelled like they're pronounced, or is it too late? Should *island* become *iland*; *laugh–laf*; *love–lov*; *restaurant–restrant*; *tough–tuf*; *you–yu*? Write what you think, and suggest words you'd like to change. Also, tell how would you make these spelling changes happen.

What the Dictionary Tells You About Words

In each entry for a word, the dictionary tells you an amazing amount about words: spelling, syllables, accent, pronunciation, part of speech, other word forms, prefixes, roots, suffixes, definition, origin (history of when the word came into English and from what language), synonyms…

Look at the words *neighbor* and *companion*:

NEIGHBOR

neigh·bor (nā′bər), *n.* **1.** a person who lives near another. **2.** a person or thing that is near another. **3.** one's fellow human being: *to be generous toward one's less fortunate neighbors.* **4.** a person who shows kindliness or helpfulness toward his or her fellow humans: *to be a neighbor to someone in distress.* **5.** (used as a term of address, esp. as a friendly greeting to a stranger): *Tell me, neighbor, which way to town?* —*adj.* **6.** situated or living near another: *one of our neighbor nations.* —*v.t.* **7.** to live or be situated near to; adjoin; border on. **8.** to place or bring near. —*v.i.* **9.** to live or be situated nearby. **10.** to associate with or as if with one's neighbors; be neighborly or friendly (often fol. by *with*). Also, esp. *Brit.,* **neigh′bour.** [bef. 900; ME; OE *neahgebūr, nēahbūr* (*nēah* NIGH + (*ge*)*būr* farmer; see BOER, BOOR); akin to D *nabuur,* G *Nachbar,* ON *nābūi*] —**neigh′bor·less,** *adj.*

COMPANION

com·pan·ion[1] (kəm pan′yən), *n.* **1.** a person who is frequently in the company of, associates with, or accompanies another: *my son and his two companions.* **2.** a person employed to accompany, assist, or live with another in the capacity of a helpful friend. **3.** a mate or match for something: *White wine is the usual companion of fish.* **4.** a handbook or guide: *a bird watcher's companion.* **5.** a member of the lowest rank in an order of knighthood or of a grade in an order. **6.** Also called **companion star, comes.** *Astron.* the fainter of the two stars that constitute a double star. Cf. **primary** (def. 19b). **7.** *Obs.* a fellow. —*v.t.* **8.** to be a companion to; accompany. [1250–1300; ME *compainoun* < AF; OF *compaignon* < LL *compānión-* (s. of *compāniō*) messmate, equiv. to *com-* COM- + *pān(is)* bread + *-iōn- -*ION; presumably as trans. of a Gmc word; cf. Goth *gahlaiba,* OHG *galeipo*] —**com·pan′ion·less,** *adj.*
—**Syn. 1.** comrade, partner, mate. See **acquaintance.**

☐ **TRY THIS**: Look at NEIGHBOR and COMPANION and write the information for each word.

SPELLING:

SYLLABLES:

ACCENT:

PRONUNCIATION:

PART OF SPEECH:

OTHER WORD FORMS:

PREFIXES:

ROOTS:

SUFFIXES:

DEFINITION:

ORIGINAL SPELLING:

ORIGIN (where):

TIME PERIOD (when):

SYNONYMS:

Amazing Dictionary Discoveries

❑ **NOW**: Discover the information for these sentences in the Dictionary.

ARMOR: The piece of armor that covers a hand is called a _ _ _ _ _ _ _ _.

ASTERISK: The little asterisk * in both Latin and Greek means _ _ _ _ _ _ _ _ _.

BASKETBALL: The basket measures _ _ inches across. The court is _ _ or _ _ feet.

CENTIPEDE is from the Latin prefix: *cent-* _ _ _ _ _ _ _ + the root: *ped-* _ _ _ _.

COMPANION comes from the _ _ _ _ _ prefix: *com-* _ _ _ _ + root: *pain-* _ _ _ _ _.
The word – *companion* originally meant *one with whom you shared bread.*

DACHSHUND: The drawing shows a dachshund stands _ _ _ inches high at the shoulders. It came
from _ _ _ _ _ roots: *dach*: _ _ _ _ _ _ + *hund*: _ _ _. Now you know where English got *hound-dog.*

HEIMLICH MANEUVER: To save someone from choking, you: _ _ _ _ _ _ _ _ _ _ _ _ _ _ _ _ _ _ _.

HIPPOPOTAMUS is from 2 _ _ _ _ _ roots. *Hippo* means _ _ _ _ _ _, and *potamos* means _ _ _ _ _ _.

HORSE: The measurement around a horse's body is called the _ _ _ _ _ _.

ICE HOCKEY: The goal area of an ice hockey rink is _ _ _ _ feet long.

MAGIC SQUARE: In a magic square, all rows are _ _ _ _ _. Draw one:

MANTA RAY: The drawing shows this ray measures _ _ _ _ feet across and _ _ _ _ feet long.

MANTIS: A mantis is an _ _ _ _ _ _, and is _ _ _ _ inches long.

MANUAL ALPHABET: Manual comes from the root *manus* which means _ _ _ _.

MORSE CODE: Write your name in Morse code: (If your dictionary has the alphabet).

MULTIPLY: is from Old French. Prefix: *multi* means _ _ _ _ + the root: *plier* means *to* _ _ _ _.

NIGHTINGALE: At night, you hear the melodious song of the _ _ _ _ nightingale wooing a mate.

PENINSULA comes from the _ _ _ _ _ prefix: *paene-* _ _ _ _ _ _ and the root: *insula-* _ _ _ _ _ _.

PNEUMONOULTRAMICROSCOPICSILICOVOLCANOCONIOSIS has _ _ _ syllables.

PORTUGUESE MAN-OF-WAR: Its float is _ _ _ _ inches long. Its tentacles hang _ _ _ _ to _ _ _ feet.

RE WORDS and **UN WORDS**: A dictionary has more words under the prefix _ _ than under _ _.

SEA HORSE originally came from the _ _ _ _ _ word: *sehors* meaning _ _ _ _ _ _. It is _ _ _ _ inches.

ST. BERNARD: This great dog that rescues people in the Swiss Alps is _ _ _ inches high at the shoulders.

VOLCANOES (If your dictionary has a list-): Mt. St. Helens in _ _ _ _ _ _ _ _ _ _ erupted in _ _ _ _ _ _.

YOLK came from an _ _ _ _ _ _ _ _ _ word before 900 A.D.: *geolu* which meant _ _ _ _ _ _.

❑ **NOW**: Use the dictionary to discover 2 interesting things you didn't know. Write these below.

296

POWER SPELLING
BOOK of LISTS

visual

clues

phonics

special Pronunciation

Rules

Roots

The Beat

THE POWER SPELLING BOOK of LISTS

The **POWER SPELLING BOOK of LISTS** is like a Learning Tree full of leaves that teach you ways to spell words forever! Each leaf is a list that shows you fun and lasting ways to use 7 great Memory Tools to remember every spelling word you meet. These 7 Memory Tools are: *POWER CLUES; PHONICS POWER and PATTERNS; POWER RULES; POWER of the BEAT and SYLLABLES; PRONUNCIATION POWER; POWER of ANCIENT ROOTS; and VISUAL POWER.*

Also, these *POWER* SPELLING LISTS help you use your hearing, seeing, feeling, and creative memory to detect and understand words. Then, these special Lists teach you the Memory Tools you need **so your brain can truly know and recall ways to spell words for the rest of your life!**

The reason the *POWER* SPELLING LISTS truly work is they match the ways your BRAIN learns:

- Your BRAIN uses HEARING, SEEING, and FEELING to take in, learn, and remember words. The Lists also use all three of your senses.

- Your BRAIN organizes information. The Lists organize spelling into 7 CATEGORIES based on the 7 *POWER* Spelling Tools: Clues; Phonics and Patterns; Rules that Work; Feeling the Beat and Syllables; Pronunciation; Ancient Roots; and Visual Power.

- Your BRAIN stores information in its memory. The Lists teach you 7 ways to use powerful MEMORY TOOLS to CONNECT the words you are learning to spell with information your BRAIN can learn and remember.

- Finally, the more you reinforce information in your BRAIN, the easier it is for your BRAIN to recall and use it. As you keep using these Lists of Memory Tools to learn and remember words, you keep strengthening the MEMORY PATHS to your BRAIN until using and recalling this information becomes automatic, like walking and talking!

Knowing these seven ways *to gain* and *retain* the BRAIN'S *POWER* to SPELL is like climbing the LEARNING TREE to the top. The Lists help you reach the top because they teach you the MEMORY TOOLS that your BRAIN needs to learn to spell and remember words forever!

So, ***LET'S GET GOING*** *and use* ***THOSE LISTS!***

LET'S CLIMB *this* ***LEARNING TREE*** *to the top!!!*

The POWER Spelling Book of Lists
(Clues and Other Tools for Remembering Every Word You Meet)

***POWER* Spelling: The Only Spelling Program That Teaches All the Spelling Skills
Plus Teaches Students Clues and Tools for Remembering Every Word They Meet!**

302

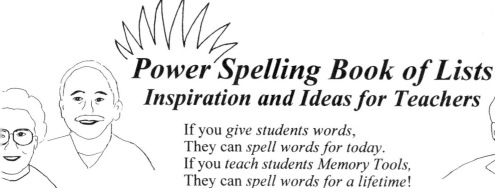

Power Spelling Book of Lists
Inspiration and Ideas for Teachers

If you *give students words*,
They can *spell words for today*.
If you *teach students Memory Tools*,
They can *spell words for a lifetime*!

The *POWER* Spelling Book of Lists is a long-time-needed, dynamic teaching resource that truly provides ways to remember every word it presents! It gives you lists of *Memory Tools* that you can use to teach your student to retain the spelling of words forever! This guide gives you ideas for introducing these Memory Tools in unique ways that will involve students. Finally, these lists can be used as spelling lessons or to enrich the lessons in *POWER* Spelling or in any other spelling program you are using.

Some of these lists use basic, established ways of remembering spelling, while others use innovative and multisensory approaches that have been developed and tested over thirty years. These tools clearly help students remember those challenging English words that have silent letters or don't follow phonics or rules. Basic lists include: Phonics *POWER*; *POWER* Rules that Work; Pronunciation *POWER*; and the *POWER* of Ancient Roots, Prefixes and Suffixes. Innovative lists include: Clues-in-a-Row; Special Phonics Pronunciations; Words that Fit a *POWER* Beat; and Visual *POWER* (Words You Can Draw, Palindromes, Reversals, Echo Words, Bookend Words...). You'll also find fun spelling games and other activities: *Rhyme Thyme*; *Building Words with Prefixes, Roots, and Suffixes*; and *Word Search*.

Enjoy using these lists as you teach your students
ways to retain words for the rest of their lives!

Tool 1: POWER Clues

Objectives: As students explore these lists of *Clues*, they'll learn to use and create different kinds of *Clues*: *Clues-in-a-Row, Letter Clues, Word Clues, Same Pattern Clues, Other Word (OWF) Clues*, and *Visual Clues*. Students will find clues fun and helpful because they teach them ways to connect words to their brain's memory triggers. (These Lists of *Clues* directly correspond to Lessons 1, 3, and 5 in *POWER* Spelling. You can find additional ideas in the *POWER* Spelling Teacher's Guide under these lessons.)

Special Clues-in-a-Row (271 words): Students particularly love *Clues-in-a-Row* since they're a great way to remember spelling and a clever play on words: *It was noticeable that my soda was not ice-able. This is so significant, please sign if I can't.* You can give students 2-3 *Clues-in-a-Row* each week, or you can take a break from regular spelling lessons by using 20-25 of these clues as a Special Lesson.

One way to introduce these *Clues* is to read *Clue-in-a-Row* sentences, and have students raise their hand as soon as they hear both the word and the *Clue-in-a-Row*: *Instead of being beaten by challenges, be a ten in over coming them* (Students would identify *beaten* and *be a ten*.) *They decided to initiate a trip to a pizza parlor, and in it I ate a lot* (*initiate* and *in it I ate*). *Even at night, in gales of wind, the nightingales sing* (*nightingales* and *night in gales*). And the list goes on.

Another approach is to put 7-10 *Clues-in-a-Row* on the board: *abundance, finished...* Then, ask your students to point out the words they see in a row, and have them create clues for these: *There was such an abundance of food, we even saw a bun dance. Once her ocean life was finished, the little mermaid said, "My fin I shed forever."*

Clues for Homophones (175 sets) and *Clues* for Confusing Words (55 sets): Both of these lists of *Clues* will help students learn and remember the differences between many homophones and confusing words. A good way to introduce either of these lists is to choose sets of words like the bold ones in the box. Write these on the board. Then, ask, "Can anyone explain the difference between one of these sets of words?" Write down student's answers. Then help students create *Clues* or use other *Tools* to retain these words. Write *their* ideas after the words (corresponds to Lesson 5 in *POWER* Spelling).

POWER CLUES FOR HOMOPHONES

1. **capital** (capital city, n.): Tallahassee is a capital.
   capital (capital letters, n.): Capital letters are tall.
   Capitol (building, n.): A Capitol has a dome-O.

2. **eight** (8, adj): My dog's weight is eight pounds.
   ate (past of eat, v.): *Anagram*: ate – eat.

3. **hangar** (for airplanes, n.): airplane hangar
   hanger (for clothes, n.): clothes hanger

4. **meat** (food, n.): You eat meat.
   meet (to see, v.): When you meet, you greet.
   mete (to measure, v.): I can mete a mile in meters.

5. **peace** (no war, n.): Each country wanted peace.
   piece (serving amount, n.): I ate a piece of pie.

6. **toe** (digit on the foot, n.): I hit my toe with a hoe.
   tow (to pull, v.): You can tow or row a boat.

POWER CLUES FOR CONFUSING WORDS

1. **pitcher** (n., ballplayer; container; n.): Can a pitcher pitch a cherry pit? pit + cher.
   picture (n.drawing;photo): Pick your picture and I'll put on my signature: pick + -ture.

2. **as-cend-ed** (v., arose): As the rocket ascended, it arose till our sight of Earth ended: as + c + ended.
   de-scend-ed (v., came down): Down to a desert we descended and ended on Earth: des + c + ended.

3. **tired** (adj., sleepy): When I get tired, my eyes are red. *SPP*: ti-red. *Rule*: tire + d = tired.
   tried (v., past of try): They lied, and tried to cover the truth *SPP*: tri-ed. *Rule*: try + i = tried.

After you have introduced one of these Lists of *Clues*, it's very helpful to give students their own lists of clues. Then, they can use the lists and mark words as they learn ways to remember them

Clues for Challenging Words (556 Words) and **Clues for Very Challenging Words** (120 Words): To introduce these words, list the bold words in the learning box on the board. Then ask, "Can anyone make up a *Clue* for one of these words?" As students create *Clues*, write these down. Then ask, "Does anyone see anything similar or different about any of these clues." Help them see the different ways they can create *Clues* and write these after the *Clues* (corresponds to Lesson 3 in *POWER* Spelling).

POWER CLUES FOR CHALLENGING WORDS

1. **athlete**: The athlete did a high leap. (One or two letter *Clue*)
2. **beginning**: At the beginning of our trip, we stayed at an inn. (*Clues* that use a word or two)
3. **courage**: It takes courage to live in our age. (Almost a *Clue*-in-a-Row)
4. **calendar** A calendar has a list and dates. (One or two letter *Clue*)
5. **column**: A columnist writes a column. (Other Word Form *Clue*)
6. **rain**: The rain in Spain falls mainly on the plains (Same Pattern *Clue*)
7. **separate**: As I tried to separate oranges and apples, a rat jumped out. (*Clues* that use a word or two)

Again, give students the lists so they can mark words they have learned to remember. Also, challenge students to create clues for other words and share these with the class.
(Have students send their *favorite Clues* to: Linda Skerbec, 230 California Ave., Suite 107, Palo Alto, CA 94306.)

Pronouncing Other Word Forms (120+ words; Corresponds to Lessons 10 and 35): Students can use *Other Word Forms* to more clearly hear letters: *metal-metallic, personal-personality, whistle-whistling.*

To introduce *OWF Clues*, list some words on the board: *column, hospital, limb, medal, receive, whistle...* Ask students, "What letters are silent or difficult to hear in these words?" Underline the letters they point out (plus any letters they miss). Then ask, "Can you think of any other forms of these words where you can better hear these letters?" Write down the *OWF's* they give you.

While students are thinking of *Other Word Forms*, point out that good dictionaries always list the other forms that a word can have. Take a few words that have silent letters or where letters are difficult to hear, and have one or more students look up a word and read the other forms of the word in a dictionary. Help students see how helpful it is to simply be able to look up *Other Word Forms*.

CLUES THAT USE OTHER WORD FORMS

column: columnist, columnar-like columns   medal: medallion
hospital: hospitality   receive: reception
limb: limber   whistle: whistling, whistler

assemble: assembles, assembled, assembling, assembler
deceive: deceives, deceived, deceiving, deceiver, deception
resign: resigns, resigned, resigning, resignation

Also, ask students for words they can think of where *Other Word Forms* help. Point out that *OWF's* provide great help for -al and -le words. (OWF Lists correspond to Lessons 1 and 35: L Endings: -al, -el, -il, and –le.)

clues

ideas

rules

WORDS

Lists

games

empowerment!

Tool 2: Phonics POWER

Objectives: Students will discover the different sounds that make up the English language. They will also learn the different ways that consonants and vowels work and how they make sounds: Single Letter Sounds, Consonant/Vowel Sounds; 2 letter sounds(digraphs). They will find out that Copy Cat Kids and Blends are not new sounds; just a copy or blend of single sounds. (These Phonics Lists correspond to *POWER* Spelling Lessons 6, 7, 13, 14, and 17-24. For additional ideas, also see Teacher's Guide.)

POWER **Spelling List of All the Phonics Sounds** (Lesson 6-7): This list provides a summary of all the different sounds that the letters in the English language make. To get your students thinking, ask, "How many different sounds do you think there are in English?" Write down their ideas. Then ask, "What kinds of letters make these sounds?" As students give answers, write the words: **All the Consonant Sounds** and **All the Vowel Sounds** on the board. Then ask questions to help students discover the information in the learning box, plus ask students to think of words for each sound. If you don't get all the sounds, simply list any remaining sounds and ask for words for these.

ALL THE CONSONANT SOUNDS

<u>15 Single Consonant Sounds</u> (Qu = single sound)

B	**J**	**N**	**T**
D	**K**	**P**	**V**
F	**L**	**Qu**	**Z**
H	**M**	**R**	

<u>2 Consonants = Own Sound and Copy a Sound</u>

G copies J   **S** copies Z

<u>2 Consonants (vowels) **W** and **Y**</u>

<u>5 Consonant Digraphs (2-Letter Teams)</u> + **NG**

CH	**TH**-not voiced
SH	**WH**
TH-voiced	**NG**

<u>1 Special Sound: **ZH**</u>

(Other ways that Consonants makes sounds that aren't different = Copy Cat Sounds and Blends)

ALL THE VOWEL SOUNDS

<u>10 Single Vowel Sounds: 5 Short; 5 Long</u>

Short Vowel Sounds	Long Vowel Sounds
A	**A**
E	**E**
I	**I**
O	**O**
U	**U**

<u>Vowel Digraphs (2 Vowels Together)</u>

<u>2 Vowel (consonants) **W** and **Y**</u>

<u>5 Special 2-Letter Vowel Sounds</u>

AU/AW (Broad O)	**OU/OW** (Broad O)
OO (as in moon)	**OO** (as in book)
OI/OY (Diphthong)	**EW** (Diphthong)

<u>5 R-Controlled Vowel Sounds</u>

AR	**AIR**
ER, IR, UR (same sound)	**EAR/EER**
OR, ORE (same sound)	

<u>1 Schwa Sound: **o** (neutral vowel sound)</u>

Again, note that Consonants can make sounds two other ways: by copying sounds (Single-Letter and Two-Letter Copy Cat Kids) or by blending sound that already exist (Beginning and Ending Blends).

- (Single Letter Copy Cats: <u>C-copies K and S</u>; <u>X-copies KS and Z</u>; <u>G copies J</u>; <u>S copies Z</u>.)
- (Two-Letters Copy Cats: <u>CH-copies K and Sh</u>; <u>GH copies F</u>; <u>PH copies F</u>; <u>Qu copies K and KW</u>.)
- (Beginning and Ending Consonants Blends: Each consonant keeps its own sound and *blends* with other sounds as you can hear in <u>blend</u> and <u>strength</u>. Note: Digraphs can be in Blends too).

(You can introduce these sounds in one lesson or add a new kind of sound each day during the week. Also, suggest that students check dictionaries to see what they say the different sounds are. Note that there are 45-55 sounds in English, depending on the source used.) Finally, give students their own: *List of All the Phonics Sounds*.

POWER Spelling Lists of Ways that Consonants Make Sounds (Lessons 6, 7, 13,14)

Let's Create the Single Consonant Sounds (Includes <u>the Consonant/Vowels: W and Y</u>: Lessons 6, 7)
6 Digraph Sounds and the Special ZH Sound (Two-Letters Make One Sound: Lesson 7)
4 One-Letter Copy Cat Kids and **4 Two-Letter Copy Cat Kids** (Letters that Copy Other Sounds: Lesson 13)
Beginning and Ending Consonant Blends (Letters that Keep Their Sound and Blend Together: Lesson 14)

The ways CONSONANTS can make sounds are: <u>Single Consonants</u> (includes <u>Qu</u>); <u>Consonant/Vowels</u>; <u>Digraphs</u>; <u>One and Two-Letter Copy Cat Kids</u>; and <u>Beginning and Ending Blends</u>. Point out that these five kinds of sounds cover all the ways that consonants can make sounds.

Depending on the list from above that you are using, write the category of consonant sounds on the board, and ask students to give you the consonants in the category. Then, ask students to give examples of words that fit the letters. The more words you get, the better. Help each student think of words that fit.

POWER Spelling Lists of Ways that Vowels Make Sounds (Lessons 6, 17-24)

Short Vowel Sounds (Lesson 17**)**
Long Vowel Sounds: Silent E Sounds (Lesson 18**)**
Long Vowel Digraphs: When 2-Vowels-Go-Walking Sound (Two letters make one sound. Lesson 19**)**
The Challenging EI and IE Vowel Sounds (Lesson 20**)**
Special 2-Vowel Combinations: Broad O Sound, Diphthongs, Double O Sound (Lesson 21**)**
R-Controlled Vowel Sounds (Lesson 22**)**
POWER Spelling List of Open Syllable Words (Short A and I; Long A, E, I, O, and U; Lesson 23**)**

The 7 lists above cover all the ways VOWELS can make sound. Each of these lists covers the ways that the vowel pattern can be spelled with many examples. Also, at the bottom of each list, students get to play the *Rhyme Thyme Game* where they choose 2-word rhymes to solve each definition. For example, a Hog Dance is a *Pig Jig*; Weak Ape – *Limp Chimp*; Endless Grin – *Mile Smile*; Hair Robbery – *Braid Raid*; Short Break – Brief Relief; Intelligent Pastry – *Smart Tart*.

Again, depending on the list you are using, write the category of vowel sounds on the board, and list the vowels in that category. Ask students for words that fit each vowel sound. The more words you get, the better. Try to involve each student in thinking of words that fit the sounds.

List: The Many Different Ways the English Language Spells Its Sounds (Lesson 24**)**
This one-page summary shows the different ways that the sounds in the English Language can be spelled. To introduce this list, copy all the vowel sounds on the list on the board. Then ask students, "How many different ways can you think of to spell each sound?" Also, suggest that students think of foreign words in English that make the different sounds: *ballet, depot, gnu*. Then, give each student a copy of the list. Point out that one reason the English Language is difficult to spell is that there are many ways to spell the same sound. At the same time, the variety of words in the English Language makes it the richest language in the world!

Tool 3: POWER Spelling Rules

Objectives: Students will build their understanding of *Rules That Work* and learn that these rules truly give them *POWER* to know how words are spelled. They will practice using the rules for some words.

Summary of *POWER* Spelling Rules that Work (one page); ***POWER* Spelling List of Rules that Work** (5 pages) Understanding and using *Rules That Work* adds a stable structure to spelling *POWER*, and clues and other tools will help with the exceptions. Give students these lists before they play their first *POWER* Spelling Game. Then, right from the start, they can use them and strengthen their understanding of the rules throughout the year. (These lists correspond to Lessons 25-30, and 33.)

Introduce *Rules That Work* by asking students, "Are there any spelling rules you know?" List the rules they share. Then say, "I want you to observe words until tomorrow and see if you can discover any more rules." During the week, build a list of the rules that students find. Show them that knowing and using the rules gives them spelling *POWER*, and that some rules have no exceptions: *Contraction Rule, Qu Rule*. Add that clues will help with the exceptions. Finally, list words like those below on the board. Ask students what rules can help with these and write the rules next to the words.

RULES THAT WORK

attend: *Prefix Rule*: Just add the prefix to the root.

frying: *Y Rule*: <u>Y</u> stays before -<u>ing</u>.

glowworm: *Compound Rule*: Just add the 2 words.

happiness: *Y Rule*: Change <u>y</u> to <u>i</u> except before -<u>ing</u>.

likable: *E Rule*: Drop <u>silent e</u> before vowel suffix.

lovely: *E Rule*: Keep <u>silent e</u> before consonant suffix.

neighbor: *IE/EI Rule*: Sounds like <u>a</u>, spelling is <u>EI</u>.

picnicking: *K Rule*: Add <u>k</u> before <u>i</u> and <u>e</u> suffixes.

referring: *Rule*: Accent on -<u>fer</u>, double final consonant.

quote: *Q Rule*: <u>Qu</u> stays together.

running: *Rule*: Double consonant to keep vowel short.

they're: *Rule*: Contraction always gets the apostrophe.

Tool 4: Feeling the Power of the Beat

Objectives: Students will practice feeling the *POWER of the Beat* and learn ways to put words to a beat. They will discover that the beat is a fun and very helpful tool for remembering words.

For some words like *rhythm, encyclopedia, singing, arithmetic, mathematics*, putting the letters or syllables to a *Beat* is a great spelling tool: *r-h-y t-h-m; e-n c-y-c l-o p-e-d-i-a; a-rith-me-tic; math-e-ma-tics*. Using the *Beat* helps students draw on their feeling sense (in addition to hearing and seeing), and it is particularly helpful for kinesthetic learners. You can also use this tool to affirm your students who play instruments, sing, etc., and to have students bring in some of their music (See Lesson 8).

To introduce the *POWER* of the *Beat*, write some of the words from the list on the board. Include some -*ing* words and double-letter words. Then ask, "Can someone choose a word and tell how you would put this word to a beat?" As students share beats, write their rhythm on the board. If students seem hesitant, take a word like *rhythm, dancing*, or *parallel*. Show students a few beats. Ask which one they like best, or if anyone has another suggestion. Do this for a few more words, and this should get students involved. Point out that some -*ing* words, double-letter words, and other words with a natural rhythm, are easy to put to a beat. Ask students to think of their own words and put these to a beat. (To increase involvement, first have students work in small groups and then work with the class.)

Tool 5: Pronunciation POWER

Objectives: Students will learn how *Pronunciation Tools* can help them retain words. **Pronunciation POWER for Spelling** will give them the correct pronunciation for 75 of the most commonly mispronounced words. **Special Phonics Pronunciations** will teach them a fun Old English way to pronounce words so that all the letters can be heard for spelling **Pronouncing Other Word Forms** will help them use other forms of words to better hear some of the letter.

Power Spelling List of Proper Pronunciations (75 words) A fun way to involve students in this lesson is to say, "I'm going to pronounce some words that are often misspelled because they're mispronounced. I'll say each word two ways, and after each set, I want you to vote on the way you think is correct. Now, is the word: *athelete* or *athlete* (vote); *bevrage* or *beverage* (vote); *candidate* or *candadate* (vote); *disastrous* or *disasterous* (vote); *jewelry* or *jewelery* (vote); *hindrance* or *hinderance* (vote)?" As students vote, ask why they chose a certain spelling. After each vote, write the correct spelling on the board. Then, help students use *Clues* and other *Tools* to retain these words. Perhaps keep an on-going list of **Proper Pronunciations** in the room and add to it each week.

Special Phonics Pronunciations (*SPP's*) (155 words; Lessons 2 and 10) This pronunciation tool can take your students back to the time of Chaucer (before A.D. 1400) when every letter was pronounced, about 600 years ago, before Columbus and Queen Elizabeth I. Tell them that once there was a time (1400 A.D. and before) when spelling was much easier because every consonant and vowel was pronounced: *climban, iland, k-not, etc.* (For more info, see: *POWER Spelling List of Events that Changed the Spelling of English.*)

A unique way to introduce this list is to write the bold words (each has silent letters) on the board. Point out that because of changes that occurred in pronunciation, or because these words are foreign, they have silent letters. Then, ask, "Who can pronounce one of these words so that every letter can be heard?" Write the pronunciations students give next to each word. Ask this question until you've covered all the words. Next, ask, "Can anyone think of another word with silent letters, and pronounce this word so all letters are heard?" Let students explore and have fun pronouncing words this special way. Then, ask, "Do you prefer regular English pronunciation or these *Special Phonics Pronunciations*?" Suggest that they call these *Special Phonics Pronunciations*: *SPP's* for short.

Special Phonics Pronunciations – *SPP's*

climb: clim-b	**often**: of-ten
every: e-ver-y	**restaurant**: res-ta-u-rant
gnome: g-nom-e	**raspberry**: ras-p-ber-ry
February: Feb-ru-ar-y	**knock**: k-noc-k
meant: me-ant	**Wednesday**: Wed-nes-day

Silent G: Try: g-nat; g-naw; g-nome; g-nu…
Silent K: Try: k-nac-k; k-ni-fe; k-nit; k-noc-k; k-not; k-no-w; k-nuc-kle…

Next, ask, "Can someone share other words that start with a <u>*silent g* or *k*?</u>" Write these on the board. Finally, ask students to create a sentence using some of the words on the board where they pronounce all the vowels and consonants, similar to the way people did with Old English: <u>The g-no-me clim-bs lim-bs e-ver-y Wed-nes-day to k-noc-k g-nats out of tre-es.</u>

Tool 6: POWER of Ancient Roots

Ancient Roots help greatly with spelling because, overall, roots and their prefixes and suffixes are consistently spelled, and the rules for adding prefixes and suffixes are consistent. Also, students learn how roots, prefixes, and suffixes work and their meanings. (Lists correspond to Lessons 11, 26-36.)

Objectives: Students will discover that knowing Latin and Greek roots, plus some Old English roots builds spelling (and vocabulary) *POWER* because the same root can be in several words, and most roots are spelled like they're pronounced. They will also learn ways to remember the spelling of challenging prefixes and suffixes.

Power Spelling Lists of Words: Star, Heart, Hand, Foot, Light, Time, and Fire: These lists of roots help students see how Greek, Latin, and Old English use different words for the same root. A good way to introduce these is to choose one of the lists and write the bold words on the board (It's fun to also draw pictures of the root on the board, i.e., stars, hearts, hands, etc., or have a student do it.). When the board's ready, ask students, "Why do you think Greek, Latin, and Old English use different words for the same root?" Then ask, "Can anyone point out the root in one of these words or a prefix or suffix that's been added?" Circle the root and put a single line under prefixes and suffixes. Then pass out the sheets, and have students do the activity. These lists can also be used as spelling lessons.

Power Spelling List of Prefix Patterns and **Power Spelling List of Suffix Patterns**
These lists build students' spelling ability by showing them more about how prefixes and suffixes work, and by giving them tools to remember some prefixes and suffixes that are challenging because they can be spelled several ways: -in, -il; -e, ex; -ar, -er, -or and others.

Power Spelling Word-Building Games with Prefixes, Roots, and Suffixes: 1, 2, and 3: Use these creative learning games to help students build words while seeing how prefixes, roots and suffixes connect. To introduce this game, simply copy the bold words from a game on the board, and give students copies of the sheet. Point out that often a root by itself is a word, and read some of the roots. Then ask, "How do prefixes, roots, and suffixes build words?" Support the answers students give. Then use the metaphor of a *word sandwich*. The root is the main part and the prefixes and suffixes act like the bread that can be on one (open-face sandwich) or both sides. Finally ask them to build some words and share these. As they give you words, briefly review the Prefix and Suffix Rules (including Silent E and Final Y) as needed to connect word parts. Also, let students know they can make up their own words as long as they define them. Students can play these games individually or in groups and see how many words they can build. (Note: Game 1 has basic Old Eng. roots; games 2 and 3 have Latin and Greek roots.)

Magical Suffixes Create Nouns, Verbs, Adjective and Adverbs: This game shows students ways to turn a root into a noun, verb, adjective, or adverb, just by adding *Magical Suffixes*. First, write some of the bold words from the game on the board, and also, list some suffixes for nouns, verbs, adjectives, and adverbs. Also, give students a list. Then, ask them to add suffixes to the roots and tell you what part of speech they have created. Let them have fun trying this out. (If students need to learn the parts of speech, *Special Lesson 3* has fun visual activities to teach them nouns, verbs, adjectives, and adverbs.)

Power Spelling List of Words and Their Roots (287 words): Knowing how these words are put together provides rich spelling help. To introduce these lists, simply write some of the words on the board, and then have students break the words down into their parts. It's helpful if students have already played the Word-Building Game. Then they can see that in the same way they built words for that game, they can also take words apart to understand the spelling and meaning of the roots, prefixes, and suffixes.

Tool 7: Visual Power

Visual Power can be a particularly effective tool because it adds another dimension of seeing to the way that students perceive words. This added dimension makes certain *visual words* easier to retain (Lists correspond to Lessons 1 and 12 and Special Lesson 1).

Objective: Students will enjoy discovering some amazing visual patterns in swords, and they will see how these patterns help with spelling: *Palindromes, Reversals, Echoes...* They can also draw words, play *Word Search*, and learn the *Sight Recognition Words*.

Words You Can See and Draw: Students seem to enjoy these a lot because these words involve their visual imagination. To introduce these, <u>print</u> the bold words below on the board (or choose other words).

balloon	kickball
eye	level
high	shampoo

Ask, "Is there anything you can see in these words that you could turn into a drawing that connects with the meaning of the word?" As students point these out, have them draw them (Ideas are: 2 sticks and 2 balloons in *balloon*; 2 eyes and a nose in *eye*; 2 chairs in *high*; 2 *kickball* kickers; a level line between the 2 l's in *level*; and 2 bubbles in *shampoo*.). Look at a few more visual words, plus ask students to come up with visual words of their own.

Palindromes, Reversals, Echoes, Bookends, and Anagrams (Corresponds to Lesson 12 and Special Lesson 1): These are a lot of fun for students and truly help them remember words for spelling.

To introduce *Palindromes*, begin by simply writing: DO GEESE SEE GOD? on the board. Then ask, "Can anyone see anything special about this sentence?" Then write another sentence: STEP ON NO PETS. Once students start noticing, acknowledge them, and say, "I want to wait a few more minutes." Add: RACECAR and KAYAK, DAD. Then, ask one of the first students who noticed something to explain what they saw. Also ask, "Can anyone think of other palindromes?" and you may get: MOM, POP, LEVEL, etc. Finally ask, "How do you think palindromes can help with spelling?" After this, hand out the list that corresponds to what you've taught, or hand out Special Lesson 1. Let students enjoy the Word Play. (On the same day, or another time, you can introduce <u>reversals</u> by writing *deer-reed*; and *drawer-reward* and on the board and wait for students to discover the pattern)

DO GEESE SEE GOD?		STEP ON NO PETS.	
KAYAK	**MOM**	**DAD**	**POP**
RACECAR	**WOW**		**LEVEL**

Searching for Words Games (*Note*: Every *POWER* Spelling Game has one or more *Word-Search Words*): These words keep your students' visual abilities sharp. Hand out these lists or every so often, write one of these words on the board and ask, "How many different words can you find in this word? (heart: a, art, he, hear ear). Then ask if anyone can create a clue using the words they see.

Sight Recognition Words and **Clues and Tools for Sight Recognition Words:** Since these words are so commonly used, it's important for students to instantly recognize them on sight. Most older students can. If you have students who struggle with these, use clues, etc., and review these words until students know them on sight. (You can also have students review these on their own or with a study partner.)

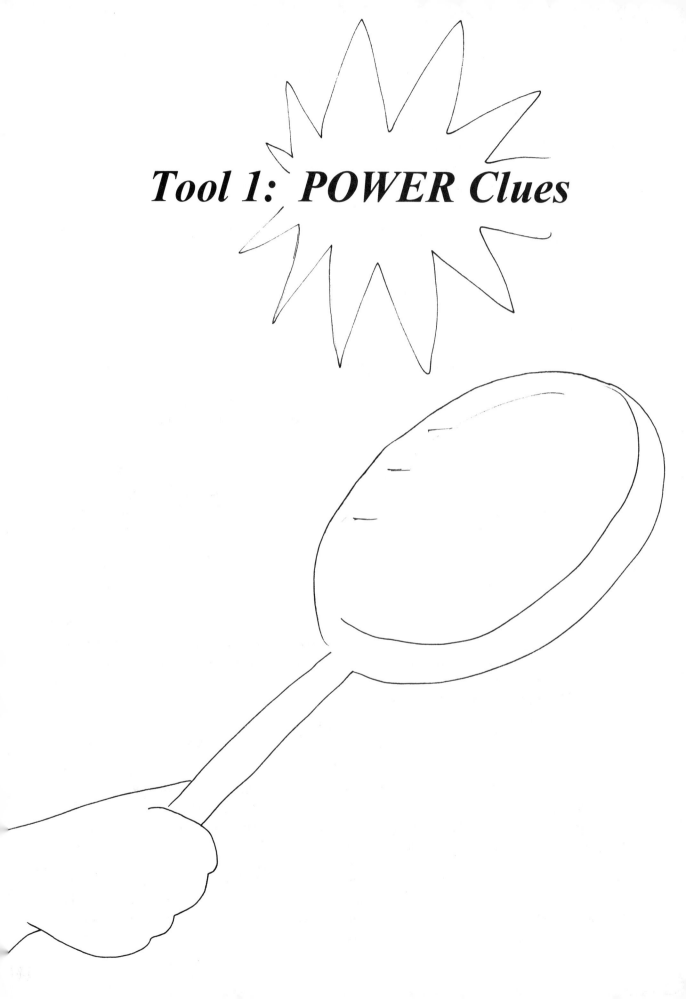

Tool 1: POWER Clues

POWER Spelling Special Clues-in-a-Row

Clues-in-a-Row make for great spelling and word play! There's always another one to find...

1. **ab-a-lo-ne**: Bea, the <u>abalone</u> felt like – <u>a B alone</u>.
2. **a-base** (to put down): Don't <u>abase</u> a ball player for not getting on <u>a base</u>.
3. **a-bun-dance**: We had such an <u>abundance</u> of food, we even got to see <u>a bun dance</u>.
4. **a-gain**: When you do something <u>again</u> and <u>again</u>, you make <u>a gain</u> in ability.
5. **al-lowed**: We <u>all owed</u> ticket money we paid to be <u>allowed</u> into the theatre.
6. **a-loud**: When he spoke <u>aloud</u>, he had <u>a loud</u> voice.
7. **al-to-get-her**: If she's an <u>alto, get her</u>; we have <u>altogether</u> too few altos (low female voices).
8. **al-ways**: She gave <u>Al ways</u> to <u>always</u> find her.
9. **a-maze**: I will try to <u>amaze</u> you with how fast I can get through <u>a maze</u>.
10. **am-i-a-ble**: <u>Am I able</u> to be <u>amiable</u>? (Fr. *ami*-friend; *amiable*-friendly)
11. **an-te-lope**: Can an <u>ant elope</u> with an <u>antelope</u>?
12. **arm-or**: I would also like some <u>armor</u> for my <u>arm or</u> leg.
13. **art-i-choke**: Alas, <u>Art, I choke</u> on an <u>artichoke</u>.
14. **at-ten-dance**: Now that I've taken <u>attendance</u> here, remember: <u>At ten dance</u>!
15. **beans-talk**: Can you hear <u>beans talk</u> on a <u>beanstalk</u>?
16. **be-gin**: Can I <u>beg in</u> before we <u>begin</u>?
17. **be-wild-er**: How kids can always <u>be wilder</u> can still <u>bewilder</u> me.
18. **buf-fa-loes**: Do <u>buffaloes</u> <u>buff aloes</u> (cacti) in their spare time on the prairie?
19. **cat-a-log**: Please order a <u>cat, a log</u>, and a flying fish from that <u>catalog</u>.
20. **dare-de-vil**: A <u>daredevil</u> like Evil Knevil has often <u>dared evil</u>.
21. **dis-cov-er-y**: We made this <u>discovery</u>: <u>Disco Very</u> Noisy!
22. **er-rand**: When you run that <u>errand</u>, please don't <u>err and</u> forget something
23. **gen-er-a-tion**: When one <u>generation</u> goes to the next, do they <u>gene ration</u>?
24. **hailed**: <u>Ha, I led</u> them to safety before it <u>hailed</u> huge ice balls.
25. **han-dled**: They <u>handled</u> our concerns so well, we felt <u>hand led</u>.
26. **hand-some**: <u>Hand some</u> sodas to those nice, <u>handsome</u> guys.
27. **her-on** (a large white bird): He put <u>her on</u> the back of the <u>heron</u>.
28. **her-ring** (a fish): That <u>herring</u> (fish) swallowed <u>her ring</u>.
29. **hon-or-a-ble**: Your <u>Honor, able</u> am I to be <u>honorable</u>.
30. **i-deal**: At work, <u>I deal</u> with <u>ideal</u> people who value high <u>ideals</u>.
31. **im-pact**: They way that <u>imp acts</u> has an <u>impact</u>.
32. **im-port-ant**: It's <u>important</u> not to <u>import ants</u> home in your picnic basket.
33. **in-i-ti-ate**: When he decided to <u>initiate</u> a trip to the pizza parlor, <u>in it I ate</u> a lot.
34. **in-nate** (existing since birth): The <u>innate</u> musical gifts <u>in Nate</u> have been there forever.
35. **in-ven-tor**: An <u>inventor</u> likes to <u>invent or</u> discover new things.
36. **i-rate** (angry): I know you feel <u>irate</u> about your score, but <u>I rate</u> you Number 1!
37. **is-land**: There <u>is land</u> on an <u>island</u>.

38. **kit-ten**: In her <u>kit, ten</u> <u>kittens</u> were curled up.

39. **les-son**: I learned the <u>lesson</u> of taking <u>less on</u> to do each day.

40. **man-i-cure**: <u>Man, I cure</u> nails with a <u>manicure</u>.

41. **meas-ure**: Please give <u>me a sure</u> <u>measure</u>.

42. **no-tice**: Did you <u>notice</u> that it was <u>not ice</u> I put down your back.

43. **no-where**: <u>Now here</u> at last are my glasses; I could find them <u>nowhere</u>.

44. **of-fice**: I advise you to build your <u>office</u> <u>off ice</u>.

45. **of-ten**: I have been there so <u>often</u>, I can think <u>of ten</u> times right now.

46. **or-bit**: In <u>orbit</u>, the astronauts sucked <u>or bit</u> food out of a tube.

47. **pas-sag-es**: We go through <u>passages</u> of time as we <u>pass ages</u> in our life.

48. **pas-times**: <u>Pa's time</u> is spent enjoying his <u>pastimes</u>.

49. **pleas-ant**: Hear my <u>pleas ants</u>, because it's not <u>pleasant</u> having you on picnics.

50. **pre-ferred**: When they asked what color I <u>preferred</u>, I said, "I <u>prefer red</u>."

51. **rob-in**: I saw <u>Rob in</u> our yard watching a <u>robin</u> with a bright red vest

52. **sail-or**: That <u>sailor</u> invited us to <u>sail or</u> swim with him today.

53. **sig-ni-fi-cant**: This agreement is so <u>significant</u>, please: <u>sign if I can't</u>. (Change y to i in signify.)

54. **sled-ding**: I got a <u>sled ding</u> while I was <u>sledding</u>.

55. **soared**: <u>So a red</u> bird <u>soared</u> into our house today.

56. **sur-geon**: <u>Surge on</u>, Oh, <u>surgeon</u>, <u>surge on</u>.

57. **ten-ants**: <u>Ten ants</u> are my <u>tenants</u>.

58. **to-geth-er**: We went <u>together</u> to school <u>to get her</u>.

59. **weath-er**: Why are <u>we at her</u> constantly over the <u>weather</u>?

60. **week-nights**: On <u>weeknights</u>, <u>wee knights</u> in tiny suits of armor spar with miniature swords.

More POWER Spelling Special Clues-in-a-Row

By popular demand, here are more *Clues-in-a-Row* for great spelling help and word play!

1. **a-ban-doned**: Ed was not <u>abandoned</u>; there was <u>a band on</u> Ed.
2. **a-bridge** (shorten): I cross <u>a bridge</u> to my work where I <u>abridge</u> dictionaries.
3. **a-cross**: He wore <u>a cross</u> <u>across</u> his chest.
4. **a-cute** (sharp: acute pain): When I had <u>acute</u> appendicitis, it was not just <u>a cute</u> little pain.
5. **ad-her-ents** (supporters): After seeing an <u>ad, he rents</u> an entire building for <u>adherents</u> of his cause.
6. **ad-o-les-cent**: Does an <u>adolescent</u> have <u>a dole scent</u> (*a dole me out money* scent)?
7. **a-lien-ate** (turn off; make hostile): The food the <u>alien ate</u> did not <u>alienate</u> me.
8. **a-lone**: <u>A lone</u> stranger was walking <u>alone</u> in the desert.
9. **a-long**: Come <u>along</u> with me on <u>a long</u> hike by the ocean.
10. **art-ist-ry** (artistic quality): To develop your own true <u>artistry</u>, what you can do with <u>art is try</u>.
11. **as-cer-tain**: I want to <u>ascertain</u> why, <u>as certain</u> children get older, they lose the joy of learning.
12. **asked**: When I <u>asked</u> to help, they said, "<u>Ask Ed</u> for a task."
13. **as-par-a-gus**: I'd enjoy <u>a spar, Agus</u>, with spears of <u>asparagus</u> (spar: sword fight; Agus: abbr. of Augustine).
14. **as-phalt**: Don't let that <u>asp halt</u> our work on the <u>asphalt</u> (asp: poisonous snake).
15. **as-sist-ants**: I <u>assist ants</u> who are <u>assistants</u> to the queen.
16. **as-ton-ished** (amazed): <u>As Toni shed</u> her feather, I was <u>astonished</u> to watch.
17. **a-stride** (with a leg on each side): I set <u>astride</u> my horse as he took <u>a stride</u>.
18. **a-tone**: Many <u>atone</u> for sin to feel <u>at one</u> with God.
19. **at-ro-phy** (decline; waste away): Don't let your skills <u>atrophy</u>, and you'll earn <u>a trophy</u>.
20. **at-tire** (n., clothes; v., dress up): <u>At tire</u> stores, you can <u>attire</u> your car with new wheels.
21. **a-void**: When they decided to <u>avoid</u> me, I felt <u>a void</u> in my life (void: emptiness).
22. **ax-is**: That <u>ax is</u> resting on the <u>axis</u> of the board (axis: center point; point on which something rotates).
23. **bar-gain**: At the sales <u>bar, gain</u> all the <u>bargain</u>s you can.
24. **bar-rage** (overwhelming amount coming at you): He wanted to halt the <u>barrage</u> of <u>bar rage</u>.
25. **beat-en**: Don't be <u>beaten</u> by hard work, but strive to <u>be a ten</u> in completing challenges.
26. **beau-ties**: The <u>beauties</u> wore <u>beau ties</u> (Fr. beau = boy).
27. **bul-let-in**: The <u>bullet in</u> the <u>bulletin</u> board was stuck in deeply.
28. **butch-er**: I like our <u>butcher</u>, <u>but Cher</u> says hers is better.
29. **cab-in**: We found a <u>cab in</u> our <u>cabin</u>.
30. **car-pet**: Our <u>car pet</u> sits on the <u>carpet</u> in our car.

31. **cab-in**: We found a <u>cab in</u> our <u>cabin</u>.

32. **can-a-pés** (crackers with caviar, etc.): <u>Can apes</u> dine on <u>canapés</u>?

33. **car-pet**: Our <u>car pet</u> sits on the <u>carpet</u> in our car.

34. **ca-pa-ci-ty**: To <u>cap a city</u> celebration, we sold-out our final show to <u>capacity</u>.

35. **car-a-van**: In our <u>caravan</u>, we had a <u>car, a van</u>, and a bus.

36. **ce-le-bra-ted**: We <u>celebrated</u> with a <u>celeb rated</u> high at the theatre.

37. **chem-is-try**: When you take <u>chemistry</u>, the best thing to do with <u>chem is try</u>.

62. **con-sci-ence**: Students of good <u>conscience</u> will not try to <u>con science</u> teachers.

63. **con-sole**: Can you <u>con sole</u> to <u>console</u> other fish that get caught?

38. **coup-on**: I have a <u>coupon</u> for a troop to perform a <u>coup on</u> our lawn (coup: brave deed in battle).

39. **de-ter-gent**: Why do dishes and <u>detergents</u> <u>deter gents</u>?

40. **de-ter-mines**: He <u>determines</u> the causes that <u>deter mines</u> from having gold: <u>deter + mines</u>.

41. **ed-i-tor**: You alone can <u>edit or</u> you can hire an <u>editor</u>.

42. **Ein-stein** (Ger. physicist, famous for Theory of Relativity): <u>Einstein</u> put his beer in <u>ein stein</u> (Ger. ein: one).

43. **en-dor-sing** (supporting): Instead of just <u>endorsing</u> groups, <u>end or sing</u> the songs you've written.

44. **er-rant** (going astray): You will <u>err, ant</u> if you become an <u>errant</u> ant (errant: straying off course).

45. **er-ror**: When you <u>err or</u> an <u>error</u> happens, you can still learn and move forward.

46. **fin-ished**: Once her ocean life was <u>finished</u>, the little mermaid said, "My <u>fin I shed</u> forever."

47. **fund-a-men-tal-ly**: <u>Fundamentally</u>, can the Census Bureau (counts people) <u>fund a men tally</u>?

48. **gal-le-on** (old sailing ship): Invite that <u>gal, Leon</u>, aboard your Spanish <u>galleon</u>.

49. **gov-ern-or**: A <u>governor</u> needs to <u>govern or</u> resign.

50. **has-ten** (to hurry): The parking attendant must <u>hasten</u> since he <u>has ten</u> cars to bring up.

51. **his-tory**: <u>Hi, Story</u> Time for <u>history</u>: Today I'll read about the Presidential Election of 2000.

52. **in-fi-nite** (unending): Since our Earth can be measure <u>in finite</u> miles, it's not <u>infinite</u>.

53. **in-form-al**: Please <u>inform Al</u> that the dress for this occasion is <u>informal</u>.

54. **in-fur-i-ate**: The cruel queen asked, "Does it <u>infuriate</u> animal lovers that dressed <u>in fur I ate</u> beef?"

64. **in-her-it**: When I study her, <u>in her it</u> is clear that we <u>inherit</u> features from our parents.

55. **in-tents** (plans; intentions): Our <u>intents</u> were to camp and sleep <u>in tents</u>.

56. **in-tim-i-da-ted**: <u>In Tim, I dated</u> a guy who never <u>intimidated</u> me.

57. **in-vests**: He <u>invests</u> <u>in vests</u> he likes or buys shoes instead.

58. **laugh**: The sound of her <u>laugh</u> was "<u>La – ugh</u>."

59. **le-gend**: A chief told a <u>legend</u> where a warrior's <u>leg ends</u> up being all that holds him to a cliff.

60. **le-thal** (deadly): The decision was to <u>let Hal</u> manage the <u>lethal</u> clean-up.

61. **log-ic-al**: I see <u>logic, Al</u>, in being <u>logical</u> as well as feeling. *Phonics*: <u>g</u> = <u>j</u>; <u>c</u> = <u>k</u>.

62. **man-i-fold** (many, adj.): <u>Man, I fold</u> <u>manifold</u> napkins for this restaurant.

63. **man-or** (estate): Does the <u>man or</u> his wife run the <u>manor</u>?

64. **man-u-script**: When I saw his great <u>manuscript</u>, I exclaimed, "<u>Man, U script</u> well."

65. **men-ace**: <u>Men, ace</u> this challenge before it becomes a <u>menace</u>.

66. **mer-chants**: While the <u>merchants</u> sailed, they sang <u>mer chants</u> to <u>mer</u>maids (Fr. mer: sea).

67. **met-al**: When I need a <u>metal</u> tool, I <u>met Al</u> who made it for me.

68. **me-te-or**: We can <u>mete or</u> measure a <u>meteor</u> (Gk. <u>meteor</u>os: raised in air).

69. **mis-spell**: <u>Miss Pell</u> said, "Please don't <u>misspell</u>." *mis-spell*

70. **mus-tache**: Your <u>mustache</u> <u>must ache</u> when people pull on it.

71. **nat-ur-al-ly**: <u>Nat, U rally</u> our team so <u>naturally</u> at all the games.

72. **night-in-gales**: Even at <u>night in gales</u> of wind, the <u>nightingales</u> sing.

73. **no-ta-ble**: We're <u>not able</u> to have a <u>notable</u> dinner since we have <u>no table</u>.

74. **noth-ing**: <u>Nothing</u> simply means <u>no thing</u> (Old Eng., nanthing: nothing).

75. **no-tice-a-ble**: It was <u>noticeable</u> that, inside the bottle, my soda was <u>not ice able</u> (Soft C Rule).

76. **nov-ice** (someone new and fresh): She's a <u>novice</u>, and she has <u>no vice</u>.

77. **o-mit-ted**: The umpire had to <u>omit Ted</u> from playing since he'd <u>omitted</u> bringing his <u>mitt</u>.

78. **o-nus** (responsibility; duty): The <u>onus</u> is <u>on us</u>.

79. **op-er-a-ted**: Since you <u>operated</u> all day, let's take a break and go to the <u>opera, Ted</u>.

80. **or-nate**: With all that jewelry, is Anne <u>or Nate</u> too <u>ornate</u>?

81. **page-ant** (contest; event): During the <u>pageant</u>, please read me each <u>page, ant</u>.

65. **pal-try** (ridiculously small): Don't have your <u>pal try</u> working for that <u>paltry</u> pay.

82. **pas-try** (dough for a pie, etc.): <u>Pa's try</u> at making <u>pastry</u> was successful.

83. **pause**: I hear <u>pa use</u> a <u>pause</u> now and then when he speaks.

84. **peas-ants**: Did the <u>peasants</u> eat <u>peas, ants</u>, and other food from the land?

85. **per-cent**: Today I pay 10,000 <u>percent</u> of the original worth <u>per cent</u> for Indian Head pennies.

86. **planned**: The <u>plan Ned</u> <u>planned</u> and built was an after-school center for kids.

87. **plea-sure**: I'm glad I asked for toys since my <u>plea sure</u> will bring the children <u>pleasure</u>.

88. **pre-par-ing**: As I'm <u>preparing</u>, and doing a surgery <u>prep, a ring</u> and jewelry are removed.

89. **pro-fit**: Is your <u>pro fit</u> and able to <u>profit</u> from experience?

90. **pros-e-cute** (bring legal charges): Don't try to <u>prosecute</u> a case with <u>prose cute</u> to your kids.

91. **pun-ished**: Should I be <u>punished</u> for every <u>pun I shed</u>?

92. **pup-pet**: My cat <u>puppet</u> has a little <u>pup pet</u>.

93. **rank-ings**: We even <u>ran kings</u> through our <u>rankings</u>.

94. **re-ar-range**: I want to <u>rearrange</u> my pots on the <u>rear range</u>.

95. **sa-lam-i**: <u>Sal, am I</u> like a <u>salami</u>?

96. **scathe** (damage; harm): "I must <u>scat," he</u> said, "before they <u>scathe</u> my reputation even more."

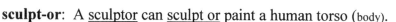

97. **sculpt-or**: A <u>sculptor</u> can <u>sculpt or</u> paint a human torso (body).

98. **sear-ing** (burning): The <u>searing</u> sun made a <u>sea ring</u> shadow around the island.

99. **seethe** (surge as if boiling): Did you <u>see the</u> volcano <u>seethe</u> with lava and erupt?

100. **soak-ing**: <u>So a king</u> walked by while you were <u>soaking</u> in your tub.

101. **soar-ing**: <u>So a ring</u> fell to Earth from the <u>soaring</u> plane.

102. **so-lace** (comfort): She was too old for an office job, <u>so lace</u>-making became her <u>solace</u>.

103. **sol-ids**: There's bacteria in our lab, <u>so lids</u> are put on samples to keep these <u>solids</u> clean.

104. **star-ring**: The <u>starring</u> actor wore a <u>star ring</u>.

105. **suc-ces-sor**: A <u>successor</u> often seeks to achieve <u>success or</u> try even harder.

106. **sum-mary**: Can you give me the <u>summary</u> <u>sum Mary</u> needs at work today?

107. **su-per-vi-sor**: My <u>supervisor</u> wears a purple <u>super visor</u>.

108. **tap-es-try** (designed wall hanging): With these <u>tapes, try</u> to mend the <u>tapestry</u>.

109. **tem-per-a-men-tal**: When you feel <u>temperamental</u>, try to <u>temper a mental</u> state with kindness.

110. **ter-mi-nate**: Since last <u>term I ate</u> too much, I decided to <u>terminate</u> midnight snacks.

111. **twin-kled**: As stars <u>twinkled</u> above, <u>Twink led</u> us safely home.

112. **u-ni-verse**: I wrote just <u>uni verse</u> about the <u>universe</u>: <u>uni</u> (one) + verse (Latin Clue-in-a-Row).

113. **van-ished**: Even my <u>van I shed</u> when I <u>vanished</u>.

114. **with-draw-al**: The <u>withdrawal</u> said: "Please <u>withdraw Al</u> from the golf tournament."

Very Challenging Clues-in-a-Row

115. **cog-i-tate** (think): I did <u>cogitate</u> and write my ideas; but in woodshop, a <u>cog, it ate</u> my paper.

116. **men-da-ci-ty** (lying): Politicians with <u>mendacity</u> can't <u>mend a city</u> and its ways.

117. **mend-i-cant** (needy person): <u>Mend I can't</u>, but I'll buy new clothes for a <u>mendicant</u>.

118. **per-fuse** (spread with light, color, etc.): It costs a lot <u>per fuse</u> to <u>perfuse</u> our entire house with light.

119. **pes-ti-lent** (deadly; annoying): The <u>pest I lent</u> the scientist can cause <u>pestilent</u> illness.

120. **o-pal-es-cent** (like opals) Although orchid have <u>opalescent</u> beauty, oft we have noted: <u>O pale scent</u>.

121. **pan-ache** (grand style; flair): With <u>panache,</u> I showed my <u>pan ache</u> from where a <u>pan</u> hit my head.

122. **pa-ren-the-sized**: He <u>parenthesized</u> the information about the <u>parent he sized</u> up.

123. **souse** (soak in a pickling solution): <u>So use</u> brine and dill to <u>souse</u> those pickles.

124. **win-now** (separate): You'll <u>win now</u> when you compete to <u>winnow</u> the wheat from the chaff

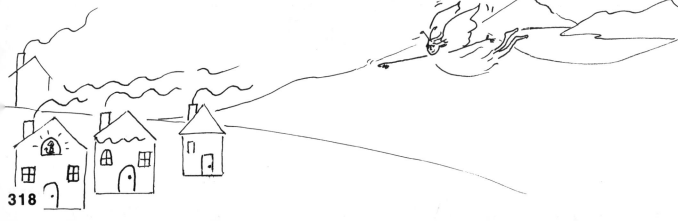

POWER Spelling Almost-Clues-in-a Row

Once you start looking, you can find lots of words you can put together in unique ways to create Almost-Clues-in-a-Row, and they sure help you remember words. Use the ones you like best.

1. **ac-quit-tal** (freed of charges): <u>A C quit</u> talking about the <u>acquittal</u>: A + C + quit + tal.
2. **ac-tu-al-ly**: <u>Act, U all</u>, and <u>actually</u> put on a play: act + U + all + y.
3. **ad-a-mant** (unyielding): He's <u>adamant</u> that there's <u>a dam ants</u> built that stops a river.
4. **ad-dress**: I put an <u>ad (for a) dress</u> in my <u>address</u> book: ad + dress.
5. **al-le-vi-ate**: <u>Al (and) Levi ate</u> papayas to <u>alleviate</u> all indigestion: Al + Levi + ate.
6. **al-li-ga-tor**: <u>Alli (the) gator</u> is my <u>alligator</u> friend: alli + gator.
7. **al-pha-bet**: <u>Alpha (and) Beta</u> are the first 2 letters of the Greek <u>alphabet</u>: Alpha +Bet~~a~~.
8. **am-a-teur**: Will <u>a mate urge</u> you to see a great <u>amateur</u> performance? a + mate + ur~~ge~~.
9. **a-poth-e-cary**: The <u>apothecary</u> makes medicine in <u>a pot he carries</u>: a + pot + he + car~~ries~~ + y.
10. **art-i-facts** (ancient pottery, etc.): <u>Art, I (learned) facts</u> about <u>artifacts</u> today: art + I + facts.
11. **as-sas-sin**: One could consider an <u>assassin</u> a double <u>ass in</u> evil: ass + ass + in.
12. **at-ten-dants**: <u>At (work I) tend (to) ants</u> who are <u>attendants</u> to the queen: at + tend + ants.
13. **ben-e-fits**: Mr. <u>Ben E. Fits</u> enjoys running <u>benefits</u>: Ben + E + Fits.
14. **bev-er-age**: They claimed you will <u>(n)ever age</u> if you drink their <u>beverage</u>: b + ~~n~~ever + age.
15. **break-fast**: When you have <u>breakfast</u>, you <u>break (your) fast</u> through the night: break + fast.
16. **can-did** (direct): I <u>can (and) did</u> what was <u>candid</u>: can + did.
17. **can-yon**: As I look at the view, I <u>can yon(der)</u> see a <u>canyon</u>: can + yon~~der~~.
18. **cas-tle**: The <u>castle cast le</u>ngths of reflection across the lake: cast + le~~ngths~~.
19. **ca-te-gor-y**: My black <u>cat (and) Egor</u> fit in the superstition <u>category</u>: cat + Egor + y.
20. **cat-er-pil-lar**: I watched a <u>caterpillar</u> <u>later</u>, crawling up a <u>pillar</u>: c + ~~l~~ater + pillar.
21. **cham-pagnes**: The <u>champ</u> opened the <u>champagnes</u> <u>Agnes</u> brought: champ + Agnes.
22. **chan-nel**: <u>Chan (and) Nel</u> swam the English <u>Channel</u>: Chan + Nel.
23. **chil-dren**: Each <u>child</u> <u>ren</u>ted a bike for <u>children</u>: child + ren(ted).
24. **cin-na-mon**: At my <u>inn, a Mon.</u> morning treat is fresh <u>cinnamon</u> rolls: c + inn + a + Mon.
25. **clas-si-cal**: <u>Classical</u> music comes in any <u>class I call</u> for, concerning the occasion: class + I + cal~~l~~.
26. **com-mit-tees**: I can <u>commit (to bringing) tees</u> for the golf <u>committees</u>: commit + tees.
27. **con-cave** (curved inward) You can <u>con (a) cave</u> to be <u>concave</u>?
28. **con-duc-tors**: <u>Conductors</u> <u>conduct</u> orchestras: conduct + or(chestras).
29. **cour-age**: It takes <u>courage</u> to live in <u>our age</u>: c + our + age.
30. **cy-clone**: The <u>cyclone</u> <u>cycl(ed) one</u> time through the air: cycl(ed) + one.

31. **de-ci-sion**: A play I made a <u>decision</u> to see in <u>Dec. is (what) I (put) on</u> my calendar: <u>Dec + is + I + on</u>.

32. **dis-con-tent**: I am feeling some <u>discontent</u> because my <u>disc (is) on (our) tent</u>: <u>disc + on + tent</u>.

33. **dog-mat-ic**: I am not <u>dogmatic</u> about the <u>dog mat I c</u>an buy: <u>dog + mat + I + c</u>.

34. **dol-lar**: For just a <u>dollar</u>, a <u>doll</u> artist painted beautiful eyes on my <u>doll</u>: <u>doll + ar</u>(tist).

35. **dor-mi-to-ry**: I can live in a <u>dorm: it or</u> an apartment near the <u>dormitory</u>: <u>dorm + it + or + y</u>.

36. **ei-ther**: It's <u>either me, it, her</u>, or the dog (or cat) who did it: ~~me~~ + <u>it + her</u>.

37. **es-car-got** (snail): The <u>escargot</u> and the <u>ES Car got</u> into a race: <u>ES + Car + got</u>.

38. **ex-or-bi-tant**: <u>Ex</u>(it from our) <u>orbit, ant</u>, your appetite is <u>exorbitant</u>: <u>ex~~it~~ + orbit + ant</u>.

39. **feath-er**: For the eagle, it was a true <u>feat (for) her</u> to keep each <u>feather</u>: <u>feat + her</u>.

40. **for-tu-nate**: You're <u>fortunate</u> that the <u>fort U (and) Nate</u> built survived the storm: <u>fort + U + Nate</u>.

41. **friend**: On <u>Fri., (the) end</u> of the school week, I see my <u>friend</u>: <u>Fri. + end</u>.

42. **fun-gus**: That <u>fungus</u> was <u>fun (for) gus</u> to look at: <u>fun + Gus</u>.

43. **gal-lant**: <u>G (gee), all ant</u>s in my garden are <u>gallant</u>: <u>G + all + ant~~s~~</u>.

44. **gel-a-tin**: Can <u>gelatin gel at (a cold temperature) in</u> a room: <u>gel + at + in</u>?

45. **germ-i-nate** (start growing): That <u>germ I (gave) Nate</u> began to <u>germinate</u>: <u>germ + I + Nate</u>.

46. **gov-ern-ment**: <u>Government</u> exists to <u>govern men</u>(t): <u>govern + men~~t~~</u>.

47. **guard**: <u>G, U ar</u>e a good <u>guard</u>: <u>G + U + ar~~e~~ + d</u>.

48. **gui-dance**: <u>G, U (and) I dance</u> well without any <u>guidance</u>: <u>G + U + I + dance</u>.

49. **gui-tar**: <u>G, U (and) I (got) tar</u> on my <u>guitar</u>: <u>G-U-I + tar</u>.

50. **heart**: <u>He (creates) art</u> when he draw the amazing <u>heart</u>: <u>he + art</u>.

51. **hes-i-tant**: I was <u>hesitant</u> that <u>he sit (with an) ant</u> at our picnic: <u>he + sit + ant</u>.

52. **i-den-ti-cal**: It's <u>identical</u> to the <u>dent I (got in) Cal</u>. (California): <u>i + dent + I + Cal</u>.

53. **im-me-di-ate-ly**: An <u>M (and) M Ed (and) I ate</u> was gone <u>immediately</u>: <u>i + M + M + Ed + I + ate + ly</u>.

54. **in-al-ien-a-ble** (unalterable): <u>In alien (countries, am I) able</u> to have <u>inalienable</u> rights: <u>in + alien + able</u>

55. **in-cu-bate**: When I came <u>in (the) cub ate</u> a lot, but we still had to <u>incubate</u> her : <u>in + cub + ate</u>.

56. **in-hib-its**: If dating <u>inhibits</u> you, know: <u>in (saying) hi, bits</u> of friendship are formed: <u>in + hi + bits</u>.

57. **in-no-cent**: <u>In no (way, not for a) cent</u>, would I harm an <u>innocent</u> person: <u>in + no + cent</u>.

58. **in-sure**: I can <u>insure</u> you that you're <u>in (for) sure</u>: <u>in + sure = insure</u>.

59. **ir-i-des-cent** (w/rainbow colors): This <u>iridescent</u> flower is so sweet, <u>I ride (its) scent</u>: <u>I + ride + scent</u>.

60. **i-so-late**: <u>I (was) so late</u> getting sick, they had to <u>isolate</u> me from the well patients: <u>i + so + late</u>.

61. **ju-di-cial**: In the <u>Judicial</u> Department, <u>Judi (was with the) CIA</u>: <u>Judi + CIA + l</u>.

62. **ken-nel**: <u>Ken (and) Nel</u> run a <u>kennel</u>: <u>Ken + Nel</u>.

63. **know-ledge**: I still <u>know (the) ledge</u> where I sat and read to gain <u>knowledge</u>: know + ledge.

64. **lei-sure**: She wore a <u>lei (for) sure</u> during her <u>leisure</u> time in Hawaii: lei + sure.

65. **lev-eled**: Since I wanted the driveway <u>level (for) Ed</u>, we <u>leveled</u> it: level + Ed.

66. **lieu-ten-ant**: The <u>lieutenant</u> commanded, " <u>Lie (down) U ten ants</u>!" lie + ù + ten + ants.

67. **ma-chines**: <u>Mac Hines</u> repairs <u>machines</u>.

68. **man-i-kin** (model): <u>Man, I ('ll show my) kin</u> the <u>manikin</u> that looks like Uncle Bob: man + i + kin.

69. **man-u-al** (by hand): <u>Man, U (and) Al</u> did a lot of <u>manual</u> work: Man + U + Al.

70. **main-te-nance**: He took care of the <u>maintenance</u> for the <u>main</u> tenants: main + tenants + ce.

71. **ma-rooned**: When I was <u>marooned</u> on an island, <u>Ma, Roo, (and) Ned</u> rescued me: Ma + Roo + Ned.

72. **med-i-cine**: A <u>medic in (th)e</u> service provides <u>medicine</u>: medic + in + the.

73. **mis-er-a-ble**: A <u>miser (is) able</u> to be <u>miserable</u> because he hordes things: miser + able.

74. **mo-men-tous**: The <u>momentous</u> storm felt like an <u>omen to us</u>: m + omen + to + us.

75. **mys-ter-y**: Where <u>my stereo</u> went is still a <u>mystery</u>: my + stereo + y.

76. **nic-kel**: The <u>elf</u> gave <u>Nick (an) elf</u> <u>nickel</u>: Nick + elf = nickel.

77. **oc-ca-sion** (*Phonics*: c = k; s = zh): <u>O, C (see) Casi on</u> this <u>occasion</u>: O + C + Casi + on.

78. **o-pened**: I <u>opened</u> the door with a <u>pen (for) Ed</u>: o + pen + Ed.

79. **or-ches-tra** (*Phonics*: ch = k.): An <u>orchestra</u> is like a group <u>or chest</u> of instruments: or + chest + ra.

80. **or-di-na-ry**: A gold coin <u>or dinar</u> is not <u>ordinary</u>: or + dinar + y (dinar: Persian coin).

81. **or-i-gin**: What's the <u>origin</u> of that <u>o(ld) rig in</u> the sea: old + rig + in? (rig: mast and sails of ship).

82. **pal-a-ces**: While gambling at Reno <u>Palaces</u>, I showed my <u>pal (the) aces</u> I was dealt: pal + aces.

83. **pan-to-mime**: For our cooking <u>pantomime</u>, I gave the role of the <u>pan to (a) mime</u>: pan + to + mime.

84. **pe-tal**: My <u>pet always</u> eats a <u>petal</u> or two: pet + al.

85. **phe-no-me-non** (feat): Our pitcher's <u>phenomenon</u> was <u>he (let) no men on</u> base: p + he + no + men + on.

86. **phil-har-mon-ic**: Since <u>Phil (loved) harmonic</u> sound, he had a <u>philharmonic</u> orchestra: phil + harmonic.

87. **pig-eon**: My <u>pigeon</u> has loved my <u>pig (for an) eon</u> (eon: long period of time): pig + eon.

88. **pitch-er** (baseball player): Can a <u>pitcher</u> pitch the <u>pit (of a) cherry</u>: pit + cherry.

89. **ques-tion**: What <u>quest I (am) on</u> is an important <u>question</u>: quest + I + on.

90. **rap-port** (understanding): To build <u>rapport</u> with dock hands, my boss liked to <u>rap (at the) port</u>: rap + port.

91. **re-veled** (celebrated): We <u>reveled</u> when <u>Eve led</u> us out of the cave: r + Eve + led.

92. **scared**: I felt <u>scared</u> when the <u>car Ed</u> drove hit mine: s + car + Ed.

93. **scarred**: When I was <u>scarred</u>, the <u>scar (turned) red</u>: scar + red.

94. **sea-son**: During the summer <u>season</u>, to the <u>sea (my) son</u> goes: sea + son.

95. **sent-i-nel** (guard): The <u>sentinel</u> and <u>I</u> <u>sent Nel</u> a message: sent + I + Nel.

96. **ser-geants**: The <u>sergeants</u> wore <u>serge</u> (p)ants: serge + ~~p~~ants (serge: wool fabric).

97. **sev-er-al**: Since I had <u>several</u> projects due, I had to <u>sever all</u> extra work: sever + al~~l~~.

98. **sher-bet**: <u>Her bet</u> was that they would have raspberry <u>sherbet</u> for dessert: s + her + bet.

99. **shrink-age**: Can a person really have <u>shrinkage</u> and <u>shrink</u> (with) <u>age</u>: shrink + age?

100. **sin-cere-ly**: <u>Since rely</u>(ing) on you is important to me, I <u>sincerely</u> need you: since + rely.

101. **so-lar**: I was exploring planets, <u>so Larry</u> came to do <u>solar</u> research: so Lar~~ry~~.

102. **soph-ists** (ancient Gk. teachers; ph = f): <u>So fists</u> (f = ph) aren't what <u>sophists</u> use to solve problems?

103. **splen-dor**: Can you <u>lend or</u> borrow <u>splendor</u>: sp + lend + or?

104. **su-per-in-ten-dents**: The <u>superintendents</u> saw <u>super dents in ten</u> buses: super + in + ten + dents.

105. **tor-na-do**: The <u>tornado</u> had <u>torn a door</u> off the shed: torn + a + do~~or~~.

106. **tra-veled**: We <u>traveled</u> where the <u>Ave. led</u>: tr + ave. + led.

107. **trag-I-cal-ly**: Although it was <u>tragic</u> (my) <u>ally</u> was there when I was <u>tragically</u> hurt: tragic + ally.

108. **us-age**: Tell <u>us</u> (the) <u>age</u> by which students should know word <u>usage</u>: us + age.

109. **ush-er**: The <u>usher</u> took <u>us</u> (with) <u>her</u> and led us to our seats: us + her.

110. **u-su-al-ly** (4 syllables; <u>S</u> = <u>zh</u>): Come with <u>us, U</u> (you) <u>all</u>, as you <u>usually</u> do: us + U + all + y.

111. **val-u-able**: <u>Val</u>, (are) <u>U able</u> to protect this <u>valuable</u> gem? Val + U + able.

112. **vic-tim**: <u>Vic</u> (and) <u>Tim</u> had each been a <u>victim</u> in the crash: Vic + Tim.

113. **voy-age**: The b<u>oy</u> was the right <u>age</u> for the <u>voyage</u>: v + ~~b~~oy + age.

114. **whim-si-cal**: <u>Whims I call</u> <u>whimsical</u> are swinging and running barefoot: whims I cal~~l~~.

POWER *Spelling Clues for Homophones*

Barefoot, I feel the very <u>soul</u>
of what I stand upon. In shoes,
I simply feel my <u>soles</u>.

Use *Clues* to learn and remember the difference between these Homophones. This will give you a lot of spelling *POWER* and put you ahead of the computer, since *Spell Check* can't check Homophones.

1. **a lot** (n., large amount): There are <u>a lot</u> of <u>hot</u> <u>spots</u> I've <u>got</u> to see. *Rule*: <u>A lot</u> is always 2 words.
   allot (v., measure out): We can <u>allot</u> one <u>ballot</u> per person.

2. **ad** (n., advertisement): That <u>ad</u> is <u>bad</u>. <u>Ad</u> is simply short for <u>ad</u>vertisement.
   add (v., add together): <u>Add</u> another <u>d</u> to <u>ad</u> and you have <u>add</u>.

3. **aid** (n., assistance): We <u>paid</u> for a first-<u>aid</u> course.
   aide (n., a helper): The school <u>aide</u> is on your <u>side</u>. *Anagrams*: aides – ideas, aside.

4. **air** (n., oxygen): The <u>air</u> was <u>fair</u> today. *Same Pattern*: fair, lair, pair, stairs…
   <u>**heir**</u> (n., one who inherits): <u>He</u> is <u>their</u> <u>heir</u> to the throne. *Same Pattern*: heir, their.
   error (n., mistake): He has a <u>terror</u> of making an <u>error</u>.

5. **aisle** (n., path): <u>Aisle</u> has <u>a(n) isle</u> in it: <u>a + isle = aisle</u>.
   I'll (contraction: I will). <u>I'll</u> still come. *Same Pattern*: you'll, he'll, she'll, we'll…
   isle (n., island): There <u>is</u> <u>land</u> on an <u>isle</u>: <u>is + le = isle</u>.

6. **all to-get-her** (*All of us* can replace *all together*): We went <u>to get her</u> all <u>together</u> (all of us).
   al-to-get-her (adv., *Entirely* can replace *altogether*): I was <u>altogether</u> (entirely) too late <u>to get her</u>.
   Compound Word Rule Exception (just one l): al~~l~~ + together = altogether.

7. **all read-y** (*All of us* can replace *all ready*): We were <u>all</u> (all of us) <u>ready</u> to go.
   al-read-y (adv., *Now* can replace *already*): I was <u>already</u> (now) home by noon. When you add <u>all</u> to a word, an <u>l</u> is dropped: al~~l~~ + ready. *Same Pattern*: almost, always.

8. **al-lowed** (v., permitted): To be <u>allowed</u> into the show, we <u>all owed</u> ticket money: all + owed.
   a-loud (adj., can be heard): An angel stood on <u>a (c)loud</u> and spoke <u>aloud</u>: <u>a + ~~c~~loud</u>.

9. **al-tar** (n., in a church): *Visual Clue*: The <u>altar</u> of many churches rises like an <u>A</u>.
   al-ter (v., to change): I wanted to <u>alter</u> the length of my <u>halter</u>.

10. **ant** (n., insect): Can an <u>ant</u> move a rubber tree <u>plant</u>? *Same Pattern*: can't, grant, pant.
    aunt (n., relative): Our <u>aunt</u> likes <u>haunted</u> houses. *Same Pattern*: dauntless (brave), gaunt (thin).

11. **arc** (n., part of a circle): Watch that <u>star circle</u> in an <u>arc</u>.
    ark (n., boat): Can you <u>park</u> an <u>ark</u> in the <u>dark</u>?

12. **as-sis-tance** (n., help): I need assis<u>tance</u> with my <u>dance</u>: assist + <u>~~d~~ance</u> = assistance.
    as-sis-tants (n., ones who help): I <u>assist ant</u> <u>assistants</u> who <u>assist</u> the queen: <u>assist + ants</u>.

13. **ate** (v., did eat): I <u>ate</u> a d<u>ate</u>. *Anagram*: <u>ate</u> = eat and tea. *Same Pattern*: fate, gate, late…
    eight (adj., number 8): The w<u>eight</u> was <u>eight</u> pounds. *Same Pattern*: freight, weight.

14. **at-ten-dance** (n., presence): After <u>attendance</u> was taken, the disc jockey announced, <u>At ten, dance!</u>
    at-ten-dants (n., escorts): I watch and <u>attend (to) ants</u> who are <u>attendants</u> to the queen: attend + an

15. **bard** (n., traveling poet) The work of a <u>bard</u> was often h<u>ard</u>. *Phonics*: <u>bar + d = bard</u>.
    barred (v., adj., having bars): We <u>barred</u> the old, <u>tarred</u> doors. *Rule*: <u>2 r's</u> keep <u>a</u> short.

16. **bare** (adj., naked): Take c<u>are</u> not to be b<u>are</u>, or someone may st<u>are</u>. *Same Pattern*: dare, fare…
    bear (n., animal; v., carry): The <u>bear</u> listened with his <u>ears</u>. *Same Pattern*: bear, pear, tear (rip).

17. **beat** (v., whip): We <u>beat</u> the cr<u>eam</u> to <u>eat</u> on shortcake.
    beet (n., vegetable): Sugar <u>beets</u> are sw<u>eet</u>.

18. **be** (v., exist): "To <u>be</u> or not to <u>be</u>?" That is the question h<u>e</u> (Hamlet) asked.
    bee (n., insect): The <u>bee</u> hive is in that tr<u>ee</u>.

19. **berry** (n., fruit): A <u>berry</u> and a ch<u>erry</u> are both fruits. *SPP*: ber-ry.
    bury (v., put in ground): The j<u>ury</u> did not <u>bury</u> the problem. *SPP*: bu-ry.

20. **berth** (n., bunk): A <u>berth</u> is a bed.
    birth (n., act of being born): I felt m<u>irth</u> (joy) at the <u>birth</u> of my son.

21. **blew** (v., past of blow) I <u>blew</u> <u>dew</u> off a f<u>ew</u> blades of grass. *Two Vowels Rule*: <u>W</u> makes <u>e</u> long.
    blue (adj., color): There's a tr<u>ue</u> <u>blue</u> h<u>ue</u> to this paint. *Two Vowels Rule*: <u>E</u> makes <u>u</u> long.

22. **board** (n., lumber): We made an <u>oar</u> out of the <u>board</u>.
    bored (n., v., adj., not interested): We got <u>bored</u> looking for m<u>ore</u> <u>ore</u> in the creek.

23. **boar** (n., wild hog): A <u>boar</u> bit through my <u>oar</u>. *Same Pattern*: roar, soar.
    bore (n., v., drill; dull person): I had to <u>bore</u> a hole in the <u>ore</u>. *Same Pattern*: core, lore, sore.

24. **bold-er** (adj., braver): The c<u>older</u> it got, the <u>bolder</u> he became.
    boul-der (n., large stone): A <u>boulder</u> is a m<u>ound</u> of stone.

25. **bough** (n., bough of a tree): The bark on the <u>bough</u> was too <u>rough</u> for climbing.
    bow (n., curtsy): She made a l<u>ow</u> <u>bow</u> to the audience.
    bow (n., front of a ship): Go n<u>ow</u> and stand on the b<u>ow</u>. (Antonym of bow = stern: back of a ship.)

26. **boy** (n., young male): The <u>boy</u> felt j<u>oy</u> as he played with a t<u>oy</u>.
    buoy (n., float): We need to <u>buy</u> a <u>buoy</u>. *SPP*: bu-<u>oy</u>.

27. **brake** (n., pedal to stop; v., stop): I put on my br<u>ake</u> by the l<u>ake</u>. *Rule*: Silent <u>e</u> makes the <u>a</u> long
    break (v., smash; split): The expression *Break bread together* means *to share a meal*.

28. **bread** (n., food): I <u>read</u> about making <u>bread</u>. *Same Pattern*: dead, head, lead, read, tread.
    bred (v., brought up; raised): F<u>red</u> was well-<u>bred</u>. *Same Pattern*: bed, fed, led, red, wed.

29. **brews** (n., drinks; v., steeps): The cr<u>ews</u> drank the <u>brews</u>.
    bruise (n., injury): We got a <u>bruise</u> from that <u>brui(n), see</u>: bru<s>in</s> + <u>see</u> (L. bruin: bear).

30. **bri-dal** (adj., for brides): A bridal shower is all for the bride: bride + all. *Silent E Rule.*
    bri-dle (n., horse headgear): Let me put the bridle on my horse. In bridling, you hear dl in bridle.

31. **buy** (v., purchase): I want to buy the guy I love a gift.
    by: (adv., prep near): We walked by my park. (Prepositions are usually short: at, by, in, of, to).
    bye (exclam., short for good-bye): I looked in his eyes to say, "Bye." *SPP:* by-e.

32. **cap-i-tal** (n., city): Tallahasee is the capital of Florida.
    cap-i-tal (n., letters): Capital letters are taller than lowercase letters.
    Cap-i-tol (n., building): Most Capitols (buildings) have a dome on top.

33. **cede** (v., grant; to yield territory): He ceded the land where the cedar trees grew.
    seed (n., part of a plant): We need to plant the seed soon.

34. **cent** (n., penny): A cent is cash (L. cent: hundredth of a dollar).
    scent (n., fragrance; smell): The scent ascended in the room (L., scent: sentir-to smell). *SPP:* s-cent.
    sent (v., did send): I sent the sentimental gift to my mom (Old Eng., sent: sendan-journey).

35. **cer-e-al** (n., rain): I eat real cereal like oats. (L., Roman Goddess of cereal was Ceres.) *SPP:* ce-re-al.
    ser-i-al (n., part of a series): She wrote a serious serial to her first book (L. series: to connect).

36. **cheap** (adj., inexpensive): That heap of clothes is really cheap.
    cheep (n., bird call): The bird made a cheep and a peep.

37. **chew** (v., use teeth): With just a few teeth, that old dog could chew any bone.
    choose (v., select): I choose that goose.

38. **chil-i** (n., pepper; Mexican dish): *Visual:* See the ili as 2 people eating a chili.
    chil-ly (adj., cold): When it's chilly out, you can get ill.

39. **chord** (n., three or notes that make same sound): The chorus sang chords. *SPP:* c-hord.
    cord (n., measure of wood; strong string; spinal cord): Please order a cord of wood tied with a cord.

40. **clause** (n., part of a sentence): I pause before I use a clause: cla + use.
    claws (n., nails on animals): Many animals have claws on their paws.

41. **close** (v., shut): Close off that hose. *Phonics:* S = z sound. *Rule:* Silent e makes the o long.
    clothes (n., garments): Clothes are made of cloth. *Phonics:* S = z sound.

42. **coarse** (adj., rough): The oar was made of coarse wood. *SPP:* co-ar-se.
    course (n., class, way; v., flows): Our course is about how courts work. *SPP:* co-ur-se.

43. **com-ple-ment** (n., completes something): A complement to a collection helps complete it.
    com-pli-ment (n., praise): I like to receive compliments on my lime pie.

44. **cores** (n., centers of fruit): As they ate more apples, they made more cores.
    corps (n., body under a leader): The corporal was head of the corps (L. corpus: body). *SPP:* cor-ps.

45. **coun-cil** (n., governing group): Most cities have a City Council. *SPP:* coun-cil.
    coun-sel (n., advice; v., advise): We selected the kind of counsel we can count on. *SPP:* coun-sel.

46. **creak** (n., creaking sound): The h<u>ea</u>vy t<u>ea</u>k door made a <u>creak</u>.
    creek (n., stream): I took my rod and <u>reel</u> to the <u>creek</u>, but, <u>eek</u>, I fell in the <u>creek</u>.

47. **crewel** (n., stitching): Her <u>crewel</u> work looked like a <u>jewel</u>.
    cruel (adj., mean): You can't be <u>true</u> to a heart that's <u>cruel</u>? *SPP*: cru-el. *Same Pattern*: duel, fuel.

48. **cur-rant** (n., small red berry) *Clue*: An <u>ant</u> ate a <u>currant</u>. *Rule*: <u>2 r's</u> keep <u>u</u> short.
    cur-rent (adj., recent; n., movement; electrical charge): My <u>current rent</u> is due. *Rule*: 2r's keep <u>u</u> short.

49. **cym-bals** (n., instruments): *Clue*: Keep <u>cymbals</u> <u>bal</u>anced as you <u>bang</u> them (L. cymbalums: hollow objects).
    sym-bols (n., signs): *Clues*: <u>Symbols</u> are often very <u>old</u>. Also, great <u>symbols</u> <u>bolster</u> (build-up) a company's image (L., G., symbolums: signs).

50. **dear** (n., loved one; treasured; greeting): She was n<u>ear</u> and d<u>ear</u> to him.
    deer (n., animal): The <u>deer</u> nibbled on a <u>reed</u>. *Reversal*: deer – reed.

51. **de-sert** (n., dry, sandy region): A desert can feel alone, like <u>one lone s</u>.
    de-sert (v., to abandon, leave alone): The <u>s</u> in <u>desert</u> is <u>one s all alone</u> and abandoned.
    des-sert (n., treat after meal): A dessert is <u>s</u>omething <u>s</u>weet like <u>s</u>trawberry <u>s</u>hortcake.

52. **dew** (n., moisture): We watched rainbows in the n<u>ew</u> <u>dew</u>.
    do (v., shall; to act): You <u>do</u> <u>so</u> well at work.
    due (adj., needed now): Sue is <u>due</u> any minute.

53. **die** (v., not live): Don't <u>die</u> from that <u>diet</u>.
    dye (n., color): I like <u>yellow</u> <u>dye</u>.
    dye-ing (n., coloring-dye): I am <u>dyeing</u> my hat <u>yellow</u>. *Phonics*: Add <u>e</u> to <u>dying</u> for <u>dyeing</u>.
    dy-ing (v., not living): He was <u>dying</u> where he was <u>lying</u>. *Rule Exception*: d~~ie~~ + y + ing = <u>dying</u>.

54. **do** (n., musical note): <u>Do</u>, re, me, fa, s<u>o</u>…
    doe (n., female deer): <u>Does</u> that <u>doe</u> have a fawn? (Does and does-female deer-have same spelling.)
    dough (n., bread mixture): That d<u>ough</u> is t<u>ough</u>. *Phonics*: Ough = long o.

55. **du-al** (adj., two): In d<u>ua</u>lity, you can hear <u>ua</u> in <u>dual</u>. *Reversal*: <u>Laud</u> spelled backwards is <u>dual</u>.
    du-el (n., formal combat; sword fight): They were <u>due</u> for a <u>duel</u> at noon (Lat. duellum: war).

56. **eave** (n., edge of a roof): Don't let your <u>eaves</u> get full of <u>leaves</u>.
    eve (n., evening): <u>Eve</u> is short for <u>evening</u>.

57. **fair** (adj., honest; exhibition): The <u>air</u> was <u>fair</u> at the <u>fair</u>.
    fare (n., cost for transportation): Take c<u>are</u>, and don't lose your <u>fare</u>!

58. **feat** (n., festive achievement): Is a gr<u>eat</u> <u>feat</u> is <u>eat</u>ing 100 pizzas?
    feet (n., plural of foot): My <u>feet</u> m<u>eet</u> the ground with each step (Old Eng. fot).

59. **fir** (n., tree): Our <u>first</u> <u>fir</u> tree has a star on top.
    fur (n., animal covering): Don't h<u>ur</u>t <u>furry</u> animals for <u>fur</u>.

60. **flea** (n., insect): <u>Ea</u>ch <u>flea</u> hid on the dog. *Same Pattern*: pea, sea, tea…
    flee (v., leave in haste): <u>Flee</u> from the <u>bees</u>. *Same Pattern*: fee, knee, see, tee, whee.

61. **flew** (v., did fly): As the wind b<u>l</u>ew, the bird <u>flew</u>. The <u>w</u> in <u>flew</u> looks like a <u>w</u>ing.
flu (n., illness): Drink <u>fl</u>uids when you have the <u>flu</u>.
flue (n., part of a chimney): The <u>flue</u> is <u>du</u>e to be cleaned.

62. **flour** (n., grain): We use <u>our</u> <u>flour</u> for making bread. *Same Pattern*: dour (gloomy), hour, our.
flow-er (n., bloom): April sh<u>owers</u> bring May <u>flowers</u>.

63. **for** (prep., to go to; pro): I'm either <u>for</u> this <u>or</u> <u>for</u> that.
fore (adj., at or toward the front): We were at the <u>fore</u>front of the race, be<u>fore</u> the other runners.
four (adj., number): <u>Four</u> is <u>our</u> favorite number.

64. **fore-word** (n., word before book; preface): You often have a <u>foreword</u> be<u>fore</u> the <u>word</u>s of a book.
for-ward (adv., frontward direction): Can I go <u>forward</u> by being <u>for</u> <u>war</u>? (L. <u>for</u>: ahead + <u>ward</u>: direction).

65. **forth**: (adv., to set off): We set <u>forth</u> <u>for</u> the adventure of a lifetime.
fourth (adj., 4th): When we were <u>four</u>, <u>our</u> friends came to <u>our</u> <u>fourth</u> birthday party.

66. **foul** (adj., bad): A <u>foul</u> attitude can cause your s<u>oul</u> pain.
fowl (n., bird): An <u>owl</u> is a member of the <u>fowl</u> family.

67. **gait** (n., walk of a horse, person...): The horse's <u>gait</u> was strong and str<u>aight</u>.
gate (n., door-like enclosure): My l<u>ate</u> d<u>ate</u> walked through the <u>gate</u>.

68. **gam-ble** (v., to take a chance): In gam<u>bl</u>ing, you hear the <u>bl</u> in <u>gamble</u>.
gam-bol (v., to frolic; play): We've like to <u>gambol</u> in the <u>ol</u>d mill stream.

69. **gilt** (v., put gold on): Can a Scotsman <u>gilt</u> his kilt with gold braid?
guilt (n., feeling from doing wrong): <u>Guilt</u> is b<u>uilt</u> by doing wrong.

70. **gnu**: (n., African antelope): The <u>gn</u>at and <u>gn</u>ome rode on the <u>gnu</u>. *SPP*: g-nu.
knew (v., did know): I <u>knew</u> you would <u>know</u>. *SPP*: k-new. *Same Pattern*: k<u>nack</u>, k<u>new</u>, k<u>now</u>.
new (adj., not used): I found rainbows in the <u>new</u> morning d<u>ew</u>. *Same Pattern*: dew, few, mew.

71. **go-ril-la** (n., ape): When our <u>gorilla</u> runs, we shout, "Go, Rilla!"
guer-ril-la (n., Sp. soldier for warfare): <u>Guerrilla</u>s can't <u>err</u> or be <u>ill</u>-prepared. *SPP*: gu-er-ril-la.

72. **grate** (v., grind): I want to <u>grate</u> some d<u>ates</u> to make d<u>ate</u> bars.
great (adj., large): They performed a <u>great</u> f<u>eat</u> (Old Eng.-great).

73. **groan** (n., moan): A <u>groan</u> is like a m<u>oan</u>. *Same Pattern*: groan, loan, moan
grown (v., matured): My bird has <u>grown</u> and fl<u>own</u> away. *Same Pattern*: blown, known, shown.

74. **guessed** (v., figured out; Scan.): If I had not <u>guessed</u>, would he have conf<u>essed</u>? *SPP*: gu-es-sed.
guest (n., company; Scan.): <u>G</u>unther is our b<u>est</u> <u>guest</u>. *SPP*: gu-est.

75. **hail** (n., balls of raining ice): We caught some <u>hail</u> in a p<u>ail</u>.
hale (adj., healthy): When you're <u>hale</u>, you're not sick and p<u>ale</u>.

76. **hair** (n., growth on head): <u>Air</u> is blowing through my h<u>air</u>. *Same Pattern*: fair, lair, pair.
hare (n., rabbit): I c<u>are</u> for my h<u>are</u>. *Same Pattern*: bare, dare, fare, mare, rare, share.

77. **hall** (n., passage way): We rolled a ball down the hall.
    haul (v., carry): Paul will haul the wood.

78. **halve** (v., cut in half): Hal and Vern shared halves. *SPP*: hal-ve.
    have (v., own): I gave you all I have. *SPP*: ha-ve.

79. **hang-ar** (n., garage for plane): Hangar with a at the end is an airplane hangar.
    hang-er (n., holder for clothes): Hanger with e at the end is a clothes hanger.

80. **hart** (n., red male deer): Don't harm the hart.
    heart (n., organ): I can hear my heart pulse with the Earth. *Anagram*: heart = Earth.

81. **hay** (n., dried grass): We lay in the hay.
    hey (exclamation to get attention): Hey, I need my key.

82. **he'll** (contraction: He will.): He'll means he will.
    heal (v., make well): He wanted to heal his heart. *Same Pattern*: deal, meal, seal, teal.
    heel (n., bottom of shoe): I could feel my heel wearing thin. *Same Pattern*: kneel, peel, reel.

83. **hear** (v., to listen): You hear with your ear.
    here (adv., this place): We go here, there, and everywhere. (All end with ere.)

84. **heard** (v., past of hear): I heard them with my ear: hear + d = heard. *SPP*: he-ard.
    herd (n., group of animals): Her deer was one of the herd.

85. **him** (pron., male): Name him Jim or name him Tim.
    hymn (n., church song): Hymns are always found in a hymnal.

86. **hoarse** (adj., husky): His hoarse voice sounded coarse.
    horse (n., animal): She cooled down her horse with a hose.

87. **hole** (n., opening): The mole went down a hole. *Rule*: Silent e makes o long.
    whole (adj., all): Who did the whole lesson? *SPP*: w-hole. *Rule*: Silent e makes o long.

88. **hour** (n., 60 minutes): Half an hour is 30 minutes (Lat and Gk., hora: time).
    our (poss. pron., belonging to us.): These are our four chairs we own.

89. **in-stance** (n., occurrence): During that instance, his stance (position) was strong. *SPP*: in-stan-ce.
    in-stants (n., moments): The ants were gone in instants.

90. **it's** (contraction: It is.): It's time for leaves to change color.
    its (poss. pron.): The animal had to use its wits to survive. *Same Pattern*: fit, lit, knit…

91. **knead** (v., work): I like to knead bread. *2 Vowels Rule*: A makes e long. *Same*: bead, lead, read.
    need (v., am required): I need to plant this seed today. *Same Pattern*: deed, feed, reed, seed…

92. **knight** (n., feudal warrior): The knight's armor was as black as night. *SPP*: k-ni-g-ht
    night (n., from evening to morning): At night the bright moon made the sky light. *SPP*: ni-g-ht.

93. **know** (v., understand): <u>Now</u> that we have talked, I <u>know</u> you better. *SPP*: k-now.
no (negative expression): <u>No</u>, don't <u>go</u>.

94. **lay** (v., reclined; set down): I <u>lay</u> in the <u>hay</u> all <u>day</u> and rested.
lei (n., Hawaiian flower necklace): During <u>lei</u>sure time in Hawaii, wear a <u>lei (for) sure</u>: lei + sure.

95. **lead** (n., graphite): She <u>read</u> what he had written in <u>lead</u>. *Same Pattern*: dead, head.
led (past tense of lead): <u>Ed</u> <u>led</u> the way to the <u>red</u> <u>shed</u>. *Same Pattern*: bed, fed, led, red, wed.
lead (v., n., show way): *Clue*: I <u>lead</u> in loving to <u>read</u>. *Same Pattern*: bead, plead. *2 Vowel Rule*.

96. **leased** (v., rented): When we <u>leased</u> the room, it <u>eased</u> our expenses.
least (adj., smallest): Drive <u>east</u> for the <u>least</u> traffic problems.

97. **li-ar** (n., untruthful person): The <u>liar</u> took the next <u>rail</u> out of town. *Reversal*: liar – rail .
lyre (n., musical instrument): He put his <u>lyre</u> on the funeral <u>pyre</u>. *Visual*: <u>Y</u> in <u>lyre</u> looks like a <u>lyre</u>.

98. **light-en-ing** (v., make lighter): I am <u>lightening</u> my <u>ten</u> suitcases. *Pronunciation*: 3 syllables.
light-ning (n., light before thunder): <u>Lightning</u> is a <u>light</u> <u>zing</u>: light + n + ~~z~~ing. *Pronunciation*: 2 sylbs.

99. **loan** (n., something borrowed): Please don't <u>groan</u> about the <u>loan</u>. *2 Vowel Rule*: <u>A</u> makes <u>o</u> long.
lone (adj., single): <u>Lone</u> means <u>one</u> all al<u>one</u>. *Silent E Rule*: <u>Silent e</u> makes <u>o</u> long.

100. **loot** (n., money; v., steal): They used a <u>tool</u> to get to the <u>loot</u>. *Reversal*: <u>loot</u> – <u>tool</u> .
lute (n., musical string instrument): You pluck strings on a <u>lute</u> and blow a <u>flute</u>.

101. **made** (v., manufactured; did): He <u>made</u> the <u>grade</u>. (Expression meaning to pass a class; test, etc.)
maid (n., girl; female servant): The <u>maid</u> brought <u>aid</u>.

102. **mail** (v., send by post): They never <u>fail</u> to deliver your <u>mail</u>. *Same Pattern*: bail, hail, jail.
male (n., adj., man): *Moby Dick* is a <u>tale</u> of a famous <u>male</u> wh<u>ale</u>. *Same Pattern*: bale, sale, tale.

103. **main** (adj., most important): Your <u>main</u> <u>gains</u> in spelling will re<u>main</u>.
mane (n., hair on a horse): The <u>mane</u> is a per<u>mane</u>nt part of a horse.

104. **man-ner** (n., way; style): In what <u>manner</u> should I hang this b<u>anner</u>?
man-or (n., estate): Does the <u>man or</u> his wife run the <u>manor</u>?

105. **man-tel** (n., shelf above fireplace): In his home, a <u>man</u> can <u>tell</u> where the <u>mantel</u> is.
man-tle (n., cloak): His <u>mantle</u> <u>let</u> down to the ground.

106. **mar-ry** (v., wed): After you <u>marry</u>, you <u>carry</u> the bride across the threshold (bottom of doorway).
Mar-y (n., name): <u>Mary</u>, <u>Mary</u>, quite cont<u>rary</u>…
mer-ry (adj., happy): I feel <u>merry</u> when I eat a ch<u>erry</u>.

107. **meat** (n., beef): They like to <u>eat</u> <u>meat</u>.
meet (n., competition; v., come upon): When I <u>meet</u> you, I'll <u>greet</u> you. *Same Pattern*: beet, feet.
mete (v., measure): You can <u>mete</u> something by using <u>mete</u>rs (a meter is .9 yards).

108. **me-dal** (n., award): A <u>medal</u>lion is a large <u>medal</u>.
med-dle (v., interfere): Don't <u>meddle</u> now or ever start <u>meddling</u> in their problems.

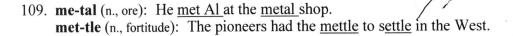

109. **me-tal** (n., ore): He <u>met Al</u> at the <u>metal</u> shop.
met-tle (n., fortitude): The pioneers had the <u>mettle</u> to <u>settle</u> in the West.

110. **moan** (n., groan): Did you <u>moan</u> and <u>groan</u> over that <u>loan</u>?
mown (v., adj., cut): After he'd <u>mown</u> the <u>lawn</u>, it was not <u>overgrown</u>.

111. **none** (pron., not one): None means not one: <u>not</u> + <del>one</del> = <u>none</u>.
nun (n., religious sister): Our <u>nun</u> made learning <u>fun</u>.

112. **oar** (n., paddle): They made an <u>oar</u> out of a <u>board</u>.
or (conj., either or): Either and <u>or</u>; neither and <u>nor</u>.
ore (n., mineral deposit): We looked for m<u>ore</u> <u>ore</u> in the vein.

113. **ov-er-do** (v., do too much): I <u>do</u> <u>overdo</u> when I search all day for 4-leaf cl<u>overs</u>?
ov-er-due (adj., past due): My <u>overdue</u> book was <u>due</u> on Tues. *Two Vowel Rule*: <u>E</u> makes <u>u</u> long.

114. **pail** (n., bucket): He put his m<u>ail</u> in a p<u>ail</u>.
pale (adj., light color): The wh<u>ale</u> was p<u>ale</u> gray.

115. **pain** (n., hurt): He felt <u>pain</u> from the spr<u>ain</u> in his leg. *Two Vowel Rule*: <u>I</u> makes <u>a</u> long.
pane (n., a strip): <u>Pane</u>s of glass often come in <u>panels</u>. *Silent E Rule*: <u>Silent e</u> makes <u>a</u> long.

116. **pair** (n., two of a kind): She had a <u>pair</u> of br<u>aids</u> in her h<u>air</u>. *Two Vowel Rule*: <u>I</u> makes <u>a</u> long.
pare (v., cut): Take c<u>are</u> when you <u>pare</u> those apples.
pear (n., fruit): A <u>pear</u> can be red, golden, or green like a <u>pea</u>.

117. **passed**: (v., went by; succeeded): Every lad and <u>lass</u> <u>passed</u> the exam. Rule: <u>Ss</u> keeps the <u>a</u> short.
past: (n., time gone; former): <u>Last</u> year is in the <u>past</u>. *Same Pattern*: cast, fast, last, mast…

118. **pa-tience** (n., composure): Their <u>patience</u> was <u>en</u>couraged. *SPP*: pa-ti-en-ce.
pa-tient (n., sick person): The <u>patient</u> wanted to <u>en</u>ter the hospital. *SPP*: pa-ti-ent.

119. **pause** (n., brief stop): After a <u>pause</u>, they gave more app<u>lause</u>.
paws (n., animal feet): An animal has <u>paws</u> and cl<u>aws</u>.

120. **peace** (n., state of contentment; no war): <u>Each</u> country wanted a <u>peace</u> tr<u>ea</u>ty.
piece (n., individual amount; a work): He ate a <u>piece</u> of <u>pie</u>.

121. **peal** (n., v., ring): A bell will <u>peal</u> when it's time for your m<u>eal</u>. *Two Vowel Rule*: <u>A</u> makes <u>a</u> long.
peel (v., take off skin): I can <u>feel</u> my skin <u>peel</u> from sunburn. *Two Vowel Rule*: <u>E</u> makes <u>e</u> long.

122. **ped-al** (n., v., ride a bike): <u>Al</u> can <u>pedal</u> fast (L. ped: foot + al: noun suffix = <u>pedal</u>).
ped-dle (v., sell place to place): The <u>ped</u>dler was <u>peddling</u> papers (Mid. Eng. pedde: basket).

123. **peer** (n., an equal; look searchingly): I want to <u>peer</u> at the <u>deer</u>. *Same Pattern*: beer, cheer, seer.
pier (n., dock): They ate <u>pie</u> by the <u>pier</u>. *Same Pattern*: pier, tier (layer).

124. **plain** (adj., simple; n., area of land): It's <u>plain</u> as <u>rain</u>. *Same Pattern*: gain, main, pain…
plane (n., flat surface; smoothing tool; flying machine): A <u>plane</u> landed in the <u>lane</u> (M. E. <u>plane</u>n: like a bi

125. **pole** (n., tall stick): He hammered a <u>pole</u> in the <u>hole</u>.
poll (n., number of votes cast; v., count): Be sure to enr<u>oll</u> to be in the <u>poll</u>,

126. **poor** (adj., having little money): The <u>poor</u> person came to our <u>door</u>.
pore (n., skin gland): That s<u>ore</u> <u>pore</u> is m<u>ore</u> swollen today.
pour (v., flow into): <u>Pour</u> <u>our</u> s<u>our</u> milk <u>out</u>.

127. **pray** (v., ask help of God): We <u>pray</u> each <u>day</u> (Ger., fragen: to beg; ask).
prey (n., the hunted; v., hunt): The <u>pre</u>dator <u>preyed</u> on its <u>prey</u> (Mid. Eng., preye: to hunt; seize).

128. **pre-sence** (n., act of being there): The re<u>ference</u> book we used made a <u>difference</u>.
pre-sents (n., gifts; v., gives): She <u>sent</u> the <u>presents</u>, and will <u>present</u> them later.

129. **prin-ci-pal** (n., chief): The <u>principal</u> was his <u>pal</u> in it.
prin-ci-ple (n., rule): A <u>principle</u> is a <u>rule</u> to live by.

130. **prof-it** (n., v., benefit; gain): We are <u>fit</u> to <u>profit</u>.
proph-et (n., speaker of truth): A <u>prophet</u> <u>lets</u> people hear truth (M.E. prophetes: speak) *Phonics*: <u>ph</u> = <u>f</u>.

131. **rain** (n., v., water from clouds): The <u>rain</u> in Spain falls m<u>ain</u>ly on the <u>plain</u>. *VV Rule*: I makes <u>a</u> long.
reign (n., period of rule; v., rule): <u>Eight</u> rulers <u>reigned</u>. *SPP*: re-ig-n.
rein (n., for a horse): She held <u>rein</u> <u>in</u> her hand near her v<u>ein</u> (L. retinere: to hold back.).

132. **raise** (v., put up): They <u>raise</u> their hands in <u>praise</u>. *SPP*: rai-s-e.
rays (n., beams): In the sun's <u>rays</u>, the cat pl<u>ays</u> with her shadow.
raze (v., tear down): I watched in a <u>daze</u> as they <u>razed</u> the homes after the fire. *SPP*: ra-ze.

133. **read** (v., past of to read): I <u>read</u> about b<u>read</u>. *Same Pattern*: head, instead, lead (pencil lead).
red (adj., color): <u>Red</u> is the color of my b<u>ed</u> (Old. Eng., red: color of blood).

134. **read** (v., to read): I like to <u>read</u> about b<u>ead</u>s. *Same Pattern*: bead, lead (verb), mead (honey wine).
reed (n., tall grass): The <u>deer</u> was nibbling on a <u>reed</u>. *Reversal*: <u>reed</u> = <u>deer</u>.

135. **real** (adj., genuine): <u>Real</u>ity is for <u>real</u>. *SPP*: re-al. *Two Vowel Rule*: <u>E</u> makes <u>a</u> long.
reel (n., spool): The <u>eel</u> is coiled up like a <u>reel</u>. *SPP*: re-el. *Two Vowel Rule*: <u>E</u> makes <u>e</u> long.

136. **right** (adj., correct): Can you <u>rig</u> that sail <u>right</u> at <u>night</u>? *Phonics*: Igh, makes long i sound.
write (v., to write): I write using my small *Nite Lite*. *Rule*: <u>Silent e</u> makes <u>i</u> long.
rite (n., ceremony) <u>Rite</u> and a <u>ritual</u> come from same root. *Rule*: <u>Silent e</u> makes <u>i</u> long.

137. **ring** (n., circular band): She has a <u>ring</u> on her <u>finger.</u>
wring (v., squeeze) <u>We</u> <u>wring</u> out the washing on <u>W</u>ednesday.

138. **road** (n., path or street): They saw a <u>toad</u> on the <u>road</u>. *Rule*: The <u>a</u> makes <u>o</u> long.
rode (v., past of ride). We <u>rode</u> in cowboy m<u>ode</u> at the <u>rode</u>o. *Rule*: <u>Silent e</u> makes <u>i</u> long.

139. **roe**: (n., fish eggs): J<u>oe</u> likes sturgeon <u>roe</u> which is caviar. *Same Pattern*: doe, foe, hoe, toe, woe.
row (v., use oars): We sat on the b<u>ow</u> of the boat while he <u>rowed</u>. Same: low, mow, stow, tow.

140. **root** (n., plant part that grows downward; v., cheer). They <u>root</u> and <u>toot</u> when the <u>root</u>s grow.
route (n., way): We took a s<u>outh</u> <u>route</u> <u>out</u> of the town: <u>r + out + e</u>. *SPP: rou-te.*

141. **rose** (n., flower): I watered my <u>rose</u> with a h<u>ose</u> (Fr., <u>rose</u>: pink + <u>s</u>). *Rule:* <u>Silent e</u> makes <u>o</u> long.
rows (n., lines; v., moves a boat): I keep my b<u>ows</u> in <u>rows</u>.

142. **rote** (n., memory): He would often qu<u>ote</u> by <u>rote</u>.
wrote (v., past of write): She <u>wrote</u> a n<u>ote</u>.

143. **sail** (n., v., go by boat): We stood by the <u>rail</u> to watch the boat <u>sail</u>. *Two Vowel Rule:* <u>I</u> makes <u>a</u> long.
sale (n., bargain): The <u>tale</u> of the wh<u>ale</u>, *Moby Dick*, was for <u>sale</u>. *Rule:* <u>Silent e</u> makes <u>a</u> long

144. **scene** (n., setting): We used <u>scene</u>ry for the <u>scene</u>. *SPP:* s-ce-ne. *Rule:* <u>Silent e</u> makes <u>e</u> long.
seen (v., viewed): Have you <u>been</u> <u>seen</u> by your dentist this year?

145. **sea** (n., ocean): Oc<u>ea</u>n is a synonym for a <u>sea</u>. *Same Pattern:* feat, heat, tea.
see (v., look at): You <u>see</u> a b<u>ee</u> with your <u>eyes</u>. *Same Pattern:* fee, gee, tee.

146. **sew** (n., v., stitch): A f<u>ew</u> ladies <u>sew</u> teddy bears.
so (conj., in order that): G<u>o</u> <u>so</u> you can play ball.
sow (n., plant): N<u>ow</u> we <u>sow</u> seeds in perfect r<u>ows</u>.

147. **shone** (v., gave forth light): The star has <u>shone</u> in <u>one</u> place. *Rule:* <u>Silent e</u> makes <u>o</u> long.
shown (v., let seen): I have <u>shown</u> you my <u>own</u> rocks. *Two Vowel Rule:* <u>W</u> makes <u>o</u> long.

148. **slay** (v., kill): He had to <u>slay</u> the giant when he <u>lay</u> sleeping (Ice., slay: strike). *Rule:* <u>I</u> makes <u>a</u> long.
sleigh (n., sled): <u>Eight</u> reindeer pull Santa's <u>sleigh</u>. *Rule:* <u>Sleigh</u> sounds like <u>a</u>, so <u>e is before i</u>.

149. **soar** (v., sly; go up): Rockets r<u>oar</u> as they <u>soar</u>ed upward. *Same Pattern:* boar, oar, roar.
sore (n., adj., pain): My muscles are too <u>sore</u> to do m<u>ore</u>. *Same Pattern:* bore, ore, more.

150. **sole** (adv., only; n., shoe sole): There's a h<u>ole</u> in the <u>sole</u> of your shoe.
soul (n., spirit): His <u>soul</u> was <u>so</u> <u>ul</u>tra fair that he brought justice to all: <u>so + ul</u>~~tra~~.

151. **some** (adj., pron., ortion): I hope <u>some</u> people c<u>ome</u>. *Same Pattern:* become, overcome, someone
sum (n., total amount): What is the <u>sum</u> of <u>gum</u> you can chew? *Same Pattern:* bum, chum, hum.

152. **son** (n., male offspring): Mom and <u>son</u> thought in un<u>ison</u>. *Same Pattern:* ton, won.
sun (n., star that heats Earth): Come r<u>un</u> in the <u>sun</u> and have f<u>un</u>. *Same Pattern:* bun, pun, spun.

153. **stairs** (n., climbing levels): I used a ch<u>air</u> to reach the attic <u>stairs</u>. *Same Pattern:* fairs, hairs, pairs
stares (n., v., looks at): Do you c<u>are</u> if he <u>stares</u>. *Same Pattern:* dares, fares, glares, hares

154. **stake** (n., post): <u>Take</u> this <u>stake</u> for a fence post. *Same Pattern:* bake, cake, lake.
steak (n., seat): Is a <u>steak</u> m<u>eat</u> you <u>eat</u>? *Same Pattern:* break.

155. **sta-tion-ary** (adj., stable): Something <u>stationary</u> is <u>stable</u> (<u>stays</u> in one place).
sta-tion-ery (n., letters): You write lett<u>ers</u> on <u>stationery</u>.

156. **straight** (adj., not crooked): The <u>train</u> went <u>straight</u>. *Phonics*: <u>Igh</u> makes <u>long a sound</u>.
strait (n., channel of water): We had to w<u>ait</u> to get through the str<u>ait</u>.

157. **tail**: (n., hindmost part of animal; tail of a kite): She likes to br<u>aid</u> her horse's <u>tail</u>.
tale (n., story): We read a <u>tale</u> of a wh<u>ale</u> in a book of t<u>all</u> <u>tales</u>.

158. **tear** (n., liquid from crying): Can you h<u>ear</u> a cl<u>ear</u> <u>tear</u> fall by your <u>ear</u>?
tier (n., one of a series of rows rising behind each other): I sat on a <u>tier</u> by the <u>pier</u> and ate <u>pie</u>.
tear (v., rip): He didn't want to w<u>ear</u> a shirt with a <u>tear</u>.

159. <u>**their**</u> (poss. pron.): <u>He</u> is <u>their</u> <u>heir</u> (one who will possess). *Note*: All 3 homophones begin with <u>the</u>.
<u>**there**</u> (adverb telling where): We looked <u>here</u> and <u>there</u>. *Phonics*: <u>Ere</u> makes an <u>air sound</u>.
they're (contraction: they are): <u>Hey</u>, <u>they</u>'re at college. (*Again Note*: All 3 homophones begin with <u>the</u>.)

160. **threw** (v., tossed): The ball he <u>threw</u> <u>blew</u> right past them.
throu<u>gh</u> (prep., finished): It's <u>rough</u> to walk <u>through</u> a door.

161. **tide** (n., ebb and flow): They liked to <u>ride</u> the <u>tide</u>.
tied (v., bound; adj., having the same score): They <u>vied</u> (competed) in chess and then <u>tied</u>.

162. **to** (prep., toward): For <u>going</u> <u>to</u> a place, use <u>to</u>: I went to the park…to school…to work…
too (adv., also, in addition): For emphasis, use <u>too</u>: You gave me <u>too</u>…much. I want to go <u>too</u>.
two (adj., number): The <u>two</u> of us have <u>two</u> children. One, <u>two</u>, three…<u>twelve</u>…<u>twenty</u>…

163. **toe** (n., digit on the foot): I hit my <u>toe</u> with a h<u>oe</u>. *Same Pattern*: doe, foe, roe (fish eggs).
tow (v., to pull): You can <u>tow</u> or <u>row</u> a boat. *Same Pattern*: bow, low, mow.

164. **vain** (adj., conceited): You do not <u>gain</u> by being <u>vain</u>. *Two Vowel Rule*: <u>I</u> makes <u>a</u> long.
vane (n., weather vane): See the weather <u>vane</u> by my <u>lane</u>. *Rule*: <u>Silent e</u> makes a long.
vein (n., tube) <u>Veins</u> <u>veer</u> <u>into</u> the heart: <u>ve~~er~~ + in</u> = <u>vein</u>. *Rule*: <u>Vein</u> sounds like <u>a</u>, so the spelling is <u>ei</u> like w<u>eigh</u>.

165. **var-y** (v., change) <u>Gary</u> can <u>vary</u> his days to match his v<u>arious</u> interests (L., vari: differing + <u>y</u> = <u>vary</u>).
ver-y (adv., extremely): <u>Every</u> time I see you, I'm <u>very</u> happy (L., <u>ver</u>: truth + <u>y</u> = <u>very</u>).

166. **wade** (v., walk in water): *Clue*: I m<u>ade</u> a pool to <u>wade</u> in. *Rule*: <u>Silent e</u> makes <u>a</u> long.
weighed (v., measured heaviness): The box <u>weighed</u> <u>eight</u> pounds. *Phonics*: <u>eigh</u> = <u>long a sound</u>.

167. **wail** (n., v., cry): When you stepped on her t<u>ail</u>, the cat gave a <u>wail</u>.
whale (n., ocean mammal): The <u>whale</u> swam in the <u>gale</u> (heavy wind).

168. **waist** (n., middle): <u>Wait</u> while I measure your <u>waist</u>. *Two Vowel Rule*: <u>I</u> makes <u>a</u> long.
waste (trash; use up) H<u>aste</u> makes <u>waste</u>. *Rule*: <u>Silent e</u> makes <u>a</u> long.

169. **ware** (n., pottery, silverware, etc.): Take c<u>are</u> when you purchase different <u>ware</u>.
wear (v., have on): There's an expression: "Some people <u>wear</u> their h<u>eart</u> on their sleeve."

170. **we've** (contraction: pron. + v., we have): <u>We</u>'ve come to h<u>ave</u> fun. *Same Pattern*: we're, we'll…
weave (v., interlace): She'd often w<u>eave</u> a design of l<u>eaves</u>. *Two Vowel Rule*: <u>A</u> makes <u>e</u> long.

171. **weak** (adj. having little strength): The bird with the broken b<u>eak</u> was <u>weak</u>.
week (n., every seven days): I pay a <u>wee</u> <u>fee</u> each <u>week</u> for fresh flowers.

172. **who's** (contraction: pron. + v., who is): <u>Who's</u> playing with <u>whom</u>? *Same Pattern*: who'll, who'd..
whose (possessive pronoun): *SPP*: <u>w</u>-hose. *Clue*: <u>Whose</u> <u>hose</u> is this? (Old. Eng., hwaes: hose.)

173. **wr̄ap** (n., v., over): <u>Wrap</u> this around your <u>wr</u>ist. *SPP*: w-rap.
rap (v., knock; talk): They gave a t<u>ap</u>, then a <u>rap</u> on the door.

174. **yoke** (n., v., harness): The ox br<u>oke</u> the <u>yoke</u>.
yolk (n., egg centers): His <u>folk</u> cooled the <u>yolk</u>.

175. **you're** (contraction: you are): <u>You're</u> my friend, L<u>ou</u>. *Same Pattern*: you'd, you'll…
your (poss. pron.): Is this <u>your</u> book or <u>our</u> book? *Visual*: <u>Your</u> has <u>our</u> in it.

POWER Spelling Clues for Confusing Words

Learning and remembering the difference between these *Confusing Words* gives you great spelling *POWER* and puts you ahead of the computer. Since *Spell Check* can't check words that are spelled correctly, but used in the wrong way, your BRAIN has to know and be able to check the words!!!

1. **ac-cent** (n., beat in a word; sound of speech): I <u>accept</u> all my friends with <u>accents</u>.
   as-cent (n., to climb up): The holiday <u>scent</u> made an <u>ascent</u> in the room.
   as-sent (v., n., consent): <u>As (I) sent</u> my dress to her, I gave her my <u>assent</u> to wear it: <u>as + sent</u>.

2. **ac-cept** (v., to agree or take): I <u>accept</u> responsibility for the <u>accident</u> (L. <u>ac</u>: to + <u>cept</u>: take = to take).
   ex-cept (prep., not take; x-ing-out): Everyone went <u>except</u> <u>E</u>d (L. <u>ex</u>: not + <u>cept</u>: take = not take).

3. **ad-vice** (n., guidance): The <u>vice</u> principal gave good <u>advice</u>.
   ad-vise (v., give guidance): Be w<u>ise</u> when you <u>advise</u>.

4. **af-fect** (n., feelings, mood): Your <u>affect</u> was full of affection. *Phonics*: <u>2 f's</u> makes <u>a</u> short.
   ef-fect (n., change; result): Th<u>e</u> <u>effect</u> was <u>e</u>xciting and <u>effect</u>ive. *Phonics*: <u>2 f's</u> keeps <u>e</u> short.

   af-fect (v., to influence): What you say ma<u>y</u> <u>affect</u> others.
   ef-fect (v. to cause; make happen): He wanted his <u>effort</u> to <u>effect</u> change.

5. **al-ley** (n. back street): Move from an <u>alley</u> into the <u>valley</u>. *Rule*: <u>Y</u> makes <u>e</u> long.
   al-ly (n., supporter): M<u>y</u> true <u>ally</u> really lo<u>ves</u> me. *Pattern*: all<u>y</u>, my, try.

6. **a-lum-na, a-lum-nae** (female graduate): Da<u>na</u> is an <u>alumna</u> (<u>a</u>: singular; <u>ae</u>: plural).
   a-lum-nus, alumni (male graduate): Augus<u>tus</u> is an <u>alumnus</u> (<u>us</u>: singular; <u>i</u>: plural).

7. **an-gel** (n., heavenly being): They made a <u>gel</u>atin <u>angel</u>. *SPP*: an-<u>gel</u>.
   an-gle (n., measurement btw. 2 lines; to fish): Let's put an <u>e</u> in the <u>angle</u> of the L. *SPP*: ang-<u>le</u>.

8. **Ant-arc-ti-ca** (opposite North Pole): <u>Antarctica</u> means <u>anti</u> (Gk., opposite) the <u>Arctic</u> (Gk, Arktos: bear): <u>anti</u> + <u>arctic</u> + a (Gk., <u>anti</u>: opposite + <u>arktos</u>: bear).

   Arc-tic (at North Pole): The <u>Arctic</u> Ocean forms an <u>arc</u> near the North Pole: <u>arc + tic</u> = <u>Arctic</u> (Gk. Arktos: The Bear, the most northern constellation).

9. **an-te** (prefix meaning before): An <u>ante</u>room is a room that comes <u>before</u> (ante) a main room.
   an-ti (prefix meaning against; not; opposite): An <u>anti</u>social person is <u>not</u> (anti) <u>social</u>.

10. **ar-e-a** (n. place): I'm in an <u>area</u> at the <u>rear</u> of the school. *2 Open Syllables*: ar-<u>e</u>-<u>a</u>.
    ar-i-a (n. melody; opera solo): <u>M</u>aria sang a beautiful <u>aria</u>. *2 Open Syllables*: ar-<u>i</u>-<u>a</u>.

11. **as-cend-ed** (v., climbed toward; <u>arose</u>): The <u>scent</u> ascended and <u>a</u>rose in the room.
    de-scend-ed (v., climbed from; went <u>down</u>): He <u>ended</u> and <u>descended</u> by climbing <u>down</u> from the hill.

12. **au-ral** (adj., hearing; L. <u>aur</u>: ear): If <u>audio</u> equipment's too loud, Au<u>nt</u> Laural has <u>aural</u> problems.
    o-ral (adj., verbal; L. <u>or</u>: mouth): When you <u>orate</u> (speak), you use your <u>oral</u> abilities.

13. **bas-es** (n., things you stand on): Can fielders <u>chase</u> runners off <u>bases</u>? *Phonics*: <u>s</u> = s; <u>s</u> = z.
   ba-sis (n., reason): The b<u>asis</u> for the reward remains <u>as is</u>: b + <u>as</u> + <u>is</u>. *Phonics*: Each <u>s</u> = s sound

14. **be-side** (prep., next to): He walked <u>beside</u> me, by my <u>side</u>. *Prefix Rule*: Add <u>be</u> + <u>side</u> = beside.
   be-sides (adv., in addition to; also): I'd like this <u>besides</u>. *Prefix Rule*: <u>be</u> + <u>sides</u> = besides.

15. **bought** (v., purchase): I <u>ought</u> to have <u>bought</u> that book. *SPP*: bo-ugh-t
   brought (v., past of to bring): I <u>ought</u> to have <u>brought</u> a book to your party. *SPP*: bro-ugh-t.

16. **breadth** (n., wid<u>th</u>): The <u>breadth</u> of <u>bread</u> is usually 6 inches: <u>bread</u> + <u>th</u>. *SPP*: bread-th.
   breath (n., act of inhaling and exhaling): Without <u>breath</u>, there is <u>death</u>.
   breathe (v., inhale and exhale): <u>He</u> cannot <u>breathe</u> and <u>eat</u> at the same time: <u>br</u> + <u>eat</u> + <u>he</u>.

17. **cen-ten-ni-al** (n., 100-year anniversary): A <u>century</u> ends with <u>centennial</u> celebrations.
   sent-i-nel (n., stands watch): <u>I</u> <u>sent</u> <u>Nel</u> a message from the <u>sentinel</u>: <u>sent</u> + <u>I</u> + <u>Nel</u>.

18. **choose** (v., pick): I will <u>choose</u> a <u>goose</u>. *Phonics*: <u>oo</u>; <u>s</u> = <u>z</u>; *Same Pattern*: loose, moose, noose...
   chose (v., selected): I <u>chose</u> a red <u>rose</u>. *Phonics*: <u>long o</u>; <u>s</u> = <u>z</u>. *Same Pattern*: close, hose, nose...

19. **close** (adv., near): It was <u>close</u> to the time for my <u>dose</u> of medicine. *Phonics*: <u>s</u> = s sound.
   close (v., shut): <u>Close</u> off that <u>hose</u>. *Phonics*: <u>s</u> = z sound. *Rule*: Silent E makes <u>o</u> long.

20. **co-ma** (n., an unconscious state): A person in a <u>coma</u> is called "<u>comatose</u>." (Gr. <u>koma</u>: deep sleep)
   com-ma (n., a punctuation mark): Before the <u>command</u>, I put in a <u>comma</u> (He said<u>,</u> "Go!").

21. **con-fi-dant** (n., friend; advisor): <u>Ant</u>'s confid<u>ant</u> was Bee. *Silent E Rule*: confid~~e~~ + <u>ant</u> = confidant.
   con-fi-dent (adj., sure): I am <u>confident</u> I made that <u>dent</u>.

22. **con-science** (n., sense of right and wrong; 2 syllables): <u>Conscience</u> has <u>science</u> in it (L. <u>con</u>: with + <u>scien</u>: knowledge + <u>s</u>: noun suffix). *SPP*: con-<u>sci</u>-en-<u>ce</u>.

   con-sci-en-tious (adj., careful; 4 syllables): I was <u>conscientious</u> in <u>science</u> class (L. <u>con</u>: with + <u>scien</u>: knowledge + <u>ious</u>: adj. suffix). *SPP*: con-<u>sci</u>-en-<u>ti</u>-ous.

   con-scious (adj., awake; 2 syllables) She was gra<u>cious</u> when she was <u>conscious</u> (L., <u>con</u>: with + <u>sci</u>: knowing + <u>ous</u>: adj. suffix). *SPP*: con-sci-ous.

23. **cos-tume** (n., special way of dressing): The <u>plume</u> for my <u>costume</u> <u>cost</u> the most: <u>cost</u> + ~~p~~lume.
   cus-tom (n., practice; habit): It's <u>customary</u> for <u>us to</u> have <u>customs</u>: <u>c</u> + <u>us</u> + <u>to</u> + <u>m</u>.

24. **de-cent** (adj., proper): That flattened <u>cent</u> is not a <u>decent</u> <u>cent</u>: <u>de</u> + <u>cent</u>.
   des-cent (n., way down from): As we made our <u>descent</u>, we smelled the <u>scent</u> of pine: <u>de</u> + <u>scent</u>.
   dis-sent (n., v., disagree): I disagreed, so I <u>sent</u> a vote of <u>dissent</u>: <u>dis</u> +<u>sent</u> (L. dis: not + sentire: feel)

25. **de-vice** (n., an item): Our new <u>device</u> makes shapes of <u>ice</u>. *Same Pattern*: dice, mice, rice...
   de-vise (v., to plan): I will <u>devise</u> a fun surpri<u>se</u>. *Same Pattern*: arise, rise, wise...

26. **e-mi-grate** (v., move away from): <u>Emile</u> and <u>Emily</u> <u>emigrated</u> (L., <u>e</u>: away from + <u>migrat</u>: move + <u>e</u>).
   im-mi-grate (v., move into): They want to <u>immigrate</u> <u>immediately</u> (L. <u>im</u>-to + <u>migrat</u>-move + <u>e</u>).

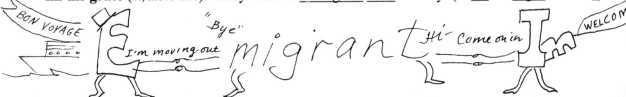

27. **em-i-nent** (adj., famous; distinguished): <u>Emile</u> is an <u>eminent</u> <u>emissary</u>: <u>e + mine + nt</u>.
    im-mi-nent (adj., any time): The opening of the <u>mine</u> is <u>imminent</u>: <u>im + mine + nt</u>.

28. **err** (v., to make a mistake): To <u>err</u> means to make an <u>error</u>.
    error (n., a mistake): I have a <u>terror</u> of making an <u>error</u>.

29. **far-ther** (adj., more distant-re: space): The city was <u>far</u> away, so <u>father</u> drove <u>farther</u>: <u>far + ther</u>.
    fur-ther (adj., more distant-re: to degree, quantity, time): A <u>future</u> time is <u>further</u> away than today.

30. **fi-na-le** (n., performance conslusion): Since <u>finale</u> is an Italian word, pronounce final <u>e</u>.
    fi-nal-ly (adv., at the end): <u>Finally</u>, <u>all</u> our <u>final</u> exams were over: <u>final + ly</u>: adv. suffix.
    fine-ly (adv., in a fine manner): We will <u>dine</u> on <u>finely</u> prepared <u>brine</u> (sea) shrimp: <u>fine + ly</u>.

31. **find-ing** (v., locating): I'm <u>finding</u> <u>bindings</u> for skis. *Same Pattern*: minding, reminding.
    fin-ing (v., making pay): He's <u>fining</u> the <u>mining</u> boss. *Rule*: <u>fine + ing</u>. *Pattern*: dining, lining.

32. **for-mal-ly** (L. adv., with ceremony): For <u>formal</u> events, dress <u>formally</u>: <u>formal + ly</u>.
    form-er-ly (O. E. adv., previously): <u>Formerly</u>, I knew you at a <u>former</u> time: <u>former + ly</u>.

33. **hos-tel** (n., youth lodging): My <u>host</u> and everyone <u>else</u> at the <u>hostel</u> were nice: <u>host + el</u>.
    hos-tile (adj., antagonistic): Crocs in the <u>Nile</u> are <u>hostile</u>. *Rule*: <u>Silent e</u> makes <u>i</u> in long.

34. **in-ter-state** (adj., between states): <u>Interstate</u> means <u>between</u> <u>states</u> with an <u>e</u> (L. inter: between).
    in-tra-state (adj., among states): <u>Intrastate</u> means <u>among</u> <u>states</u> with an <u>a</u> (L. intra: among).

35. **la-ter** (adj., after a time): We <u>ate</u> <u>later</u>. *Rule*: Silent <u>e</u> makes <u>a</u> long. *Same Pattern*: cater, hater.
    lat-ter (adj., second; near end): A <u>latter</u> <u>batter</u> hit a run. *Rule*: -<u>tt</u> makes <u>a</u> short. *Pattern*: hatter, matter.

36. **loose** (adj., not tight; got away): The <u>goose</u> and <u>moose</u> got <u>loose</u>.
    lose (v., misplace; not win): It's hard to <u>lose</u> your <u>nose</u>.

37. **meant** (v., intended): She <u>meant</u> to find <u>me</u> and <u>ant</u>, meant to be friends: <u>me + ant</u>. *SPP*: me-ant.
    met (v., saw; was introduced to): I <u>met</u> a great <u>pet</u> at the store. *Same Pattern*: get, let, set, vet.

38. **min-ute** (n., 60 seconds): To spell <u>minute</u>, think of *minute* (tiny), and hear the <u>long i</u> and <u>u</u>.
    mi-nute (adj., tiny): A <u>minute</u> item is <u>miniature</u> and <u>cute</u>. *Rule*: <u>Silent e</u> makes <u>u</u> long.

39. **mor-al** (n., lesson; adj., having virtue): A <u>moral</u> person has good <u>morality</u> (L., <u>moral</u>: virtue)
    mor-tal (n.; adj., human; won't live forever): All <u>mortal</u> people face <u>mortality</u> (L., <u>mort</u>: death)

40. **pa-tient** (n., ill person; calm): If <u>Pa</u> ties a <u>tie</u>, he is <u>patient</u>: <u>Pa + tie + nt</u>. *SPP*: pa-ti-ent.
    pa-tience (n., bearing with): <u>Pat, I</u> <u>enchant</u> with <u>patience</u>: <u>Pat + I + enchant + e</u>. *SPP*: pa-ti-en-ce.

41. **per-son-al** (adj., private): My <u>personal</u> friend has a great personality.
    per-son-nel (n., part of an org. concerned with people): <u>Nel</u> is the <u>person</u> running <u>personnel</u>.

42. **pic-ture** (n., drawing or photograph): <u>Pick</u> the <u>picture</u> where you want my <u>signature</u>: <u>pick + ture</u>.
    pitch-er (n., baseball player; container): Can a <u>pitcher</u> <u>pitch</u> the <u>pit</u> (of a) cherry: <u>pit + cherry</u>.

43. **pre-cede** (v., go before): I'll <u>precede</u> you and try to inter<u>cede</u> (<u>pre</u>: before + <u>cede</u>: go = <u>precede</u>: go before).
pro-ceed (v., move forward): <u>Proceed</u> through life, and let kindness ex<u>ceed</u> wealth. *Phonics*: <u>Ee</u> = long e

44. **psy-chi-a-try** (practiced by M.D.): <u>I</u> gave <u>psychiatry</u> <u>a try</u>: <u>psych</u> + <u>I</u> + <u>a</u> + <u>try</u> (Gk. <u>sych</u>: spirit; ps = s).
psy-chol-o-gy (practiced by Ph.D.): <u>Psyche</u> (Gk. mind; spirit; <u>ps</u> = <u>s</u>) + <u>ology</u> (Gk., study of) = <u>psychology</u>.

45. **qui-et** (adj., not noisy): The night was tran<u>quil</u> and <u>quiet</u>. *Qu Rule*: Q is followed by <u>u</u>
(except at end of a word). *Other Word Forms*: <u>qui</u>escence; <u>qui</u>etude (L. quiesc: quiet). *Quit it*
quit (v., stop): <u>Quit</u> <u>it</u>! *Qu Rule*: qu = together. *Same Pattern*: bit, kit, sit.
quite (adv., rather): *Clue* and *Rule*: Quit + <u>silent e</u> = <u>quite</u>. *Same Pattern*: bite, kite, site.

46. **re-cent** (adj., not long ago): I found a <u>cent</u> with a <u>recent</u> date: <u>re + cent</u>. *Phonics*: <u>C</u> = s sound.
re-sent (v., to feel indignant): I <u>resent</u> fake <u>sent</u>iment. *Phonics*: <u>S</u> = z sound.
re-sent (v., sent again): When I <u>resent</u> the package, I sent it again: <u>re + sent</u>. *Phonics*: <u>S</u> = z sound.

47. **speak** (v., say words): I was too w<u>eak</u> to sp<u>eak</u>. *Same Pattern*: beak, leak, teak, weak
speech (n., a talk): Don't sp<u>eed</u> through your sp<u>eech</u>. *Same Pattern*: beech (tree), leech

48. **stat-ue** (n., carving; mold): The <u>stature</u> of the <u>statue</u> was true. *Two Vowel Rule*: E makes <u>u</u> long.
sta-tute (n., law): We will not dispute a <u>statute</u> of the <u>state</u>. *Silent E Rule*: state + ute = <u>statute</u>.

49. **than** (conj., for comparison): We took more <u>than</u> our <u>hands</u> could hold. *Same Pattern*: can, fan, man…
then (adv., at that time): <u>Then</u> the <u>hen</u> laid an egg. *Same Pattern*: glen, men, when, wren…

50. **thor-ough** (adj., complete): It was <u>rough</u>, but he did a <u>thorough</u> job. *SPP*: tho-rough.
though (conj., even): Even <u>though</u> it's <u>tough</u>, I'll see it through. *SPP*: tho-ugh.
thought (n., idea): I <u>thought</u> about what I <u>ought</u> to do. *SPP*: tho-ugh-t. *ti + re*

51. **tired** (adj., sleepy): When I'm t<u>ired</u>, my eyes are <u>red</u>.
SPP: ti-<u>red</u>. *Rule*: tire + d = <u>tired</u>. *tri + ed*

tried (v., past of try): <u>I</u> tried to reach <u>Ed</u>. *SPP*: tri-<u>ed</u>.
Rule: tr<del>y</del> + i = <u>tried</u>. *Same Pattern*: cried, fried, tried.

52. **ve-ra-cious** (adj., truthful): Truth is <u>veracious</u> and <u>very</u> <u>gracious</u> (L. vera: truth).
vo-ra-cious (adj., greedy): My <u>voracious</u> pig is not <u>gracious</u>: <u>vora</u> + <del>gra</del>cious.

53. **we're** (contraction: we <u>are</u>): <u>We're</u> at home. *Same Pattern*: we'll, we've.
were (v., past of are): We <u>were</u> going <u>here</u> and t<u>here</u>. *Same Pattern*: were, here.
where (adv., what place): <u>Where</u> <u>were</u> you – over t<u>here</u> or <u>here</u>? *Same Pattern*: here, there.

54. **weath-er** (n., climate): <u>We</u> <u>eat</u> <u>her</u> food outside when the w<u>eather</u> is nice: <u>we-at-her</u>.
whe-ther (conj., if): They did not know <u>whether</u> or not to use <u>ether</u>: <u>wh + ether</u>.

55. **which** (adj., pron., what): <u>Which</u> person is <u>rich</u>? *Same Pattern*: enrich, rich, which.
witch (n., sorceress): The <u>witch</u> had an <u>itch</u>. *Same Pattern*: ditch, hitch, pitch, stitch.

56. **write** (v., to put down ideas): I <u>write</u> about my <u>white</u> <u>kite</u>. *Same Pattern*: kite, quite, site. *I wrot*
wrote (v., did write): I <u>wrote</u> a <u>note</u>. *Same Pattern*: dote (care for), tote (carry), wrote. *a not*

338

POWER Spelling Clues for Challenging Words

1. **a-ble**: Are you <u>able</u> to set the <u>table</u>? *Other Word Forms*: In <u>ably</u>, you hear the <u>bl</u> in <u>able</u>.

2. **a-bout**: The cat was <u>about</u> to go <u>out</u>: <u>a + bout</u>.

3. **ab-sent**: When I was <u>absent</u>, the school <u>sent</u> my homework to me: <u>ab + sent</u>.

4. **ac-cep-tance**: She gave him her <u>acceptance</u> for the <u>dance</u>. *Phonics*: <u>c</u> = <u>k</u> and <u>c</u> = <u>s</u> sound.

5. **ac-ci-dent**: Did <u>I dent</u> my car in the <u>accident?</u> (L. <u>ac</u>: to + <u>cid</u>: befall + <u>ent</u>). *Phonics*: <u>c</u> = <u>k</u>; <u>c</u> = <u>s</u>

6. **ac-cuse**: To <u>accuse</u> means to call to <u>account</u> (L. <u>ac</u>: to + <u>cuse</u>: call to account). *Phonics*: <u>2 c's</u> = <u>k</u>.

7. **ac-tors**: I hope you'll <u>act (in our play)</u> or come see the <u>actors</u>: <u>act + or +s</u>.

8. **ad-di-tion-al**: <u>Add</u> the <u>additional</u> things <u>on Al</u>'s list: <u>add + iti + on + Al</u>.

9. **ad-dress**: <u>Add</u> my <u>address</u> to your <u>address</u> book (Old Fr. addresser: address).

10. **ad-van-ta-ge**: At my <u>age</u>, it's an <u>advantage</u> to have a <u>van</u>. *Rule*: <u>Silent e</u> makes <u>a</u> long; keeps g soft.

11. **ad-ver-tise**: <u>Advertise</u> well, and get a <u>rise</u> out of people. *Rule*: Silent <u>e</u> makes <u>i</u> long.

12. **af-firm**: <u>After</u> working for a <u>firm</u>, I can <u>affirm</u> my own ability: <u>after</u> + <u>firm</u> (<u>af</u>: to make + <u>firm</u>).

13. **a-gainst**: I want to box <u>against</u> the bag <u>again</u>. *Phonics*: <u>again + st</u> = <u>against</u>.

14. **al-bum**: <u>Al</u> did not make an <u>album</u> for a <u>bum</u>: <u>al + bum</u> (L. albus: white).

15. **al-ge-bra**: <u>Al</u> and <u>Geb</u> raced to <u>algebra</u>: <u>Al + Geb + ra</u>. *Phonics*: g = <u>j</u> sound.

16. **al-monds**: <u>Almonds</u> are <u>almost</u> oval: <u>al-most</u> + nd. *Same Pattern*: balmy, calm, palm, psalm…

17. **al-though**: <u>Although</u> it was <u>tough</u>, I did it. *Phonics*: <u>ough</u> = <u>long o</u>. *Rule*: When you add <u>all</u>, drop an l.

18. **al-tos**: <u>Halt</u> the <u>altos</u> for the <u>solos</u>: <u>halt</u> + os (Italian musical words end in s: sopranos, pianos, solos…)

19. **am-bu-lance**: Like a <u>lance</u> (sword), the <u>ambulance</u> raced to the <u>hospital</u> (Fr. ambulance-walking hospital).

20. **a-mong**: I am <u>among</u> her <u>long</u>-time friends. *Same Pattern*: along, song, wrong.

21. **a-mount**: My <u>amount</u> of ice cream rose up like <u>a mountain</u>: <u>a + mountain</u>.

22. **a-muse-ment**: <u>A muse</u> creates <u>amusement</u>: <u>a + muse + ment</u> (L. musa:art, poetry. Gk. mousa: entertainers).

23. **a-mu-sing**: I'm <u>using</u> an <u>amusing</u> joke in my talk. *Rule*: Drop <u>Silent e</u> before vowel: <u>a + muse + ing</u>.

24. **an-cient**: <u>An ancient</u> citizen <u>entered</u> the hall: <u>an + ci + ent</u>. *Phonics*: <u>c</u> = <u>sh</u> sound.

25. **an-i-mal**: An <u>animal</u> is a <u>mammal</u>: <u>ani + mal</u> = animal (L. <u>anim</u>: alive + <u>al</u>: noun suf.).

26. **an-nu-al**: <u>Ann</u> put her photographs in her <u>annual</u>. *SPP*: an-nu-al. *Same Pattern*: annually.

27. **ans-wered**: <u>Were</u> your questions ans<u>wered</u>: <u>ans + were + d</u>?

28. **an-ti-dote**: I wr<u>ote</u> a n<u>ote</u> for an <u>antidote</u> (Gk. <u>anti</u>: against + <u>dote</u>: something given against germs, poison, etc.)

29. **a-pol-o-gy**: I made an <u>apology</u> for not playing <u>a polo</u> game: <u>a + polo + gy</u>. *Phonics*: g = <u>j</u> sound.

30. **ap-pear**: The magician made an <u>apple</u> and a <u>pear</u> <u>appear</u> from his <u>ear</u>: <u>ap + pear</u>.

31. **ap-point**: Don't <u>appoint</u> a "bad apple." *Two Vowels Rule*: <u>I</u> makes the <u>o</u> long.

32. **a-quar-i-um**: My <u>aquarium</u> water was <u>aqua</u>: <u>aqua + rium</u> (<u>aqua</u>: water + <u>rium</u>: n. suffix).

33. **aren't** (contraction: are not): <u>Aren't</u> you going to c<u>are</u> for your horse?

34. **arg-u-ment**: It's hard to have an argument with gum in your mouth: ar + gum + ent.

35. **a-rith-me-tic**: He worked with me on arithmetic: a + r + ~~with~~ + me + tic = arithmetic.

36. **ar-ma-dil-lo**: My armadillo is mad and ill: ar + mad + ill + o (Sp. little armed man or little warrior).

37. **ar-riv-al**: Upon arrival, Bar had a rival in the valley: ~~B~~ar + rival.

38. **as-tro-naut**: It takes a strong person to be an astronaut (Gk. astro-star + naut-sailor = star sailor).

39. **as-tron-o-mers**: Astronomers have a strong scientific interest in stars: a + stron + o + mers.

40. **ath-lete**: The athlete did a high leap: athlete.

41. **at-ten-tion**: At ten, the students come to attention: at + ten + tion.

42. **at-ti-tude**: It takes a great attitude to clean an attic: at + ti + tude. *Rule*: Silent e makes u long.

43. **au-di-ence**: The audience entered the auditorium through a fence: audi + ence (ones who hear).

44. **au-thor**: The author wrote about Thor, the Scandinavian God of Thunder: au + thor.

45. **au-to-graph**: The author signed her autograph: *Gk. Compound*: auto: self + graph: map = autograph

46. **au-to-ma-tic**: My auto has a mat and automatic brakes: auto-self + mat-moving + ic-adj. suf.

47. **au-tumn**: November is the last month of autumn. *SPP*: au-tum-n. *Same Root*: autumnal…

48. **a-ver-age**: Sixteen is a ver(y) average age to get a car: a + ver(y) + age = average.

49. **a-while**: Smile awhile. (Old Eng. anshwile: period of time).

50. **ba-gel**: I fed the bagel from my bag (to the) elephant (Yiddish 1930, bagel{ beygl): bag + el(ephant).

51. **bal-ance**: For her dance, she had to balance on one foot (ba: pair of + lance: metal dishes = balance).

52. **bal-my**-mild: The palm tree sways in a calm, balmy breeze. Visual: The l's tall like a palm.

53. **beach**: Each of us likes the beach. A beach is land by the sea (perhaps O. E. bece-stream).

54. **beau-ti-ful**: Be a beautiful person. *Roots and Y Rule*: beau~~ty~~ + i + ful = beautiful (Fr. beaute).

55. **be-cause**: I am thankful because I can use a scooter. *Same Pattern*: clause, pause, applause.

56. **be-come**: How did I become me? (Danish: become-bekomen) *SPP*: be-co-me.

57. **been**: I have been there and have seen the sights.

58. **be-fore**: I made more than before (Old Eng. beforen). *Compound Rule*: be + fore = before.

59. **beg-gar**: The beggar lived in a garret (attic) and looked in garbage. *Rule*: 2 g's keep e short.

60. **be-gin-ning**: At the beginning of our trip, wc stayed at an inn. *Rule*: 2 n's keep i short.

61. **be-lieve**: Don't believe a lie. *Same Pattern*: grieve relieve

62. **be-low**: We sat in the row below the stage for the show. *2 Vowels Rule*: W makes o in low long.

63. **be-neath**: They like to eat beneath the umbrella. *Same Pattern*: beneath, eat, wreath

64. **bi-cy-cle**: It's hard to ride a bicycle on icy streets (Gk. bi-two + cycle-wheel = bicycle).

65. **bird**: A golden bird was chirping in a fir tree.

66. **birth-day**: I felt mirth (joy) on my birthday. *Compound Word Rule*: birth + day = birthday.

67. **blan-ket**: An E.T. was drawn in the blank space on her blanket: blank + ET.

68. **blaze**: We like to gaze at the blaze in our fireplace. *Rule*: Silent e makes a long.

69. **bleach-ers**: <u>Each</u> set of <u>bleachers</u> needs to be opened up.

70. **blend**: Please <u>lend</u> me your <u>blender</u>?

71. **both**: <u>Both</u> <u>moths</u> have wings of velvet cl<u>oth</u>. *Same Letter Pattern*: doth, froth, moth...

72. **bou-quet**: Your <u>bouquet</u> is <u>bound</u> to thrill the <u>queen</u> (Old Fr. <u>bouquet</u> "a piece of woods").

73. **braid**: A <u>maid</u> with hair in <u>braids</u> <u>laid</u> and read. *Same Pattern*: aid, paid, staid (serious; settled).

74. **brass**: We played our <u>brass</u> instruments in cl<u>ass</u>.

75. **brook**: L<u>ook</u>! A <u>brook</u>! *Same Pattern*: book, brook, cook, hook, look, shook...

76. **brought**: I <u>ought</u> to have br<u>ought</u> the book that I <u>bought</u>. *Phonics*: <u>ough</u> = aw sound.

77. **bub-ble**: They <u>blew</u> <u>bubbles</u>. *Visual*: The <u>b's</u> look like bubble blowers. *Rule*: <u>2 b's</u> keep <u>u</u> short.

78. **built**: We <u>bu-ilt</u> a <u>bug</u> house. *SPP*: <u>bu</u>-ilt. *Visual*: The <u>u</u> looks like a bag to put nails in.

79. **bunch**: I eat a <u>bunch</u> for <u>lunch</u>. *Same Pattern*: crunch, hunch, munch, punch...

80. **bur-glar**: The <u>burglar</u> stole <u>fur</u> and <u>art</u>: <u>burg</u> + <u>lar</u>.

81. **bus-i-ness**: I need a <u>bus in</u> my <u>business</u>. *SPP*: bus-<u>i</u>-ness. *Y Rule*: <u>bus~~y~~</u> + <u>i</u> + <u>ness</u> = <u>business</u>.

82. **buy-er**: That <u>guy</u> is the <u>buyer</u>. *Rule*: When y follows a vowel, keep the y: <u>buy</u> + <u>er</u> = <u>buyer</u>.

83. **cal-en-dar**: A <u>calendar</u> has a list of <u>dates</u>.

84. **calf, calves**: <u>Alfie</u>, my <u>calf</u> is h<u>alf</u> a year old. *SPP*: c<u>al</u>-f. *Same Pattern*: dwarf, scarf, wharf...

85. **calm**: To feel c<u>al</u>m, rest under a p<u>al</u>m or use a soothing b<u>al</u>m.

86. **cam-el**: I <u>came</u> on a <u>camel</u>: <u>came</u> + <u>l</u>.

87. **can-di-date**: Our <u>candidate</u> was <u>candid</u> and <u>ate</u> before he spoke: <u>can</u> + <u>did</u> + <u>ate</u> (L. candidates-white robed).

88. **can-dle**: A <u>candle</u> <u>lets</u> light into a room.

89. **can-dy**: They sent me a can of <u>candy</u> (Arabic: kand: candy).

90. **ca-noe-ing**: He rested his t<u>oes</u> while they were <u>canoeing</u>. (Keep <u>e</u> for *pronunciation*.)

91. **cap-ture**: Whcn you go out to <u>capture</u> things, wear a <u>cap</u> for s<u>ure</u>: <u>cap</u> + <u>ture</u>.

92. **ca-reer**: I <u>care</u> about my <u>career</u>: <u>career</u>

93. **car-riage**: <u>Carri</u> is the right <u>age</u> to try a <u>carriage</u> (Celtic: <u>carr</u>-wheeled vehicle). *Y Rule*: <u>carr~~y~~</u> + i + <u>age</u>.

94. **car-ry-ing**: Don't <u>tarry</u> when <u>carrying</u> pianos. *Rule*: Keep y before -ing: <u>carry</u> + <u>ing</u> = <u>carrying</u>.

95. **catch**: My <u>cat</u> can <u>catch</u> a <u>cherry</u>: <u>cat</u> + <u>ch</u>. *Same Pattern*: batch, hatch, latch, match...

96. **caught**: When the <u>cat</u> <u>caught</u> me, I yelled, "<u>Ugh</u>!": c<u>at</u> + <u>ugh</u> + t. *Phonics*: augh = short a.

97. **cau-tion** (*Anagram*: auction): At an <u>auction</u> bid with <u>caution</u> (L. <u>caut</u>-taking care + <u>ion</u>-n. suf.).

98. **ceil-ing**: You fac<u>e</u> the <u>ceiling</u> when you look up. *2 Vowel Rule*: The i makes e long.

99. **cel-lo**: She played a <u>cello</u> while eating <u>Jello</u>. *Phonics*: In Italian, <u>c</u> is often pronounced <u>ch</u>.

100. **cemetery**: I yelled, "Eeek," in the c<u>e</u>m<u>e</u>t<u>e</u>ry. How many <u>meters</u> in this c<u>e</u>m<u>e</u>t<u>e</u>ry? *Visual*: 3 e's.

101. **cer-tain**: It is <u>certain</u> to <u>rain</u>. *Phonics*: <u>c</u> = <u>s</u>.

102. **chief**: The <u>chief</u> said, "<u>Hi</u>.": <u>c</u> + <u>hi</u> + <u>ef</u>. *Same Pattern*: mischief, mischievous.

103. **chime**: Our bells <u>chime</u> on <u>time</u>: <u>ch</u> + <u>ime</u>.

104. **cit-i-zen**: The <u>city</u>'s oldest <u>citizen</u> teaches <u>Zen</u>. *Rule*: Change y to i: <u>city</u> + i + <u>zen</u> = <u>citizen</u>.

105. **climbed**: He was <u>limber</u> and <u>climbed</u> to the top of the tree: c + limber (Old English: climban).

106. **clouds**: <u>Clouds</u> with thunder seem <u>loud</u>. *Phonics*: <u>s</u> = <u>z</u>; <u>ou</u> as in <u>out</u>.

107. **coil**: When the snake saw <u>oil</u>, it started to <u>coil</u>. *Same Pattern*: boil, foil, recoil, soil.

108. **cold**: Out in that <u>cold</u>, I felt b<u>old</u>. *Same Pattern*: bold, cold, gold, hold, old, sold, told.

109. **col-lect**: <u>Colleen</u> <u>collects</u> art to show at her <u>lectures</u>: col + lect. *Rule*: 2 l's keep <u>o</u> short.

110. **col-lege**: They had to <u>collect</u> my <u>college</u> tuition. *Phonics*: c = k; g = j. *Rule*: 2 l's keep <u>o</u> short.

111. **col-umn**: The <u>columnist</u> wrote a <u>column</u>.

112. **comb**: I <u>comb</u> my <u>bangs</u>. *SPP*: com-<u>b</u> (Old English: com<u>b</u>).

113. **com-for-ta-ble**: Up in our <u>fort, (we're) able</u> to feel <u>comfortable</u>: com + fort + able (able with strength).

114. **com-ing**: My h<u>oming</u> pigeons were c<u>oming</u> home. *Rule*: Drop <u>silent e</u>: before a vowel: come + ing

115. **com-pa-ny**: I used a <u>pan</u> to cook for <u>company</u>: com + pan + y (company-have bread with).

116. **com-pete**: <u>Pete</u> got to <u>compete</u>: com + Pete (with striving). *Same Root*: competent, competently.

117. **com-pose**: Please <u>compose</u> a song for a r<u>ose</u>. *Rule*: Silent <u>e</u> makes <u>o</u> in pose long.

118. **con-cen-tra-tion**: I don't pay a <u>cent (for a) ration</u> of <u>concentration</u>: con + cent + ration (with centering).

119. **con-cert**: He was <u>certain</u> to go to the <u>concert</u>: con + cert (con-with + cert-agreement; altogether).

120. **con-trolled**: The <u>troll</u> <u>controlled</u> the bridge: con + troll + ed. *Rule*: Accent on -trol, <u>double the l</u>.

121. **con-ver-sa-tion** (*Anagram*-voices rant on): When I <u>converse</u>, I have a <u>conversation</u>: convers<s>e</s> + ation.

122. **cough**: I have a r<u>ough</u> c<u>ough</u>. *Same Pattern*: gh = f: enough, tough…

123. **could**: I <u>could</u>, if I w<u>ould</u>, and I sh<u>ould</u>! *SPP*: cou<u>l</u>-d. *counselor ~ roles*

124. **coun-sel-or**: A coun<u>selor</u> plays many <u>roles</u>-5 letters reversed: <u>counsel</u>-advise + <u>or</u>-one who = <u>counselor</u>

125. **coun-tries**: I <u>count</u> the <u>countries</u> on each continent: count + ries. *Rule*: <u>country</u> + i + <u>es</u> = <u>countries</u>.

126. **cous-in**: Our <u>cousin</u> is with <u>us</u> <u>in</u> the <u>company</u>: <u>Co.</u>+ us + in. *Phonics*: <u>C</u> = k; <u>s</u> = z.

127. **creed** (set of beliefs): Do we all n<u>eed</u> a <u>creed</u> to live by? *Same Pattern*: deed, feed, heed.

128. **cried**: I <u>cried</u> when I fr<u>ied</u> onions. *Y Rule*: <u>cry</u> + i + ed = <u>cried</u>. *Same Pattern*: dried, tried…

129. **croc-o-dile**: <u>Croco</u>, the <u>crocodile</u> swam down the N<u>ile</u>: Croco + dile. *Rule*: Silent <u>e</u> makes <u>i</u> long.

130. **cry-ing**: She was <u>crying</u> while fr<u>ying</u> onions. *Y Rule*: Keep y before -ing: drying, trying…

131. **crys-tal**: I saw a <u>crystal</u> <u>stal</u>actite hanging from the cave's ceiling: cry + stal (Gk. krystal-clear ice).

132. **cus-to-mer**: Her <u>custom</u> is to s<u>erves</u> the <u>customer</u>: custom + er (L. consueltudo-one's own way + er).

133. **cute**: What a <u>cute</u> little fl<u>ute</u>. *Phonics*: <u>E</u> turns <u>cut</u> into <u>cute</u>. *Same Pattern*: lute, mute…

134. **dai-ly**: She got <u>daily mail</u>. *Y Rule*: Change <u>y</u> to <u>i</u>, except before -ing: <u>day</u> + i + ly = <u>daily</u>.

135. **dance**: <u>Dan (and)</u> Celia love to <u>dance</u>: Dan + Ce. *Same Pattern*: chance, glance, lance-sword.

136. **deaf**: When you are <u>deaf</u>, your <u>ear</u> can't <u>hear</u> correctly: d + ea + f (Old Eng. de-af).

137. **de-ci-sion**: A <u>decision</u> was made that <u>Dec. is</u> now the 12th month on the calendar: Dec + is + i + on.
 (On the Roman Calendar, Dec. had been the 10th month. Dec- means 10 in Latin.)

138. **de-fense**: <u>De</u>fense <u>serves</u> <u>security</u>. *Same Pattern*: incense, license, pretense, sense, suspense...

139. **def-i-nite**: Something <u>definite</u> has <u>finite</u> boundaries: <u>de + finite</u> (<u>de</u>-of + <u>finite</u>-finished; end).

140. **de-moc-ra-cy**: I watched fire <u>crackers</u> and a <u>demo</u> on <u>democracy</u> on July 4th: <u>demo + crac + y</u>.

141. **den-tist**: A <u>dentist</u> never puts a <u>fist</u> in your mouth: <u>dent + ist</u>? (Lat. <u>dent</u>-tooth + <u>ist</u>-noun suf).

142. **de-pend-able**: You are <u>able</u> to <u>depend</u> on a <u>dependable</u> person: <u>depend + able</u>.

143. **des-cend**: I can <u>describe</u> the <u>end</u> of the view as I <u>descend</u>: <u>descr̶ib̶e + end</u> (L. descend-climb away from).

144. **de-sign**: I will <u>design</u> a <u>sign</u> for you: <u>de + sign</u>. *SPP*: de-sig-n.

145. **desk**: I study <u>skills</u> at my de<u>sk</u> (Old Ital. <u>desco</u>-table).

146. **des-per-ate**: After the <u>person ate,</u> he no longer felt desperate: <u>des + per + ate</u> (L. desperare-w/out hope).

147. **de-stroy**: Greece's <u>destiny</u> was to <u>destroy</u> <u>Troy</u> with the Trojan Horse: <u>des + Troy</u>.

148. **de-ter-mine**: Nothing can <u>deter</u> (stop) me as I <u>determine</u> if this <u>mine</u> had gold: <u>deter + mine</u>.

149. **dia-mond**: What's the <u>diameter</u> of a <u>diamond</u>? (*I love* in French and Latin is <u>amo</u>: <u>Diamonds</u> are for love).

150. **dif-fer-ent** (3 syllables): I pay a <u>different</u> <u>rent</u>. *Rule*: Accent on 1st syllable, don't double the <u>r</u>.

151. **di-no-saur**: <u>Dino</u>, our <u>dinosaur</u> <u>sa</u>(ves) <u>ur</u>chins (bratty boys): <u>Dino</u> (terrible) + <u>sav̶es̶</u> + <u>ur̶c̶hins</u> (lizard).

152. **dis-a-gree**: I <u>disagree</u> on the shade of <u>green</u>. *Rule*: Just add prefix: <u>dis</u> (pre-not) + <u>agree</u> = <u>disagree</u>.

153. **dis-co-ver**: I can <u>discover</u> you hiding under the <u>cover</u>: <u>dis</u> (under) + <u>cover</u> = <u>discover</u>.

154. **dis-cuss**: Don't <u>cuss</u> when you <u>discuss</u>: <u>dis</u> (not) + <u>cuss</u> (strike) = <u>discuss</u> (not strike-talk instead).

155. **di-vide**: Take <u>divid</u> (palindrome: same both ways) + <u>e</u>: <u>divid + e</u> = <u>divide</u> (Lat. dividere-to divide).

156. **di-vi-dend**: Take <u>divid</u> (palindrome) + <u>end</u>: <u>divid + end</u> (end result from dividing).

157. **diz-zy**: Did that <u>fizzy</u> drink make you <u>dizzy</u>? (Old Eng. ysig - foolish). *Beat*: d-i-z-z-y.

158. **doc-tor**: My <u>doctor</u> is a doc concerned with the <u>torment</u> of disease: <u>doc + tor</u>.

159. **does**: Two <u>does</u> (female deer) are in <u>does</u> (He does it). *Same Pattern*: goes, hoes, foes, toes...

160. **doubt**: I have <u>double</u> <u>doubt</u> about that plan. *SPP*: dou-<u>b</u>-t.

161. **dough**: It's not <u>tough</u> to make <u>dough</u>. *Phonics*: O<u>ugh</u> = long <u>o</u>.

162. **dread-ful**: I <u>read</u> a <u>dreadful</u> tale. *Rule*: Drops an <u>l</u> when full is a suffix: dread + ful̶l̶ = dreadful.

163. **dumb**: <u>Dumbo</u> – The Flying Elephant – was not <u>dumb</u>.

164. **dwarves**: Did the 7 <u>dwarves</u> <u>carve</u> their beds? *Same Pattern*: scarves, wharves (Old English plurals).

165. **ea-gle**: The mother <u>eagle</u> watched over her <u>eaglets</u> (baby eagles). *OWF*: Hear <u>gl</u> in eagle in eaglet.

166. **ear-ly**: He got up <u>early</u> to h<u>ear</u> the birds sing: <u>h̶ear + ly</u> (Old Eng. aerlic: early).

167. **Earth** (anagram: heart): He put his <u>ear</u> to the <u>earth</u> to hear its h<u>ear</u>t beat: <u>ear + th</u> = <u>earth</u>.

168. **el-e-phant**: The <u>elephant</u> has an <u>ant</u> on its back: <u>eleph + ant</u> = <u>elephant</u> (Gk. elephas; ph = f)

169. **e-le-ven**: <u>Seven</u> and <u>Eleven</u> are not <u>even</u> numbers: el<u>even</u>.

170. **em-brace**: Let's <u>race</u> to see who can <u>embrace</u> Mom first: <u>em</u> (prefix-with) + <u>brace</u> (L. <u>bracela</u>: two arms).

171. **en-gi-neer**: The <u>engineer</u> must st<u>eer</u> the train.

172. **e-nough**: <u>Enough</u> of the <u>rough</u> stuff! *Phonics*: Greek: <u>gh</u> = <u>f</u> sound.

173. **en-ter-tain**: We will <u>enter</u> and <u>entertain</u>: <u>enter + tain</u>. *2 Vowel Rule*: The i makes <u>a</u> long in -<u>tain</u>.

174. **e-qual-ly**: <u>All</u> the gifts are <u>equally</u> divided. *Rule*: Qu = 1 letter. *Suffix Rule*: <u>equal + ly = equally</u>.

175. **e-ra-ser**: An <u>eraser</u> serves for <u>erasing</u> black boards: era<u>ser</u>. *Rule*: Silent <u>e</u> makes <u>a</u> long in <u>erase</u>.

176. **es-capes**: Superman <u>escapes</u> in his <u>S</u> (es) <u>capes</u>: <u>es + capes</u> (es-away from + capa: Sp.-hooded cloak).

177. **eve-ning**: That <u>evening</u> the sky was <u>even</u> scarlet. *Suffix Rule*: <u>even + ing = evening</u>.

178. **ex-act-ly**: The play's first <u>act</u> began <u>exactly</u> at eight p.m: <u>ex + act + ly</u>.

179. **ex-am-ple**: My <u>exam</u> will be comple<u>te</u> once I give an <u>example</u>: <u>exam + ple</u>.

180. **ex-ceed**: Don't <u>exceed</u> the <u>speed</u> limit. *Two Vowel Rule*: <u>2 e's</u> create a long e: <u>exceed</u>.

181. **ex-er-cise**: Walking in a <u>city</u> is a <u>wise</u> <u>exercise</u>. *Phonics*: C = s; s = z. (L. exercitium-to train)

182. **ex-haust**: <u>Ha</u>, don't <u>exhaust</u> <u>us</u> when we work for you: <u>ex + ha + us + t</u> (L. exhaustus-emptied out; drained)

183. **ex-pla-na-tion**: He told them the <u>plan</u> in his <u>explanation</u>: <u>ex + plan + ation</u>.

184. **ex-plor-a-tion**: He took <u>rations</u> (measures of food) on his <u>explorations</u>. *Rule*: <u>explore + ation</u>.

185. **fa-ble**: I'm <u>able</u> to read you a <u>fable</u> with a <u>f</u>amous moral: <u>f + able</u>.

186. **fa-mil-i-ar**: It is not good to be <u>familiar</u> with a <u>liar</u>. *Y Rule*: famil<u>y</u> + i + ar = <u>familiar</u>.

187. **fa-ther**: She helped <u>her</u> <u>father</u> at her home: <u>f + at + her</u> (Old Eng. Faeder).

188. **Feb-ru-ar-y**: <u>R U</u> (Are you) ready for February to come? <u>Feb + RU + ary</u>.

189. **fawn**: A <u>fawn</u> was standing on our <u>lawn</u>.

190. **field**: The <u>elder</u> farmers planted the <u>field</u>. *Same Pattern*: field, shield, wield, yield

191. **fiend**: That was the <u>end</u> of the <u>fiend</u>: <u>fiend</u>.

192. **fierce**: The <u>fierce</u> giant yelled, "<u>Fie</u>…": <u>fierce</u>.   *Fie fierce fiend* (handwritten)

193. **fin-a-lize**: We need to <u>finalize</u> your <u>size</u>: <u>final + ize = finalize</u> (<u>fin</u>: Lat.-end + <u>al</u>-adj. suf + <u>ize</u>-v. suf).

194. **fin-ger**: She put a <u>ring</u> on <u>her</u> <u>finger</u>.

195. **fin-ish**: <u>Finish</u> your <u>dish</u> (<u>fin</u>-Lat. finire-to end + <u>ish</u>-adj. suf). *Same Pattern*: fish, swish, wish…

196. **flight**: *Phonics*: Letters -<u>igh</u> = <u>I</u> sound I took a <u>night</u> <u>flight</u>. *Same Pat*: light, night, plight…

197. **flute**: She played a <u>lute</u> and a <u>flute</u>. *Silent E Rule*: E makes u in long. *Same Pat*: mute, cute…

198. **foal**: The little <u>foal</u> was the color of <u>coal</u>.

199. **for-eign**: Be<u>fore</u> he came to America, he lived in a <u>foreign</u> country. *Phonics*: -<u>eig</u> = short i

200. **for-feit**: He had to <u>forfeit</u> <u>it</u>.

201. **for-ty**: The <u>fort</u> was <u>forty</u> years old. *Same Pattern*: Mort, port, sort…

202. **fought**: You <u>ought</u> not to have <u>fought</u>.

203. **foun-da-tion**: He wanted to <u>found</u> <u>a</u> <u>foundation</u> (<u>found</u>-establish + <u>ation</u>-noun suffix).

204. **foun-tain**: The water fell from the <u>fountain</u> fell like <u>rain</u> like <u>rain</u> on a <u>mountain</u>.

205. **fra-grant**: His <u>grant</u> researches what people find <u>fragrant</u>: <u>fra + grant</u>. My pet <u>ant</u> is <u>fragrant</u>.

206. **freight**: He sent <u>eight</u> pounds by freight.

207. **frog**: The <u>frog</u> was with a <u>dog</u> on a <u>log</u> in the <u>fog</u>. *Compound Word*: frog + man = <u>frogman</u>.

208. **fudge**: The <u>d</u> in <u>fudge</u> is for <u>d</u>ivine. *SPP*: fud-ge. *Phonics*: <u>G</u> = *j* sound. *Same Pattern*: grudge…

209. **gal-ax-y**-system of stars: They want the best <u>gala</u> (showy party) in the <u>galaxy</u>.

210. **gar-land**: She made a <u>garland</u> from flower growing on her <u>gar</u>(den) <u>land</u>: <u>gar + land</u>.

211. **germs**: <u>Germs get</u> in and cause diseases (L. <u>germen</u>-bud). *Phonics*: g = j

212. **get-ting**: I keep <u>getting wet setting</u> sprinklers. *Rule*: <u>2 t's</u> keep the e short: betting, letting…

213. **ghost**: A <u>ghost</u> was my <u>host</u>: <u>g + host</u>. *SPP*: g-host. *Same Pattern*: most, post.

214. **gi-ant**: A <u>giant</u> is the largest kind of <u>ant</u>. *Phonics*: g = <u>j</u> sound.

215. **gi-raffe**: Does having a long neck <u>affect giraffes</u>? *SPP*: gi-raf-fe. *Phonics*: g = <u>j</u> sound.

216. **give**: They l<u>ive</u> to <u>give</u> (Since no Eng. word ends in <u>v</u>, <u>e</u> completes <u>give</u> without making the <u>i</u> long. Also: love…)

217. **glade** (meadow): Each bl<u>ade</u> of grass in the <u>glade</u> felt soft.

218. **glist-en**: <u>Listen</u> and watch the <u>ten</u> colored lights <u>glisten</u> to the beat. SPP: glis-ten.

219. **g-naw**: Don't <u>gnaw</u> on my s<u>aw</u>. *SPP*: g-naw. *Same Pattern*: gnat, gnome, gnu…

220. **g-nome**: I know a <u>gnome</u> whose <u>home</u> is <u>Nome</u> (in Alaska). *SPP*: g-nome.

221. **gob-let**: Let me put a <u>gob</u> of chocolate pudding in this <u>goblet</u>: <u>gob + let</u>.

222. **goes**: When he <u>goes</u> driving, d<u>oes</u> he go to the beach?

223. **gram-mar** (*Palindrome*: <u>rammar</u>): <u>Ma</u> gave us a <u>gram</u> of <u>grammar</u> a day. *Rule*: <u>2 m's</u> keep <u>a</u> short.

224. **gray** (color, adj.): The <u>ray</u> couldn't cut through <u>gray</u> sky. *Same Pattern*: bay, say…(Grey, Gray-last names).

225. **grief, grieve**: Don't <u>gripe</u> over <u>grief</u>; <u>grieve</u> instead.

226. **ground**: She drew a <u>round</u> drawing on the <u>ground</u> (Old English: grund).

227. **group**: The group ate s<u>oup</u> (Italian: gruppo).

228. **growl**: We heard the wolves h<u>owl</u> and <u>growl</u>. *SPP*: grow-<u>l</u>.

229. **guard**: <u>G, U</u> work h<u>ard</u> as a <u>guard</u>: <u>GU + ard</u>.

230. **guess**: <u>G, U</u> made a good <u>guess</u>, but it's <u>less</u> than the amount: <u>GU + ess</u>.

231. **half, halves**: My c<u>alf</u>, Alfie, is half a year old. *SPP*: hal-f.

232. **har-bor**: The boats <u>bordered</u> the <u>harbor</u>.

233. **harm-ful**: Sound an al<u>arm</u> if something <u>harmful</u> is near. *Same Pattern*: charm, farm, harm…

234. **harp**: I played A <u>sharp</u> on my <u>harp</u>: ~~sharp~~.

235. **have**: I g<u>ave</u> you what I <u>have</u>. (Silent <u>e</u> doesn't make <u>a</u> in <u>have</u> long. Since no Eng. word ends in <u>v</u>, it just ends have.)

236. **heard**: I <u>heard</u> them with my <u>ear</u>: <u>heard</u> (past of <u>hear</u>. Add <u>d</u> to get <u>heard</u>).

237. **hearth**: The bricks on the <u>hearth</u> were made from <u>earth</u>: <u>hearth</u>.

238. **heav-en**: <u>Eaves</u> are high like <u>heaven</u>. *Same Pattern*: leaven, heavy…

239. **height**: He has a <u>height</u> of <u>eight</u> feet: <u>height</u>.

240. **hon-est**: Bees make <u>honest</u> honey: <u>hon + e~~y~~ + st</u>.

241. **hos-pi-tal**: The <u>a</u>mbulance raced to the <u>hospital</u>

242. **house**: Come see a m<u>ouse</u> at our <u>house</u> (house-hus-Old English before 900).

(garden gnome ⤳)

243. **huge**: I want a <u>huge</u> <u>hug</u>. *Phonics*: <u>G</u> = <u>j</u> sound. *Rule*: Silent <u>e</u> turns <u>hug</u> into <u>huge</u>.

244. **hug-ged**: He b<u>ugged</u> her until she <u>hugged</u> him. *Rule*: <u>2 g's</u> keeps <u>u</u> short

245. **hun-dred**: I held a <u>hundred</u> <u>red</u> balloons: hun + <u>dred</u>.

246. **i-de-a**: Her <u>idea</u> for a <u>deal</u> was great. *Phonics*: Hear each vowel: <u>i-de-a</u>.

247. **ig-loo**: The m<u>oo</u>n rose above the <u>igloo</u>.

248. **im-ag-i-na-tion**: I want to go to the <u>Imagi Nation</u>. *Rule*: Drop Silent E: <u>imagi</u> + n<u>e</u> + ation.

249. **in-crease**: <u>Increase</u> your income with <u>ease</u>: in + cr + ease.

250. **in-debt-ed**: <u>Deb</u> (and) <u>Ted</u> were inde<u>bt</u>ed to each other: in + Deb + Ted = inde<u>bt</u>ed.

251. **in-di-vid-u-al**: An <u>individual</u> can play <u>dual</u> roles: <u>in + di + vi + dual</u>. *Visual*: <u>3 i's</u>.

252. **in-for-ma-tion**: I'm <u>in for</u> citizens having <u>information</u> about our n<u>ation</u>: <u>in + for + m + ation</u>.

253. **in-spect**: He put his <u>spect</u>acles on to <u>inspect</u> the project: <u>in + spect</u>…

254. **in-stead**: He r<u>ead</u> <u>instead</u>. *Same Pattern*: bread, lead (pencil), tread (walk)…

255. **in-stinct**: <u>In</u> case of <u>stings</u>, a<u>ct</u> by <u>instinct</u> and pull out the stinger: <u>in + sting + act</u> = <u>instinct</u>.

256. **in-struc-tor**: The <u>instructor</u> will <u>instruct or</u> give orders.

257. **in-stru-ments**: You <u>strum</u> some <u>instruments</u>: <u>in + strum + ents</u>.

258. **in-tel-li-gent**: <u>In</u> a moment, <u>I</u> can <u>tell</u> you that <u>gent</u> is <u>intelligent</u>: <u>in + tell + I + gent</u>.

259. **in-ter-est-ing**: When <u>Tere</u> got a <u>sting</u>, it was <u>interesting</u> for her to learn about it: <u>in + Tere + sting</u>.

260. **inter-rupt**: To <u>interrupt</u> is to <u>err</u> or <u>rupt</u>ure conversation (<u>inter</u>-between + <u>rupt</u>-break apart).

261. **in-tro-duc-tion**: At the <u>Intro</u>, they showed a new duct (pipe carrying water, air…): <u>intro</u> + <u>duc</u> + t + io…

262. **jewel-ry**: She looked in her <u>jewelry</u> for the <u>l</u>ost <u>r</u>ing: jewel<u>ry</u>. *Pronunciation*: 2 syllables.

263. **jour-neys**: My <u>journal</u> describes <u>our journeys</u> through the Florida K<u>eys</u>.

264. **judgment**: I trust the <u>judgment</u> of a good <u>m</u>an.

265. **juice**: I like <u>ice</u> in my <u>juice</u>.

266. **ka-yak** (palindrome): <u>Kay</u> was rowing the <u>kayak</u>.

267. **kick-ball**: <u>N</u>ick and <u>R</u>ick play <u>kickball</u>. *Compound Rule*: Just add: <u>kick</u> + <u>ball</u> = <u>kickball</u>.

268. **kin-der-gar-ten**: There were <u>ten</u> children in the <u>kindergarten</u> (Ger. <u>kinder</u>-child + <u>garten</u>-garden).

269. **knave**: The *k*nave gave away the tarts. *SPP*: <u>k</u>-na-ve.

270. **knee**: He banged his *k*nee on a tr<u>ee</u>. *SPP*: <u>k</u>-nee.

271. **knife**: His *k*nife saved his l<u>ife</u>. *Rule*: <u>Silent E</u> make the <u>i</u> in *k*nife long.

272. **la-bor**: I <u>labor</u> on work at my <u>lab or</u> office: <u>lab + or</u>.

273. **laid**: The m<u>aid</u> <u>laid</u> the cups on the table. *Same Pattern*: aid, raid, said…

274. **lamb**: A <u>lam</u>*b* is a <u>b</u>aby sheep.

275. **lamp**: She turned on the <u>lamp</u> to read at c<u>amp</u>. *Same Pattern*: camp, damp, ramp, stamp…

276. **lan-tern**: The wick is in the cen<u>ter</u> of the <u>lantern</u>: lan + <u>tern</u> (Gk. lampter-light; lamp).

277. **la-zy**: He felt too <u>lazy</u> to even do a m<u>aze</u>. *Same*: crazy, hazy… (For <u>laziness</u>, change y to <u>i</u> + <u>ness</u>).

278. **leaves**: <u>Leaves</u> collect in the <u>eaves</u>: <u>l</u> + <u>eaves</u>.

279. **leg-al**: There's no <u>legal</u> law for how fast a <u>gal</u> can run: le + gal (L. leg: law + al-adj. suffix).

280. **li-brar-y**: You can find <u>rare</u> books in the <u>library</u>: <u>li</u> + <u>b</u> + <u>rare</u> + <u>y</u>. *Pronounce* 2 r's: li-b<u>r</u>ar-y.

281. **li-cense**: You get a <u>license</u> for a <u>c</u>ar. *Same*: defense, incense, intense, sense, suspense, tense…

282. **lim<u>b</u>**: It helps to be <u>limb</u>er when you c<u>limb</u> a <u>limb</u>.

283. **li-mit**: The store had a <u>limit</u> on <u>limes</u>: <u>lim~~es~~</u> + <u>it</u> = <u>limit</u>.

284. **lis-ten**: <u>Listen</u> for <u>ten</u> minutes: <u>lis</u> + <u>ten</u> = <u>listen</u>.

285. **lit-er-a-ture**: Our <u>era</u> has good children's <u>literature</u> for s<u>ure</u>: <u>lit</u> + <u>era</u> + <u>ture</u>.

286. **li-zard**: My <u>lizard</u>, <u>Liz</u>, has a <u>hard</u> shell: <u>Liz</u> + ~~hard~~ = lizard.

287. **lla-ma**: We saw a <u>mama</u> <u>llama</u> with her babies (Sp. llama).

288. **loaves, loaf**: He <u>loves</u> fresh-baked <u>loaves</u>. Put <u>a</u> in the middle of <u>love</u> + <u>s</u>: <u>lo-a-ve</u> + <u>s</u> = lo<u>a</u>ves.

289. **love**: A d<u>ove</u> is a symbol of <u>love</u> (Old Fr. luve).

290. **loy-al**: A friend who is <u>loyal</u> is <u>al</u>ways true: loy + al~~ways~~ *Same Pattern*: loyal-loyalty, royal-royalty

291. **mag-a-zine**: This is <u>a</u> <u>fine</u> <u>magazine</u>: mag + a + z<u>ine</u> (Arabic: makzan-a storehouse).

292. **maj-es-ty**: The <u>jester</u> did tricks for his <u>majesty</u> the king: <u>ma</u> + <u>jest~~er~~</u> + <u>y</u>.

293. **man-a-ge-ment**: That <u>man</u> has the <u>age</u> and skills to <u>manage</u> <u>men</u>: <u>man</u> + <u>age</u> <u>men</u> + t.

294. **ma-ny**: <u>Many</u> a <u>man</u> hasn't <u>any</u> hobby. (Old Eng. manig: many).

295. **mar-ri-age**: I am the <u>age</u> for <u>marriage</u>. *Rule*: Change y to i except before -ing : <u>marr~~y~~ + i + age</u>.

296. **men-i-al**-lowly, servant-like: The <u>men, I, (and) Al</u> did the <u>menial</u>, clean-up work: <u>men</u> + <u>I</u> + <u>Al</u>.

297. **math-e-mat-ics**: <u>Ma (has) them at</u> school learning <u>mathematics</u>: <u>ma</u> + <u>them</u> + <u>at</u> + ics.

298. **mes-sag-es**: Since I've had this <u>mess (for) ages</u>, I can't find my <u>messages</u>: <u>mess</u> + <u>ages</u>.

299. **might've** (contraction-might have): I <u>might</u>'ve done it <u>right</u>. *Phonics*: <u>Igh</u> = <u>long i</u> (bright, sight).

300. **mi-nus**: <u>Linus</u> is never <u>minus</u> his blanket. *Phonics*: One <u>n</u> keeps the <u>u</u> long.

301. **mis-take**: Don't m<u>ake</u> the same <u>mistake</u> (Lat. prefix: <u>mis</u>-wrongly + <u>take</u>).

302. **mis-treat**: Don't <u>mistreat</u> your body; <u>eat</u> good food: mis + tr<u>eat</u> (Lat. prefix: <u>mis</u>-wrongly + <u>treat</u>).

303. **mod-el**: <u>Del</u> is a <u>model</u>: mo<u>del</u>.

304. **moon-light**: Moonlight is not at n<u>oon</u>, but at n<u>ight</u>. *Phonics*: <u>Igh</u> = <u>i</u> sound. *Rule*: Add <u>moon</u> + <u>light</u>.

305. **more**: The <u>more</u> I w<u>ore</u> it, the <u>more</u> it t<u>ore</u>. *Same Pattern*: core, fore, lore (literature), sore…

306. **mor-sel**: She <u>selected</u> a <u>select</u> <u>morsel</u> of fish for her cat.

307. **mort-gage**: <u>Mort</u> had to <u>gage</u> the value of the <u>mortgage</u> on his house: <u>Mort</u> + <u>gage</u>.

308. **mos-qui-toes**: <u>Most</u> of the <u>mosquitoes</u> <u>quit</u> biting my <u>toes</u>: <u>mos~~t~~</u> + <u>qui~~t~~</u> + <u>toes</u>. *Phonics*: qu = k.

309. **most**: Do <u>most</u> people believe in g<u>host</u>s? *Same Pattern*: ghost, host, lost, post.

310. **mo-ther**: She wanted no <u>other</u> <u>mother</u> than her own: <u>m</u> + <u>other</u> (Old Eng. mother-modor).

311. **moun-tains**: <u>Out</u> in the <u>mountains</u>, it often r<u>ains</u>: <u>moun</u> + <u>tains</u>

312. **mouth**: He yelled out, "<u>south</u>." with his <u>mouth</u>: <u>mouth</u> *SPP*: mo-u<u>th</u>.

"SOUTH!"

313. **mus-cle**: I likes to clench my muscle: mus-clench (Lat. musculus-little mouse: bulge resembled this)

314. **mu-se-um**: Use the museum: museum (muse-entertainer + um-n. suf). *Bookend Word*: mu-se-um.

315. **mu-si-cian**: A musician plays music (Lat. musica-art of muse + ian-adj suf.) *SPP*: mu-si-ci-an.

316. **mustn't**: (contraction-must not) I mustn't crash in the dust. *Same Pattern*: gust, just, lust, rust…

317. **naugh-ty**: I caught that naughty mosquito: n + eaught + y. *Phonics*: augh = short a sound.

318. **near-ly**: Since my early years, I had loved him nearly and dearly (Old Eng. near-nigh).

319. **ne-ces-sary**: Time for recess is necessary at school: n +re-cess + ary = necessary.

320. **neigh-bor**: Eight neighbors were born today: n + eight + born = neighbor (OE. *nigh-ge-bur-near by farm*

321. **neph-ew**: I have a few nephews: ne + phew (Ph = f in Gk.).

322. **nev-er-the-less**: Nevertheless never has any vowel except eeee… *Visual*: 4 e's in nevertheless.

323. **niece**: My niece is nice. To create niece, put e in the middle of nice: ni + e + ce = niece.

324. **nim-bus** (cloud): The dark nimbus cloud looked to him like a bus: nim + bus.

325. **nine-ty** (90): That pine is ninety years old. *Rule*: Keep Silent e before vowel suffix: nine + ty.

326. **ninth**: He received ninth place in this marathon: n + in + th. *SPP*: nin-th.

327. **oc-curred**: O, C (see) what occurred in the current: O C + *Rule*: Accent on cur, double r.

328. **o-cean**: Ocean and sea are synonyms: ocean (Lat. oceanus; Gk. okeanus). *SPP*: o-ce-an.

329. **oint-ment**: They gave me ointment at my appointment.

330. **op-er-a**: Our time is a popular era for opera: pop + era (L. opera-work).

331. **op-por-tun-i-ty**: He had an opportunity to give port (workers) unity: op + port + unity.

332. **orange**: An orange is in the range of citrus fruit: o + range = orange (Sanskrit. naranga-orange tree).

333. **or-i-gin**: He knew about the origin of the rig in the port: o + rig + in (rig-sails, mast, etc. of a ship).

334. **or-phan**: The orphan held a beautiful fan. (Change the f to ph and you have or-phan.)

335. **ought**: O, ugh, I ought not to have bought that dessert: o + ugh + t . *Phonics*: ough = short a.

336. **out-rage-ous**: I felt rage about the outrageous lie: out + rage + ous. *Rule*: E keeps g soft.

337. **oy-sters**: The boys and their sisters found some oysters: boy + sisters = oysters.

338. **paid**: I paid for first aid. *Exception*: Y Rule: Change y to i : pay + i + d = paid.

339. **par-a-chute**: I saw them parachute at the parade. *Phonics*: ch = sh. *Rule*: Silent e makes u long.

340. **par-al-lel**: On a par (are) all three l's in parallel are par + all + el. *Visual*: Three parallel l's.

341. **part-ner**: He wanted his partner to choose a good part in the play: partner.

342. **peach**: Each peach is easy to reach: peach *Two Vowel Rule*: The a makes the e long in peach.

343. **ped-al**: The pedal always turns the wheel on a bike: ped (foot) + al (adj suf) = pedal.

344. **pen-cil**: With pen and pencil, he'd stencil cilia for biology: pen-cilia. *Phonics*: C = s sound.

345. **peo-ple**: People, don't pick the peonies please: pe-o + ple.

346. **per-cus-sion**: No person can cuss our percussion section: per + cuss + ion (L. percuss-strike + ion-n. suf

347. **per-form**: I want every person to perform with correct form: per + form.

348. **per-form-ance**: She will <u>perform</u> a d<u>ance</u> for h<u>er</u> <u>performance</u>: <u>per + form + ~~d~~ance</u>.

349. **per-ma-nent**: A <u>mane</u> is a <u>permanent</u> part of a horse: <u>per + mane + nt</u>.

350. **phan-tom**: <u>Tom</u> was a <u>phantom</u> for Halloween: <u>phan + Tom</u>. *Phonics*: Greek: Ph = f.

351. **pi-a-no, pi-a-nos**: <u>Pia</u> played the <u>piano</u>: <u>Pia</u> + no (Italian musical words: pianos, solos…end in s.)

352. **pierce**: <u>P</u>ierce the <u>pie</u> with a knife: <u>pierce</u>.

353. **pint**: She gave her <u>pinto</u> a <u>pint</u> of water: <u>pint</u>~~o~~ *Exception* to Short Vowel Rule.

354. **pla-net**: From our <u>plane</u>, we saw a <u>planet</u>: <u>planet</u>.

355. **played**: <u>Ed</u> <u>played</u> and st<u>ayed</u> all d<u>ay</u>. *Rule* (Keep <u>y</u> when it follows a vowel: playing, prayed, stayed…)

356. **plum**: She chewed pl<u>um</u> g<u>um</u>. *Same Pattern*: bum, glum, hum, rum, strum…

357. **plumb-er**: The <u>plumber</u> used <u>lumber</u> for his repairs. *SPP*: plum-<u>b</u>er:

358. **plume**: She held a <u>plum</u>-colored <u>plume</u>. *Silent E Rule*: The e makes the u before it long.

359. **poise**: We ate <u>poi</u> with <u>poise</u>: *SPP*: <u>poi</u>-se (poi: Hawaiian dish made from pounded tarot roots) .

360. **por-poise**: The <u>porpoise</u> made a high-pitched n<u>oise</u> and jumped with <u>poise</u>: <u>por + poise</u>.

361. **pos-ses-sion**: A <u>posse</u> set out to take <u>possession</u> of the bandit: <u>posse</u>ssion.

362. **pos-si-ble**: Is it <u>possible</u> for your <u>siblings</u> to come? pos + si – bl~~ings~~ + e (In possibly, you hear <u>bl</u>).

363. **po-ta-toes**: <u>Potatoes</u> have <u>toes</u> and <u>eyes</u>. *Roots*: (Spanish-Indian). *Same Pattern*: tomatoes.

364. **pow-er**: He wanted <u>power</u> n<u>ow</u>: <u>pow + er</u>. *Same Pattern*: bower, shower, tower…

365. **pre-serve**: <u>Preserve</u> the earth, and it will <u>serve</u> you: <u>pre + serve</u>. (Lat. pre-before + <u>serve</u>-watch over):

366. **pres-i-dent**: The <u>president</u> will <u>reside</u> in Wash. D.C.: <u>president</u>.

367. **pres-sure**: Be s<u>ure</u> to <u>press</u> and check the <u>pressure</u>. *Rules*: 2 s's keep <u>e</u> short. <u>E</u> makes <u>u</u> long.

368. **priest**: A <u>priest</u> often prays in <u>p</u>rivate. *SPP*: <u>pri + est</u>.

369. **prin-ce** (princes): <u>S</u>ince the <u>prince</u> like m<u>ince</u>, he won't w<u>ince</u> (draw back) at the pie: <u>prince</u>.

370. **prin-ces-ses**: Do <u>princesses</u> live on ex<u>cesses</u> (too much) ? *Pron*: For plural, add <u>cs</u>: prin<u>cesses.</u>

371. **priv-i-lege**: Don't give a <u>privilege</u> to a <u>vile</u> person: pri<u>vile</u>ge. *SPP*: priv-i-lege.

372. **pro-bab-ly**: The <u>baby</u> <u>probably</u> did it. *SPP*: pro-bab-ly. *Beat*: p-r-o b-a-b l-y.

373. **prom**: They came <u>from</u> the <u>prom</u> at midnight.

374. **pro-mise**: For a <u>promise</u> <u>see</u> that you don't com<u>promise</u>: <u>pro + mi + se</u>~~e~~ (O. E. promisse-send forth).

375. **pro-mo-tion**: We set her <u>promotion</u> in <u>motion</u>. *Rule*: Drop <u>Silent e</u> before vowel suf: <u>promot</u>~~e~~ + <u>ion.</u>

376. **pro-nounce**: We learn to <u>pronounce</u> the name of each noun. *SPP*: pro-noun-ce (bounce, ounce, pounce).

377. **pro-nun-ci-a-tion**: We were taught <u>pronunciation</u> by a <u>nun</u>: pro<u>nun</u>ciation

378. **pro-pos-al**: They <u>saluted</u> <u>Sal</u>'s <u>proposal</u>.

379. **prove**: Can you pr<u>ove</u> l<u>ove</u>? (Since no word in English ends in v, silent e is added to complete the word.)

380. <u>psalm</u> (a psalm is like a prayer): I held a <u>psalm</u> book in my <u>palm</u> (Gk. psalmos-song: ps = f).

381. **pump-kin**: We like to carve pum<u>p</u>kins with our <u>kin</u>. *SPP*: pump-<u>kin</u>.

382. **pu-pils**: That <u>pup</u> is not one of my <u>pupils</u>: pu-pils (L. pupillus). *Rules*: Single <u>p</u> keeps <u>u</u> long.

383. **pure**: I want to find a <u>pure</u> <u>cure</u>. *Rule*: <u>Silent</u> <u>e</u> makes <u>u</u> long. *Same*: purer, purest, endure, lure.

384. **pur-pose**: Does my <u>purpose</u> for choosing <u>purple</u> <u>pose</u> a problem? pur~~ple~~ + pose = <u>purpose</u>.

385. **quaint**: Now, <u>aint</u> that qu<u>aint</u>! <u>qu</u> + <u>aint</u> *Rules*: Qu = one letter. *2 Vowels*: <u>I</u> makes <u>a</u> long.

386. **quar-ter**: *Clue*: A qu<u>art</u>er of his wealth was for <u>art</u> : <u>quarter</u> (Lat. quartus-fourth + <u>er</u>-n. suffix).

387. **quar-tet**: The <u>quartet</u> (4 singers) sang for a <u>quarter</u>-hour: <u>quarte~~r~~</u> + <u>t</u> (Lat. quartus-four + <u>et</u>-n. suf).

388. **quote**: He wr<u>ote</u> down his favorite <u>quote</u> (L., quotare-divide into verses). *Qu and Silent E Rules*.

389. **rasp-ber-ry**: When I gra<u>sp</u>ed the <u>raspberry</u>, I felt the <u>raspy</u> (rough like a saw) vines.

390. **reached**: <u>Each</u> child <u>reached</u> for a <u>peach</u>: <u>p</u> + <u>each</u> = peach.

391. **re-a-lize**: I <u>realize</u> you want a <u>deal</u> in the right <u>size</u>. (F. real~~is~~ -real + <u>ize</u>-v. suf.). *OWF*: realization.

392. **re-cess**: We made a m<u>ess</u> during <u>recess</u>. <u>re</u> (again) + <u>cess</u> (stop) = <u>recess</u>. *OWF*: cessation.

393. **re-ci-tal**: At the <u>recital</u>, <u>I</u> (saw) talent: recital *Rule*: Drop Silent <u>e</u> before vowel suf: <u>recit~~e~~ + al</u>

394. **re-cog-nize**: I <u>recognize</u> my dog by his <u>size</u>: <u>re + cog + nize</u>. *Same Root*: cognizant-knowing.

395. **re-coil** (draw-back; coil up again): The snake saw <u>oil</u> and began to <u>recoil</u>. *Same Pattern*: foil, toil…

396. **re-com-mend** (or: rec-om-mend): I <u>recommend</u> you for <u>compass</u> <u>mend</u>ing: <u>re + com + mend</u>.

397. **re-lief, relieve**: Telling a <u>lie</u> gives no <u>relief</u>: <u>re + lie + f</u> = relief. *Same Pattern*: brief, grief…

398. **re-mem-ber**: <u>Remember</u> the snow of December. *Same Pattern*: ember, September, November…

399. **rep-re-sen-ta-tive**: A <u>representative</u> can <u>represent</u> (a person) at a l<u>ive</u> meeting.

400. **re-sign**: When you <u>resign</u>, you need to <u>sign</u> a number of forms: re<u>sign</u>. *SPP*: re-sig-n.

401. **res-tau-rant** (or res-taurant): I <u>rest</u> at a <u>restaurant</u> with my ant: <u>rest + a + ur + ant</u>. *SPP*: res-ta-u-rant.

402. **re-turn**: <u>Return</u> means to <u>turn</u> again: <u>re + turn</u>. *Prefix Rule*: <u>re + turn = return</u>.

403. **re-ward** (Reversal: reward – drawer): A <u>reward</u> was in his <u>drawer</u> (M.E. orig. reward was regard).

404. **rhyme**: <u>Rhyme</u> and thyme (green herb) rhyme. *Rule*: Silent e makes y long.

405. **rhy-thm**: *Visual*: Just one vowel; h in each syllable: <u>rhy</u> - <u>thm</u>. *Beat*: R – H – Y   T – H – M

406. **ri-val**: The <u>rival</u> in the <u>valley</u> caused <u>rivalry</u>: <u>ri + val~~ley~~</u> (L. rivalis: living on other side of the river).

407. **ro-bot**: <u>Robo,</u> our <u>robot</u>, can do a <u>lot</u>: <u>Robo + t</u> (Czech. robota-forced labor).

408. **ro-de-o**: He <u>rode</u> his horse in the <u>rodeo</u>: <u>rode + o</u> (Sp. rodear-to go around).

409. **ro-ses**: I water my <u>roses</u> with h<u>oses</u> (Fr. roses-pink). *Phonics*: <u>s</u> = <u>z</u>. *Rule*: Silent <u>e</u> makes <u>o</u> long.

410. **rough**: My c<u>ough</u> felt <u>rough</u>. *Phonics*: gh=f. *Same Visual Pattern*: enough, rough, tough

411. **said**: He <u>said</u> he <u>paid</u> for the book. *SPP*: <u>sa</u>-<u>id</u>. *Same Pattern*: aid, laid, paid, maid, raid.

412. **sand-wich**: Please spill no <u>t</u> (tea) on my <u>sandwich</u>. *SPP*: san<u>d</u>-wich (fr. Earl of Sandwich).

413. **scar-let** (bright red): For the color of my <u>car</u> – <u>let</u> me paint it <u>scarlet</u>: <u>s + car + let</u>.

414. **schol-ar**: A <u>scholar</u> can learn <u>art</u> at sch<u>oo~~l~~</u> (L. <u>schola</u> + <u>r</u>-noun suf. = <u>scholar</u>).

415. **school**: At nursery <u>school</u>, I played with <u>choo</u> <u>choo</u> trains: <u>s + choo + l</u> (L. schola; Gk. skhole).

416. **sci-ence**: We built a <u>fence</u> in <u>science</u>: <u>sci</u> + ~~fence~~ = <u>science</u>. (Gk. sci-knowledge + <u>ce</u>-n suf)

417. **scis-sors**: <u>Scott</u> won't <u>miss</u> or get cuts with <u>scissors</u>: <u>sc</u> + ~~miss~~ + <u>or</u> + <u>s</u>. *Phonics*: s = z sound.

418. **score**: They earned m<u>ore</u> points for their <u>score</u>.

419. **scream**: "Ice <u>cream</u>, ice <u>cream</u>…We all <u>scream</u> for ice <u>cream</u>!": <u>s + cream</u>. *Rule*: E makes a long.

420. **screech**: We began to <u>screech</u> when we saw the <u>leech</u>: <u>screech</u>. *Same Pattern*: b<u>eech</u>, l<u>eech</u>, scr<u>eech</u>.

421. **scrip-tures**: The <u>script (s)ure</u> was written by hand in ancient <u>scriptures</u>: <u>script + sure</u>.

422. **sec-re-tary**: My <u>secretary</u> can keep a <u>secret</u>: <u>secretary</u>. *OWF*: In secret<u>a</u>rial you hear the <u>a</u>.

423. **seize**: <u>See</u> him <u>seize</u> it (Old Fr. seiser: seize).

424. **sense**: Sense is an *Echo Word* with <u>se</u> echoed at the end: <u>se</u> – n – <u>se</u> = <u>sense</u>.

425. **sep-a-rate**: When I tried to sep<u>arate</u> the oranges and apples, <u>a rat</u> jumped out: <u>sep + a + rat + e</u>.

426. **sev-en**: <u>Seven</u> and el<u>even</u> are not <u>even</u> numbers: s<u>even</u>.

427. **sha-dow**: I <u>had</u> a good <u>shadow</u>, <u>now</u> that the sun was out: <u>s + had + ow</u>. (shadow-Old Saxon-skadowan).

428. **shark**: <u>Hark</u>, a <u>shark</u> is in the p<u>ark</u> lake: <u>shark</u>.

429. **shel-tered**: <u>Help</u> me build a <u>shelter</u>. *Rule*: Simply add the suffix: <u>shelter</u> + <u>ed</u> = <u>sheltered</u>.

430. **shep-herd**: A <u>shepherd</u> <u>herds</u> sh<u>ee</u>p. *Exception*: E is dropped in sheep: <u>shee + p</u> and <u>her + d.</u>

431. **shield**: The <u>elder</u> of the tribe carried a <u>shield</u>. *SPP*: shi-eld.

432. **shoul-der**: <u>Should</u> you <u>shoulder</u> so much responsibility? <u>shoulder</u>.

433. **sho-vel**: We had to <u>shovel</u> snow so <u>Velda</u> could find her house: sho<u>vel</u>. *Beat*: s-h-o v-e-l

434. **show-boat**: Look <u>how</u> we fl<u>oat</u> on the <u>showboat</u>. *Compound Rule*: show + boat = <u>showboat</u>.

435. **shriek**: She gave a <u>shrill</u> <u>shriek</u>: <u>Ek</u>!: shri<del>ll</del> + <u>ek</u> = <u>shriek</u>.

436. **sig-na-ture**: When you give your <u>signature</u>, you <u>sign a</u> s<u>ure</u> symbol of yourself.

437. **si-lent**: Please be <u>silent</u> when you <u>enter</u> the library.

438. **sim-ple**: <u>Simon</u> made a simple <u>plea</u>: <u>Sim<del>on</del></u> + <u>plea</u> = <u>simple</u>. (In <u>simply</u>, you hear the <u>pl</u> in <u>simple</u>.)

439. **since**: <u>Since</u> I like m<u>ince</u> pie, I don't w<u>ince</u> when I eat it. *SPP*: sin-ce.

440. **skate**: <u>Kate</u> loved to <u>skate</u>: <u>skate</u>. *Rule*: Silent <u>e</u> makes th<u>e</u> <u>a</u> in skat<u>e</u> long.

441. **sketch** (draw): Do you <u>etch</u> when you sketch? *SPP*: sk<u>e-t-ch</u>. (etch-engrave w/acid; outline clearly).

442. **ski-ing**: You need both i's (eyes) for skiing.

443. **sleigh**: <u>Eight</u> reindeer pull Santa's <u>sleigh</u>. *Rule*: <u>Sleigh</u> sound like <u>a</u>, so <u>e comes before i</u>.

444. **slow-ly**: He liked to <u>slowly</u> bl<u>ow</u> huge bubbles. *Same Pattern*: flow, glow, know, low, mow…

445. **smiles**: I'd walk a hundred <u>miles</u> for one of your <u>smiles</u> . *Rule*: Silent <u>e</u> makes the <u>i</u> long.

446. **smooth**: The dentist made my t<u>ooth</u> <u>smooth</u>. *Same Pattern*: booth, forsooth, smooth, tooth.

447. **snack**: He put a <u>snack</u> in his p<u>ack</u>. *Same Pattern*: back, lack, pack, snack…

448. **snor-kel**: Can you <u>snorkel</u> in <u>kel</u>p (seaweed)?

449. **some-time**: I want to visit <u>sometime</u>, and c<u>ome (at a) time </u>that is f<u>ine</u> for you.

450. **speak**: <u>Speak</u> up for those who are w<u>eak</u>. *Same Pattern*: beak, creak, peak, teak…

451. **speech**: Don't sp<u>eed</u> through your <u>speech</u>.

452. **splen-did**: <u>Did</u> you wear that <u>splendid</u> dress to the dance?

453. **splurge**: I have an <u>urge</u> to spl<u>urge</u>. *Roots*: <u>Splurge</u> is perhaps a blend of <u>splash</u> and <u>surge</u>.

454. **sports**: He enjoyed all <u>sorts</u> of <u>sports</u>.

455. **spurn**: To <u>spurn</u> means to t<u>urn</u> someone away (O. E. spurnan-to kick)

456. **square**: The 4 sides of a <u>square</u> <u>are</u> <u>equal</u>: squ<u>are</u>.

457. **squeezes**: His chest <u>squeezes</u> when he sn<u>eezes</u>. *Rule*: Qu = 1 letter (breezes, freezes, wheezes…)

458. **star**: The <u>star</u> twinkled in the d<u>ark</u>.

459. **sten-cil**: I made <u>ten</u> <u>stencil</u> drawing of <u>cilia</u> with my <u>pencil</u>: s + ten + cil<del>ia</del> = stencil. (cilia-eyelashes).

460. **ster-e-os**: <u>Steve</u> played <u>stereos</u> in the <u>stern</u> of his boat. *Rule*: <u>Stereos</u> (Gk.), a musical word, ends in -

461. **stit-ch, stit-ches**: She took the <u>stitch</u> and removed <u>it</u> (from his) <u>chest</u>: <u>st + it + chest</u> = <u>stitches</u>. (itche

462. **store**: She <u>tore</u> through the <u>store</u> to buy m<u>ore</u>.

463. **strange**: Stories of ghosts fit into the <u>range</u> of "<u>strange</u>."

464. **street**: He liked to <u>greet</u> strangers on his <u>street</u>. *Same Pattern*: beet, feet, meet, street.

465. **strength**: A <u>strong</u> <u>engine</u>'s <u>strength</u> can pull a train. *Pronounce Blends and Digraphs*: <u>str-eng-th</u>

466. **strike**: He did not mean to <u>strike</u> <u>Mike</u> with his <u>trike</u>.

467. **strings**: Violins and other <u>string</u> instruments seem to <u>ring</u>: <u>string</u>. *Same*: dings, sings, wings.

468. **stu-dent**: A <u>Students</u> need to <u>study</u> to <u>enter</u> my class: stud<del>y</del> + ent<del>er</del> = student

469. **stud-y-ing**: <u>Ying</u> was <u>studying</u>. *Rule*: Keep Final <u>y</u> before suffix, ing: study + ing = <u>studying</u>.

470. **sug-ar**: Can you grow <u>sugar</u> cane in your <u>garden</u>. *Phonics*: S = sh sound.

471. **sum-mit**: That <u>summer</u>, I climbed to the <u>summit</u> to see <u>it</u>: sum<u>mit</u>. *Rule*: <u>2 m's</u> keep <u>u</u> short.

472. **sure**: Are you <u>sure</u> that this water is <u>pure</u>? *Rule*: Silent <u>e</u> makes the <u>u</u> long in <u>sure</u>.

473. **sure-ly**: When you are <u>sure</u> of something, you can <u>surely</u> <u>rely</u> on it: <u>su + rely</u>.

474. **sur-face**: The <u>surface</u> is the <u>face</u> of the water (<u>sur</u>-above + <u>face</u>-Mid. Eng.-facen). *SPP*: sur-<u>fa-ce</u>.

475. **sur-prise**: It was a <u>surprise</u> to see a whale <u>surface</u> and <u>rise</u>: <u>sur + p + rise</u>.

476. **sur-roun-ded**: We were <u>surrounded</u> on the <u>ground</u>. *Suffix and Prefix Rules*: <u>sur + round + ed</u>.

477. **sur-vive**: Those who <u>surface</u> al<u>ive</u> will <u>survive</u>: <u>sur + vive</u> (<u>sur</u>-beyond, above + <u>vive</u>-live).

478. **sus-pense**: The <u>suspense</u> felt t<u>ense</u>. *Same Pattern*: 7 words end in -<u>se</u>: defense, incense, intense, license, sense, suspense, tense. The rest end in -ce.

479. **swears**: When someone <u>swears</u>, it sounds bad to my <u>ears</u>: sw<u>ears</u>.

480. **sweat**: We like to <u>sweat</u> off what we <u>eat</u>: sw<u>eat</u>.

481. **swirl**: She liked to <u>swirl</u> and tw<u>irl</u> and wh<u>irl</u> (The Scandinavian word: *svirla* means <u>swirl</u>.)

482. **sword**: He bet his <u>word</u> on his <u>sword</u>: <u>sword</u>. *SPP*: s-<u>word</u>.

483. **sym-pho-ny**: A great <u>symphony</u> is not <u>phony</u> (Gk. <u>symphon</u>: harmonious + <u>y</u>-n. suf.). *Phonics*: <u>ph</u> = <u>f</u>.

484. **sys-tem**: A flower <u>system</u> has a <u>stem</u>, leaves, and a flower.

485. **teach-er**: Can a <u>teacher</u> <u>reach</u> <u>each</u> student?

486. **tem-per-a-ture** (4 syllables): I lost my <u>temper</u> at the time our <u>temperature</u> was 110: <u>temper + a + ture</u>.

487. **the-a-ter** (theatre): Does the <u>theater</u> have a good <u>heater</u>? *Two Vowel Rule*: <u>A</u> makes <u>e</u> long.

488. **them-selves** (plural pronoun): They, <u>themselves</u> play with the <u>elves</u>. *Same Pattern*: delves, shelves.

489. **they**: (contraction-they would): <u>Hey</u>, <u>they</u> like to go biking: <u>they</u>. *Same Pattern*: hey, prey.

490. **thieves** (thief): <u>Thieves</u> usually steal in the <u>eves</u>: thi<u>eves</u> (Old English: theofian).

491. **thirst**: I <u>first</u> needed water for my <u>thirst</u>: th + irst = <u>thirst</u> (Lat. thyrstan-thirst).

492. **thought**: They <u>ought</u> not to be <u>thought</u>. *Suffix Rule*: Just add: <u>thought</u> + <u>less</u>.

493. **thread**: Can you <u>read</u> the label on the <u>thread</u>? *Same Pattern*: bread, dread, head, lead, read...

494. **ther-mos**: She put <u>her mos</u>(t) loved drink in a <u>thermos</u>: t + her + most = thermos

495. **threat**: Facing <u>thre</u>(e) <u>at</u> once was a <u>great</u> <u>threat</u>: <u>three</u> + <u>at</u> (O. E. threat-pressure, oppression).

496. **thumb**: <u>Thumb</u>elina was no bigger than a <u>thumb</u>. *SPP*: thum-<u>b</u>.

497. **ti-tle**: What is the <u>title</u> of a <u>legend</u> you love? (Old Eng. titul-title).

498. **to-ma-toes**: He squished the <u>tomatoes</u> between his <u>toes</u> (Spanish-Indian).

499. **tongue**: He had a "<u>ton</u>" of <u>gum</u> on his <u>tongue</u>. *SPP*: ton-gue.

500. **to-night**: <u>Tonight</u> the <u>bright</u> moon makes the sky <u>light</u>. *SPP*: to-ni-g-ht.

501. **ton-sils**: <u>Tonsils</u> are <u>on</u> (each) <u>si</u>de of your throat.

502. **tor-na-does**: In the center of <u>tornadoes</u>, <u>does</u> the air stay still? <u>torn</u> + <u>a</u> + <u>does</u> (Sp. twist + thunderstorm)

503. **tor-pe-does**: When a ship is hit by <u>torpedoes</u>, <u>does</u> it always sink? <u>tor</u> + <u>pe</u> + <u>does</u>.

504. **to-ward** (or toward): Don't move <u>to war</u>; go <u>toward</u> peace: <u>to</u> + <u>war</u> + <u>d</u>. *SPP*: To spell, say <u>to-ward</u>.

505. **towel**: <u>To wel</u>(come) our guest, we put a welcome <u>towel</u> out: <u>to</u> + <u>wel</u>(come).

506. **tra-ge-dy**: I felt <u>rage</u> at the villain in the <u>tragedy</u>.

507. **trag-ic**: Their attempt at <u>magic</u> resulted in a <u>tragic</u> accident.

508. **trea-sure**: The <u>treasure</u> is a <u>treat</u> for <u>sure</u>: <u>treat</u> + <u>sure</u> = treasure. *Phonics*: <u>s</u> = <u>zh</u>: pleasure...

509. **tru-ly**: <u>July</u> is a <u>truly</u> hot month. *Exception*: <u>True</u> drops an e: true + <u>ly</u> = <u>truly</u>. *Same*: duly, unruly...

510. **trum-pet**: His <u>pet</u> blew a <u>trumpet</u>.

511. **truth**: <u>Ruth</u> spoke the <u>truth</u> (Old Eng., treowth: truth).

512. **tun-nel**: <u>Nel</u> likes the <u>fun</u> of a <u>tunnel</u>. *Rule*: The <u>2 n's</u> keep <u>u</u> short. *SPP*: tun-<u>nel</u>.

513. **tur-tle**: My <u>turtle</u> <u>left</u> lettuce in her bowl. <u>Turt led</u> the way to the <u>turtle</u> pond. *Beat*: t-u-r t-l-e.

514. **twelfth**: T.W. was the <u>twelfth</u> <u>elf</u>: <u>TW</u> + <u>elf</u> + <u>th</u>. *Pronounce* all consonants: t-w-el-f-th.

515. **twen-ti-eth**: I <u>went</u> to the movie for the <u>twentieth</u> time: *Y Rule*: t-wenty + i + eth = <u>twentieth</u>.

516. **ty-phoon**: A <u>typhoon</u> struck the sea at <u>noon</u> (Gk. typhoon: violent wind). *Phonics*: Ph = f in Greek.

517. **um-brel-la**: Did Cind<u>erella</u> lose an <u>umbrella</u>? (L. <u>umbra</u>: shade + <u>umbel</u>: flower w/stalks extending out).

518. **um-pire**: You <u>hire</u> an <u>umpire</u> to make calls for a game (<u>um</u>: not + <u>pire</u>: peer = not a peer).

519. **un-fair**: The <u>air</u> was <u>unfair</u> at the <u>fair</u>.

520. **va-cant**: An <u>ant</u> lives in the <u>vacant</u> house: <u>va</u> + <u>c</u> + <u>ant</u> = <u>vacant</u>.

521. **vac-uum**: A <u>vacuum</u> goes ...uuu<u>uum</u>: <u>vac</u> + <u>uum</u> = <u>vacuum</u>.

522. **val-leys**: Get out of the <u>alleys</u> and into the <u>valleys</u> (Old French valles). *Rule*: <u>2 l's</u> keep a short.

523. **vege-table**: We put our <u>vegetables</u> on the <u>tables</u>: <u>vege + tables</u> = vegetables. *SPP*: ve-ge-ta-ble.

524. **ve-ry**: E<u>very</u> time I see you, I'm <u>very</u> happy (<u>ver</u>: L.verus-truth + <u>y</u>-adv. suffix = <u>very</u>).

525. **vil-lage**: At what <u>age</u> did you build that <u>villa</u> in your <u>village</u>? *Same Root*: villagers

526. **vil-lain**: The <u>villain</u> was <u>in</u> the <u>villa</u>: <u>villa + in</u>.

527. **vi-o-lin**: <u>Linda</u> studies <u>violin</u>: <u>vi + o + Linda</u>. *Pronounce* every vowel: vi-o-lin.

528. **vit-a-mins**: Be sure to take your <u>vitamins</u> and <u>minerals</u>: <u>vita + mins</u> = <u>vitamins</u>.

529. **vol-ca-noes** (also, volcanos): Can you row <u>canoes</u> through <u>volcanoes</u>? (Latin).

530. **vowels**: *SPP*: vo<u>w</u>-els. He <u>vowed</u> to learn the sound of <u>vowels</u>.

531. **want**: I w<u>ant</u> this <u>ant</u> for a pet: <u>w + ant</u> = <u>want</u>.

532. **wasp**: Both a <u>wasp</u> and an <u>asp</u> (poisonous snake) are dangerous: <u>w + asp</u> = <u>wasp</u>.

533. **watch**: *SPP*: wa-t-ch. <u>Watch</u> me <u>catch</u> the ball. *Same Pattern*: catch, hatch, match...

534. **wealth**: <u>We</u> <u>all</u> wanted to gain <u>wealth</u>: <u>we + al(l) + th</u> (Also: <u>weal</u>-old word that means "prosperity.")

535. **weird**: <u>We</u> are weird: <u>weird</u>.

536. **wharf**: You can find a <u>wharf</u> (place to anchor boats) at a <u>harbor</u>: w<u>harf</u>. *SPP*: w-harf.

537. **wheel-bar-row**: He had a <u>arrow</u> in his <u>wheelbarrow</u>. *Compound Rule*: <u>wheel + barrow</u>.

538. **when**: <u>When</u> does your <u>hen</u> lay eggs? *Same Pattern*: den, glen, men, pen, ten, then...

539. **while**: <u>While</u> I'm cooking, please say <u>hi</u> to the guests. *SPP*: <u>wh</u>-ile (Old Eng. hwil: away).

540. **whis-tle**: Can you say br<u>istle</u>, th<u>istle</u> and <u>whistle</u> while <u>whistling</u>? *SPP*: whist-le.

541. **whol-ly**: Some people <u>wholly</u> use <u>holly</u> for decorating: <u>w + holly</u>.

542. **womb**: The woman had a <u>baby</u> in her <u>womb</u> (Old Eng. wamb). *SPP*: wom-<u>b</u>:

543. **wo-men** (O. E. plural for woman): The <u>women</u> knew the <u>omen</u> was not truth: <u>w + omen</u>.

544. **won-der-ment**: The <u>wonder</u> of reaching the moon awed the <u>men</u> with <u>wonderment</u>: (O. E. wonder).

545. **word**: An honest <u>word</u> has great <u>worth</u> (Old Eng. woord). *Pattern*: cord, Ford, lord...

546. **worse**: My hole got <u>worse</u> as I <u>wore</u> my jeans (O. E. wyrsa). *SPP*: wor-se. *Pattern*: horse, Norse.

547. <u>w</u>**reath**: They kissed undern<u>eath</u> a <u>wreath</u> of mistletoe. *SPP*: w-reath. *Rule*: <u>A</u> makes <u>e</u> long.

548. **wrench**: A <u>wren</u> was sitting on the <u>wrench</u> when he went to fix the <u>bench</u>.

549. <u>w</u>**rist**: Athletes often <u>w</u>rap their <u>wrists</u>. *Same Pattern*: fist, list, mist, twist...

550. **writ-ten**: My <u>kitten</u> had <u>written</u> <u>ten</u> prints: <u>wr + kitten</u>. *Rule*: <u>2 t's</u> keep the <u>i</u> short.

551. **wrong**: Did I sing the <u>wrong</u> <u>song</u>? *SPP*: <u>w</u>-rong.

552. **xy-lo-phone**: I can play the <u>xylophone</u> while talking on a <u>phone</u> (Gk. <u>xylo</u>: wood + <u>phone</u>: sound. Ph = f).

553. **yel-low**: Y<u>ell</u>, "Ow!" if you like mellow <u>yellow</u>. *Same Pattern*: bellow, fellow, mellow.

554. **yield**: I always <u>yield</u> to my <u>elders</u>: <u>yi + elders</u> = yield.

555. **young**: <u>You</u> are <u>young</u>: <u>you + ng</u> (O. E: geong-young).

556. **youth**: <u>You</u> both are seeking <u>youth</u>: <u>you + both</u> = youth. *Same Pattern*: couth, mouth, south...

POWER Spelling Clues for Very Challenging Words

1. **ab-surd** (senseless): It's <u>absurd</u> to leave milk out unless you want c<u>urd</u>: ab + s + <s>c</s>urd.

2. **ac-ci-dent-al-ly** (<u>c</u> = <u>k</u>; <u>c</u> = <u>s</u>): <u>I</u> <u>accidentally</u> got a <u>dent</u> on my <u>ally</u>'s car: acc + i + dent + ally.

3. **ac-com-mo-date**: <u>A.C.</u> chose a <u>common</u> <u>date</u> to <u>accommodate</u> us: A.C. + commo<s>n</s> + date.

4. **ac-cum-u-late**: Do <u>cumulus</u> clouds <u>accumulate</u> water <u>late</u>?: ac + cumul + ate (cumul: heap).

5. **ac-cus-tomed**: I've grown <u>accustomed</u> to your <u>custom</u>: ac + custom + ed (L. <u>ac</u>: to + <u>custom</u>: ways + ed).

6. **a-chieve-ment**: I said <u>hi</u> to <u>men</u> on the <u>eve</u> of my <u>achievement</u>: ac + hi + eve + men + t.

7. **ac-quaint-ance**: <u>A. C.</u> "<u>ain't</u>" an <u>acquaintance</u> I d<u>ance</u> with: A.C. + qu + aint + <s>d</s>ance.

8. **ac-quire**: I need to (<u>ac</u>) <u>acquire</u> a t<u>ire</u>: ac + quire (search for). *Silent E* and *Qu Rules.*

9. **ac-tu-al-ly**: Can you <u>actually</u> <u>act</u> like <u>U</u> are my <u>ally</u>? act + U + ally. *SPP*: ac-tu-al-ly.

10. **al-li-ance** (formal agreement to unite): <u>Alli</u> ran a d<u>ance</u> <u>alliance</u>: alli + <s>d</s>ance. *Y Rule*: all<s>y</s> + i + ance.

11. **an-chor**: C<u>an</u> <u>chorus</u> groups sing *Anchors Away*? <s>c</s>an + chor<s>us</s> = <u>anchor</u> (O. E. ancor).

12. **a-noint** (bless with oil): You use <u>an oil</u> to <u>anoint</u> a person: an + oi<s>l</s> + nt = <u>anoint</u>

13. **ap-paloo-sa** (a horse): I fed my <u>appaloosa</u> an <u>apple</u> and fixed <u>a loose</u> stirrup: appl<s>e</s> + a + loos<s>e</s> + a.

14. **ap-pear-ance**: They made an <u>appearance</u> as an <u>apple</u> and <u>pear</u> at the <u>dance</u>: appl<s>e</s> + pear + <s>d</s>ance.

15. **au-di-tory**: Most teachers teach his<u>tory</u> in <u>auditory</u> ways: audi + tory (audi: hearing + <u>tory</u>).

16. **au-ral**: Aunt L<u>aural</u> had <u>aural</u> problems. *Roots*: L., <u>aur</u>: concerning the ear + <u>al</u>: adj. suffix = <u>aural</u>.

17. **be-nign**: Her words were <u>benign</u> (M.E., <u>bene</u>: good + <u>ign</u>). *Phonics*: <u>ig</u> = <u>long i</u>. *SPP*: be-nig-n.

18. **buoy-ant**: Let's <u>buy</u> a <u>buoyant buoy</u> for that <u>ant</u> to float on: bu-o-y + ant. *SPP*: <u>bu</u>-oy-ant

19. **bu-reau**: My <u>burgundy</u> <u>bureau</u> is from my b<u>eau</u> (boyfriend): bur + <s>b</s>eau (Fr. <u>bureau</u>: desk).

20. **caf-feine**: The Co<u>ffee</u> that is m<u>ine</u> has <u>caffeine</u> in it: ca + ffe<s>e</s> + ine. *SPP*: caf-fe-in-e.

21. **can-celed**: I <u>canceled</u> my <u>celery</u> order: can + celer<s>y</s> + d. *Rule*: Accent on <u>can</u>, don't double <u>l</u>.

22. **ce-le-bra-tions**: My <u>celebrations</u> have carrots, <u>celery</u> and other <u>rations</u>: celer<s>y</s> + b + rations.

23. **cha-rac-ters**: For <u>charades</u>, we <u>acted</u> out <u>characters</u>: char + acte<s>d</s> + ers. *Phonics*: <u>ch</u> and <u>c</u> = <u>k</u>; <u>s</u> = <u>z</u>.

24. **chor-e-o-gra-phy**: Is <u>choreography</u> a <u>chore</u>? (Gk. <u>chore</u>: <u>chorea</u>: disease w/movement + <u>o</u> + <u>graph</u>: map + <u>y</u>).

25. **com-pelled** (forced): The robber <u>compelled</u> the t<u>eller</u> to give him cash. *Rule*: 2 <u>l</u>'s keep <u>e</u> short.

26. **con-ceit-ed**: She had no <u>concept</u> of <u>it, Ed</u> – of how to act <u>conceited</u>: conce<s>pt</s> + it + Ed.

27. **con-fer-ence**: A <u>conference</u> and a <u>reference</u> made a di<u>fference</u> (L. <u>con</u>: with + <u>fer</u>: bear + ence).

28. **con-grat-u-la-tions**: <u>Congratulations</u> with <u>gratitude</u> and a<u>dulations</u>: con + grat + <s>a</s>dulations.

29. **con-sol-id-ate**: My body can <u>consolidate</u> the <u>solid</u> food I <u>ate</u>: con + solid + ate.

30. **cri-ti-cis-m**: A <u>critic is</u> behind every <u>criticism</u>: critic + is + m (G. <u>kritic</u>: judge). *Phonics*: <u>c</u> = <u>k</u>, <u>s</u>.

31. **cu-ri-os-i-ty**: I had <u>curiosity</u> about the <u>curios</u> (items to view) in the <u>city</u>: curios + ~~e~~ity.

32. **cur-rent-ly**: The <u>rent</u> is <u>currently</u> due: <u>cur + rent +ly</u> (L. <u>curren</u>: course of time, water, etc.; now).

33. **de-mean-or**: She could not tell if his <u>demeanor</u> was <u>mean or</u> kind: de + mean + or.

34. **de-nial**: He wanted to <u>deny all</u> in a <u>denial</u>. *Y Rule*: <u>den~~y~~ + i + al = denial</u>.

35. **di-gest**: I <u>dig est</u>imating the time to <u>digest</u> food? <u>dig + est</u> (M.E. digesten: dissolve).

36. **di-lem-ma**: <u>Emma</u> had a <u>dilemma</u> (Gk. dilemma-confusion). *Beat*: d-i-l-e-m-m-a.

37. **dil-i-gent, dil-i-gence**: He was a <u>diligent gent</u>: <u>dili + gent = diligent</u>. *SPP*: dil-<u>i</u>-<u>gen</u>-<u>ce</u>.

38. **di-sas-trous** (3 syl.): The storm is <u>as troubling</u> and <u>disastrous</u> as the flood: <u>dis + as + trou~~bling~~ + s</u>.

39. **dis-ci-pline**: He had the <u>discipline</u> to stay in <u>line</u>. *Phonics*: <u>c</u> = <u>s</u>. *Visual*: Notice <u>3 i's</u>.

40. **do-cents** (guides in museums): <u>Do docents</u> work for <u>cents</u>? *Roots*: <u>doc</u> (L. teacher) + <u>ent</u> (noun. suf).

41. **ec-o-nom-ical-ly**: <u>Economically</u> our <u>economic</u> system is an <u>ally</u>: economic + ally.

42. **e-con-o-mize**: Let's <u>economize</u> to a budget my <u>size</u>. *Y Rule*: econom~~y~~ + ~~s~~ize = economize.

43. **en-vi-ron-ment**: <u>Men</u> mine <u>iron</u> in the <u>environment</u>: <u>env + iron + men + t</u> (Fr. <u>en</u>: in + <u>virons</u>: a circle).

44. **e-quiv-a-lent**: Is a heart the <u>equivalent</u> of a <u>valentine</u>? <u>equi + valent~~ine~~</u>.

45. **es-tab-lish-ment**: My <u>tab</u> (bill) I <u>wish</u> to pay to the <u>men</u> in the <u>establishment</u>: es + tab + l~~wish~~ + ment.

46. **ex-<u>h</u>aust**: <u>Ha,</u> you did not <u>exhaust us</u>: ex + ha + us + t. *Same Pattern*: exhale, exhibit.

47. **ex-<u>h</u>ort** (urge; advise): Dr. Seuss had to <u>exhort Hort</u>on to sit on the egg: <u>ex + Hort</u>.

48. **Fahr-en-heit**: My <u>Fahrenheit</u> pen thermometer hit a <u>height</u> of 99 degrees: <u>Fahr + ~~pen~~ + height</u>.

49. **fre-quent-ly**: <u>Frequently</u> I <u>fret</u> over the <u>rent</u>: <u>fre~~t~~ + qu + ~~r~~ent + ly</u>. *Qu Rule*: <u>Qu</u> = one letter.

50. **ha-rass**: <u>Ha,</u> don't <u>harass</u> me, or I'll wrestle you to the <u>grass</u>: ha + <u>~~g~~rass</u> = harass (harassment).

51. **hin-drance**: It was a <u>hindrance</u> when the <u>hind</u> (deer) <u>ran</u> onto the road: <u>hind + ran + ce</u>.

52. **hors-d'oeu-vre**: My <u>hors(e,) doe, (and) Uvre</u> enjoy an <u>hors d'oeuvre</u>: <u>hors~~e~~ + doe + Uvre = hors d'oeuvres</u> (French, <u>hors</u>: outside + <u>de</u>: of + <u>oeuvre</u>: main course; apostrophe replaces <u>e</u>: hors d'oeuvre).

53. **hun-dredth**: He wrote <u>hundredth</u> in <u>red</u>. *Phonics*: <u>hundred + th</u> (ending for fourth, tenth…).

54. **il-lit-er-ate**: If you are <u>illiterate</u>, you are not (il) able to read <u>literature</u>: <u>il + literat~~ure~~ + ate</u>.

55. **il-log-i-cal**: I see <u>logic, Al,</u> in a <u>log</u> having rings: <u>il (not) + logic + Al</u>. *Phonics*: <u>g</u> = <u>j</u>; <u>c</u> = <u>k</u>.

56. **il-lum-i-nate**: When he was <u>ill, Nate</u> watched the sun <u>illuminate</u> his room: <u>ill + um + i + Nate</u>. *Visual*: See 4 or more candles in <u>illuminate</u>.

57. **im-ma-ture**: <u>I'm</u> the kid <u>Ma</u> <u>turn</u>ed into being <u>mature</u>: I'm + ma + turn~~ed~~ + e: (im: not + mature: grown).

58. **in-an-i-mate**: <u>Animate</u> means alive, like an <u>animal</u>. <u>Inanimate</u> means in (not) + animate.

59. **in-ci-den-tal-ly**: <u>Incidentally</u>, my <u>dent</u> is <u>all</u> out: <u>in + ci + dent + all + y</u> = incidentally.

60. **in-e-vi-ta-ble**: <u>In Evi</u>'s house, it's <u>inevitable</u> that we'll study at the <u>table</u>: <u>in + Evi + table</u>.

61. **i-ni-tials**: While the cement was still wet, <u>in it</u> <u>Al</u> and <u>I</u> wrote our <u>initials</u>: <u>in + it + I + Al</u>.

62. **in-ter-ces-sion**: <u>Intercession</u>: pro<u>cess</u> of going between people to help: <u>inter</u>: between + <u>cess</u>: go.

63. **in-ter-ces-sor**: This <u>intercessor</u> will solve this m<u>ess or</u> get more help: <u>inter + c + ~~m~~ess + or</u>.

64. **jea-lou-sy**: He felt <u>jealousy</u>, but knew it was <u>a lousy</u> emotion: <u>j + ~~he~~ + a + lousy</u> = jealousy.

65. **la-ti-tude**: <u>Fl</u>at <u>latitude</u> lines run around the Earth, parallel to the equator: <u>~~fl~~at + it + ude</u>.
    Roots: <u>lati</u> (L. high) + <u>tude</u> (n. suf).

66. **li-a-ble** (likely; legally responsible): I'm <u>liable</u> to do the good I'm <u>able</u> to do: <u>l + I + able</u> (L. <u>li</u>: legal + <u>able</u>).

67. **lim-pid** (clear): She forgot her <u>limp</u> as she swam in the <u>limpid</u> pool.

68. **lon-gi-tude**: <u>Long</u> <u>longitude</u> lines connect 2 <u>lo</u>w temperature areas -- North and South Pole. The 1st <u>longitude</u> line goes through <u>Lon</u>don (Greenwich: where 1ˢᵗ time zone begins): <u>long + it + ude</u> (L. length).

69. **mag-ni-fi-cent**: <u>Magnify</u> one <u>cent</u>, and see a <u>magnificent</u> face of Lincoln. *Y Rule*: <u>magnif~~y~~ + i + cent</u>.

70. **main-te-nance**: He took care of the <u>maintenance</u> for the <u>main</u> <u>tenants</u>: <u>main + tenan~~ts~~ + ce</u>.

71. **ma-neu-ver**: I can <u>maneuver</u> my horse by his <u>mane</u> for <u>U</u>: <u>mane + U + ver</u> (O. E. manuver: hand work).

72. **man-i-kin** (model): <u>Man, I</u> will show my <u>kin</u> the <u>manikin</u> that's like Uncle Bob: <u>man + i + kin</u>.

73. **man-u-al** (by hand): Ancient <u>manuscripts</u> were <u>all</u> done <u>manually</u>: <u>manu + all + y</u>. (L. manus: hand + al).

74. **mar-ga-rine**: <u>Margaret</u> cut <u>margarine</u> into <u>fine</u> slices: <u>margar + ~~f~~ine</u> (Gk. margaron: pearl; g = j sound).

75. **ma-trix**: A <u>matrix</u> is a *math concept* or means *origin*: <u>mat~~h~~ + rix</u>. (L. <u>matr</u>e: mother; origin + <u>ix</u>: n. suf.).

76. **mi-rage**: At what <u>age</u> did you see that <u>mirage</u>? (L. <u>mir</u>ari: wonder at + <u>age</u>: n. suf).

77. **nau-se-a**: To avoid <u>nausea</u>, <u>use a</u> seasickness patch: <u>na + use + a</u> (Gk. nau: sea + ea).

78. **nour-ish**: <u>Nourish</u> y<u>our</u>selves with a healthy d<u>ish</u>: <u>n + our + ~~d~~ish</u> (L. <u>nour</u>: feed + <u>ish</u>).

79. **nuc-lei** (plural: nucleus): Can you put a <u>lei</u> on a <u>nuclei</u> (L. <u>nuc</u>: little nut; core + <u>lei</u>: n. suf. = nuclei)

80. **o-be-di-ent**: <u>To bed I went</u> to try to be <u>obedient</u>! <u>~~T~~o + bed + I + ~~w~~ent</u> = obedient.

81. **ob-sta-cle**: <u>Sta(y) clear</u> of the <u>obstacle</u>, so you can get in: <u>ob + sta~~y~~ + clea~~r~~</u> = obstacle.

82. **oc-cur-rence**: <u>O, C</u> (the) <u>curren~~t~~</u> + ce = occurrence. *Rule*: Accent on <u>cur</u>; double the <u>r</u>.

83. **of-fered**: I will <u>offer Ed</u> a good price: <u>offer + Ed</u>. *Rule*: Accent on first syllable; don't double <u>r</u>.

84. **on-o-mat-o-poe-ia**: Edgar Allen <u>Poe</u> wrote <u>poems</u> with <u>onomatopoeia</u>: <u>on + o + mat + o + Poe + ia</u>.

85. **on-to-lo-gi-cal**: Shall I share my <u>ontological</u> argument or shall we go <u>on to</u> (more) <u>logical</u> things?

86. **op-po-nent**: My <u>opponent</u> was on the <u>opposite</u> side of the <u>net</u>: <u>oppo + nent</u> (<u>op</u>: against + <u>pon</u>: set up).

O + C + current + ce = occurrence

35

87. **op-tic** (vision): He was a to<u>p</u> <u>optic</u> specialist (Gk. optikos-vision). *Same Pattern*: hop, top…

88. **par-a-digm**: I <u>dig</u> <u>my</u> new <u>paradigm</u>: <u>para + dig + my</u> (<u>paradigm</u>: pattern). *SPP*: par-a-dig-m.

89. **pas-teur-ize**: <u>Pasteurize</u> comes from Louis <u>Pasteur</u>: <u>pasteur</u> + <u>ize</u>. *SPP*: pas-te-ur-ize.

90. **pa-vil-ion** (building): By the <u>pavilion</u>, on the <u>pavement</u>, <u>I</u> saw 2 <u>lions</u>: <u>pav + I + lion</u> = pavilion.

91. **pen-guin**: <u>G, U in</u> the <u>penguin</u> suit, can I borrow your <u>pen</u>? : <u>pen + G + U + in</u> (Welsh: pengywn).

92. **pen-i-cill-in**: Don't <u>panic</u> when you're <u>ill inside</u>; <u>penicillin</u> can help: <u>pen + ic + ill + in</u> = penicillin.

93. **pen-in-su-la**: A <u>pen (fit) in</u> the map's <u>peninsula</u>: <u>pen + in + sula</u> (<u>pen</u>: almost + <u>insula</u>: island).

94. **per-i-pa-te-tic** (traveling about; itinerant): Being <u>peripatetic</u> is not <u>pathetic</u>: <u>peri + pathetic</u>.

95. **per-pet-u-al-ly** (continually): A <u>pet U all</u> should have <u>perpetually</u>: <u>per + pet + u + all + y</u>.

96. **pe-ruses**: We <u>peruse</u> the cupboard to see what each <u>person uses</u>: <u>person</u> + <u>uses</u> = <u>peruses</u>.

97. **pes-tle** (pounding tool): Don't be a <u>pest</u>; <u>let</u> me grind with this <u>pestle</u>: <u>pest + let</u> (<u>trestle</u>, <u>wrestle</u>).

98. **pi-geon**: *Phonics*: g = j. *Clue*: My <u>pigeon</u> has loved my <u>pig (for an) eon</u> = <u>pigeon</u> (M. Fr. pijon).

99. **pneu-mon-ia**: <u>Pneu</u> had <u>pneumonia</u> on <u>Mon</u>.: <u>Pneu + Mon + ia</u> (Gk. pneumonia: lung disease).

100. **poin-set-ti-a**: My <u>tia</u> (Sp. aunt) <u>set</u> the <u>poinsettia</u> <u>in</u> water: <u>po + in + set + tia</u> = poinsettia.

101. **pur-sue**: *SPP*: pur-su-<u>e</u>. *Clue*: <u>Pursue</u> the thief and get <u>Sue</u>'s <u>purse</u>: <u>pur + Sue</u> = pursue.

102. **pro-fes-sor**: Students call the <u>professor</u> who gave the <u>lesson</u>, "<u>Prof</u>.": <u>prof + lesson + r</u>.

103. **pseu-do**: I'll <u>se(e if) U do</u> this in a <u>pseudo</u> way: <u>p + see + U + do</u> = pseudo (Gk. pseudo: false. Ps = s).

104. **quartz**: <u>Quartz</u> is a <u>quiet</u> <u>art</u> of nature: <u>qu + art + z</u>. *Phonics*: <u>quartz</u> = <u>quarts</u>. *SPP*: qu-art-z.

105. **re-ce-ding**: As <u>cedar</u> trees died, the base line was <u>receding</u>: <u>re + cedar + ing</u> = <u>receding</u>.

106. **re-hear-sal**: We <u>hear Sal</u> sing at each <u>rehearsal</u>: <u>r + we + hear + Sal</u> = <u>rehearsal</u>.

107. **res-cu-ing**: <u>U (and) I</u> are cuing and <u>rescuing</u> people: <u>res + c + U + Ing</u> and <u>res + cuing</u>.

108. **rhu-barb**: <u>Barb</u> gave us a <u>huge</u> stalk of <u>rhubarb</u>: <u>r + huge + Barb</u> = rhubarb. *SPP*: r-hu-barb.

109. **sar-ca-sm**: <u>Sarcasm</u> says <u>something mean</u>. (Gk. sarkazmos: tear flesh) *Phonics*: <u>s</u> = <u>s</u>; <u>c</u> = <u>k</u>; <u>s</u> = <u>z</u>.

110. **sat-el-lite**: <u>Sa(m will) tell (s)ites</u> he saw from the <u>satellite</u>: <u>Sam + tell + sites</u> = satellites.

111. **sched-ules**: For his schedules at <u>school</u>, <u>he'd</u> follow <u>rules</u>: <u>sc + he'd + rules</u>. *SPP*: sc-hed-ules.

112. **seis-mic**: <u>Seismic</u> jolts can <u>separate</u> land. *Roots*: seism (Gk. seismos: quake) + ic (adj. suf.).

113. **sen-si-ble**: It's <u>sensible</u> to get along with <u>siblings</u>: <u>sen + siblings + e</u>. *Rule*: <u>sense + ible</u> = <u>sensible</u>.

114. **sim-i-lar**: Some small squirrels look <u>similar</u> to <u>large</u> mice.

115. **sin-cere-ly**: *Clue-in-a-Row* (almost): <u>Since (I) rely</u> on you, I <u>sincerely</u> trust you: <u>since + rely</u>.

116. **skein** (n., of yarn; geese in flight; succession): I'll <u>sketch</u> a <u>skein</u> in flight: <u>sketch + in</u> = <u>skein</u>.

117. **sol-diers**: <u>Old</u> <u>soldiers</u> never <u>die</u>: s + ol~~d~~ + die + rs = soldiers. *SPP*: sol-di-er.

118. **sta-lac-tites**: <u>Stalactites</u> hang from the ceiling <u>tightly</u>: stalac + tites = stalactites.

119. **sta-lag-mites**: Do <u>Stalagmites</u> <u>lag</u> in growing up <u>mightily</u>? sta + lag + mites = stalagmites.

120. **sta-ture**: The <u>state</u> of his <u>stature</u> great for s<u>ure</u>: stat~~e~~ + ure = stature (Lat. status-stand + <u>ure</u>-n. suf.).

121. **sub-lime** (inspiring awe): The <u>lime</u> you brought was <u>sublime</u>: sub + lime = sublime.

122. **sub-tle**: He explained the <u>subtle</u> meaning in the <u>subtitle</u>: sub + ~~title~~ = <u>subtle</u>. *SPP*: sub-tle.

123. **sus-tain**: Do you <u>sustain</u> the strength you m<u>ust</u> (g)<u>ain</u> for a marathon? s + ~~must~~ + ~~g~~ain = sustain.

124. **syl-la-bles** (3 syllables): Hearing <u>syllables</u> makes us <u>able</u> to spe<u>ll</u> more easily: <u>syll</u> + <u>able</u>.

125. **sym-me-try**: Let <u>me try</u> to create <u>symmetry</u>: <u>sym</u> + me + try (Gk. <u>sym</u>: same + <u>meter</u>: measure + <u>ry</u>).

126. **ther-mom-e-ter**: <u>Her mom</u> read a <u>thermometer</u>: t + her + mom + eter (Gk. thermometer: heat measure).

127. **tour-na-ment**: Please put <u>our name</u> on the <u>tournament</u> roster: t + our + name + nt.

128. **trag-i-cal-ly**: It was <u>tragic, (but my) ally</u> was there when I was <u>tragically</u> hurt: tragic + ally.

129. **tran-quil-li-ty**: Writing poems with my <u>quill</u> (feather pen), I feel <u>tranquility</u>: tran + quill + ity.

130. **tres-tle** (frame to support trains, roses...): <u>Trains</u> usually <u>rest level</u> on a <u>trestle</u>: t + rest + le~~vel~~.

131. **vi-si-ble**: <u>Vi</u> and other <u>siblings</u> (brothers, sisters) were <u>visible</u> in the photo. (L. <u>visi</u>: vision + <u>ble</u>: adj. suf).

132. **wres-tle**: To <u>wrestle</u> him, I'll <u>wrest</u> (his) <u>leg</u> behind him: <u>wrest + le~~g~~</u>. *Same Pattern*: nestle, trestle.

133. **Xe-rox**: I now have z<u>ero</u> left to <u>Xerox</u>: x + (~~z~~)ero + x. *Phonics*: <u>x</u> = <u>z</u>; <u>x</u> = <u>ks</u>.

134. **ya~~cht~~**: <u>You all-Come</u> <u>h</u>op on the <u>yacht</u>. *SPP*: ya-ch-t. (Danish: Jacht for jachtschip: hunting ship).

Space to Save Your Clues

Save *all* the *Clues you create and discover that work for you.* Add more paper so you won't miss one!

Tool 2: Phonics POWER

POWER Spelling List of All the Phonics Sounds

26 LETTERS exist in English: **19 CONSONANTS, 5 VOWELS, 2 CONSONANT/VOWELS.**
These 26 letters and their combinations create all the different sounds in the English Language.
15 CONSONANTS MAKE THEIR OWN SOUND – B D F H J K L M N P R T V Z and **Qu.**
2 CONSONANTS: G and **S** make their own sound; and **G** copies **J** (gem); **S** copies **Z** (sunrise).
 CONSONANTS: C just copies **K** (cat) and **S** (city). **X** just copies **KS** (box) and **Z** (xylophone).
4 SOUNDS: W and **Y** are **CONSONANT/VOWELS** – w in wind/ bow – y in yes/sky; bunny.

5 SHORT VOWELS		CLOSED SYLLABLES		OPEN SYLLABLES
a	/ă/ as in baa	cat	apple	acorn
e	/ĕ/ as in eh…	bed	elephant	
i	/ĭ/ as in ick	pin	igloo	divide
o	/ŏ/ as in ah	frog	octopus	
u	/ŭ/ as in ugh	sun	umbrella	

5 LONG VOWELS		SILENT-E	2 VOWELS	OPEN SYLLABLES	
ā	/ā/ as in ace	face	rain	table	
ē	/ē/ as in bee	theme	peach	zero	
ī	/ī/ as in ice	kite	pie	tiger	
ō	/ō/ as in oak	rose	boat	banjo	
ū	/ū/ as in cube	flute	fruit	music	(few)

5 R-CONTROLLED VOWEL SOUNDS (ire: like long i: fire; ure: like long u: lure)

ar /är/	as in star				
er /ėr/	as in fern	**ir** /ėr/	as in bird	**ur** /ėr/	as in turtle
or /ôr/	as in horn	**ore** /ôr/	as in ore		
air /âr/	as in hair	**are** /âr/	as in square		
ear /ēr/	as in tear	**eer** /ēr/	as in deer		

1 BROAD O VOWEL SOUND

au /ô/	as in auto	**aw** /ô/	as in saw	**al** /ô/	as in ball

1 SPECIAL VOWEL COMBINATIONS – DIPHTHONGS

ou /ou/	as in cloud	**ow** /ou/	as in owl
oi /oi/	as in coil	**oy** /oi/	as in boy

2 DOUBLE O SOUNDS

oo /o͞o/	as in moon	**u** /o͞o/	as in ruler
oo /o͝o/	as in book	**u** /o͝o/	as in bush

SCHWA SOUND /ə/ (Unaccented Neutral Vowel Sound in parade, poem, pencil, lemon, circus)

5 CONSONANT DIGRAPHS (2 CONSONANTS = ONE SOUND: Together Teams You Never Separate)

CH as in chair	beach		
SH as in shell	flash		
TH as in three	path	(voiced: with breath)
TH as in feather	smooth	(unvoiced: without breath)
WH as in wheat	what	(HW sound)
1 NG as in song	engine	(1 sound in song; 2 in engine)
1 ZH as in treasure (not spelled zh)	vision, azure (blue), mirage (not real).	

Hearing the Sounds of Phonics Game

Let's play a game that really help you hear the *sounds* of Phonics. It's called *ONOMATOPOEIA*. What? Sounds like Greek to me. Actually, *onomatopoeia* is Greek for *sound* words like *ah choo*. *Onomatopoeia* means: *to make words* (*-poeia*) where the *name of the word* (*onoma-*) *is the same as the sound*: *bong, blat, crash, choo choo, cuckoo, roar, zoom...*

❑ **NOW**: Write each *onomatopoeia* word next to its matching vowel sound: **baa**, **bark**, **blare**, **bong**, **bow** wow, **burp**, **caw**, **chug**, **clip**, **clop**, **croak**, **eek**, **eh**, **grate**, **groan**, **growl**, **meow**, **oink**, **patter**, **pitter**, **purr**, **roar**, screech, **snort**, **tick**, **tock**, **toot**, **whir**, **woof**, **yuck**, **zoom**. Also, add sound words you like.

Short Vowel Sounds
ă   as in **a**pple   *ah choo*
ĕ   as in **e**lephant   *eh...eh*
ĭ   as in **i**gloo
ŏ   as in **o**ctopus   sn**o**w
ŭ   as in s**u**n

Long Vowel Sounds
ā   as in f**a**ce   r**ai**n
ē   as in **ee**k   p**ea**ch
ī   as in **i**ce   k**i**te
ō   as in **oa**k   r**o**se
ū   in **u**nicycle   c**u**be

R-Controlled Vowel Sounds
är   as in st**ar**   *arf*
ér   as in f**er**n   b**ir**d   t**ur**tle
ôr   as in h**or**n   **or**e
âr   as in h**air**   squ**are**
ēr   as in t**ear**   d**eer**
īr   as in f**ire**   (long i + r)
ūr   as in l**ure**   (long u + r)

Special Vowel Combinations
au   as in **au**to   s**aw**   b**a**ll
ou   as in cl**ou**d   fl**ow**er
oi   as in c**oi**l   b**oy**
ōō   as in m**oo**n   r**u**ler
ŏŏ   as in b**oo**k   b**u**sh

Consonant Vowel: y as in sk**y**, **eye**

Finally, list sounds that these living things and objects make. Write them next to their vowel sound.
people   animals   birds   reptiles   insects   cars/trains   bells/instruments   other

Creating and Feeling the Single Consonant Sounds
Single Consonant and Consonant/Vowel Sounds

Have fun <u>feeling</u> how consonant sounds are formed. There are 15 consonants (includes Qu) that make their own sound; 2 consonant/vowels (W, Y) 2 consonants (G, S) that make their own sound and copy a sound; and 2 consonants (C, X) that only copy sounds. As you say the words for each consonant, touch your Adam's apple and feel the sound vibration. Also, feel how your lips, tongue, and mouth help form each sound.

B (ball, boy) — Feel how you bump your LIPS together. Then blow them apart with your VOICE.

C (cat, city) — C is a total Copy Cat without its own sounds. C copies K and S.

D (door, dad) — Feel your TONGUE behind your upper TEETH. Now blow your TONGUE down.

F (fish, farm) — Feel your top TEETH over your lower LIP. Now blow out AIR with no VOICE.

G (goose, go) — Bring your LIPS together in a circle. Blow out AIR with VOICE. G also copies J (gem).

H (horse, hat) — Say *ha, ha*. Feel AIR come out through your MOUTH. H is formed by AIR.

J (jazz, jet) — Feel your TEETH together and use VOICE to push the sound out of your MOUTH.

K (kite, kick) — Say *kick*. Feel the K sound at the back of your THROAT. Now push it out.

L (lion, lamb) — Feel your TONGUE up behind your TEETH. Now hum out the L sound.

M (music, mom) — Say *mom*. Feel a HUM come out your NOSE as your LIPS open and close.

N (nest, nun) — Feel your TONGUE touch the front roof of your mouth and feel the HUM of the N sound come out your NOSE, like you did for M, but with your MOUTH opened.

P (pine, pep) — Feel your LIPS together, and then just blow them apart with a kind of POP sound.

Qu (queen, quilt) — Qu works as a single consonant. Say K + W to make the KW sound in *queen* and *quilt*.

R (rain, roar) — Feel your TONGUE pulled back and raised against the roof of your MOUTH as you make a kind of ERRR... sound at the back of your MOUTH.

S (sun, sis) — Feel your TONGUE and TEETH hiss the S sound out. S also copies Z.

T (tiger, tent) — Say *tent*. Feel your TONGUE behind your TEETH and blow it down.

V (vine, vest) — Feel your TEETH over your lower LIP and make a HUM. Compare this to B.

W (window, wow) — Say *wow*. Feel your LIPS pursed together and let a little AIR out. (vowel sound = blow).

X (x-ray, ox) — X is a total Copy Cat without its own sound. X copies K and S together (KS in x-ray, ox) and also makes the Z sound (xylophone).

Y (yo-yo, yell) — Say *yo-yo* and *yell*. Feel your LIPS part as the Y sound comes from the back of your THROAT. (Remember: Y also has a vowel sound: toy, play).

Z (zipper, zoo) — Feel your LIPS and TEETH clenched as you create a BUZZZZZ... sound with AIR.

5 Consonant Digraphs and NG
Digraph (Greek, di: two + graph: letters) = *one sound*

Just like the consonants, each Digraph creates its own single sound. For this reason, we call Digraphs *TOGETHER TEAMS YOU NEVER SEPARATE.* These pairs stay together to create one sound. Most of the time, NG works like a Digraph (song, ringing), but NG can also be 2 sounds as in *engine, language.*

CH as in **ch**air: <u>ch</u>ild, <u>ch</u>ime, <u>ch</u>oose, <u>ch</u>ose, <u>ch</u>ur<u>ch</u>, bea<u>ch</u>, pit<u>ch</u>er, tea<u>ch</u>

SH as in **sh**ell: <u>sh</u>adow, <u>sh</u>ark, <u>sh</u>one, <u>sh</u>own, <u>sh</u>ould, da<u>sh</u>, establi<u>sh</u>, fla<u>sh</u>

TH as in **th**umb: <u>th</u>ank, <u>th</u>eater, <u>th</u>ink, <u>th</u>ought, <u>th</u>ousand, <u>th</u>ump, pa<u>th</u> (voiced: with breath)

TH as in fea**th**er: <u>th</u>aw, <u>th</u>ere, <u>th</u>in, <u>th</u>ough, <u>th</u>us, a<u>th</u>lete, bo<u>th</u>, smoo<u>th</u> (unvoiced: no breath)

WH as in **wh**eat: <u>wh</u>at, <u>wh</u>eel, <u>wh</u>en, <u>wh</u>ich, <u>wh</u>ite, <u>wh</u>orl (circular coil), <u>wh</u>y

NG as in ri**ng**:   alo<u>ng</u>, si<u>ng</u>, so<u>ng</u>, danc<u>ing</u>, ring<u>ing</u> (Ex.: *engine, ginger, etc.*)

Just as you were able to FEEL the individual consonant sounds, you can also feel the sounds of the digraphs and NG. As you say each two-consonant sound below, try to feel a sound vibration. Also, feel how your lips, tongue, mouth, and breath make the different digraph sounds.

CH   Say *beach*. Feel the your TONGUE on the roof of your MOUTH and a little air between your LIPS.

SH   Say *dash*. Feel your TONGUE near the roof of your MOUTH as your breath makes a *sh...* sound between your TEETH.

TH   Say *thumb*. Feel your TONGUE touch your top TEETH and AIR burst out as you voice the *th...* sound.

TH   Say *that*. Again, feel your TONGUE touch your top TEETH and feel a slight bit of AIR come <u>out</u>.

WH   Say *what*. Feel your LIPS round and then open more fully as they release AIR to make the *wh...* sound.

NG   Say *ring*. Feel your TONGUE round toward the roof of your MOUTH as the *ng...* sound is made in your THROAT.

One Special ZH Sound

There's also a special <u>ZH</u> sound that work like a digraph, although the sound is not spelled with <u>ZH</u>. You just hear the sound of these letters. Say this sound and feel it, just like you did for the digraph.

ZH as in trea**s**ure: a<u>z</u>ure, divi<u>s</u>ion, mira<u>g</u>e, lei<u>s</u>ure, mea<u>s</u>ure, plea<u>s</u>ure (su, si, zu, ge = ZH sound).

ZH   Say *mirage*. Feel a hushed BREATH stream between your TEETH, and feel your MOUTH slightly opened and rounded as the *zh...* sound comes out.

Four One-Letter Copy Cat Kids: C, G, S, and X

4 SINGLE LETTERS THAT SOMETIMES COPY OTHER SOUNDS: C, G, S and X

Call Cisco Cat. He Cycles in the City:
C copies **K**: cat, comic, curl.
C copies **S**: city, circle, cycles.

GIDGET Girl Goes to a Gym.: G makes its own **G** sound: gal, gets, girl, goal, gum...
G copies **J**: gem, ginger, gym.

SUSANNAH Sure Sings Songs.: S makes its own **S** sound: sand, seal, sister, some, sun...
S copies **Z**: as, has, scissors...
S copies **SH**: sugar, sure...
S copies **ZH**: division, leisure, measure, pleasure, treasure.

ALEXI Exuberantly Excels on Xylophones.:
X copies **Z**: index, Xerox (ks)...
X copies **KS**: box, galaxy.

Four Two-Letter Copy Cat Kids: Ch, Gh, Ph, and Qu

4 DOUBLE-LETTERS THAT CAN COPY OTHER SOUNDS: CH, GH, PH, and QU

CHRISTY Teaches a Children's Orchestra.:
CH copies **K**: ache, architect, chaos, character, chorus, chord, chemistry, mechanic, monarch, orchestra
CH copies **SH**: chef, chapeau (French cap).
(CH also makes its own **CH** sound: chance, child, chug, inches, merchant, reached, teach...)

ROUGHY'S Rough and Tough.:
GH copies **F** at the end of a few words: cough, enough, laugh...

KRISTOPH is Phenomenal at Phonics.:
PH copies **F**: phantom, phenomenon, phonics, phone, physical, gopher, nephew, paragraph, triumph...

RACQUEL Quotes Quite Eloquently.:
QU copies **KW**: quack, queen, quite, quotes, acquaint, equal, frequent, eloquently, liquid, squirrel.
QU copies **K**: picturesque, technique, unique...

POWER *Spelling List of Beginning Consonant Blends*

❑ **TRY THIS:** For these Blends, write some Tongue Twisters, like: *Blue blossoms blend and blur into blankets* or *Gradually green grapes and grasses grew.* If you need more blend words, just look in the dictionary under the blend. Write your Tongue Twisters by their Consonant Blend.

❑ **BL CONSONANT BLEND:** *Blue blossoms blend and blur into blankets.*

black	blend	bloom	blue	ably	nimbly
blanket	blimps	blossom	blur	emblem	resembling
bleach	blind	blow	blush	humbling	tumbler

CL CONSONANT BLEND

clam	clay	clever	close	cluster	eclipse
clap	clean	cliff	clothes	cyclone	exclaim
classy	cleats	climb	cloud	declare	include

FL CONSONANT BLEND

flash	flew	float	flow	flute	inflatable
flavor	flight	flock	flower	flying	influence
fleet	flip	flour	fluffy	conflict	reflection

GL CONSONANT BLEND

glad	glamorous	gleam	glimpse	glittering	bugling
glade	glass	glider	glisten	glows	snuggly

PL CONSONANT SOUND

place	plane	platform	plow	apply	multiply
plaid	planets	player	plus	employ	reply
plain	plant	pleasant	applaud	explain	supply

SL CONSONANT BLEND

slant	sleek	slices	slimy	slope	asleep
sled	slept	slide	slippery	slow	grandslam

BR CONSONANT BLEND

brain	bread	bridge	broad	celebrate	librarian
branch	breath	bright	broken	cobra	vibrate
brave	breeze	bring	brother	daybreak	zebra

CR CONSONANT BLEND

crayon	create	cried	crouching	crown	decree
cream	creek	cross	crowd	crucial	microscope

DR CONSONANT BLEND

dragon	dream	drip	drew	drum	cathedral
drama	drench	drive	drop	dry	children
draw		droop	drove	address	dewdrops

FR CONSONANT BLEND

fraction	free	fresh	frost	fruit	bullfrog
fragile	freedom	friend	frozen	fry	leapfrog
fragrant	French	frisky	frugal	befriend	refresh

GR CONSONANT BLEND

gradually	grapes	great	grew	grow	engrave
grain	grass	green	grin	agree	hungry
grand	gravity	greet	ground	degree	program

PR CONSONANT BLEND

practice	present	pristine (pure)	program	provide	improve
pray	prince	probably	propeller	approach	supreme
prepare	print	products	prove	express	surprise

TR CONSONANT BLEND

track	trail	travel	true	contrast	extra
tractor	train	triangle	trying	country	sentry (guard)
trade	trampoline	trick	attract	entry	subtract

WR CONSONANT BLEND

wrap	wreath	wrestle	wrist	written	playwright
wrapper	wren	wriggle	writing	wrote	unwrap

SC CONSONANT BLEND

scallop	scared	scatter	scissors	score	scuba
scan	scarf	science	scoop	scout	telescope

SK CONSONANT BLEND

skate	skiing	skip	skylark	basket	dusky
sketch	skimming	skunk	asked	brisker	muskrat

SM CONSONANT BLEND

small	smell	smile	smolder	smooth	blacksmith
smart	smelt	smitten	smooch	smudge	resmooth

SN CONSONANT BLEND

snack	sneakers	sniff	Snoopy	snore	snowflake
snail	sneeze	snip	snooze	snorkel	snug

SP CONSONANT BLEND

space	speak	spell	spin	spring	respect
spark	special	spider	sports	inspire	respond

SQU CONSONANT BLEND

squad	square	squeak	squelch (crush)	squiggle	squirt
squall (storm)	squash	squeeze	squid	squirrel	squish

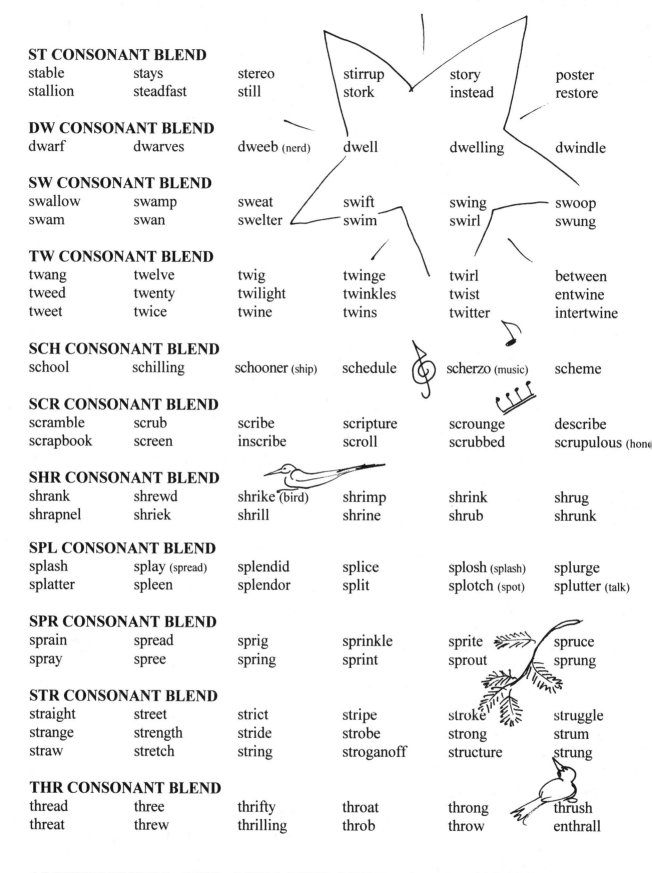

ST CONSONANT BLEND
stable	stays	stereo	stirrup	story	poster
stallion	steadfast	still	stork	instead	restore

DW CONSONANT BLEND
dwarf	dwarves	dweeb (nerd)	dwell	dwelling	dwindle

SW CONSONANT BLEND
swallow	swamp	sweat	swift	swing	swoop
swam	swan	swelter	swim	swirl	swung

TW CONSONANT BLEND
twang	twelve	twig	twinge	twirl	between
tweed	twenty	twilight	twinkles	twist	entwine
tweet	twice	twine	twins	twitter	intertwine

SCH CONSONANT BLEND
school	schilling	schooner (ship)	schedule	scherzo (music)	scheme

SCR CONSONANT BLEND
scramble	scrub	scribe	scripture	scrounge	describe
scrapbook	screen	inscribe	scroll	scrubbed	scrupulous (hone

SHR CONSONANT BLEND
shrank	shrewd	shrike (bird)	shrimp	shrink	shrug
shrapnel	shriek	shrill	shrine	shrub	shrunk

SPL CONSONANT BLEND
splash	splay (spread)	splendid	splice	splosh (splash)	splurge
splatter	spleen	splendor	split	splotch (spot)	splutter (talk)

SPR CONSONANT BLEND
sprain	spread	sprig	sprinkle	sprite	spruce
spray	spree	spring	sprint	sprout	sprung

STR CONSONANT BLEND
straight	street	strict	stripe	stroke	struggle
strange	strength	stride	strobe	strong	strum
straw	stretch	string	stroganoff	structure	strung

THR CONSONANT BLEND
thread	three	thrifty	throat	throng	thrush
threat	threw	thrilling	throb	throw	enthrall

4-LETTER BLENDS: SCHL, SCHM, SCHN, SCHW (These are Yiddish Words.)
schlep (carry)   schmuck (pest)   schmooze (chatter)   schnauzer (dog)   schwa (neutral vowel)

POWER Spelling List of Final Consonant Blends

❑ **NOW:** Build some words with these Ending Blends by rhyming words with the words below, or take: A Single Consonant, Consonant; Digraph (ch, sh, th, wh); or Beginning Blend + a Vowel + a Final Blend and build words: milk, silk, calm, palm, chomp, stomp, stump, jump, bunk junk; skunk, stunk.

L- ENDING BLENDS

LD: child, mild, wild * field, shield, yield * bold, cold, gold, hold, mold, old, scold, sold told

LK: balk, chalk, stalk, talk, walk * bulk, hulk, sulk *

LM: balm, calm, palm, psalm *

LP: help, kelp, yelp (animal bark or cry) *

LT: fault, halt, malt, salt * belt, dwelt, knelt, melt, smelt (fish) * built, gilt, jilt, kilt, quilt, stilt, tilt *

LTH: health, stealth, wealth

M- ENDING BLEND (also conte**mp**t)

MP: camp, champ, cramp, damp, ramp, scamp, stamp, tramp * blimp (weak), chimp, crimp, primp, skimp * bump, champ, clump, dump, hump, jump, lump, plump, pump, rump, slump *

N- ENDING BLENDS

NC(e): chance, dance, France, glance, lance, prance, stance, trance * mince, prince, since, wince

NCH: bench, clench (hold tightly), drench, French, quench, stench, trench, wench, wrench * brunch, bunch, crunch, hunch, munch, punch *

ND: band, bland, brand, gland, hand, land, sand, stand, strand (string of beads, etc.) * bend, blend, end, fend (fight off), lend, mend, send, spend, tend, trend, wend (proceed; go) bind, blind, find, grind, hind, kind, rind, wind * bond, fond, frond, pond * ground mound, pound, round, sound *

NGTH: length, strength *

NK: bank, blank, clank, crank, dank, drank, flank, plank, rank, sank, tank, thank, yank * blind, brink, chink, clink, drink, link, mink, pink, rink, shrink, sink, stink, think, wink * bonk, honk * bunk, chunk, drunk, dunk, funk, hunk, junk, plunk, punk, shrunk, spunk, stunk, sunk, trunk *

NT: ant, can't, chant, grant, pant, plant, rant, slant * glint, hint, lint, mint, splint, sprint, squint, tint. bent, cent, dent, gent, lent, rent, scent, sent, spent, tent, vent, went * fount, mount *

❑ *PLAY RHYME THYME:* Fill in the blanks with words that end with the letters in parentheses.

Gentle Kid: _ _ _ _ _ _ _ _ _ (LD)

Icy Metal: _ _ _ _ _ _ _ _ (LD)

Moving Conversation: _ _ _ _ _ _ _ _ (LK)

Cry for Aid: _ _ _ _ for _ _ _ _ (LP)

Stop for a Soda: _ _ _ _ for a _ _ _ _ (LT)

Weak Shellfish: _ _ _ _ _ _ _ _ _ _ _ (MP)

Grasp a Tool: _ _ _ _ _ _ a _ _ _ _ _ _ (NCH)

Chew Noon-Meal: _ _ _ _ _ _ _ _ _ _ (NCH

Accidental Look: _ _ _ _ _ _ _ _ _ _ _ _ (Nce)

Nice Brain: _ _ _ _ _ _ _ _ (ND)

Crooked Penny: _ _ _ _ _ _ _ _ (NT)

Green Shade: _ _ _ _ _ _ _ _ (NT)

R- ENDING BLENDS (The rest of these blends are covered under R-Controlled Vowels.)

RD: bard (poet), card, guard, hard, lard, shard, yard * bird, third * cord, chord, ford, sword, word *

RK: ark, bark, dark, hark, lark, mark, park, shark, spark, stark *

RL: burl, churl, curl, furl, hurl, purl *

RN: fern, tern, stern * born, corn, horn, morn, scorn, shorn, thorn torn, worn *

RT: art, cart, chart, dart, mart, part, smart, start, tart *

RTH: birth, girth (horse measurement), mirth *

S- ENDING BLENDS

SK: ask, cask, flask, mask, task * desk * brisk, disk, frisk, risk, whisk * dusk, musk, tusk *

SP: asp, clasp, gasp, grasp, hasp, rasp * crisp, lisp, wisp *

ST: blast, cast, fast, last, mast, past, vast * best, blest, chest, crest, guest, jest, lest, nest, pest, quest (search), rest, test, vest, west, wrest (wrestle from) * fist, grist, list, mist, twist, wrist * boast, coast, roast, toast * host, ghost, most, post; cost, lost * bust, crust, dust, gust, just, lust, must, rust, thrust, trust *

T- ENDING BLENDS

CT: act, fact, pact, tact

FT: aft, craft, draft, graft, shaft, waft (carry through the air) * deft (skillful), heft, cleft, left, theft * drift, gift, lift, rift, shift, sift, swift, thrift * oft (often), loft, soft *

PT: crept, kept, slept, swept, wept *

TCH: batch, catch, hatch, latch, match, patch, scratch, thatch, watch * etch, fetch, sketch, wretch * ditch, hitch, pitch, stitch, switch, witch * blotch, botch, notch * clutch, crutch, Dutch, hutch *

W- ENDING BLENDS

WD and WL: crowd * awl, bawl, brawl, crawl, drawl, shawl, scrawl, trawl * fowl, growl, howl, owl, jowl, prowl, scowl *

WN: brawn, dawn, drawn, fawn, lawn, pawn, prawn, spawn, yawn * brown, crown, down, drown, frown, gown, town * blown, flown, grown, known, mown, own, shown, sown, thrown *

❏ **PLAY RHYME THYME**: Fill in the blanks with words that end with the letters in parentheses.

Tough Sentry: _ _ _ _ _ _ _ _ _ (RD)

Hidden Predator: _ _ _ _ _ _ _ _ _ (RK)

Quick Toot: _ _ _ _ _ _ _ _ _ (ST)

Greatest Search: _ _ _ _ _ _ _ _ (ST)

Cook Bread : _ _ _ _ _ _ _ _ _ (ST)

Spirit Welcomer: _ _ _ _ _ _ _ _ _ (ST)

Boat Wind: _ _ _ _ _ _ _ _ _ (FT)

Skillful Robbery: _ _ _ _ _ _ _ _ _ (FT)

Fast Present: _ _ _ _ _ _ _ _ _ (FT)

Grasp a Lighter: _ _ _ _ _ a _ _ _ _ _ (CH)

Hen Frown: _ _ _ _ _ _ _ _ _ (WL)

Deer Sigh: _ _ _ _ _ _ _ _ (WN)

ANSWERS: Hard Guard; Dark Shark; Fast Blast; Best Quest; Roast Toast; Ghost Host; Raft Draft; Deft Theft; Swift Gift; Catch a Match; Fowl Scowl; Fawn Yawn.

The Many Ways the Different Consonant Sounds Are Spelled

<u>Single Consonants</u>, Consonant/Vowels, and <u>Digraphs</u> create the Different Consonant Sounds in the English language. These Consonant Sounds are usually spelled according to Phonics Rules, but there are also a number of *exceptions* (in parentheses). Note: *C and X are not different sounds; they copy* sounds. Also, *Blends do not create a different sound*, but *blend* consonants or consonants and digraphs.

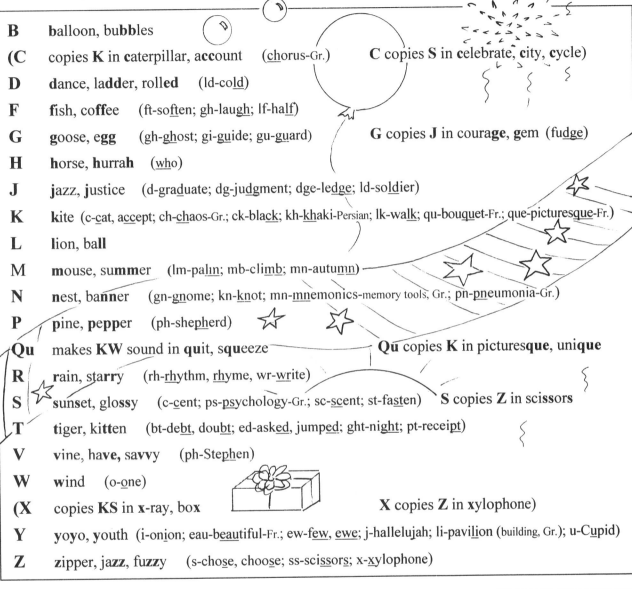

B	**b**alloon, **b**ubbles
(C	copies **K** in **c**aterpillar, a**cc**ount (<u>ch</u>orus-Gr.) **C copies S in c**elebrate, **c**ity, **c**ycle**)**
D	**d**ance, la**dd**er, roll**ed** (ld-co<u>ld</u>)
F	**f**ish, co**ff**ee (ft-so<u>f</u>ten; gh-lau<u>gh</u>; lf-ha<u>lf</u>)
G	**g**oose, e**gg** (gh-<u>gh</u>ost; gi-<u>g</u>uide; gu-<u>g</u>uard) **G copies J in** coura**g**e, **g**em (fu<u>dge</u>)
H	**h**orse, **h**urrah (<u>wh</u>o)
J	**j**azz, **j**ustice (d-gra<u>d</u>uate; dg-ju<u>dg</u>ment; dge-le<u>dge</u>; ld-so<u>l</u>dier)
K	**k**ite (c-<u>c</u>at, a<u>cc</u>ept; ch-<u>ch</u>aos-Gr.; ck-bla<u>ck</u>; kh-<u>kh</u>aki-Persian; lk-wa<u>lk</u>; qu-bou<u>qu</u>et-Fr.; que-pictures<u>que</u>-Fr.)
L	**l**ion, ba**ll**
M	**m**ouse, su**mm**er (lm-pa<u>lm</u>; mb-cli<u>mb</u>; mn-autu<u>mn</u>)
N	**n**est, ba**nn**er (gn-<u>gn</u>ome; kn-<u>kn</u>ot; mn-<u>mn</u>emonics-memory tools, Gr.; pn-<u>pn</u>eumonia-Gr.)
P	**p**ine, **p**epper (ph-she<u>ph</u>erd)
Qu	makes **KW** sound in **qu**it, s**qu**eeze **Qu copies K in** pictures**qu**e, uni**qu**e
R	**r**ain, sta**rr**y (rh-<u>rh</u>ythm, <u>rh</u>yme, wr-<u>wr</u>ite)
S	**s**unset, glo**ss**y (c-<u>c</u>ent; ps-<u>ps</u>ychology-Gr.; sc-<u>sc</u>ent; st-fa<u>st</u>en) **S copies Z in** sci**ss**ors
T	**t**iger, ki**tt**en (bt-de<u>bt</u>, dou<u>bt</u>; ed-ask<u>ed</u>, jump<u>ed</u>; ght-ni<u>ght</u>; pt-recei<u>pt</u>)
V	**v**ine, ha**v**e, sa**vv**y (ph-Ste<u>ph</u>en)
W	**w**ind (o-<u>o</u>ne)
(X	copies **KS** in **x**-ray, bo**x** **X copies Z in x**ylophone**)**
Y	**y**oyo, **y**outh (i-on<u>i</u>on; eau-b<u>eau</u>tiful-Fr.; ew-f<u>ew</u>, <u>ew</u>e; j-hallelujah; li-pavil<u>i</u>on (building, Gr.); u-C<u>u</u>pid)
Z	**z**ipper, ja**zz**, fu**zz**y (s-cho<u>s</u>e, choo<u>s</u>e; ss-sci<u>ss</u>ors; x-<u>x</u>ylophone)

CH	**ch**ild (c-<u>c</u>ello-Ita.; t-fu<u>t</u>ure; tch-ca<u>tch</u>) **(CH copies K: ch**ord, **ch**orus-Gr.**)**
SH	**sh**ell, hu**sh** (c-o<u>c</u>ean, ch-ma<u>ch</u>ine, s-<u>s</u>ugar; sci-con<u>sci</u>ence)
TH	**th**at, pa**th** (voiced: air)
TH	**th**in, smoo**th** (voiceless: little air)
WH	**wh**eat, **wh**istle, **wh**y (also called <u>HW</u> sound)
NG	ri**ng**, si**ng**ing (ngue-to<u>ngue</u>) (NOTE: <u>NG</u> can also be 2 separate sounds: e<u>ng</u>ine, la<u>ng</u>uage)
ZH	(special sound: a**z**ure, divi**s**ion, mira**g**e, trea**s**ure)

3

POWER Spelling List of Short Vowel Sounds

❑ **TRY THIS**: Below are some of the most common sets of words that follow the Short Vowel Rule. Under each set, put two or more words together to make one or more rhymes.

A as in cat: bat, brat, chat, fat, flat, gnat, hat, mat, pat, rat, sat * cab, crab, grab, jab, lab, tab * back, black, knack, pack, sack, snack, track * dad, fad, glad, had, lad, mad, sad * clam, cram, dam, ham, jam, scram, slam, swam, yam* camp, champ, cramp, lamp, ramp, stamp * band, hand, land, sand, stand * bank, blank, plank, prank, sank, tank, thank, yank * cap, clap, gap, lap, map, nap, rap, snap, tap, trap, wrap, yap *

E as in egg: beg, leg, peg * bed, fed, fled, led, red, shed, sled, sped * bell, cell, dwell, fell, sell, shell, swell, tell, well, yell * den, glen, hen, men, pen, ten, then, when, wren * bend, blend, end, lend, mend, send, spend, trend * bent, cent, dent, gent, lent, rent, sent, scent, spent, tent, went * bless, chess, dress, guess, less, mess, press, stress * best, chest, guest, nest, pest, quest, rest, test, vest, west, zest * bet, get, jet, let, met, net, pet, set, vet, wet, yet *

I as in pin: chin, fin, grin, kin, shin, skin, spin, tin, thin, twin, win * brick, chick, click, flick, kick, pick, quick, sick, stick, thick, trick, wick * bid, did, grid, hid, kid, rid, skid, slid * big, dig, fig, jig, pig, rig, twig, wig * bill, chill, drill, grill, hill, ill, quill, skill, spill, still, thrill, will * brim, dim, grim, rim, slim, swim, trim, whim * hint, mint, print, sprint, squint, tint * chip, clip, dip, drip, flip, grip, hip, lip, ship, sip, skip, slip, snip, tip, trip, zip *

O as in frog: "Ribbit!" bog, dog, fog, hog, jog, log, smog * blob, cob, job, knob, mob, rob, sob, snob * block, clock, dock, flock, knock, lock, rock, shock, sock * clod, cod, nod, plod, pod, rod, sod, trod * bong, dong, gong, long, song, strong, thong, wrong * chop, cop, crop, drop, hop, mop, pop, prop, shop, stop, top * blot, cot, dot, got, hot, jot, knot, lot, not, plot, pot, rot, shot, slot, spot, tot, trot *

U as in sun: bun, fun, pun, run, spun, stun, sun * club, cub, grub, rub, scrub, sub, tub * bug, dug, hug, jug, mug, plug, rug, shrug, slug, smug, snug, tug * bum, chum, drum, gum, hum, plum, sum * bump, dump, grump, jump, lump, plump, pump, thump * brunch, bunch, crunch, hunch, lunch, munch, punch * blush, brush, crush, gush, hush, mush, plush, rush, slush * crust, dust, gust, just, must, rust, trust *

❑ **RHYME THYME GAME**: To play, just fill in the blanks below.

Arithmetic Anger: _ _ _ _   _ _ _ _ _ (ATH)

Cozy Insect Mat: _ _ _ _   _ _ _   _ _ _ (UG)

Rained-on Doctor: _ _ _   _ _ _ (ET)

Endless Tune: _ _ _ _   _ _ _ _ (ONG)

Fat Crab: _ _ _ _ _   _ _ _ _ (UMP)

Heated Tie: _ _ _   _ _ _ _ (OT)

Hog Dance: _ _ _   _ _ _ (IG)

Imp Conversation: _ _ _ _   _ _ _ _ (AT)

Money Run: _ _ _ _   _ _ _ (ASH)

Only Believe: _ _ _ _   _ _ _ _ _ (UST)

Sailing Journey: _ _ _ _   _ _ _ _ (IP)

Scarlet Glider: _ _ _   _ _ _ _ (ED)

Spaniel Run: _ _ _   _ _ _ (OG)

Taxi Bill: _ _ _   _ _ _ (AB)

This is answers printed upside down at bottom.

72

ANSWERS: Math Wrath; Snug Bug Rug; Wet Vet; Long Song; Plump Grump; Hot Knot; Pig Jig; Brat Chat; Cash Dash; Just Trust; Ship Trip; Red Sled; Dog Jog; Cab Tab.

POWER Spelling List of Long Vowel Sounds with Silent E

TRY THIS: Under each set of Silent E Words, put two or more words together to make rhymes.

A + Consonant + E as in face: brace, grace, lace, pace, place, race, space, trace * blade, fade, glade, grade, jade, made, wade, shade, trade * bake, cake, fake * bale, gale, male, pale, sale, scale, tale, whale * blame, came, dame, fame, flame, frame, game, lame, name, same, shame, tame * crane, lane, mane, pane, plane, sane, vane * cape, drape, grape, scrape, shape, tape * haste, paste, taste, waste * crate, date, fate, gate, grate, late, mate, plate, rate, skate, state * brave, cave, crave, gave, pave, rave, save, shave, wave * blaze, craze, daze, faze, gaze, glaze, graze, haze, maze *

E + Consonant + E as in athlete: compete, complete, concrete, Crete (island near Greece), delete (take out), deplete (use up) * concede, recede, secede * extreme (strong), scheme, supreme (highest), theme (main idea) * mete(measure) * obsolete (out of date) * discrete (careful) * these *

I + Consonant + E as in kite: bite, mite, quite, site, sprite, white, write * bribe, scribe, tribe * dice, ice, lice, mice, nice, price, rice, slice, twice, vice * knife, life, strife, wife * bike, hike, like, spike, strike * file, mile, pile, smile, tile, while * chime, crime, dime, lime, mime, prime, time * dine, fine, line, mine, nine, pine, tine, shine, shrine, spine, swine, pine, whine, wine * pipe, ripe, stripe * fire, hire, spire, tire, wire * rise, wise * alive, dive, drive, five, hive, jive, live, strive, thrive *

O + Consonant + E as in rose: chose, close, hose, nose, pose, prose * robe, globe, probe * abode, code, mode, rode * hole, mole, pole, role, stole, whole * dome, gnome, home, Nome, Rome * bone, clone, cone, hone, lone, phone, shone, stone, tone, zone * cope, grope, hope, mope, nope, pope, rope, scope, slope * note, quote, vote, wrote * clove, dove (dive), cove, grove, stove, wove *

U + Consonant + E as in flute: brute, chute, cute, lute, mute; commute, parachute, salute * cube, lube, tube * crude, dude, rude, prude * duke, nuke, fluke * mule, rule, Yule * dune, June, prune, tune; attune * fuse, muse, use; excuse, refuse *

RHYME THYME GAME: To play, just fill in the blanks below:

Bell Hour: _ _ _ _ _   _ _ _ _ (IME)   Italian Dwelling: _ _ _ _   _ _ _ _ (OME)

Excellent Polish: _ _ _ _   _ _ _ _ _ (INE)   Kind Rodents: _ _ _ _   _ _ _ _ (ICE)

Flower Poetry: _ _ _ _   _ _ _ _ _ (OSE)   Long Grin: _ _ _ _   _ _ _ _ _ (ILE)

Green Grass: _ _ _ _   _ _ _ _ (ADE)   Mammal Story: _ _ _ _ _   _ _ _ _ (ALE)

Highest Idea: _ _ _ _ _ _ _   _ _ _ _ _ (EME)   Summer Song: _ _ _ _   _ _ _ _ (UNE)

Impolite Guy: _ _ _ _   _ _ _ (UDE)   World Search: _ _ _ _ _   _ _ _ _ _ (OBE)

373

POWER Spelling List of Long Vowel Sounds with Digraph.

❑ **TRY THIS**: These words follow the When Two Vowels Go Walking…Rule which means the second vowel makes the first vowel long. Put two or more of these words together to make rhymes.

AI as in braid: aid, laid, maid, paid, raid; mermaid * bail, fail, hail, jail, mail, nail, pail, quail, rail, sail, snail, tail, trail, wail; prevail * brain, chain, drain, grain, main, pain, plain, rain, vain; again, remain, sustain * faint, paint, quaint, saint, taint; acquaint * gait, plait (to braid), trait, wait *

AY as in ray: bay, clay, day, gay, gray, hay, jay, lay, May, nay, pay, play, pray, ay, slay, spray, stray, sway, tray, way; away, betray, castaway, essay, holiday, stingray, today *

EA as in sea: flea, pea, plea, tea * beach, bleach, each, peach, preach, reach, teach * bead, knead, lead, read, plead * beak, creak, leak, peak, sneak, speak, squeak, teak (wood), weak * deal, heal, meal, peal, real, seal, squeal, teal (blue-green), zeal; reveal, conceal * beat, cheat, feat, heat, meat, neat, seat, treat, wheat; repeat * breathe, wreath, underneath *

EE as in bee: "bzzz" fee, free, gee, glee, knee, see, tree * deed, feed, heed, reed, seed, weed, bleed, breed, creed, freed, greed, speed, steed * cheek, creek, Greek, leek, meek, peek, seek, sleek, week * beep, cheep, creep, deep, jeep, keep, peep, sheep, sleep, steep, sweep, weep * bees, cheese, fees, frees, glees, knees, sees, trees * beet, feet, fleet, greet, meet, sheet, sleet, street, sweet, tweet *

IE as in pie: die, fie, lie, tie, vie * died, dried, fried, lied, tied * dies, cries, dries, flies, fries, lies, pies, skies, ties, tries, vies *

OA as in coach: poach (way of cooking), roach; encroach * load, road, toad * coal, foal (baby horse), goal, shoal (sandbank) * foam, loam, roam * groan, loan, moan * boast, coast, roast, toast * boat, coat, float, goat, moat, oat, throat *

OE as in does: foes, floe (sheet of floating ice), hoes, roes (fish eggs), toes, woes, cargoes, echoes, goes, heroes, oboes, tomatoes, potatoes, zeroes *

OW as in blow: crow, flow, glow, grow, know, low, mow, row, show, sow, throw, tow; elbow * blown, flown, grown, known, mown, shown, sown, thrown; unknown *

UE as in glue: blue, cluc * cruel, duel, flue, fuel * cue, hue, rue, Sue, true; ensue (happen), rescue *

❑ **RHYME THYME GAME**: Just fill in the blanks below:

Animal Clothing: _ _ _ _ _ _ _ _ (OA) Hair Robbery: _ _ _ _ _ _ _ _ _ (AI)

Bird Hello: _ _ _ _ _ _ _ _ _ _ (EE) Honest Color: _ _ _ _ _ _ _ _ (UE: genuine)

Bird Display: _ _ _ _ _ _ _ _ (OW) Insect Carriage: _ _ _ _ _ _ _ _ _ _ (OA)

Digit (finger; toe) Sadness: _ _ _ _ _ _ (OE) Insect's Joint: _ _ _ _ _ _ _ _ _ (EE)

Evil Fencing: _ _ _ _ _ _ _ _ _ (UE) Lost Beam: _ _ _ _ _ _ _ _ (AY)

Fast Horse: _ _ _ _ _ _ _ _ _ _ (EE) Slow Letter: _ _ _ _ _ _ _ _ (AI)

ANSWERS: Goat Coat; Tweet Greet; Crow Show; Toe Woe; Cruel Duel; Speed Steed; Braid Raid; True Blue; Roach Coach; Bee's Knees, Stray Ray; Snail Mail.

POWER Spelling List of IE and EI Vowel Sounds

I before E
Except after C (When C sounds like S),
Or when sounded as A
As in neighbor, their, or weigh (A sound <u>always</u> spelled EI).

❏ **NOW**: IE and EI Vowel Sounds are very challenging to spell because they can make so many different sounds. EI can even make a <u>long a</u> sound. Each list will help you see IE and EI words that have the same sound and spelling pattern. For each list, put 2 or more words together to make rhymes.

IE (Long <u>e</u> sound) in: belief, chief, grief, thief; belief, relief, handkerchief, unbelief * field, shield, wield (use), yield (surrender) * shriek * achieves, believes, disbelieves, grieves, relieves, reprieve, retrieve, thieves * piece * lien (legal claim on property) *

IER (Long <u>er</u> sound) in: pier * fierce, pierce * hieroglyphics *

IES (Long <u>i</u> sound spelled: <u>ies</u>.) in: cries, dies, lies, pies, ties, vies (competes), allies, solidifies *

EI (Short <u>un</u> sound) in: foreign sovereign * (Short <u>it</u> sound) in: counterfeit, forfeit *

EI (Long <u>e</u> sound) in: sheik * caffeine, codeine, protein * heinous (evil) *

EI (Long <u>i</u> sound) in: Einstein, stein * seismic (earthquakes)* feisty (spirited), heist (robbery)* Fahrenheit *

CEI (Long <u>e</u> sound) in: conceit, deceit, receipt * conceive, deceive, perceive, receive *

CIE (Long <u>she</u> sound) in: ancient, patient, quotient * efficient, deficient, omniscient (all-knowing), quotient (answer in division), recipient, sufficient *

CIE (Short <u>shu</u> sound) in: conscience, conscious * (Long <u>i</u> sound) as in science *

EI/EIG (Long <u>a</u> sound) in: skein(of geese), rein, vein, chow mein * feign (pretend), reign;* beige * leisure *

EIGH (Long <u>a</u> sound) in: sleigh, weigh; neighbor, inveigle (lure by flattery) * eight, freight, weight *

EIR (Long <u>air</u> sound) as in heir, their *

❏ ***RHYME THYME GAME***: To play, just fill in the blanks below:

Surrender the Land: _ _ _ _ _ the _ _ _ _ _ (IE)

Main Opinion: _ _ _ _ _ _ _ _ _ _ _ (IE)

Quick Help: _ _ _ _ _ _ _ _ _ _ _ (IE)

Trusts Stealers: _ _ _ _ _ _ _ _ _ _ _ _ _ _ _ (IE)

Ferocious Stab: _ _ _ _ _ _ _ _ _ _ _ _ (IER)

Use a Piece of Armor: _ _ _ _ _ a _ _ _ _ _ _ (IE)

Vanity and Dishonesty: _ _ _ _ _ _ _ and _ _ _ _ _ _ (EI)

Scientist's Beer Mug: _ _ _ _ _ _ _ _ _'_ _ _ _ _ _ (EI)

Old Sick Person: _ _ _ _ _ _ _ _ _ _ _ _ _ _ (CIE)

Heaviness of Load: _ _ _ _ _ _ of _ _ _ _ _ _ _ (EIGH)

Pretend to Rule: _ _ _ _ _ a _ _ _ _ _ (EIGN)

They Own the Successor: _ _ _ _ _ _ _ _ _ (EIR)

ANSWERS: Yield the Field; Chief Belief; Brief Relief; Believes Thieves; Fierce Pierce; Wield a Shield; Conceit and Deceit; Einstein's Stein; Ancient Patient; Weight of Freight; Feign a Reign; Their Heir.

375

POWER Spelling List of Special Two-Vowel Sounds

Broad O: au, aw (al); **Diphthongs:** ew, oi and oy; ou and ow; **Double O:** oo and oo

❏ **NOW:** Under each set of Special Two-Vowel Sounds, put 2 or more words together to make rhymes.

AU as in auto: aught, caught, fraught, naught, taught; * haul, maul, Paul * haunch (hip), launch, paunch (stomach), staunch (steadfast) * fault, vault * flaunt (show off), gaunt (thin), haunt, jaunt (short run), taunt (tight) * cause, clause, pause * (Spelling is AU when you hear more than one consonant after the vowel.)

AW as in saw: caw, claw, draw, flaw, gnaw, jaw, law, paw, raw, saw, slaw, straw * bawl, brawl, crawl, drawl, scrawl, shawl, trawl * brawn, dawn, drawn, fawn, lawn, pawn, prawn, spawn, yawn *

AL as in ball: all, call, fall, gall, hall, mall, pall, small, squall, stall, tall, wall * balk, chalk, talk, walk * balm, calm, palm, psalm, qualm * halt, malt, salt * awl, bawl, brawl, crawl, drawl, trawl *

OI as in coil: boil, broil, foil, soil, spoil, toil; recoil, turmoil * choice, voice; rejoice * coin, groin, join, loin * joint, point; ointment * foist, hoist, joist (support beam), moist * noise, poise; turquoise *

OY as in boy: coy, joy; ploy, Roy, soy, toy; ahoy, annoy, decoy, employ, enjoy, oyster, royal *

OU as in cloud: loud, proud * couch, grouch, ouch, pouch, slouch, vouch * bounce, pounce, trounce (defeat); announce, pronounce * bound, found, ground, hound, mound, pound, round, sound, wound * count, fount, mount; fountain, mountain * douse (put out fire), house, louse, mouse, spouse * bout, clout (strong influence), pout, scout, shout, snout, spout, sprout, stout, trout * mouth, south.

OW as in owl: "WHOO?" fowl, growl, howl, jowl, owl, prowl, scowl * bow, brow, chow, cow, how, now, plow, row (fight), sow, vow; allow * brown, clown, crown, down, drown, frown, gown, town; renowned *

EW as in ewe: blew, brew, crew, dew, few, flew, hew, knew, mew, new, pew, phew; crewel (sewing) *

OO as in moon: coon, croon, loon, noon, soon, spoon, swoon * boo, coo, moo, shoo, too, woo, zoo; bamboo, cuckoo, shampoo, yahoo * cool, fool, pool, tool, school, spool, stool * bloom, boom, broom, doom, gloom, groom, loom, room, zoom * droop, hoop, loop, scoop, sloop (sailboat), snoop, stoop, swoop, troop * goose, loose, moose, noose * boot, hoot, loot, root (cheer), toot, scoot, shoot *

OO as in book: brook, cook, crook, hook, look, nook, shook, took * good, hood, stood, wood * (*Exceptions:* Could, should, and would also make oo sound, but they're spelled ou.)

❏ **RHYME THYME GAME:** To play, just fill in the blanks below:

Bird Cry: ___ ____ (OW)   Nice Lumber: ____ ____ (OO)

Black Colt: ____ ____ (OA)   Noisy Cumulus: ____ _____ (OU)

Crabby Sofa: _____ _____ (OU)   Nose Power: _____ _____ (OU)

Group Drink: ____ ____ (EW)   Quiet Tree: ____ ____ (AL)

Little Storm: _____ _____ (ALL) Shy Lad: ___ ___ (OY)

Lunch Utensil: ____ _____ (OO)   Stream Lure: _____ ____ (OO)

POWER Spelling List of Powerful R-Controlled Vowel Sounds

NOW: Notice the strong effect that **R** has on the sound of words. It can change *cat* to *cart*, *bit* to *bird*. Put two or more words together to create rhymes for these **R-Controlled Words**.

AR as in star: bar, car, far, jar, mar, par, scar, spar, tar; party, sparkle * bard, card, guard, hard, shard (broken piece), yard; garden * barge, charge, large * bark, dark, hark, lark, mark, park, shark, spark, stark (bare) * arm, charm, farm, harm; alarm * barn, darn, yarn * harp, tarp, sharp * harsh, marsh * cart, chart, dart, mart, part, smart, start, tart *

ER as in fern: tern (bird), stern (back of boat; strict); lantern * her; mermaid, monster, perfect, verdict * merge, serge (wool), verge (on the edge) * berm (part of a beach), germ, term * nerve, serve, swerve *

IR as in bird: gird, third * fir, sir, stir, whir; circle, circus, squirrel, stirrup, thirteen, thirty * girl, twirl, swirl * firm, squirm; affirm, infirm (sick) * dirt, flirt, shirt, skirt, squirt * birth, girth (measurement around horse), mirth (joy), birthday *

OR as in horn: born, corn, morn, sworn, thorn, torn, worn; acorn, adorn * for; forest, forty, glory, orbit * force * porch, torch, scorch * cord, ford, lord, chord, sword * cork, fork, pork, stork * dorm, form, norm, storm; transform, uniform * horse * forth, north *

UR as in turn: burn, churn, spurn (turn away) * blur, burr (weed), fur, purr, slur, spur; murmur * hurdle, purple, turtle * burl (knot), curl, furl, hurl, purl (knit) * curse, nurse, purse * curt (rude), hurt, blurt, spurt *

AIR as in hair: air, chair, fair, flair (style), hair, lair, pair, stair * dairy, hairy, repair *

ARE as in square: bare, blare, care, dare, fare, flare, glare, hare, mare, pare, rare, scare, share, snare, spare, stare, ware; barren * baring, blaring, caring *

EAR as in ear: clear, dear, fear, gear, hear, near, rear, sear (burn), spear, tear (cry), year, weary *

EER as in deer: beer, cheer, jeer, leer, peer, queer, seer, sneer, steer; musketeer, engineer *

IRE as in fire: dire, hire, mire, sire, spire (top pf bldg.), tire; aspire, retire * brier, crier, drier, flier *

ORE as in shore: bore, chore, core, fore, more, ore, pore, score, snore, sore, store, swore, tore, wore; before, ignore *

URE as in lure: cure, pure, sure; endure, insure, leisure, measure, pleasure, treasure *

RHYME THYME GAME: To play, just fill in the blanks below:

Animal Drink: _ _ _ _ _ _ _ _ (EER)

Arrival Joy: _ _ _ _ _ _ _ _ _ (IR)

Big Boat: _ _ _ _ _ _ _ _ _ (AR)

Bird Greenery: _ _ _ _ _ _ _ _ (ER)

Burning Wheel: _ _ _ _ _ _ _ _ (IRE)

Close Weapon: _ _ _ _ _ _ _ _ _ (EAR)

Combed Style: _ _ _ _ _ _ _ _ _ (AIR)

Distant Heavenly Body: _ _ _ _ _ _ _ (AR)

Doorway Light: _ _ _ _ _ _ _ _ _ (OR)

Intelligent Pastry: _ _ _ _ _ _ _ _ (AR)

Naked Rabbit: _ _ _ _ _ _ _ _ (ARE)

Work Shop: _ _ _ _ _ _ _ _ _ (ORE)

ANSWERS: Deer Beer; Birth Mirth, Large Barge; Term Fern; Fire Tire; Near Spear; Hair Flair; Far Star; Porch Torch; Smart Tart; Bare Hare; Chore Store.

LIST OF VOWEL + R WORDS—AR, ER, IR, OR, and UR

ar	er	ir	or	ur
arm	berth	birch	aorta	blur
bard	fern	bird	actor	blurt
bark	germ	birth	alligator	burn
burglar	her	chirp	born	church
car	merge	dirt	cord	churn
cart	nerve	fir	cork	curl
char	serf	firm	corn	curt
charm	serve	first	fork	fur
dark	stern	flirt	forth	furl
far	swerve	gird	horn	hurl
guard	term	girl	lord	hurt
harsh	tern (a bird)	irk	north	lurk
jar	verb	mirth	porch	nurse
lard	verge	quirk	pork	slur
Mars	were	shirt	scorch	spur
march	carpenter	sir	scorn	spurn
marsh	chowder	skirt	sport	turn
par	December	smirk	stork	absurd
park	eager	squirm	storm	blurring
scar	entertain	squirt	sword	burden
shard	hero	stir	thorn	burlap
sharp	imperfect	third	torch	burrow
smart	interpret	twirl	absorb	disturb
snarl	lantern	affirm	acorn	flour
spar	monster	birdbath	category	furnish
star	November	birthday	distort	further
tarp	October	birthrate	export	hour
tart	panther	circle	forest	hurdle
yard	partner	circus	forgave	murder
yarn	reader	confirm	formula	murmur
artist	remainder	dirty	forty	purple
garden	rooster	firmly	glory	return
garlic	September	girdle	history	Saturday
harvest	sister	infirm	horizon	sour
marble	sooner	reaffirm	hornet	sturdy
market	speaker	skirmish	memory	suburb
marlin	sweater	skirted	morning	surfer
marvel	termite	squirrel	oarsman	surplus
party	thunder	stirrup	organic	surprise
popular	tiger	stirring	orbit	survive
scarlet	under	thirteen	platform	Thursday
sparkle	usher	thirsty	porcupine	turnips
target	verdict	thirty	record	turbulent
tarnish	western	whirlpool	transport	turtle
varnish	yesterday	whirlwind	uniform	usurp

Starring Letter R in the Art of Musical Story Telling

<u>R</u> Rules!!! Its rrrr…sound is so powerful that it can change *at* into *art*; *bad* into *bard* (singing poet); *her* into *here*; *lye* into *lyre*. As you read *Starring R: Bards, Wandering Minstrels, and Troubadours*, you will see and hear some <u>R</u>-Words that are used to tell you about the art of musical story telling, popular in the Middle Ages (from A.D. 1100 –1400). As you read this <u>R</u>-Article, you'll discover more about the sounds <u>R</u> creates when it comes after vowels.

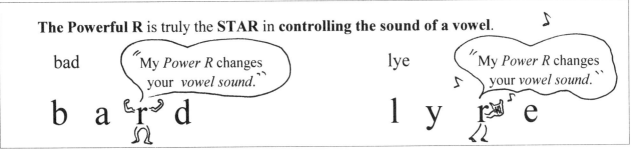

The Powerful R is truly the **STAR** in **controlling the sound of a vowel**.

bad   "My *Power R* changes your *vowel sound*."   lye   "My *Power R* changes your *vowel sound*."

b a **r** d   l y **r** e

When R follows a vowel, it has <u>5 R-Controlled Vowel Sounds</u> of its own: <u>Short Vowel Sounds:</u> <u>ar, er, and or</u>, and <u>Long Vowel Sounds: air and ear</u>. Short <u>ir</u> and <u>ur</u> make the same sound as <u>er</u>; <u>or</u> and <u>ore</u> have the same sound; and <u>ire</u> and <u>ure</u> keep their same long vowel sound. All of these R-vowel sounds, however, can be spelled in several ways, so R-Words can be very challenging.

Some <u>R</u>-Words You'll Meet in *Starring R* and the Different Ways <u>R</u>-Words Can Be Spelled

<u>3 Short Vowel Sounds (er, ir, ur = same)</u>

ar: star: <u>far</u>, <u>art</u>, b<u>ar</u>d, h<u>ar</u>p, ch<u>ar</u>med
er: fern: h<u>er</u>bal sing<u>er</u>, sev<u>er</u>al, prefe<u>rr</u>ed, v<u>er</u>ses
(**ir**: bird same as <u>er</u>): f<u>ir</u>, th<u>ir</u>st, b<u>ir</u>d, v<u>ir</u>tues
or: horn: f<u>or</u>, f<u>or</u>mal, l<u>or</u>ds, st<u>or</u>y, troubad<u>our</u>
(**ur**: turtle same as <u>er</u>): p<u>ur</u>pose, c<u>ur</u>rently, fl<u>our</u>ished

<u>2 Long Vowel Sound (ore = same as or; ire, ure = long)</u>

air: hair, square: sh<u>are</u>, b<u>ear</u>ers, h<u>eir</u>, v<u>ar</u>ious, wh<u>ere</u>
ear: dear, deer: h<u>ere</u>
(**ire**: fire same as long <u>i</u>): de-s<u>ire</u>s, <u>Ire</u>land, l<u>yre</u>
(**ore**: like <u>or</u>): ore (Final e can't make ore long), c<u>our</u>ting
(**ure**: pure same as long <u>u</u>): c<u>ure</u>s, d<u>ur</u>ing, pleas<u>ure</u>s

Starring R: Bards, Wandering Minstrels, and Troubadours

❏ **NOW**: Read *Starring R*, and underline the syllables where R follows a vowel.

The art of musical storytelling, that of being a wandering composer and singer of poems and stories, flourished during the Middle Ages (particularly 1100 – 1400). These entertainers and important bearers of news were known by various names throughout Europe: bards, minstrels, troubadours. In the Celtic lands, Ireland, Scotland, and Wales, Bards sang and recited epic poems and songs of national heroes, oft while playing the harp or lyre. In England, Wandering Minstrels played and sang, entertaining villagers and lords and ladies. These songsters were expected to know and preserve the folk tales; share all the court scandals; be versed in herbal cures; and, of course, at a moment's notice, compose formal verses for courting, while playing several instruments currently preferred by the court. In France, Troubadours charmed the royalty who yearned to hear their rich and varied wails and tales of romantic love. Called "chansons d'amor," these love songs celebrated the pure virtues of love, as well as its physical desires and pleasures.

POWER Spelling List of Open Syllable Words

Knowing about Open Syllables gives you valuable Spelling *POWER*. It helps you to be able to hear where one syllable ends and the next begins. Also, being able to hear Open Syllables helps you know if a word has a Double-Letter or Open Syllable. Listen: aggravate – aglow; ally – aloft; apex – apple.

OPEN SYLLABLE
LONG A SOUND
ACCENTED
agent
apex (very top)
April
banal (trivial)
basic
basin
basis
craven (cowardly)
David
hatred
label
latent (not developed yet)
matrix (math concept)
naked
native
nature
rabid (having rabies)
raven
sacred (holy)
saline (having salt)
stamen (flower part)
vacate

OPEN SYLLABLE
SHORT A SOUND
UNACCENTED
abide
abode
abolish
about
abuse
abut (touch against)
across
adapt
adopt
adept (skilled)
adult

afloat
aflutter (excited)
against
agenda
aglow
aglitter
agleam
agree
aground
alike
Alaska
alive
aloft
alone
along
aloof
amazing
amend
amuse
apiece
apology
arise, arose
atone (make amends)
awhile
awake, awoke
canal
charade
China
delta
dogma (a belief)
extra
Japan
llama
majestic
ninja
parole
stanza
stigma
trapeze
ultra

vista (a view)

OPEN SYLLABLE
LONG E SOUND
be
below
begin
behave
belong
betrothed
between
beyond
categories
celebrate
decided
defend
define
defrost
defunct (not existing)
depend
deposit
depot (station)
desist (to stop)
devote
edict (proclamation)
ego
elect
elope
erupt
event
feline
female
frequent
he
hello
hero
Korea
me
misbehave
precede

predict
preferred
pretend
prevent
rebate
receipt
regret
reject
relief
remote
repent (to confess)
repetition
respect
respond
result
review
revise
secret
she
vegetable
veto
we
Xerox
Zero

OPEN SYLLABLE
LONG I SOUND
ACCENTED
biped (two-footed)
bicycle
bisect
china
climax
crisis
dialect
digest
dilute
disquiet
giant
hi

hi fi
I
ibex (wild goat)
icon (image)
idea
iris
Irish
item
license
mica
minus
nitrate
nitric
quiet
shining
silent
similar
sinus
siren
stipend
strident (harsh)
tirade (rage)
tricycle
trident (3-pronged spear)
tripod (camera stand)
trisect
vibrate
vitamin

OPEN SYLLABLE I UNACCENTED
altitude
Africa
antidote
candidate
captivate
complicate
compliment
condiment (seasoning)
confident
culminate (result in)
cultivate
diligent
divest (to take away)
divide
dividend
divine

dominate
emigrate
estimate
fabricate
illicit (not lawful)
indicate
imitate
immigrant
implicate
inhibit
investigate
litigate (take to court)
medicate
mobilize
obligate
optimistic
physical
platinum
privilege
science
sensitive
sentiment
skiing
silicon (man-made rock)
similar
stabilize
substitute
sugar
ventilate

OPEN SYLLABLE LONG O SOUND
abdomen
absolute
accolade (award)
annotate (make notes)
aristocrat
banjo
bingo
bogus (false)
bonus
broken
coconut
cogent (forceful)
coma (unconscious)
comma
crocus (flower)

diagnosis
diorama (tiny scene)
diploma
dislocate
donate
focus
frozen
go
gusto
halo
hoping
hotel
hypocrite
isolate
isometric (even; equal)
limbo (in waiting)
locate
mimosa (flower: lily)
moment
motel
nitrogen (a gas)
no
oasis
October
oboe
omen (predicting sign)
open
over
November
photo
piano
poem
polite
potato
potent (powerful)
profile
program
protect
proton
provide
robot
rodents (rat family)
rotate
silo
sloping
soda
solo

spoken
stiletto (small dagger)
tempo
thorax (human chest)
tomato
tomorrow
totem
violent
violin

OPEN SYLLABLE LONG U SOUND
accumulate
aluminum
calculate
cubic
cumulus (puffy clouds)
Cupid
duplex
duel
duo (twosome)
February
fuel
futile (useless)
genuine
human
humid
impudent (rude)
July
menu
music
mutate (to change)
peninsula
potato
puma (cougar)
pupil
student
stupid
tumult (disturbance)
tunic
Ulysses
unicorn
unicycle
unit
unite
valuable
Zulu (live in S. Africa)

List of the Many Ways Vowel Sounds Are Spelled in English

Below, you can see the many ways sounds in English are spelled today. Although challenging for th speller, this variety shows that many cultures have added to the rich vocabulary of English.

(*Note*: Exceptions to Basic Phonics Spelling are in parentheses.)

Aa
Short Vowel: **ant**, **cat**, **baaa**   (pl**ai**d, h**a**lf, l**augh**)
Long Vowel: **ace** **rain**, **hay**, **table**   (g**au**ge, br**ea**k, v**ei**n, th**ey**, ball**et**-Fr., bouqu**et**-Fr.)
Short Vowel + R: **star** **garden**   (h**ea**rt, s**er**geant-Fr., baz**aar**-marketplace-Fr., biz**arre**-strange-Per.)
Long Vowel + R: **hair** **square**   (pr**ay**er, p**ear**, th**eir**, th**ere**, th**ey're**, v**ery**)
Broad O: **au** in v**au**lt; **aw** in s**aw**; **al** in b**al**l   (same as **short o** sound: c**au**ght, br**oa**d, s**ou**ght)
Schwa Sound: **ago**, **alike**

Ee
Short Vowel: **egg** **elephant**   (m**a**ny, s**ai**d, s**ay**s, r**ea**d-past, l**eo**pard)
Long Vowel: th**e**se, tr**ee**, p**ea**ch, rec**ei**ve, **e**qual   (p**eo**ple, k**ey**, f**ie**ld, na**ï**ve-Fr, sk**i**, am**oe**ba, qu**ay**-Sp.)
Short Vowel + R: **fern**, **mermaid**   (same as **ur sound**)   (l**ear**n)   (coy**o**te-Sp.)
Long Vowel + R: **hear**, **deer**   (h**ere**, p**ier**, f**ier**ce)
Schwa Sound: **eleven**   EW Sound: **few**   LE Sound: **candle**
Silent E as in **love** (The *e* completes the *v*, without making the o long)

Ii
Short Vowel: **pin**, **igloo**   (g**y**m, s**ie**ve, for**eig**n, mount**ai**n, w**o**men, b**ui**ld, b**u**siness, b**ee**n)
Long Sound: **kite**, **pie**, **tiger**   (l**igh**t, **ai**sle, st**ei**n-mug, h**eigh**t, k**i**nd, b**uy**)
Short Vowel + R: **bird**, **circle** (same as **ur**)
Long Vowel + R: **fire**   (ch**oir**)
Schwa Sound: **divide**   IL Sound: **pencil**

Oo
Short Vowel: **clock**, **octopus**   (c**ou**gh, br**oa**d, **au**thor, w**a**tch, y**a**cht-Dan., **ah**, s**aw**)
Long Sound: **rose**, **boat**, **bow**, **open**   (g**oe**s, s**ew**, **oh**, y**o**lk, b**eau**-Fr, br**oo**ch-Fr.)
Vowel + R: **horn**, **ore**: (same short and long)   (din**o**saur, d**oor**, qu**ar**ter)
OU Sound (Dipthong): **cloud**, **bough**   OW Sound: **owl**, **flower**   (s**au**erkraut)
OI Sound   (Dipthong): **oil**   (Iroqu**oi**s)   OY Sound: **boy**   (b**uoy**)
Double O: **moon** (same as long u)   (tr**u**th, gl**ue**, m**o**ve, gr**ew**, can**oe**)
Double O: **book**   (w**o**lf, c**ou**ld, f**u**ll)
Schwa Sound: **canyon**

Uu
Short Vowel: **sun**, **umbrella**   (fl**oo**d, tr**ou**ble, s**o**n, s**o**me, d**oe**s, w**a**s)
Long Vowel: **flute**, **fruit**, **music**   (b**eau**ty, f**ew**, h**uge**, v**iew**, **y**ou, **y**ule, thr**ough**)
Short Vowel + R: **turn**, **turtle**   (l**ear**n, t**er**m, **err**, th**ir**sty, w**or**k, p**urr**)
Long Vowel + R: **lure** (same as long u)
Schwa Sound: **circus**   UL Sound: **awful**

Ww   Sound: **bow** (same as long o)   **few**, **ewe** (same as long u)
Yy   Sound: **eye**, **sky**, **lyre** (same as long i)   **bunny**   (same as long e)   (s**a**yonara-Japanese)

Tool 3: POWER Rules

POWER Spelling Summary of Rules That Work

Apostrophe-Contraction Rule – When you have a set of homophones with a contraction (pronoun + verb) *and* a possessive: *it's – its*; *they're – their*; *you're – your*; *who's – whose*; the contraction ALWAYS gets the apostrophe. The possessive NEVER does. This rule ALWAYS works.

Qu Rule – Q is ALWAYS followed by <u>u</u>, except at the end of a word: quail, queen, quit, quote, Iraq.

Short Vowel Rule – A single vowel stays short when it's followed by one consonant without a vowel coming right after the consonant: *cat, apple, net, pin, top, octopus, up, umbrella...* Also, it usually stays short when it's followed by more than one consonant: *band, list, end, cloth, bunt...*

Silent E Rule – When Silent E comes right after a single consonant, it usually makes the vowel before that consonant long: *face, these, kite, rose, flute, graceful...* Exceptions: *come, have, love...*

When Two Vowels Go Walking Rule – When two vowels go walking, the first vowel does the talking, and says its own name. The second vowel makes the first vowel long: *rain, boat, fruit...*

I Before E Rule – <u>I before E</u> (*believe, friend, grief, niece, piece*), <u>except after C</u> (when c sounds like s: *ceiling, deceive, receive*), <u>or when sounded as A</u>, as in *neighbor* and *weigh*: (*vein, sleigh*).

Solid Compound Word Rule – To create solid compound words, add two words together without making any changes to make a new word: <u>fire + works</u> = *fireworks*; <u>race + car</u> = *racecar*.

Prefix Rule – When you add a prefix to a word, <u>simply fasten it in front of the word</u>. Don't take out letters and don't add letters. Just spell the prefix and then the word: *disease, enjoy, submarine...*

Suffix Rule – When a suffix is <u>added to the end of a word</u>, it changes not only the meaning, but it can also turn the word into a noun, verb, adjective, or adverb: *darkness, enjoyment, runs, fastest, slowly, snowing...* The rest of the rules explain how you add suffixes to words.

Silent E Rule Before Suffixes – <u>When a consonant comes before Silent E</u>, keep Silent E before a suffix that begins with a consonant: *hopeful, likeness*. Drop Silent E before a suffix that begin with a vowel: *exciting*. <u>When a vowel precedes Silent E</u>, keep Silent E before all suffixes: *hoeing, freeing*.

Rule for Final Y before a Suffix – <u>Words ending in y preceded by a consonant</u> change the y to i before all suffixes except <u>-ing</u>: *carried, carrying; tried, trying*. <u>Most words ending in y preceded by a vowel do not drop the y</u>: *enjoyment, enjoying; canoed, canoeing*. Exceptions: *rescuing, truly...*

Inserted K Rule – Words that end in <u>hard c (k sound)</u> insert <u>k</u> before suffixes that begins with <u>e, i, or y</u> to keep the k sound: *frolic-frolicked; panic-panicky; picnic-picnicking...*

Doubling Final Consonants Rule for One-Syllable Words.
1. If a word has <u>one</u> syllable, and
2. If a word <u>ends with a consonant,</u> and
3. If the <u>consonant</u> has a <u>single vowel</u> before it: *run, swim...*, then:
<u>Double the final consonant before a suffix that begins with a vowel</u> (-ed, -er, -ing): *running, swimming...*

Doubling Final Consonants Rule for Words with More than One Syllable.
1. If a word has more than <u>one</u> syllable, and
2. If a word <u>ends in a single consonant,</u> and
3. If a <u>single short vowel</u> comes before the consonant: *admit, occur, travel...*, and
4. If, <u>in the completed word</u>, the <u>accent falls on the last syllable of the original word</u>, then:
<u>Double the final consonant before a suffix that begins with a vowel</u>: *admitted, occurred, traveler...*

POWER Spelling List of Rules That Work

Apostrophe-Contraction Rule – When you have a set of homophones with a contraction (pronoun + verb) *and* a possessive: <u>it's – its</u>; <u>they're – their</u>; <u>you're – your</u>; <u>who's – whose</u>; the <u>contraction ALWAYS gets the apostrophe.</u> <u>The possessive NEVER does.</u> This rule ALWAYS works.

1. **it's** (It is-): <u>It's</u> time for the sun to shine its (possessive) rays.
   its (poss): My pet is taking <u>its</u> catnap.
2. **they're** (they are): <u>Hey</u>, <u>they're</u> coming too. *Same Pattern*: hey, prey, they…
   their (poss): Inside, <u>their</u> has <u>heir</u> (a possessive word).
3. **you're** (you are): <u>You're</u> the first person here with your (possessive) project.
   your (poss): Inside, <u>your</u> has <u>our</u> (a possessive word).
4. **who's** (who is): <u>Who's</u> going kayaking on the lake today?
   whose (poss): <u>Whose</u> hose is this?
5. **could've**: (could have) I <u>should've</u> come, and I <u>would've</u> if I <u>could've</u> (Use <u>could have</u>, not could of).
6. **don't** (do not); **won't** (will not): <u>Don't</u> worry – they <u>won't</u> get there before us.
7. **o'clock** (of the clock): At six <u>o'clock</u> chimes ring at the <u>dock</u>. *Same Pattern*: knock, lock, rock.
8. **she'd** (she would): <u>He</u> and <u>she'd</u> like to go biking. *Same Pattern*: he, she, we.
9. **we'll** (we will): <u>We'll</u> come riding with you. *Same Pattern*: he'll, she'll, you'll.

Qu Rule – Qu always stays together and functions as a single consonant.

1. **quake**: <u>Qu</u> works as one letter. Silent <u>e</u> makes the <u>a</u> in <u>quake</u> long.
2. **ques-tion**: <u>Qu</u> = one letter, so the 2nd vowel: <u>e</u> does not makes 1st vowel: <u>u</u> long.
3. **quit**: <u>Qu</u> works as one letter, so i does not make the <u>u</u> long. The <u>i</u> is short.
4. **quite**: <u>Qu</u> = one letter so it is necessary to add a Silent <u>e</u> to make the <u>i</u> long.
5. **quo-te**: <u>Qu</u> works as one letter. Silent <u>e</u> makes the <u>o</u> in <u>quote</u> long.

Short Vowel Rule – A single vowel stays short when it's followed by one consonant without a vowel coming right after the consonant: *cat, apple, net, pin, top, octopus, up, umbrella…* Also, it usually stays short when it's followed by more than one consonant: *band, list, end, cloth, bunt…*

1. **blank-et**: <u>A</u> and <u>e</u> are followed by one or more consonant without a vowel right after the consonant.
2. **drummed**: *Double m* keeps the <u>u</u> short.
3. **hopped**: *Double p* keeps the <u>o</u> short. Without <u>pp</u>, the word is <u>hoped</u>: cop-cope; mop-mope…
4. **mag-net**: Each syllable follows *Short Vowel Rule*.
5. **splash**: *Same Pattern*: cash, dash, gash, mash, smash, splash.

Some Exceptions: bind, find, hind, mind, wind; pint; ghost, host, post; bright, fight, light, night, sight…

Silent E Rule – When Silent E comes right after a single consonant, it makes the vowel before that consonant long: *face, these, kite, rose, flute, graceful...* Some of the exceptions are: *come, have, love...*

1. **airp-lane**: Silent e change plan to plane. Then add: air + plane = airplane.
2. **a-lone**: Silent e makes the o in lone long. Then connect prefix: alone.
3. **cube**: Silent e changes cub to cube: *Same Pattern*: cut-cute; hug-huge; tub-tube...
4. **love**: *Exception*: Silent e does not make o long (E is added because no Eng. word ends in –v) above, dove.
5. **make**: Silent e makes the a long in make: *Same Pattern*: bake, cake, lake, take, wake...
6. **mi-cro-scope**: Silent e makes the o long in scope. Then add Roots: microscope: cope, hope...
7. **stare**: Silent e changes star to stare. *Same Pattern*: care, fare, hare, mare, pare, ware...
8. **theme**: Silent e changes them to theme. *Same Pattern*: her-here, met-mete; pet-Pete...
9. **um-pire**: Silent e makes i in pire long + prefix-um = umpire. *Same Pattern*: fire, sire, tire...
10. **write** (to write, verb): Silent e changes writ to write. *Same Pattern*: bite, ignite, site...

Some Exceptions: eye; gone, one, some; give, have, love; are, before, figure, sure; there, where...

When Two Vowels Go Walking Rule – When two vowels go walking, the first vowel does the talking, and says its own name. The 2nd vowel makes the 1st vowel long: *rain, boat, fruit...*

1. **foal** (baby horse): 2 vowel-a makes 1st vowel-o long: foal. *Same Pattern*: coal, goal...
2. **maid-en**: 2nd vowel-i makes 1st vowel-a long: maid. *Same Pattern*: laid, paid, raid...
3. **show-boat**: W makes o long: show. A makes o long: boat. *Same Pattern*: bow, glow...coat, goat..
4. **play-day**. Y makes a long in play and day: play + day. *Same Pattern*: bay, hay, pray, say...
5. **quaint**: I makes the a long in quaint. *Same Pattern*: faint, paint, saint...

Exceptions: There are a number of exceptions. Lesson 19 has a complete list of these with clues.

I Before E Rule – I before E (*believe, friend, grief, niece, piece*), except after C (when c sounds like s: *ceiling, deceive, receive*), or when sounded as A, as in *neighbor* and *weigh*: (*vein, sleigh*).

1. **believe**: I before E.
2. **fierce**: I before E.
3. **niece**: I before E.
4. **shield** I before E.
5. **receive**: Except after C (c = s).

6. **ceiling**: Except after C (c = s sound: ei.)
7. **conscience**: Unless c = sh sound: then ie.)
8. **efficient**: Unless c = sh sound; then ie.)
9. **neighbor**: Or when sounded as A.
10. **sleigh**: Or when sounded as A.

List of IE/EI Words with the Same Vowel Sound and Pattern:

ield, ief, ieve (long e): field, shield, wield, yield * belief, grief, relief, thief * achieves, believes, grieves, relieves, thieves *
ier, ierce (long e): pier * fierce, pierce *;   ier (long i): hieroglyphics *
ei, eign (short i): forfeit * foreign, sovereign, sovereignty *
eik, ein, eine (long e): sheik * heinous (evil), protein * caffeine, codeine *
ein, eis, eist, eit (long i): Einstein, stein (Ger. beer mug) * seismic * feisty (spirited), heist (robbery) * Fahrenheit *
ceit, ceive (long e): conceit, deceit, receipt * conceive, deceive, perceive, receive* (Reception, deception... help with spelling.)
cience, cient, scient (sh): conscience * ancient, efficient, patient, quotient, sufficient * omniscient ; cie (long i): science *
ei, eigh (long a): beige * eight, freight, neighbor, reign, sleigh, weight * feign (pretend), reign * veil * rein, vein * leisure *
eir (air): heir, their *

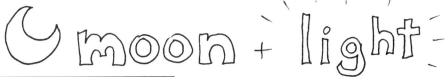
moon + light

Solid Compound Word Rule: To create solid compound words, just add the two words together, without making any changes: cup + cake = cupcake; moon + light = moonlight; race + car = racecar.

1. **birth + day**: Add: birth + day = birthday. *Same Pattern*: Mayday, payday, Thursday.
2. **drift + wood**: Add: drift + wood = driftwood. *Same Pattern*: hardwood, heartwood
3. **lamp + lighter**: Add: lamp + lighter = lamplighter (-igh = long i): *Same Pattern*: starlight.
4. **news + stand**: Add: news + stand = newsstand (Add both complete words. Notice 2 s's).
5. **sea + shore**: Add: sea + shore = seashore. *Clue*: An ocean is a place to search for sea lore.

Also, look for Latin and Greek Compound Words. They follow the same rule: *astronaut, photograph.*

6. **astro + naut**: Add astro (G. star) + naut (G. sailor) = astronaut (astro (G. star) + naut (G. sailor).
7. **audio + visual**: Add audio (L. hearing) + visual (L. seeing) = audiovisual (hearing/seeing). *seagull*

Exceptions: A few words drop a letter: *alphabet, pastime, shepherd.*
Also, words: *all, full, till, well, etc.* use just one *l* in compound words: *also, careful, until, welcome.*

8. **al + ways**: *Exception*: Add: all + ways = always *Same Pattern*: almost, also, although.
9. **past + time**: *Exception*: Add: past + time = pastime (Pa's time is spent enjoying pastimes.)
10. **wel-come**: *Exception*: Add: well + come = welcome. *Same Pattern*: welfare.

sea shore

STARFISH

Prefix Rule – When you add a prefix to a word, simply fasten it in front of the word. Don't take out letters and don't add letters. Just spell the prefix and then the word: *disease, enjoy, submarine.*

1. **bi-cycle**: Add prefix before root: bi (prefix: two) + cycle (Gk. root: wheel) = bicycle.
2. **sub-marine**: Add prefix before root: sub (prefix: under) + marine (L. root: water) = submarine.

Prefixes with Different Forms: ad-, com-, ex-, and in-: These prefixes have different forms depending on the root to which they're added. *One-Plus-One Rule*: When the prefix ends with same letter with which root begins, make sure to write the double letter.

Ad- (to, toward) has the forms: ab-, ac-, al-, an-, ap-, as-, and at-: absent, allow, announce, appear.
3. **ac-cident**: ac (prefix: to) + cide (L. root cidere-befall) + nt (noun suffix).

Com- (with, together) has the forms: col-, con-, and cor: collect, connect, correct.
4. **com-fort**: com (prefix: with) + fort (L. root: fortis-strength) + able (adj. suffix).

Ex (out of, from, beyond): has forms ex- (before c, f, h, q, p, s, t): exhale, erase, and e-: emigrate, emit.
5. **e-migrate**: e (prefix: from) + migra (L. root: migra-to move) + te (verb suffix) = emigrate.

In- (not, in, into), has three forms: il-, im-, and ir-: illiterate, immature, important, irregular.
6. **im-migrate**: im (prefix: into) + migra (L. root: migra-to move) + te (verb suffix) = immigrate.

prae → fixus

Suffix Rule – When a suffix is <u>added to a root</u>, it not only changes the meaning of the word, but also turns the word into a noun, verb, adjective or adverb. Like prefixes, just add a suffix to the word. Exceptions are: Words Ending in Silent E and Words Ending in Final Y (See Rules below).

1. **accident + al + ly**: Add each suffix: <u>accide</u> + <u>nt</u> (n. suf.) + <u>al</u> (adj. suf) + <u>ly</u> (adv. suf.) = <u>accidentally</u>.
2. **cloud + less**: When a root ends in a consonant, just add suffix to root: <u>cloud</u> + <u>less</u> = <u>cloudless</u>.
3. **easy + ly**: If the root ends with a <u>y</u>, change the <u>y</u> to <u>i</u> except before -ing: <u>easily</u>.
4. **excite + ment**: If root ends with silent <u>e</u>, just add consonant suffix: <u>excite</u> + <u>ment</u> = <u>excitement</u>.
5. **four + th**: Just add -th to numbers: <u>fourth</u>, <u>eighth</u>, <u>hundredth</u> (exceptions: <u>fifth</u>, <u>ninth</u>, <u>twelfth</u>).
6. **peaceful + ness**: Just add consonant suffixes: <u>peace</u> + <u>ful</u> = <u>peaceful</u> + <u>ness</u> = <u>peacefulness</u>.

Silent E Rule Before Suffixes – When a consonant precedes silent <u>e</u>: Keep silent <u>e</u> before a suffix beginning with a consonant: *hopeful, likeness*. Drop silent <u>e</u> before suffix that begin with a vowel: *exciting*. <u>When a vowel precedes Silent E, keep Silent E before all suffixes</u>: *hoeing, freeing*.

<u>When CONSONANT precedes Silent E, keep Silent E before a consonant suffix</u> (-ly, -ment, -r, ty):

1. **achieve + ment**: Keep <u>silent e</u> before a consonant suffix: <u>achieve</u> + <u>ment</u> = <u>achievement</u>.
2. **love + ly**: Keep <u>silent e</u> before suffix beginning with a consonant: <u>love</u> + <u>ly</u> = <u>lovely</u>, likely.
3. **nine + ty**: Keep <u>silent e</u> before suffix that begins with a consonant: <u>nine</u> + <u>ty</u> = <u>ninety</u>.
4. **provide + r**: Keep <u>silent e</u> before a consonant suffix: <u>provide</u> + <u>r</u> = <u>provider</u> (driver, glider, rider).
Exceptions: awful, daily, judgment, wisdom, wholly, ninth (fifth, twelfth), argument (rescuing, truly, duly).

<u>Drop Silent E before suffix that begins with vowel</u> (-ed, -ing, -able): *natural, pleasure, writing*.

5. **have + ing**: Drop <u>silent e</u> before suffix beginning with vowel: <u>have</u> + <u>ing</u> = <u>having</u>, giving, loving.
6. **please + ant**: Drop <u>silent e</u> before suffix beginning with vowel: <u>please</u> + ant = <u>pleasant</u>.
7. **like + able**: Drop <u>silent e</u> before suffix beginning with vowel: <u>like</u> + <u>able</u> = <u>likable</u>, usable.
Exceptions: *Soft C and G*: <u>Silent e is needed to keep c and g soft before a and o</u>: traceable (<u>c</u> = <u>s</u>); <u>courageous</u> (g = j). Silent <u>e</u> is not needed before -ing: <u>tracing</u>, <u>changing</u> (since i keeps <u>c</u> and g soft).

8. **advantage + ous**: <u>Silent e</u> keeps <u>g</u> soft (j sound) before -<u>ous</u>: <u>advantage</u> + <u>ous</u> = <u>advantageous</u>.
9. **notice + able**: Silent <u>e</u> keeps <u>c</u> soft (s sound) before -<u>able</u>: <u>notice</u> + <u>able</u> = <u>noticeable</u>.

<u>When a VOWEL precedes Silent E, keeo Silent E before all suffixes</u>: *freedom, canoeing, seeing*.

10. **free + dom**: <u>free</u> + <u>dom</u> = freedom.
11. **shoe + ing** (shoeing a horse): <u>shoe</u> + <u>ing</u> = <u>shoeing</u>. *Same Pattern*: canoeing, hoeing, toeing.
12. **see + ing**: <u>see</u> + <u>ing</u> = <u>seeing</u>: *Same Pattern*: agreeing, freeing, teeing (in golf).
Exceptions: argument, rescuing, cuing, truly; dying (<u>Die</u> changes to a Final <u>Y</u> word): dying, lying, tying.

Rule for Final Y before a Suffix – Words ending in y preceded by a consonant change the y to i before all suffixes except -ing: *carried, carrying*; *tried, trying*. Most words ending in y preceded by a vowel do not drop the y: *enjoyment, enjoying*; *canoed, canoeing*. Exceptions: *arguing, rescuing, truly*.

1. **economy + ic**: Change y to i before all suffixes except -ing: econom~~y~~ + i + c = economic.
2. **harmony + ca**: Change y to i before all suffixes except -ing: harmon~~y~~ + i + ca = harmonica.
3. **lonely + ness**: Change y to i before all suffixes except -ing: lonel~~y~~ + i + -ness = loneliness.
4. **mystery + ous**: Change y to i before all suffixes except -ing: myster~~y~~ + i + ous = mysterious.
5. **try + ing**: Change y to i before all suffixes except -ing: try + ing = trying (tried, trial; frying, crying).

Words ending in y, preceded by a vowel, keep the y before all suffixes: staying, buying, toyed, toying.

6. **enjoy + ed**: Change y to i before all suffixes except -ing: enjoy + ed = enjoyed-enjoying, enjoys.
7. **play + ed**: Change y to i before all suffixes except -ing: play + ed = played-playing, player, plays.
8. **volley + ed**: Change y to i before all suffixes except -ing: volley + ed = volleyed-volleying, volleys.
Exceptions: lay-laid; pay-paid; say-said; slay-slain; day-daily.

Inserted K Rule: Words that end in hard c (k sound) insert a k before suffixes that begins with e, i, or y to keep the k sound: *frolic-frolicked*; *mimic-mimicked*; *panic-panicky*; *picnic-picnicking*; *shellac-shellacking*; *traffic- trafficked*.

colic – colicky	**picnic** – picnicked, picnicking, picnicker
frolic – frolicked, frolicking	**politic** – politicking
mimic – mimicked, mimicking	**shellac** – shellacked, shellacking
panic – panicking, panicky	**traffic** – trafficked, trafficking

THE PICNIC KING!

Doubling Final Consonants Rule for One-Syllable Words.

4. If a word has <u>one</u> syllable, and
5. If a word <u>ends with</u> a <u>consonant,</u> and
6. If the <u>consonant</u> has a <u>single vowel</u> before it: *run, swim*..., then:

Double the final consonant before a suffix that begins with a vowel (-ed, -er, -ing): *running, swimming*.

Double the final consonant for the words: star-starred;   rid-ridding;   mop-mopped
Do not double consonant for the words: stare-stared;   ride-riding;   mope-moped

<u>a</u>: bar-barred   tape-taped   fin-finned   slime-slimed   rob-robbed
bare-bared   wag-wagged   fine-fined   strip-stripped   robe-robed
mat-matted   wage-waged   grip-gripped   stripe-striped   slop-slopped
mate-mated   <u>e</u>: her-here   gripe-griped   <u>o</u>: cop-copped   slope-sloped
rat-ratted   cede-cede   pin-pinned   cope-coped   <u>u</u>: cub-cube
rate-rated   mete-meted   pine-pined   dot-dotted   cut-cute
scrap-scrapped   them-theme   rip-ripped   dote-doted   hug-huge
scrape-scraped   <u>i</u>: din-dinned   ripe-ripen   hop-hopped   run-rune
tap-tapped   dine-dined   slim- slimmed   hope-hoped   tub-tube

Doubling Final Consonants Rule for Words with More than One Syllable.

1. If a word has more than <u>one</u> syllable, and
4. If a word <u>ends in</u> a <u>single consonant,</u> and
5. If a <u>single short vowel</u> comes before the consonant: *admit, occur, travel*..., and
4. If, <u>in the completed word,</u> the <u>accent falls on the last syllable of the original word,</u> then:

Double the final consonant before a suffix that begins with a vowel (-ed, -en, -ence, -er, -ing): *written, traveled*.

acquitted   deterred   forgetting   possessing   scattered
admitting   dispelled   happening   preferred   submitting
annulled   embedded   inferred   propelling   transferred
beginning   entrapped   occurred   recurring   transmitted
compelled   equipped   omitting   referred   tunneled
conferred   excelling   patrolled   regretting   upsetting
deferred   forbidding   permitted   remitted   written

If, when you have a completed word, the <u>accent does not fall on the last syllable of the original word, then:</u>
<u>Do not double the final consonant</u> before suffixes that begin with a vowel (-ed, -en, -ence, -er, -ing).

offered   differed   limiting   piloted   suffering
benefiting   entering   offering   profiting   traveled
canceled   happened   opened   reference   thundering
conference   leveled   preference   shivering   visiting

Follow Contraction Rules
with Bigfoot and the Abominable Snowman

❑ **NOW**: Underline the correct homophones as you read this adventure story.

Since the late 1800, hundreds of people have reported seeing the Bigfoot or some of (it's, its) footprints. Depending on the story (you're, your) reading, Bigfoot is described as being between seven and ten feet tall and weighing up to 500 pound. The person (who's, whose) seen Bigfoot usually reports that (it's, its) footprints are about six inches wide and sixteen inches long.

These hairy, human-like creatures are reported to make (they're, their, there) home in the mountains of California, Oregon, and Washington. Sometimes (they're, their, there) spotted as far north as British Columbia, Canada. (They're, Their, There) the Canadians call (they're, their, there) mysterious creature *Sasquatch*.

(It's, Its) interesting that when people tell (they're, their, there) Bigfoot stories, (they're, their, there) descriptions are very similar to those told about the Abominable Snowman. This creature (who's, whose) said to live on Mount Everest and on other mountains in the Himalayans, is described as big, hairy, and tall, just like Bigfoot. Since (you're, your) going to Mount Everest soon, you wonder what you'll discover. (You're, your) camera and gear are packed, and (you're, your) ready for adventure!

Before you know it, (you're, your) at the base of Mount Everest, ready to begin (you're, your) trek to the summit. (It's, Its) a clear day for climbing, and (you're, your) Sherpa guides from Nepal are ready and waiting. Above all, (you're, your) ready, and (you're, your) almost hoping to see an Abominable Snowman, a *Yeti*. Your Sherpas eagerly share stories about *Yeti* (who's, whose) name originally meant *The All Devouring One*, and (who's, whose) fearful reputation is known by all the local people. (There, They're, Their) excited to tell you *Yeti's* size and height, and about giant footprints they've seen in the snow. (You're, Your) interested; but, at the same time, you wonder if the sun can melt normal footprints into larger ones.

Now (it's, its) time to climb Mount Everest. As you begin (you're, your) ascent, you wonder what (your, you're) stories will be like when you return – that is, if you return. Is (there, they're, their) an Abominable Snowman living on this mountain? Perhaps, (it's, its) all just imagination. (You're, Your) just not sure, but now (it's, its) (you're, your) turn to truly find out for yourself!

Exceptions to the Short Vowel Rule

There are three groups of words with a Short Vowel Pattern that don't make a Short Vowel sound:
- Short Vowel Pattern with Long Vowel Sounds
- Short Vowel Pattern with R-Controlled Sound
- Short Vowel Pattern with Special Vowel Sound

Short Vowel Pattern with Long Vowel Sound

-ig words: **-igh**: high, nigh, sigh, thigh * **-ight**: bright, fight, flight, fright, knight, light, might, night, plight (problem), right, sight, tight * **-ign**: sign, design

-ild words: child, mild, wild

-inct words: (long e sound): distinct, extinct, instinct, precinct, succinct

-ind words: behind, bind, blind, find, grind, hind, kind, mind, rind, wind (wrap),

-ink words: (long e sound): blink, brink, chink, mink, pink, rink, shrink, slink, stink, wink

-int word: pint

-old words: bold, cold, fold, gold, hold, mold, old, scold, sold, told * **-oll**: knoll, scroll, toll, troll * **-olt**: bolt, colt, dolt, jolt, molt, volt

-ont words: don't, won't

-os words: **-oss**: gross * **-ost**: ghost, host, most, post

-oth words: both, loth (loathe, hate), quoth (quotes), troth

-uth words: Ruth, truth

Short Vowel Pattern with R-Controlled Vowel Sounds

The letter R is so powerful that it changes the sound of all the short vowels it follows.

-ar words: star, garb, arch, card, dwarf, shark, snarl, farm, barn, sharp, march, cart

-er words: her, herb, perch, herd, serf, berg, jerk, term, fern, pert, berth (sleeping spot), beryl

-ir words (er): fir, birch, bird, irk (bother), twirl, firm, chirp, first, dirt, birth

-or words: for, porch, chord, word, work, fork, whorl, world, form, corn, corps, fort, north

-ur words (er): fur, curb, church, curd (made into cheese), surf, lurk, curl, turn, burp, burst, hurt

Short Vowel Pattern with Special Vowel Sounds

Some words with a *Short Vowel Pattern* make an *ah, um, oom,* or *oosh* sound.

-al words: **-ald**: bald * **-alk**: balk (resist), chalk, stalk (follow), talk, walk * **-all**: ball, call, fall, hall, stall, tall, squall (storm), wall * **-alm**: balm, calm, palm, psalm, qualm (worry) * **-alt**: halt, malt, sa

-amp words: swamp

-ant word: want

-asp word: wasp

-at words: swat, what * **-acht**: yacht (boat): * **-atch**: watch, swatch (cloth sample)

-aw words: caw, claw, draw, flaw, gnaw, jaw, law, maw, paw, raw, saw * **-awk**: awkward, gawk, hawk, squawk * **-awl**: awl, bawl, brawl (fight), crawl, drawl (draw out vowel sound), scrawl (scribble), sprawl (laze) * **-awn**: dawn, fawn, lawn, pawn, prawn, spawn (fish eggs)

-om words: from * **-omb**: tomb, womb *

-ush words: bush, push

Exceptions to the Final Silent E Rule

You have learned that when <u>final e</u> follows a single consonant, it makes the vowel right before the consonant long: <u>stage</u>, <u>theme</u>, <u>kite</u>, <u>globe</u>, <u>cube</u>... There are, however, some words where <u>final e</u> follows a single consonant, but can't make the vowel before it long: <u>have</u>, *here*, <u>give</u>, <u>come</u>, <u>sure</u>... (*Note*: Up until 1500, <u>final e</u> was still pronounced, but then it became SILENT forever! *Since e is silent*, final <u>e</u> words that don't follow the rule are challenging to spell. Exceptions are below.)

<u>One word that end in **-ace**</u>:	surface
<u>Unaccented **-ate** syllables</u>:	accurate, chocolate, considerate, delicate, desperate, fortunate, separate…
<u>One word that end in **-ave**</u>:	have
<u>One word that end in **-eye**</u>:	eye (long <u>i</u> sound)
<u>Unaccented **-ice** syllables</u>:	cowardice, licorice, notice, office, precipice (cliff), police, prejudice
<u>Some words that end in **-ive**</u>:	give, live
<u>Some words that end in **-ome**</u>:	come, some; become, worrisome.
<u>Some words that end in **-one**</u>:	done, gone, none, one; redone, undone.
<u>Some words that end in **-ove**</u>:	dove (bird), glove, love, move, prove, shove; above, beloved.

(<u>*Note for -ve*</u>: For some *-ve* words the vowel before *-ve* is often short: *give, have, prove*. <u>Since no English words end in v, *so final e* ends these words</u>. Words like *gave, alive*... have a long vowel.)

<u>Words that end in **-are**</u>:	are, bare, care, dare, fare, glare, hare, mare, pare, rare, share, ware…
<u>Words that end in **-ere**</u>:	ere, here, there, where
<u>Words that end in **-ore**</u>:	core, fore, lore, more, pore, shore, sore, tore, wore, yore, explore
<u>Some words that end in **-ure**</u>:	sure; ensure, figure, insure, measure, overture, pleasure, treasure

(<u>*Note for -re*</u>: *R is a very powerful vowel*. It can take a word where <u>*final e*</u> has made the vowel long, and *take the long sound away*: *thee-there, whee-where, foe-fore, Sue-sure*.)

There are some <u>words with</u> <u>two consonants before final e</u> where the <u>final e syllable is not pronounced</u>.
<u>Words that end in **-dge**</u> (dg = j sound): edge, hedge, ledge; bridge, ridge; dodge, lodge; fudge, judge.
<u>Words that end in **-nce**</u>: chance, dance, glance, entrance; fence, hence, sentence, prince, since; once.
<u>Words that end in **–nse**</u>: defense, dense, incense, license, suspense, tense; rinse
<u>Words that end in **-rce, -rse**</u>: farce; merge, verge; fierce, pierce; horse, worse; purse, urge.
<u>Words that end in **-rge**</u>: barge, charge, large; enlarge; merge, verge, forge, gorge, surge.

There are some <u>words that end in -ceive and -ieve</u> where the <u>*final e*</u> ends the word.
<u>Words that end in **-ceive**</u>: conceive, deceive, perceive, receive
<u>Words that end in **-ieve**</u>: believe, achieve, grieve, relieve, retrieve

"Alas, Silent e can't ALWAYS make vowels long

Follow the IE/EI Rule and Play Memory Tool Scramble

"After you!"   *O No, No! After...*

I before E
Except after C (When C sounds like S),
Or when sounded as A
As in neighbor, their, or weigh (A sound <u>always</u> spelled EI).

☐ **NOW:** Fill in EI or IE and List the *Memory Tool* you use to remember the word: *Clue, SPP, Rule…*

1. f<u>ie</u>rce: *Clue:* <u>Fierce</u> giant said, "Fie on the fiend!"
2. fr_____nd:
3. sc_____nce
4. h_____ght
5. ch_____f
6. bel_____ve, bel_____f
7. _____ther, n_____ther
8. n_____ghbor
9. gr_____ve, gr_____f
10. w_____gh
11. n_____ce
12. br_____f
13. _____ght
14. p_____ce
15. sl_____gh
16. p_____r
17. c_____ling
18. th_____f, th_____ves
19. th_____r
20. h_____r

21. anc<u>ie</u>nt: *SPP:* <u>an-ci-ent</u>
22. caff<u>ei</u>ne: *Clue:* Co<u>ffe</u>e with <u>caffeine</u>.
23. v_____n:
24. w_____rd
25. r_____gn
26. v_____l
27. s_____ze
28. perc_____ve
29. b_____ge
30. f_____sty
31. al_____n
32. sh_____ld
33. ach_____vement
34. forf_____t
35. quot_____nt
36. prot_____n
37. conc_____ve
38. retr_____ver
39. dec_____ve, dec_____t
40. rec_____ve, rec_____pt

List of *IE/EI* Words with the Same Vowel Sound and Pattern:

<u>ield, ief, ieve</u> (long e): field, shield, wield, yield * belief, grief, relief, thief * achieves, believes, grieves, relieves, thieves *
<u>ier, ierce</u>: pier * fierce, pierce *   <u>ier</u> (long i): hieroglyphics *
<u>ei, eign</u> (short i): forfeit * foreign, sovereign, sovereignty *
<u>eik, ein, eine</u> (long e): sheik * heinous (evil), protein * caffeine, codeine *
<u>ein, eis, eist, eit</u> (long i): Einstein, stein (Ger. beer mug) * seismic * feisty (spirited), heist (robbery) * Fahrenheit *
<u>ceit, ceive</u> (long e): conceit, deceit, receipt * conceive, deceive, perceive, receive* (Reception, deception… help with spelling.)
<u>cience, cient, scient</u> (sh sound): conscience * ancient, efficient, patient, quotient, sufficient * omniscient (all knowing) *
<u>cie</u> (long i): science *
<u>ei, eigh</u> (long a): beige * eight, freight, neighbor, reign, sleigh, weight * feign (pretend), reign * veil * rein, vein * leisure *
<u>eir</u> (air): heir, their *

Tool 4: POWER of the Beat
and
Syllables

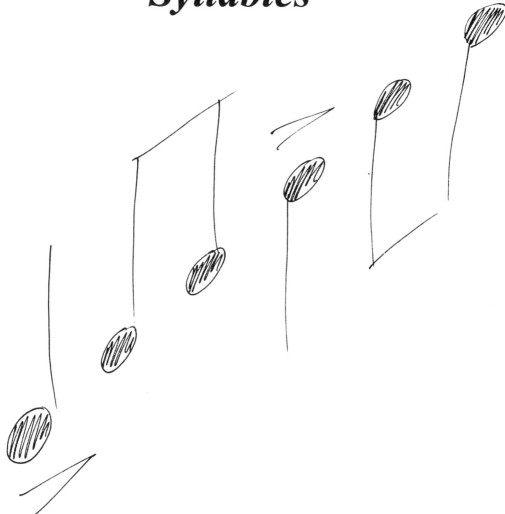

POWER Spelling List of Words That Fit a Beat

Feeling the *POWER* of the BEAT inside is a great way to learn certain words. When you feel the beat you add feeling to hearing and seeing words. You get the RHYTHM of the word inside of you.

a – rith – me – tic (4 syllable beats)

$\frac{2}{4}$ C-R-I S-I-S

a-c c-o-m-m o-d-a-t-e

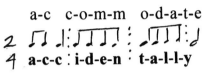

$\frac{2}{4}$ a-c-c i-d-e-n t-a-l-l-y

a-l-u-m n-u-s

a-n t-e c-e d-e

a-n-n u-a-l

A-r-c t-i-c

$\frac{4}{4}$ a-r-e-n '(a-pos-tro-phe) -t

b-a n-a n-a

b-a-l a-n-c-e

b-e c-a u-s-e

b-e-g-i n-n-i-n-g

$\frac{2}{4}$ ***b-u-s-y i-n-g***

b-u-z-z-i-n-g...

c-e-r t-a-i-n

c-h-o c-o l-a t-e

c-o-m-m i-t-t-e-e

c-o-n-c-e-r-t

d-e c-i s-i o-n

d-e-s-s e-r-t

d-i-a-m-o-n-d

d-i-s c-u-s-s

d-i-z-z-y

d-r-u m-m-e-d

e-c-h o-e-s ... ...

e-c-o n-o-m i-c-a l-l-y

e-m-b a-r-r a-s-s m-e-n-t

e-n-c-y-c-l-o-p-e-d-i-a

e-n-e-r g-i-z-e

e-r u-p-t

$\frac{6}{8}$ *e-s-s-e-n-c-e*

e-x c-e l-l e-n-t

e-x-a-m p-l-e

e-x-p-e-r I-e-n-c-e

f-i-n-a-l-l-y

f-o-u-n   t-a-i-n

g-i-r-a-f-f-e

$\frac{2}{4}$ G-U : a-r-d

h-a-p-p   i-l-y

h-i-e-r o-g-l-y p-h-i-c-s

$\frac{2}{4}$ h-i   pp-o : p-o-t-a : m-u-s

h-i-c c-u-p

h-o-r-s d'-o-e-u v-r-e-s

h-u-g-g i-n-g

h-u-r-r-y I-n-g

i-n t-e-r-r u-p t-e d

i-m-p o-s-s i-b-i l-i-t-y

i-n f-i n-i t-y

J – A – Z – Z

J-U-M-P I-N-G

k-i-s-s i-n-g

light-en-ing (3 beats-to lighten)

light--ning (2 beats-*zing of light*)

l-i-s t-e-n

l-o-v-a b-l-e

l-u-c-k i-l-y

m-a g-a z-i n-e

m-a-r-r i-a-g-e

math – e – ma – tics (4 syllable beats)

M-i-c k-e-y : M-o-u-s-e

m-i-d d-l-e

m-i-r r-o-r.

M-i-s-s i-s-s i-p-p-i

m-n-e m-o n-i c-s (memory tools)

m-u s-i c-i a-n

m-u s-i-c

n-e-w-s s-t-a-n-d

N-I-N E-T-Y

n-i-n-t-h

N-O-N S-E-N-S-E

n-o-t a-b-l-e

o-c-c-u r-r-e-d

$\frac{4}{4}$ o-c-e-a-n

o-c-t-o p-u-s

o-f-t-e-n

o-r-i g-i-n

p-e-o p-l-e

"see you next week"

39

P-h-i-l h-a-r m-o-n-i-c

p-i-a-n-o

p-n-e-u m-o-n-i-a.

p-o-ss e-ss

p-r-o b-a-b-l-y

p-u-r p-l-e

q-u-e-s t-i-o-n

R–H–Y T–H–M

r-h-y-m-e

r-e-c e-i-v-e

r-o b-o-t

r-u-m b-l-e

2/4 *r-u-s-h i-n-g*

s-c-i-s s-o-r-s

S-E-I-Z-E

S-Q-U-A
Q R
U-A-R-E

s-e-v-e-r-a-l

s-h-o v-e-l

s-u-b t-l-e

s-u-c-c e-s-s f-u-l-l-y

s-y-l-l a-b-l-e

4/8 t-e-r-r- i-b-l-e

t-h-o-u g-h-t

t-r-o t-t i-n-g

t-u-r t-l-e

t-y – p-h-o-o-n

t-y-r a-nn-o s-a-u r-u-s

u-s-u-a-l-l-y

v-o-l c-a-n-o

v-o-w e-l-s

w-r-i-t t-e-n

X-E R-O-X

y-a c-h-t

Feeling the Power of the Beat

Let's put some more words to the *POWER of the Beat*. Also, put the syllables of the three *longest words* in the English language to a beat, and you'll see how easy and fun it is to say them.

C-R-A-Z-Y

i-n t-e-r   c-e-s-s i-o-n

g-i-r a-f-f-e

a-t-t   r-a-c-t

c-i-n-n   a-m-o-n

a-p-p-l-e

l-l-a-m-a

B-U-F-F   A-L-O

s-q-u-i   r-r-e-l

W-A-F   F-L-E

g-a-z   e-l-l-e

p-o-o   d-l-e

p-o-p-p-y

s-u-n   s-e-t

v-a-c   u-u-m

j-i-n g-l-e b-e-l-l-s

pneu-mo-no ul-tra mi-cro-scop-ic si-li-co vol-ca-no co-ni-o-sis
(Longest Word in English! This disease is caused by inhaling ultra-microscopic silica dust; 1835)

floc-ci   nau-ci ni-hil-i pil-i-fi ca-tion (2nd! flocci + nauci + nihili + pili each mean worthless; 1735)

an-ti dis-es-tab-lish men-tar-i-a-ni-sm (3rd! opposition to state withdrawal of support for a church; 1800's)

su-per-cal-i fra-gi-lis-tic ex-pi-al-I do-cious (Mary Poppins's word for *good*)

Tik-ki tik-ki tem-bo no-sa rem-bo cha-i bar-i ru-chi pip per-i pem-bo (Chinese name)

Tool 5: Pronunciation POWER

POWER Spelling Pronunciation POWER

Pronunciation POWER is a great *POWER Spelling Tool* because lots of words get misspelled simply because people don't learn to pronounce them correctly. They leave out a letter, or substitute one letter for another, or even add syllables that don't belong. NOW, carefully read the words below and mark the ones you mispronounce. Then use *Clues* and other *Tools* to remember the pronunciation.

Correct Pronunciation	Mispronunciation	POWER Clues and Tools for Remembering Pronunciation
ac-ci-dent-**al**-ly:	*accidently*	When I was <u>accidentally</u> hit, I needed <u>dental</u> work.
Ant-arc-ti-ca:	*Antartica*	*Roots*: <u>ant</u> (opposite) + <u>arctic</u> + <u>a</u> = <u>Antarctica</u> (opposite Arctic).
Arc-tic:	*Artic*	The <u>Arctic</u> Ocean forms an <u>arc</u> around part of the North Pole.
a-rith-**me**-tic	*arithemetic*	Work w<u>ith me</u> on <u>arithmetic</u>: <u>a</u> + <u>r-~~w~~ith</u> + <u>me</u> + <u>tic</u>. (4 Beats).
ar-tis-tic-**al**-ly	*artisticly*	When I want to be <u>artistic</u>, she's my <u>ally</u>: <u>artistic</u> + <u>ally</u>.
asked:	*ast*	*Clue-in-a-Row*: When I <u>asked</u> for help, they said, "<u>Ask Ed</u>."
ath-lete	*athalete*	The <u>athlete</u> did a <u>high leap</u>: at<u>hl</u>ete (2 syllables)
a-ve-**r**age	*average*	Sixteen is <u>a very average age</u> to drive: <u>a</u> + <u>ver~~y~~</u> + <u>age</u>.
bev-**e-rage**	*bevrige*	Drink our <u>beverage</u> and n<u>ever age</u>: <u>B</u> + <u>~~n~~ever</u> + <u>age</u>.
boun-da-ry	*boundry*	It's hard to find the <u>boundary</u> in the <u>dark</u>: <u>boun</u> + <u>dar~~k~~</u> + <u>y</u>.
can-**di**-date	*canadate*	The <u>candidate</u> was <u>candid</u> (open) and <u>ate</u>: <u>can</u> + <u>did</u> + <u>ate</u>.
ca-**val**-ry	*calvary*	<u>Valiant</u> men in the <u>cavalry</u> fought on horseback: ca<u>val</u>ry.
con-grat-u-late	*congradulate*	<u>Congratulate</u> us with <u>gratitude</u>: <u>con</u> + <u>grat</u> + <u>u</u> + <u>late</u>.
de-scribe	*disscribe*	*Roots*: <u>de</u>(not) + <u>scribe</u> (L. write) = <u>describe</u> (not write; tell).
de-spair	*disspair*	*Roots*: <u>de</u> (not) + <u>spair</u> (L. spirit) = <u>despair</u> (not have spirit).
dif-**fer**-ence	*diffrence*	*Roots*: <u>differ</u> + <u>ence</u> (state of) = <u>difference</u> (state of difference).
dis-appoint	*dissappoint*	*Roots*: <u>dis</u> (not) + <u>appoint</u> = <u>disappoint</u> (not appoint).
dis-as-**trous**	*disasterous*	<u>Disastrous</u> winds are <u>as troubling</u> as waves: <u>dis</u> + <u>as</u> + <u>trous</u>.
em-pa-the-tic-**all**y	*empatheticly*	Be an <u>empathetic ally</u> for people: <u>empathetic</u> + <u>ally</u>.
en-vir-**on**-ment	*envirement*	We found <u>iron</u> in the <u>environment</u>: envir<u>on</u>ment.
e-spe-cial-ly	*espeshly*	*Roots*: <u>e</u> (above) + <u>special</u> (L. unique) + <u>ly</u> = <u>especially</u>.
ex-**act**-ly	*exatly*	The first <u>act</u> began <u>exactly</u> on time: <u>ex</u> + <u>act</u> + <u>ly</u>.
ex-per-i-ment-**all**y	*eksspiramentally*	When I feel <u>experimental</u>, he's my <u>experimental ally</u>.
fa-**mi**-liar	*fermiliar*	It's not good to be <u>familiar</u> with a <u>liar</u>. *Y Rule*: fami<u>l~~y~~</u> + liar.
fi-**nal**-ly	*finely*	With my <u>fin(e) ally</u>, we fin<u>ally</u> did <u>all</u> the work: <u>fin~~e~~</u> + <u>ally</u>.
fund-a-ment-**all**y	*fundemently*	*Clue-in-a-Row*: <u>Fundamentally</u>, we need to <u>fund a men</u> tally.

sand-**wich**	*sanwitch*	Please spill no <u>t</u> (tea) on my <u>sandwich</u>.
sep-**a**-rate	*seperate, seprate*	When I tried to <u>separate</u> oranges and apples, <u>a rat</u> jumped out.
sig-**na**-ture	*signiture*	I use my <u>signature</u> to <u>sign a</u> note: <u>sign + a + ture</u>.
soph-**o**-more	*sophmore*	*Say*: <u>soph-o-more</u>. The <u>sophomore</u> liked choc<u>o</u>late.
strict-ly	*strickly*	He ran the troops <u>strictly</u> to get a <u>victory</u>: str<u>ictly</u>.
su-per-in-ten-d**e**nt	*superintendant*	*Pronunciation*: 4 words: <u>super + in + ten + dent</u>.
sur-**geon**	*sirjin*	*Clue-in-a-Row*: <u>Surge on</u>, oh, <u>surgeon</u>, <u>surge on</u>.
sur-prise	*suprise*	What a <u>surprise</u> to see whales <u>surface</u> and <u>rise</u>: <u>sur + p-rise</u>.
tem-**per**-a-ment	*temprament*	*CNR*: <u>Temper a ment</u>al state to have good <u>temperament</u>.
tem-**per**-a-ture	*temprature*	Keep your <u>temper at</u> cool levels to have it <u>temperate</u>.
tra-**ge**-dy	*tradegy*	I felt <u>rage</u> at the villain in the <u>tragedy</u>: <u>t + rage + dy</u>.
um-**brel**-la	*umberella*	<u>umbr</u> (L. umbra: shade) + <u>elle</u> (Fr. n. suf) = <u>umbra + elle + a</u>.
u-su-**al**-ly	*usully*	<u>Us U all</u> <u>usually</u> see: <u>us + u + all + y</u> = <u>usually</u>.
val-**u**-a-ble:	*valuble*	*CNR*: <u>Val, are U able</u> to protect a <u>valuable</u> gem?
whe-ther	*wether*	*CNR*: I'll <u>whet her</u> interest on <u>whether</u> or not *ET's* exist.
with-draw-**al**	*withdrawl*	*CNR*: The <u>withdrawal</u> said, "<u>Withdraw Al</u>, please."

POWER Spelling Special Phonics Pronunciations

Special Phonics Pronunciations (SPP's) will truly help with these words because they are not spelled like they're commonly pronounced. *SPP's* provide a way to pronounce <u>all the letters in these word like people pronounced all the vowels and consonants in Old English.</u> Use *SPP's*, plus *Clues, Roots,* and *Other Tools,* and you'll be able to spell and remember these words forever!

Words	Common Pronunciations	Special Phonics Pronunciations	Clues and Other Tools for Remembering Words
ache	*ake*	ac-he	He had <u>a chest</u> ache: <u>a</u> + <u>chest</u> = <u>ache</u>.
acquaintance	*aquaintans*	ac-qu-aint-ance	<u>A. C.</u> (is a) <u>quaint</u> acquaintance: <u>A.C.</u> + <u>quaint</u> + ~~dance~~.
adjective	*adjetive*	ad-jec-tive	*Pattern*: <u>adjective</u>, obj<u>ective</u> (Silent <u>e</u> doesn't make <u>i</u> long).
again	*agin*	a-gain	You <u>gain</u> in ability if practice again: <u>a</u> + <u>gain</u>.
allegiance	*alejens*	al-le-gi-ance	Say <u>all</u> 4 syllables: <u>al-le-gi-ance</u> (as in d<u>ance</u>)
almond	*amond*	al-mond	The <u>almond</u> was <u>almost</u> oval: <u>almost</u> + <u>nd</u>.
ancient	*anshent*	an-ci-ent	*Phonics*: <u>ci</u> = <u>sh</u>. <u>An</u>cestors can be <u>an-ci-ent</u>
answered	*anserd*	an-s-wer-ed	<u>Were</u> you there when I <u>answered</u>: ans + <u>wered</u>.
autumn	*autum*	au-tum-n	<u>N</u>ovember's the last month of <u>autumn</u>; autum<u>n</u>al
auxiliary	*augzilry*	aux-il-i-a-ry	*Root*: <u>auxili</u> (L. aid; help) + <u>ary</u> (n. suf.) = <u>auxiliary</u>
balance	*balens*	ba-lan-ce	Keep your balance when you spar with a lance (sword).
ballet	*ballay*	bal-let	Instead of soft<u>ball, let</u> me do <u>ballet</u>.: bal~~l~~ + let.
benign	*benine*	be-nig-n.	Read the <u>benign</u> sign: ben~~e~~ + ~~sign~~ (bene: good).
brilliant	*brilyant*	bril-li-ant.	*Visual*: four candles (<u>illi</u>) in <u>brilliant</u>.
brought	*brout*	brou-g-ht	I <u>ought</u> to have <u>brought</u> a book I <u>bought</u>: br + ought.
buffet	*buffay*	buf-fet	<u>Let</u> me <u>buff</u> the tables for the <u>buffet</u>: buff + ~~l~~et.
business	*biznis*	bus-i-ness	I need a <u>bus in</u> my <u>business</u>: bus + in + ess.
calendar	*calendr*	cal-en-dar	A <u>calendar</u> has a list of <u>dates</u>: calen<u>dar</u>.
carriage	*carrig*	car-ri-age	*Y Rule*: Change y to i: carr~~y~~ + <u>i</u> + <u>age</u> = <u>carriage</u>.
castle	*cassel*	cast-le	The <u>castle cast</u> lengths of reflection on the water.
caught	*caut*	ca-ug-ht	When my <u>cat caught</u> me, I said <u>ugh</u>!: ca + ugh + t.
cereal	*seryal*	cer-e-al	<u>Ceres</u> is the Roman goddess of <u>real cereal</u> and grain.
champagne	*champain*	cham-pag-ne	The <u>champ</u>ion team opened <u>champagne</u>.
chocolate	*choklut*	cho-co-la-te	*Roots*: Use the Spanish pronunciation: <u>cho-co-la-te</u>.
chord	*cord*	c-hord	I could hear the <u>chords</u> <u>ch</u>ime in <u>ch</u>urch.
climate	*climut*	cli-ma-te	<u>I</u> moved my <u>mate</u> to a cooler <u>climate</u>.
climb	*clime*	clim-b	You need to be <u>limber</u> to <u>climb</u> on that <u>limb</u>.
colonel	*kernel*	co-lo-nel	The <u>colonel</u> helped <u>el</u>ders in the <u>colony</u>: colon~~y~~ + el.
con-ta-gious	*contajus*	con-ta-gi-ous	<u>G.I.</u> was <u>contagious</u> on <u>contact</u>: <u>G.I.</u>+ conta~~ct~~ + g…
corps	*cor*	corps	*Roots*: <u>corps</u> (Latin, corpus: body). Corp~~us~~ = <u>corps</u>.
could	*cwud*	coul-d	Put <u>u</u> in <u>cold</u>: <u>co-u-ld</u> (should, would).
courageous	*coragjus*	cou-ra-ge-ous	In <u>our age</u>, be <u>courageous</u>: <u>our</u> + <u>age</u> + <u>ous</u> (E keeps g soft)
cousin	*cuzin*	co-us-in	<u>Our</u> <u>cousin</u> is with <u>us</u> in the <u>Co</u>.: Co + us + in.

— Brilliant — Ballet !

Word	Pronunciation	Syllables	Sentence
cro**chet**	*croshay*	cro-chet	<u>Chet</u> wanted someone to <u>crochet</u> a sweater.
cro**quet**	*crokay*	cro-<u>quet</u>	Do I play <u>croquet</u> with a rac<u>quet</u>? *SPP*: <u>cro-qu-et</u>.
crow**d**	*crou*	crow-<u>d</u>	My <u>crow</u> was in the <u>crowd</u>: <u>crow</u> + <u>d</u> (O. E. crow<u>dan</u>
cru**e**l	*crule*	cru-<u>e</u>l	Can you be <u>true</u> to someone who's <u>cruel</u>?
cupboard	*cubbard*	cup-board	A <u>cupboard</u> is a <u>board</u> where you place <u>cups</u>.
de**cisio**n	*desijun*	de-<u>ci</u>-<u>si</u>-on.	<u>Dec. is</u> when many gift <u>decisions</u> are made.
de**po**t	*depo*	de-pot	We found a <u>pot</u> at the train <u>depot</u>: <u>de</u> + <u>pot</u>.
de**tour**	*deture*	de-<u>to</u>-<u>ur</u>	During <u>our</u> <u>tour</u>, we' ll take a <u>detour</u>: <u>de</u> + <u>t</u> + <u>our</u>.
dia**mo**nd	*dimond*	di-<u>a</u>-mond	A <u>diamond's</u> has a <u>diameter</u>. *Amo* (I love) is in <u>diamond</u>.
dis**ho**nest	*disonest*	dis-h-on-est.	Bees never make dis<u>honest</u> honey? <u>dis</u> + <u>hone</u>y̶ + <u>t</u>.
echoes	*ekkos*	ec-hoe̶s	Each of the <u>echoes</u> goes back: <u>ech</u> + g̶oes = echoes
ef**fici**ent	*efishent*	ef-fi-<u>ci</u>-ent.	They <u>lent</u> me <u>Effi's</u> efficient robot: <u>Effi</u> + <u>ci</u>-l̶ent.
eno**ugh**	*enuf*	e-no-ug-h	<u>Enough</u> of the <u>rough</u> stuff! *Phonics*: Gk.: gh = <u>f</u>.
eve**ry**	*evry*	e-<u>ve</u>-ry	Does <u>every</u> princess live happily <u>ever</u>? <u>every</u>.
every**bo**dy	*evrybuddy*	e-ve-ry-bo-dy	<u>Everybody</u> here has a <u>very</u> strong <u>body</u>: <u>e</u> + <u>very</u> + <u>body</u>
ex-**ha**ust	*egsast*	ex-<u>ha</u>-ust.	<u>Ha</u>, don't <u>exhaust</u> <u>us</u> when we work: <u>ex</u> + <u>ha</u> + <u>us</u> +
ex-**hi**-bit	*egszibit*	ex-<u>hi</u>-bit	I put a <u>bit</u> of <u>history</u> in the <u>exhibit</u>: <u>ex</u> + <u>hi</u> + <u>bit</u>.
fa**wn**	*faun*	faw̲-n	We saw a <u>fawn</u> on our <u>lawn</u> at dawn.
February	*Febuary*	Feb-r̲u-ar-y	<u>RU</u> and Mary ready for <u>February</u>: <u>Feb</u> + <u>RU</u> + <u>Mary</u>?
fiery	*firey*	fi-<u>er</u>-y	The giant yelled, "<u>Fie</u>," at the <u>fiery</u> dragon: <u>Fie</u> + <u>ry</u>.
finan**cially**	*financhuly*	fi-nan-<u>ci</u>-al-ly	Add <u>i</u> to keep <u>c</u> soft' then add -ally: <u>finance</u> + <u>i</u> + <u>all</u>
fo**l**k	*fok*	fol-k	My <u>folk</u> ate the whites and the <u>yolk</u>.
for**eig**n	*forun*	fore-<u>ig</u>-n	Be<u>fore</u> here, I lived in a <u>foreign</u> country: <u>fore</u> + <u>ign</u>.
fu**dg**e	*fuj*	fud-ge	<u>D</u> in <u>fudge</u> is for delicious. *Phonics*: g = <u>j</u>: fud-ge.
gauge	*gaj*	ga-u-ge	I can <u>gauge</u> that my <u>game</u> fish is <u>huge</u>: <u>ga</u> + h̶uge.
genu**ine**	*genuine*	gen-u-in-e	The gold was <u>fine</u> and <u>genuine</u>.
ghost	*gost*	g-<u>host</u>	A <u>ghost</u> was my <u>host</u>: <u>ghost</u>.
gla**cie**r	*glaysher*	gla-<u>ci</u>-er	We drank <u>cider</u> and watched the <u>glacier</u>.
gli**st**en	*glissen*	glis-<u>ten</u>	<u>Ten</u> lights began to <u>glisten</u> to the music: <u>glis</u> + <u>ten</u>.
gnaw	*naw*	g-naw	The <u>gnat</u> started to <u>gnaw</u> on my <u>saw</u>.
gra**ciou**sly	*grashusly*	gra-<u>ci</u>-<u>ous</u>-ly	Add <u>i</u> to keep <u>c</u> soft. Then add =ly: <u>grace</u> + <u>I</u> + <u>ous</u> + ly
guard	*gard*	gu-ard	<u>G</u>, <u>U</u> (work) <u>hard</u> as a <u>guard</u>: <u>G</u> + <u>U</u> + h̶ard = <u>guard</u>.
guess	*ges*	gu-ess	<u>G</u>, <u>U</u> (m)<u>ess</u> up a room fast: <u>G</u> + <u>U</u> + m̶ess = <u>guess</u>.
gui-tar	*gitat*	gu-i-tar	<u>G</u>, <u>U</u> (and) <u>I</u> (got) <u>tar</u> on my <u>guitar</u>: <u>G-U-I</u> + tar.
half, halves	*haf, haves*	hal-f, hal-ves	This <u>half</u> is for my c<u>alf</u>, <u>Alfie</u>.
handkerchief	*hankerchief*	hand-ker-chief	<u>Hand</u> the <u>chief</u> a <u>handkerchief</u> to wave <u>hi</u>.
hand**so**me	*hansum*	hand-so-me̲	<u>Hand some</u> food to that <u>handsome</u> guy: <u>hand</u> + <u>some</u>.
herbal	*erbul*	h-erb-al	<u>Her</u> balance of <u>herbal</u> teas kept her strong: <u>her</u> + <u>ba</u>
honesty	*onesty*	<u>h</u>-on-est-y	<u>Ester's</u> bees made <u>honest</u> honey: <u>hon</u> + <u>Ester̶</u>.
illu**si**on	*ilujun*	il-lu-<u>si</u>-on.	He was <u>ill</u>, and told <u>us</u> his <u>illusions</u>: <u>ill</u> + <u>us</u> + <u>ions</u>.

go-**vern**-ment	*goverment*	A <u>government</u> exists to <u>govern men</u>: <u>govern + ment</u> + t.
hin-**drance**	*hinderance*	A <u>hind</u> (deer) <u>ran</u> through the <u>hindrance</u>: <u>hind + ran + ce</u>.
his-**tor-y**	*histry*	*Clue-in-a-Row*: <u>Hi</u>, <u>story</u> time today is about <u>history</u>.
hun-**dred**	*hundrid*	We had a <u>hundred red</u> balloons: <u>hund + red</u>.
hur-**ry**-ing	*hurring*	*Y Rule*: Keep <u>y</u> before -<u>ing</u>: <u>hurry + ing</u> = <u>hurrying</u>.
in-**stinct**	*instink*	<u>In</u> case of <u>stings</u>, a<u>ct</u> by <u>instinct</u>: <u>in + sting + act</u>.
in-**ter**-est-ing	*intresting*	It was <u>interesting</u> that <u>Tere</u> had no <u>sting</u>: <u>in + Te-re + sting</u>.
jewel-**ry**	*jewelery*	She looked in her <u>jewelry</u> for the <u>l</u>ost <u>r</u>ing: jewe<u>lry</u>.
kin-der-**gar-ten**	*kindergarden*	<u>Ten</u> tots are in <u>kindergarten</u> (Ger. <u>kinder</u>: child + <u>garten</u>: garden).
light**n**ing	*lightening*	<u>Lightning</u> is a <u>light zing</u>: <u>light + n + zing</u> = <u>lightning</u>.
lit-**er**-a-ture:	*litrature*	The <u>literature</u> in our <u>era</u> is <u>sure</u> great: <u>lit + era + t + sure</u>.
math-**e**-ma-tics	*mathmatics*	<u>Ma the</u> (good) <u>ma</u> helped with <u>ma + the + ma + tics</u> (4 Beats)
mi-ni-**a**-ture	*minature*	I saw a <u>mini</u> horse <u>at</u> the <u>Miniature</u> Show: <u>mini + at + ure</u>.
mis-chie-**vous**	*mischievious*	The <u>mischievous</u> <u>chief</u> was ner<u>vous</u>: <u>mis + chief + vous</u>.
na-tu-**ral**-ly	*naturly*	*Clue-in-a-Row*: <u>Nat, U rally</u> our team so <u>naturally</u>.
ne-ces-**sar**-y	*ne-ce-sary*	<u>Recess</u> is <u>necessary</u> at school: <u>n + recess + ary</u>.
numb	*num*	What <u>number</u> of fingers are <u>numb</u>?
oc-ca-sion-**al**-ly	*ocasionly*	<u>O, C</u> (see) <u>Casi on all occasions</u>: <u>OC + Casi + on + all + y</u>.
op-**por-t**un-it-y	*oppertunity*	It's an <u>opportunity</u> to build <u>port unity</u>: <u>op + port + unity</u>.
op-**ti**-mist	*optomist*	<u>Tim is</u> an <u>optimist</u>: <u>op + tim + is + t</u> = op<u>tim</u>ist.
par-tic-u-lar	*perticular*	This is the particular part I want in the play.
part-ner	*pardner*	My <u>partner</u> wants to play the <u>part</u> of the <u>nerd</u>: <u>part + nerd</u>.
per-form	*preform*	Can each <u>person</u> <u>perform</u> with good <u>form</u>? <u>person + form</u>.
per-spir-a-tion:	*prespiration*	If a <u>person</u> climbs <u>spires</u>, he <u>perspires</u> and get <u>perspiration</u>.
pes-**si**-mist	*pessamist*	I con<u>fess, I'm</u> a <u>pessimist</u>: <u>p + fess + I'm + ist</u>.
pre-scrip-tion	*perscription*	*Roots*: <u>pre</u> (before) + <u>script</u> (L. write) + <u>ion</u> = <u>prescription</u>.
prim-**i**-tive	*primative*	*See* <u>3 i's</u>. There's no <u>limit I've</u> set on <u>primitive</u> isles to find.
priv-**i**-lege	*privlege*	Don't give a <u>privilege</u> to a <u>vile</u> person.
prob-**a-bly**	*probally, probly*	You <u>probably</u> will do it <u>ably</u>.
rec-**og**-nize	*reconize*	I <u>recognize</u> that <u>cog</u> by its <u>size</u>: <u>re + cog + n-size</u>.
re-com-mend	*reccommend*	*Roots*: <u>re</u> (again) + <u>commend</u> (L.) = <u>recommend</u>.
re-mem-**brance**:	*rememberance*	What <u>brand</u> of <u>Remembrance</u> Cards do you buy?

Two fingers and one thumb

judi**cial**	*judishal*	ju-di-<u>ci</u>-al	<u>Judi</u> worked for the <u>judicial</u> CIA: <u>Judi</u> + CIA + l.
knead	*need*	<u>k</u>-ne-ad	He r<u>ead</u> about how to <u>k</u>nead bread: <u>kn</u> + ead.
knee	*nee.*	<u>k</u>-nee	She banged her <u>knee</u> on a tr<u>ee</u>: <u>kn</u> + ~~tree~~.
knight	*nite*	<u>k</u>-nig-<u>h</u>-t	Can a <u>knight</u> in black be seen at <u>night</u>? <u>k</u> + <u>night</u>.
knives	*nives*	<u>k</u>-ni-ves	I've used <u>knives</u> to carve. (M.E. k-nif).
know**l**edge	*nollege*	<u>k</u>-now-le<u>d</u>-ge	I <u>know</u> (a) <u>ledge</u> where I read to get <u>knowledge</u>.
known	*nowan*	<u>k</u>-now-<u>n</u>	I have <u>known</u> you <u>now</u> for a year: <u>k</u> + <u>now</u> + n.
labo**r**atory	*labratory*	la-b<u>o</u>r-a-tor-y	I <u>labor</u> in a <u>lab or at</u> home: <u>lab</u> + <u>or</u> + <u>at</u> + <u>or</u> + <u>y</u>.
langu**age**	*languij*	lan-gu-age	*Roots*: <u>langu</u> (Fr. tongue) + <u>age</u> (n. suf) = <u>langu</u> + <u>age</u>.
lau**gh**	*laf*	la-<u>ug</u>-h	<u>Laura's laugh</u> goes *la-ugh*! *Phonics*: <u>gh</u> = <u>f</u>.
launch	*lawnch*	la-<u>un</u>-ch.	I sat on my h<u>aunch</u>es to eat <u>lunch</u> at the <u>launch</u>.
li**cor**ice	*likrish*	li-<u>co</u>-rice	Does your <u>Co</u>. make <u>licorice rice</u>? <u>li</u> + <u>Co</u>.+ rice.
lis-**t**en	*lissen*	lis-ten.	I had to <u>listen</u> for <u>ten</u>. <u>l</u> + <u>is</u> + <u>ten</u>.
loaves	*loves*	<u>lo</u>-a-<u>ves</u>	Put <u>a</u> in <u>loves</u> to get <u>loaves</u>: <u>lo</u> + <u>a</u> + <u>ves</u>.
lunch**e**on	*lunchen*	lun-ch-e-<u>on</u>	My <u>lunch</u> (with) Leon was a <u>lunch</u> + ~~Leon~~ (luncheon).
marri**age**	*marrige*	mar-ri-age	Am <u>I</u> the <u>age</u> for <u>marriage</u>. *Y Rule*: marr~~y~~ + i + age.
mea**nt**	*ment*	me-<u>ant</u>	They <u>meant</u> to walk with <u>me</u> (and) <u>ant</u>: <u>me</u> + <u>ant</u>.
mus**c**les	*mussels*	mus-<u>c</u>les	I <u>must clench</u> my <u>muscle</u>: <u>must</u> + <u>cle</u>~~nch~~ = <u>muscle</u>.
musi**c**ian	*muzishen*	mu-si-<u>ci</u>-<u>an</u>	*Roots*: <u>music</u> (L. music) + <u>ian</u> (n. suf.) = <u>musician</u>.
nigh**t**	*nite*	nig-<u>h</u>-t	We made a <u>night</u> fl<u>ight</u>. *Phonics*: igh = <u>long i</u>.
ni**n**th	*nineth*	ni-<u>n</u>-<u>th</u>	The <u>ninth</u> <u>month</u> is September: <u>ni</u> + ~~month~~.
noti**c**eable	*notisable*	no-ti-<u>ce</u>-a-ble	It was <u>noticeable</u> that his soda was <u>not ice able</u>.
nu**i**sance	*nusans*	nu-<u>i</u>-san-<u>ce</u>	<u>Is</u> that <u>nuisance</u> going to <u>dance</u>? <u>nu</u> + <u>is</u> + ~~d~~ance.
occu**rr**ed	*okurred*	<u>oc</u>-cur-<u>red</u>	<u>O</u>, <u>C</u> what <u>occurred</u> in the <u>current</u>: <u>OC</u> + <u>curre</u>~~nt~~ + d.
o-**ce**an	*oshun*	o-<u>ce</u>-an	An <u>ocean</u> and a <u>sea</u> are synonyms: <u>ocean</u>.
offi**c**ial	*ofishal*	of-fi-ci-al	I took <u>off</u> my <u>official</u> <u>CIA</u> badge: <u>off</u> + <u>I</u> + <u>CIA</u> + <u>l</u>.
often	*offen*	of-ten	I am <u>often</u> one <u>of ten</u> who exercise: <u>of</u> + <u>ten</u>.
omi**ss**ion	*omishen*	o-mis-<u>si</u>-on	If you're <u>on</u> a <u>mission</u>, make no: <u>o</u> + <u>miss</u> + ~~i~~n + on.
orange	*ornge*	o-r<u>a</u>n-ge	Is <u>orange</u> in the <u>range</u> of bright colors: <u>o</u> + <u>range</u>.
ordinarily	*ordinarly*	or-di-nar-<u>i</u>-ly	*Roots and Rule*: <u>ordinar</u>~~y~~ (L. usual) + <u>i</u> + <u>ly</u> (adv. suf
outra**geou**s	*outrajous*	out-ra-<u>ge</u>-<u>ous</u>	He felt <u>outrage</u> (batting) <u>out</u>: <u>out</u> + <u>rage</u> + <u>ou</u>~~t~~ + s.
pal**m** (tree; hand)	*pam*	pal-m	*Visual*: An <u>l</u>'s ta<u>ll</u> like a <u>palm</u> (balm, calm, psalm).
parliament	*parlament*	par-li-a-ment	*Roots*: <u>parle</u>~~y~~ (talk) + <u>ia</u> + -ment (n. suf) = <u>parliament</u>.
phy**s**i**c**ian	*fazition*	phy-<u>si</u>-<u>ci</u>-an	*Root*: <u>physic</u> (G. natural science; ph=f) + <u>ian</u> = <u>physician</u>.
picture**sque**	*picheresk*	pic-tur-es-<u>que</u>	Carefully say: pic-tur-es-que (statuesque).
pig**e**on	*pijun*	pig-<u>e</u>-<u>on</u>	My <u>pigeon</u> has loved my <u>pig</u> (for an) <u>eon</u>: <u>pig</u> + <u>eon</u>
pitcher	*picher*	pit-cher	Can a <u>pitcher</u> pitch the <u>pit of a cherry</u>: <u>pit</u> + <u>cher</u>~~ry~~
plea**s**ure	*plezhure*	ple-a-<u>s</u>ure	My <u>plea</u> (was) <u>sure</u> to bring kid's pleasure: <u>plea</u> + <u>sure</u>.
plumb**er**	*plummer*	plum-<u>b</u>er	*Roots*: <u>plumb</u> (L. plumbum: lead weight) + er = <u>plumber</u>.
pneumo**nia**	*numoania*	<u>p</u>-neu-mo-<u>ni</u>-a	*Roots*: <u>pneumon</u> (Gk. pneumon: lung. pn = n) + <u>ia</u> (n. suf.)

psalm	*salm*	p-sal-m	That <u>p</u>salm brought c<u>al</u>m (balm, palm).
pseudo	*sudo*	p-seu-do	I <u>see U do</u> dress in a <u>pseudo</u> way: p + see + U + do.
pum**p**kin	*pumkin*	pump-kin	I'll carve a <u>pumpkin</u> with my <u>kin</u>: pump + kin.
qual**m**	*quam*	qual-m	He didn't feel c<u>al</u>m about lying; he felt a <u>qualm</u>.
ras**p**berry	*razberry*	rasp-berry	The <u>raspberry</u> vines were <u>raspy</u> (rough like a saw).
re-si**g**n	*resine*	re-sig-n	Please <u>sign</u> this to <u>resign</u>: re + sign.
restaurant	*restrant*	res-ta-u-rant	I <u>rested</u> with an <u>ant</u> at a <u>restaurant</u>: rest + aur + ant.
Salmon	*samun*	sal-mon	<u>Sal</u>ly ordered <u>sal</u>ami and <u>sal</u>mon.
sche**d**ules	*skedules*	s-ched-u-les	Use <u>rules</u> and <u>schedules</u> at school, <u>Ed</u>: sch + Ed + rules.
scheme	*skeme*	s-che-me	He played a <u>scheme</u> (<u>E</u> makes <u>e</u> long) on <u>me</u> at school.
ser**geant**	*sarjent*	ser-ge-ant	See the <u>ant</u> on the <u>sergeant's</u> serge pants: serge + ant.
sophomore	*safmor*	soph-o-mo-re	The <u>sophomore</u> likes choc<u>o</u>late. *Phonics*: ph = f.
spa**gh**etti	*spagetti*	spa-g-het-ti	<u>G, Hetti</u>, at our <u>spa</u> I love <u>spaghetti</u>: spa + G + Hetti.
squir**rel**	*squirl*	squir-rel	<u>Squir (and) Rel</u> are my pet <u>squirrels</u>: Squir + rel.
strength	*strenth*	stren-g-th	The Little <u>Engine</u> found <u>strength</u>: str + Engine + th.
stre**tch**	*strech*	str-et-ch	<u>Stretch</u> your fingers before you s<u>ketch</u>.
subtle	*suttle*	sub-tle	A <u>subtitle</u> stated the book's <u>subtle</u> meaning: subtitle.
suffi**ci**ent	*sufficient*	suf-fi-ci-ent	*Phonics*: ci = sh. *SPP*: Say 4 syllables: <u>suf-fi-ci-ent</u>.
sur**ge**on	*surgen*	sur-ge-on	<u>Surge on</u>, Oh <u>surgeon</u>. *Ph.* g = j (surgeon = go nurse).
sword	*sord*	s-word	He bet his <u>word</u> on his skill with a <u>sword</u>: s + word.
techni**que**	*tekneak*	tech-ni-qu-e	*Phonics*: que = k: techni + que = technique.
temperament	*temprament*	tem-per-a-ment	<u>Temper a mental</u> to keep a good <u>temperament</u>.
toni**ght**	*tonite*	to-ni-g-ht	*Same Pattern*: <u>ight</u> = <u>long i</u>: bright, light, night…
tou**gh**	*tof*	tou-g-h	*Same Pattern*: gh = f sound: cou<u>gh</u>, enou<u>gh</u>, rou<u>gh</u>.
toward	*tward*	to-war-d	I walked <u>toward</u> the door <u>to (his) ward</u>: to + ward.
towel	*towl*	to-wel	I put out a new <u>towel</u> to welcome her: to + welcome.
tragi**cally**	*tragicly*	tra-gic-al-ly	He's my <u>ally</u> if I am <u>tragically</u> hurt: tragic + ally.
twe**lfth**	*twelf*	twel-f-t-h	<u>TW</u> is the <u>twelfth</u> <u>elf</u>: TW + elf + TH.
uni**que**	*unik*	u-ni-qu-e	*Roots*: <u>uni</u> (one) + <u>que</u> (n. suf.) = <u>unique</u>.
veracious	*verashus*	ve-ra-ci-ous	*Roots*: <u>verac</u> (L. veracity: truth) + <u>-ious</u> (adj. suf.).
wealth	*welth*	we-al-th	<u>We all</u> thought of ways to gain wealth: we + al + th
Wednesday	*Wensday*	Wed-nes-day	Birds <u>wed</u> in a <u>nest</u> on <u>Wednesday</u>: Wed + nest + day.
wharf	*worf*	w-harf	A <u>wharf</u> and a <u>harbor</u> are both boat docks for.
wom**b**	*woom*	wom-b	A <u>woman</u> carries a <u>baby</u> in her womb (O.E.: wamb).
wreath	*reeth*	w-reath	The <u>wrens</u> kissed undern<u>eath</u> a <u>wreath</u>.
wrench	*rench*	w-ren-ch	A <u>wren</u> was sitting on the <u>wrench</u> on the <u>bench</u>.
wristwatch:	*ristwach*	w-rist-wat-ch	*Phonics*: Say all silent letters: w-rist + wat-ch.
wrong:	*rong*	w-rong	What's <u>wrong</u> with your <u>wrist</u>?
yolks	*yoke*	yol-ks	My f<u>olks</u> eat egg <u>yolks</u>.

POWER Spelling Pronouncing Other Word Forms

Pronouncing *Other Word Forms* can be a great *POWER Spelling Tool*. Sometimes there are other forms of a word where you can hear letters, or the order of letters, you couldn't hear in the original word. For example, Dumbo lets you hear **b** in dum**b**; lim**b**er-lim**b**; re**ce**ption-re**cei**ve. Now try these:

1. a-li**gn**: Please align my ligaments when you set my leg. *Same Pattern*: benign (good)
2. am-bu-l**a**nce (walking hospital before cars): Hear -**a** in ambulance in ambulatory (able to walk).
3. au-di-**t**ion: Hear -**t** in audition in audit.
4. an-gu-l**ar**: Hear -**ar** in angular in angularity.
5. at**h**-lete: Hear -**hl** in athlete in athletic.
6. au-th**or**: Hear -**or** in author in authority.
7. au-tum**n**: I love autumn since I love autumnal colors. (You can say *autumn* colors.)
8. bom**b**: His attitude was like a bomb, bombastic and explosive.
9. cir-cu-l**ar**: Hear -**ar** in circular in circularity.
10. col-um**n**: The columnist was writing her column.
11. com-ple-**t**ion: Hear the -**t** in complete in completion
12. con-**cei**ve: Hear -**ce** in conceive in conception. *Same Pattern*: deceive, receive…
13. conce**pt**: You can better hear -**pt** in concept in conceptual.
14. con-dem**n**: You can hear -**n** in condemn in condemnation.
15. con-g**rat**-u-la-tions: You can better hear -**at** in congratulations in gratitude.
16. con-**science**, conscious: Science helps you hear -**sci** in conscience and conscious.
17. de**bt**: When you are in debt, you have a debit (amount you owe).
18. de-**cei**ve: Hear -**ce** in deceive in deception.
19. de-fen**se**: In defensive, you can hear -**s** in defense.
20. de-si**gn**: In designation, you can hear -**n** in design and sign.
21. des-per-**a**te: In desperation, hear -**a** in desperate.
22. dis-sol**ve**: You can better hear -**ve** in dissolve in solvent.
23. doc-t**or**: In doctoral, you can hear -**or** in doctor.
24. dum**b**: Dumbo *The Flying Elephant* was not dumb.
25. ed-it-**or**: In editorial, you can hear -**or** in editor.
26. eve-**r**y: In ever, hear -**er** in every.
27. ex-**h**il-a-rate: In hilarious you can hear -**h** in exhilarate (ex-more than + hilarate-cheerful).
28. fa-mil-**i**-ar: Hear the -**liar** in familiar in familiarity
29. for-**eig**n: Before we came here, we lived in a foreign country.
30. has-**t**en: Hear -**t** in hasten in haste.
31. hea**l**th: Heal helps you hear the letters in health.
32. hym**n**: A hymn is found in a hymnal.

33. hy-po-cri-sy: You can hear -o and -i in hypocrisy in hypocrit.
34. in-fi-nite (having no limits): In finite, you can hear the long i's in infinite.
35. in-tro-duce: In intro or introduction, hear the letters in introduce.
36. limb: In limber, hear -b in limb.
37. li-brar-y: Hear both r's in library in librarian.
38. li-cense: In licensure, you can hear -cens in license.
39. man-a-ger: Hear -er in manager in managerial.
40. mem-o-ry: Hear -or in memory in memorial.
41. mus-cu-lar: Hear -ar in muscular in muscularity.
42. nom-i-na-tion: Hear -t in nomination in nominate.
43. non-sense: Hear both s's in nonsense in nonsensical.
44. oc-cur-rence: You can better hear -re in occurrence in current.
45. of-fense: Hear -s in offense in offensive.

46. pas-tor: Hear -or in pastor in pastoral.
47. pe-cu-li-ar: Hear -liar in peculiar in peculiarity.
48. pop-u-lar: In popularity, you can hear -ar in popular.
49. ra-di-ance: Hear the -a in radiance in radiate.
50. re-ceipt: Hear -ce and -p in receipt in reception.
51. re-ceive: You can better hear -ce in receive in reception.
52. re-cog-nize: Hear -cog in recognize in cognizant (knowing).
53. reg-u-lar: Hear -ar in regular in regularity.
54. re-pre-sen-ta-tive: In presentation, you can hear -a in representative.
55. re-sign: When you resign you hand in a resignation.
56. re-serve: You can better hear -ser in reserve in reservation.
57. re-ver-ence: Hear the e's in reverence in revere.
58. schol-ar: Hear -ar in scholar in scholastic
59. sen-a-tor: Hear -or in senator in senatorial.
60. sense: Hear both s's in sense in sensation and sensitive.
61. sign: You can hear -g in sign in signature.
62. sim-i-lar: You can better hear -ilar in similar in similarity.
63. soft-en: In soft, you can hear -t in soften.
64. sol-emn (formal seriousness): You can hear -n in solemn in solemnity.
65. spe-cial: In speciality (Brit. pronun.), you can hear -cial in special.

66. tol-er-ance: Hear -a in tolerance in tolerate.
67. thumb: Thumbelina was no bigger than a thumb.
68. tol-er-ance: Hear -a in tolerance in tolerate.
69. tu-tor: In tutorial you can hear the -or in tutor.
70. val-u-a-ble: Hear -a in valuable in evaluate.

POWER Spelling Pronouncing Other Word Forms
for -al, -el, and -le words

Pronounce these *Other Word Forms* to hear the vowel or order of letters for -al, -el, and -le words.

1. ac-tu-**al**: Hear the -al in actual in actuality.

2. an-**gle**: Hear the -gl in angle in angling.

3. as-sem-**ble**: Hear the -bl in assemble in assembling and assembler.

4. cas-**tle**: You can hear the tl in castle in castling

5. crum-**ble**: When cookies crumble, they're crumbly.

6. cud-**dle**: Hear the -dl in cuddle in cuddly.

7. dis-ci-**ple**: You can hear the -pl in disciple in discipling.

8. du-**al** (two): In duality, you can hear -ual in dual. (Homophone is duel: sword fight.)

9. ea-**gle**: The mother eagle watched over her eaglet.

10. fa-mil-i**ar**: In familiarity you can hear the -liar in familiar.

11. fa-**tal**: Hear the -al in fatal in fatality.

12. fi-**nal**: A finale is like a final finality.

13. gam-**ble**: Hear the -bl in gamble in gambling.

14. gen-er-**al**: When you reply in a general way, it's called a generality.

15. gen-**tle**: In gently you can hear the -tl in gentle.

16. gig-**gle**: Hear the -gl in giggle in giggling.

17. han-**dle**: Hear the -dl in handle in handling.

18. hon-or-a-**ble**: Hear the -bl in honorable in honorably.

19. hos-pi-**tal**: We appreciated the hospitality at the hospital.

20. hur-**dle**: Don't get hurt while hurdling over each hurdle.

21. im-ag-i-na-**ble**: You can hear the -a in imaginable in imagination

22. im-pos-si-**ble**: Hear the -bl in impossible in impossibly

23. jug-**gle**s: That juggler juggles like he's been juggling for years.

24. man-u-**al**: Hear -al in manual in manually.

25. mar-**ble**: The marbling on some marble is often beautiful.

26. me-d**al** (award): A medallion is a large medal.

27. me-**tal**: Something made from metal is metallic.

28. mod-**el**: What mode (style) of dress will the model wear for the show?

29. mor-**al**: Hear the -al in moral in morality.

30. mul-ti-**ple**: I will multiply these multiple numbers.

nothin' to it!

410

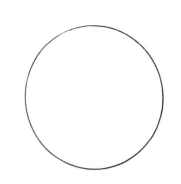

31. na-tion-**al**: Hear the -al in national in nationality.

32. na-tur-**al**: The naturalist loved all natural things.

33. nau-ti-c**al**: Hear the -al in nautical in nautically.

34. neu-tr**al**: Hear the -al in neutral in neutrality.

35. no-**ble**: Hear -ble in noble in nobler and noblest.

36. nom-in-n**al**: Hear the -a in nominal in nominate.

37. nor-m**al**: Hear the -al in normal in normality.

38. nov-**el**: A novella is a short novel.

39. oc-ca-sion-**al**: You can hear the -al in occasional in occasionally,

40. o-r**al**: In orate (speak), you can hear the a in oral (L., or: mouth).

41. o-ri-gi-n**al**: Hear the -al in original in originality.

42. pan-**el**: To panel the room, I used wooden panes.

43. pen-**cil**: Say penciling slowly and hear the -cil in ptencil.

44. per-son-**al**: Hear the -al in personal in personality.

45. prac-ti-c**al**: You can hear the -al in practical in practicality.

46. puz-**zle**: Hear the -pl in puzzle in puzzling and puzzler.

47. reb-**el**: Hear the -el in rebel in rebellion.

48. re-ci-t**al**: In recitation you can hear the -a in recital.

49. rus-**tle**: Hear the -tl in rustle in rustling.

50. shov-**el**: I had to shove the shovel into the snow.

51. sim-i-l**ar**: Hear the -ar in similar in similarity.

52. sim-**ple**: You can hear the -pl in simple in simply

53. spc-**cial**: Hcar thc -cial in spccial in speciality.

54. sten-**cil**: Say stenciling slowly and hear the -cil in stencil.

55. strug-**gle**: Hear the -gl in struggle in struggling.

56. ta-**ble**: A tablet is like a table you write on.

57. ter-ri-**ble**: Hear the -bl in terrible in terribly

58. to-t**al**: You can hear the -al in total in totality

59. tri-b**al**: Hear the -al in tribal in tribally.

60. tri-vi-**al**: Hear the -al in trivial in triviality.

61. trou-**ble**: You can hear the -bl in trouble in troubling.

62. twin-**kle**: In twinkling you hear the -kl in twinkle.

63. vi-t**al**: Hear the -al in vital in vitality.

64. whis-**tle**: Hear the -tl in whistle in whistling.

65. wrin-**kle**: You hear the -kl in wrinkle in wrinkly.

Tool 6: POWER of Ancient Roots

Roots: POWER Spelling List of Star Words

AST, ASTRO: Greek Root for *Star*

aster – flower that *looks like a star* with rays; n.

asterisk – * small *star-like symbol* used in writing; n.

disaster – misfortune; event is *not right with stars*; n.

asteroid – small planet, up to 600 miles in diameter; n.

astrodome – aircraft navigational dome; (*star dome*); n.

astrologist – one who tells *effect of stars on affairs*; n.

astronaut – one trained for space flight; *star sailor*; n.

astronomical – concerning astronomy; enormous; adj.

astronomer – person who *studies stars*, planets; n.

STELLA: Latin Root for *Star*

constellation – *a group with stars*; n.

Estelle – name meaning like a *star*; n.

interstellar – *between stars* like *interstellar* communication; adj.

Stella – name meaning *star*; n.

stellar – outstanding; *like a star* in brilliance *pertaining to the stars*; adj.

STEORRA: Old English Word for *Star*;   **STERRE**: Middle English Word for *Star*

star-crossed – opposed by stars (star-crossed lovers); adj.

stardom – fame where *one becomes a star*; n.

starfish – ocean creature with rays in a star shape; n.

starlight – *light from the stars*; n.

starred – *was the star* in a play or show, etc.; v.

starry-eyed – romantic; stars in ones eyes; adj.

Starry Night – painting by Vincent van Gogh; n.

Stars and Stripes – name for American flag; n.

star-shaped – shaped like a star; adj.

Star-Spangled Banner – U. S. National Anthem

❑ **TRY THIS**: Complete these sentences by using the words above.

Two other names for the American flag are the _ _ _ _ _ _ _ _ _ _ _ _ _ _ and *Old Glory*.

Our National Anthem is the _ _ _ _ - _ _ _ _ _ _ _ _ _ _ _ _ _ _.

I watched each _ _ _ _ _ _ _ _ _ prepare for the space flight.

The _ _ _ _ _ _ _ _ _ _ scientifically studied and searched the heavens for new stars and planets.

To help with celestial navigation, the pilot looked through the _ _ _ _ _ _ _ _ _.

After the pianist's _ _ _ _ _ _ _ performance, the audience applauded for five minutes.

An _ _ _ _ _ _ _ _ _ _ _ wants to know the effect the stars have on people.

Ceres, which is the largest _ _ _ _ _ _ _ _ (about 600 miles across) was discovered on January 1, 1801.

The price of that racecar is _ _ _ _ _ _ _ _ _ _ _ _.

Shakespeare's play *Romeo and Juliet* is about two _ _ _ _ - _ _ _ _ _ _ _ lovers hurt by family strife.

The word _ _ _ _ _ _ _ _ means misfortunate occurrence, an event that is *not right with the stars*.

The _ _ _ _ _ _ _ *Night*, painted by Vincent van Gogh, has swirls of dark sky filled with stars.

STAR: Stars and Stripes; Star-Spangled Banner; astronaut; astronomer; astrodome; stellar; astrologist; asteroid; astronomical; star-crossed; disaster; Starry.

413

Roots: POWER Spelling List of Heart Words

CARD, COR, CORD, COUR – Latin Roots for *Heart*

cardiac – *concerning the heart*; adj.

cardiac arrest – *sudden stopping of the heart*; n.

cardiologist – *doctor who cares for the heart*; n.

cardiology – *medical study of the heart*; n.

cardiovascular – *affecting heart* and blood vessels; adj.

cardiopulmonary – *affecting heart* and lungs; adj.

electro-cardiogram – *write-out of the heartbeat*; n.

courage – *quality of heart* to face difficulty; n.

accord – be in harmony (toward the heart), n.

accordance – act of being in agreement; n.

coronary – concerning the *health of the heart*; ad

cordial – friendly; *invigorating the heart*; adj.

cordialness, cordiality – *heartfelt acts*; n.

discordant – not in harmony (*not with the heart*); adj.

record – enter by writing; to tape; (*again in heart*); v

courageous – *having heart*; brave, adj.

HEORTE, HERTE – Old and Middle English Words for *Heart*

dishearten – *to depress ones heart* or hope; v.

heart attack – *damage to heart* from lack of oxygen; n.

heartbeat – the *beat of the heart*; n.

heartbreak – great sorrow (*feels like heart is breaking*); n.

heartwarming – *warming to the heart*; adj.

heartwood – wood in center (*heart*) of a tree; n.

heartless – unfeeling; *without heart*, adj.

heartfelt – *felt in the heart*; adj.

heartily – genuinely; *with heart involved*; adv.

hearty, heartier, heartiest – jovial; *with heart*; a

❑ **NOW**: Complete these sentences by using the words above.

The doctor read my _ _ _ _ _ _ _ - _ _ _ _ _ _ _ _ _ to see how my heartbeat looked.

The strange tones of that music sound very _ _ _ _ _ _ _ _ _ _ and lacking in harmony.

Did my criticism depress or _ _ _ _ _ _ _ _ _ _ you?

When you moved so far away that we couldn't go out together, I felt great _ _ _ _ _ _ _ _ _ _.

With a heart, the Cowardly Lion became very _ _ _ _ _ _ _ _ _ _.

At the Peace Conference, the nations reached an _ _ _ _ _ _.

By writing them down, I _ _ _ _ _ _ my tender, _ _ _ _ _ _ _ _ _ feelings in my journal.

My _ _ _ _ _ _ _ _ _ _ _ _ examined my heart to see if it was healthy.

I have a _ _ _ _ _ _ _ _ _ _ _ _ _ _ problem, involving both my heart and blood vessels.

_ _ _ _ _ _ _ _ _ _ is the medical study of the heart.

Since the fire did not reach the _ _ _ _ _ _ _ _ _ of the tree, the sequoia was still able to grow.

My heart was touched by your _ _ _ _ _ _ _ _ _ _ _ _ fire and the heartfelt stories you shared.

Roots: POWER Spelling List of Hand Words

MAN, MANU: Latin Root for *Hand*

manacle – restraint for *hands*; *handcuff*; n.,v.

manage – to take charge of (*care for by hand*); v.

manager – one who takes charge of (*by hand*); n.

maneuver – regulate movement or operate (by hand)

manicure – beauty treatment *for hands* and nails; n.

manicurist – one doing beauty treatment *for hands*; n.

manipulate – unfairly manage; skillfully manage; v.

manual – done by hand, adj.; hand booklet, n.

manual alphabet – hand alphabet; sign language; n.

manual training – act of training by hand; n.

manufacture – to make (used to be by hand); v.

manuscripts – documents written *by hand*; n.

HAND: Old and Middle English Word for *Hand*

handbag – *hand-held* bag for *hand items*; n.

handbook – *hand* guide for school, a car, work; n.

handcuffs – device around wrists to lock *hands*; n

handle, handling – touch, touching *with hands*; v.

handicrafts – art or trade done *by hand;* n.

handmade – clothing, books created *by hand*; adj.

hand-off – player *hands* object to teammate; n.

hand-out – food, clothing *handed* to the needy; n.

handprint – print made by *pressing down a hand*; n.

hand puppets – puppets that *fit over the hand*; n.

handshake – greeting made by *gripping hands*; n.

handstands – acts of *balancing on the hands*; n.

hands-on – personal (*hands-on*) participation; adj.

handy, handier, handiest – capable with hands; adj.

❏ **TRY THIS:** Complete these sentences by using the words above.

Another name for the _ _ _ _ _ _ _ _ _ _ _ _ _ _ is sign language.

She asked the _ _ _ _ _ _ _ _ _ _ to do a _ _ _ _ _ _ _ _ that polished and decorated her nails with stars.

The quarterback made a _ _ _ _ – _ _ _ to his teammate, a running back.

We visited a shop that had _ _ _ _ _ _ _ _ _ _ _ made by people from many nations.

Ancient scribes wrote their _ _ _ _ _ _ _ _ _ _ _ on papyrus (bark) or parchment (prepared skin of sheep).

The Blue Angels _ _ _ _ _ _ _ _ _ _ their planes into a perfectly patterned position.

Life-saving classes are _ _ _ _ _ - _ _ because you practice the life-saving techniques on classmates.

Skilled carpenters once _ _ _ _ _ _ _ _ _ _ _ made all furniture (made it by hand).

It's good to skillfully _ _ _ _ _ _ _ _ _ _ an object, like a car; but not good to _ _ _ _ _ _ _ _ _ people.

People used to reach agreements with a _ _ _ _ _ _ _ _ _; but now, most agreements require contracts.

I created my own _ _ _ _ _ _ _ _ _ _ _ to put on plays for my friends.

I love doing _ _ _ _ _ _ _ _ _ _ and cartwheels on a lawn.

Roots: POWER Spelling List of Foot Words

PED, PEDE: Latin Root for *Foot*

biped – animal that *walks on 2 feet*; n.

centipede (*100 feet*) – insect with 15-173 legs; n.

impede – hinder in movement; (*put a foot against*); v.

millipede (*1,000 feet*)– insect with 20-100 segment, each with 2 legs; n.

pedal – *foot-operated* mechanism for car, bike; n.

pedestal – the base of a column or building; n.

pedestrian – person who *travels on foot*; n., adj.

pedicure, pedicurist– beauty treatment for toenails and feet; n

POD: Greek Root for *Foot*

cephalopods – class of mollusks with tentacles (like *hands and feet*) attached to head; includes octopus, squid;

podiatrist – doctor *who cares for feet*; n.

podium – platform for a conductor or speaker; n.; base (*at the foot*) of a building; n.

tripod – stand or stool with *3 legs* (*means 3 feet*); n.

FOT: Old and Middle English Word for *Foot*

footage – *measurement in feet* of material, lumber; n.

football – game played with a *football*; n.

footed, footing – paid or settled a bill; v.

footbridge – bridge made for people *on foot*; n.

footman – man *helping feet* in or out of a carriage; n.

footlocker – trunk to be kept *at foot* of a bed; n.

footloose – free to *travel about on foot*; adj.

footnote – note at bottom (*the foot*) of a paper; n.

footprint – *print made by foot* of animal, person; n.

footsie – act of *flirting by touching feet*; n.

footstep – *step made by a foot*; n.

footwork – *use of feet* in dancing, boxing; n.

❑ **TRY THIS**: Complete these sentences by using the words above.

Milli- means *a thousand*, but a _ _ _ _ _ _ _ _ _ usually only has between 40 and 200 feet.

Most speakers feel more comfortable if they are standing behind a _ _ _ _ _ _ .

The two students were playing _ _ _ _ _ _ _ under the table.

As we walked across the wonderful old _ _ _ _ _ _ _ _ _ _ , we looked down at the stream below.

Overall, do you prefer being a _ _ _ _ _ _ _ _ _ _ or do you prefer driving?

During the summer they felt _ _ _ _ _ _ _ _ _ and fancy free.

Do you know why photographers set their cameras on a _ _ _ _ _ _ to take pictures of fireworks?

To build a bookcase that reached the ceiling, we needed a large _ _ _ _ _ _ _ of lumber.

A human being is a _ _ _ _ _ , and so is a penguin, because they both walk on two feet.

_ _ _ _ _ _ _ , meaning a servant *who helps feet* get in or out of a carriage, is a word from 1250.

When the _ _ _ _ _ _ _ _ _ gave her a _ _ _ _ _ _ _ _ , she asked for cherry red polish.

He never let a challenge _ _ _ _ _ _ his dream of being a pilot.

FOOT: millipede; podium; footsie; footbridge; pedestrian; footloose; tripod; footage; biped; footman; pedicurist, pedicure; impede.

Roots: *POWER* Spelling List of Fire Words

PYR: Greek Root for *Fire*   **PYR**: Latin Root for *Fire*

pyramids (L., Gk.: pyramis) – ancient Egyptian tombs constructed with sloping sides meeting at an apex; n. Perhaps they were called pyramids because they *looked like huge rising flames.*

pyre – heaps of wood or other material *that fire can burn*; pyres were *burned in funeral rites*

pyrography – art of decorating wood or leather *using a heated point or flame*

pyromania, pyromaniac – one with a compulsion to *set things on fire*

pyrotechnician – specialist in *determining the origins of fires* and their control

pyrotechnics – the *art of making fireworks*

Pyrenees – high mountain range between Spain and France – *perhaps looked like tall flames*

pyrite – brassy mineral that looked like gold called *fool's gold*; Indians used it to make fire

pyrope – brassy red garnet; gemstone for January (Gk. pyropos: fire-eyed; Lat. pyropus: gold bronze)

FYR: Old English and Middle English Word for *fire*

fiery – *containing fire*; intensely strong; adj.

fire alarm – calls fire station when a *fire starts*; n.

fire ant – South American ant w/a *fiery sting*

fire drill – practice drill *in case of a fire*; n.

fire engine – truck equipped for *firefighting*; n.

fire extinguisher – contains chemical to stop fires; n.

fireball – sun; shooting star; or *fiery meteor*; n.

firebird – bird *w/golden plumage like fire*; n.

Firebird Suite – Russian ballet music by Stravinsky; n.

fireboat – vessel that *fights fires on boats*; n.

firebreak – burned land that *checks spread of a fire*; n.

firecrackers – gunpowder-filled noise makers; n.

fire-eater – entertainer who *eats fire*; n.

firefly – beetle w/*light that glows* from abdomen; n.

fireproofing – coating to *protect materials from fire*

fireworks – explosive display of *fiery lights*; n.

❑   **TRY THIS**: Complete these sentences by using the words above.

For mating, the male _ _ _ _ _ _ _ puts out a light signal, and the female _ _ _ _ _ _ _ returns her signal.

A _ _ _ _ _ _ _ _ _ _ _ _ _ is trained in determining just how a fire started and how to control it.

The firemen dug a _ _ _ _ _ _ _ _ _ to prevent the fire from spreading.

The Great _ _ _ _ _ _ _, on the bank of the Nile, contains 2 million stone blocks, 2 ½ tons each.

A _ _ _ _ _ _ _ is a brightly burning meteor that plunges through the earth's atmosphere.

_ _ _ _ _ _ _ _ _ _ _ is used to protect material and building products from burning.

A _ _ _ _ _ _ _ _ _ _ is a person who is driven by mentally unhealthy compulsions to start fires.

Iron _ _ _ _ _ _ is a brassy mineral called fool's gold. It was used by the Indians to start fires.

As the sun sets, the _ _ _ _ _ _ _ _ Mountains look like flames, creating a divider between Spain and France.

FIRE: firefly, firefly; pyrotechnician; firebreak; Pyramid; fireball; fireproofing; pyromaniac; pyrite; Pyrenees

Roots: POWER Spelling List of Time Words

TEMP: Latin Root for *Time*

contemporary – with the *same time period*; adj.

contemporaries – people *living at same time*; n.

tempo – the musical *time beat*; n.

temporal – concerned with *this time or world*; adj.

temporarily – for a *short period of time*; adv.

temporary – not forever; adj; short-term worker; n.

CHRON: Greek Root for *Time*

anachronism – item not in its proper *time period*; n.

chronic – lasting over a *long period of time*; adj.

chronicle – *record over time*, v; history; journal; n.

chronology – the order in which events occurred; n.

chronological – arranged *according to time*; adj.

chronometer – instrument *for measuring time*; n.

TIMA: Old and Middle English Word for *Time*

daytime – *time during day* (playtime, springtime); n.

pastime – activity; interest *you spend time on*; n.

time capsule – contains items *from a specific time period that will be opened at a future time*; n.

time limit – *time in which action must be done*; n.

time machine – machine for *traveling in time*; n.

time-honored – lasted and *respected over time*; adj.

timeless – *no beginning or end time*; eternal; adj.

timely – occurring *at a suitable time*; adj. (untimely)

timeout – break in activity; *interruption of time*; n.

time zones – 24 divisions of globe with their time coinciding in hours with Greenwich, England

ahead of time – done in advance

behind the times – old-fashioned; out of date

for the time being – for now; *for this time*

keep time – *record time*; keep beat.

kill time – occupy oneself *to make time pass*

make time – move quickly to *gain extra time*

pass the time of day – converse with someone

take one's time – be slow or leisurely; dawdle

time flies – *time goes fast*

time of one's life – an *extremely enjoyable time*

❑ **TRY THIS**: Complete these sentences by using the words above.

California is in the Pacific _ _ _ _   _ _ _ _, and New York is in the Eastern _ _ _ _   _ _ _ _.

A wristwatch is a kind of _ _ _ _ _ _ _ _ _ _ because it's an instrument that measures time.

Have friends or family put timely items in a _ _ _ _   _ _ _ _ _ _ _ , and then open it 20 years later.

I connect the word _ _ _ _ _ with the musical _ _ _ _ _ of jazz and the _ _ _ _ _ of my heartbeat.

Asthma is a _ _ _ _ _ _ _ disease because it usually lasts over many years.

Many people think of their time on Earth as _ _ _ _ _ _ _ _ _ or not forever.

Pa's time carving furniture is his favorite _ _ _ _ _ _ _.

Marriage is a _ _ _ _ - _ _ _ _ _ _ _ ceremony which has lasted over centuries.

I put the birthdays of my friends in _ _ _ _ _ _ _ _ _ _ _ _ _ order so I would remember them.

8

TIME: Time Zone; Time Zone; chronometer; time capsule; tempo, tempo; chronic; temporary; pastime; time-honored; chronological.

Roots: POWER Spelling List of Light Words

LUC, LUM: Latin Root meaning *Light*

bioluminescence – *light given off by fireflies*; n., or *emitted by creatures at cold ocean temperatures.*

elucidate – make clear; take *light from*; v.

translucent – allowing some *light to go across*; adj.

illuminate – cast *light on*; brighten up; v.

illumination – something that *light is cast on*; n.

lucid – clear; filled with *light*; adj.

luminous – *radiating or reflecting light*; adj.

luminary – important person; *one who sheds light*; n.

Lucille, Lucy – name means *Bringer of Light*; n.

PHOTO: Greek Root meaning *Light*

photography – process of *taking pictures with light*: photo: *light* + graph: *map*; n.

photograph – camera picture; a *light map*; n.

photo – short for photograph: *light map*; n.

photographer – one who takes *light maps*; n.

photographic – having to do with *light maps*; adj.

photosynthesis – *sunlight* lets plant use chlorophyll; n.

phototherapy – *light therapy* for depression or skin; n.

photothermic – *involving light* and heat; adj.

LEOHT, LIHT: Old and Middle English Words for *Light*

headlights – *lights on front* of car, plane, truck; n.

light, lighter, lightest – *degrees of being light*; adj.

lighted – *having light on it*; adj.

lighten – *to make lighter* in color or weight; v.

lightening – *making lighter*; v.

lighthouse – *tower flashing light* to guide ships; n.

lightning – *a light zing* before thunder; n.

light show – *show with light patterns* and music; n.

limelight – center of attention; *light* at stage front; n.

moonlight – *light from the moon*; n.

spotlight – *light focusing on spots* on a stage; n.

starlight – *light from the stars*; n.

❑ **TRY THIS:** Complete these sentences by using the words above.

A glowing light _____ the room. A beautiful smile _____ her face (same word).

The spelling lesson was so _____ and clear, I could understand every word.

They enjoyed the attention of being in the _____, the center of attention.

Both fireflies and tiny creatures deep in the ocean glow with their own _____.

Egyptians built the tallest _____ (Pharos of Alexandria, 400 feet, guided ships for 1,500 years; 246 B.C.)

A _____ means a *light map* because it's made by light and outlines things like a map.

She was _____ her clothes by bleaching them out in the sun.

Benjamin Franklin flew a kite with a metal key during a storm to show that _____ was electrical.

A _____ is a person who attains excellence in an area or is an inspiration to others.

The golden glass was _____ because some light could pass through it and color the room gold.

LIGHT: illuminates; lucid; limelight; bioluminescence; lighthouse; photograph; lightening; lightning; luminary; translucent.

41

Roots: POWER Spelling List of Dark Words

OBSCURUS: Latin Root meaning *Dark*

obscure – not clear; vague; *in darkness*; adj.

obscured – unable to be understood; *in darkness*; adj.

obscurity – state of being unknown, *state of darkness*; n.

ECLIPSE: Greek Root relating to *Dark*

eclipse – Earth *blocks light* btw, moon and sun; n.

eclipsed – *lost light*; lost importance; v,

DEORC, DERK: Old and Middle English Words for *dark*

dark, darker, darkest – *having little or no light*; adj.

Dark Ages (476-1000) – *dark period* lacking in skills, education, or knowledge of Greek or Roman classics; n.

dark horse – unknown horse (in the *dark*) who wins; person unexpectedly nominated at a convention; n.

darken, darkened – made *darker*; v.

darkening – making *darker*; v.

darkness - state of being *without light*

dark room – a *darkened room* where film film is developed and printed; n.

Roots: POWER Spelling List of Day and Night Words

DIURN: Latin Root for *Day*

diurnal – concerning *day*, active during the *day*

NOC: Latin Root for *Night*

nocturnal – concerning *night*, active at *night*

nocturne – music to be played in evening or at *nigh*

DAEG: Old and Middle English Word for *Day*

daily – each day; adj.

day care – daytime care for preschoolers, elderly; n.

daybook – book for business of the day; journal; n.

daydream – think of fantasies during day; v.

daylight savings time: states *save daylight*; n.

daystar: a morning star; the sun before A.D.1000; n.

NIHT: Old and Middle English Word for *Night*

night crawler – an earthworm (crawls in dark); n.

night person – one who *functions best at night*; n.

nightingale – bird (Male sings at night during mating season

nightlife – *night activities*: nightclub, theatre, etc.; n

nightly – *each night*, adv.

nightmare – terrifying dream *during the night*; n

❑ **NOW**: Complete these sentences by using the words above.

This author's writing is so _ _ _ _ _ _ _ that I can't even begin so understand it.

Since nobody knew this man had composed music, his memory sank into _ _ _ _ _ _ _ _ _.

The Arabian stallion that so suddenly won the race was truly a _ _ _ _ _ _ _ _ _.

Animals active at night are _ _ _ _ _ _ _ _ _, while animals active during the day are _ _ _ _ _ _ _.

The _ _ _ _ _ _ _ _ was a time when the learning and art skills of Greece and Rome seemed lost.

Every summer, most of the United States goes on _ _ _ _ _ _ _ _ _ _ _ _ _ _ _ _ _ _ _.

Even at night, in gales of wind, the _ _ _ _ _ _ _ _ _ _ _ _ sing for a mate.

In the evening, I especially enjoying listening to a _ _ _ _ _ _ _ _ composed by Chopin.

A _ _ _ _ _ _ _ _ _ is not a special kind of female horse.

DARK; DAY and NIGHT: obscure; obscurity ;dark horse; nocturnal, diurnal; Dark Ages; Daylight Savings Time; nightingale; nocturne; nightmare.

Word-Building with Prefix, Root, and Suffix Blocks: 1

❑ **TRY THIS GAME**: How many words can you build using Old English word blocks? Choose a Root block and then discover which Prefix blocks and/or Suffix blocks you can connect to it that make sense. Also, try adding two Suffix blocks onto a Root block. Write down every word you can make, from short to long. Also, feel free to invent words of your own and to define what these words mean. *Note*: *Y Rule* for *happy*: happy̶ + i + ness = happiness; happy̶ + i + est = happiest.

PREFIXES	ROOTS	SUFFIXES.
mis- (wrong, not)	**dark** (O.E. not light)	**-ed** , **-s** (verb suffixes)
over- (too much)	**friend** (O.E. buddy)	**-en** (to make; v. suf.)
re- (again)	**hand** (O.E. fingers, thumb)	**-er** (person who; n. suf. more; adj. suf.)
un- (not)	**happy** (O.E. cheerful)	**-est** (most; adj. suf.)
under- (under)	**kind** (O.E. warm-hearted)	**-ful** (full of; adj. suf.)
	light (O.E. not dark)	**-ing** (continuing action; v. suf.)
	soft (O.E. gentle)	**-less** (without; adj. suf.)
	take (Old Norse: grasp; lead)	**-ly** (adjective and adverb suffix)
	thought (O.E. idea)	**-ness** (state or quality; n. suf.)
	throw (O.E. hurl; toss)	**-ship** (state or quality; n. suf.)
		-s (plural noun suffix)

LIST WORDS HERE: *darkens* (dark + en + s), *lights* (light + s), *retaken* (re + take + n), *thoughtlessly, happiest*

re + turn + ing

Word-Building with Prefix, Root, and Suffix Blocks: 2

❑ **TRY THIS GAME**: See how many words you can build using Latin Word Part Blocks. Choose a Root Block and then discover which Prefix Blocks and/or Suffix Blocks you can connect to it that make sense. Also, try adding two Suffix Blocks to a Root Block. Write down every word you make, from short to long. Also, feel free to add any Prefixes, Roots, and Suffixes you'd like, plus feel free to invent and define your own words. With all the words you can build, you may need more paper!

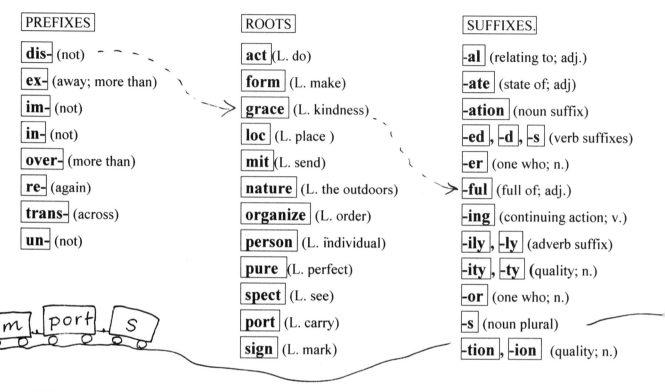

PREFIXES	ROOTS	SUFFIXES
dis- (not)	**act** (L. do)	**-al** (relating to; adj.)
ex- (away; more than)	**form** (L. make)	**-ate** (state of; adj)
im- (not)	**grace** (L. kindness)	**-ation** (noun suffix)
in- (not)	**loc** (L. place)	**-ed**, **-d**, **-s** (verb suffixes)
over- (more than)	**mit** (L. send)	**-er** (one who; n.)
re- (again)	**nature** (L. the outdoors)	**-ful** (full of; adj.)
trans- (across)	**organize** (L. order)	**-ing** (continuing action; v.)
un- (not)	**person** (L. individual)	**-ily**, **-ly** (adverb suffix)
	pure (L. perfect)	**-ity**, **-ty** (quality; n.)
	spect (L. see)	**-or** (one who; n.)
	port (L. carry)	**-s** (noun plural)
	sign (L. mark)	**-tion**, **-ion** (quality; n.)

LIST WORDS HERE: *locate* (loc + ate), *reorganizing* (re + organize + ing), *submit*

Word-Building with Prefix, Root, and Suffix Blocks: 3

❑ **TRY THIS GAME**: See how many words you can build using Latin and Greek Word Part Blocks. Choose a Root Block and then discover which Prefix Blocks and/or Suffix Blocks you can connect to it that make sense. Also, try adding two Suffix Blocks to a Root Block. Write down every word you make, from short to long. Also, feel free to add any Prefixes, Roots, and Suffixes you'd like, and feel free to invent and define your own words. You may need more paper to build more words!

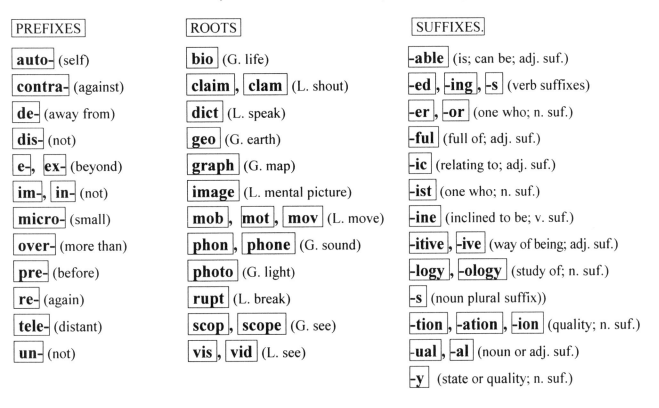

PREFIXES	ROOTS	SUFFIXES
auto- (self)	**bio** (G. life)	**-able** (is; can be; adj. suf.)
contra- (against)	**claim**, **clam** (L. shout)	**-ed**, **-ing**, **-s** (verb suffixes)
de- (away from)	**dict** (L. speak)	**-er**, **-or** (one who; n. suf.)
dis- (not)	**geo** (G. earth)	**-ful** (full of; adj. suf.)
e-, **ex-** (beyond)	**graph** (G. map)	**-ic** (relating to; adj. suf.)
im-, **in-** (not)	**image** (L. mental picture)	**-ist** (one who; n. suf.)
micro- (small)	**mob**, **mot**, **mov** (L. move)	**-ine** (inclined to be; v. suf.)
over- (more than)	**phon**, **phone** (G. sound)	**-itive**, **-ive** (way of being; adj. suf.)
pre- (before)	**photo** (G. light)	**-logy**, **-ology** (study of; n. suf.)
re- (again)	**rupt** (L. break)	**-s** (noun plural suffix))
tele- (distant)	**scop**, **scope** (G. see)	**-tion**, **-ation**, **-ion** (quality; n. suf.)
un- (not)	**vis**, **vid** (L. see)	**-ual**, **-al** (noun or adj. suf.)
		-y (state or quality; n. suf.)

LIST WORDS HERE: *automotive* (auto + mot + ive), *diction* (*speech*: dic + ion), *biography*

POWER Spelling List of Prefix Patterns

Prefixes with Different Forms that Match the Root

The sets of prefixes below have different forms depending on the letter with which the root begins. As you read each set, add any words or any other forms of a words you think of.

ad- (to; toward): **Ad-** has the forms: **ab-, ac-, al-, an-, ap-, ar-, as-,** and **at-** to match roots that begin with the letters: **b, c, d, l, n, p, qu, r, s, t. Ab-** goes before **b** and sometimes before **d** and **s**.

ab-	:	abbreviate, abdicate (to leave position as ruler), absence, absolute
ac-	:	accept, accident, account, accurate, accuse, accustom
ac + qu	:	acquaint, acquaintance, acquire, acquit (free from a charge)
ad-	:	addendum (appendix to a book), address, addict, additional
al-	:	allegiance, alley (narrow street), allow, allowance, ally (unite)
an-	:	annex (add), announce, annually (yearly), annul (end)
ap-	:	appear, appoint, appreciate, approach, approve
ar-	:	arrange, arrest, arrive, arrogant (acting superior)
as-	:	ascend (to go up), aspect (viewpoint), assess, assistant
at-	:	attend, attitude, attract, attune

e + qua- (means equal and is part of the word): equal, equaled, equalize, equalizing, equation, equator

e + qui- (means equal; used for compound words): equidistant, equilibrium, equinox, equity (just), equivalent

com- (together; with): **Com-** has the forms: **col-, com-, con-,** and **cor-** that match roots that begin with the letters: **l, m, p, n,** and **r**.

col-	:	collaborate (to work together,) collage, collect, collection, college, collide
con-	:	connect, connection, connive (secretly plan), connote (to suggest an another meaning)
com-	:	(before m, p and rest of consonants): combine, compare, compete, computer
cor-	:	correct, correspond, corroborate (to strengthen; support), corrode (to wear away), corrosion

ex- (out of, from, beyond): **Ex-** goes before **c, f, q, p, s,** and **t** (**E-** goes before the rest of the consonants.)

ex-	:	examine, example, exercise, exfoliate (remove surface skin), explain, exquisite, extra
ex + h	:	exhale, exhaust, exhaustion, exhibit, exhort (to strongly urge)
e-	:	(out, away from): e + migrate = emigrate (move out), emit (send out), emission, erase

in- (not, in, into): **In-** has the forms: **il-, im-, in-, ir-** to match roots that begin with **l, m, n, p,** and **r**.

il-	:	illegal, illegible, llicit (not lawful), illiterate (not able to read), illusion (not real)
im-	:	immediate, immigrate (to move into), immobile, immortal (not dying), immune
im-	:	(Form: im is used before p.) impatient, important, impossible, improper, impure
in-	:	innate (inborn), inner, innocent, innovate (do something new), innumerable
ir-	:	irrational (not clear thinking), irrecoverable, irregular, irremovable, irreversible

24

Prefixes with Different Forms Because of Meaning

The prefixes below have different forms that are added to roots because each form has a different meaning. Once you clearly understand the differences, you will have no trouble spelling them.

ante- (L. or; before): ante̲date (before the date); ante̲meridian (before noon); ante̲room (room before)

anti- (Gk. against): anti̲biotics (against antibodies); anti̲freeze (against freezing); anti̲septic (against infection)

de- (L. down; away from): de̲fend (strike down); de̲flate (blow out from); de̲scend (climb down); de̲scribe (write down)

dis- (L., not): dis̲appear (not appear); dis̲pleasure (not pleasure); dis̲service (not service); dis̲similar (not similar)

dys- (G. concerns illness: bad or ill): dys̲pepsia (bad stomach); dys̲rhythmia (bad rhythm: disturbance in rhythm of brain waves resulting in bad speech); muscular dys̲trophy (bad development)

for- (means: for): forget, forgive, forward, forbid, forfeit, forbearance, format, fortitude (strength).

fore- (before, earlier, front, previous): forearm, forecast, foretold, foreword, forefinger, forehead, forefathers

intra- (L. among; within): intrastate (within the state); intramurals (within same walls); intravenous (within veins)

inter- (L. between): intercede (to go btw. for someone); intercollegiate; interstate; interfere (to come between)

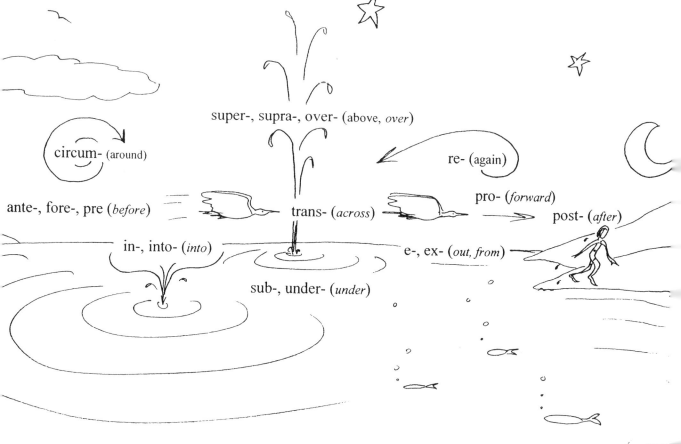

circum- (*around*)

super-, supra-, over- (above, *over*)

re- (*again*)

ante-, fore-, pre (*before*)

trans- (*across*)

pro- (*forward*)

post- (*after*)

in-, into- (*into*)

e-, ex- (*out, from*)

sub-, under- (*under*)

POWER Spelling List of Suffix Patterns

Soft C and Soft G Patterns before Suffixes

Soft C Pattern: To stay soft (s sound), c *must* be followed by e or i; so, keep silent e before –able: noticeable, peaceable, pronounceable, replaceable, traceable. Also, c stays soft (s sound) if it is followed by -ious and -ible: gracious, precious; invincible, legible; efficient, sufficient.

Soft G Pattern: To stay soft (j sound) g *must* be followed by e or i; so keep silent e before -able, -on, and -ous: changeable, knowledgeable, manageable; pigeon, dungeon; advantageous, courageous, gorgeous. Also, g stays soft (j sound) if it is followed by -ion and -ous: contagious, religion.

Suffixes Patterns: -able, -ible

-able: If you're left with a complete word when you drop the suffix (or just a silent e or l has been dropp the spelling is usually -able:

acceptable	desirable	likable	reliable
amiable (friendly)	detectable	lovable	salable
available	drinkable	manageable (soft g)	seasonable
avoidable	eatable	measurable	serviceable (soft c)
believable	excusable	noticeable (soft c)	sizable
breakable	fashionable	perishable	sociable
capable	favorable	pleasurable	transportable
changeable (soft g)	imaginable	predictable	usable
comfortable	inflammable	presentable	valuable
correctable	knowledgeable (soft g)	profitable	vulnerable
dependable	laughable	readable	workable

-ible: If you are not left with a complete word when you drop the suffix, the spelling is usually -ible. Also, if -ion can be added to the base and make sense, as in collection, the spelling is -ible.

audible	edible	incomprehensible	producible
compatible	eligible	invisible	reducible
contemptible	flexible	invincible	resistible
convincible	forcible	irresistible	reversible
credible	gullible	legible	sensible
dirigible (blimp)	horrible	negligible	susceptible
discernible	illegible	plausible	terrible
divisible	impossible	possible	visible

collectible-collection	divisible-division	intelligible-intelligent	responsible-respons
convertible-conversion	destructible-destruction	invisible-vision	reversible-reversion
digestible-digestion	horrible-horrific	permissible-permission	terrible-terrific

Suffixes Patterns: -al, -el; -le, -il

The -al, -el; -le, and -il suffixes are very difficult to spell because they all sound so much alike. Below, there are some *Other Word Forms* that will help you with each of these suffixes.

-al The -al suffix changes a word into a noun or adjective (meaning *concerning*). After the al suffix, you can add -ity or -ly, or sometimes both and hear -al. For a few al words, after a you can add -tion

1. ac-tu-**al**: actuality
2. an-gu-l**ar**: angularity
3. bru-t**al**: brutality
4. fa-t**al**: fatality
5. fi-n**al**: finality, finale
6. gen-er-**al**: generality
7. hos-pi-t**al**: hospitality
8. in-di-vi-du-**al**: individuality
9. le-g**al**: legality, legally
10. log-i-c**al**: logically
11. ma-gic-**al**: magically
12. man-u-**al**: manually (by hand).
13. me-chan-i-c**al**: mechanically
14. me-d**al**: medallion (large medal)
15. me-t**al**: metallic
16. mor-**al**: morality
17. mus-ic-**al**: musically, musicality
18. na-tion-**al**: nationality
19. nat-u-r**al**: naturally
20. nau-ti-c**al**: nautically
21. neu-tr**al**: neutrality
22. nom-i-n**al**: nomination
23. nor-m**al**: normality
24. oc-ca-sion-**al**: occasionally
25. o-rig-i-n**al**: originality
26. per-son-**al**: personality
27. prac-tic-**al**: practicality
28. prin-ci-p**al**: principally, principality
29. re-ci-t**al**: recitation
30. ri-v**al**: rivalry
31. re-g**al**: regally
32. sig-n**al**: signaling
33. spe-**cial**: speciality
34. tri-vi-**al**: triviality
35. to-t**al**: totality, totally
36. vi-t**al**: vitality, vitally

-el For some -el words, you can add -ing to better hear -el. Also, a few -el words contain *Other Words Forms*: *model-mode*; *panel-pane*; *shovel-shove*.

1. can-c**el**: canceling
2. chan-n**el**: channeling
3. coun-s**el**: counseling, counselor
4. fun-n**el**: funneling
5. ken-n**el**: kenneling
6. le-v**el**: leveling
7. mod-**el**: modeling (*OWF*: Mode is in model.)
8. nic-k**el**: nickeling
9. nov-**el**: novella (short novel)
10. pan-**el**: paneling (*OWF*: Pane is in panel.)
11. par-c**el**: parceling
12. quar-r**el**: quarreling, quarrelers
13. re-b**el**: rebelling, rebellion
14. shov-**el**: shoveling (*OWF*: Shove is in shovel.)
15. swiv-**el**: swiveling
16. tow-**el**: toweling
17. tra-v**el**: traveling, travelers.
18. tun-n**el**: tunneling

-le For -le verbs, you can drop e and add -er or -ing to better hear consonants that come before silent e: *chuckling*; *giggling*. For -le nouns and adjectives: drop e and add y to hear consonant + ly: *able-ably*

a-**ble**: ably

an-**gle**: angling, angler

au-di-**ble**: audibly

bat-**tle**: battling

be-live-a-**ble**: believably

bun-**dle**: bundling

cap-a-**ble**: capably

cra-**dle**: cradling

cud-**dle**: cuddling, cuddly

dan-**gle**: dangling

de-ni-a-**ble**: deniably

de-pend-a-**ble**: dependably

dou-**ble**: doubling, doubly

ex-cit-a-**ble**: excitably

fid-**dle**: fiddling, fiddler

fum-**ble**: fumbling, fumbler

gam-**ble**: gambling, gambler

gen-**tle**: gently, gentler

gig-**gle**: giggling, giggly

han-**dle**: handling, handler

hon-or-a-**ble**: honorably

hum-**ble**: humbling, humbly

hur-**dle**: hurdling, hurdler

i-**dle**: idling, idly

im-pos-si-**ble**: impossibly

jin-**gle**: jingling

jug-**gle**: juggling, juggler

kin-**dle**: kindling

mis-er-a-**ble**: miserably

mul-ti-**ple**: multiply

nes-**tle**: nestling

no-**ble**: nobler, noblest, nobly

not-a-**ble**: notably

no-tice-a-**ble**: noticeably

pos-si-**ble**: possibly

pur-**ple**: purpling, purplish

puz-**zle**: puzzling, puzzler

re-sem-**ble**: resembling

rum-**ble**: rumbling

rus-**tle**: rustling

ter-ri-**ble**: terribly

sam-**ple**: sampling, sampler

sen-si-**ble**: sensibly

sim-**ple**: simply, simpler

squig-**gle**: squiggling

sta-**ple**: stapling, stapler

strug-**gle**: struggling, struggler

ta-**ble**: tablet, tabling

tic-**kle**: tickling, tickly

trou-**ble**: troubling

tum-**ble**: tumbling

twin-**kle**: twinkling

vis-i-**ble**: visibly

waf-**fle**: waffling

whistle: whistling, whistler

wrin-**kle**: wrinkling, wrinkly

-il: Since it's found in only 5 words, il words are easy to learn: 2 concern writing: *stencil* and *pencil*; 2 involve citizens: *civil* and *council*, and the last word says: *Live* not by *evil* (*Live* = reverse of *evil*.)

(These sets of al, el, le, and -il words are further explained in *Lesson 35* in *POWER Spelling* and also under *Clues for Other Word Forms* in this *POWER Spelling Book of Lists*.)

Suffixes Patterns
(-ance, -ant, -iance, -iant; -ence, -ent; -ience, -ient, -ense)

The words below are challenging because they're pronounced the same way, but since they're used so often, it's important to learn and store correct spelling in your mind. Carefully look at each word. Underline clue words you find in words like: <u>lance</u>, <u>dance</u>, <u>ran</u>, and <u>tan</u>. Also, think of *OWFs* you can use that help you better hear letters in the words, like: <u>elegant</u>, <u>cell</u>, <u>confide</u>, <u>interfere</u>, and <u>reside</u>.

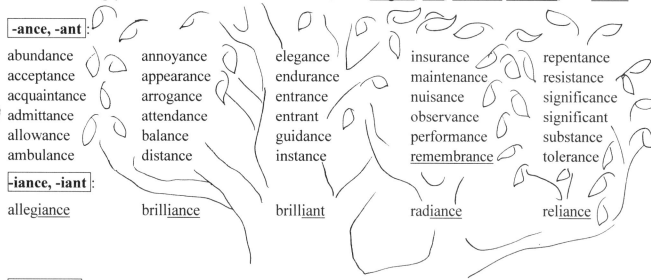

-ance, -ant:

abundance	annoyance	elegance	insurance	repentance
acceptance	appearance	endurance	maintenance	resistance
acquaintance	arrogance	entrance	nuisance	significance
admittance	attendance	entrant	observance	significant
allowance	balance	guidance	performance	substance
ambulance	distance	instance	remembrance	tolerance

-iance, -iant:

allegiance   brilliance   brilliant   radiance   reliance

-ence, -ent: Note that words with pattern of <u>current</u> or <u>conference</u> are *always* spelled <u>-ent</u> and <u>-ence</u>. OWF's in the words can help with some: co<u>here</u>, coinci<u>de</u>, comple<u>te</u>, confi<u>de</u>, inter<u>fere</u>.

abhorrence (hatred)	conference	eloquence	innocence	recent
absence	confidence	evidence	insistence	recurrence
adolescence	consequence	excellence	intelligence	reference
circumference	correspondence	existence	interference	residence
coherence	current	fence	occurrence	reverence
coincidence	dependence	impatience	permanence	sentence
competence	deference (yield)	incident	preference	silence
completion	difference	independence	presence	transference
concurrent	diligence	influence	prudence	violence

-ience, -ient:

audience	convenience	experience	obedience	patience
conscience	convenient	impatient	obedient	patient

-ense: Just a few -ense words exist. OWFs can help you better hear some letters: conden<u>s</u>ation.

condense - condensation	immense (Use sense)	license – licensure	sense – sensation (echo)
defense – defensive	incense – incensing	offense – offensive	suspense – suspension
expense – expensive	intense - intensive	pretense (Use	tense – tension

Suffixes Pattern (-ar, -er, -or)

-ar : (Note: You can add -ity to some -ar words. If you can, the spelling is always -ar before -ity.)

altar (church)	cellar	hangar (plane)	particular	similar
angular	circular	jugular	peculiar	singular
beggar	collar	liar	pillar	spectacular
burglar	dissimilar	lunar	polar	sugar
calendar	dollar	molar	popular	vehicular (car)
caterpillar	familiar	muscular	regular	vinegar
cedar	grammar	nectar	scholar	vulgar

When you create an OWF by adding <u>-ity</u>, you can more clearly hear <u>-ar</u>: *popular-popularity.*

an-gu-lar: angularity	mus-cu-lar: muscularity	reg-u-lar: regularity
cal-en-dar: calendarian	par-tic-u-lar: particularity	sim-i-lar: similarity
cir-cu-lar: circularity	pe-cul-i-ar: peculiarity	sing-u-lar: singularity
fa-mil-i-ar: familiarity	po-lar: polarity	tri-an-gu-lar: triangularity
jug-u-lar: jugulate	pop- u -lar: popularity	vul-gar: vulgarity

-er :

alter (change)	brother	father	mother	singer
announcer	carrier	further	observer	sister
baker	debater	hanger (clothes)	officer	soldier
beginner	defender	jeweler	partner	speaker
believer	diameter	lawyer	passenger	speller
bolder	disaster	manager	preacher	teacher
border	employer	messenger	prisoner	traveler
boulder	farther	minister	provider	writer

-or : (Note: After <u>-t</u>, the spelling is usually <u>-or</u>.)

actor	conductor	educator	janitor	radiator
alligator	conqueror	elevator	governor	sailor
anchor	contributor	emperor	legislator	sculptor
auditor	counselor	escalator	major	senator
author	creditor	factor	minor	suitor
aviator (pilot)	debtor	governor	motor	superior
bachelor	dictator	harbor	neighbor	supervisor
behavior	director	humor	odor	tailor
benefactor	distributor	inferior	pastor	tenor
collector	doctor	inventor	professor	traitor
competitor	editor	investigator	protector	visitor

-ard or ards: In the set *downward, downwards* the word, *downward*, is used for an adjective (a *downward* look) and both *downward* and *downwards* can be used as an adverb. The recommended spelling is *downward* (no *s*) because it's right both as an adjective and adverb, and because it's shorter.

-ary: adversary, commentary, culinary (concerning cooking), customary, dictionary, elementary, secondary, secretary, stationary (stable; in one place), temporary...

-ery: cemetery, confectionery, distillery, millinery (concerning hats), monastery, stationery (for letters)

-cy: consistency, democracy, infancy, frequency, secrecy, sufficiency.

-sy: ecstasy, heresy (believing other doctrine), hypocrisy (falseness; appearing to have principles, but not), idiosyncrasy (personal habit; quirk), jealousy.

Some Challenging Verb Suffixes (-ick, -ise, -ize, -yze)

The Inserted K Rule

-ic to –ick: The Inserted K Rule: If a suffix beginning with <u>e</u>, <u>i</u>, or <u>y</u> was added to a words that ended in a hard <u>c</u> (c with a <u>k sound</u>), the <u>c</u> would change to a <u>soft s</u> sound. Before these suffixes, <u>k</u> is inserted after the <u>c</u> so that the word will continue to have the <u>hard k sound</u>.

colic – colicky	**picnic** – picnicked, picnicking, picnicker
frolic – frolicked, frolicking	**politic** – politicking
mimic – mimicked, mimicking	**shellac** – shellacked, shellacking
panic – panicking, panicky	**traffic** – trafficked, trafficking

Words that End in -ise, -ize, and -yze

There's a small group of *-ise* words; four *-yze* words; and then several hundred *-ize* words.

-ise: *Note*: <u>Surprise</u> has <u>ise</u>: The <u>surprise</u> gave me a <u>rise</u>.   <u>Prize</u> has <u>ize</u>: I'm <u>prizing</u> the <u>zing</u> I feel.

cise:	circumcise, exercise	**mise**:	compromise, promise
prise:	enterprise, surprise	**tise**:	advertise, chastise,
rise:	arise, moonrise, sunrise	**vise**:	advise, advertise, supervise, supervision

-yze: There are only four words: **analyze**   **catalyze**   **electrolyze**   **paralyze**.

-ize: Several hundred remaining words end in **-ize**. *Other Word Forms* help you hear the <u>z</u>.

authorize – authorization	**prize** – prizing (I'm pri<u>zing</u> the <u>zing</u> I feel.)
computerize – computerization	**popularize** – popularization, popularity
energize – Energizer	**realize** - realization, reality
finalize – finalization, finality	**visualize** – visualization, visualizing

Some Challenging Noun Suffixes: -sion, -tion, -eption

Words with the suffixes -sion and -tion are challenging because they're pronounced the same way: *tension, caution, cushion,* and *fashion.* Below are a few that you can visually reinforce. Underline words for *Clues* or use *Other Word Forms* or *Special Phonics Pronunciations* for challenging words.

-sion : Look for words like mission and tension in -sion words and *OWFs* that help with letters. If verb ends in -de, add -sion for the noun: exclude-exclusion; include-inclusion; suspend-suspension…

admission: admissive	exclusion: exclusive	inclusion: inclusive	session: 3 s's
compassion: passion	extension: extensive	pretension: pretense	suspension: suspense
compulsion: compulsive	incision: *SPP:* in-ci-si-on	remission: remiss	tension: intensive

-tion : Look for letters like -ation, and words inside -tion words and *OWFs* that help with letters.

action: Act I on	creation: create	fascination: fascinate	intention: *Clue:* In tent I
addiction: Ad (on) diction	desperation: desperate	imagination: imaginative	limitation: Limit a(c)tio
addition: Add it I on	examination: exam I nation	initiation: *Clue:* In it I ate	medication: medic at I
completion: complete	explanation: explanatory	inspiration: Inspire a(c)tion	separation: separate

-eive to -eption : conceive-conception; deceive-deception; perceive-perception, receive-reception.

Nouns with the Same Plural Suffix Patterns

-oes *Nouns Ending in -oes (often American Indian or Spanish):* does (deer), foes, hoes, roes, toes, woes; canoes, cargoes, echoes, heroes, mosquitoes, potatoes, tomatoes, tornadoes, vetoes, volcanoes.

-oes *Verbs Endling in -oes:* hoes, echoes, vetoes; also does, goes.

-os *Plurals for Italian Musical Words:* always end in os: altos, banjos, cantos, concertos, contraltos, pianos, quartos, solos, sopranos (Also, include: discos and studios which relate to music).

-os *Other Words Endling in -os:* dynamos, Eskimos, hellos, momentos, silos, zeros (or zeroes)…

is to -ses (Greek): axis-axes; basis-bases; crisis-crises; oasis-oases; parenthesis-parentheses; thesis-these

-um to -a (Latin): criterion-criteria; datum-data; medium-media (*exception:* alumna-*sing* and alumnae-plural

-us to -ii (Latin): alumnus-alumni; focus-foci; radius-radii; stimulus-stimuli

-f to -ves (Old English pattern for words ending in f and lf): calf-calves, elf-elves, half-halves, knife-knives, leaf-leaves, loaf-loaves, scarf-scarves, self-selves, sheaf-sheaves, shelf-shelves, thief-thieves, wife-wives, wolf-wolves.

-f to fs (Old English pattern for the rest of the words ending in f, you just add -s): belief-beliefs, cliff-cliffs, cuff-cuffs, dwarf-dwarfs, gulf-gulfs, roof, roofs.

One Truly Challenging Adverb Pattern

-ue to -uly : For words with UE, drop e and add the adverb suffix: -ly: due-duly, true-truly, unruly.

truly unruly!

POWER Spelling Word Building with Magical Suffixes

You have the *POWER* to build nouns, adjectives, verbs, and adverbs by adding *Magical Suffixes* to words. See how *courage* can become all four parts of speech, depending on the suffixes that are added.

NOUN: It takes *courage* to climb a mountain at our age.
ADJECTIVE: We are *courageous* kids who carefully climb mountains.
VERB: We *were encouraging* them to climb the mountain. (En-, a prefix, is also added.)
ADVERB: We climbed *courageously* up the mountain.

❑ **TRY THIS GAME**: Try adding noun, adjective, verb, and adverb suffixes to the words below until you build a word that makes sense. Also, check your words to make sure they make sense in the spaces. See how many words you can build! Good dictionaries always list all the *Other Forms of the Word*.

NOUN -ant, -ion, -ness, -er, -y (Person, place, thing, feeling) The _____	ADJECT: -ful,-ing, -y, -er, -est (Describes a noun, pronoun) The _____ person	VERB (Do 2): -e, -s, -ed, -ing (Action or state of being) I _____. You _____.	ADVERB: -ly (Describes verb's action) We worked_____.
completion	*complete*	*completes, completed*	*completely*
confidant	*confident*	*confide, confiding*	*confidently*
determination			
excitement			
imagination, image			
criticism, critic			
desire			
description			
continuation			
possession			
deceiver, deception			
impression			
necessity			
intention			
persistence			
practice, practicality			

Magical Suffixes Create Nouns, Verbs, Adjectives, and Adverbs

You have the *POWER* to build nouns, adjectives, verbs, and adverbs by adding *Magical Suffixes* to words. See how <u>help</u> can become all four parts of speech, depending on the suffixes that are added.

NOUN: A child needs <u>help</u> with his balloon.
ADJECTIVE: When the balloon escaped, he made a <u>helpless</u> cry.
VERB: We *were* <u>helping</u> him get the balloon out of the tree.
ADVERB: He cried <u>helplessly</u> when we saw the balloon in a tree.

❑ **TRY THIS GAME:** Try adding noun, adjective, verb, and adverb suffixes to the words below until you build a word that makes sense. Also, check your words to make sure they make sense in the spaces. See how many words you can build! Good dictionaries always list all the *Other Forms of the Word.*

<u>NOUN</u> -ion, -ness, -er, -y (Person, place, thing, feeling…) The _____	<u>ADJECT</u>: -ful,-ing, -y, -er, -est (Describes a noun, pronoun) The _____ person	<u>VERB</u> (Do 2): -s, -ed, ing (Action or state of being) I _____. You ____.	<u>ADVERB</u>: -ly (Describes action of verb) We worked _____.
act (in a play); **action**	*active*	*act, acting*	*actively*
beauty			
business			
dream, dreamer	*dreamy*	*dream, dreamed…*	*dreamily*
freedom			
enjoyment			
laughter			
love, loveliness			
play, playfulness			
rest, restfulness	*restful*	*rested, resting*	*restfully*
surprise			
sleep, sleepiness			
prayer			
care, carefulness			

Adding Nouns, Verbs, Adjectives, and Adverbs Game

❑ **TRY THIS**: For this game, suffixes have turned the same roots into all four parts of speech when possible: *free, freedom, frees, freely*. Since all you need for a sentence is a noun and a verb, let's see what kind of sentences you can make: *Play, played; Thoughts think*. Then you can add adjectives to nouns and adverbs to verbs (and also put a determiner before the noun): *His playful play plays playfully*; *My thoughtful thought thinks thoughtfully*.

To play this game, choose a word from each of the 5 lists and put them together to create sentences. You can use the same root for all four parts of speech or choose different roots. Have fun experimenting and putting words together you've never tried before. Write ten or more sentences.

Determiners and Possessive Words	Adjectives	Nouns	Verbs	Adverbs
the	dreamy	dream	dreamed	dreamily
a	laughing	laugh, laughter	laughed	laughingly
an	cheerful	cheer	cheered	cheerfully
my	excited	excitement	excited	excitedly
our	romantic	romance	romanced	romantically
your	playful	play, players	played	playfully
his	beautiful	beauty	beautified	beautifully
her	careful	care	cared	carefully
their	active	act, action, actors	acted	actively
	thoughtful	thought	thought, thinks	thoughtfully
	free	freedom	freed	freely
	quiet	quietness	quieted	quietly
	lively	life	lived	lively
	brave	brave, bravery	braved	bravely
	icy	ice, icicle	iced	icily
	imaginative	imagination	imagined	imaginatively
	joyful	joy	joys, (enjoyed)	joyfully
	lovely, loving	love. lovers	loved	lovingly
	mysterious	mystery	mystified	mysteriously
	powerful	power	powers (empowers)	powerfully
	sleepy	sleep, sleepers	sleeps, slept	sleepily
	timely	time, timers	timed	timely
	busy	business	busies, busied	busily
	helpful	help	helps, helped	helpfully
	sad	sadness	saddens	sadly
	light, lighter...	light	lights, lightens	lightly
	dark, darker...	darkness	darkens	darkly
	weary	weariness	wearies, wearied	wearily
	quick	quickness	quickened	quickly

POWER Spelling List of Words and Their Roots

Discovering and learning about a word's ROOTS is very helpful to spelling because you can see how each word is built. What does the root mean? Does the word contain prefixes (syllables added before the root)? How about suffixes (syllables added after a root)? Also, as you learn howl Greek, Latin, Old English... words are built, you can build your vocabulary and even learn about how people thought and lived in those times.

1. **ac-a-dem-ic**: academ (G. Academius) + ic (adj. suf.) = academic. Academius had an Academy with a grove where Plato and Aristotle walked and talked.

2. **ac-cede**: ac (L. prefix: to, toward) + cede (L. root: go; accept) = accede (to go to and accept).

3. **ac-ci-dent**: ac (L. prefix: to) + cide (L. root: cidere-befall) + nt (n. suf.) = accident (to befall).

4. **ac-cord**: ac (L. prefix: toward) + cord (L. root: cord-heart) = accord (toward the heart; of one heart).

5. **ac-cum-u-late**: ac (L. pre: to) + cumul (L. root: cumul-heap) + ate (v. suf.) = accumulate (to heap).

6. **ac-quire**: ac (L. prefix: to) + quire (L. root: search for) = acquire. *Same Pattern*: inquire

7. **ad-o-les-cent**: adolesc (L. root: growing up) + ent (n. suf: one who) = adolescent (one growing up).

8. **ag-o-ny**: agon (G. root: agon-suffering in a contest like ancient Olympic games) + y (n. suf.) = agony

9. **ag-o-ra-pho-gi-a**: gora (G. root: agora-market place or open place) + phobia (Gk. fear).

10. **al-bum**: album (Lat. root: albus-white. Albus came to mean album, and many albums are white.)

11. **al-pha-bet**: Alpha (and) Beta are the first 2 letters of the Greek alphabet: Alpha +Beta.

12. **a-muse-ment**: a (pre: to) + muse (L. musa; G. mousa) + ment (n. suf.) = amusement (art, poetry, music).

13. **an-i-ma-tion**: anima (L. root: anima-alive) + tion (n. suf.) = animation (alive) (Inanimate: not alive).

14. **an-nounce-ment**: an (L. pre: toward) + nounce (L. root: messenger) + ment (n. suf.) = announcement.

15. **Ant-arc-ti-ca** (S. Pole): Ant (pre: opposite) + arctic (G. root: Arktos-bear) + a = Antarctica (opposite Arctic).

16. **an-te-ce-dent**: ante (pre: before) + cedent (L. root: cede-come) = antecedent (comes before). *Visual*: 4 e's.

17. **an-ti-dis-es-tab-lish-men-tar-i-an-ism**: anti + dis (L. prefixes) + establish (L. root: establish) + ment + arian, and ism (noun suffixes).

18. **an-ti-sep-tic**: anti (pre: against) + sept (G. root: septos-rotted) + ic (n. suf.) = antiseptic (against what rotted).

19. **an-y-bod-y**: any (Old Eng. anig: one) + body (Old Eng. root: bodig-body) = anybody (anigbodig).

20. **a-phro-di-si-ac** (love potion): Aphrodisiac come from the goddess Aphrodite (Gk. goddess of love).

21. **a-pos-tro-phe**: apo (pre: away; from) + strophe (G. to turn) = apostrophe (when actor in Greek plays *turned* from the audience to address one person). Later, apostrophe also meant the sign that *turns to the left*.

22. **ap-plause**: ap (prefix: to) + plause (L. root: plaudels-praise) = applause (to praise).

23. **ap-pre-ci-ate**: ap (pre: to) + preci (L. root: preci-value) + ate (v. suf.) = appreciate (to value as precious).

24. **ar-chae-o-lo-gy**: arche (G. root: archaeo-ancient things) + logy (G. study of) = archaeology.

25. **Arc-tic**: Arctic (G. arktos: Bear-most northern constellation) Arctic Ocean forms arc around N. Pole.

26. **ar-rive**: ar (pre: to) + rive (L. root: ripa-come ashore) = arrive (come ashore from travel by ship).

27. **a-scend**: a (L. pre: a: to; toward) + scend (L. root: scendere: climb) = ascend (to climb toward).

28. **as-sem-ble**: as (pre: toward) + sem (L. root: simu-same time) + ble (v. suf) = assemble (go toward at same time).

29. **as-ter-isk** (*): aster (L. root: aster-star) + isk (n. suf) = asterisk (astericus: little star).

30. **as-tro-naut**: astro (L. root: astro-star) + naut (G. root: naute-sailor) = astronaut (star sailor).

31. **at-las** (globe; strongman): <u>atlas</u> (Gk. Atlas: the strongman who held the world on his back).

32. **a-tone-ment**: <u>atone</u> (L. root: adun-at one) + <u>ment</u> (n.. suf) = <u>atonement</u> (at-one-ment with God).

33. **au-di-ence**: <u>audi</u> (L. root: audi-hear) + <u>ence</u> (n. suf: ones who) = <u>audience</u> (ones who hear).

34. **au-to-graph**: <u>auto</u> (G. root: authos-self) + <u>graph</u> (G. root: graph-writing; map) = <u>autograph</u> (self-map).

35. **au-to-ma-tic**: <u>auto</u> (G. authos-self) + <u>mat</u> (G. root: matos-moving) + <u>ic</u> (adj. suf) = <u>automatic</u> (self-moving).

36. **a-vi-a-tor**: <u>avi</u> (L. root: avi-bird) + <u>ate</u> (v. suf) + <u>or</u> (n. suf.) = <u>aviator</u> (Aviators are involved with flying).

37. **bal-ance**: <u>ba</u> (M.E. bi-two; pair of) + <u>lance</u> (M. E. root: lanx-metal dishes) = <u>balance</u> (pair of metal dishes).

38. **beau-ti-ful-ly**: <u>beauty</u> + <u>i</u> (O. Fr. root: beaute-beauty) + <u>ful</u> (adj. suf.) + <u>ly</u> (adv. suf.) = <u>beautifully</u>.

39. **ben-e-fits**: <u>bene</u> (L. root: good) + <u>fits</u> (L. root: deed) = <u>benefits</u>.

40. **bi-cycle**: <u>bi</u> (Gk. prefix: bi-two) + <u>cycle</u> (Gk. root: cycle-wheel) = <u>bicycle</u>.

41. **bi-ol-o-gy**: <u>bio</u> (Gk. root: bio-life) + <u>logy</u> (Gk. root: logy-study of) = <u>biology</u> (study of life).

42. **black**: <u>black</u> (M.E. blak; O. E. root: blae k-ink) = <u>black</u>: *Clue:* In my backpack, black ink spilled.

43. **blue**: <u>blue</u> (Old Eng. blewe-angry or disclored. Later, <u>blah + hue</u> was blended into <u>blue</u>): <u>blah</u> + <u>hue</u> = <u>blue</u>.

44. **branch**: <u>branch</u> (Lat. root: branca-paw of an animal.)

45. **cal-cu-late**: <u>calcul</u> (Lat. root: calculus-small stones for counting) + <u>ate</u> (v. suf.) = <u>calculate</u>.

46. **cat-er-pil-lar**: <u>cater</u> (O. Fr. root: chate-cat) + <u>pillar</u> (O. Fr. root: pelose-hairy) = <u>caterpillar</u> (hairy cat).

47. **cede** (Lat. root: to yield territory, land, etc.): He <u>ceded</u> the land where the <u>cedar</u> treesgrew.

48. **cen-ti-me-ter**: <u>centi</u> (L. one hundredth) + <u>meter</u> (L. root: meter-measure .9 yards) = <u>centimeter</u> (centimeter = one hundredth of a meter, approximately .4 of an inch). *Phonics:* <u>c</u> = <u>s</u>.

49. **cent-i-pede**: <u>cent</u> (L. prefix-hundred) + <u>ped</u> (L. root: foot) = centipede (hundred feet).

50. **ce-re-al**: <u>cere</u> (L. root: The Roman Goddess of <u>cereal</u> was <u>Ceres</u>) + al (n. suf.) = <u>cereal</u>.

51. **cha-o-tic**: <u>chaos</u> (Gk. root: chaos-unformed matter) + <u>tic</u> (adj. suf.) = <u>chaotic</u>.

52. **chess**: (Persian, <u>shah</u>-king + <u>mat</u>-is dead = <u>shah-mat</u>-the king is dead (*Shah-mat* has now become *check mate*).

53. **cho-re-og-ra-phy**: <u>chore</u> (Gk. root: chore-movement illness) + <u>ography</u> (Gk. root: graphy-map) = <u>choreography</u>.

54. **ci-vi-li-za-tion**: <u>civil</u> (L. root: civ-citizen) + <u>ize</u> (v. suf) + <u>ation</u> (n. suf-organization) = <u>civilization</u> (org. of citizens).

55. **claus-tro-pho-bi-a**: <u>claustro</u> (G. root: enclosed like a clause) + <u>phobia</u> (G. root: fear) = <u>claustrophobia</u> (fear of enclosed places). I earned a <u>trophy</u> for healing my <u>claustrophobia</u>.

56. **col-or-ful**: <u>color</u> (L. root: color or hue) + <u>ful</u> (adj. suf: full of) = <u>colorful</u> (full of color).

57. **com-fort-a-ble**: <u>com</u> (pre: with) + <u>fort</u> (L. root: fortis-strength) + <u>able</u> (adj. suf) = <u>comfortable</u> (able with strength).

58. **com-pan-ion**: <u>com</u> (pre: with) + <u>pan</u> (L.root: pan-bread) + <u>ion</u> (n. suf) = <u>companion</u> (one you share bread with).

59. **com-par-i-son**: <u>com</u> (L. pre: with) + <u>pari</u> (L. root: pari-on a par; matched) + <u>son</u> = <u>comparison</u> (matched with).

60. **com-pose**: com (Lat. pre-com-with) + pose (Lat. root: poser-put together) = <u>compose</u> (put together with).

61. **com-pu-ter**: <u>com</u> (L. pre-with) + <u>pute</u> (L. root: puta; counting, thinking) + <u>r</u> (n. suf) = <u>computer</u> (with thinking).

62. **con-cede**: <u>con</u> (Lat. pre-with) + <u>cede</u> (Lat. root: ced-to yield): = <u>concede</u> (to act with yielding).

63. **con-cen-tra-tion**: <u>con</u> (with) + <u>centr</u> (L. root: center) + ate (v. suf) + ion (n. suf) = <u>concentration</u> (centering).

64. **con-duc-tor**: <u>con</u> (pre: with) + <u>duct</u> (L. root: ducere-lead) + <u>or</u> (n. suf: one) = <u>conductor</u> (one with leading).

65. **con-grat-u-la-tions**: <u>con</u> (pre: with) + <u>grat</u> (L. root: gratus-thanks, pleasing) + ulate (v. suf) + <u>tions</u> (n. suf).

66. **con-science**: <u>con</u> (pre: with) + <u>scien</u> (L. root: scien-knowing) + <u>ce</u> (n. suf.) = <u>conscience</u> (with knowing).

67. **con-tem-por-a-ry**: con (pre-with) + tempo (L. root: time) + rary (adj. suf) = <u>contemporary</u> (with same time).

68. **con-ver-sa-tion**: <u>con</u> (pre: with) + <u>verse</u> (L. root: associate) + <u>ation</u> (n. suf.) = <u>conversation</u> (associate with).

69. **co-op-er-ate**: <u>co</u> (pre: with) + <u>oper</u> (L. root: oper: work) + <u>ate</u> (verb suf.) = <u>cooperate</u> (with work).

70. **co-or-di-nate**: <u>co</u> (pre: with) + <u>ordin</u> (L. root: same order) + <u>ate</u> (v. suf.) = <u>coordinate</u> (with order).

71. **cour-te-ous**: <u>courte</u> (Fr. root: courte) + <u>ous</u> (adj. suf.) = <u>courteous</u> (Be <u>courteous</u> in <u>court</u>: court + eous)

72. **cor-rect**: <u>cor</u> (with) + <u>rect</u> (L. root: rect-means to <u>correct</u>; take direction) = <u>correct</u> (with correct direction)

73. **cri-sis**: cri (Gk. root: <u>kri</u>-to judge; decide) + <u>sis</u> (n. suf.) = <u>crisis</u>. There's a <u>crisis rising</u> over oil.

74. **dai-ly**: <u>day</u> (O. E. root: daeg-day) + <u>i</u> + <u>ly</u> (adv. suf) = <u>daily</u>.

75. **de-rive**: <u>de</u> (pre: from) + <u>riv</u> (L. root: riv-river) + <u>e</u> (v. suf) = <u>derive</u> (draw from river or from another source).

76. **de-scend**: <u>de</u> (L. pre: de-away from) + <u>scend</u> (L. root: scendere-limb) = <u>descend</u> (to climb away from).

77. **de-scribe**: <u>de</u> (pre: not) + <u>scribe</u> (L. root: scribus-write) = <u>describe</u> (not write; to tell). <u>Describe</u> the <u>scribe</u>.

78. **de-si-ra-ble**: <u>desire</u> (M. E. root: desiren) + <u>able</u> (adj. suf.) *Rule*: Drop silent <u>e</u>: desire + able = <u>desirable</u>.

79. **des-pair**: <u>de</u> (pre: de-from; without) + <u>spair</u> (L. root: spairare: spirit) = <u>despair</u> (to be without spirit).

80. **des-per-ate**: <u>de</u> (pre: de-without) + <u>sper</u> (L. root: sperare- hope) + te (v suf.) = <u>desperate</u> (without hope)

81. **des-sert**: <u>dessert</u> (French: root: desservir-to clear the table. Then you have <u>dessert</u>) = <u>dessert</u>.

82. **de-stroy**: <u>de</u> (pre: de-not) + <u>stroy</u> (L. root: build) = <u>destroy</u> (not build) <u>Troy</u> was destroyed with the Trojan Horse.

83. **de-vel-op-ment**: <u>de</u> (pre: de-not) + <u>velop</u> (O. Fr. root: veloper-wrapping things up) + <u>ment</u> (n. suf.) = <u>development</u> (not just wrapping things up).

84. **dic-tion-ar-y**: <u>diction</u> (L. diction-spoken word) + ary (n. suf-place for) = <u>dictionary</u> (place for spoken word). *Same Root*: <u>bene</u> (well) + <u>diction</u> (speak) = <u>benediction</u>; <u>contra</u> (against) + <u>diction</u> (speak) = <u>contradiction</u>.

85. **dif-fer-ence**: <u>dif</u> (pre: dif-away from) + <u>fer</u> (L. root: fer-bear) + <u>ence</u> (n. suf) = <u>difference</u> (bear away from).

86. **di-no-saur**: *2 Roots*: <u>dino</u> (G. root: deinos-terrible) + <u>saur</u> (G. root: saurus-lizard) = <u>dinosaur</u> (terrible lizard).

87. **dis-as-ter**: <u>dis</u> (pre-not; away from) + <u>aster</u> (L. astrum; Gk. astron-stars) = <u>disaster</u> (away from; not by the stars).

88. **dis-cuss**: <u>dis</u> (pre:dis- not) + <u>cuss</u> (L. root: cutere-strike) = <u>discuss</u> (not strike) Don't start <u>cussing</u>, discuss.

89. **dis-ease**: <u>dis</u> (pre: dis-not) + <u>ease</u> (L. root: comfort) = <u>disease</u> (not at ease) You feel <u>dis-ease</u> with a <u>disease</u>.

90. **dis-solve**: <u>dis</u> (pre: away from) + <u>solve</u>(L. root: solve-free; loosen). Will that <u>solvent dissolve</u> this cloth

91. **dor-mi-to-ry**: <u>dormi</u>: (L. root: dormire-sleep) + <u>tor</u> (L. forium-room) + y (n. suf) = dormitory (sleeping room).

92. **dur-ing**: <u>dur</u> (O. Fr. root: durer-last) + <u>ing</u> (suf.) = <u>during</u> *Same Root*: durable, enduring, endurance.

93. **e-co-nom-ic**: <u>econom</u> (Gk. root: economos -manager of the house) + ic (adj. suffix) = <u>economic</u>.

94. **el-bow**: <u>el</u> (O. E. root: ell-measurement from bend of elbow to fingertip) + <u>bow</u> (bend) = <u>elbow</u> (measure of bend).

95. **em-brace**: <u>em</u> (pre: em-with) + <u>brace</u> (L. root: bracela-two arms) = <u>embrace</u> (with two arms).

96. **e-mit**: <u>e</u> (pre: e-from) + <u>mit</u> (L. root: mittere-send) = <u>emit</u> (send from). *Reversal*: <u>emit</u> = <u>time</u>.

97. **en-cy-clo-pe-di-a**: <u>en</u> (in) + <u>cyclo</u> (G. root: well-rounded) + <u>ped</u> (G. root: child) + <u>ia</u> (suf.) = <u>encyclopedia</u>.

98. **en-force-able**: <u>en</u> (pre: in) + <u>force</u> (ME root: forcen-strength) + <u>able</u> (adj. suf) = <u>enforceable</u> (able in strength).

99. **en-sem-ble**: <u>en</u> (pre: in) + <u>sem</u> (L. root: simu: same time) + <u>ble</u> (n. suf) = <u>ensemble</u> (in together at same time-Group of musicians, actors…who perform at same time). *Same Root*: assemble, resemble…

100. **en-thu-si-as-tic**: <u>enthusi</u> (G. root: entheos-in God) + <u>astic</u> (adj. suf.) = <u>enthusiastic</u> (having God within).

101. **en-ve-lope**: <u>en</u> (pre: in) + <u>velop</u> (O. Fr. root: wrap up) + <u>e</u> (n. suf) = envelope. *Same Root*: <u>development</u>.

102. **e-nor-mous**: <u>e</u> (pre: e-beyond) + <u>normous</u> (L. root: what's normal). Look at that <u>enormous mouse</u>!

103. **e-pi-der-mis**: <u>epi</u> (pre: epi-above) + <u>dermis</u> (Gk.root: dermis-skin) = <u>epidermis</u> (above the skin).

= *ensemble* (tres bien!)

104. **e-rupt**: <u>e</u> (pre: e-beyond) + <u>rupt</u> (L. root: ruptus-breaking) = <u>erupt</u> (beyond breaking). <u>erupt</u>ion, <u>rupt</u>ure.

105. **es-caped**: <u>es</u> (pre: es-away from) + <u>cape</u> (Sp. capa-hooded cloak) + ed (v. suf) = <u>escape</u> (away from cloak).

106. **es-tab-lish**: <u>establ</u> (Lat. root: establire-stable) + <u>ish</u> (adj. suf.) = <u>establish</u>.

107. **ex-cep-tion-al**: <u>ex</u> (pre: out from) + <u>cept</u> (take) + <u>tion</u> (n. suf.) + <u>al</u> (adj. suf.) = <u>exceptional</u> (take out).

108. **ex-cess**: <u>ex</u> (pre-beyond) + <u>cess</u> (root: cede-to go) = <u>excess</u> (that which goes beyond).

109. **ex-ci-ted**: <u>ex</u> (pre: above; thoroughly) + <u>cite</u> (L. root: set in motion) + <u>d</u> (v. suf.). = <u>excited</u> (set in motion).

110. **ex-hil-a-rate**: <u>ex</u> (pre: from; above) + <u>hilar</u> (L. root: hilarus-cheer) + <u>ate</u> (v suf.) = <u>exhilarate</u> (above cheer).

111. **fan-tas-tic**: <u>fantasy</u> (Gk. phantasia-appearance from imagination) + ic (adj. suf.) = <u>fantastic</u>.

112. **fin-al**: <u>fin</u> (L. root: finis-end) + <u>al</u> (adj. suffix) = <u>final</u> (end).

113. **fra-gile**: <u>frag</u> (L. root: fragilus-break; g = j sound) + <u>ile</u> (adj suf) = <u>fragile</u>. *Clue*: A <u>rag</u> is not <u>fragile</u>.

114. **ge-og-ra-phy**: <u>geo</u> (G. root: earth) + <u>graph</u> (G. root: graphos-map) + <u>y</u> (n. suf.) = <u>geography</u> (earth map).

115. **ge-ol-o-gy**: <u>geo</u> (G. root: earth) + <u>log</u> (G. root: logy-study of) + y (n. suf.)= <u>geology</u> (study of earth).

116. **grate-ful**: <u>grate</u> (Lat. root: gratis-thanks) + <u>ful</u> (adj. suf-full of) = <u>grateful</u> (full of thanks).

117. **green**: <u>green</u> (O. E. root: grene) = <u>green</u> (grass color).

118. **ham-bur-ger**: <u>hamburg</u> (from <u>Hamburg</u>, <u>Ge</u>rmany) + er (n. suf.). Short Vowel Rule for each syllable.

119. **harp-si-chord**: <u>harp</u> (OE. root: hearpe) + <u>si</u> (and) + <u>chord</u> (G. root: chorde-instrument string) = <u>harpsichord</u>.

120. **hel-i-cop-ter**: <u>heli</u> (G. root: helix-to turn; spiral) + <u>copter</u> (G. root: with wings) = <u>helicopter</u>.

121. **he-ro-ic**: hero (Gk. root: heroikos-hero) + ic (adj. suf.) = <u>heroic</u>

122. **hi-er-o-glyph-ics**: <u>hiero</u> (G. sacred) + <u>glyphics</u> (G. root: carvings; writing) = <u>hieroglyphics</u> (sacred carvings).

123. **hip-po-pot-a-mus**: <u>hippo</u> (G. root: hippos-river) + <u>potamus</u> (G. root: potamos-horse) = <u>hippopotamus</u>.

124. **hoof**: hoof (Old Eng. root: hof). *Plural*: Change the *f* in hoof to *v* + *es* = hooves.

125. **hors-d'oeu-vre**: <u>hors</u>: (Fr. outside) + <u>d'</u> (Fr. ' replaces e-of) + <u>oeuvre</u> (main course) = horsd'oeuvre.

126. **hum-ble**: <u>hum</u> (L. root: humus-earth) + <u>ble</u> (adj. suf.) = <u>humble</u> (idea of bending down to the earth).

127. **il-le-gal**: <u>il</u> (pre: not) + <u>legal</u> (L. root: law) = <u>illegal</u> (not the law) *Clue*: For a <u>gal</u> to get <u>ill</u> is not <u>illegal</u>.

128. **il-log-i-cal**: <u>il</u> (il-not) + <u>logic</u> (G. root: logicos-reason) + <u>al</u> (adj. suf.) = <u>illogical</u>.

129. **im-i-ta-tion**: <u>imitate</u> (L. root: imitari-to copy) + <u>ion</u> (n. suf.) = <u>imitation</u>.

130. **im-mor-tal**: <u>im</u> (pre: not) + <u>mort</u> (L. root-dying) + <u>al</u> (adj. suf.) = <u>immortal</u> (not mortal).

131. **im-pa-tient**: <u>im</u> (pre: not) + <u>patient</u> (L. root: patiens-to bear) = <u>impatient</u> (not bear).

132. **im-po-lite**: im (pre: not) + polite (L. root: politus-polished) = <u>impolite</u> (not polished in manners).

133. **im-por-tant**: <u>im</u> (pre: to) + <u>port</u> (L. root: carry weight) + <u>ant</u> (adj. suf.) = <u>important</u> (to carry weight).

134. **im-pro-vise**: <u>im</u> (pre: not) + <u>prov</u> (L. root: provide) + <u>ise</u> (v. suf.) = <u>improvise</u> (not provide beforehand).

135. **in-an-i-mate**: <u>in</u> (pre: not) + <u>anima</u> (L. root: anima-alive) + <u>te</u> (adj. suf.) = <u>inanimate</u> (not alive).

136. **in-cred-i-ble**: <u>in</u> (pre: not) + <u>cred</u> (L. root: cred-believe) + <u>ible</u> (adj. suf.) = <u>incredible</u> (not believe).

137. **in-de-pen-dence**: <u>in</u> (pre: not) + <u>depend</u> (L. root: depend on) + <u>ence</u> (n suf) = <u>independence</u> (not depend on).

138. **in-fin-ite**: <u>in</u> (pre: not) + <u>finite</u> (L. root: finitus-stopped; limited) = <u>infinite</u> (not limited; endless).

139. **in-for-ma-tion**: <u>in</u> (pre: not) + <u>form</u> (L. root: ideas formed in the mind) + <u>ation</u> (n. suf.) = <u>information</u>.

140. **in-ter-cede**: <u>inter</u> (pre: between) + <u>cede</u> (L. root: cede-go; yield) = <u>intercede</u> (go between to help).

141. **In-ter-net**: <u>inter</u> (pre: between) + <u>net</u> (O. E. root: netten-net) = <u>Internet</u> (communication btw. networks).

ad infinitum!

216. **pro-vi-de**: <u>pro</u> (for; before) + <u>vide</u> (L. root: videre-see) = <u>provide</u> (see before; look after). Provide ride.

217. **psy-chi-a-try**: <u>psych</u> (G. root: psyche-spirit; mind) + <u>iatry</u> (re: medicine) = <u>psychiatry</u> (M.D.'s care of mind).

218. **psy-cho-lo-gy**: <u>psych</u> (G. root: psyche-mind) + <u>ology</u> (root: study of) = <u>psychology</u> (study of the mind)

219. **pur-ple**: <u>purple</u> (O.E. purple; K. purpure-purple shellfish known for purple dye) = <u>purple</u>.

220. **pyr-a-mid**: <u>pyramid</u> (G. root: pyramis-fire. It is thought the pyramids looked like huge rising flames.)

221. **quo-ta-tion**: <u>quota</u> (L. root: quotare-divide into verses) + tion (n. suf.) = <u>quotation</u> (part of a verse)

222. **read-i-ly**: <u>ready</u> + <u>i</u> (O.E. root: roedi-prompt) + <u>ly</u> (adv. suf.) = <u>readily</u> (promptly).

223. **re-cede**: <u>re</u> (pre: re-back; again) + <u>cede</u> (L. root: cede-move; go) = <u>recede</u> (to move back).

224. **rec-og-nize**: <u>re</u> (pre: re-again) + <u>cogni</u> (L. root: know) + <u>ze</u> (v. suf.) = <u>recognize</u> (again know).

225. **re-cord-ed**: <u>re</u> (pre: re-again) + <u>cord</u> (L. root: heart) = <u>record</u> (remembered in the heart).

226. **rec-re-a-tion**: <u>re</u> (pre: re-again) + <u>create</u> (L. root: creatus-make) + <u>ion</u> (n. suf.) = <u>recreation</u>.

227. **red**: <u>red</u> (Old Eng. red; Danish <u>rood</u>-color of blood).

228. **re-gal** (word both ways): <u>reg</u> (L. root: royal) + <u>al</u> (adj. suf) = <u>regal</u>. *Reversal*: regal = lager (aged beer).

229. **rel-a-tive**: <u>relate</u> (L. root: relatus-to carry back) + <u>ive</u> (n. suf.) = <u>relative</u>. *Same Root*: relate, relationship.

230. **re-mem-ber**: <u>re</u> (again) + <u>member</u> (L. root: mindful) = <u>remember</u> (again mindful) Remember September.

231. **re-mind-ful**: <u>re</u> (pre: re-again) + <u>mind</u> (O. E. root: gemynd-mind) + <u>ful</u> (adj. suf) = <u>remindful</u>.

232. **re-new**: re (pre: again) + new (O. E. root: neowe-new) = <u>renew</u> (new again).

233. **re-vi-ver** (palindrome): <u>re</u> (pre-again) + <u>vive</u> (L. root: vivere-live) + <u>r</u> (n. suf.) = <u>reviver</u> (help live again).

234. **rhi-no-cer-os**: <u>rhino</u> (G. root: rhinos-nose) + <u>ceros</u> (G. root keras-horn) That <u>rhino</u> <u>cer</u>tainly is huge.

235. **ring-ing**: <u>ring</u> (O. E. hringan-ring) + <u>ing</u> (v. suffix) = <u>ringing</u>.

236. **roy-al-ty**: <u>roy</u> (L. root: <u>roy</u>-king) + <u>al</u> (adj. suf.) + <u>y</u> (noun suf.) *Clue*: <u>Roy</u> felt l<u>oy</u>alty to the r<u>oy</u>alty.

237. **sand-wich**: (First eaten in 18th century by Earl of <u>Sandwich</u> in Kent, who once gambled for 24 hours eating only the beef he put between slices of bread.) You don't put <u>t</u> (tea) in a sandwich.

238. **sax-o-phone**: <u>sax</u> (Sax family-19th century Belgian instrument makers) + <u>o</u> + <u>phone</u> (Gk. root: sound).

239. **sched-ule**: <u>sched</u> (L. root: scheda- paper) + <u>ule</u> (n. suf.) = <u>schedule</u>.

240. **scho-lar-ship**: <u>school</u> (L. root: schole-school) + <u>ar</u> (suf) + <u>ship</u> (n. suf-help shape) = <u>scholarship</u> (help w/school).

241. **se-cede**: <u>se</u> (apart) + <u>cede</u> (L.root: cede-to move) = <u>secede</u> (move apart from; nations seceded during Civil War.)

242. **sec-re-tary**: <u>secret</u> (L. root: secretum-secret) + <u>ary</u> (n. suf. <u>Secretary</u> once meant one trusted with secret matters).

243. **seis-mic** (earth fibrations): <u>seism</u> (G. root: seismos-shake; quake) + ic (adj. suf.) = <u>seismic</u> (re: quakes).

244. **se-ren-i-ty**: <u>seren</u> (L. root: tranquil; peaceful) + <u>ity</u> (n. suf: state of) = <u>serenity</u> (state of peacefulness).

245. **sig-na-ture**: <u>sign</u> (L. root: signare-mark with a sign; inscribe) + <u>ate</u> (adj. suf.) + <u>ure</u> (n. suf.) = <u>signature</u>.

246. **si-rens**: <u>sirens</u> (G. root: sirens-In Greek mythology, the high singing of the <u>Sirens</u> lured sailors to destruction.)

247. **snoop-y** (prying): <u>snoop</u> (Danish root: snoepen-take food on the side) + y (adj. suf). Is <u>Snoopy</u> a <u>snoopy</u> beagle?

248. **soph-ist** (philosopher): <u>soph</u> (G. root: wise) + <u>ist</u> (n. suf: one who) = <u>sophist</u> (one who is wise).

249. **spec-i-al**: <u>species</u> (L. root: species-unique) + <u>al</u> (adj. suf.) = <u>special</u> (unique).

250. **stam-pede**: <u>stamp</u> (Sp. root: estamp-stamp) + <u>ede</u> (n. suf.) = <u>stampede</u>.

251. **sub-mar-ine**: <u>sub</u> (pre: under) + <u>marine</u> (L. root: marinus; Fr. root: marine-sea) = <u>submarine</u> (under the sea).

252. **sub-tle** (easily missed; finely spun): <u>ub</u> (pre-sub-beneath) + <u>tle</u> (L. tilis-web) = <u>subtle</u> (finely spun like a web)

179. **pal-in-dromes**: <u>palin</u> (L. again back) + <u>dromes.</u> (L. running) = <u>palindrome</u> (running-back again).

180. **par-a-chute**: <u>para</u> (Fr. pre: guard against) + <u>chute</u> (Fr. root: falling) = <u>parachute</u> (guard against falling).

181. **par-a-digm**: <u>para</u> (pre: side by side) + <u>digm</u> (G. root: deigma-pattern) = <u>paradigm</u> (a pattern; a standard).

182. **par-al-lel**: <u>para</u> (pre: beside) + <u>all</u> + <u>el</u> (G. root: allele-each other). *See* <u>3 parallel lines</u> *beside each other.*

183. **pen-in-su-la**: <u>pen</u> (prefix. almost) + <u>insula</u> (L. root: island) = <u>peninsula</u> (almost an island).

184. **per-cep-tion**: <u>per</u> (L. per: thoroughly) + <u>cep</u> (L. root: ceptus-take in) + <u>tion</u> (n. suf.) = <u>perception</u>.

185. **per-i-pa-te-tic**: <u>peri</u> (G. peri-around) + <u>pate</u> (G. root-walk) + <u>tic</u> (adj. suf.) = peripatetic (walk around; wander; Aristotle's walking about discussing philosophy). Being <u>peripatetic</u> isn't <u>pathetic</u>: <u>peri</u> + <u>pathetic</u>.

186. **per-mis-sible**: <u>per</u> (pre: to) + <u>miss</u> (L. root: miss-let; allow) + <u>ible</u> (adj. suf.) = <u>permissible</u>.

187. **per-pe-tu-al**: <u>perpetu</u> (L. root: uninterrupted) + <u>al</u> (adj. suf.) + <u>ly</u> (adv. suf.) = <u>perpetually</u>.

188. **pes-si-mism**: <u>pessim</u> (L. root: worst) + <u>ism</u> (n. suf.) = <u>pessimism</u>. *Clue:* I confess, I'm feeling <u>pessimism</u>.

189. **phan-tom**: <u>phantom</u> (G. root: phantasm-image; vision; bring before the mind. Ph = f.) = <u>phantom</u>.

190. **phar-ma-cy**: pharmac (G. root: pharmakia-drugs; ph=f) + y (n. suf.) = <u>pharmacy</u>.

191. **phe-no-men-on**: <u>phenomenon</u> (G. Root: phainomenon-feat, miracle. Ph = f.) = <u>phenomenon</u>.

192. **phil-har-mon-ic**: <u>phil</u> (G. root: love. Ph=f) + <u>harmonic</u> (G. root: harmonica-harmony) = <u>philharmonic</u>

193. **phi-los-o-phy**: (2 G. roots): <u>philo</u> (philos-love) + <u>soph</u> (sophie-wisdom) + <u>y</u> (n. suf.) = <u>philosophy</u>

194. **pho-nics**: <u>phon</u> (G. root: phon-sound) + <u>ics</u> (n. suf.) = <u>phonics</u> (study of sound).

195. **pho-no-graph**: (2 G. roots): <u>phono</u> (phono-sound. Ph=f) + <u>graph</u> (graph-written) = <u>phonograph.</u>

196. **pho-to-graph**: (2 G. roots): <u>photo</u> (photo-light) + <u>graph</u> (graph-map; written) = <u>photograph</u> (light map)

197. **phys-i-cal**: <u>physic</u> (G. root: physic-re: medicine. Ph=f) + <u>al</u> (adj. suf.) = <u>physical</u>.

198. **pic-ture**: <u>pict</u> (L. root: pictus-painting) + <u>ure</u> (n. suf.) = <u>picture</u> (painting).

199. **pla-gia-rize** (present another's work as yours): plagia (L. root: plagiun-kidnap) + ize (v. suf.) = <u>plagiarize</u>.

200. **plane** (flying machine): <u>plane</u> (M. E. <u>planen</u>-like a bird; to soar).

201. **pneu-mon-ia**: <u>pneumon</u> (G. root: lungs) + <u>ia</u> (n. suf.) = <u>pneumonia</u>. <u>Pneu</u> got <u>pneumonia</u> on <u>Mon</u>day.

202. **pos-ses-sion**: <u>possess</u> (M. E. root: possess-gain; win) + <u>ion</u> (n. suf.) = <u>possession</u> (that which is gained).

203. **post-script**: <u>post</u> (pre: after) + <u>script</u> (L. root: scriptum-writing) = <u>postscript</u> (comes after the writing.)

204. **pre-ce-dent**: <u>pre</u> (before) + <u>cedent</u> (L. root: cede-go) = <u>precedent</u> (go before-Courts follow precedents).

205. **pre-his-tor-ic**: <u>pre</u> (before) + <u>history</u> (G. root: historia-knowing) <u>i</u> + <u>c</u> (adj. suf) = <u>prehistoric</u>.

206. **pre-fix**: <u>pre</u> (before) + <u>fix</u> (M.E. root: fixen: fix; attach) = <u>prefix</u> (You attach a <u>prefix</u> before a word).

207. **pre-pare**: <u>pre</u> (before) + <u>pare</u> (M.E. root: paren-make ready: trim) = <u>prepare</u> (make ready before).

208. **pre-scribe**: <u>pre</u> (before) + <u>scribe</u> (L. root: scriptue-write) = <u>prescribe</u> (write before, i.e. prescription).

209. **pre-serve**: <u>pre</u> (prefix-before) + <u>serve</u> (L. root: severe-watch over) = <u>preserve</u> (watch over before).

210. **pres-i-dent**: <u>presid</u> (L. root: presidere-preside; govern) + <u>ent</u> (adj. suf.) = <u>president</u> (one who governs).

211. **prim-i-tive**: <u>prime</u> (L. root: first of its kind) + <u>itive</u> (adj. suf.) = <u>primitive</u> (first of its kind).

212. **pro-cess**: <u>pro</u> (pre: forward) + <u>cess</u> (L. root: cede-moving) = <u>process</u> (moving forward...).

213. **pro-fes-sion-al**: <u>pro</u> (for) + <u>fess</u> (L. root: vow of profession) + <u>ion</u> + <u>al</u> (suffixes) = <u>professional</u>.

214. **pro-phet**: <u>pro</u> (prefix: for) + <u>phet</u> (G. root: phetes-to speak) = <u>prophet</u> (to speak for God).

215. **pro-vi-de**: <u>pro</u> (for; before) + <u>vide</u> (L. root: videre-see) = <u>provide</u> (see before; look after). Provide ride.

441

216. **psy-chi-a-try**: <u>psych</u> (G. root: psyche-spirit; mind) + <u>iatry</u> (re: medicine) = <u>psychiatry</u> (M.D.'s care of mind)

217. **psy-cho-lo-gy**: <u>psych</u> (G. root: psyche-mind) + <u>ology</u> (root: study of) = <u>psychology</u> (study of the mind).

218. **pur-ple**: <u>purple</u> (O.E. purple; K. purpure-purple shellfish known for purple dye) = <u>purple</u>. ♪

219. **pyr-a-mid**: <u>pyramid</u> (G. root: pyramis-fire. It is thought the pyramids looked like huge rising flames.)

220. **quo-ta-tion**: <u>quota</u> (L. root: quotare-divide into verses) + <u>tion</u> (n. suf.) = <u>quotation</u> (part of a verse).

221. **read-i-ly**: <u>ready</u> + <u>i</u> (O.E. root: roedi-prompt) + <u>ly</u> (adv. suf.) = <u>readily</u> (promptly).

222. **re-cede**: <u>re</u> (pre: re-back; again) + <u>cede</u> (L. root: cede-move; go) = <u>recede</u> (to move back).

223. **rec-og-nize**: <u>re</u> (pre: re-again) + <u>cogni</u> (L. root: know) + <u>ze</u> (v. suf.) = <u>recognize</u> (again know).

224. **re-cord-ed**: <u>re</u> (pre: re-again) + <u>cord</u> (L. root: heart) = <u>record</u> (remembered in the heart). ♪

225. **rec-re-a-tion**: <u>re</u> (pre: re-again) + <u>create</u> (L. root: creatus-make) + <u>ion</u> (n. suf.) = <u>recreation</u>.

226. **red**: <u>red</u> (Old Eng. <u>red</u>; Danish <u>rood</u>-color of blood).

227. **re-gal** (word both ways): <u>reg</u> (L. root: royal) + <u>al</u> (adj. suf) = <u>regal</u>. *Reversal:* regal = lager (aged beer).

228. **rel-a-tive**: <u>relate</u> (L. root: relatus-to carry back) + <u>ive</u> (n. suf.) = <u>relative</u>. *Same Root:* relate, relationship

229. **re-mem-ber**: <u>re</u> (again) + <u>member</u> (L. root: mindful) = <u>remember</u> (again mindful) Remember September.

230. **re-mind-ful**: <u>re</u> (pre: re-again) + <u>mind</u> (O. E. root: gemynd-mind) + <u>ful</u> (adj. suf) = <u>remindful</u>.

231. **re-new**: <u>re</u> (pre: again) + <u>new</u> (O. E. root: neowe-new) = <u>renew</u> (new again).

232. **re-vi-ver** (palindrome): <u>re</u> (pre-again) + <u>vive</u> (L. root: vivere-live) + <u>r</u> (n. suf.) = <u>reviver</u> (help live again).

233. **rhi-no-cer-os**: <u>rhino</u> (G. root: rhinos-nose) + <u>ceros</u> (G. root keras-horn) That <u>rhino</u> certainly is huge.

234. **ring-ing**: <u>ring</u> (O. E. hringan-ring) + <u>ing</u> (v. suffix) = <u>ringing</u>.

235. **roy-al-ty**: <u>roy</u> (L. root: roy-king) + <u>al</u> (adj. suf.) + <u>y</u> (noun suf.) *Clue:* <u>Roy</u> felt <u>loyalty</u> to the <u>royalty</u>.

236. **sand-wich**: (1st eaten in 18th century by Earl of <u>Sandwich</u> in Kent, who once gambled for 24 hours eating only the beef he put between slices of bread.) You don't put <u>t</u> (tea) in a sandwich.

237. **sax-o-phone**: <u>sax</u> (Sax family-19th century Belgian instrument makers) + <u>o</u> + <u>phone</u> (Gk. root: sound).

238. **sched-ule**: <u>sched</u> (L. root: scheda- paper) + <u>ule</u> (n. suf.) = <u>schedule</u>.

239. **scho-lar-ship**: <u>school</u> (L. root: schole-school) + <u>ar</u> (suf) + <u>ship</u> (n. suf-help shape) = <u>scholarship</u> (help w/school).

240. **se-cede**: <u>se</u> (apart) + <u>cede</u> (L.root: cede-to move) = <u>secede</u> (move apart from; nations seceded during Civil War.)

241. **sec-re-tary**: <u>secret</u> (L. root: secretum-secret) + <u>ary</u> (n. suf. <u>Secretary</u> once meant one trusted with secret matters).

242. **seis-mic** (earth fibrations): <u>seism</u> (G. root: seismos-shake; quake) + <u>ic</u> (adj. suf.) = <u>seismic</u> (re: quakes).

243. **se-ren-i-ty**: <u>seren</u> (L. root: tranquil; peaceful) + <u>ity</u> (n. suf: state of) = <u>serenity</u> (state of peacefulness).

244. **sig-na-ture**: <u>sign</u> (L. root: signare-mark with a sign; inscribe) + <u>ate</u> (adj. suf.) + <u>ure</u> (n. suf.) = <u>signature</u>.

245. **si-rens**: <u>sirens</u> (G. root: sirens-In Greek mythology, the high singing of the <u>Sirens</u> lured sailors to destruction.)

246. **snoop-y** (prying): <u>snoop</u> (Danish root: snoepen-take food on the side) + y (adj. suf). Is <u>Snoopy</u> a <u>snoopy</u> beagle?

247. **soph-ist** (philosopher): <u>soph</u> (G. root: wise) + <u>ist</u> (n. suf: one who) = <u>sophist</u> (one who is wise).

248. **spec-i-al**: <u>species</u> (L. root: species-unique) + <u>al</u> (adj. suf.) = <u>special</u> (unique).

249. **stam-pede**: <u>stamp</u> (Sp. root: estamp-stamp) + <u>ede</u> (n. suf.) = <u>stampede</u>.

250. **sub-mar-ine**: <u>sub</u> (pre: under) + <u>marine</u> (L. root: marinus; Fr. root: marine-sea) = <u>submarine</u> (under the sea).

251. **sub-tle** (easily missed; finely spun): <u>ub</u> (pre-sub-beneath) + <u>tle</u> (L. tilis-web) = <u>subtle</u> (finely spun like a web)

252. **suc-cess**: <u>suc</u> (pre-from under) + <u>cess</u> (L. ced-move out; prosper) = <u>success</u> (move out from under…).

253. **suc-ces-sion**: <u>suc</u> (from under) + <u>cess</u> (L. root: cede-move) + <u>ion</u> (n. suf.) = <u>succession</u> (move out from under).

254. **su-per-sede**: <u>super</u> (above) + <u>sede</u> (L. root: sede-sit) = supersede (sit above) Only <u>supersede</u> ends in <u>sede</u>.

255. **sym-me-try**: <u>sym</u> (G. root: sym-same) + <u>met</u> (G. root: meter-measure) + <u>ry</u> (n. suf.) = <u>symmetry</u> (same measure).

256. **sym-pho-ny**: <u>sym</u> (G. root: harmonious) + phony (G. root: sound.) = <u>symphony</u> (concert; harmonious sound).

257. **tel-e-phone**: <u>tele</u> (pre-far) + <u>phone</u> (G. root: phone-sound) = <u>telephone</u>. *Phonics*: <u>Ph</u> in Greek = <u>f</u>.

258. **ther-mom-e-ter**: <u>thermo</u> (G. root: thermos-heat) + <u>meter</u> (G. root: metron-measure) = <u>thermometer</u>.

259. **ther-mo-stat**: <u>thermo</u> (G. root: heat) and <u>stat</u> (G. root: stabalizer) = <u>thermostat</u>. *Root*: thermos, thermal.

260. **thun-der**: <u>thun</u> (O. E. Thunor: god of thunder; Norse-Thor: god of thunder;) + <u>der</u> (n. suf.) = <u>thunder</u>.

261. **tide**: <u>tide</u> (Old. Eng. tid: time). *Clue*: Then, and now, <u>time</u> is still often told by the <u>tide</u>.

262. **tor-na-do**: <u>tornar</u> (Sp. root: to twist) + <u>tronada</u> (Sp. root: thunder storm) = <u>tornado</u> (twisting storm; tornadoes).

263. **tra-ge-dy**: <u>trag</u> (G. root: tragos: goat) + <u>edy</u> (G. root edie; oide: song) = <u>tragedy</u> (goat song). Some historians say that *goat song* came to mean *tragedy* because songs were sung over goats sacrificed to gods.

264. **trans-form**: trans (pre: change) + form (L. root: form-structure) = <u>transform</u> (change structure).

265. **trans-late**: <u>trans</u> (pre: across) + <u>late</u> (L. root: carry; transfer) = <u>translate</u> (carry from one language across to another.)

266. **trans-port**: <u>trans</u> (L. prefix-across) + <u>port</u> (L. root: port-carry) = <u>transport</u> (carry across).

267. **tur-quoise**: Turquoise came from <u>Turkish</u> (stone) + <u>oise</u>. *Phonics*: Later, <u>k</u> became <u>qu</u> = <u>turquoise</u>.

268. **ty-ran-no-saur-us rex**: <u>tyrant</u> (L. root: total ruler) + <u>no</u> + <u>saurus</u> (L. root: lizard) + <u>rex</u> (L. root: king).= <u>tyrannosaurus</u> <u>rex</u>.

269. **um-brel-la**: <u>umbra</u> (L. root: umbra-shade) + <u>umbel</u> (L. root: flower with stalks extending from center) + <u>elle</u> (Fr. noun suffix) = <u>umbrella</u> (shade flower).

270. **um-pire**: <u>um</u> (prefix-not) + <u>pire</u> (a peer; equal) = <u>umpire</u> (role not equal to others because he makes calls).

271. **un-a-ware**: <u>un</u> (pre: not) + <u>aware</u> (O. E root: gewaer-watchful) = <u>unaware</u> (not watchful).

272. **un-con-di-tion-al**: <u>un</u> (not) + <u>condition</u> (L. root: influence) + <u>al</u> (adj. suf) = <u>unconditional</u> (not by influence).

273. **un-der-stand**: <u>under</u> (pre: beneath) + <u>stand</u> (L. root: standan-support) = <u>understand</u>.

274. **u-ni-corn**: <u>uni</u> (pre: one) + <u>corn</u> (L. root: cornu-horn) = <u>unicorn</u> (one horned).

275. **u-ni-cy-cle**: <u>uni</u> (L. pre: one) + <u>cycle</u> (L. root: cycle-wheel) = <u>unicycle</u> (one wheel).

276. **u-nique**: <u>uni</u> (L. uni-one) + <u>que</u> (adj. suf. que = k) = <u>unique</u> (unicus-one of a kind). *SPP*: u-ni-qu-e.

277. **u-ni-verse**: <u>uni</u> (pre: one; united) + <u>verse</u> (L.root: versus-turned) = universe (all turned into one; entire).

278. **un-na-tur-al**: <u>un</u> (not) + <u>nature</u> (L. root: natus-born; natural order) + <u>al</u> (adj. suf) = <u>unnatural</u> (not by nat. order).

279. **un-nec-es-sa-ry**: <u>un</u> (prefix: not) + <u>necess</u> (L. necess-needful) + <u>ary</u> (n. suf) = <u>unnecessary</u>.

280. **u-ra-ni-um**: <u>uran</u> (<u>Uran</u>us: supreme Gk. god) + <u>ium</u> (n. suf.) = <u>uranium</u> (element used for nuclear fuel).

281. **ver-dict**: <u>ver</u> (L. root: ver-truth) + <u>dict</u> (L. root: dictus-speak) = <u>verdict</u> (speak truth).

282. **ve-ry**: <u>ver</u> (L. root: verus-truth) + <u>y</u> (adv. suf) = <u>very</u> (truth).

283. **vice-president**: <u>vice</u> (L. in place of) <u>presid</u> (L. root: praesidere-sit in front; preside) + <u>ent</u> (n. suf-one who) = <u>vice president</u> (one who presides...

284. **vi-de-os**: <u>vide</u> (L. root: videre-to see) + <u>o</u> (L. root: audio-to hear) = <u>video</u> (<u>videos</u>-Ital. music words-add -<u>s</u>).

285. **wheel-bar-row**: <u>wheel</u> (O.E. root: hweol-wheel) + <u>barrow</u> (O.E. root: barrow-cart with handles at each end).

286. **white**: <u>white</u> (Lat. root: albus-white. Albus later came to mean album, and many albums are <u>white</u>.)

287. **yellow**: <u>yellow</u> (O.E. root: geolu-yolk; <u>yellow</u> came from the deep color of the yolk).

Tool 7: Visual POWER

POWER Spelling Visual Words You Can Draw

1. **al-tar**: The <u>altar</u> area of many churches rises up like an <u>A</u>.

2. **bi-cy-cle**: Find 2 wheels and a pedal in <u>bicycle</u>: <u>c y c</u>.

3. **bril-li-ant**: There are 4 candles (<u>illi</u>) in the middle of <u>brilliant</u>.

4. **bub-ble**: The <u>3 b</u>'s look like <u>bubble</u> <u>b</u>lowers.

5. **bulb**: The <u>b</u>'s look like <u>bulbs</u> growing up, and <u>u</u> and <u>l</u> are 3 stems.

6. **buz-zing**: The <u>2 z</u>'s look and feel like a <u>buzzing</u> motion: <u>b-u-z-z-i-n-g</u>.

7. **can-yon**: The <u>y</u> goes down like a <u>canyon</u>: <u>y</u>.

8. **col-lege**: See the 2 pi<u>ll</u>ars in <u>college</u>: <u>ll</u>.

9. **col-or**: See (<u>olo</u>) in <u>color</u> as 2 paint jars with an easel in between them: <u>olo</u>.

10. **col-um<u>n</u>**: See 1 tall <u>column</u> (<u>l</u>) and 7 small <u>columns</u> (<u>u m n</u>).

11. **flew**: The <u>w</u> in <u>flew</u> look like 2 birds that flew together: <u>w</u>.

12. **gi-raffe**: See the 2 <u>giraffes</u>: <u>f f</u>.

13. **hic-cup**: See and feel a <u>hiccup</u> in: <u>hic-cup</u>.

14. **high**: See 2 chairs (<u>h h</u>) you can use to climb up <u>high</u>.

15. **hole**: See 1 large <u>hole</u> (<u>o</u>) and a small <u>hole</u> (<u>e</u>) in <u>hole</u>.

16. **ig-loo**: <u>Igloo</u> is shaped like an <u>igloo</u>.

17. **kick-ball**: See the 2 <u>kickers</u> (<u>k k</u>) in <u>kickball</u>.

18. **lar-go**: <u>Largo</u> looks, sounds, and feels slow: <u>largo</u>.

19. **laz-i-ness**: The letters in l-a-z-i-n-e-s-s look and feel lazy.

20. **le-vel**: Notice it's level in between the l's in: l e v e l.

21. **lug-gage**: See 3 g's hanging down (g g g) like luggage and 1 sack (u).

22. **merry-go-round**: Merry-go-round goes around with go in the center.

23. **par-al-lel**: See 3 parallel l's.

24. **pen-i-cil-lin**: See 5 penicillin shots: iilli.

25. **peo-ple**: See the rounded letters as faces of 5 people.

26. **race-car**: Racecar looks long and low like a racecar.

27. **shoe-ing**: See the bottom of a hoof (o) and a horseshoe (e) in shoeing.

28. **splash**: See the letters in splash go: splash.

29. **squig-gles**: The 2 g's look like squiggles: g g.

30. **stac-ca-to**: The letters in staccato look fast like cats: s-t-a-c-c-a-t-o.

31. **sub-mar-ine**: See a long submarine with the b like a periscope.

32. **swim-ming**: See the wave motions in swimming.

33. **ty-phoon**: Phoon looks like wind blowing in typhoon.

34. **wheels**: See 2 wheels (e e) in the middle of wheels

35. **world**: The o in world is round, like a globe.

36. **zoom-ing**: See the wheels (o o) of a zooming racecar.

More POWER Spelling Visual Words You Can Draw

1. **an-gle**: Can you see there's an <u>angle</u> in which to put <u>e</u>: <u>angle</u>.

2. **bal-loon**: In <u>balloon</u>, see two sticks (<u>ll</u>) and two balloons (<u>o o</u>).

3. **bed**: See the headboard and footboard in <u>bed</u>, and it's flat in between.

4. **build**: <u>Build</u> has a sack (<u>u</u>) to put the nails (<u>il</u>) in: <u>build</u>.

5. **call**: The <u>C</u> is a mouth, and you can <u>call</u> <u>all</u> your friends: <u>C + all</u>.

6. **climbed**: You can <u>climb</u> up and over the <u>bed</u>.

7. **cy-cle**: <u>Cycle</u> has two wheels and a seat and pedals: <u>cycle</u>.

8. **eye**: See each <u>eye</u>, plus the rest of the face in the middle: <u>e y e</u>.

9. **feet**: <u>Feet</u> has two slippers (<u>e e</u>) which your <u>feet</u> can slip on..

10. **food**: See the two plates (o o) in the middle of food.

11. **gig-gling**: See the four <u>giggling g</u>'s and laugh with them.

12. **globe**: See the <u>globe</u> (<u>o</u>) in the center of <u>globe</u>.

13. **hum-ming**: <u>Humming</u> looks like it keeps right on <u>hummmming</u>…

14. **hush**: <u>Hush</u> looks and feels and sounds like <u>hush</u>…shhhh…

15. **il-lum-i-nate**: See 2 tall candles (<u>ll</u>) and lots of small ones in <u>illuminate</u>.

16. **lit-tle**: The letters in <u>little</u> make the word look very <u>little</u>.

17. **look**: There are 2 eyes in <u>look</u>: <u>o o</u>.

18. **mir-ror**: See 1 double <u>mirror</u> (<u>m</u>), 3 hand-<u>mirrors</u> (<u>r r r</u>), and one more <u>mirror</u> (<u>o</u>).

19. **mo-not-o-nous**: <u>Monotonous</u> goes <u>on</u> and <u>on</u> in the same <u>monotonous</u> way.

20. **moun-tain**: <u>Mountain</u> goes up and down like a <u>mountain</u>.

21. **palm** (tree; palm of hand): The l's tall like a palm: l.

22. **pil-lar**: There are 2 large pillars (l l) and 1 small pillar (i) in pillar.

23. **pools**: See 3 pools (p o o), a diving board (l), and a water slide (s) in pools.

24. **pop-ping**: See 3 popping p's popping all over.

25. **pup-pet**: Find 3 pet puppets (p p p) in puppet.

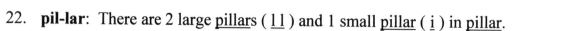

26. **res-cu-ing**: See a person (i) we're rescuing and warming-up in a sleeping bag: u.

27. **riv-er**: See 3 water ways (r v r) that narrow and empty into a river.

28. **school**: See the train that went choo choo at school.

29. **sees**: Find 2 eyes (e e) and 2 ears (s s) in the letters in sees.

30. **sham-poo**: Notice the bubbles in shampoo: oo.

31. **ski-ing**: Find 2 poles (i i) in the middle of skiing.

32. **sleep**: See two eyes (e e) that sleep soundly.

33. **speak**: K is like an opened mouth ready to speak each word.

34. **spring**: The g at the end of spring looks like a spring.

35. **squir-rel**: Look for two little squirrel friends (r r), "Squir and "Rel."

36. **too**: See too stretch out and say, "You gave me toooo….much."

37. **twin-kle**: Just watch the letters twinkle and wink too: twinkle.

38. **um-brel-la**: See the 2 l's that go up like umbrella sticks (l l).

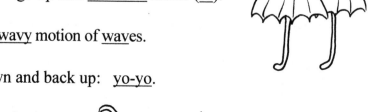

39. **wa-vy**: Wavy looks like the wavy motion of waves.

40. **yo-yo**: See 2 yo-yos go down and back up: yo-yo.

POWER Spelling List of Palindromes

Total Palindromes

civic: *Clue*: It's your civic duty to be civil.

eye: *Visual*: See each eye, nose, and eye.

kayak: *Clue*: Kay was rowing the kayak.

level: *Visual*: The letters inside of level are level.

madam: *Clue*: Madam, I am Adam (sentence palindrome).

racecar: *Compound Word Rule*: Just add race + car = racecar.

radar: *Acronym*: First letters spell RADAR: Radio Detecting and Range.

refer: *Clue*: I'll be your reference when I refer you to her.

reviver: *Rule*: The silent e makes the i in revive long.

rotator: *Rule*: Drop silent e before a vowel suffix: rotate + or.

sagas: *Clue*: Sages (wise ones) of old told sagas (stories or legends).

sees: *Clue*: The bear sees bees and honey trees.

solos: *Rule*: Plural of Italian musical words ends with -s: solos.

toot: *Phonics*: Toot makes the oo sound you hear in moon.

dad	mom	Anna	Eve
deed	peep	Aviva	Hannah
gig	pop	Bob	Otto

Inside Palindromes

banana: *Inside Palindrome*: b-**anana**. *Visual*: See and hear 3 open syllables: ba-na-na.

divide: *Inside Palindrome*: **divid**-e. *Rule*: Silent e makes the second i long in divide.

grammar: *Inside Palindrome*: g-**rammar**: *Clue*: Ma gave me a gram of grammar a day.

igniting: *Inside Palindrome*: i-**gniting**. *Rule*: Drop silent e before vowel suffix: ignite + ing.

monotonous: *Inside Palindrome*: m-**onotono**-us. *Visual*: 4 o's in a row + us: mo-no-to-no + us.

recognizing: *Inside Palindrome*: reco-**gnizing**. *Rule*: Drop silent e before vowel: recognize + ing.

synonym (same name): *Inside Palindrome*: s-**ynony**-m *Roots*: syn (same) + o + nym (name) = synonym.

Phrase and Sentence Palindromes

A man, a plan, a canal – Panama.

Do geese see God?

Niagara, O roar again.

No lemons, no melon.

In a regal age ran I.

Draw, O coward.

Red rum, sir, is murder.

Madam, I'm Adam.

Rise to vote, Sir.

Never a foot too far, even.

Too hot to hoot.

Step on no pets.

Live not on evil, madam. Live not on evil.

Cigar, toss it in a can. It is so tragic.

The POWER Spelling List of Reversals
A Word Both Forwards and Backwards

deer	–	reed:	The deer nibbled on a reed (music pipe, tall grass).
deliver	–	reviled:	He began to deliver a speech that reviled (put down) his opponent.
denim	–	mined:	They wore denim when they mined for gold.
desserts	–	stressed:	We were too stressed for desserts.
dial	–	laid:	I went to dial the phone and then laid it down.
dog	–	God:	Does a dog have unconditional love like God?
Don	–	nod:	Don gave a nod of his head.
doom	–	mood:	Can thinking of doom cause a bad mood?
drab	–	bard:	That bard was not drab (boring) in his poem.
drawer	–	reward:	A reward in my drawer?
edit	–	tide:	I edit tide tables.
faced	–	decaf:	He faced each day with decaf.
gnat	–	tang:	We found a gnat in our Tang.
gum	–	mug:	It's gum on my mug!
hoop	–	Pooh:	Winnie the Pooh plays with a hoop (-oo in moon).
keels	–	sleek:	The keels guide my boat through sleek (smooth) water.
lap	–	pal:	My lap has room for a pal.
Leon	–	Noel:	Leon sang *The First Noel*.
lever	–	revel:	I revel (celebrate) that my lever worked.
liar	–	rail:	The liar took the next rail out of town.
live	–	evil:	Live not on evil (sentence palindrome).
loop	–	pool:	I swam the loop around the pool.
loot	–	tool:	The burglar used a tool to steal the loot.
naps	–	span:	What span of time do most naps last?
not	–	ton:	The young whale did not weigh a ton.
net	–	ten:	I caught ten fish in my net.
now	–	won:	Now, I finally have won!
peek	–	keep:	Keep quiet and peek at the sleeping baby.
pets	–	step:	Step on no pets (sentence palindrome).
pools	–	sloop:	I sail my sloop (sailboat) through pools of clear sea.
pot	–	top:	Keep the top on your pot.
regal	–	lager:	The regal ruler drank his lager (beer).
saw	–	was:	In Rome, everything I saw was amazing.
stew	–	wets:	I wet vegetables for stew to keep them fresh.
sleep	–	peels:	Skin burned in the tropics even peels while you sleep.
snoops	–	spoons:	She snoops for old spoons at garage sales.
stop	–	pots:	Stop the pots from boiling over.
time	–	emit:	In time, he would emit (send forth) wisdom.
tub	–	but:	I'd fill the tub, but the water is cold.
wonder	–	red now:	It's no wonder my hands are red now from painting.

"Live not on Evil!"

POWER Spelling List of Echo Words

Echo Words are words where you can hear the letters at the beginning of the word repeated in the same order at the end. Echoes truly help with spelling since the letters at the end of the word echo back the same letters at the beginning. NOW: For fun, cover the clues. Look, listen and think, and see how many words you can figure out on your own. Then check the clues for additional help.

1.	e d __ e d	bordered
2.	M I __ M I	city in Florida
3.	o n __ o n	vegetable with strong odor
4.	s a __ s a	Mexican sauce made from tomatoes, onions…
5.	s e __ s e	seeing is one; hearing is another…
6.	c h __ __ __ c h	place where some people worship
7.	d e __ __ d e	ten-year period
8.	d e __ __ d e	reach a decision
9.	d e __ __ d e	decipher or unscramble a message
10.	e d __ __ e d	read, checked and corrected errors
11.	E I N __ __ __ E I N	physicist who developed Theory of Relativity
12.	e m __ __ e m	badge; symbol
13.	e r __ __ __ e r	used to rub out writing
14.	G E __ __ G E	male name meaning "farmer"
15.	o r __ __ __ o r	skilled speaker
16.	r e __ __ r e	highly respect
17.	r e __ __ r e	end working, usually at an older age; go to bed
18.	t o __ __ t o	round and red and used in salads
19.	i n __ __ __ __ i n	hormone that controls the body's sugar balance
20.	l e __ __ __ l e	clear; easily read
21.	r e __ __ __ __ r e	need; demand; I _____ that you do this
22.	r e __ __ __ __ r e	bring back to original condition
23.	T O __ __ __ __ T O	capital of Ontario, Canada
24.	e d __ __ __ __ __ e d	schooled
25.	h e __ __ __ __ __ h e	pain in the head
26.	e s __ __ __ __ __ __ e s	calculates approximately
27.	m e __ __ __ __ __ __ m e	device that beats out the rhythm for music
28.	s t __ __ __ __ __ __ s t	steady; loyal
29.	t e __ __ __ __ __ __ t e	bring to an end
30.	u n d __ __ __ __ __ __ u n d	below the top of the earth

4

POWER Spelling List of Bookend Words

Bookend Words are words where the letters at the front of the word are reversed at the end of the word. In this kind of word play, the letters at each end of the word are like matching bookends. NOW: Cover the clues. Look, listen and think, and see how many words you can figure out on your own. Then check the clues for additional help (Note: Find and star the Bookend Palindromes).

1.	c i __ i c	concerning city government and/or citizens
2.	k a __ a k	watertight, Eskimo canoe
3.	l e __ e l	flat, even surface
4.	m a __ a m	title for a woman
5.	s a __ a s	ancient stories; tales or legends
6.	s o __ o s	song sung by one person
7.	s t __ t s	short for the word "statistics"
8.	d e __ __ e d	pushed in from an accident or blow
9.	d e __ __ e d	declare as untrue; past of deny
10.	e n __ __ n e	the part of a car, train… that runs it
11.	e v __ __ v e	change or develop over time
12.	m u __ __ u m	houses objects of historical, artistic and scientific value
13.	n o __ __ o n	fanciful idea; whim; an item like needles, thread…
14.	r e __ __ e r	one who loves books
15.	s e __ __ e s	You have 5: hearing, seeing, feeling, tasting, smelling.
16.	s t __ __ t s	long poles with raised foot rests that you use for walking
17.	s t __ __ t s	skillful, daring, or dangerous acts; feats
18.	d e __ __ __ e d	made a decision
19.	n e __ __ __ e n	men who report the news
20.	r e __ __ __ e r	come back in again; spacecrafts _____ the Earth's atmosphere
21.	r e __ __ __ e r	put new fabric on a couch, chair, etc.
22.	s t __ __ __ t s	narrow channels that join bodies of water
23.	s u __ __ __ u s	amount that is in excess of what is needed
24.	t h __ __ __ h t	something you think; idea
25.	s t __ __ __ __ t s	those who attend school
26.	r e __ __ __ __ e r	jog ones memory
27.	s w __ __ __ __ w s	passes through mouth and throat and into stomach
28.	f o __ __ __ __ __ o f	designed so that it can't be broken into
29.	r e __ __ __ __ __ e r	answer in subtraction; amount that is left in division
30.	s e __ __ __ __ __ e s	beaches; areas of land by the ocean

POWER Spelling List of Anagrams
Anagrams or Ars Magna (Latin)

Anagrams are words, phrases, or sentences that are formed by *rearranging* their letters into another word, phrase, or sentence where the meaning connects both of them.

an-a-gram = <u>ars</u> <u>magna</u> (L. great art): *Roots*: <u>ana</u> (Gk. again) + <u>gram</u> (Gk. things written) = <u>anagram</u>.

as-tron-o-mers = <u>moon</u> <u>starers</u>: *Roots*: <u>astro</u> (Gk. star) + <u>nomy</u> (Gk. management of: n. suf.) + <u>ers</u> (n. suf).

committees = <u>cost me time</u>: *Visual*: See 3 sets of double letters: <u>co-mm-i-tt-ee</u>.

con-si-der-ate = <u>care is needed</u>: *Clue*: They were considerate in the rate they charge.

con-ver-sa-tion = <u>voices rant on</u>: *Rule*: Drop silent <u>e</u> before vowel suffix: <u>converse</u> + <u>ation</u> (n. suf.)

dor-mi-tory = <u>dirty room</u>: *Visual*: <u>Dormitory</u> has 3 words-in-a-row: <u>dorm + it + or + y</u>.

en-dear-ment = <u>tender</u> <u>name</u>: *Clue*: He whispered an <u>endearment</u> in her <u>ear</u>.

float = <u>aloft</u>: *Clue*: A <u>goat</u> was <u>afloat</u> on the <u>boat</u>.

heart = <u>earth</u>: *Clue*: I put my <u>ear</u> close to the <u>earth</u> to hear its <u>heart</u> beat.

measured = <u>made sure</u>: *Clue*: After you've <u>made sure</u>, please give <u>me a sure</u> <u>measure</u>.

moonlight = <u>thin gloom</u>: *Clue*: <u>Soon</u>, in the <u>night</u>, we'll have <u>moonlight</u>.

nu-cle-ar = <u>unclear</u>: Reverse <u>nu</u> in <u>nuclear</u> and you have <u>unclear</u>. *Same Pattern*: dear, hear, tear…

pal-in-drome = <u>splendor am I</u>: *Clue*: There's a <u>pal</u> <u>in</u> <u>palindrome</u>.

post-poned = <u>stopped</u> <u>on</u>: *Clue*: He <u>postponed</u> the test for us to <u>bone</u> up and <u>hone</u> (sharpen) our skills.

puns-ter = <u>run</u> <u>pest</u>: *Clue*: There's the <u>punster</u> whose <u>puns</u> terrorized my ears.

rescue = <u>secure</u>: *Clue*: They gave us a <u>cue</u> on how to <u>rescue</u> them. ☆

separation = <u>one is apart</u>: *Clue*: When they did a <u>separation</u> of the fruit, <u>a rat</u> jumped out.

sig-na-ture = <u>a true sign</u>: *Clue*: Is that my <u>signature</u> for <u>sure</u>?

snoozed = <u>dozes on</u>: *Clue*: The <u>Snoo (and) Zed</u> <u>snoozed</u> together.

sur-geon = <u>go nurse</u>: *Clue-in-a-Row*: My <u>surgeon</u> will <u>surge on</u> through the <u>surgery</u>.

teas (drinks) = <u>east, eats, seat, sate</u> (to satisfy): *Clue*: I enjoys different <u>teas</u> when I <u>eat</u>.

Anagram Phrases

the eyes — <u>They see.</u>

Morse code — <u>Here come dots.</u>

Statue of Liberty — <u>built to stay free</u>

Anagrams — <u>ars magna</u> (Latin for *great art*)

an aisle — <u>is a lane</u>

Valentine poem — <u>pen mate in love</u>

POWER Spelling List of Visual Discoveries

When you start looking at words, there are some pretty amazing Visual Discoveries you can make. Just look below at: *facetious* (not serious), *loaves, sequoia,* and *staccato*!!!

1. **aard-vark**: Notice <u>aa</u> at the beginning of <u>aardvark</u> and another <u>a</u> later (Danish, <u>aarde</u>: earth + <u>varken</u>: pig).

2. **au-di-to-ri-um**: See 5 two-letter syllables: <u>au-di-to-ri-um</u> (L., <u>audi</u>: hear + <u>torium</u>: n. suf.).

3. **ba-na-na**: See <u>3 a's</u>, <u>2 n's</u>, and 3 two-letter syllables in the word: <u>ba-na-na</u>.

4. **church**: <u>Church</u> is an *Echo Word*. The <u>ch</u> at the beginning is echoed at the end: <u>ch-ur-ch</u>.

5. **civ-i-li-za-tion**: See <u>4 i's</u> in <u>civilization</u> and <u>3 i's</u> in <u>civilize</u>.

6. **com-mit-tee**: See 3 double letters in <u>committee</u>: c-o-<u>mm</u>-i-<u>tt</u>-<u>ee</u>.

7. **di-vide**: Look for <u>divid</u>, a palindrome inside of <u>divide</u>. Add <u>e</u> to make the <u>i</u> in <u>divide</u> long.

8. **e-le-ven**: See <u>3 e's</u>, in between single consonants in <u>eleven</u>.

9. **ex-cel-lent**: Look for <u>3 e's</u> and a <u>cell</u> in <u>excellent</u>.

10. **ex-per-i-ence**: Help <u>Eri</u> find <u>4 e's</u> and <u>one i</u> in <u>experience</u>.

11. **for-ty**: Notice that <u>forty</u> contains no <u>u</u> or <u>four</u>, but <u>four</u>, <u>four</u>teen, and twenty-<u>four</u> all do.

12. **fa-ce-tious** (not serious): See a <u>face</u> and the vowels (<u>a-e-i-o-u</u>) in order in <u>facetious</u>.

13. **gag-gle** (a group of geese): See <u>3 g's</u> gaggling with <u>gle</u>e in <u>gaggle</u>.

14. **gig-gling**: See: <u>4 g's</u> that like to <u>gig</u>gle in <u>giggling</u>.

15. **in-de-pen-dence**: See <u>4 e's</u> in <u>dependence</u>. Add prefix <u>in</u> + <u>dependence</u> = <u>independence</u>.

16. **in-dis-crim-i-na-tion**: See 7 words-in-a-row in <u>indiscrimination</u>: <u>in</u> - <u>disc</u> - <u>rim</u> – <u>in</u> - <u>at</u> - <u>I</u> - <u>on</u>.

17. **in-fi-ni-ty**: See <u>3 i's</u> and 3 words-in-a-row in <u>infinity</u>: <u>in</u> - <u>fin</u> - <u>it</u> - y (L., <u>in</u>-not + <u>finite</u>: ending + <u>y</u>).

18. **lim-it-ing**: See <u>3 i's</u> in between single consonants in <u>limiting</u>.

19. **lla-ma**: See the <u>double l</u> (<u>ll</u>) at the beginning of <u>llama</u>.

20. **loaves**: Notice that if you take <u>a</u> out of <u>loaves</u>, you have <u>loves</u>.

21. **mid-dle**: Notice that <u>middle</u> has <u>dd</u> in the <u>middle</u>: mi – <u>dd</u> – le.

22. **lul-la-by**: See the 3 l's that <u>lull</u> you to sleep in <u>lullaby</u>: <u>l</u>-u-<u>l</u>-<u>l</u>-a-b-y.

23. **Mis-sis-sip-pi**: See <u>4 i's</u> and 3 double letters in <u>Mississippi</u>: M-<u>i</u>-<u>ss</u>-<u>i</u>-<u>ss</u>-<u>i</u>-<u>pp</u>-<u>i</u>.

24. **mo-no-to-nous**: See <u>4 monotonous o's</u> in between single consonants in: <u>mo</u>-<u>no</u>-<u>to</u>-<u>no</u> + <u>us</u>.

25. **mur-mur**: See 3 repeated letters in <u>murmur</u>: <u>mur</u> - <u>mur</u>.

26. **never-the-less**: See <u>4 e's</u> and 3 words-in-a-row in <u>nevertheless</u>: <u>never</u> - <u>the</u> - <u>less</u>.

27. **ninth**: You find only 1 vowel and no nine in <u>ninth</u>. The <u>i</u> in <u>ninth</u> should really be short.

28. **pop-ping**: See <u>3 popping p's</u> in <u>popping</u>.

29. **pre-ferred**: See: <u>3 e's</u> and <u>3 r's</u> in <u>preferred</u>: p-<u>r</u>-<u>e</u>-f-<u>e</u>-<u>rr</u>-<u>e</u>-d. Also, we <u>prefer red</u>.

30. **pos-ses-sion**: See 2 sets of <u>ss</u> in <u>possession</u>: p-o-<u>ss</u>-e-<u>ss</u>-i-o-n.

31. **ref-er-ence**: See <u>4 e's</u> in <u>reference</u>. Also, <u>4 e's</u> are in <u>preference</u> and <u>deference</u>.

32. **re-mem-ber**: See <u>3 e's</u> with consonants in between in <u>r-e-m-e-m-b-e-r</u> and De<u>cember</u>.

33. **re-pe-ti-tion**: See the <u>repetition</u> of <u>e's</u> and <u>ti's</u>: <u>re + pe + ti + ti + on</u> = <u>repetition</u> (Also, find <u>pet</u>).

34. **rhy-thm**: Notice, there's just one vowel and each 3-letter-syllable has an <u>h</u> in <u>rhythm</u>: <u>rhy</u> - <u>thm</u>.

35. **scis-sors**: See the <u>silent c</u> and <u>4 s's</u> in <u>scissors</u>: <u>s</u>-c-i-<u>s</u>-<u>s</u>-o-r-<u>s</u>. Now, hear <u>3 s's</u> make a <u>z sound</u>.

36. **se-quoi-a**: Notice that the great <u>Sequoia</u> has all 5 vowels: <u>Sequoia</u>: <u>e</u>-<u>u</u>-<u>o</u>-<u>i</u>-<u>a</u>.

37. **stac-ca-to** (quick notes): Find a palindrome in <u>staccato</u> and each <u>cat</u> back to back: <u>s-taccat-o</u>.

38. **strength**: <u>Strength</u> is the English word with the most consonants per vowel: 7 to 1.

39. **su-per-in-ten-dent**: See 4 words-in-a-row in superintendent: <u>super</u> - <u>in</u> - <u>ten</u> - <u>dent</u>.

40. **un-no-tice-a-bly**: Start with <u>a</u>, and find all the vowels in reverse order (<u>uoiea</u>) in <u>unnoticeably</u>

41. **un-u-su-al**: See <u>3 u's</u> in <u>unusual</u>: <u>u</u>-n-<u>u</u>-s-<u>u</u>-a-l.

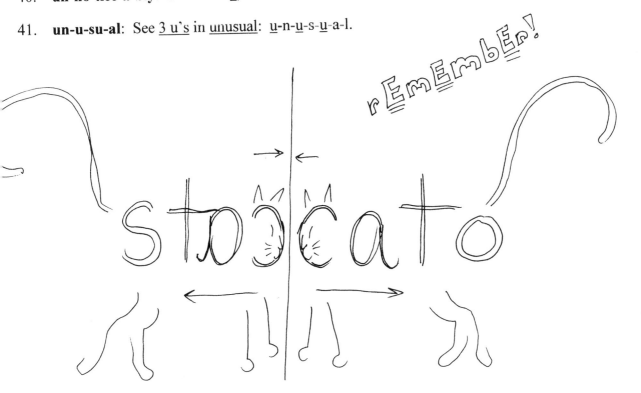

POWER Spelling Searching for Words: Game 1

The *Searching for Words Game* helps develop your visual abilities in spelling. Cover the answers, and write each word on a sheet of paper. Then, go through the word alphabetically, and see how many words you can find. Once you see the words inside, you can create clues if you'd like.

a-mused: Find 10 words: <u>a</u>, <u>am</u>, <u>amuse</u>, <u>amused</u>, <u>Ed</u>, <u>muse</u>, <u>mused</u>, <u>us</u>, <u>use</u>, <u>used</u>.

ap-peared: Find 9 words: <u>a</u>, <u>an</u>, <u>appear</u>, <u>are</u>, <u>ear</u>, <u>eared</u>, <u>pea</u>, <u>pear</u>, <u>red</u>.

be-gin-ning: Find 8 words: <u>be</u>, <u>beg</u>, <u>begin</u>, <u>gin</u>, <u>I</u>, <u>in</u>, <u>inn</u>, <u>inning</u>. *Clue:* In the <u>beginning</u>, I lived at an i

be-lieve: Find 6 words: <u>be</u>, <u>belie</u>, <u>Eli</u>, <u>eve</u>, <u>I</u>, <u>lie</u>. *Clue:* Don't <u>believe</u> a <u>lie</u>.

braid-ed: Find 10 words: <u>a</u>, <u>aid</u>, <u>aide</u>, <u>aided</u>, <u>bra</u>, <u>braid</u>, <u>Ed</u>, <u>I</u>, <u>raid</u>, <u>raided</u>.

com-for-ta-ble: Find 9 words: <u>a</u>, <u>ab</u>, <u>able</u>, <u>comfort</u>, <u>for</u>, <u>fort</u>, <u>or</u>, <u>tab</u>, <u>table</u>.

cup-board: Find 7 words: <u>a</u>, <u>board</u>, <u>boar</u>, <u>boa</u>, <u>cup</u>, <u>oar</u>, <u>up</u>.

de-sired: Find 8 words: <u>desire</u>, <u>Ed</u>, <u>I</u>, <u>ire</u>, <u>red</u>, <u>sir</u>, <u>sire</u>, <u>sired</u>.

flow-ered: Find 12 words: <u>Ed</u>, <u>ere</u>, <u>Flo</u>, <u>flow</u>, <u>flower</u>, <u>low</u>, <u>lower</u>, <u>lowered</u>, <u>ow</u>, <u>owe</u>, <u>red</u>, <u>were</u>.

grow-ing: Find 9 words: <u>grow</u>, <u>I</u>, <u>in</u>, <u>ow</u>, <u>owing</u>, <u>row</u>, <u>rowing</u>, <u>win</u>, <u>wing</u>.

heart: Find 5 words: <u>a</u>, <u>art</u>, <u>ear</u>, <u>he</u>, <u>hear</u>. *Clue:* Can you <u>hear</u> my <u>heart</u>?

im-por-tant: Find 9 words: <u>a</u>, <u>an</u>, <u>ant</u>, <u>I</u>, <u>I'm</u>, <u>imp</u>, <u>import</u>, <u>or</u>, <u>port</u>, <u>tan</u>. *Clue:* An <u>ant</u> is <u>important</u>.

lan-tern: Find 5 words: <u>a</u>, <u>an</u>, <u>ant</u>, <u>ante</u>, <u>tern</u> (bird).

knowl-edge: Find 10 words: <u>Ed</u>, <u>edge</u>, <u>know</u>, <u>knowledge</u>, <u>led</u>, <u>ledge</u>, <u>no</u>, <u>now</u>, <u>on</u>, <u>owl</u>.

lone-li-ness: Find 7 words: <u>Eli</u>, <u>I</u>, <u>in</u>, <u>line</u>, <u>lone</u>, <u>one</u>, <u>on</u>.

nar-rowed: Find 10 words: <u>a</u>, <u>arrow</u>, <u>Ed</u>, <u>ow</u>, <u>owe</u>, <u>owed</u>, <u>row</u>, <u>rowed</u>, <u>wed</u>, <u>we</u>.

pal-a-ces: Find 8 words: <u>a</u>, <u>ace</u>, <u>aces</u>, <u>Al</u>, <u>lace</u>, <u>laces</u>, <u>pa</u>, <u>pal</u> (My pal drew an <u>ace</u> at the <u>Palace</u>).

pan-thers: Find 10 words: <u>a</u>, <u>an</u>, <u>ant</u>, <u>anther</u>, <u>anthers</u>, <u>her</u>, <u>hers</u>, <u>pan</u>, <u>pant</u>, <u>the</u>.

pleased: Find 10 words: <u>a</u>, <u>as</u>, <u>ease</u>, <u>eased</u>, <u>Ed</u>, <u>lease</u>, <u>leased</u>, <u>plea</u>, <u>pleas</u>, <u>please</u>.

rank-ings: Find 9 words: <u>a</u>, <u>an</u>, <u>I</u>, <u>in</u>, <u>kin</u>, <u>king</u>, <u>kings</u>, <u>ran</u>, <u>rank</u>.

sea-shore: Find 9 words: <u>a</u>, <u>as</u>, <u>ash</u>, <u>ashore</u>, <u>or</u>, <u>ore</u>, <u>sea</u>, <u>seas</u>, <u>shore</u>.

sled-ding: Find 7 words: <u>din</u>, <u>ding</u>, <u>Ed</u>, <u>I</u>, <u>in</u>, <u>led</u>, <u>sled</u>.

space-ship: Find 13 words: <u>a</u>, <u>ace</u>, <u>aces</u>, <u>hi</u>, <u>hip</u>, <u>I</u>, <u>pa</u>, <u>pace</u>, <u>paces</u>, <u>ship</u>, <u>spa</u>, <u>space</u>, <u>spaces</u>.

sparked: Find 9 words: <u>a</u>, <u>ark</u>, <u>Ed</u>, <u>pa</u>, <u>par</u>, <u>park</u>, <u>parked</u>, <u>spa</u>, <u>spark</u>.

su-per-in-ten-dent: Find 12 words: <u>den</u>, <u>dent</u>, <u>end</u>, <u>I</u>, <u>in</u>, <u>intend</u>, <u>per</u>, <u>super</u>, <u>superintend</u>, <u>tend</u>, <u>ten</u>, <u>up</u>.

teach-ing: Find 8 words: <u>a</u>, <u>aching</u>, <u>chin</u>, <u>each</u>, <u>I</u>, <u>in</u>, <u>tea</u>, <u>teach</u>.

twin-kled: Find 9 words: <u>Ed</u>, <u>I</u>, <u>in</u>, <u>ink</u>, <u>led</u>, <u>twin</u>, <u>twinkle</u>, <u>win</u>, <u>wink</u>.

throw-ing: Find 9 words: <u>I</u>, <u>in</u>, <u>ow</u>, <u>owing</u>, <u>row</u>, <u>rowing</u>, <u>throw</u>, <u>win</u>, <u>wing</u>.

un-der-stand-ing: 13 words: <u>a</u>, <u>an</u>, <u>and</u>, <u>din</u>, <u>ding</u>, <u>I</u>, <u>in</u>, <u>Stan</u>, <u>stand</u>, <u>standing</u>, <u>tan</u>, <u>under</u>, <u>understand</u>.

your-self: Find 7 words: <u>elf</u>, <u>our</u>, <u>ours</u>, <u>self</u>, <u>you</u>, <u>your</u>, <u>yours</u>.

NOW: Choose a few of your own words and list the words you see inside of them.

POWER Spelling Searching for Words: Game 2

❏ **Searching for Words Game**: This game helps develop your ability to look closely at words. To play, simply write a *Search Word* on a piece of paper. Then go through the word alphabetically and list the words you find beginning with a. Once you see all the words inside, it's easy to create *Clues*.

ad-o-les-cent: Find 8 words: <u>a</u>, <u>ad</u>, <u>ado</u>, <u>cent</u>, <u>do</u>, <u>dole</u>, <u>ole</u>, <u>scent</u>.

ad-van-tage-ous: Find 9 words: <u>a</u>, <u>ad</u>, <u>age</u> <u>an</u>, <u>ant</u>, <u>tan</u>, <u>us</u>, <u>van</u>, <u>vantage</u>.

an-i-mat-ed: Find 13 words: <u>a</u>, <u>an</u>, <u>anima</u>, <u>animate</u>, <u>at</u>, <u>ate</u>, <u>Ed</u>, <u>I</u>, <u>ma</u>, <u>mat</u>, <u>mate</u>, <u>mated</u>, <u>Ted</u>.

as-pir-at-ed (made h sound): Find 15 words: <u>a</u>, <u>as</u>, <u>asp</u>, <u>aspirate</u>, <u>at</u>, <u>ate</u>, <u>Ed</u>, <u>I</u>, <u>Ira</u>, <u>irate</u>, <u>pirate</u>, <u>pirated</u>, <u>rat</u>, <u>rated</u>, <u>Ted</u>.

as-sis-tant: Find 11 words: <u>a</u>, <u>an</u>, <u>ant</u>, <u>as</u>, <u>ass</u>, <u>assist</u>, <u>I</u>, <u>is</u>, <u>sis</u>, <u>Stan</u>, <u>tan</u>. *Clue*: My <u>assistant</u> was an <u>ant</u>.

can-di-date: Find 10 words: <u>a</u>, <u>an</u>, <u>and</u>, <u>ate</u>, <u>can</u>, <u>candid</u> (direct), <u>date</u>, <u>did</u>, <u>id</u>, <u>I</u>.

chal-len-ging: Find 10 words: <u>a</u>, <u>Al</u>, <u>all</u>, <u>Allen</u>, <u>gin</u>, <u>ha</u>, <u>hall</u>, <u>I</u>, <u>in</u>, <u>Len</u>.

com-pas-sion-ate: Find 15 words: <u>a</u>, <u>as</u>, <u>ass</u>, <u>at</u>, <u>ate</u>, <u>compass</u>, <u>compassion</u>, <u>I</u>, <u>ion</u>, <u>Nat</u>, <u>Nate</u>, <u>pass</u>, <u>passion</u>, <u>passionate</u>, <u>on</u>.

com-pe-tent: Find 5 words: <u>compete</u>, <u>pet</u>, <u>Pete</u>, <u>ten</u>, <u>tent</u>.

dis-cour-aged: 14 words: <u>a</u>, <u>age</u>, <u>aged</u>, <u>courage</u>, <u>disc</u>, <u>discourage</u>, <u>Ed</u>, <u>I</u>, <u>is</u>, <u>our</u>, <u>rag</u>, <u>rage</u>, <u>raged</u>, <u>scour</u>.

es-tab-lish-ment: Find 9 words: <u>a</u>, <u>ab</u>, <u>establish</u>, <u>I</u>, <u>is</u>, <u>me</u>, <u>men</u>, <u>stab</u>, <u>tab</u>.

ex-per-i-men-tal-ly: Find 14 words: <u>a</u>, <u>Al</u>, <u>ally</u>, <u>experiment</u>, <u>experimental</u>, <u>I</u>, <u>I'm</u>, <u>me</u>, <u>men</u>, <u>mental</u>, <u>per</u>, <u>rime</u> (tale), <u>tall</u>, <u>tally</u>.

im-me-di-ate: Find 8 words: <u>a</u>, <u>at</u>, <u>ate</u>, <u>Ed</u>, <u>I</u>, <u>me</u>, <u>med</u>, <u>mediate</u> (settle a dispute).

im-mi-gra-te: Find 14 words: <u>a</u>, <u>at</u>, <u>ate</u>, <u>Ed</u>, <u>grate</u>, <u>grated</u>, <u>I</u>, <u>immigrate</u>, <u>migrate</u>, <u>migrated</u>, <u>rat</u>, <u>rate</u>, <u>rated</u>, <u>Ted</u>. *Clue*: When I <u>immigrate</u>, <u>I'm</u> <u>migrating</u> to a new place.

in-ci-den-tal-ly: Find 14 words: <u>a</u>, <u>Al</u>, <u>all</u>, <u>ally</u>, <u>den</u>, <u>dent</u>, <u>dental</u>, <u>I</u>, <u>id</u>, <u>in</u>, <u>incident</u>, <u>incidental</u>, <u>tall</u>, <u>tally</u>.

in-de-pen-dent: Find 6 words: <u>den</u>, <u>dent</u>, <u>dependence</u>, <u>end</u>, <u>in</u>, <u>pen</u>.

in-ter-est-ing: Find 8 words: <u>ere</u>, <u>I</u>, <u>in</u>, <u>interest</u>, <u>resting</u>, <u>rest</u>, <u>sting</u>, <u>tin</u>.

o-rig-i-nal: Find 9 words: <u>a</u>, <u>Al</u>, <u>Gina</u>, <u>gin</u>, <u>I</u>, <u>in</u>, <u>or</u>, <u>origin</u>, <u>rig</u>. *Clue*: I saw the <u>original</u> <u>rig in Al</u>'s yard.

op-er-ated: Find 12 words: <u>a</u>, <u>at</u>, <u>ate</u>, <u>Ed</u>, <u>era</u>, <u>opera</u>, <u>operate</u>, <u>per</u>, <u>rat</u>, <u>rate</u>, <u>rated</u>, <u>Ted</u>.

pa-ren-the-ses: Find 11 words: <u>a</u>, <u>are</u>, <u>aren't</u>, <u>he</u>, <u>he's</u>, <u>pa</u>, <u>parent</u>, <u>rent</u>, <u>the</u>, <u>these</u>, <u>theses</u>.

phe-no-me-non: Find 8 words: <u>he</u>, <u>hen</u>, <u>me</u>, <u>men</u>, <u>no</u>, <u>non</u>, <u>omen</u>, <u>on</u>.

sat-is-fac-tion: Find 11 words: <u>a</u>, <u>at</u>, <u>act</u>, <u>action</u>, <u>fact</u>, <u>faction</u>, <u>I</u>, <u>is</u>, <u>on</u>, <u>tis</u>, <u>sat</u>.

search-ing: Find 11 words: <u>a</u>, <u>arc</u>, <u>arch</u>, <u>arching</u>, <u>chin</u>, <u>ear</u>, <u>I</u>, <u>in</u>, <u>sea</u>, <u>sear</u> (burn), <u>search</u>.

sig-ni-fi-cant: Find 8 words: <u>a</u>, <u>an</u>, <u>ant</u>, <u>can</u>, <u>can't</u>, <u>I</u>, <u>if</u>, <u>sign</u>. *Clue*: This is <u>significant</u>, so <u>sign</u> <u>if</u> <u>I</u> <u>can't</u>.

the-a-ter: Find 8 words: <u>a</u>, <u>at</u>, <u>ate</u>, <u>eat</u>, <u>eater</u>, <u>heat</u>, <u>heater</u>, <u>the</u>.

yearn-ing: Find 8 words: <u>a</u>, <u>ear</u>, <u>earn</u>, <u>earning</u>, <u>I</u>, <u>in</u>, <u>year</u>, <u>yearn</u>. *Clue*: This <u>year</u>, <u>I'm</u> <u>yearning</u> for a dog.

NOW: Choose a few of your own words and list the words you see inside of them.

POWER Spelling List of Sight-Recognition Words

These words are so commonly used that they need to be recognized on sight. Also, since some of these words are irregular and don't follow the rules of phonics, they *must* be learned and memorized. Use *Clues* and *Tools* so you can know and recognize *all* these words forever!

a	began	different	from	in
about	begin	do	get	into
above	being	does	girl	is
add	below	don't	give	island
adjective	between	door	go	it
after	big	down	good	it's
again	book	each	got	its
air	both	earth	great	just
all	boy	eat	group	keep
almost	bread	end	grow	kind
along	but	enough	had	know
also	by	even	hand	land
although	call	every	hard	large
always	came	example	has	last
an	can	eyes	have	late
and	car	face	he	learn
animal	carry	family	head	leave
another	catch	far	hear	left
answer	change	father	help	let
any	child	feather	her	letter
are	children	feet	here	life
around	chose	few	high	light
as	city	find	him	like
ask	cold	first	his	line
away	color	follow	home	list
back	come	food	house	listen
be	could	for	how	little
because	country	form	I	live
become	cut	found	idea	long
been	day	four	if	look
before	did	friends	important	love

made	oil	science	the	want
make	old	sea	their	was
man	on	second	them	watch
many	once	see	then	water
may	one	seem	there	way
me	only	sentence	these	we
mean	open	set	they	well
measure	or	should	they're	went
men	other	show	thing	were
might	our	side	think	what
mile	out	sign	this	when
miss	over	small	those	where
more	own	so	though	which
most	page	some	thought	while
mother	paper	something	three	white
mountain	part	sometimes	through	who
move	people	song	time	whose
much	picture	soon	to	why
must	piece	sound	today	will
my	place	spell	together	with
name	plant	start	too	without
near	play	state	took	woman
need	point	still	tree	women
never	put	stop	try	words
new	read	story	turn	work
next	really	stretch	two	world
night	right	study	under	would
no	river	such	until	write
not	run	sure	up	year
now	said	take	us	you
number	same	talk	use	young
of	saw	tell	usually	your
off	say	than	very	you're
often	school	that	walk	youth

MOUNTAIN

I did it!

45

Visual Tools and Clues for Sight Recognition Words

Sight Recognition Words need to be recognized on sight because they're words you see and use all the time; plus, some of them can't be sounded out. Use *Visual Tools*, *Clues*, and *Same Pattern* to learn these very important words now. Then reading and writing will come be much easier for you.

1. **a-bout**: *See*: <u>out</u> in <u>about</u>. *Clue*: The cat was <u>about</u> to go <u>out</u>: <u>a</u> + b + <u>out</u>.

2. **a-bove**: *Visual*: <u>a + bove</u> = <u>above</u>. *Clue*: I see <u>a dove</u> flying <u>above</u>. *Same Pattern*: dove, love.

3. **add** (v., add together): *Visual*: <u>Add</u> a <u>d</u> to <u>ad</u> (advertisement)and you have <u>add</u>.

4. **af-ter**: *Roots*: <u>aft</u> (O. Fr., back part of boat) + <u>er</u> (suf.) = <u>after</u> (behind; in back).

5. **a-gain**: *Visual*: <u>a + gain</u> = <u>again</u>. *Clue-in-a-Row*: Do it <u>again</u> and <u>again</u> and make <u>a gain</u>.

6. **air**: *Clue*: The <u>air</u> was <u>fair</u> today. *See Same Pattern* in: air, fair, hair, pair.

7. **al-most**: *Visual*: <u>al + most</u> = <u>almost</u>. *Rule*: <u>All</u> always drops <u>one l</u>: al̶l̶ + <u>most</u> = <u>almost</u>.

8. **a-long**: *Visual*: <u>a + long</u> = <u>along</u>. *Clue-in-a-Row*: Come <u>along</u> on <u>a long</u> trip with us.

9. **al-so**: *Rule*: <u>All</u> always drop <u>one l</u>: al̶l̶ + <u>so</u> = <u>also</u>. *See Same Pattern*: also, almost.

10. **al-though**: *Visual*: <u>thou + gh</u> = <u>though</u>. *Rule*: <u>All</u> drops <u>one l</u>: al̶l̶ + <u>though</u> = <u>although</u>.

11. **al-ways**: *Clue-in-a-Row*: I gave <u>Al ways</u> to <u>always</u> find me. *Rule*: Drop <u>one l</u>: al̶l̶ + <u>ways</u>.

12. **and**: *Visual*: <u>an + d</u> = <u>and</u>. *Phonics*: See and *say* the *Blend*: <u>a-n-d</u>.

13. **an-i-mal**: *See*: <u>I</u> and <u>ma</u> in <u>animal</u>. *Clue*: <u>I</u> took <u>ma</u> an <u>animal</u> (L. <u>anim</u>: alive + <u>al</u>: suf. = <u>animal</u>).

14. **a-no-ther**: *Visual*: <u>an + other</u> = <u>another</u>. *Clue-in-a-Row*: <u>Another</u> means *an other*.

15. **ans-wered**: *See*: <u>were</u> in <u>answered</u>. *Clue*: <u>Were</u> your questions <u>answered</u>?

16. **an-y**: *Visual*: <u>an + y</u> = <u>any</u>. *Clue*: Since I don't have <u>many</u> books, <u>any</u> would be great.

17. **are**: *Visual*: <u>are + a</u> = <u>area</u>. *Clue*: I c<u>are</u> that you <u>are</u> here in the <u>area</u>.

18. **a-round**: *Phonics*: See *Blend*: <u>rou + n-d</u>. *Same Pattern*: around, found.

19. **asked**: *See*: <u>ask</u> + <u>Ed</u>. *Clue-in-a-Row*: When I <u>asked</u> to help, he said, "<u>Ask Ed</u> for a t<u>ask</u>."

20. **a-way**: *Visual*: <u>a + way</u> = <u>away</u>. *Clue-in-a-Row*: While we're <u>away</u>, I need <u>a way</u> to get my mail.

21. **back**: *See*: <u>c</u> and <u>k</u> in <u>back</u>. *See Same Pattern*: back, lack, Mack, sack, tack (O.E. bac: back).

22. **be-cause**: *Visual*: <u>be + cause</u>. *SPP*: be-ca-<u>use</u>. *Same Pattern*: because, cause, pause.

23. **be-come**: *See*: <u>be + come</u> = <u>become</u>. *Clue*: How did I <u>become me</u>? *SPP*: be-co-me.

24. **been**: *See*: <u>bee</u> in <u>been</u>. *Clue*: That <u>bee</u> has <u>been</u> sleeping on my flower. *Same Pattern*: been, seen.

25. **be-fore**: *See*: <u>be + fore</u> = before. *Compound Rule*: <u>be</u> + <u>fore</u> = <u>before</u>. *Pattern*: fore, core, more.

26. **be-gan**: *Visual*: <u>beg + an</u> = <u>began</u>. *Clue*: We <u>began</u> to help our <u>gander</u> fly again.

27. **be-gin**: *Visual*: <u>be + gin</u> = <u>begin</u>. *Clue-in-a-Row*: Can I <u>beg in</u> before we <u>begin</u>?

28. **be-low**: *Clue*: I sat in the <u>row</u> <u>below</u>. *VV Rule*: W makes <u>o</u> long. *Pattern*: below, bestow (give).

29. **be-neath**: *Clue*: We like to <u>eat</u> <u>beneath</u> a wr<u>eath</u>. *Same Pattern*: beneath, eat, wreath.

30. **bet-ter**: *See*: <u>ette</u> in b-<u>ette</u>-r. *Rule*: <u>2 t's</u> keep <u>e</u> short. *Same Pattern*: better, letter, wetter.

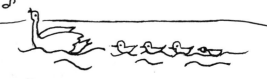

31. **be-tween**: *See*: <u>be</u> and <u>wee</u> in <u>between</u> . *Clue*: Let my seat <u>be</u> <u>between</u> the <u>wee</u> people.

32. **big**: *Clue*: Di<u>g</u> a <u>big</u> hole. *See Same Pattern*: big, dig, fig, gig, jig, pig, wig.

33. **book**: *Visual*: <u>Book</u> has 2 eyes (o o) with which to read. Same *Pattern*: cook, look, took.

34. **both**: *Clue*: <u>Both</u> m<u>oths</u> have wings like c<u>loth</u>. *Same Visual Pattern*: both, cloth, moth.

35. **boy**: *Clue*: The <u>boy</u> felt j<u>oy</u> with his t<u>oy</u>. *See Same Pattern*: boy, joy, toy.

36. **bread**: *See* <u>read</u> in <u>bread</u>. *Clue*: I <u>read</u> a book on making <u>bread</u>. *SPP*: bre-ad.

37. **but**: *Reversal*: <u>but</u> – <u>tub</u>. *Clue*: C<u>ut</u> snowflakes, <u>but</u> don't get c<u>ut</u>. *Same Pattern*: cut, hut.

38. **by**: *Clue*: We walked <u>by</u> <u>my</u> park. *Same Pattern*: by, my, why.

39. **call**: *See*: <u>all</u> in c<u>all</u>. *Clue*: They <u>call</u> the game F<u>all</u> B<u>all</u>.

40. **came**: *Visual* and *Rule*: <u>Silent e</u> turns <u>Cam</u> into <u>came</u>. *Clue*: You called my n<u>ame</u> and I c<u>ame</u>.

41. **can**: *Visual*: <u>c</u> + <u>an</u> = <u>can</u>. *Phonics*: <u>c</u> = <u>k</u>. *Clue*: <u>Can</u> that m<u>an</u> get a t<u>an</u>?

42. **car**: *Clue*: I drive f<u>ar</u> in my <u>car</u>. *See Same Pattern*: car, far, star.

43. **carry**: *Visual*: <u>car</u> + <u>ry</u> = <u>carry</u>. *See Same Pattern*: carry, Larry, marry, tarry (go slowly).

44. **catch**: *See*: <u>cat</u> + <u>ch</u> (digraph) = <u>catch</u>. *Clue*: My <u>cat</u> can <u>catch</u> a <u>ch</u>erry. *Same Pattern*: latch, match.

45. **change**: *SPP*: chan-ge. *Digraph*-<u>ch</u> in <u>change</u>. *Same Pattern* in: change, range, strange.

46. **child**: *See*: <u>hi</u> in c<u>hi</u>ld. *Clue*: Say <u>hi</u> to your <u>child</u>.

47. **chil-dren**: *Visual*: <u>child</u> + <u>ren</u> = <u>children</u>. *Clue*: Each <u>child</u> counted to t<u>en</u>.

48. **choose**: *Clue*: <u>Choose</u> a g<u>oose</u>. *Phonics*: <u>oo</u> sound; <u>s</u> = <u>z</u>; *Same Pattern*: choose, loose, moose.

49. **chose**: *See*: <u>hose</u> in c<u>hose</u>. *Clue*: I <u>chose</u> a r<u>ose</u>. *Phonics*: <u>s</u> = <u>z</u>. *Same Pattern*: hose, rose.

50. **ci-ty**: *Find* <u>it</u> in the middle of c<u>it</u>y. *Phonics*: <u>c</u> = <u>s</u>. *Same Pattern*: city, pity.

51. **cold**: *See*: <u>old</u> in c<u>old</u>. *Clue*: When it's <u>cold</u>, I feel b<u>old</u>. *Rule Ex*: <u>co</u> + <u>ld</u> = cold (long <u>o</u>).

52. **col-or**: *See*: <u>olo</u> as 2 jars of paint color with an easel between them: c-<u>olo</u>-r.

53. **come**: *See*: <u>me</u> in co<u>me</u>. *Clue*: Little kids say, "me come too." *Same Pattern*: come, some.

54. **could**: *Visual*: Put <u>u</u> in <u>cold</u> to make <u>co-u-ld</u>. *SPP*: <u>co-uld</u>. *Same Pattern*: should, would.

55. **coun-try**: *See*: <u>count</u> in <u>country</u>. *Clue*: I find and <u>count</u> each <u>country</u>.

56. **cut**: *Clue*: The snowflakes you <u>cut</u> are <u>cut</u>e. *Same Pattern*: but, cut, hut.

57. **day**: *Clue*: Let's pl<u>ay</u> all <u>day</u>. *VV Rule*: <u>Y</u> makes <u>a</u> long. *Same Pattern*: bay, may, say.

58. **did**: *Visual*: See <u>did</u> is a palindrome (same spelling both ways). *Same Pattern*: bid, did, hid.

59. **dif-fer-ent**: *See*: <u>ere</u> in diff<u>ere</u>nt. *Clue*: I pay a <u>different</u> r<u>ent</u>. *Rule*: Accent on <u>dif-</u>, don't double <u>r</u>.

60. **does**: *See*: <u>does</u> (female deer) in <u>does</u> (He <u>does</u> it). *Same Pattern*: goes, hoes, toes…

61. **don't**: *Contraction*: <u>Don't</u> = <u>do not</u>. *See Same Pattern*: don't, won't.

62. **door**: *See*: 2 round <u>doors</u> that swing <u>open</u>: <u>d-o o-r</u>. Same Pattern: door, poor

63. **down**: *Visual*: <u>d</u> + <u>own</u> = <u>down</u>. *Clue*: The clown walked <u>down</u> town.

64. **each**: *Clue*: I can r<u>each</u> and <u>eat</u> <u>each</u> p<u>each</u>. *Phonics*: Hear *Digraph* <u>ch</u> in p<u>each</u>.

65. **earn**: *Visual*: <u>ear</u> + <u>n</u> = <u>earn</u>. *Clue*: I use <u>each</u> <u>ear</u> to <u>earn</u> money at the phone company.

46

66. **earth** (anagram: heart): *See* <u>ear</u> + <u>th</u> in <u>earth</u>. *Clue*: I put my <u>ear</u> to the <u>earth</u> to h<u>ear</u> its h<u>eart</u> beat.

67. **eat**: *Visual*: <u>e</u> + <u>at</u> = <u>eat</u>. *Clue*: We <u>eat</u> at noon. *VV Rule*: <u>A</u> makes <u>e</u> long.

68. **ei-ther**: *Clue*: See <u>it</u> and <u>her</u> in <u>either</u>. *Clue*: It's <u>either</u> me, it, (or) her: ~~me~~ + it + her.

69. **end**: *Visual*: <u>N</u> turns *Ed* into <u>end</u>. *Clue*: <u>Ed</u> had to <u>end</u> the letter. *Same Pattern*: bend, end..

70. **e-nough**: *Visual*: <u>eno</u> + <u>ugh</u> = eno<u>ugh</u>. *Phonics*: Gk: <u>gh</u> = <u>f</u>. *Clue*: <u>Enough</u> of the r<u>ough</u> stuff!

71. **e-ven**: *Visual*: <u>eve</u> + <u>n</u> = <u>even</u>. *Clue*: Are s<u>even</u> and el<u>even</u> <u>even</u> numbers?

72. **eve-ry**: *See*: <u>ever</u> and <u>very</u> in <u>every</u>. *Clue*: Does <u>every</u> prince live happily <u>ever</u> after?

73. **ex-act-ly**: *Find*: <u>act</u> in <u>exactly</u>. *Clue*: The first <u>act</u> began <u>exactly</u> at noon.

74. **ex-am-ple**: *Visual*: <u>exam</u> + <u>ple</u> = <u>example</u>. My <u>exam</u> is comp<u>le</u>te once I give an <u>example</u>.

75. **eyes**: *Visual*: <u>e</u> + <u>yes</u> = <u>eyes</u>. Also, see 2 <u>eyes</u> and a nose: <u>e y e</u> + s. *Phonics*: <u>s</u> = <u>z</u>.

76. **face**: *See*: <u>ace</u> in <u>face</u>. *Clue*: Her <u>face</u> has gr<u>ace</u> like l<u>ace</u>. *Phonics*: <u>c</u> = <u>s</u>. *Rule*: <u>E</u> makes <u>a</u> long.

77. **fa-mi-ly**: *Find* <u>am</u> and <u>I</u> in <u>family</u>. *Clue*: <u>Am I</u> in a <u>family</u>? (<u>Ami</u>: Fr. for friend is in family).

78. **far**: *Visual*: <u>fa</u> + <u>r</u> = <u>far</u>. *Clue*: I go <u>far</u> in my c<u>ar</u>. *Same Pattern*: far, jar, star.

79. **fa-ther**: *Find* <u>at</u> and <u>her</u> in <u>father</u>. *Clue*: She helped <u>her</u> <u>father</u> <u>at</u> <u>her</u> home.

80. **feath-er**: *Clue-in-a-Row*: The eagle's true <u>feat</u> (was for) <u>her</u> to keep each <u>feather</u>: <u>feat</u> + <u>her</u>.

81. **feet**: *Visual*: <u>See</u> 2 slippers in the middle of <u>feet</u> (<u>e e</u>). *Same Pattern*: feet, meet, sweet.

82. **few**: *Clue*: I saw rainbows in a <u>few</u> drops of d<u>ew</u>. *Same Pattern*: dew, few, new.

83. **find**: *Visual*: <u>fin</u> + <u>d</u> = <u>find</u>. *Clue*: Can you <u>find</u> a m<u>ind</u>? *Pattern*: find, mind.

84. **first**: *Visual*: <u>fir</u> + <u>st</u> = <u>first</u>. *Clue*: The <u>first</u> year, our <u>fir</u> tree grew a foot: <u>fir</u> + <u>st</u>.

85. **fol-low**: *See*: <u>ollo</u> (palindrome) inside of <u>follow</u>. *Same Pattern*: follow, hollow.

86. **food**: *Visual*: See two plates (<u>o o</u>) in the middle of <u>food</u>.

87. **for** (prep., to go to): *Visual*: <u>f</u> + <u>or</u> = <u>for</u>. *Clue*: I'm either <u>for</u> this <u>or</u> <u>for</u> that.

88. **form**: *Visual*: <u>for</u> + <u>m</u> = <u>form</u>. *See Same Pattern*: dorm, form.

89. **found**: *Visual*: <u>U</u> turns *fond* into <u>found</u>. *Clue*: I <u>found</u> something r<u>ound</u> on the gr<u>ound</u>.

90. **four**: *Visual*: <u>f</u> + <u>our</u> = <u>four</u>. *Clue*: <u>Four</u> is <u>our</u> favorite number. *See Same Pattern*: pour, our.

91. **friend**: *Clue-in-a-Row*: On <u>Fri., (the) end</u> of the week, I see my <u>friend</u>.

92. **from**: *Visual*: <u>From</u> has the same letters as <u>form</u>. *Clue*: We walked home <u>from</u> the p<u>rom</u>.

93. **get**: *Clue*: I b<u>et</u> you'll <u>get</u> the job. *See Same Pattern*: bet, get, let, set, wet.

94. **girl**: *Visual*: <u>R</u> turns *gil* into <u>girl</u>. *See Same Pattern*: girl, swirl, twirl. *Phonics*: See *Blend*: gi-r

95. **give**: *Clue*: They l<u>ive</u> to <u>give</u> (No Eng. word ends in <u>v</u>; <u>ve</u> just ends <u>give</u> without making <u>i</u> long.)

96. **goes**: *See*: <u>go</u> in <u>goes</u>. *Clue*: I want to <u>go</u> where he <u>goes</u>. *Phonics*: <u>s</u> = <u>z</u>. *Same Pattern*: does, goes

97. **good**: *Visual*: <u>goo</u> + <u>d</u> = <u>good</u>. *Clue*: <u>Goo</u> can mean <u>good</u> to a baby. *Same Pattern*: good, stood

98. **got**: *Visual*: <u>go</u> + <u>t</u> = <u>got</u>. *Clue*: It <u>got</u> h<u>ot</u> today. *Same Pattern*: got, hot, lot.

99. **great**: *See*: <u>eat</u> in <u>great</u>. *Clue*: Your food is <u>great</u> to <u>eat</u>. *SPP*: gre-at.

100. **group**: *Find*: <u>up</u> in <u>group</u>. *SPP*: gro-up. *Clue*: The <u>group</u> ate <u>up</u> the s<u>oup</u>: <u>gro</u> + <u>up</u>.

101. **grow**: *Visual*: g + row = grow. My flowers grow in a row. *Rule*: W makes o long in grow.

102. **had**: *Visual*: h + ad = had. *Clue*: That soda I had was bad. *Same Pattern*: glad, had, rad..

103. **hand**: *Visual*: h + and = hand. *Clue*: Give the band a hand. *Same Pattern*: hand, land, sand.

104. **hard**: *Visual*: R turns *had* into hard. *Clue*: I had hard work to do.

105. **has**: *Visual*: h + as = has. *Clue*: She has as much as he has.. *Phonics*: s = z.

106. **have**: *Visual*: h + ave = have. *Clue*: I have run down this ave. (A isn't long; e just ends have.)

107. **head**: *Visual*: he + ad = head. *Clue*: He had ideas for an ad in his head. *SPP*: he-ad.

108. **hear** (v., listen): *Visual*: H + ear = hear. *Clue*: I hear with my ear. *See Same Pattern*: dear, tear.

109. **heard** (v., past of hear): *Find* hear in heard. *Clue*: I heard with my ear. *SPP*: he-ard.

110. **help**: *Visual*: he + lp = help. *Phonics*: *Blend*: he-l-p. *Same Pattern*: help, kelp, yelp.

111. **her**: *Visual*: he + r = her. *Clue*: Does he know her?

112. **here** (adv., this place): *Find* ere (before)in here. *Clue*: I go here, there, everywhere. (All end in ere.)

113. **high**: *Visual*: See h's as chairs to climb on to be up high. *Phonics*: igh = long i.

114. **him**: *Visual*: hi + m = him. *Clue*: I said hi to him.

115. **his**: *Visual*: hi + s = his. *Phonics*: s = z. *Clue*: This is his.

116. **home**: *Visual*: ho + me = home. *Clue*: Our home has a dome. *Rule*: E makes o long.

117. **house**: *Visual*: ho + use = house. *Clue*: See the mouse use our house.

118. **how**: *Visual*: h + ow = how. *Same Pattern Clue*: How now brown cow.

119. **i-de-a**: *See* and *hear* 3 *Open Syllables* in i-de-a. *Clue*: Her idea for a deal was ideal.

120. **im-port-ant**: *See*: port + ant. *Clue-in-a-Row*: It's important not to import ants in picnic baskets.

121. **is-land**: *See*: is + land = island. *Clue-in-a-Row*: There is land on islands. *Phonics*: *Blend*: la-nd.

122. **it's**: *Contraction*: it's = it is. *Clue*: It's good to use your wits when climbing a mountain.

123. **its** (poss. pron.): *Clue*: An animal uses its wits to survive. *See Same Pattern*: its, pits, wits.

124. **just**: *Find*: us in the middle of just. *Clue*: I just must try for us. *Phonics*: *Blend*-st in ju-s-t.

125. **keep**: *Visual*: 2 eyes asleep in keep (e e). *Rule*: 2 e's = long e. *See Same Pattern*: deep, peep.

126. **kind**: *Visual*: kin (relatives) + d = kind. *Clue*: My kin are kind. *Blend*-nd: ki-n-d.

127. **know**: *Visual*: k + now = know. *Clue*: I know you better now. *SPP*: k-now.

128. **land**: *Visual*: l + and = land. *Clue*: I'll jump and land in sand. *Blend* -nd is in la-nd.

129. **large**: *Clue*: I saw a large barge. *SPP*: lar-ge. *See Same Pattern*: barge, charge, large, Marge.

130. **last**: *Find*: as inside last. *Clue*: Did I run as fast as last time? *Blend* -st: la-s-t.

131. **late**: *Visual*: l + ate = late. *Clue*: We ate late. *Rule*: Silent e makes a long. *Pattern*: gate, late.

132. **learn**: *Visual*: R turns *lean* into learn. *Clue*: I can learn to earn money. *Blend* –rn in lea-rn.

133. **leaves**: *See*: eaves in leaves. *SPP*: le-a-ves. *Clue*: Leaves collect in eaves. *Plural*: leaf + v + es.

134. **left**: *Visual*: F turns *let* into left. *Phonics*: *See* and *hear* *Blend* le-ft.

135. **let**: *Clue*: I bet you'll let me win. *See Same Pattern*: bet, let, met, set.

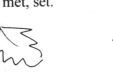

136. **life**: *Visual*: F makes *lie* life. *Clue*: Don't lie; get a life! *SPP*: li-fe. *Rule*: E makes i long.

137. **light**: *Clue*: It's light out tonight. *Phonics*: igh = long i. *Same Pattern*: bright, night, sight.

138. **like**: *Visual*: K turn *lie* into like. I don't like to tell a lie. *Same Pattern*: bike, like, Mike.

139. **line**: *See* in inside line. *Rule*: Silent e makes i long. *See Same Pattern*: fine, line, mine.

140. **list**: *See* is in the middle of list. *Blend*: li-st. *See Same Pattern*: fist, insist, mist, wrist.

141. **lis-ten**: *See* is + ten in listen. *Clue*: Listen: Is ten minutes up? l + is + ten.

142. **lit-tle**: Little *looks* little. *OWF Clue*: The Littlest Angel was little. *Rule*: 2 t's keep i short.

143. **live**: *See* v turn *lie* into live. *Reversal*: live - evil. *Clue*: Live to give; not for evil.

144. **long**: *See* n turns *log* into long. *Clue*: I sat on a long log. *See Same Pattern*: gong, long song.

145. **look**: *See* 2 eyes in l-o o-k. *Clue*: Look in a book. *See Same Pattern*: book, cook, took.

146. **love**: *Clue*: A dove is a symbol of love (O. Fr. luve)s. *SPP*: lo-ve. *See Same Pattern*: dove, shove.

147. **made**: *Visual and Rule*: Silent e turns *mad* into made. *Clue*: He made the grade (passed class).

148. **make**: *Find* ma in make. *Clue*: Ma makes cakes. *SPP*: ma-ke *Rule*: Silent e makes a long.

149. **ma-ny**: *Visual*: man + y = many. *Clue*: Many a man hasn't any hobby.

150. **may**: *Visual*: ma + y = may. *Clue*: Ma may visit today. *2-Vowel Rule*: Y makes a long.

151. **mean**: *Visual*: me + an = mean. *Clue*: That bean's really mean. *2-Vowel Rule*: A makes e long

152. **meas-ure**: *See* me, a, and sure in measure. *Clue-in-a-Row*: Please give me a sure measure.

153. **meet**: *Visual*: E turns *met* into meet. *Rule*: 2 e's = long e. *See Same Pattern*: beet, feet, meet.

154. **men**: *Visual*: me + n = men. *See Same Pattern* in: men, omen, women.

155. **might**: *Clue*: I might go out tonight. *Phonics*: igh = long i. *See Same Pattern*: light, right, tight

156. **mile**: Her smile was a mile long. *Rule*: Silent e makes i long. *See Same Pattern*: file, mile, tile.

157. **miss**: *See* miss + is + sip in Mississippi. *Rule*: 2 s's keep i short. *Beat*: m-i-s-s i-s-s i-p-p-i.

158. **more**: *See* ore in more. *Clue*: There's more ore in the core. *Same Pattern*: core, fore, more.

159. **most**: *Clue*: I like that host the most. *Phonics*: *Blend*: mo + s-t. *See Same Pattern*: host, ghost.

160. **mo-ther**: *See* her in mother. *Clue*: We want her, and no other mother (OE mother: modor).

161. **moun-tain**: *Find*: a, I, in, and mount. *Clue*: Mount a (rope) in this mountain crag.

162. **move**: *Clue*: Can I move over by the person I love. *Same Pattern*: love, prove.

163. **much**: *See* and hear *Digraph* -ch in mu-ch. *See Same Pattern*: much, such.

164. **must**: *See* us in must. *Clue*: I must just do it. *Phonics*: Hear *Blend*: mu + s-t.

165. **name**: *See* am in name. *Clue*: We have the same name. *Rule*: E makes a long.

166. **near**: *See* ear in near. *Clue*: Dear, speak near to my ear. *Same Pattern*: fear, tear

167. **need**: *See* ee in need Rule: 2 e's = long e. *Clue*: I need to plant a seed today.

168. **nev-er**: *Visual*: Never has eve in the middle. *Clue*: Never ever.

169. **next**: *Visual*: X turns *net* into next. *Clue*: Take the next exit. *Say Blend*: ne + x-t.

170. **night**: *Clue*: I use a n<u>igh</u>t l<u>igh</u>t. *Phonics*: igh = <u>long i</u>. *See Same Pattern*: flight, night, might.

171. **none**: *Visual*: <u>non + e</u> = <u>none</u>. *Clue*: <u>None</u> means <u>not ~~one~~</u> = <u>none</u>.

172. **not**: *Visual*: <u>no + t</u> = <u>not</u>. *Clue*: It's <u>not</u> <u>hot</u> today.

173. **noth-ing**: *Visual*: <u>no + thing</u> = <u>nothing</u>. *Clue-in-a-Row*: <u>Nothing</u> simply means <u>no thing</u>.

174. **now**: *Visual*: <u>n + ow</u> = <u>now</u>. *Same Pattern Clue*: H<u>ow</u> n<u>ow</u> br<u>ow</u>n c<u>ow</u>?

175. **num-ber**: *See Blend*: <u>nu + m-b + er</u>. *See Same Pattern*: lumber, slumber.

176. **of**: *Visual*: <u>off – f</u> = <u>of</u>. *Clue*: *Phonics*: <u>of</u>: <u>f</u> = <u>v</u> sound (<u>off</u>: <u>f</u> = <u>f</u> sound).

177. **off**: *Visual*: <u>of + f</u> = <u>off</u>. *Clue*: Build your <u>off</u>ice <u>off</u> ice. *Rule*: 2 f's keep <u>o</u> short in <u>off</u>.

178. **of-ten**: *Visual*: <u>of + ten</u> = <u>often</u>. *Clue-in-a-Row*: I am <u>often</u> one <u>of ten</u> who help.

179. **oil**: *Clue*: The <u>oil</u> went through a c<u>oil</u>. *See Same Pattern* in: coil, oil, toil.

180. **old**: *Clue*: He is <u>old</u> and b<u>old</u>. *See Blend*: <u>o + l-d</u>. *See Same Pattern*: bold, cold.

181. **once**: *Visual*: <u>C</u> turns *one* into <u>once</u> (one time). *SPP*: Say <u>on-ce</u>. *Phonics*: <u>once</u> = <u>wuns</u>.

182. **one**: *Visual*: <u>on + e</u> = <u>one</u>. *Clue*: <u>One</u> is <u>one</u> and all al<u>one</u>.

183. **on-ly**: *Visual*: on + ly = <u>only</u>. *Roots*: <u>on~~e~~</u> (OE, an: one) + <u>ly</u> (suf.) = <u>only</u> (means one + ly).

184. **o-pen**: *See* Open Syllable (vowel or ends in vowel) <u>o</u> in <u>o-pen</u>. *Clue*: Can I <u>open</u> my <u>O-Pen</u>, please.

185. **or** (conj., either-or): *Rule*: Use either-<u>or</u>; neither-nor. *See Same Pattern*: for, nor, or.

186. **oth-er**: *See* <u>the</u> in <u>other</u>. *Clue*: Where is <u>the</u> <u>other</u> br<u>other</u>?

187. **our** (pron. belonging to us.): *Visual*: <u>U</u> turns *or* into <u>our</u>. *Clue*: These are <u>our</u> <u>four</u> books.

188. **out**: *Clue*: Sh<u>out</u> <u>out</u> l<u>out</u>d for our team. *See Same Pattern*: about, out, pout.

189. **o-ver**: *Visual*: <u>R</u> + <u>over</u> = <u>Rover</u>. *Clue*: M<u>ove</u> <u>over</u>, <u>Rover</u>. *Same Pattern*: clover, Rover.

190. **own**: *Visual*: <u>W</u> turns *on* into <u>own</u>. *Clue* Can you <u>own</u> a t<u>own</u>? *See Blend*: <u>o + w-n</u>.

191. **page**: *Visual*: <u>p + age</u> = <u>page</u>. *Clue*: What <u>age</u> is a <u>page</u>? *Phonics*: <u>g</u> = <u>j</u>. *Rule*: <u>E</u> makes <u>a</u> long.

192. **pa-per**: *See* <u>ape</u> in <u>paper</u>. *Clue*: Our <u>ape</u> is in the <u>paper</u>. *Same Pattern*: caper, taper.

193. **part**: *Visual*: <u>R</u> turns *pat* into <u>part</u>. *Phonics*: *Say Blend*: <u>pa + r-t</u>.

194. **peo-ple**: *See*: 5 faces of people in: <u>p-e-o-p…e</u>. *Clue*: I like <u>people</u> to pick my p<u>eo</u>nies.

195. **pic-ture**: *Clue*: <u>Pick</u> a <u>picture</u>, and show me where you want my signa<u>ture</u>: <u>pic~~k~~ + ture</u>.

196. **piece**: *See*: <u>pie</u> in <u>piece</u>. *Clue*: I ate a <u>piece</u> of <u>pie</u>. *Same Pattern*: niece, piece.

197. **place**: *Visual*: <u>pl + ace</u> = <u>place</u>. *Phonics*: Say the *Blend*: <u>pl-ace</u>. *Rule*: <u>Silent e</u> makes <u>a</u> long.

198. **point**: *See* <u>poi</u> in <u>point</u>. *Clue*: <u>Point</u> to the <u>poi</u> (pounded tarot root). *Phonics*: *Blend*: <u>poi-n-t</u>.

199. **quite**: *Visual* and *Rule*: <u>Silent e</u> turns <u>quit</u> into <u>quite</u>. *See Same Pattern*: bite, quite, site.

200. **read** (v., past of read): *Visual*: <u>A</u> turns <u>red</u> into <u>read</u>. *Clue*: I <u>read</u> about b<u>read</u>. *Pattern*: head, read.

201. **real-ly**: *Find* <u>ally</u> (supporter) in <u>really</u>. *Clue*: Are you <u>really</u> my <u>ally</u>? *VV Rule*: <u>A</u> makes <u>e</u> long.

202. **ride**: *Visual* and *Rule*: <u>Silent e</u> turns <u>rid</u> into <u>ride</u>. *Clue*: <u>Ride</u> by my s<u>ide</u>. *Pattern*: hide, tide.

203. **right**: *Clue*: I can <u>rig</u> my sail <u>right</u> at n<u>igh</u>t. *Phonics*: <u>igh</u> = long <u>i</u>. *Pattern*: right, night.

204. **ri-ver**: *See* <u>ive</u> in the middle of <u>river</u>. *Clue*: <u>I've</u> been on this <u>river</u> forever.

205. **said**: *Visual*: <u>I</u> turns *sad* into <u>said</u>. *Y Rule*: sa~~y~~ + i + d = <u>said</u>. *Same Visual Pattern*: paid, said.

206. **same**: *Visual* and *Rule*: <u>Final e</u> turns <u>Sam</u> into <u>same</u>. *Clue*: I have the <u>same</u> name.

207. **saw**: *Reversal*: <u>saw</u> – <u>was</u>. *Clue*: I <u>saw</u> he <u>was</u> here. *See Same Pattern*: law, paw, raw, saw.

208. **say**: *2 Vowel Rule*: <u>Y</u> makes <u>a</u> long. *See Same Pattern*: bay, day, lay, may, pay, way…

209. **school**: *See* <u>choo</u> in <u>school</u>. *Clue*: We played <u>choo choo</u> train at school. *Phonics*: <u>s + ch</u> (digraph)

210. **sci-ence**: I built a <u>fence</u> in <u>science</u>: <u>sci</u> + ~~f~~<u>ence</u>. (Gk. <u>scien</u>: knowledge + <u>ce</u>: n. suf).

211. **sea**: *Clue*: <u>Sea</u> and oc<u>ea</u>n are synonyms. *VV Rule*: <u>A</u> makes <u>e</u> long. *Same Pattern*: pea, tea.

212. **se-cond**: *Find* <u>econ</u> in <u>second</u>. *Clue*: I go to <u>econ</u> (economics class) in <u>seconds</u>: <u>s + econ + ds</u>.

213. **see**: *Clue*: I <u>see</u> a b<u>ee</u> tree. *Rule*: <u>2 e's</u> = long <u>e</u>. *See Same Pattern*: bee, see, tee.

214. **seem**: *Visual*: <u>See</u> + <u>m</u> = <u>seem</u>. *Clue*: I <u>see</u> that you <u>seem</u> happy. *Rule*: <u>2 e's</u> = long <u>e</u>.

215. **sen-tence**: *See* <u>ten</u> in <u>sentence</u>. *SPP*: sen-<u>ten</u>-ce. *Visual* and *Beat*: <u>s-e-n   t-e-n   c-e</u>. ♪

216. **set**: *Clue*: Who's part of the *Jet Set*? *See Same Pattern*: bet, jet, let, met, set, wet.

217. **should**: *Clue*: I w<u>ould</u> if I c<u>ould</u>, and I <u>should</u>. *SPP*: sh<u>o</u>-uld. *See Same Pattern*: could, would.

218. **show**: *Visual*: <u>s + how</u> = <u>show</u>. *Clue*: <u>How</u> was the <u>show</u>? 2-Vowel Rule: <u>W</u> makes o long.

219. **side**: *Clue*: R<u>ide</u> by my <u>side</u>. *Rule*: <u>Silent e</u> makes i long. *See Same Pattern*: hide, ride, side.

220. **sign**: *Visual* and *OWF*: See and hear <u>sign</u> in <u>signal</u>. *Phonics*: s<u>ign</u> = long <u>i</u>.

221. **small**: *Visual*: <u>s + all</u> = <u>small</u>. *Clue*: We <u>all</u> are <u>small</u>. *Same Pattern*: ball, call, fall, tall.

222. **some**: *Visual*: <u>so + me</u> = <u>some</u>. *SPP*: so-<u>me</u>. *Clue*: The baby said, "<u>So me</u> get <u>some</u> too."

223. **song**: *See* <u>on</u> in <u>song</u>. *Clue*: The s<u>ong</u> went <u>on</u>... *Phonics*: *Digraph*: <u>so + ng</u>. *Pattern*: long song.

224. **soon**: *Visual*: <u>O</u> turns *son* into <u>soon</u>. *Clue*: <u>Soon</u> the m<u>oon</u> came up. *Pattern*: moon, spoon.

225. **sound**: *Phonics*: *See* and *hear Blend*: <u>sou</u> + <u>n-d</u>. *Same Pattern*: ground, sound, found.

226. **spell**: *Visual*: Letter <u>p</u> turns *sell* into <u>spell</u>. *Same Pattern*: bell, fell, sell, spell, tell.

227. **start**: *Visual*: <u>st + art</u> = <u>start</u>. I <u>start</u> <u>art</u> today: *Phonics*: See *Blends*: <u>st + a + rt</u>.

228. **state**: *Visual*: <u>st + ate</u> = <u>state</u>. *Rule*: <u>Silent e</u> makes <u>a</u> long. *Same Pattern*: late, rate, state.

229. **still**: *Visual*: <u>st + ill</u> = <u>still</u>. *Clue*: Are you <u>still ill</u>? *Phonics*: See and say *Blend*: <u>s-t</u> + ill

230. **stop**: *Visual*: <u>st + op</u> = <u>stop</u>. *Reversal*: stop - pots. *Blend*-st: <u>s-t-op</u>. *Pattern*: hop, stop. top.

231. **stor-y**: *See* <u>or</u> in <u>story</u>. *Clue*: I know a <u>story</u> of a <u>stork</u>. *Phonics*: Say the *Blend*: <u>s-t + ory</u>.

232. **stretch**: *Visual*: <u>str + etch</u> = <u>stretch</u>. *Phonics*: Say *Blends* and *Digraph*: <u>s-t-r + e + t-ch</u>.

233. **stud-y**: *Visual*: <u>stud + y</u> = <u>study</u>. *Phonics*: *Blend*: <u>s-t + udy</u>. *Same Pattern*: student, studying.

234. **such**: *Phonics*: *See* and *say Digraph*: <u>su + ch</u>. *See Same Pattern*: much, such.

235. **sure**: *Visual*: <u>R</u> turns *Sue* into <u>sure</u>. *Clue*: We need a <u>sure</u> c<u>ure</u>.

236. **take**: *Rule*: <u>Silent e</u> makes <u>a</u> long. *SPP*: ta-<u>ke</u>. *See Same Pattern*: lake, sake, take, wake.

237. **talk**: *Phonics*: *See* and *say Blend*: <u>ta-l-k</u>. *See Same Pattern*: chalk, talk, walk.

238. **tell**: *See Same Pattern*: bell, fell, sell, spell, tell, well.

239. **than**: *Visual*: <u>th + an</u> = <u>than</u>. *Clue*: We took more <u>than</u> our <u>han</u>ds could hold.

240. **that**: *Visual*: <u>th + at</u> = <u>that</u>. *Clue*: I want <u>that hat</u>. *Same Pattern*: cat, hat, mat, sat, that.

241. **their**: *See* <u>heir</u> in <u>their</u>. *See* <u>their</u>, <u>there</u>, and <u>they're</u> begin with <u>the</u>. *Clue*: <u>He</u> is <u>their heir</u>.

242. **them**: *Visual*: <u>the + m</u> = <u>them</u>. *Clue*: Please tell <u>them</u> to fix that <u>hem</u>.

243. **then**: *Visual*: <u>t + hen</u> = <u>then</u>. *Clue*: <u>Then</u> the <u>hen</u> laid an egg. *Pattern*: hen, men, then.

244. **there**: *Visual*: <u>R</u> turns *thee* into <u>there</u>. *Clue*: Look <u>here</u> and <u>there</u>. *See Same Pattern*: ere, where.

245. **these**: *See* <u>he</u> in <u>these</u>. *Clue*: <u>He</u> needs <u>these</u>. *Blend*: <u>s-t + op</u>. *Rule*: <u>Silent e</u> makes <u>e</u> long.

246. **they**: *See* <u>hey</u> in <u>they</u>. *Clue*: <u>Hey</u>, <u>they</u> might go too. *Phonics*: ey = long a. *Pattern*: hey, prey, they.

247. **they're**: *Contraction*: <u>they're</u> = <u>they are</u>. The <u>'</u> replaces <u>a</u> in <u>are</u>: <u>they're</u>. *Pattern*: they'd, they'll.

248. **thing**: *Visual*: <u>thin + g</u> = <u>thing</u>. *Phonics*: Say the *Digraph* + ng: <u>th + i + ng</u>.

249. **think**: *Visual*: <u>thin + k</u> = <u>think</u>. *Phonics*: Say *Digraph*: <u>th</u> and *Blend*: <u>th + i + n-k</u>.

250. **this**: *Visual*: <u>t + his</u> = <u>this</u>. *Clue*: <u>This is his</u> book. *Phonics*: Say *Digraph*: <u>th-is</u>.

251. **those**: *Visual*: <u>t + hose</u> = <u>those</u>. *Clue*: I have a <u>hose</u> for <u>those</u> roses. *Rule*: <u>Silent e</u> makes <u>o</u>.

252. **though**: *Visual*: <u>thou + gh</u> = <u>though</u>. *Clue*: <u>Thou</u> came, <u>though</u> it was <u>tough</u>. *SPP*: tho-ugh.

253. **thought**: *Visual*: <u>th + ought</u> = <u>thought</u>. *Clue*: I <u>ought</u> to have <u>thought</u> first. *Bookend*: <u>thought</u>.

254. **through**: *Find* <u>rough</u> in <u>through</u>. *Clue*: It's <u>rough</u> to walk <u>through</u> a door.

255. **to** (prep. <u>to</u> a place): *Visual*: <u>To</u> is short. *Pronunciation*: Say <u>to</u> quickly like *ta*: <u>to</u> school, <u>to</u> work.

256. **to-geth-er**: *Find* <u>to</u>, <u>get</u>, and <u>her</u> in <u>together</u>. *Clue-in-a-Row*: We went <u>together</u> to + get + her.

257. **too** (adv. also; in addition): *Visual*: <u>Too</u> stretches out: *Say*: I ate <u>too</u>...much. I want to go <u>toooo</u>...

258. **took**: *Visual*: <u>too + k</u> = <u>took</u>. *See Same Pattern*: book, cook, look, took.

259. **to-ward**: *Find* <u>to</u> and <u>war</u> in <u>toward</u>. *Clue*: Don't move <u>to war</u>: to + war + d. *SPP*: <u>to-ward</u>.

260. **tree**: *Clue*: This is a b<u>ee</u> <u>tree</u> with honey inside. *See Same Pattern*: bee, gee, see, tee, tree.

261. **try**: *See Same Pattern*: cry, dry, fry, try.

262. **turn**: *Visual*: <u>t + urn</u> = <u>turn</u>. *See Same Pattern*: burn, churn, turn, urn

263. **two** (number): *See* <u>w</u> in the middle of <u>two</u>. *Same Pattern*: <u>two</u>... <u>tw</u>elve...<u>tw</u>enty...

264. **un-der**: *See Same Pattern*: blunder, plunder, thunder, under.

265. **un-til**: *See* just <u>one l</u> in -til. *Prefix Rule*: <u>un + till</u> = <u>until</u> (Till drops an l).

266. **use**: *Visual* and *Rule*: <u>Silent e</u> turns <u>us</u> into <u>use</u>. *Clue*: Can you <u>use us</u>? *Phonics*: <u>s</u> = <u>z</u>.

267. **u-su-al**: *See* <u>us</u>, <u>U</u> (you), and <u>Al</u> in <u>usual</u>: <u>us + U + Al</u>. *Phonics*: <u>su</u> = <u>zhoo</u>. *Rule*: <u>use + ual</u> = <u>usual</u>

268. **ver-y**: *Clue*: <u>Ev</u>ery time I see you, I'm <u>very</u> happy. *Roots*: <u>ver</u> (L. <u>ver</u>: truth) + <u>y</u> (suf.) = <u>very</u>.

269. **walk**: *Phonics*: See and say *Blend-<u>lk</u>*: <u>wa-l-k</u>. *Same Visual Pattern*: chalk, talk, walk.

270. **want**: *See* <u>ant</u> in <u>want</u>. *Clue*: I w<u>ant</u> this <u>ant</u> for a pet: <u>w + ant</u>. *Phonics*: *Blend*: <u>wa + n-t</u>.

271. **was**: *Reversal*: <u>was</u> – <u>saw</u>. *Visual*: <u>W</u> turns <u>as</u> into <u>was</u>. *Clue*: He <u>was</u> just <u>as</u> good. *Phonics*: <u>s</u> = <u>z</u>.

272. **watch**: *SPP*: wa-t-ch. <u>Watch</u> me <u>catch</u> the ball. *Same Pattern*: catch, hatch, match…

273. **wa-ter**. *Visual*: See <u>ate</u> in the middle of <u>water</u>. *Clue*: You don't say, I <u>ate</u> <u>water</u>.

274. **way**: *VV Rule*: <u>Y</u> makes <u>a</u> long. *See Same Pattern*: lay, may, pay, say, way.

275. **we're**: *Contraction*: <u>we're</u> = <u>we are</u>. *See Same Pattern*: we'd, we'll.

276. **well**: *See Same Pattern*: bell, fell, sell, spell, tell, well.

277. **went**: *Phonics*: See and say *Blend*: <u>we-n-t</u>. *See Same Pattern*: bent, dent, gent, sent.

278. **were**: *Visual*: <u>R</u> turns *wee* into <u>were</u>. We <u>were</u> <u>here</u>. *Same Visual Pattern*: here, there, were.

279. **what**: *Visual*: <u>w + hat</u> = <u>what</u>. *Clue*: <u>What</u> <u>hat</u> did I wear? *Phonics*: Say *Digraph*: <u>wh -at</u>.

280. **when**: *Visual*: <u>w + hen</u> = <u>when</u>. *Phonics*: *Digraph*: <u>wh + en</u>. *Same Pattern*: hen, then.

281. **where**: *Visual*: <u>R</u> turns *whee* into <u>where</u>. *Same Pattern*: here, there, where.

282. **which**: *Phonics*: Say *Digraphs*: <u>wh, ch</u>: <u>wh + i + ch</u>. *See Same Pattern*: rich, which, sandwich.

283. **while**: *Phonics*: See <u>hi</u> in <u>while</u>. *Clue*: <u>While</u> I cook, say <u>hi</u> for me. *Phonics*: *Digraph*: <u>wh + ile</u>.

284. **white**: *Visual*: <u>whit</u> (nothing) + <u>e</u> = <u>white</u>. *See Same Pattern*: kite, site, white.

285. **who**: *Visual*: <u>w + ho</u> = <u>who</u>. *Phonics*: <u>who</u> (silent w) = <u>hoo</u> sound.

286. **who's**: *Contraction*: <u>who's</u> = <u>who is</u>. *Clue*: <u>Who's</u> <u>hol</u>ding a book? *Same Pattern*: who'll, who…

287. **whose** (poss. pron.): *Visual*: <u>w</u> + <u>hose</u> = <u>whose</u>. *SPP*: <u>w</u>-hose. *Clue*: <u>Whose</u> <u>hose</u> is this?

288. **why**: *Phonics*: See and say *Digraph*: <u>wh + y</u>. *See Same Pattern*: shy, thy, why

289. **will**: *Visual*: <u>w + ill</u> = <u>will</u>. *See Same Pattern*: bill, fill, ill, mill, till, will.

290. **with**: *Visual*: <u>wit + h</u> = <u>with</u>. *Clue*: Use <u>wit</u> <u>with</u> kindness. *Phonics*: See *Digraph*: <u>wi + th</u>.

291. **wo-man**: *Visual*: <u>wo + man</u> = <u>woman</u>. *SPP*: wo-man. *See Same Pattern*: man, yeoman.

292. **wo-men**: *Visual*: <u>w + omen</u> = <u>women</u>. *See Same Pattern*: men, omen, women.

293. **word**: *Clue*: An honest <u>word</u> has great <u>worth</u>. *Phonics*: <u>or</u> = <u>er</u>. *Same Pattern*: cord, word.

294. **work**: *Visual*: <u>R</u> turns *wok* into <u>work</u>. *Phonics*: <u>or</u> = <u>er</u>. *Same Visual Pattern*: cork, fork, work.

295. **world**: *Visual*: <u>L</u> turns *word* into <u>world</u>. <u>O</u>'s round like world. *Clue*: Here's my <u>word</u> on the <u>world</u>.

296. **worse**: *Visual*: <u>S</u> turns *wore* into <u>worse</u>. *Clue*: The hole got <u>worse</u> when you <u>wore</u> the jeans.

297. **would**: *Clue*: I <u>would</u> if I <u>could</u>, and I <u>should</u>. *SPP*: wo-uld. *Same Pattern*: could, should.

298. **write**: *Visual*: <u>writ</u> (sealed order) + <u>e</u> = <u>write</u>. *See Same Pattern*: bite, kite, write

299. **year**: *Visual*: <u>y + ear</u> = <u>year</u>. *VV Rule*: <u>A</u> makes <u>e</u> long. *Same Pattern*: dear, fear.

300. **you**: *Visual*: <u>yo + u</u> = <u>you</u>. *Clue*: <u>You</u> and <u>Lou</u> can swing on the rope..

301. **you're**: *Contraction*: <u>you're</u> = <u>you are</u>. *See Same Pattern*: you'd, you'll, you're.

302. **young**: *Visual*: <u>you + ng</u> = <u>young</u>. *Clue*: <u>You</u> are <u>young</u>. *Phonics*: <u>you + ng</u>.

303. **your** (poss. pron.): *Visual*: <u>Y</u> turns <u>our</u> into <u>your</u>. *Clue*: Is this <u>your</u> dog or <u>ours</u>?

304. **youth**: *Visual* and *Digraph*: <u>you + th</u> = <u>youth</u>. *Clue*: <u>You</u> both want <u>youth</u>: you + both.

POWER Spelling Special Lists

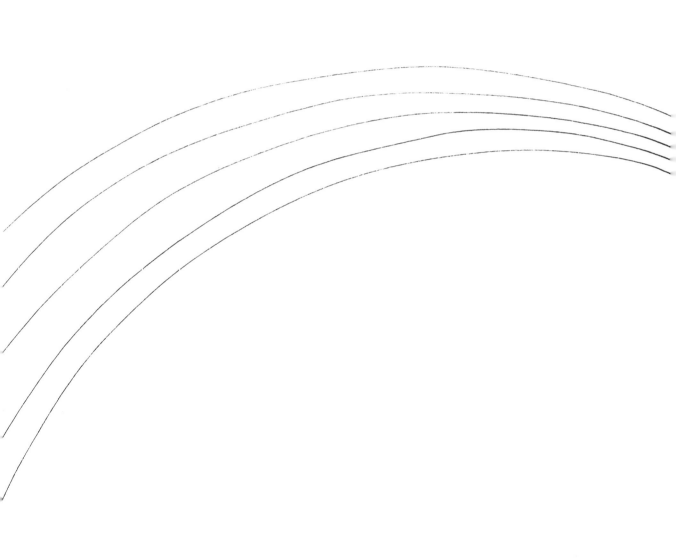

POWER Spelling 1,000 Most Commonly Used Words

One-third of the words used in written materials in English come from words 1-25 in this list; half of the words come from words 1-100; sixty-five percent of the words come from words1-300; and ninety percent of the words in written material come from words 1-1,000. You gain tremendous spelling *POWER* by learning to spell these words and by using *Tools* to remember them forever!

1-25	can	could	thing	big	America
the	said	people	our	even	World
of	there	my	just	such	
and	use	than	name	because	**201-300**
a	an	first	good	turn	high
to	each	been	sentence	here	every
in	which	call	man	why	near
is	she	who	think	ask	add
you	do	oil	say	went	food
it	how	its	great	men	between
he	their	now	help	read	own
was	if	find	through	need	below
for	will	long	much	land	country
on	up	down	before	different	plant
are	other	day	line	home	last
as	about	did	right	us	school
with	out	get	too	move	father
his	many	come	mean	try	keep
they	then	made	old	kind	tree
I	them	may	any	picture	never
at	so	part	same	again	start
be	some		tell	change	city
this	her	**101-200**	boy	off	earth
have	would	over	follow	play	eye
from	make	new	came	spell	light
or	like	take	want	air	thought
	him	only	show	away	head
26-100	into	little	also	animal	under
one	time	work	around	house	story
had	has	know	form	point	saw
by	look	place	three	page	left
word	two	year	small	letter	don't
but	more	live	set	mother	few
not	write	me	put	answer	while
what	go	back	does	found	along
were	see	give	another	study	might
we	number	most	well	still	close
when	no	very	large	learn	something
your	way	after	must	should	seem

470

next	facet	didn't	true	box	system
hard	watch	friends	hundred	finally	behind
open	far	easy	against	wait	ran
example	Indian	heard	pattern	correct	round
begin	really	order	numeral	oh	boat
life	almost	red	table	quickly	game
always	let	door	north	person	force
those	above	sure	slowly	became	brought
both	girl	become	money	shown	understand
paper	sometimes	top	map	minutes	warm
together	mountain	ship	farm	strong	common
got	cut	across	pulled	verb	bring
group	young	today	draw	stars	explain
often	talk	during	voice	front	dry
run	soon	short	seen	feel	though
important	list	better	cold	fact	language
until	song	best	cried	inches	shape
children	being	however	plan	street	deep
side	leave	low	notice	decided	thousands
feet	family	hours	south	contain	yes
car	it's	black	sing	course	clear
mile		products	war	surface	equation
night	**301-400**	happened	ground	produce	yet
walk	body	whole	fall	building	government
white	music	measure	king	ocean	filled
sea	color	remember	town	class	heat
began	stand	early	I'll	note	full
grow	sun	waves	unit	nothing	hot
took	question	reached	figure	rest	check
river	fish	listen	certain	carefully	object
four	area	wind	field	scientists	am
carry	mark	rock	travel	inside	rule
state	dog	space	wood	wheels	among
once	horse	covered	fire	stay	noun
book	birds	fast	upon	green	power
hear	problem	several		known	cannot
stop	complete	hold	**401-500**	island	able
without	room	himself	done	week	six
second	knew	toward	English	less	size
later	since	five	road	machine	dark
miss	ever	step	halt	base	ball
idea	piece	morning	ten	ago	material
enough	told	passed	fly	stood	special
eat	usually	vowel	gave	plane	heavy

4

fine
pair
circle
include
built

501-600
can't
matter
square
syllables
perhaps
bill
felt
suddenly
test
direction
center
farmers
ready
anything
divided
general
energy
subject
Europe
moon
region
return
believe
dance
members
picked
simple
cells
paint
mind
love
cause
rain
exercise
eggs
train
blue

wish
drop
developed
window
difference
distance
heart
sit
sum
summer
wall
forest
probably
legs
sat
main
winter
wide
written
length
reason
kept
interest
arms
brother
race
present
beautiful
store
job
edge
past
sign
record
finished
discovered
wild
happy
beside
gone
sky
glass
million
west

lay
weather
root
instruments
meet
third
months
paragraph
raised
represent
soft
whether
clothes
flowers
flour
shall
teacher
held
describe
drive

601-700
cross
speak
solve
appear
metal
son
either
ice
sleep
village
factors
result
jumped
snow
ride
care
floor
hill
pushed
baby
buy
century

outside
everything
tall
already
instead
phrase
soil
bed
copy
free
hope
spring
case
laughed
nation
quite
type
themselves
temperature
bright
lead
everyone
method
section
lake
consonant
within
dictionary
hair
age
amount
scale
pounds
although
per
broken
moment
tiny
possible
gold
milk
quiet
natural
lot

stone
act
build
middle
speed
count
cat
someone
sail
rolled
bear
wonder
smiled
angle
fraction
Africa
killed
melody
bottom
trip
hole
poor
let's
fight
surprise
French
died
beat
exactly
remain
dress
iron
couldn't
fingers

701-800
row
least
catch
climbed
wrote
shouted
continued
itself

else
plains
gas
England
burning
design
joined
foot
law
ears
grass
you're
grew
skin
valley
cents
key
president
brown
trouble
cool
cloud
lost
sent
symbols
wear
bad
save
experiment
engine
alone
drawing
east
pay
single
touch
information
express
mouth
yard
equal
decimal
yourself
control

practice	flow	indicate	major	born	allow
report	lady	except	observe	level	fear
straight	students	expect	tube	triangle	workers
rise	human	flat	necessary	molecules	Washington
statement	art	seven	weight	France	Greek
stick	feeling	interesting	meat	repeated	women
party		sense	lifted	column	bought
seeds	**801-900**	string	process	western	led
suppose	supply	blow	army	church	march
woman	corner	famous	hat	sister	northern
coast	electric	value	property	oxygen	create
bank	insects	vague	particular	plural	British
period	crops	wings	swim	various	difficult
wire	tone	movement	terms	agreed	match
choose	hit	pole	current	opposite	win
clean	and	exciting	park	wrong	doesn't
visit	doctor	branches	sell	chart	steel
bit	provide	thick	shoulder	prepared	total
whose	thus	blood	industry	pretty	deal
received	won't	lie	wash	solution	determine
garden	cook	spot	block	fresh	evening
please	bones	bell	spread	shop	nor
strange	tail	fun	cattle	suffix	rope
caught	board	loud	wife	especially	cotton
fell	modern	consider	sharp	shoes	apple
team	compound	suggested	**901-1000**	actually	details
God	mine	thin	company	nose	entire
captain	wasn't	position	radio	afraid	corn
direct	fit	entered	we'll	dead	substances
ring	addition	fruit	action	sugar	smell
serve	belong	tied	capital	adjective	tools
child	safe	rich	factories	fig	conditions
desert	soldiers	dollars	settled	office	cows
increase	guess	send	yellow	huge	track
history	silent	sight	isn't	gun	arrived
cost	trade	chief	southern	similar	located
maybe	rather	Japanese	truck	death	sir
business	compare	stream	fair	score	seat
separate	crowd	planets	printed	forward	division
break	poem	rhythm	wouldn't	stretched	effect
uncle	enjoy	eight	ahead	experience	underline
hunting	elements	science	chance	rose	view

WHEW!

POWER Spelling Most Commonly Misspelled Words
Basic List

Learn these basic words and you'll conquer a lot of spelling challenges. Many of these words are not pronounced like they're spelled, so *POWER Spelling Tools* can truly help you remember these.

about	come	give	making	receive	tonight
across	coming	goes	many	remember	too
address	cough	government	maybe	restaurant	toys
adjective	could	grammar	measure	right	train
advice	country	great	minute	rough	traveling
advise	course	group	month	route	tried
again	cousin	guard	morning	said	trouble
all right	cupboard	guess	mother	says	truly
almost	dairy	half	mountain	school	Tuesday
along	dance	handkerchief	neither	science	two
already	dear	haven't	nice	several	uncle
although	decorate	having	ninth	shoes	until
always	design	hear	noisy	since	used
among	didn't	heard	none	skiing	usually
answer	division	heart	notice	skis	vacation
any	doctor	height	o'clock	some	very
arithmetic	does	here	off	something	watch
around	dollar	hospital	often	soon	water
athlete	don't	hour	once	store	wear
aunt	early	house	only	straight	we're
awhile	earth	hundred	orange	stretch	weather
balloon	easy	instead	other	studying	Wednesday
because	edge	island	outside	sugar	weigh
been	either	it's	party	summer	welcome
before	else	its	peace	suppose	were
believe	enough	jewelry	people	sure	when
blue	every	kind	picture	surely	where
bought	everybody	knew	piece	surprise	which
bread	example	know	pint	surrounded	white
brought	eyes	laid	played	swimming	whole
build	father	later	please	taught	who's
built	favorite	latter	poison	tcacher	whose
business	feather	laugh	possible	tear	women
busy	February	learn	practice	terrible	words
buy	fierce	leave	pretty	their	world
catch	find	left	principal	there	would
character	first	lessons	pumpkin	they	write
children	forty	letter	purple	they're	writing
chocolate	fourth	listen	quarter	though	written
choose	friend	little	quiet	thought	wrote
chose	frighten	live	quit	through	you
climbed	from	loose	quite	tired	you're
close	fuel	lose	raise	today	young
color	getting	loving	read	together	your

74

POWER Spelling List of Commonly Misspelled Words
Advanced List

Learn these words now by using *POWER Spelling Tools* to remember the correct spelling forever!

absence	answered	career	decision
absolutely	anxious	carrying	defendant
abundance	apology	carriage	deferred
accede	apostrophe	cashier	definitely
acceptable	apparent	ceiling	democracy
accessible	appearance	celebrate	dependent
accidentally	appointment	cemetery	descend
accommodate	appreciate	certainly	describe
accompanying	approach	changeable	description
accomplish	architect	chief	desirable
accumulate	arctic	college	despair
accurate	arguing	colossal	desperate
ache	argument	column	development
achieve	arrangement	comfortable	different
acknowledgment	article	committee	dilemma
acquaintance	ascend	competitor	diligence
acquire	asphalt	complete	disappearance
actually	assignment	concede	disappoint
adequately	assistance	conceivable	disastrous
adjournment	asterisk	conceive	disciple
admissible	attendance	conceive	discussion
admittance	audible	condemn	dissatisfied
adolescence	author	confident	divided
advantageous	banquet	conquer	ecstasy
advertisement	bargain	conscience	efficient
advice	basically	conscientious	eighth
advise	battery	conscious	eligible
against	beginning	consistent	eliminate
aggravate	believable	continually	embarrass
aggressive	beneficial	controlling	emigrate
alignment	benefited	controversy	eminent
allotted	bicycle	convenience	emphasize
altogether	boundary	council	endeavor
amateur	breathe	counselor	enthusiasm
ambition	brilliant	counterfeit	environment
amendment	brochure	courageous	equipped
amusing	bulletin	courteous	especially
analysis	bureau	courtesy	essential
analyze	calendar	criticism	evidently
ancient	campaign	criticize	exaggerate
anecdote	canceled	curiosity	exceed
announces	cancellation	curious	excellent
annually	candidate	deceive	except

exhausted
exhibit
existence
experience
explanation
extraordinary
extremely
familiar
fascinate
favorite
finally
foreign
formerly
fulfill
gaiety
gauge
genuine
government
governor
grieve
guarantee
guarded
guidance
happened
harass
hesitate
hindrance
honorable
humorous
hurrying
hypocrite
illegible
illiterate
imaginary
immediately
immigrant
indelible
independent
individual
interest
interrupt
irrelevant
irresistible
jealousy
jeopardize
judgment
knowledge
labeling
laboratory

leisure
library
license
lightning
likable
liquid
listener
literature
luxury
magnificent
maintenance
manageable
maneuver
marriage
mathematics
meant
medicine
miniature
miscellaneous
mischievous
misspelled
mortgage
movable
muscle
mysterious
necessary
nickel
niece
ninety
ninth
noticeable
nuisance
occasionally
occurred
occurrence
omitted
opportunity
opposite
pamphlet
panicky
parallel
particular
pastime
patient
peculiar
performance
permanent
permissible
personally

personnel
persuade
physician
picnicking
pneumonia
possession
practical
precede
precious
preference
preferred
prejudice
presumptuous
prevalent
privilege
probably
procedure
proceed
profession
professor
prominent
pronunciation
propeller
publicly
pursue
pursuing
quantity
realize
receipt
recognize
recommend
reference
referral
referred
rehearsal
relevant
relief
renowned
repetition
responsible
rhyme
rhythm
ridiculous
salable
salary
sandwich
satisfactory
schedule
scheme

scissors
secretary
seize
sensible
separate
siege
significance
similar
sincerely
sophomore
source
sovereign
specifically
speech
strength
substantial
subtle
succeed
success
sufficient
summary
superintendent
supersede
surgeon
susceptible
technique
televise
temperament
theory
therefore
toward
tragedy
transferred
twelfth
unusual
using
vacuum
vegetable
vengeance
villain
visible
weird
whether
wholly
yacht
yield
youth
zealous
zenith

The POWER Spelling List of Names
with Roots and Meanings

The spelling and meaning of names is fascinating and gives rich information about the cultures that have contributed to the development of the English language. The names below come from: Arabic (Ar), French (Fr), Gaelic (G), Greek (Gr), Hebrew (H), Hungarian (Hg), Irish (Ir), Italian (It), Celtic-Breton and Welsh (K), Latin (L), Old English (OE), Old French (OF), Persian (Per), Russian (Rus), Scandinavian (Scan), Sanskrit-India (Skt), Slavic-Czech/Polish/Russian (Sl), Spanish (Sp), Teutonic-Old German (T), Yiddish (Y), Welsh (W).

The POWER Spelling List of Female Names

Abigail, Abbie, Abby: Father's Joy (H)
Ada: Joyful (H)
Adele, Adeline: Noble Origin (Fr)
Agatha: Good, Kind (Gr)
Agnes: Pure; Holy; A Lamb (Gr)
Aileen: Irish form of Helen (Ir)
Aimee: Beloved (L)
Alberta: Noble; Bright; Illustrious (T)
Alethea: Truth (Gr)
Alexandra, Alex: Helper of Mankind (Gr)
Alice: Noble Cheer (T)
Alicia: Spanish form of Alice: Noble Cheer (Sp)
Allannah: Fair One (G)
Allison, Alli: Little Truthful One; Nobility (Old Ger)
Alma: Apple, Loving (H); Alma: Nourishing, Kind (L)
Almira: Princess (Ar)
Althea: To Heal (G)
Amanda: Lovable (L)
Amaryllis: With Sparkling, Twinkling Eyes (Gr)
Amelia: Busy Working, Energetic (T)
Amy: Beloved One (L)
Anastasia: Resurrection, Rebirth (L)
Andrea: Warrior; Womanly (Gr)
Angela, Angeline: Messenger, Angel (Gr)
Anika: Very Beautiful; Sweet Faced (African)
Anita: Graceful One (H)
Ann, Anna: Grace, Mercy (H)
Annabel: Grace and Beauty (H and L)
Anne: Grace; God has Favored (H)
Annette: Graceful One (Fr)
Antoinette: Worthy of Praise (Fr)
Antonia: Deserving praise (L)
April: Born in April; To Open Up (L)
Ariane, Arleen: A pledge (K)
Ashley: From the Ashwood Meadow (OE)
Astra: Star-like (Gr)
Astril: Fair, Beautiful (Scan)
Astrid: Love (Scan)
Athena: Wisdom (Gr)
Audrey: Nobel Counsel (OE)
Aura: Gentle Breeze; A Radiating Influence (Gr)
Aurelia: Golden (L)
Aurora: The Dawn (L)
Ava: A Bird (T)
Aviva: Spring (H)

Barbara: Stranger; Patron of Architects (Gr)
Bathsheba: Daughter of an Oath; 7th Daughter (H)
Beatrice (Dante's Guide)**:** One Who Blesses; Brings Joy (L)
Bella, Belle (from Isabella)**:** Beautiful (It)
Berith: Covenant (H)
Bernadette: Brave as a Bear (T)
Bernice: Bringing Victory (Gr)
Bess, Beth (from Elizabeth)**:** Oath of God (H)
Betty, Betsy: Consecrated to God (from H)
Beverly: Meadow of The Beavers; Beaver Stream (OE)
Blanche: White, Fair (Fr)
Blossom: Flowers of a Fruit Tree (OE)
Blythe: Happy, Carefree (OE)
Bonnie: Pretty (Scot)
Brenda: A Sword; Fiery (Old Norse)
Bridget: Strength (Ir)
Brook: Stream (OE)
Candice, Candy: Fire White (Gr)
Cara, Carly: Beloved (It) Cara: Friend (Ir and G)
Carmel: A Fruitful Field; Garden (H)
Carmen: Song (Sp)
Carol: A Song of Joy (Gr)
Caroline, Carolyn: Strong, Vigorous (Gr)
Cassandra, Cassie: Helper of Men (Gr)
Catharine, Catrina: Pure (Old Fr)
Cecelia: Blind, Humble Spirit; Patron Saint of Music (L)
Celeste: Heavenly (Fr)
Celine: Heaven (Fr)
Chantal: Singer (Fr)
Charlotte (feminine of Charles)**;** Little Womanly One (Fr)
Cherie, Cher: Dear; Darling (Fr)
Cheryl: from Charlotte: Little Womanly One (Fr)
Chloe: Springtime; Verdant (Gr)
Christina, Christine, Tina: Follower of Christ (Gr)
Cicely, (Ceclia): Blind, Humble; Patron Saint of Music (L)
Cindy (Cynthia): Goddess of the Moon (Gr)
Clara, Claire, Clarice: Bright, Illustrious (L)
Cleo: Famed, Renowned (Gr)
Clover: From the Plant, Clover (OE)
Colette: From Nicole (Fr)
Colleen: Irish for "Girl" (Ir)
Constance, Connie: Firm, Dependable (L)
Corinne, Cora: Maiden or Girl (Gr)
Cynthia: The Moon; Diana (Gr)
Daisy: From Flower-poetically named Day's eye (OE)

Dana: Pure as Day (L)
Danielle: God Is My Judge (H)
Daphne: The Laurel, Bay Tree (Gr)
Dara: Possessing Good (Per) Pearl of Wisdom (H)
Darlene, Darla: Dearly Beloved; Little Dear One (Eng)
Dawn: Dawn of the Day; Enlightenment
Deborah, Debra: The Bee (H)
Dee (from Dorothy): Gift of God (Gr)
Delores: Dolor-Sorrows (L)
Denise: From Dionysus, Grecian God of Wine (Gr)
Desiree: Desired; Given to Longed-For Child (Fr)
Diana: Goddess of Moon and Hunt; Emblem of Faith (L)
Diane: Divine One (L)
Donna: A Lady (L)
Doris, Dora: A Gift, Bountiful (Gr)
Doris: Noble, Courageous (L)
Dorothy, Dottie: Gift of God (Gr)
Edith: Rich Gift (T)
Edna: Pleasure, Rejuvenation (H)
Eileen: Light (Ir)
Eleanor: Light (Gr)
Electra: Amber-Hued (Gr)
Elizabeth, Elisa, Elissa, Libby: Worshipper of God (H)
Ellen: Bright One, from Helen (Gr)
Emily, Emilia: Industrious (L and T)
Emma: Aunt; Nurse; Grandmother (T)
Enid: Soul, Life (K)
Erica: Ever Mighty (T)
Erma: Renowned, Honored (T)
Esmerelda: An Emerald (Gr)
Estelle: A Star (L)
Esther: A star (H)
Eugenia: Well-Born (Gr)
Evangeline: Bearer of Good Tidings (Gr)
Eve, Eva: Full of Life (H)
Evita (From Eve): Full of Life,
Faith: Faith-Belief in God; One of the Seven Virtues (L)
Fanny (from Frances): Free (T)
Fawn: A Young Deer (T)
Felice (Felicia): Happy (L)
Fern: From the Fern Plant (OE)
Fiona: White; Fair (G)
Flora: A Flower (L)
Florence: Flourishing (L)
Frances, Fran: From Country of France (L)
Gail: Joy (H)
Georgia: Female of George-Farmer (Gr)
Gertrude: Spear-maiden (T)
Ginger (from Virginia): Spice (L)
Glenda: Making Glad (T)
Gloria: Glory (L)
Golda, Goldie: Gold (Y)
Grace, Gracie: Blessing, Thanksgiving (L)
Greer: Wakeful Mother (Gr)
Greta, Gretel (from Margaret): Pearl (Gr)
Guinevere: Blessed and Soft; Wife of King Arthur (W)
Gwen: White, Fair, Pleasant, Blissful (W)
Halley: Holy (T)
Harriet: Home and Ruler (T)

Hazel: Hazel Tree; Emblem of Beauty and Magic (T)
Heather: Heath Flower; Emblem of Wholesome Beauty
Heidi: Nobleness (T)
Helen, Helena, Helene: Light, Sunlight (Gr)
Helga: Holy, Peaceful (Scan)
Hilary: Cheerful (L)
Hilda: Battle, or Leader in Battle (T)
Holly: From Holly Tree-Emblem of Yuletide (T)
Hope: The Virtue of Hope (OE)
Ida: Happy; also farseeing (T)
Ingrid: Beautiful (Scan)
Irene: Peace (Gr)
Iris: The Rainbow (Gr)
Irma: Whole, Universal (T)
Isabel: Pure, Consecrated to God (H)
Isolde: Vision of Beauty (K)
Jacqueline, Jacqui: One who Replaces (Fr)
Jane, Janet, Janice: Gracious Gift of the Lord (H)
Jasmine: Jasmine Flower (Per)
Jean, Jeanette, Jeanne: Gracious Gift of the Lord (H)
Jennifer, Jenny, Jenna: White Wave (K)
Jessica: Wealthy One (H)
Jewel, Jewell: Precious or a Gem (OF)
Jill: Youthful One (L)
Joan: Gracious Gift of the Lord (H)
Jocelyn: Joyful (L)
Jodi, Jodie (from Judith): Praised of God (H)
Josephine, Josie: God Shall Add (H)
Joy: Joyful in God, Glad (OF)
Joyce: Merry; also Joyful (L)
Judith: Praised of God (H)
Julie, Julia, Juliana: Youthful One; From July (L)
Justine: Just; Honest (L)
Kai: Ocean (Hawaiian)
Kara: Full of Justice Dear, Beloved One (Gr)
Karen: Pure One (Gr)
Katharine, Kathryn, Katrina: Pure One (Gr)
Kathleen: Pure One (Ir)
Katie (from Katherine): Pure One (Gr)
Kelly: Warrior or possibly Church (Ir)
Kimberly, Kim: From Royal Meadow; (Kimberly, S. Af
Kiri: Bark of a Tree (Maori Name from New Zealand)
Kirsten, Kristen, Kris (Christina): Anointed, baptized (G
Kylie: Boomerang (Australian Aboriginee)
Lana: Wool; Emblem of Innocence (L)
Lani: Sky (Hawaiian)
Larissa: Laughing and Cheerful (L)
Laura, Laurel: Laurel-crowned (L)
Layla: Wine (Ar)
Leah: Weary One (H)
Lenora: Light, Bright One (Gr)
Libby (from Elizabeth): Consecrated to God (H)
Lily: Brightly Colored, Magnificence (Gr)
Linda: Pretty One (Sp)
Lisa (from Elizabeth): Consecrated to God (H)
Lois: Agreeable, or Warrior Maid (Gr)
Loretta: Laurel-Sign of Victory (L)
Lorraine: Famed in War (T)
Louisa, Louise: Famous in Battle (T)

Lucille, Lucy: Light; Bringer of light (L)
Lynn, Lynette: Lake, Pool, Brook, Waterfall (K and T)
Mabel: Amiable, Lovable (L)
Madeline: Elevated (H)
Magdalene: Elevated (H)
Mahalah, Mahala: Tenderness (H)
Marcella: Related to Mars, or War (L)
Margaret: A Pearl (Gr)
Mara: Myrrh (H)
Maria, Marie: Wished-For Child (H and Fr)
Marina, Mara: Lover of the Sea; "Born at Sea" (L)
Martha: Lady of the House (Aramaic)
Mary, Marilyn: Bitterness of a Healing Herb (H)
Mathilda: Mighty in Battle (T)
Maureen: Myrrh (Ir)
Maxine: Greatest (L)
Maya: Great (Gr)
Meg: from **Margaret:** Pearl (Gr)
Melanie: Black, Dark-Haired (Gr and Fr)
Melinda: Sweet as Honey; Related to Melissa (Gr)
Melissa: Honeybee (Gr)
Mia: Mine (Sp)
Michele: Who Is Like God? (H)
Mildred: Mild Counsel (OE)
Minerva: Daughter of Wisdom (L)
Molly: from **Mary:** Myrrh (H)
Mona: Noble (K); **Mona:** Moon (OE)
Monica: To Advise (L)
Muriel: Bright and Sea (G)
Myna: The Moon (OE)
Myrna: Loving; Gentle (K)
Nadia: Hope (Rus)
Nancy (from Ann): Virtue of Grace (H)
Natalie, Talia: Birthday of Christ (L) Plentiful (Fr)
Natasha: Russian for Natalie (Rus)
Nellie (from Helen): Sunlight (Gr)
Nicole: Victory of the People (Gr)
Nora: Honor, Noble (L)
Norma: Model, or Standard (L)
Olive: Olive Tree or Branch-Symbol of Love and Peace (L)
Ophelia: Help, Service, Benefit (Gr)
Oprah: Fawn (H)
Page, Paige: Attendant (L)
Pamela: All Honey (Gr)
Pandora: All-Gifted (Gr)
Patience: Forbearance, Endurance, Perseverance (L)
Patricia: Noble Lady (L)
Paula: Little One (L)
Pearl: "Pearl of Great Price," Emblem of Truth (L)
Peggy (from Margaret): A Pearl (Gr)
Penelope, Penny: A Weaver (Gr)
Phaedra: Bright One (Gr)
Phoebe: Shining; the Moon (Gr)
Phillis, Phyllis: Green Foliage (Gr)
Poppy: From the Flower, Poppy (OE)
Portia: From Shakespeare: Resourceful Jurist (L)
Priscilla: Ancient Birth and Lineage (H)
Prudence: Virtue of Prudence (L)
Rachel: Little Lamb; Emblem of Gentleness (H)

Rebecca: Yoke; Captivating (H)
Renee: Born Again (L)
Rhoda: A Rose (Gr)
Rhona: A River (Gr)
Rita: Proper; Bright; Honest (Skt)
Robin (fr. Robin-bird and Robert): Shining with Fame (G)
Rosalind: Horse (T)
Rose, Rosa: White Rose (L)
Ruby: From the Jewel: Ruby Red-for Good and Love (L)
Rufara: Happy One, Swahili
Ruth: Friend, Companion (H)
Sally (from Sarah): Princess (H)
Sandra (fr. Alexandra): Defender; Helper of Mankind (Gr)
Sara, Sarah: Princess (H)
Selena: The Moon (Gr)
Shannon: Little Wise One (H)
Sharon, Shari: A Great and Fertile Plain (H)
Sheila: Heavenly (Ir)
Shirley: From a Bright Forest Clearing (OE)
Silvia: Woods (L)
Sonia: Wisdom (Gr)
Sophia: Wisdom (Gr)
Stella: Star (L)
Stephanie: Crown, wreath (Gr)
Susan: Lily or Graceful Lily (H)
Silvia: Woods (L)
Sonia: Wisdom (Gr)
Sophia: Wisdom (Gr)
Stella: Star (L)
Stephanie: Crown, wreath (Gr)
Susan: Lily or Graceful Lily (H)
Sylvia: Forester (L)
Tamar, Tammy; Tamara: Palm Tree (H and R)
Teresa: Harvester, Reaper (Gr)
Thelma: A Nurse (Gr)
Theresa: Harvester (Gr)
Tiffany: God appear (Gr)
Tova: Good (H)
Tracy: To Reap (L)
Trisha: Noble One (L)
Trudy: Strength (T)
Ursula: Little Bear (L)
Valerie: Strong (L)
Veronica: True Image of Christ (Gr)
Victoria, Vicki: Victory (L)
Violet: Violet Flower; Modesty (L)
Virginia: Spring (regeneration); Maidenly (L)
Vivian: Lively (L)
Wanda: Wanderer (T)
Wendy: Wanderer (T)
Wilma: Helmet of Steadfastness (T)
Winifred: Friend of Peace, White Wave (T)
Winona: First-Born Daughter;
Name of Hiawatha's Mother (American Indian)
Yoko: Good (Japanese)
Yolanda: The Violet (Gr)
Yvette: Bow-Bearer, Archer (T)
Yvonne: Courageous Heart (T)
Zoe: Life (Gr)

The POWER Spelling List of Male Names

Aaron: Light Bringer (H)
Abbott: Head of an Abbey (OE)
Abel: Breath; Stood for Charity, Love of Neighbor (H)
Abner: Father of Light (H)
Abraham: Father of a Multitude (H)
Adam: A Man of the Earth (H)
Adolf: Nobel Wolf (T)
Alan: Bright, Clear, Handsome, Amiable, Glorious (K)
Albert: Nobel and Bright (T)
Aldo: Old and Wise (T)
Alexander, Alec, Alex: Helper of Men (Gr)
Alfred: Elf and Counsel (OE)
Ali: Exalted, (Ar)
Allen: Bright, Clear, Handsome, Amiable (K)
Alvin: Loved by All (T)
Amadeus: Love of God (L)
Ambrose: Immortal (Gr)
Amos: Bearer of a Burden (H)
Andrew, Andre: Strong, Manly (Gr)
Angelo: Angel Messenger (L)
Anthony, Antonio: Deserving Praise (L)
Apollo: The Sun, Both as Lifegiver and Destroyer (Gr)
Aram: High, Exalted (Per)
Ariel: Lion of God; Also, Consecrated Hearth or Alter (H)
Arnold, Arne: Strong as an Eagle (T)
Artemas: Pure, Entire (Gr)
Arthur: Brave as a Bear; Noble (K)
Asa: Physician (H)
Augustine, Augustus: Exalted, Worthy of High Respect (L)
Austen, Austin: Exalted, Worthy of High Respect (L)
Barry: Blessed (H)
Barry: Straight-Shooter (K)
Bartholomew, Bart: Son of a Farmer (H)
Beau: Handsome (Fr)
Benjamin, Ben: Son of Right Hand; True, Good (H)
Bernard: Bold as a Bear (T)
Bertrand, Bertram, Bert: Bright Shield (T)
Bill: from William: Resolute Protector (T)
Bo: Householder (Sean) (Ir)
Bob: from Robert: Bright; Shining with Fame (T)
Bogart: Strong Bow (Ir)
Boyd: Yellow-Haired (K)
Brad: Someone from the Broad Meadow (OE)
Brandon: From the Beacon (L)
Brent: Lofty, Steep (OE)
Brian, Bryan: Strong (K)
Bruce: Dweller at the Thicket (OF)
Buddy, Bud: Brother (OE)
Byron: Bear; Full of Strength (T)
Caesar: Hairy (L)
Calvin: Bald (L)
Carl: Manly, Strong, Vigorous (T)
Cecil: Blind, Humble (L)

Charles, Chuck: Manly, Strong, Vigorous (T)
Christopher: Christ-Bearer (Gr)
Clarence: Illustrious (L)
Clark: Learned (L)
Claude: Lame (L)
Clifford: Town on a Cliff (OE)
Clyde: River Clyde (Scot)
Colbert: Fellow-Freeman (L)
Colton: Town Where Colts Are Bred (OE)
Connor: Love of Hounds (G)
Conrad: Bold Counsel (T)
Cornelius: Powerful; Cornu (horn) for Power of Truth
Craig: A Rock or Dweller at the Crag (K)
Curtis: Courteous (Fr)
Cyril: Lordly, Masterly (Gr)
Cyrus: Throne, Sun (Per)
Dale: Valley (OE)
Daniel: God Is My Judge; Spirit of All Prophecy (H)
Darius: Preserver, Restrainer (Per)
Darren: Little Great One (OE)
Daryl: Beloved One (OF)
David: Beloved (H)
Dean: A Dense or Wooded Valley (OE)
Dennis: From Dionysius, God of Wine (Gr)
Denzil: High Stronghold (Eng)
Derek: A Way; Pat; Mode of Life (H)
Dexter: Right Hand (L)
Dick (from Richard): Stern and Powerful Ruler (T)
Diego: Sp. for James: One Who Overthrows (Sp)
Dominic, Dominique: Belonging to the Lord (L)
Donald: World Mighty, World Ruler (K)
Douglas: Dark Stream, Seeker of Light (K)
Duane: Poet; Song (K)
Duke: Leader (L)
Dustin: Brave Fighter (T)
Dwight: White or Blond One (F)
Dylan: Sea (W)
Earl: Nobleman, Leader, Truth (T)
Ebenezer: Stone of Help (H)
Ed: Happy (T)
Edgar: Prosperous Spearman (T)
Edmund: Rich Protection; Cheerful (T)
Edward: Rich; Guardian (T)
Eivind: Lasting Friend (Scan)
Eli: Height or Elevated (H)
Elijah: My God Is the Lord (H)
Eliot, Elliot: From Elijah: God Is My Help (H)
Elmer: Noble Fame (T)
Elmo: Amiable (Gr)
Elvin: Elf-Friend, Meaning Wise Friend (T)
Emil, Emile: Industrious (L and T)
Ephraim: Fruitful (H)
Erasmus: Amiable (Gr)

Eric: Stranger (T)
Ernest: Earnest, Sincere (T)
Eugene: Well-Born; Noble (Gr)
Evan: Welsh for John: The Lord Is Gracious (W)
Everett: Strong as a Wild Boar (T)
Favell: Brave (Ir)
Felix: Happy (L)
Ferdinand: Adventurous Life; Daring (T)
Fess: Steadfast (L)
Floyd: Gray-Haired One (W)
Forrest: Woodsman (OE)
Frank: Free Man (T)
Frederic: Peaceful Ruler (T)
Gabriel: Gabe Man of God (H)
Gail: Joy (H)
Galahad: Head (W)
Gale: Valor, Virtue (K)
Galen: Calm, Gentle (Gr)
Gareth: Gentle; One of Knights at Round Table (W)
Garry: A Gardener, Gentle (K)
Garth: A Gardener; Also, Field, Enclosure (T)
Gavin: Battle Hawk (K)
Gene: Well-Born; Noble (Gr)
George: Earthman; Farmer (Gr)
Gerald: Spear Power (T)
Gideon: Tree-Feller; Bold Warrior (H)
Glen, Glynn: A Valley (K)
Goeffrey: God's Peace and Traveler (T)
Gordon: From the Great Hill; Ascended One (T)
Grant: Great One (L)
Greg: A Watchman (Gr)
Gus: Staff (T)
Guy: Warrior (L)
Hamlet: A Little Home (T)
Harold: Army Ruler (T)
Harrison: Son of Harry; Battle Worthy (T)
Harry: Ruler of the Home (T)
Harvey: Warrior (T)
Henry: Ruler of The Home (T)
Herbert: Bright Warrior (T)
Herman: Warrior (T)
Homer: A Security, Pledge (Gr)
Howard: Chief, Sword-Guardian (OE)
Hugh: Heart; Mind, Thought (T)
Hugo (from Hugh) =: Heart (T)
Humphrey: Support of Peace (T)
Ian: Scottish for John: God's Gracious Gift (Scot)
Icabod: Where Is The Glory (H)
Immanuel: God with Us (H)
Ira: Watchful (H)
Irving: Sea Friend (T)
Isaac: Laughter (H)
Isaiah: Salvation of the Lord (H)
Ishmael: Heard of God (H)
Israel: A Prince, or Champion, of God (H)
Ivan: Russian for John: God Is Gracious (Ru)
Jack (from John): God Is gracious (H)
Jacob: One Who Overthrows (H)

Jamal: Handsome (Ar)
James: English for Jacob: One Who Overthrows (H)
Jared: He Descends (H)
Jason: Healer; on Quest for Golden Fleece (Gr)
Jeffrey: God's Peace (T)
Jeremiah: Exalted of the Lord (H)
Jeremy: Appointed by God (H)
Jerome: Holy Name (G)
Jesse: The Lord Is God Exists (H)
Joel: The Lord Is God (H)
John, Jon: The Lord Is Gracious, Merciful (H)
Jonah: A Dove (H)
Jonathan: Gift of the Lord (H)
Joseph: He Shall Add; Also, Spiritual Progress (H)
Joshua: The Lord Is Salvation (H)
Juan: John The Lord Is Gracious (Sp)
Julius: Youthful One (L)
Kahali: Good Friend (Ar)
Kalil, Kahlil: Complete; Perfect (H)
Kai: Ocean (Hawaiian)
Keith: Wood (Celtic and Scottish)
Kelsey: Victory (OE)
Kenneth: Handsome, First Born (K and Scot)
Kent: A Headland Hill (K)
Kevin: Handsome (G)
Kingsley: Kings Meadow (OE)
Kirk: Dweller at The Church (Gr)
Knute, Knut: Knot (OE)
Kurt: from Conrad: Bold Counselor (T)
Kwame, Kwami: Born on Saturday (African)
Kyle: Narrow Piece of Land (Scot)
Lambert: Brightness of the Land (T)
Lance: Spear, Spearman (L)
Lancelot: Servant, Follower (L)
Laurence, Lawrence: Laurel-Crowned (L)
Lee: From the Meadow (T)
Leo, Leon: A Lion (Gr)
Leonard, Leonardo: Strong as a Lion (Gr and I)
Leopold: People and Bold (T)
Leroy: The King (L)
Lewis: Eng. Form of Louis: Renowned in Battle (T)
Linus: Flaxen Haired (G)
Lorenzo (from Laurence): Laurel-Crowned (Sp and It)
Louis: Renowned in Battle (T)
Lucas: Light (L)
Ludwig: Famous in Battle (T)
Luke: Bringer of Light or Knowledge (L)
Lyndon: Hill of Linden Trees (OE)
Lynn: Sea, Lake, Pool, Brook, or Waterfall (K and T)
Mac: Son of ... (Scot)
Manfred: Man and People (T)
Manuel: God Is with Us (Sp)
Marcellus: Named for Mars – God of War (L)
Mark: From Mars, Roman God of War (Eng)
Marcus: Latin form of Market (L)
Mars: God of War (Eng)
Marshall: Master of the Horses (OF)
Martin: Warlike (L)

Matthew: Gift of The Lord (H)
Max: Greatest (L)
Melvin: Gentle Chief (Ir and G)
Melvin: One Who Ministers (K)
Merlin: Small Falcon; Sea; Advisor of King Arthur (K)
Michael: Who Is Like Unto God? (H)
Mickey (from Michael): Who Is Like Unto God? (Ger)
Mikhail: Michael: Who Is Like Jehovah (Ru)
Miles: Soldier (L)
Mitchell: Who Is Like God? (H)
Morgan: Circle (W)
Moses: Taken Out of the Water; Saved: Deliverance (H)
Muhammad: Praised (Ar)
Murray: A Seaman; Merry (Ir)
Nathaniel, Nathan: Gift of God (H)
Neal: A Champion (K)
Nelson: Son of a Champion (Scan)
Nicholas: Victory of the People (Gr)
Noah: Rest, Comfort (H)
Noel: Christmas (L)
Norris: Norseman (T)
Oliver: The Olive Tree (L)
Omar: Eloquent (H)
Orion: Son of Light (Gr)
Oscar: Deer and Friend: Divine Spear (Ir)
Oscar: Divine Spear (T)
Otto: Rich, Happy (T)
Owen: A Youth (W)
Pablo: Sp. Paul: Small in Human Strength (Sp)
Paine: Country Man (OF)
Patrick: Of Nobel Birth (L)
Paul: Little, Powerful in God (L)
Perry: Pear Tree (OE)
Peter: A Rock; Faith (Gr)
Philip: Lover of Horses (Gr)
Plato: Broad-Shouldered, Powerful (Gr)
Ralph: Wolf or Wolf-Shield (T)
Randolph, Randal, Randy: Shield Wolf (T)
Raphael: God Has Healed (H)
Rasheed: Mature (Ar)
Raymond: Wise Protection (T)
Reginald: Ruling Power (T)
Rene: Reborn (L)
Reuben: "Behold, A Son;" Under-Standing (H)
Rex: King (L)
Richard: Powerful Ruler (T)
Rick: Strong Ruler (OF)
Robert: Bright Fame (T)
Rock, Rocky: Stability; Reliable (OE)
Rodney: Cleared Land Near Water (OE)
Roger: Famous Spear Man (T)
Roland: Fame of the Land (T)
Ronald: Ruling Power (T)
Roy: Red, Kingly (K and L)

Rufus: Man with Red Hair (L)
Russell: One with Red Hair (OF)
Ryan: Little King (Ir)
Salvadore: Savior (S)
Samson: Splendid Sun (H)
Samuel: Heard of God (H)
Saul: Prayed For (H)
Scott: From Scotland (Scot)
Scott: Scotsman (OE)
Sean: The Lord Is Gracious; Merciful (Ir)
Siegfried: Victorious Peace (T)
Simon: Hearing (H)
Sinon: Wise (Ir)
Skip: Shipmaster (Old Nose)
Stanislaus: Standing Glory (Sl)
Stanley: From the Stony Meadow (OE)
Stephen: Crown, Wreath (Gr)
Steven, Steve (from Stephen): Crown; Wreath (Gr)
Stewart: Caretaker, Steward (OE)
Ted (from Theodore): Gift of God (Gr)
Terence, Terry: Polished; Reaper (L)
Thaddeus, Ted, Thad: Valiant, Courageous (H)
Theodore: Gift of God (Gr)
Thomas: A Twin (H)
Timothy: God-Fearing (Gr)
Todd: Fox (Scot)
Tony: from Anthony: Deserving Praise (L)
Travis: From The Crossroads; To Journey (OE)
Trevor: Large Village (W)
Troy: At the Place of the Curly Haired People (Gr)
Tyler: Industrious One (K)
Tyson, Ty: Firebrand (OF)
Uri: Light (H)
Valentine: Healthy, Well (L)
Vaughan: Small (K)
Vernon: Of the Springtime; Flourishing (L)
Victory: Conqueror (L)
Vincent, Vince: Conquering (L)
Virgil: Strong (L)
Vladimir: Ruling in Peace (Sl)
Wade: The Advancer (T)
Wallace: Man from Wales (T)
Walter: Powerful Warrior (T)
Ward: Guardian, or Guarded (T)
Warren: Protecting Friend (OE)
Wayne: Wagon Maker (T)
Wendel: Wandering (T)
Wilbur: Resolute Protection (T)
William: Resolute Protect (T)
Winston: Friend or Friendly Store (T)
Wynn, Wynne: Friend (OE)
Yuri: George in Russian: Men of the Earth (Ru)
Zachariah, Zack, Zachary: Lord Has Remembered (H)
Zane (from Shane): means John: Lord Is Gracious (Ir)

Timeline of the English Language and Its Spelling
List of People and Events that Shaped the Words, Alphabets, and Spelling

This timeline traces the development of the words, alphabets, and spelling for the English Language. It can help you see why English has so many words from other languages and why some words are not spelled like they sound. Most of all, as you learn about the adventurous, amazing history of English, you may find yourself more willing to discover ways to remember its challenging words.

Although archeologists think mankind began 2,500,000 years ago, 2,215,000 years went by before ancient people created drawings and art (35,000 B.C.-18,000 B.C.), and 2,495,000 years passed before hieroglyphics and the first alphabets were carved (3,000 B.C.). Then it took until 450 A.D. for English to have its own language (then called *Anglo-Saxon*), and it took until 597 A.D. for the English Language to have an alphabet that the common people could use. So, out of the 2,500,000 years that mankind has existed, English has only had an alphabet that the common people could use for 1,604 years. Also, spelling standards only began around 1596 (just 405 years ago). Pretty amazing!

2,500,000 B.C. **BEGINNING of MANKIND:** Archeologists think fossils show that man began then.
400,000-250,000 B.C. **MANKIND** controls fire, builds shelters, buries the dead, but no art or alphabets.
35,000-18,000 B.C. **CAVE ART and CARVINGS:** Fossils show that ancient people carved ivory and bone animals, and painted animals and symbols on walls and ceilings deep inside of caves.
8000–2000 B.C. **EARLY SETTLERS in ENGLAND LEFT NO RECORD of LANGUAGE.**

8000 BC **OLD STONE AGE ENDS:** Scholars have learned that during the Old Stone Age, primitive people lived in caves in Britain. This Age ended in 8,000 B.C.
8000–3000 B.C. **PEOPLE from SPAIN and BRITANNY** (N.W. France), who lived in England, grew crops, raised cows and sheep, made pottery, used flint tools, but recorded no language.
2000 B.C. **STONEHENGE:** People from Germany (perhaps Celts) came to England and probably were the people who built monuments like Stonehenge, yet no language was ever found.

3000–700 B.C. **SPREAD of EARLY ALPHABETS**
3000–1000 B.C. **EGYPTIANS** develop Hieroglyphics, a picture-writing alphabet of about 700 signs.
SEMITES (Hebrews, Babylonian, and others in the Eastern Mediterranean area) develop alphabets. Earliest alphabet perhaps developed by Hebrews who inhabited the Sinai Peninsula.
1, 500 B.C. **PHOENICIAN TRADERS** develop an alphabet of 22 symbols for consonants sounds.
1,000-8,000 B.C. **GREEKS** learn the idea of having symbols for sounds, probably from Phoenician traders.
700-600 B.C. **ROMANS** learn Greek alphabet and perfect their 25-letter Roman alphabet by A.D.114.

500 B.C.-A.D.1066 **TRIBES and CONQUERORS BRING THEIR LANGUAGES to ENGLAND**

500 B.C.-A.D.43 **CELTS:** Tribes of Celts (Gaels, Britons) cross the English Channel and invade England. The Gaels settle in Great Britain, and the Britons (in the Legends of King Arthur) settle in England and Wales. These Celtic tribes lived in England for over 1,000 years and were the first known people to speak a language in England. In 449 A.D., when the Angles and Saxons drove them into Ireland, their Celtic language went with them.
1st Century B.C. **ROMAN SOLDIERS in GERMANY:** Roman soldier bring items to Germany that the Germans have never seen. When the Germans "buy" these, they call them by the Latin words the soldiers used. In this way, Latin words: *butter, cheese, chest, inch, mile, pillow, table, street...* were added to Anglo-Saxon before it became England's language.
A.D. 43 – 410 **ROMANS CONQUER ENGLAND:** Roman soldiers conquer England in A.D. 43, and stay and build roads, walls, and forts; and protect the Britons and Celts. In A.D. 410, they return to Rome. Since the Celts never spoke Latin, it leaves England with the Romans.

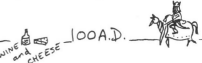

1000 B.C.E. ———— 500 B.C.E. ———— 100 A.D. ————

WINE and CHEESE

A.D. 410 – 449 **SAXONS, ANGLES, and JUTES INVADE ENGLAND:** After the Romans left, thre
German tribes invaded England. The Saxons came first – to protect the Britons and th
Celts from their enemies. Later, though, the Saxons invited the Angles and Jutes to joi
them. Then, these three tribes forced the Britons to flee to the mountains of northerr
England, and the Celts to flee to Ireland. By 449, the Angles and Saxons had becom
the two most powerful tribes in England and together were called the *Anglo-Saxons.*

A.D. 450 – 1066 **OLD ENGLISH**

A.D. 450 **ANGLO-SAXON BECOMES the LANGUAGE of ENGLAND**: By 450, Anglo-Saxon
(language of the Angles and Saxons) had begun to be spoken in England and by A.D. 1000, it
was spoken throughout England. From Anglo-Saxon, English has gained many of its
most basic words: the word, *the*; pronouns: *I, you, me, he, she, it;* verbs: *is, can, will,*
eat, sleep, drink... and other basic words: *after, in, of, for, with, and, but*... Also, this
language of the farm and kitchen has given us: *barn, cow, calf, earth, grass, hand, home,*
oven, pig, pot, seed, sheep, stove, water... and nouns for people: *child, brother, father,*
friend, heaven, love, man, mother, neighbor, sister, woman... Although, many words
have also been added from French, Latin, Greek and other languages; today, half the
words in most English sentences are still based on Anglo-Saxon words. Also, the 100
most common words in English are still from Anglo-Saxon.

ANGLO-SAXON ALPHABET: Anglo-Saxon had an alphabet, but only the pries
could use it. It was made of straight letters called runes that were carved or scratched c
stone. Rune means *secret*, and the priests used these letters for their secret rituals ar
spells. They prevented the common people from having an alphabet with which to writ

A.D. 597 **THE ROMANS RETURN to ENGLAND:** Rome made its greatest contribution to
English starting in 597 A.D. when St. Augustine and Christian missionaries from Rome
came to England. They established schools and churches, and also added many new
Latin words for things to English: *alms, altar, candle, creed, disciple, music*...

THE GIFT of the ROMAN ALPHABET: Since only the priests could use the Angl
Saxon alphabet, missionaries taught the common people to write Anglo-Saxon with th
Roman alphabet. Using this alphabet to spell Anglo-Saxon words wasn't easy, so the fir
spelling problem entered English. Since the Roman alphabet did not have enoug
vowels for the sounds of Anglo Saxon, vowel sound that were one-letter in the Angl
Saxon alphabet needed two in the Roman alphabet: *ae, ea, eo, oe*. Also, the consonar
sounds: *ng, ch,* and *th*, which were one-letter in Anglo-Saxon, were 2 letters (digraphs) i
the Roman alphabet. Still, the Anglo-Saxons had an alphabet they could use for writing
and Anglo-Saxon words were spelled like they were pronounced. This balance of Lati
and Anglo-Saxon lasted for 450 years until the Normans invaded England in 1066.

A.D. 700 <u>**BEOWULF**</u> **WRITTEN IN ANGLO-SAXON:** The first great English book, *Beowulf*
(author unknown), was written in Anglo-Saxon. It described the adventures of the mighty
warrior, Beowulf, who slew the monster, Grendel, for his king and people. Beowulf ha
all the qualities that the Anglo-Saxons admired: courage, generosity, loyalty, and strength

A.D. 750 – 1050 **THE VIKINGS INVADE ENGLAND:** Meanwhile, from 750 – 1050, Vikings (from
Denmark and Norway) invaded and settled in England. They added close to 1,500 words
from their Norse language: *dazzle, freckle, get, hit, husband, leg, scream, shirt, trust,*
skin, sky... They also added important pronouns: *they, them,* and *their.*

BARN
COW
Candle
ALTAR
1000 A.D.
freckle
1066 A.D. NORMAN INVASION
MOU
500 A.D.
DISCIPLE
DAZZLE
Liberty

A.D. 1066 – 1400 MIDDLE ENGLISH

NORMAN FRENCH enters the ENGLISH LANGUAGE, and is spoken by the ruling class. The COMMON PEOPLE and CHAUCER use ANGLO-SAXON so both languages last.

A.D. 1066 – 1204 NORMANS INVADE ENGLAND and BRING THEIR FRENCH LANGUAGE:
In 1066, the Normans, led by the fierce invader, William the Conqueror, sailed across the water from Normandy (now France), conquered England at the Battle of Hastings, and established their kingdom. From 1066 until 1204, the Normans ruled England. This educated class spoke an elegant French language that came from Latin. Among the words they brought into English were: *ballet, beautiful, constitution, elegant, equality, fashion, government, feminine, jury, liberty, mountain, magnificent, marriage, masculine, palace, soldier, state, throne,* and *triumph*. These French words are very different than the basic Old English (Anglo-Saxon) words, and much more difficult to spell.

ANGLO-SAXON STILL SPOKEN IN ENGLAND: The steadfast language of the Anglo-Saxons remained strong in England, however, because the common people spoke it. Therefore, at least 4,500 Anglo-Saxon words have remained in English. Also, since both the common people and the conquerors kept their own language, each group often had a word for the same thing. Therefore, English has many Anglo-Saxon and French synonyms: *home* and *mansion*; *work* and *labor*; *love* and *adore*; *hearty* and *cordial*...

A.D. 1387 – 1400 CHAUCER WRITES <u>THE CANTERBURY TALES</u> IN ANGLO-SAXON: Another reason that Anglo-Saxon words stayed so strongly rooted in English was that Chaucer, the greatest writer of his time, wrote in Anglo-Saxon. From 1387 until his death in 1400, Geoffrey Chaucer worked on his masterpiece, <u>The Canterbury Tales</u>, writing it in this language of the common people. In this great book about a journey from London to Canterbury, Chaucer has his characters, like the knight, the parson, and the plowman, tell tales that show what their daily life was like and what they believed.

What is important about Chaucer's English is that at the time he wrote, words in English were spelled like they were pronounced. Every vowel and consonant was spoken which meant there were no silent letters. For years after Chaucer died in 1400, writers copied his spelling, even though the way English was pronounced had changed.

A. D. 1400 – 1600 FROM MIDDLE ENGLISH TO MODERN ENGLISH

IMMIGRATION, PRINTING PRESS, RENAISSANCE, DICTIONARIES, and WORDS from OTHER LANGUAGES affect the spelling of English words. Pronunciation was changing at the same time that permanent spelling standards were being established.

During this period, many new words came into English; but, things also happened that caused English to have many words that were no longer spelled like they were pronounced. In 1400, when Chaucer died, people still pronounced all the consonants and vowels, including *final e*. By 1500, though, the *final e* had become silent, along with other vowels and consonants in words like *climb, love,* and *neighbor*. As more and more books were printed in English, spelling stayed the same, even though pronunciation was changing. Letters once pronounced: *b, e, g, h, k, l, t, w...* became *silent*

IMMIGRATION and THE GREAT VOWEL SHIFT: From 1400 – 1600, numerous young immigrants poured into London, and the way long vowels were pronounced shifted to a higher sound. This Great Vowel Shift began in London and then spread throughout England. No one knows for sure why this happened.

CANTERBURY TALES
1400 A.D.

THE GREAT VOWEL SHIFT....
1500 A.D.
(the silence of the E)

200 A.D.

4

1476	**THE PRINTING PRESS:** When William Caxton set up the first printing press in England in 1476, he kept much of the spelling that Chaucer had used even though the pronunciation of many words had changed in England. As the printing press produced more and more books, people got used to this spelling.
1495	**PAPER MILL:** John Tate established the first paper mill in England in 1495. This event was significant because now both writers and the printing press had a cheap, durable surface on which to print numerous books.
1400 – 1600	**THE RENAISSANCE in ENGLAND** **THE RENAISSANCE and LATIN:** During this time in history, which was still going on when Queen Elizabeth I ruled England (1558-1603), people became passionate about reading and using Latin. They got so excited, they even decided to change some simple words into Latin spelling which added more *silent letters*: dette became *de<u>b</u>t*; dout – *dou<u>b</u>t*; iland – *i<u>s</u>land*; rime – *r<u>h</u>yme*; sissors – *s<u>c</u>issors*...
1546 – 1616	**WILLIAM SHAKESPEARE and LATIN:** New words were added to English because great writers like William Shakespeare (1546-1616) used words from Latin to express their ideas: *alter*-to change, *amorous*-loving, *image*, *scribe*, and *verse*... Also, Shakespeare created over 2,000 new words like *hurry* and *leapfrog*..., and phrases like: *to be or not to be*, and *vanish into thin air*...
	THE RENAISSANCE and GREEK: Also, during the Renaissance, people in England began discussing the writing of the Greek philosophers Plato and Aristotle (400 B.C.), and English gained many words from Greek: *apothecary* (pharmacist), *phantom*, *photograph*... Words in math and science also came from Greek: *arithmetic*, *pneumonia*, *psychology*... Since Greek spells *n-pn*, *f-ph*, and *s-ps*, more silent letters were added to English.
1582 – 1788	**EARLY ENGLISH and AMERICAN DICTIONARIES**
1582	**MULCASTER:** Before the first English dictionary was published in 1582 (Time when Queen Elizabeth I was ruling and Shakespeare was writing plays), scholars and writers in England had been using Latin dictionaries. Also, the way words were spelled was not consistent. These educated people now wanted a dictionary for the spelling of English words. To meet this need, in 1582, Richard Mulcaster collected and organized the English words of his day. Then, he put 8,000 of these words into his book and recommended how they should be spelled. Instead of deciding to spell each word like it was pronounced, Mulcaster chose to use the common spelling, printed in books, that was already familiar to scholars and writers.
1596	**COOTE:** In 1596, Edmunde Coote, another English schoolmaster, published *The Englishe Schoole-maister*. Like Mulcaster, Coote also wrote a spelling dictionary for the common people of England. Even though Coote wanted words to be spelled like they were spoken, like Mulcaster, he chose the spelling that people already knew. Coote's dictionary was so popular that it set a spelling standard for people from all walks of life and for the schools in England. This dictionary, which also contained synonyms, remained in print for nearly 200 years.
1604	**CAWDREY:** Then, in 1604 (eight years after Coote's dictionary), Robert Cawdrey wrote *A Table Alphabetical*. Although it was less than a hundred pages with only 3,000 English words, this book is often called *the first true dictionary* since Cawdrey both spelled and defined his words. He also used the spelling that was familiar to people.

ueen Elizabeth

⊕ CAWDREY's *A Table Alphabetical*

1604 A.D.
SHAKESPEARE

1755 A.D. Samuel Johnson's *Dictionary of the* ENGLISH LANGUAG

1596 – 1640	**PRINTING PRESS and DICTIONARIES ESTABLISH SPELLING STANDARDS:** During the years following these dictionaries *the way words should be spelled* became more and more established. Coote's spelling continued to be taught in English schools, and the printing press continued pouring out books. By 1640, over 20,000 different books had been published in English, plus all the copies of these books. The printing press and early dictionaries were establishing spelling standards for the people of England.

As spelling was becoming consistent, in some areas of England, people were judged as *educated* or *uneducated* according to whether or not they used the *proper spelling taught in school.* Now there was a demand in England for a dictionary that would define words and set permanent spelling standards. |
| **1747** | **JOHNSON:** In 1747, Samuel Johnson, a struggling writer, who was blind in one eye, was the one hired to write the defining English dictionary. For eight years, he worked in an attic room, defining the meaning and establishing the spelling for **43,000** English words. To show the meaning and use of words, Johnson chose thousands of quotations from books by the best English writers. Finally, in June 1755, Johnson's *Dictionary of the English Language* was published. His grand masterpiece captured the majesty of the English language and set such permanent standards for the use and spelling of English words, that these crossed the ocean to America, where they were used by Webster. |
| **1788** | **WEBSTER:** When Johnson published his dictionary in 1755, Noah Webster had not yet been born. By 1788, though, at age 30, Webster had completed a small school dictionary, *The American Spelling Book.* It contained both familiar spelling and some words Webster simplified, plus definitions. Webster spelled and defined American words for two main reasons. One, he was patriotic. Encouraged by Benjamin Franklin, and other leaders, he wanted to set a standard for American English to show that it was as good as British English. Also, Webster was a school teacher who wanted his students to have better textbooks. so he wrote his own for spelling, grammar, and reading.

The American Spelling Book was so popular, it soon became a household book. Except for the Bible, it was the best-selling book in American history. Webster later worked tirelessly to complete his *American Dictionary of the English Language* (1828) with **70,000** defined words. (Today, Webster's Third International Dictionary has **450,000** words.) |
| **1879 – 1915** | **MURRAY:** A true hero in the history of the dictionary is James Augustus Henry Murray. After being chosen in 1879 *to spell and define every English word since 1150*, A. H. Murray worked non-stop for 36 years (until his death in 1915) to bring together, spell, and define **414,825** words. With sheer effort and commitment, Murray was able to produce *The Oxford English Dictionary*, the dictionary considered *the greatest dictionary of all time*! Today it contains over 615,000 words… (and, it is now organized by computers!) |
| **1600 – present** | **EXPLORATION, COLONIZATION, and WORDS from OTHER LANGUAGES:** During the 1600s, as the English explored and established colonies, many new words were brought in from other languages. From the Canadian and American Indians, English welcomed: *chipmunk, moccasin, moose, potato, powwow, raccoon, skunk, squash, tepee, toboggan, tomahawk…* From the Mexican-Spanish influence, we gained: *bronco, cafeteria, chili, cigar, corral, mosquito, patio, quesadilla, ranch, rodeo, tomato, vanilla…*

Since English keeps the spelling of words from other language, more *silent letters* kept coming into English. From Greece, we received: *Psychology, pneumonia…*; from Spain: *bomb, chocolate…*; from France: *ballet, champagne…*; from South Africa : *gnu. Bagel* and *chutzpah* (impudence) came from Yiddish; and the list goes on… |

moccasin

Ballet

'O.A.D.

1900 A.D. *Oxford English Dictionary* 2000 A.D.
Murray's

List of Some English Words from Foreign Languages

The English language has borrowed words throughout the world. From Ethiopia, we have *zebra*; from Australia, *boomerang*, *koala*, and *kangaroo*; *limbo* (How low can you go dance) from Jamaica; *bazaar* from Persia; *taboo* from Polynesia... Although English has been greatly enriched by these words, the sounds of many of them are spelled differently than English words.

AFRICA: *banana, gnu* (antelope) *, marimba, safari, samba, tangerine* (from Morocco), *yam, zombie*

AFR.-AMER: *blues, hip hop, jazz, Johnny cakes, rap, ragtime, soul, spirituals, sweet potato pie*

ARABIA: *algebra, artichoke, chemistry, coffee, kebab, magazine, monsoon, sofa, zero*

CHINA: *chow* (hello), *chow mein, mahjongg* (game), *soy, tea, tofu, typhoon, won tons, wok*

DUTCH: *cookie, pickle, Santa Claus, skate, sketch, skipper, sled, stove, wagon, yacht*

EAST INDIA: *candy, cashmere, catamaran* (sailboat w/2 floats), *cheetah, curry, jungle, pajamas, shampoo, shawl, verandah* (kind of porch)

ENGLAND: *flat* (apartment), *frock* (dress), *holiday* (vacation), *lorry* (truck), *mackintosh* (raincoat), *nappy* (diaper), *pence* (penny), *pram* (baby buggy), *tube* (subway)

FRANCE: *attorney, ballet, bizarre, boulevard, carousel, chef, crime, democracy, fiancé, jury, government, lieutenant, migraine, picturesque, restaurant, ticket, verdict*

GERMANY: (since 1600): *delicatessen, ecology, frankfurter, hamburger, kindergarten, noodle, pretzel, quartz, sauerkraut, stein* (beer mug), *waltz*

ITALY: *alto, aria* (opera solo), *balcony, carnival, cello, colonel, gondola, macaroni, mustache, opera, pasta, piano, soprano, solo, spaghetti, trio, volcano*

JAPAN: *bonsai* (miniature tree), *futon* (bed), *Go* (game), *haiku, judo, karate, kimono, origami, sukiyaki, teriyaki.*

RUSSIAN: *balalaika* (guitar-like instrument), *cosmonaut, czar, parka* (jacket), *samovar* (tea holder)

SCOTTISH: *bagpipes, bonny* (handsome), *brae* (hillside), *kilts, laddie, loch* (narrow arm of sea)

TURKISH: *sherbet, shish kebab, yogurt*

YIDDISH: *bagel, chutzpah* (rudeness), *kibbutz, klutz, nosh* (snack), *pastrami, schlep* (carry), *schmooze,* (talk), *schmuck* (pest), *schmaltz* (exaggerated feelings)

The English language continues to grow as new words are come in from technologies, like the space industry (*astronaut, satellite*) and computers (*debug, joystick, microchip*). Who knows what words will be added tomorrow – as discoveries are made and new sciences are developed? In time, we'll see how English will keep being enriched, for it is truly a melting pot of words from many languages and cultures.

POWER Spelling

Certificate of Achievement

for _____

Awarded to

_____

on the _____ day of _____ , 20 ____

_____
Teacher

POWER Spelling
Certificate of Achievement

for _____

Awarded to

_____

on the _____ day of _____, 20 _____

_____
Teacher

POWER Spelling
Certificate of Achievement

for _____

Awarded to _____

on the _____ day of _____, 20 _____

_____
Teacher

INDEX for *POWER* Spelling and The Book of Lists